A
Shakespeare Commentary

Dates of Composition and First Publication ; Sources of the Plots and Detailed
Outlines of the Plays; together with the Characters, Place-names, Classical,
Geographical, Topographical and curious Historical and Folk
Allusions, with glosses ; to which are added Appendices,
giving Extracts from Holinshed, Plutarch, and
the various Romances, Novels, Poems
and Histories used by Shakespeare in the formation
of the Dramas.

ARTHUR E. BAKER

Author of

" A Brief Account of the Public Library Movement in Taunton."
" A Concordance to the Poetical and Dramatic Works of Alfred, Lord Tennyson."
'' A Tennyson Dictionary : the Characters and Place-names arranged alphabetically
and described, with synopses of the Poems and Plays."
" Official Guide to Taunton."
" A Concordance to Tennyson's ' The Devil and the Lady,' " etc., etc.

PART II

FREDERICK UNGAR PUBLISHING CO.
NEW YORK

Original printing 1938

Republished 1957

Third American Printing
1971

ISBN 0-8044-2020-3   *Vol. I*
ISBN 0-8044-2021-1   *Vol. II*
ISBN 0-8044-2018-1   *Set*

Printed in the United States of America

Library of Congress Catalog Card Number 57-9168

The First Part of King Henry the Fourth

Written. 1596–1597.

Published 1598.   Mention is made of the Play by Meres in his *Palladis Tamia, Wit's Treasury.*   It was registered in the Stationers' Register under date of February 25th, 1598, and bore the following title : " Andrew Wisse : a booke intituled the Historye of Henry iiiith., with his battaile at Shrewsburye against Henry Hottspurre of the Northe, with the conceipted Mirthe of Sir John Ffalstoff."   It was reprinted in 1599, 1604, 1608, 1613, 1622, 1632, and 1639.

Source of the Plot.   The Play consists of a Comedy and a History fused together. For the historical scenes the poet's authority is Holinshed, whose *Chronicles*[1] at that time formed the book for English History, but some of the material for the comic scenes is thought to have been obtained from an old Play—*The Famous Victories of Henry V., containing the honourable battle of Agincourt*[2]—very popular at the time this play was written, though the greater portion of the humorous part is considered to be original.

    In the original draft Sir John Falstaff was called Sir John Oldcastle, but exception being taken by Henry Brooke, Lord Cobham to the character of Oldcastle being travestied after his death by the anti-Lollard party, the name was changed.   Sir John Oldcastle, Lord Cobham was the famous Lollard leader, who was condemned as a heretic and burned to death in 1417.

Outline of the Play.   The play, which continues the story of Bolingbroke opened in *The Tragedy of King Richard the Second,* and which covers a period of about ten months from the battle of Holmedon Hill on September 14th, 1402, to the battle of Shrewsbury, on July 21st, 1403, opens in King Henry's Palace in London.

    The king, addressing the nobles present, rèjoices that as the civil strife is now at an end—although before the scene closes, the seeds of discord, which give birth to another civil war are apparent—he can undertake a pilgrimage to the Holy Land— a pilgrimage he had projected some twelve months previously, when the news of Richard's murder was brought to him :

> Therefore, friends,
> As far as to the sepulchre of Christ,
> Whose soldier now, under whose blessed cross
> We are impressed and engaged to fight,
> Forthwith a power of English shall we levy ;
> Whose arms were moulded in their mothers' womb
> To chase these pagans in those holy fields
> Over whose acres walk'd those blessed feet,
> Which fourteen hundred years ago were nail'd
> For our advantage on the bitter cross.

The king then inquires of Lord Westmoreland what preparations have been made by the Council " in forwarding this dear expedience " and Westmoreland replies that the question was discussed but no action was taken, consequent upon news being

---

1. *See* Appendix I.   2. *See* Appendix II.

received that Owen Glendower a Welshman, had raised the standard of rebellion in Wales, and that the English forces under the command of Edmund Mortimer had been defeated with great slaughter, Mortimer himself being taken prisoner :

> My liege, this haste was hot in question,
> And many limits of the charge set down
> But yesternight : when all athwart there came
> A post from Wales loaden with heavy news ;
> Whose worst was, that the noble Mortimer,
> Leading the men of Herefordshire to fight
> Against the irregular and wild Glendower,
> Was by the rude hands of that Welshman taken,
> A thousand of his people butchered ;

" It seems then that the tidings of this broil Brake off our business for the Holy Land," rejoins Henry, and this decision is solidified by Westmoreland further announcing that a large Scottish army under the command of Archibald Earl of Douglas has crossed the border and been routed at Holmedon hill by Harry Hotspur, many of the Scottish knights being taken prisoner :

> Here is a dear, a true industrious friend,
> Sir Walter Blunt, new lighted from his horse,
> Stain'd with the variation of each soil
> Betwixt that Holmedon and this seat of ours ;
> And he hath brought us smooth and welcome news.
> The Earl of Douglas is discomfited :
> Ten thousand bold Scots, two and twenty knights,
> Balk'd in their own blood did Sir Walter see
> On Holmedon's plains.   Of prisoners, Hotspur took
> Mordake the Earl of Fife, and eldest son
> To beaten Douglas ; and the Earl of Athol,
> Of Murray, Angus, and Menteith :
> And is not this an honourable spoil ?
> A gallant prize ? ha, cousin, is it not ?

" In faith, It is a conquest for a prince to boast of," replies Westmoreland.   The news, however, is not altogether pleasing to Henry, his fear being that it will enhance the prestige of the house of Percy, and at the same time he is envious of Hotspur, as his only son Prince Hal—the future Henry V.—is causing him much anxiety by his wanton living and his frequenting of taverns in dissolute company, and the king wishes that some fairy had changed them when they lay in their cradles :

> Yea, there thou makest me sad and makest me sin
> In envy that my Lord Northumberland
> Should be the father to so blest a son,
>   .   .   .
> Whilst I, by looking on the praise of him,
> See riot and dishonour stain the brow
> Of my young Harry.   O that it could be proved
> That some night-tripping fairy had exchanged
> In cradle-clothes our children where they lay,
> And call'd mine Percy, his Plantagenet !
> Then would I have his Harry, and he mine.

The king then announces that Hotspur refuses to surrender any of the prisoners he has taken except Mordake Earl of Fife :

>   What think you, coz,
> Of this young Percy's pride ? the prisoners,
> Which he in this adventure hath surprised,
> To his own use he keeps ; and sends me word,
> I shall have none but Mordake Earl of Fife.

" This is his uncle's teaching : this is Worcester," interposes Westmoreland ; but, continues Henry, I have summoned Hotspur to appear before a Council at Windsor to answer for this refusal, and in consequence the expedition to the Holy Land must be postponed :

> But I have sent for him to answer this ;
> And for this cause a while we must neglect
> Our holy purpose to Jerusalem.
> Cousin, on Wednesday next our council we
> Will hold at Windsor ; so inform the lords :
> But come yourself with speed to us again ;
> For more is to be said and to be done
> Than out of anger can be uttered.

Cf. *Extract* 1 from Holinshed.

An apartment of the Prince of Wales in London supplies the next scene, where Sir John Falstaff seated at ease asks " what time of day is it, lad," to which his royal host retorts, " What a devil hast thou to do with the time of the day ? " and reproaches him in unflattering terms, saying he is so " fat-witted," with drinking that he has " forgotten to demand that truly which thou wouldst truly know," for " Unless hours were cups of sack, and minutes capons, and clocks the tongues of bawds, and dials the signs of leaping-houses, and the blessed sun himself a fair hot wench in flame-coloured taffeta, I see no reason why thou shouldst be so superfluous to demand the time of the day." But Falstaff's self-complacence is not to be disturbed, and in a half-sleepy manner he tells the Prince that when he is king he must not treat " squires of the night's body " as " thieves of the day's beauty " : but as " Diana's foresters, gentlemen of the shade, minions of the moon," so that men can say that " we be men of good government," but the prince who has accompanied Falstaff and other merry thieves on many nocturnal escapades retorts by reminding him how lavishly he spends the money which he has obtained by highway robbery : " for proof, now : a purse of gold most resolutely snatched on Monday night and most dissolutely spent on Tuesday morning " ; and Falstaff very conveniently diverts the conversation by referring to the mistress of the tavern they frequent : " By the Lord, thou sayest true, lad. And is not my hostess of the tavern, a most sweet wench ? " The two engage in a series of coarse jokes, and Falstaff, reverting to the previous conversation, asks the Prince whom he addresses as ' sweet wag,'—" whether there will be gallows standing in England when he becomes king " and implores him never to " hang a thief " when he ascends the throne, to which the Prince replies that he will appoint him hangman, and Falstaff begins to brag that he will be a " brave judge " but the Prince reminds him that he has already " judged falsely " as he shall have the " hanging of the thieves " and not be created a judge. Being under the influence of wine he then declares he will reform and lead a virtuous life, claiming that he was totally ignorant of wrong-doing, before becoming acquainted with the prince, whom he describes as a " most comparative, rascalliest, sweet young prince," who uses " similes of a most unsavoury kind," for " Thou hast done much harm upon me, Hal ; God forgive thee for it ! Before I knew thee, Hal, I knew nothing ; and now am I, if a man should speak truly, little better than one of the wicked. I must give over this life, and I will give it over : by the Lord, an I do not, I am a villain " ; but the prince turns the conversation by asking Falstaff : " Where shall we take a purse to-morrow, Jack ? " and Falstaff is so eager to participate in any expedition of a thieving or rascally nature that he forgets his promise to reform, and when the prince remarks : I see a good amendment of life in thee ; from praying to purse-taking, Falstaff observes : " Why, Hal, 'tis my vocation, Hal ; 'tis no sin for a man to labour in his vocation." Poins now enters and is greeted by both the prince and Falstaff, the former remarking : " Good morrow, Ned," to which Poins replies : " Good morrow, sweet Hal," and then turning to Falstaff mirthfully asks : " What says Monsieur Remorse ? what says Sir John Sack and Sugar ? Jack ! how agrees the devil and thee about thy soul, that thou soldest him on Good Friday last for a cup of Madeira and a cold capon's leg ? " Poins then informs them that a number of pilgrims and traders will pass through Gadshill on the morrow on their way to Canterbury, and suggests that they waylay and rob them : " But, my lads, my lads, to-morrow morning, by four o'clock, early at Gadshill ! there are pilgrims going to Canterbury with rich offerings, and traders riding to London with fat purses : I have vizards for you all ; you have horses for yourselves : Gadshill lies to-night in Rochester : I have bespoke supper to-morrow night in Eastcheap : we may do it as secure as sleep. If you will go, I will stuff your purses full of crowns ; if you will not, tarry at home and be hanged." Falstaff is delighted at the prospect of way-laying the travellers : " Hear ye, Yedward ; if I tarry at home and go not, I 'll hang you for going," but expresses disappointment when the prince refuses to accompany them : " *Fal.* Hal, wilt thou make one ? *Prince.* Who, I rob ? I a thief ? not I, by my faith," and Falstaff remarks " There's neither honesty, manhood, nor good fellowship in thee, nor thou camest not of the blood royal, if thou darest not stand for ten shillings," and threatens to be a traitor when the prince becomes king. Poins, however, declares that if left alone with the prince, he might be able to persuade him to accompany them, and so Falstaff leaves forthwith, the prince remarking as he does so : " Farewell, the latter spring ! farewell, All-hallown summer ! " When he has gone, Poins suggests playing a trick on Falstaff and the other highwaymen, proposing that after the thieves have robbed the travellers, the prince and himself under disguise shall surprise and rob them. Knowing that valour is not a strong characteristic in Falstaff and his friends, he anticipates no trouble in this respect, for they are " true-bred cowards " but the " virtue of the jest will be, the incomprehensible lies that this same fat rogue will tell us when we meet at supper : how thirty, at least, he fought with ; what wards, what blows, what extremities he endured ; and in the reproof of this lives the jest." The prince promises to join Poins in this adventure, remarking : " Well, I 'll go with thee " : and Poins departs. When he has gone the prince soliloquises on how he will " imitate the sun " which shines at the right moment in all its glory, although the " contagious clouds " sometimes " smother up his beauty," and contrasts his present " loose behaviour " which he will throw off, with the regal dignity he will assume, when he ascends the throne, for :

> I'll so offend, to make offence a skill ;
> Redeeming time when men think least I will.

We return to the King's Palace in London, where a Council is being held as indicated at the end of the first scene. Henry declares that he has hitherto been too patient at the indignity shown him :

> My blood hath been too cold and temperate,
> Unapt to stir at these indignities,
> And you have found me ; for accordingly
> You tread upon my patience :

but in future he will be master of his own house :

> but be sure
> I will from henceforth rather be myself,
> Mighty and to be fear'd, than my condition ;
> Which hath been smooth as oil, soft as young down,
> And therefore lost that title of respect
> Which the proud soul ne'er pays but to the proud.

Worcester flatly tells Henry that his House does not deserve such censure, and reminds the king that he owes his exalted position to the assistance he has received from the Percys :

> Our house, my sovereign liege, little deserves
> The scourge of greatness to be used on it ;
> And that same greatness too which our own hands
> Have holp to make so portly.

and the king peremptorily dismisses him from court : " Worcester, get thee gone ; for I do see Danger and disobedience in thine eye " : for your " presence is too bold and peremptory," adding " when we need Your use and counsel, we shall send for you." Turning to Northumberland, Henry asks for an explanation of his son's refusal to surrender the prisoners captured by him at Holmedon, to which Northumberland replies that the prisoners were not refused with that " strength " it had been reported to him, which statement is confirmed by Hotspur : " I did deny no prisoners," adding, that after the fight was over he was leaning on his sword " breathless and faint," when a " certain lord, neat and trimly dress'd, Fresh as a bridegroom ; and his chin new reap'd Show'd like a stubble-land at harvest-home ; . . . perfumed like a milliner, And 'twixt his finger and his thumb he held A pouncet-box, which ever and anon He gave his nose and took 't away again " ; approached him. Smiling and chattering, this fellow " as the soldiers bore dead bodies by," " called them untaught knaves, unmannerly, To bring a slovenly un-handsome corse Betwixt the wind and his nobility." In this affected manner, continues Hotspur, he questioned me and demanded " My prisoners in your majesty's behalf," but " smarting with my wounds being cold," and so angry at being " pestered with a popinjay, I answer'd neglectingly I know not what," . . . for he made me mad, " talking like a waiting-gentlewoman of guns and drums and wounds,"—Therefore my liege " I beseech you," not to let his report be considered as " an accusation Betwixt my love and your high majesty." But, pleads Sir Walter Blunt under such circumstances, and at " such a time and place " hasty words " may reasonably die " and be overlooked if only Hotspur is ready to recall his words :

> Whate'er Lord Harry Percy then had said
> To such a person and in such a place,
> At such a time, with all the rest re-told,
> May reasonably die and never rise
> To do him wrong, or any way impeach
> What then he said, so he unsay it now.

but Henry, in angry tones, replies that Hotspur refuses to surrender the prisoners, except on condition that Mortimer—Hotspur's brother-in-law—now a prisoner in Glendower's hands, be ransomed :

> Why, yet he doth deny his prisoners,
> But with proviso and exception,
> That we at our own charge shall ransom straight
> His brother-in-law, the foolish Mortimer ;

Henry denounces Mortimer as a traitor, only fit to starve on the mountains :

> Shall our coffers, then,
> Be emptied to redeem a traitor home ?
> Shall we buy treason ?
> .　　　.　　　.　　　.
> No, on the barren mountains let him starve ;

declaring, that any one who asks for one penny to ransom home revolted Mortimer is no friend of his.　Hearing Mortimer denounced as a traitor, Hotspur in anger exclaims : " Revolted Mortimer !　He never did fall off, my sovereign liege," and goes on to describe how bravely Mortimer fought with Glendower on the " gentle Severn's sedgy band, In single opposition, hand to hand," but Henry replies that Mortimer never did fight with Glendower :

> Thou dost belie him, Percy, thou dost belie him ;
> He never did encounter with Glendower :

declaring that he had " wilfully betray'd the lives of those that he did lead to fight " if the news was true that he had married the daughter of Glendower, that " damn'd magician " :　and addressing Hotspur as " sirrah " declares he will not hear him speak again of Mortimer, at the same time ordering him to send the Scottish prisoners to London speedily, or he shall hear of it, in " such a kind from me As will displease you " :

> Let me not hear you speak of Mortimer :
> Send me your prisoners with the speediest means,
> Or you shall hear in such a kind from me
> As will displease you.

Giving Northumberland and his son leave to depart, and with the words " Send us your prisoners, or you will hear of it," the king leaves the room.　The king having gone, Hotspur in a rage vows he will not surrender the prisoners :

> An if the devil come and roar for them,
> I will not send them :

and declaring he will " ease his heart " at the risk of losing his head, would have followed the king and told him so to his face, but is restrained from so-doing by his father, who exclaims : " What, drunk with choler ?　stay and pause a while " :　just as Worcester—Hotspur's uncle—enters.　" Speak of Mortimer ! " repeats Hotspur in angry tones, " 'Zounds, I will speak of him," asserting that he will shed every drop of his blood to raise " down-trod Mortimer As high in the air as this unthankful king, As this ingrate and canker'd Bolingbroke."　Turning to Worcester, Northumberland remarks : " Brother, the king hath made your nephew mad," but on learning that the king refuses to ransom Mortimer, Worcester replies that he cannot blame him, for was not Mortimer true heir to the crown, being next of blood to Richard : " for was not Mortimer proclaimed by Richard before setting forth on his Irish expedition."　" Did King Richard then Proclaim my brother Edmund Mortimer Heir to the crown ? " asks Hotspur, and Northumberland replies : " He did ; myself did hear it," to which Hotspur observes : " Nay, then I cannot blame his cousin king, That wish'd him on the barren mountains starve," and turning to Northumberland and Worcester indignantly asks whether they will allow themselves to be treated with contempt by the man whom they have placed on the throne.　But Worcester tells him to be quiet, and under secrecy reveals to him a scheme " full of peril and adventurous spirit," as walking over a " current roaring loud On the unsteadfast footing of a spear."　" If he fall in, good night ! " observes Hotspur, who longs for

" perilous adventure," but Worcester turns the conversation by asking : " Those same noble Scots That are your prisoners,"—and Hotspur swears " By God," he will not surrender one single Scot, not " if a Scot would save his soul," because the king " would not ransom Mortimer," forbad him even to speak of Mortimer, and continues : " I'll have a starling shall be taught to speak Nothing but ' Mortimer ' and give it him, To keep his anger still in motion." Hotspur becomes so excited that Worcester attempts to leave the room, saying :

> Farewell, kinsman : I'll talk to you
> When you are better temper'd to attend.

to which Northumberland adds :

> Why, what a wasp-stung and impatient fool
> Art thou to break into this woman's mood,
> Trying thine ear to no tongue but thine own !

This calms Hotspur a little, who replies that he is " whipp'd and scourged with rods, Nettled, and stung with pismires, when I hear Of this vile politician, Bolingbroke," but breaks out again when he remembers the homage he first paid to " this king of smiles, this Bolingbroke " before Berkeley castle. Reverting again to the Scottish prisoners, Worcester unfolds his plot, that they shall set free without ransom all the prisoners, and form an alliance with the Douglas against Henry :

> Thence once more to your Scottish prisoners.
> Deliver them up without their ransom straight,
> And make the Douglas' son your only mean
> For powers in Scotland ;

and that Northumberland shall solicit the aid of the powerful Archbishop of York —Richard Scroop—who " bears hard his brother's death, the Earl of Wiltshire, whom Bolingbroke caused to be put to death at Bristol :

> You, my lord,
> Your son in Scotland being thus employ'd
> Shall secretly into the bosom creep
> Of that same noble prelate, well beloved,
> The archbishop.

Hotspur then suggests that when the scheme has matured, the two forces shall unite with Glendower and Mortimer, a plan which Worcester himself undertakes to arrange when the time is ripe :

> When time is ripe, which will be suddenly,
> I'll steal to Glendower and Lord Mortimer ;
> Where you and Douglas and our powers at once,
> As I will fashion it, shall happily meet,
> To bear our fortunes in our own strong arms,
> Which now we hold at much uncertainty.

to which Hotspur excitedly, exclaims :

> O, let the hours be short
> Till fields and blows and groans applaud our sport !

Cf. *Extract 2* from Holinshed.

The second Act opens in an Inn Yard at Rochester.   It is early morn, and the carriers with lanterns enter to make preparations to set out for London :

> *First Car.*   Heigh-ho ! an it be not four by the day, I'll be
> hanged : Charles' wain is over the new chimney, and
> yet our horse not packed.   What, ostler !
> *Ost.*   [Within.]   Anon, anon.
> *First Car.*   I prithee, Tom, beat Cut's saddle, put a few
> flocks in the point ; poor jade, is wrung in the withers
> out of all cess.

A second carrier enters, who complains that the horses' food is so wet that it is likely to give the " poor jades the bots," and describes the Inn as the " most villainous house in all London road for fleas," for " I am stung like a tench," to which the first carrier adds that there never was a Christian king who was more severely bitten than he had been since the " first cock."

Gadshill—one of the highwaymen—enters, and endeavours to borrow a lantern :

> *Gads.*   I prithee, lend me thy lantern, to see my gelding
> in the stable.
> *First Car.*   Nay, by God, soft ; I know a trick worth two
> of that, i' faith.
> *Gads.*   I pray thee, lend me thine.
> *Sec. Car.*   Ay, when ? can't tell ?   Lend me thy lantern,
> quoth he !   marry, I'll see thee hanged first.

His request being unsuccessful, Gadshill next enquires the time they intend setting out for London, only to receive the answer : " Time enough to go to bed with a candle, I warrant thee.   Come, neighbour Mugs, we 'll call up the gentlemen : they will along with company, for they have great charge," and the carriers forthwith hasten away to rouse the merchants and pilgrims who wish to travel by the coach. A chamberlain of the inn now enters, who confides to Gadshill the amount of money in the possession of one of the travellers : " there 's a franklin in the wild of Kent hath brought three hundred marks with him in gold : I heard him tell it to one of his company last night at supper ; a kind of auditor ; one that hath abundance of charge too, God knows what.   They are up already, and call for eggs and butter : they will away presently," to which Gadshill observes that he will be surprised if they do not meet with " Saint Nicholas' clerks."   The chamberlain warns Gadshill to beware of the hangman, and Gadshill facetiously tells him that " if I hang, I 'll make a fat pair of gallows ; for if I hang, old Sir John hangs with me, and thou knowest he is no starveling," and reminds the chamberlain that his company is not composed of " foot land-rakers," " long-staff sixpenny strikers," and " mad mustachio purple-hued malt-worms " ; but of " nobility and tranquility, burgomasters and great oneyers," who will " strike sooner than speak, and speak sooner than drink, and drink sooner than pray," adding, " We steal as in a castle, cock-sure ; we have the receipt of fern-seed, we walk invisible," a statement which the chamberlain questions : " I think you are more beholding to the night than to fern-seed for your walking invisible."   Promising the chamberlain a " share of the spoils " Gadshill bids the ostler bring his horse, and bidding his informer : " Farewell, you muddy knave," forthwith departs.

A Highway near Gadshill supplies the next scene.   The Prince and Poins arrive at the spot, and taking advantage of the darkness, Poins untethers Falstaff's horse, and fastens it a little farther down the road : " I have removed Falstaff's horse, and he frets like a gummed velvet."   Falstaff enters, and enquiring for Poins is told by the Prince that he has " walked up to the top of the hill " : adding, " I 'll go seek him."

The Prince having departed, Falstaff resents the removal of his horse : " the rascal hath removed my horse, and tied him I know not where," declaring that although he has vowed many times to rid himself of Poins, he is still " bewitched with his company : " " I have forsworn his company hourly any time this two and twenty years, and yet I am bewitched with the rogue's company," for " Eight yards of uneven ground is threescore and ten miles afoot with me ; and the stony-hearted villains know it well enough : a plague upon it when thieves cannot be true one to another ! " At this point the Prince and Poins whistle from their hiding-place behind the hedge, and Falstaff remarks : " Whew ! A plague upon you all ! Give me my horse, you rogues ; give me my horse, and be hanged ! " asserting that " when a jest is so forward, and afoot too ! I hate it." " Lie down," commands the Prince, and lay thine ear close to the ground and listen if thou canst hear the travellers approaching, and Falstaff asks him if he has got a lever to lift him up again, adding : " Good Prince Hal, help me to my horse, good king's son." " Out, ye rogue ! shall I be your ostler ? " sternly replies the Prince, and Falstaff retorts by telling him to go and hang himself in his " own heir-apparent garters."

Gadshill, Bardolph, and Peto now enter : " On with your vizards," exclaims Bardolph, " there's money of the king's coming down the hill ; 'tis going to the king's exchequer," to which Falstaff rejoins : " You lie, you rogue ; 'tis going to the king's tavern " ; and after they have disguised themselves each proceed to their positions as arranged. Gadshill, Bardolph, Peto and Falstaff are to waylay the travellers in the narrow lane, and the Prince and Poins are to hide a little farther down the road and pounce upon any who may escape. [This is contrary to Poins' scheme as outlined in I. ii. 159–165.] The travellers appear, and on the suggestion of one of them, dismount, while the horses are led down the steep hill : " Come, neighbour : the boy shall lead our horses down the hill ; we 'll walk afoot awhile, and ease our legs." Immediately, the highwaymen spring from behind the thicket, and call upon the travellers to stand and deliver : " Strike ; down with them ; cut the villains' throats : ah ! whoreson caterpillars ! bacon-fed knaves ! they hate us youth : down with them ; fleece them," exclaims Falstaff. Their victims cry : " we are undone," and as they are quickly bound and robbed, Falstaff in his usual vivacious manner cries out : " Hang ye, gorbellied knaves, are ye undone ? No, ye fat chuffs ; I would your store were here ! On, bacons, on ! What, ye knaves : young men must live. You are grandjurors, are ye ? we 'll jure ye, 'faith." Having robbed and bound the travellers, the thieves disappear in the darkness, and the Prince and Poins, disguised, re-enter, the former remarking : " The thieves have bound the true men. Now could thou and I rob the thieves and go merrily to London, it would be argument for a week, laughter for a month and a good jest for ever " ; but " Stand close " ; observes Poins, " I hear them coming," and the four thieves return and seat themselves by the roadside to divide the spoil : " Come, my masters, let us share and then to horse before day," and at the same time Falstaff calls the Prince and Poins cowards : " An the Prince and Poins be not two arrant cowards, there 's no equity stirring : there 's no more valour in that Poins than in a wild-duck." They are in the act of sharing the spoil when the Prince and Poins rush out from the thicket. " Your money," shouts the Prince, to which Poins adds : " Villains ! " Being taken by surprise, Falstaff and his companions scramble to their feet and scuttle away, leaving the booty scattered on the ground : " The thieves are all scatter'd and possess'd with fear So strongly that they dare not meet each other " ; as " Each takes his fellow for an officer " exclaims the Prince, adding that " Falstaff sweats to death, And lards the earth as he walks along " ; to which Poins adds : " How the rogue roar'd ! "

The next scene is Warkworth Castle. It opens with Hotspur reading a letter—in dramatic fashion—which warns him that considering the opposition he is likely to encounter, the course he is pursuing is dangerous and the friends he is counting upon for support are very uncertain : " The purpose you undertake is dangerous ; the friends you have named uncertain ; the time itself unsorted ; and your whole plot too light for the counterpoise of so great an opposition." Hotspur, who considers his plot " is a good plot as ever was laid," and his " friends true and constant," as they include Mortimer, the Archbishop of York, Glendower and the Douglas, breaks out into a passion, and describes the writer of the letter as a " frosty-spirited rogue," and threatens if he had " hold of the rascal " to dash out his brains with his " lady's fan." Lady Percy enters, and he informs her that he will be leaving her in two hours' time. To this his wife remarks that for some time past he has had the semblance of being troubled in mind, and in his sleep has cried : " Courage ! to the field ! " and talked of " sallies and retires, of trenches, tents, Of palisadoes, frontiers, parapets, Of basilisks, of cannon, culverin, Of prisoners' ransom, and of soldiers slain, And all the currents of a heady fight." She asks what is the meaning of it all : " O, what portents are these ? Some heavy business hath my lord in hand, And I must know it, else he loves me not." " What, ho ! " exclaims Hotspur, just as a servant enters, whom he asks if his groom has " brought those horses from the sheriff ? "

Hot.	Hath Butler brought those horses from the sheriff ?
Serv.	One horse, my lord, he brought even now,
Hot.	What horse ? a roan, a crop-ear, is it not ?

and uttering his famous battle-cry " O esperance ! " the motto of the House of Percy, declares that " That roan shall be his throne." The servant gone, his wife asks for what purpose he must go, saying that she will know his business, and at the same time hinting that she is aware of the matter he has in hand :

> In faith,
> I'll know your business, Harry, that I will.
> I fear my brother Mortimer doth stir
> About his title, and hath sent for you
> To line his enterprise :

holding him by his little finger which she threatens to break, if he will not " tell her all things true." Hotspur, however, refuses to take his wife into his confidence, and tells her he does not love her : " Away, you trifler ! Love ! I love thee not, I care not for thee, Kate : this is no world To play with mammets and to tilt with lips " : " Do you not love me ? do you not, indeed ? Well, do not then ; for since you love me not, I will not love myself. Do you not love me ? Nay, tell me if you speak in jest or no," asks Lady Percy, and Hotspur replies that when he is on horseback he will swear to love her infinitely, at the same time she must not question him as to the enterprise he has in hand, assuring her " she will not utter that which she does not know " ; adding that she is to follow him on the morrow :

> But hark you, Kate :
> Whither I go, thither shall you go too ;
> To-day will I set forth, to-morrow you.
> Will this content you, Kate ?

to which she replies " It must of force." Cf. *Extracts* 3 and 4 from Holinshed.

The fourth scene is enacted at the Boar's-Head Tavern in Eastcheap, whither the Prince and Poins have proceeded directly after putting Falstaff and his companions to flight. It opens with the Prince telling Poins that he has been in the cellar of the tavern amongst " three or fourscore hogsheads " drinking with " three or four loggerheads " where he has " sounded the very base-string of humility," and so intimate has he become with three of the waiters, that he can now " call them all by their christen names, as Tom, Dick, and Francis." The waiters, he explains " take it already upon their salvation," and call him the " king of courtesy," and tell him " flatly that he is no proud Jack, like Falstaff, but a Corinthian, a lad of mettle, a good boy, ... They call drinking deep, dyeing scarlet ; and when you breathe in your watering, they cry ' hem ! ' and bid you play it off. To conclude, I am so good a proficient in one quarter of an hour, that I can drink with any tinker in his own language during my life." Telling Poins that he has " lost much honour " in not being with him " in this action," he hands him a " pennyworth of sugar," which was " clapped into his hand by an under-skinker," adding " Score a pint of bastard in the Half-moon, or so." The Prince then suggests that they pass away the time by amusing themselves at the expense of one of the waiters,—Francis : " But, Ned, to drive away the time till Falstaff come, I prithee, do thou stand in some by-room, while I question my puny drawer to what end he gave me the sugar ; and do thou never leave calling ' Francis,' that his tale to me may be nothing but ' Anon. ' " The result is that a comical scene ensues, for while the Prince holds the waiter in conversation, Poins plays the rôle of an impatient customer, and keeps shouting from the next room " Francis, Francis," to which Francis answers " Anon, anon, sir." The vintner enters, and orders the waiter to attend to the customers : " What, standest thou still, and hearest such a calling ? Look to the guests within," and turning to the Prince, says : " My lord, old Sir John, with half-a-dozen more, are at the door : shall I let them in ? " " Let them alone awhile, and then open the door," replies the Prince, and flinging himself into a chair he and Poins resume their conversation, the Prince entertaining the latter with a description of Hotspur, the hard-working soldier : " I am not yet of Percy's mind, the Hotspur of the north ; he that kills me some six or seven dozen of Scots at a breakfast, washes his hands, and says to his wife ' Fie upon this quiet life ! I want work,' " but " I prithee, call in Falstaff," and the fat knight, accompanied by Gadshill, Bardolph and Peto enter, followed by Francis carrying wine. " Welcome, Jack " : says Poins, " where hast thou been ? " " A plague of all cowards, I say, and a ven- geance too ! marry, and amen ! Give me a cup of sack, boy." . . . " You rogue, here's lime in this sack, too : there is nothing but roguery to be found in villanous man " : replies Falstaff, adding in a sentimental manner that " there lives not three good men unhanged in England ; and one of them is fat, and grows old " : Falstaff cannot overlook his supposed desertion by the Prince and Poins, and threatens to drive the Prince " out of his kingdom with a dagger of lath, and drive all his subjects afore him like a flock of wild-geese," and goes on to say that " four of us here have ta'en a thousand pound this day morning," and being asked where it is, replies that it was taken from them by a hundred men. " What, a hundred, man ? " cries the Prince in astonishment, and Falstaff goes on to describe in a boastful manner how valiantly he fought with a dozen rogues for two hours : " I am a rogue, if I were not at half-sword with a dozen of them two hours together. I have 'scaped by miracle. I am eight times thrust through the doublet, four through the hose ; my buckler cut through and through ; my sword hacked like a hand-saw—ecce signum ! I never dealt better since I was a man : all would not do. A plague of all cowards." The Prince appeals to the others to relate their story and all proceed to tell a boastful concocted tale. " We four set upon some dozen—" says Gadshill, " Sixteen at least, my lord," ejaculates Falstaff. " And bound them," adds Gadshill. " No, no, they were not bound," replies Peto, to which Falstaff adds " You rogue, they were bound,

every man of them ; or I am a Jew else, an Ebrew Jew." " As we were sharing,"
continues Gadshill, " some six or seven fresh men set upon us—" to which Falstaff
adds " And unbound the rest, and then come in the other." " What, fought you
with them all ? " exclaims the Prince in astonishment, and Falstaff improving upon
his story says that if he did not fight with fifty he is a bunch of radish, and in the
next breath says that if there were " not fifty-two or three then he is no two-legged
creature," adding " I have peppered two of them ; two I am sure I have paid, two
rogues in buckram suits. I tell thee what, Hal, if I tell thee a lie, spit in my face,
call me horse. Thou knowest my old ward ; here I lay, and thus I bore my point.
Four rogues in buckram let drive at me—" " What, four ? thou saidst but two
even now," enjoins the Prince. " Four, Hal ; I told thee four. These four came
all afront, and mainly thrust at me. I made me no more ado but took all their seven
points in my target, thus," " Seven ? why, there were but four even now," ejaculates
the Prince, to which Falstaff replies " Seven, by these hilts, or I am a villain else."
" Prithee, Let him alone ; we shall have more anon," and Falstaff goes on to enlarge
the number to nine and eventually to eleven, who were followed by three knaves
dressed in Kendal green who let drive at him for owing to the darkness he was unable
to see his own hand. " These lies are like their father that begets them ; gross as
a mountain, open, palpable," replies the Prince for " how couldst thou know these
men in Kendal green, when it was so dark thou couldst not see thy hand ? " and asks
for an explanation. No explanation is forthcoming, and the Prince demands that
his story be heard, and proceeds to give an account of what really happened, that
only himself and Poins had taken part in it, to which Falstaff replies that he knew it
was the Prince, and only ran away because he did not want to kill the heir-apparent
and so became " a coward by instinct." At this point the Hostess enters and announces " there is a nobleman of the court at door would speak with you · he says
he comes from your father," and the Prince, who does not wish to be disturbed, tells
the hostess to " give him a ' tip ' and send him back again to his mother." Falstaff
volunteers to deliver the message, and leaves the room with the words " I 'll send
him packing." During Falstaff's absence, Bardolph acknowledges that he ran away
when he saw the others run, and Peto relates how Falstaff had hacked his own sword
with his dagger, and " persuaded them to do the like," to which Bardolph adds :
" Yea, and to tickle their noses with spear-grass to make them bleed," and to
" beslubber their garments with the blood," to make believe it was done in the fight.
They are chuckling over the story, when Falstaff re-enters, and is greeted by the
Prince with : " Here comes lean Jack, here comes bare-bone. How now, my sweet
creature of bombast ! How long is 't ago, Jack, since thou sawest thine own knee ? "
in ridicule of Falstaff's stoutness, to which Falstaff replies : " when I was about thy
years, Hal, I was not an eagle's talon in the waist ; I could have crept into any
alderman's thumb-ring : a plague of sighing and grief ! it blows a man up like a
bladder." But, adds Falstaff, " There's villanous news abroad " : the " messenger
was Sir John Bracy, sent by your father ; you must to the court in the morning,"
for that " mad fellow of the North, Percy, and Glendower of Wales, that gave Amamon
the bastinado, and made Lucifer cuckold, and swore the devil his true liegeman upon
the cross of a Welsh hook—, his son-in-law Mortimer, old Northumberland, and the
Douglas, that runs o' horseback up a hill perpendicular," and " who afoot will not
budge a foot—" " Yes, Jack, upon instinct," ejaculates the Prince. " I grant ye,
upon instinct," replies Falstaff, and " he is there too, and one Mordake, and a thousand
blue-caps more ; Worcester is stolen away to-night ; thy father's beard is turned
white with the news : you may buy land now as cheap as stinking mackerel," adding :
" art thou not horribly afraid ? " to which the Prince retorts : " Not a whit, i' faith ;

I lack some of thy instinct." Falstaff warns the Prince that his father intends giving him a severe reprimand, and implores him to prepare his answers, volunteering to represent the king : " Well, thou wilt be horribly chid to-morrow when thou comest to thy father : if thou love me, practice an answer." Although the news brought by the king's messenger of the rising in the North is very serious, the Prince cannot resist the temptation of setting Falstaff in a chair as monarch, and a burlesque scene is enacted, in which Falstaff, after drinking a cup of sack, chastises the Prince for leading such a dissipated life, finally warning him against all his inordinate com-panions, except one, " a virtuous man, . . . but I know not his name, . . . A goodly portly man, i' faith, and a corpulent ; of cheerful look, a pleasing eye, and a most noble carriage ; and, as I think, his age some fifty, or, by 'r lady, including to three score ; and now I remember me, his name is Falstaff." They then change places and the Prince gives Falstaff a sound rating, calling him " That villanous abominable misleader of youth, Falstaff, that old white-bearded Satan," and Falstaff advises the Prince to " banish Peto, banish Bardolph, banish Poins," but " banish not old Jack Falstaff from thy Harry's company : banish plump Jack, and banish all the world." As the fun is at its height, a knock is heard at the door, and the Hostess, in an agitated manner enters, exclaiming : " O Jesu, my lord, my lord !—" Heigh, heigh ! the devil rides upon a fiddlestick : what 's the matter ? " asks the Prince, to which she replies : " The sheriff and all the watch are at the door : they are come to search the house." Falstaff is thrust behind the arras to evade the sheriff, who enters accompanied by the robbed carrier : " Now, master sheriff, what is your will with me ? " asks the Prince, to which the sheriff replies : " A hue and cry Hath follow'd certain men unto this house. One of them is well known, my gracious lord, A gross fat man," to which the carrier adds : " As fat as butter." The Prince, knowing to whom the sheriff refers, answers that the man they seek is not there, adding that he himself will be responsible for his appearance on the morrow, and when the sheriff remarks : " There are two gentlemen Have in this robbery lost three hundred marks," the Prince again assures him that he will hold himself respon-sible, and bidding the Prince " Good night, my noble lord," the sheriff leaves the room. The sheriff gone, the Prince remarks : " This oily rascal is known as well as Paul's. Go, call him forth," and the arras being pulled aside, Falstaff is dis-covered asleep and snoring loudly : " Falstaff !—Fast asleep beside the arras, and snorting like a horse." " Search his pockets," whispers the Prince, and on doing so, no money, only papers are found, among which is a tavern-bill for a large quantity of drink, and only for one half-penny worth of bread :

Item, A capon,	2	2
Item, Sauce,	0	4
Item, Sack, two gallons,	5	8
Item, Anchovies and sack		
after supper,	2	6
Item, Bread,	ob.	

Describing the thing as " monstrous " the Prince declares he will to the wars, and procure " this fat rogue a charge of foot," and adding that the money which was stolen shall be paid back with interest, bids Peto " good morrow " and departs.

The third Act opens at the Archdeacon's house at Bangor, where we find Hotspur, Worcester, Mortimer and Glendower—who have formed an alliance against the king—in secret conclave, the primary object of the meeting being the division of the kingdom

into three parts after they have met and defeated the king. So far everything has
been a success :

> *Mort.*   These promises are fair, the parties sure,
>   And our induction full of prosperous hope.

Addressing Mortimer, Glendower and Worcester, Hotspur bids them to be seated,
adding : " a plague upon it ! I have forgot the map." " No, here it is," observes
Glendower, " Sit, cousin Percy ; sit, good cousin Hotspur, For by that name as oft
as Lancaster Doth speak of you, his cheek looks pale, and with A rising sigh he wisheth
you in heaven." " And you in hell, as oft as he hears Owen Glendower spoke of,"
replies Hotspur. " I cannot blame him," retorts Glendower, for " at my nativity
The front of heaven was full of fiery shapes, Of burning cressets ; and at my birth
The frame and huge foundation of the earth Shaked like a coward," but Hotspur
contemptuously declares it would have been the same " if his mother's cat had but
kittened, though himself had never been born." " I say," repeats Glendower excitedly, " the earth did shake when I was born." " Then the earth was not of my
mind if it shook for fear of you," responds Hotspur. " The heavens were all on fire,
the earth did tremble," puts in Glendower, to which Hotspur retorts that the " earth
shook to see the heavens on fire and not in fear of his nativity," adding that " diseased
nature oftentimes breaks forth in strange eruptions." Glendower remarks that he
does not allow many men to address him in that fashion : " Cousin, of many men I
do not bear these crossings," and again repeats the miraculous happenings at his
birth, for " all the courses of his life did show that he was not in the roll of common
men," claiming further that he can call up spirits from the mystic deep. " So can I,
or so can any man ; But will they come when you do call for them ? " jeers Hotspur.
Telling Hotspur that he can teach him how to " command the devil," to which
Hotspur replies that he can " teach Glendower how to shame the devil by speaking
the truth," the argument, which threatens to develop into a quarrel is cut short by
Mortimer remarking :

> Come, come, no more of this unprofitable chat.

Glendower reminds Hotspur that Bolingbroke has thrice advanced a power against
him, and thrice he has sent him " Bootless home and weather-beaten back." " Home
without boots, and in foul weather too ! " retorts Hotspur, how, in the " devil's
name, does he 'scape the ague ? " and Glendower, seeing Hotspur's obstinacy picks
up a map of England, and invites the latter to " divide our right According to our
threefold order ta'en." But Mortimer reminds them that the Archdeacon of Bangor
has already divided the realm into " three limits very equally." To the Mortimers,
as successors to the crown, the whole of England south of the river Trent, and east
of the river Severn :

> England, from Trent and Severn hitherto,
> By south and east is to my part assign'd :

Glendower is to have his native Wales :

> All westward, Wales beyond the Severn shore,
> And all the fertile land within that bound,
> To Owen Glendower :

and to the Percys is assigned all the territory north of the river Trent to the Scottish
border :

> and, dear coz, to you
> The remnant northward, lying off from Trent.

adding, that the " indentures tripartite are drawn " and that on the morrow all their forces—with the exception of Glendower's, who is not yet ready, and whose help they will not need for at least a fortnight—will proceed towards Shrewsbury and unite with Northumberland and the Scottish power. As they are about to part, Hotspur, who is in a disagreeable mood, asserts that he has been allotted the smallest of the three divisions of the kingdom :

> Methinks my moiety, north of Burton here,
> In quantity equals not one of yours :

for the river, owing to its winding, cuts off a large slice of the more fertile land :

> See how this river comes me cranking in,
> And cuts me from the best of all my land
> A huge half-moon, a monstrous cantle out,

and declares that he will have the river diverted so as to run straight : " I 'll have the current in this place damn'd up : And here the smug and silver Trent shall run In a new channel, fair and evenly ; It shall not wind with such a deep indent, To rob me of so rich a bottom here." " Not wind ? " replies Glendower, " it shall, it must ; you see it doth." Mortimer shows another bend of the river which equalises what the first bend takes from Hotspur, while Worcester on the other hand remarks that but a little cost will cut the channel straight and meet Hotspur's claim. Glendower will not however hear of the river being diverted. " Who shall say me nay ? " demands Hotspur. " Why, that will I," retorts Glendower. " Let me not understand you, then ; speak it in Welsh, replies Hotspur in an excited manner, and Glendower tells Hotspur he can speak English as well as he can, having been " train'd up in the English court ; Where, being but young, he framed to the harp Many an English ditty lovely well, And gave the tongue a helpful ornament, A virtue that was never seen in him." " Marry, I am glad of it with all my heart," retorts Hotspur, adding that he would " rather be a kitten and cry mew Than one of these same metre ballad-mongers," for there was nothing in the world as set his teeth on edge as mincing poetry. Seeing Hotspur intractable, Glendower, in the interests of peace, yields to Hotspur's demands : " Come, you shall have Trent turn'd," to which Hotspur replies that he does not care, for he is willing to give thrice as much land to any well-deserving friend, but in the way of bargaining he is prepared to dispute to the " ninth part of a hair," adding : " Are the indentures drawn ? shall we be gone ? " and Glendower replies : " The moon shines fair ; you may away by night " : and promising to hurry up the scrivener who is drawing up the indentures, and to inform their wives that they are departing, forthwith leaves the room. Glendower having gone, Mortimer remonstrates with Hotspur for " crossing his father " but the latter replies he cannot help it, for " he is tedious As a tired horse, a railing wife : Worse than a smoky house : I had rather live With cheese and garlic in a windmill, far, Than feed on cates and have him talk to me In any summer-house in Christendom." " But," replies Mortimer," he is a worthy gentleman, Exceedingly well read, and profited In strange concealments ; valiant as a lion, And wondrous affable, and as bountiful As mines of India," and one who " holds your temper in a high respect," and here the discussion is cut short by the entrance of their wives escorted by Glendower. Strangely enough Mortimer cannot speak Welsh, and his wife—Glendower's daughter—cannot speak English :

> This is a deadly spite that angers me ;
> My wife can speak no English, I no Welsh,

so Glendower is called upon to act as interpreter. After a little amorous dallying between Mortimer and his wife, she invites her husband to lie down on the grass and put his head upon her lap while she sings him to sleep :

> Glen.   She bids you on the wanton rushes lay you down
> And rest your gentle head upon her lap,
> And she will sing the song that pleaseth you,
> And on your eyelids crown the god of sleep,

to which Mortimer replies : " With all my heart I 'll sit and hear her sing."   Their attitude proves highly amusing to Hotspur, who invites his wife to do likewise :

> Come, Kate, thou art perfect in laying down : come,
> quick, quick, that I may lay my head in thy lap,

to which Lady Percy replies : " Go, ye giddy goose."

The music plays, and after listening to the lady sing a Welsh song, Hotspur invites his wife to sing also, but Lady Percy refuses.   " 'Tis the next way to turn tailor, or be red-breast teacher," rejoins Hotspur, adding that as the " indentures are drawn," he will away within two hours' time, and forthwith takes his departure. Turning to Mortimer, Glendower tells him that he is as slow as " hot Lord Percy is on fire to go," and bidding him " to horse immediately," Mortimer too takes his leave.   Cf. *Extract* 5 from Holinshed.

The King's Palace in London supplies the next scene.   The King dismisses the lords as he wishes to have a private audience with his son :

> Lords, give us leave ; the Prince of Wales and I
> Must have some private conference : but be near at hand,
> For we shall presently have need of you.

When they are alone, the king, remembering his usurpation of the crown, is inclined to look upon the Prince's remissness as the " hot vengeance and the rod of heaven " to punish him for his past misdeeds :

> I know whether God will have it so,
> For some displeasing service I have done,
> That, in his secret doom, out of my blood
> He'll breed revengement and a scourge for me ;
> But thou dost in thy passages of life
> Make me believe that thou art only mark'd
> For the hot vengeance and the rod of heaven,
> To punish my mistreadings.

Gravely reproving his son for his " inordinate and low desires " and the " rude society " he frequents, which brings in its train such " mean attempts and barren pleasures " he reminds him of his princely position, and the responsibilities it carries with it :

> Tell me else,
> Could such inordinate and low desires,
> Such poor, such bare, such lewd, such mean attempts,
> Such barren pleasures, rude society,
> As thou art match'd withal and grafted to,
> Accompany the greatness of thy blood,
> And hold their level with thy princely heart ?

The Prince, although he refutes many of the charges brought to the king by

" smiling pick-thanks and base newsmongers " humbly accepts his father's reproof, and craves pardon for his remissness :

> So please your majesty, I would I could
> Quit all offences with as clear excuse
> As well as I am doubtless I can purge
> Myself of many I am charged withal :
> .　　.　　.　　.　　.　　.
> I may, for some things true, wherein my youth
> Hath faulty wander'd and irregular,
> Find pardon on my true submission.

" God pardon thee ! " replies his father, and then tells him his younger brother— Clarence—has taken his place on the Council :

> Thy place in council thou hast rudely lost,
> Which by thy younger brother is supplied,

and begs of him to try to win the good-will of the people, in like manner as he— Henry—did, when he was acclaimed with loud shouts and salutations by the people of London even in the presence of Richard.   The Prince promises amends : " I shall hereafter, my thrice gracious lord, Be more myself," and the King then draws his attention to the fact that the positions he (the prince) and Hotspur occupy are similar to those once held by Richard and himself :

> For all the world
> As thou art to this hour was Richard then
> When I from France set foot at Ravenspurgh,
> And even as I was then is Percy now.

The King, greatly moved, proceeds to remind his son that his crown may be disputed by Hotspur who had already gathered around him powerful forces :

> And what say you to this ?   Percy, Northumberland,
> The Archbishop's grace of York, Douglas, Mortimer,
> Capitulate against us and are up,

adding :

> Thou that art like enough, through vassal fear,
> Base inclination and the start of spleen,
> To fight against me under Percy's pay,
> To dog his heels and curtsy at his frowns,
> To show how much thou art degenerate.

" Do not think so ; you shall not find it so " ; is the Prince's passionate rejoinder, and " God forgive them that so much have sway'd Your majesty's good thoughts away from me ! " and being much roused at his father's earnest admonition again promises to redeem his past : " for the time will come, That I shall make this northern youth exchange His glorious deeds for my indignities," and begging his father to overlook his misdeeds, in the " name of God " promises reformation, promising to die a hundred thousand deaths before he will break his vow.   Clasping his son's hand the King remarks : " A hundred thousand rebels die in this : Thou shalt have charge and sovereign trust herein."   This private audience having concluded satisfactorily, Sir William Blunt enters with the news that Douglas and Percy will be at Shrewsbury on the " eleventh of this month."   On receiving these tidings—already five days old— the King gives orders for the Earl of Westmoreland and Lord John of Lancaster to

proceed forthwith to Bridgenorth, promising to meet them with his son—Harry—
at that place " some twelve days hence," and the scene closes with the words :

> Our hands are full of business : let's away ;
> Advantage feeds him fat, while men delay.

Cf. *Extract* 6 from Holinshed.

In the concluding scene of this Act we are again at the Boar's-head Tavern in
Eastcheap. It opens with Falstaff telling Bardolph that he has grown so thin his
skin hangs about him like an old lady's loose gown.   Bardolph considers that Falstaff
is " so fretful he cannot live long," and Falstaff asks him to make him merry by
singing a " bawdy song," to which Bardolph replies that he is so fat he is out of all
due proportion. This is not pleasing to Falstaff, who makes uncomplimentary
comments on Bardolph's red nose : " Do thou amend thy face, and I 'll amend my
life : thou art our admiral, thou bearest the lantern in the poop, but 'tis in the nose
of thee ; thou art the Knight of the Burning Lamp."   A lively passage of words
ensues, which is cut short by the entrance of the hostess, " How now, Dame Partlet
the hen ! have you enquired yet who picked my pocket ? " asks Falstaff, but on the
hostess telling him she does not keep thieves in her house, Falstaff swears his pocket
was picked and tells her to go. " Who, I ? no ; I defy thee : God's light, I was
never called so in mine own house before."   " Go to, I know you well enough,"
exclaims Falstaff, to which the hostess replies : " You do not know me, Sir John, I
know you," and claims the money he owes her for the garments he wears : " I bought
you a dozen of shirts to your back," as well as the money he owes for his board and
drink, and the money she has lent him : " You owe money here besides, Sir John, for
your diet and by-drinkings, and money lent you, four and twenty pound."   Falstaff
in reply asks her if she wants to make a " younker " of him, and whether he cannot
take his ease in her house without having his pocket picked ?   " I have lost a seal-
ring of my grandfather's worth forty mark," but the hostess informs him that the
Prince declared it was only copper, and of no value. Falstaff then describes the
Prince as a " Jack, a sneak-cup," and threatens to " cudgel him like a dog " if he
were present, when Prince Hal enters accompanied by Peto, and Falstaff advances
towards them playing on his truncheon like a fife. On Falstaff complaining that he
was robbed when asleep behind the arras the other night, the Prince insists that he
shall give a detailed account of his lost valuables, after which the Prince confesses
it was he himself who rifled Falstaff's pockets. Hearing this, Falstaff forgives the
hostess : " Hostess, I forgive thee : go, make ready breakfast ; love thy husband,
look to thy servants, cherish thy guests : thou shalt find me tractable to any honest
reason : thou seest I am pacified still. Nay, prithee, be gone."   The Hostess having
departed, Falstaff inquiries how the Gadshill robbery has been settled, to which the
Prince replies that the money taken from the travellers has been paid back, to which
Falstaff observes : " I do not like that paying back ; 'tis a double labour."   The
Prince then informs Falstaff that he and his father are now reconciled, and that he
has obtained for Falstaff " a charge of foot," to which the latter remarks he wishes
it had been one " of horse."   Handing two latters to Bardolph which he bids him
to deliver : " Go bear this letter to Lord John of Lancaster, to my brother John ;
this to my Lord of Westmoreland," the Prince calls for his horse : " Go, Peto, to
horse, to horse ; for thou and I have thirty miles to ride yet ere dinner time," and
after giving Falstaff orders to meet him in the Temple hall on the morrow, where
" thou shalt know thy charge," for " The land is burning ; Percy stands on high ;

And either we or they must lower lie," the Prince departs. " Rare words ! brave world ! Hostess, my breakfast, come ! O, I could wish this tavern were my drum ! " is Falstaff's comment, and he too leaves the scene.

The fourth Act opens in the Rebel Camp near Shrewsbury. All is not well. Hotspur, Worcester and Douglas are in conversation when a messenger enters with a letter from Northumberland, intimating that he is sick and cannot join his son :

> What letters hast thou there ?—I can but thank you.
> *Mess.* These letters come from your father.
> *Hot.* Letters from him ! why comes he not himself ?
> *Mess.* He cannot come, my lord ; he is grievous sick.

This news is very depressing, Hotspur enquiring " how has he the leisure to be sick In such a justling time ? " Worcester describes it as a " main to them," while Hotspur considers it " A perilous gash, a very limb lopp'd off." This news is followed by the entry of Sir Richard Vernon with tidings that the Earl of Westmoreland and Prince John are actually approaching with an armed force, to be followed by more troops under the command of the King :

> *Ver.* Pray God my news be worth a welcome, lord.
> The Earl of Westmoreland, seven thousand strong,
> Is marching hitherwards ; with him Prince John.
> *Hot.* No harm : what more ?
> *Ver.*   And further, I have learn'd,
> The king himself in person is set forth,
> Or hitherwards intended speedily,
> With strong and mighty preparation.

Hotspur next inquires where the Prince of Wales is : " Where is his son, The nimble-footed madcap Prince of Wales, And his comrades, that daff'd the world aside, And bid it pass ? " only to be told by Vernon—who had passed the royal army on his way to Shrewsbury—that the Prince was marching forward clad in all the trappings of war :

> I saw young Harry, with his beaver on,
> His cuisses on his thighs, gallantly arm'd,
> Rise from the ground like feather'd Mercury,
> And vaulted with such ease into his seat,
> As if an angel dropp'd down from the clouds,
> To turn and wind a fiery Pegasus,
> And witch the world with noble horsemanship.

" No more, no more " : interposes Hotspur who considers Vernon's praises of the Prince are " worse than the sun in March," which gives one the " ague," but " Let them come " ; he excitedly exclaims, for I will sacrifice all to the god of war, mentioning the Prince in particular, with whom he is anxious to fight : " They come like sacrifices in their trim, And to the fire-eyed maid of smoky war All hot and bleeding will we offer them : The mailed Mars shall on his altar sit Up to the ears in blood. I am on fire To hear this rich reprisal is so nigh And yet not ours. Come, let me taste my horse, Who is to bear me like a thunderbolt Against the bosom of the Prince of Wales : Harry to Harry shall, hot horse to horse, Meet and ne'er part till one drop down a corse." These fiery words are ended by the remark : " O that Glendower were come ! " but Vernon tells him that the Welshmen cannot join them for at least a fortnight. Douglas declares these are the worst tidings they have yet heard, to which Worcester adds " that it bears a frosty sound." Hotspur next inquires " What

may the king's whole battle reach unto ? " and being told " thirty thousand,"
Hotspur, who is mad for battle, replies :

> Forty let it be :
> My father and Glendower being both away,
> The powers of us may serve so great a day.
> Come, let us take a muster speedily :
> Doomsday is near ; die all, die merrily.

but Douglas tells him to " Talk not of dying " ; for he himself has lost all fear of
death.   Cf. *Extracts* 7 and 8 from Holinshed.

The next scene is a public road near Coventry.   Falstaff orders Bardolph to press
on before him and get him a bottle of sack : " Bardolph, get thee before to Coventry ;
fill me a bottle of sack : " while he trudges forward with his men consisting of rogues
and vagabonds, and " ne'er-do-wells " whom he has pressed into the king's service.
He has sadly misused the king's licence having made huge sums of money by letting
off those who could afford to pay in lieu of service : " I have misused the king's press
damnably.   I have got, in exchange of a hundred and fifty soldiers, three hundred
and odd pounds," in consequence of which his army consists of " slaves as ragged as
Lazarus in the painted cloth, where the glutton's dogs licked his sores ; . . .   cankers
of a calm world and a long peace, ten times more dishonourable ragged than an old-
faced ancient : and such have I, to fill up the rooms of them that have bought out
their services, that you would think I had a hundred and fifty tottered prodigals
lately come from swine-keeping, from eating draff and husks," and so ashamed is he
of them that he will not march them through the streets of Coventry : " I'll not
march through Coventry with them, that's flat " : for " There's not a shirt and a
half in all my company ; . . .   but that's all one ; " they'll find linen enough on
every hedge."   He is overtaken by the Prince and Westmoreland, the former greeting
him as " blown Jack."   Both leaders are highly amused at Falstaff's ragged men,
the Prince remarking : " Jack, whose fellows are these that come after ? I did never
see such pitiful rascals."   " Tut, tut " ; replies Falstaff, " good enough to toss ;
food for powder, food for powder ; they'll fill a pit as well as better : tush, man,
mortal men, mortal men."
    The scene concludes with the Prince telling Falstaff to " make haste " as " Percy
is already in the field," and Falstaff remarks that it is better for a dull fighter with
a keen appetite to reach the battle-field when the fighting is nearly over, and the
feast is about to begin :

> Well,
> To the latter end of the fray and the beginning of a
>   feast
> Fits a dull fighter and a keen guest.

We return to the Rebel Camp near Shrewsbury in the next scene.   It opens with
Hotspur discussing with the other leaders the prospect of engaging the king's forces.
There is a difference of opinion in this respect.   Hotspur is in favour of fighting the
same day : " We'll fight with him to-night," in which he is supported by Douglas.
Worcester and Vernon, however, counsel delay until they are reinforced, and are
charged by Douglas with being afraid.   Vernon indignantly denies that he is afraid,
and expresses astonishment that " men of such great leading as they are, That they
foresee not what impediments Drag back our expedition " : and urges upon them
not to fight until their forces have been augmented, as the troops under the king

greatly exceed their army in number.   At this juncture a trumpet sounds a parley, and Sir Walter Blunt enters :

> I come with gracious offers from the king,
> If you vouchsafe me hearing and respect.

Hotspur bids him welcome.   Blunt then announces that the king has sent him to inquire why they take up arms against the crown, and bids them to " name their griefs " which will be remedied, and " pardon absolute " if they will only return to their allegiance :

> The king hath sent to know
> The nature of your griefs, and whereupon
> You conjure from the breast of civil peace
> Such bold hostility, teaching his duteous land
> Audacious cruelty.   If that the king
> Have any way your good deserts forgot,
> Which he confesseth to be manifold,
> He bids you name your griefs ; and with all speed
> You shall have your desires with interest,
> And pardon absolute for yourself and these
> Herein misled by your suggestion,

" The king is kind," observes Hotspur, " and well we know the king Knows at what time to promise, when to pay," and then informs Blunt that the king owes his crown to the house of Percy : " My father and my uncle and myself Did give him that same royalty he wears " ;   and that when he landed " Upon the naked shore at Ravenspurgh " he came only to claim his rightful inheritance : " And when he heard him swear and vow to God He came but to be Duke of Lancaster, To sue his livery and beg his peace, With tears of innocency and terms of zeal, My father, in kind heart and pity moved, Swore him assistance and perform'd it too."   " Tut," answers Blunt, " I came not to hear this."   " Then to the point," excitedly exclaims Hotspur and goes on to say that Henry, after deposing Richard, deprived him of his life, and further, by refusing to ransom Mortimer had forced them to take up arms.   But when Blunt asks " Shall I return this answer to the king ? " Hotspur promises to consider the king's offer and to send an answer by his uncle on the morrow :

> *Hot.*   Not so, Sir Walter : we 'll withdraw a while.
>   Go to the king ; and let there be impawn'd
>   Some surety for a safe return again,
>   And in the morning early shall mine uncle
>   Bring him our purposes : and so farewell.
> *Blunt.*   I would you would accept of grace and love.
> *Hot.*   And may be so we shall.
> *Blunt.*   Pray God you do.

Cf. *Extract* 9 from Holinshed.

The last scene of this Act shows us the Archbishop's palace at York.   The archbishop is sceptical as to the success of the enterprise, and writes letters which are to be used to raise reinforcements to assist the conspirators.   Handing them to his friend,—Sir Michael—he charges him to deliver them without delay :

> Hie, good Sir Michael ; bear this sealed brief
> With winged haste to the lord marshal ;
> This to my cousin Scroop, and all the rest
> To whom they are directed.   If you knew
> How much they do import, you would make haste,

and when Sir Michael hints that he can " guess their tenour," the archbishop replies :

" Like enough you do," and orders him to hasten to Shrewsbury, for owing to Northumberland being ill, and Glendower having failed to redeem his promise, the forces at Hotspur's command are too weak to " wage an instant trial with the king." But Sir Michael tells the archbishop that he " need not fear ; There is Douglas and Lord Mortimer," " No, Mortimer is not there," interposes the archbishop. " But there is Mordake, Vernon, Lord Harry Percy, And there is my Lord of Worcester and a head Of gallant warriors, noble gentlemen," adds Sir Michael. " And so there is," rejoins the archbishop, but as the " king hath drawn The special head of all the land together," the royal forces greatly outnumber Hotspur's army. He therefore bids him proceed with haste because if Hotspur is defeated, the king, who has heard that they are implicated in the rebellion, will march with his army to York :

> And, to prevent the worst, Sir Michael, speed :
> For if Lord Percy thrive not, ere the king
> Dismiss his power, he means to visit us,
> For he hath heard of our confederacy,
> And 'tis but wisdom to make strong against him :
> Therefore make haste. I must go write again
> To other friends ; and so farewell, Sir Michael.

The King's Camp near Shrewsbury provides the opening scene of the fifth Act. It opens with the king remarking : " How bloodily the sun begins to peer Above yon busky hill ! the day looks pale At his distemperature," to which the Prince adds that the " southern wind Doth play the trumpet to his purposes, And by his hollow whistling in the leaves Foretells a tempest and a blustering day." A trumpet sounds, and Worcester and Vernon, bringing Hotspur's answer, ride into the royal camp. Henry greets them in a haughty manner, and reproaches Worcester for his unfaithfulness : " How now, my Lord of Worcester ! 'tis not well That you and I should meet upon such terms As now we meet. You have deceived our trust, And made us doff our easy robes of peace, To crush our old limbs in ungentle steel : This is not well, my lord, this is not well. What say you to it ? " Worcester replies that his opposition to the king is not of his own seeking. " You have not sought the day of this dislike ! how comes it, then ? " to which Falstaff enjoins : " Rebellion lay in his way, and he found it." " Peace, chewet, peace ! " demands the Prince, and Worcester goes on to remind Henry of the services the house of Percy have rendered him ; of the oath he swore at Doncaster that he had returned to England to claim nothing more than the title and inheritance of the Dukedom of Lancaster ; and of his promises unfulfilled, adding that since his accession he has by his " dangerous countenance " violated all " faith and troth " :

> It pleased your majesty to turn your looks
> Of favour from myself and all our house ;
> And yet I must remember you, my lord,
> We were the first and dearest of your friends.
> For you my staff of office did I break
> In Richard's time ; and posted day and night
> To meet you on the way, and kiss your hand,
>
> .   .   .   .   .   .
>
> Forgot your oath to us at Doncaster ;
> And being fed by us you used us so
> As that ungentle gull, the cuckoo's bird,
> Useth the sparrow ;
>
> .   .   .   .   .   .
>
> Whereby we stand opposed by such means
> As you yourself have forged against yourself,
> By unkind usage, dangerous countenance,
> And violation of all faith and troth
> Sworn to us in your younger enterprise.

To this Henry rejoins that the grievances which they have " set forth in the articles "
and which they have " Proclaim'd at market crosses, read in churches," are only a
cloak to cover their rebellion :

> These things indeed you have articulate,
> Proclaim'd at market crosses, read in churches,
> To face the garment of rebellion
> With some fine colour that may please the eye
> Of fickle changelings and poor discontents,
> Which gape and rub the elbow at the news
> Of hurlyburly innovation :
> And never yet did insurrection want
> Such water-colours to impaint his cause ;
> Nor moody beggars, starving for a time
> Of pellmell havoc and confusion.

The Prince, standing beside his father enjoins that in the king's, as well as in the
rebels' armies, many a " soul will pay dearly for this encounter, If once they join in
trial," and challenges Hotspur—whom he compliments on his chivalry—to meet him
in a single combat and thus decide the quarrel, to avoid unnecessary bloodshed :

> Tell your nephew,
> The Prince of Wales doth join with all the world
> In praise of Henry Percy :
>
> Yet this before my father's majesty—
> I am content that he shall take the odds
> Of his great name and estimation,
> And will, to save the blood on either side,
> Try fortune with him in a single fight.

The king, having commented on the brave words of the Prince, reiterates his offer
of unconditional pardon :

> Both he and they and you, yea, every man
> Shall be my friend again and I'll be his :
> So tell your cousin, and bring me word
> What he will do : but if he will not yield,
> Rebuke and dread correction wait on us
> And they shall do their office. So, be gone ;
> We will not now be troubled with reply :
> We offer fair ; take it advisedly.

and Worcester and Vernon depart.   After they have gone, the Prince turning to his
father, remarks that the offer will not be accepted, as Hotspur and Douglas are too
confident of their success : " It will not be accepted, on my life : The Douglas and
the Hotspur both together Are confident against the world in arms," and the king
forthwith gives orders for " every leader to his charge," to be in readiness to attack
the rebels if they do not submit.   The king having gone, the Prince and Falstaff
indulge in a few witticisms, and the Prince takes his departure, after reminding
Falstaff that he " owes God a death."   Left alone, Falstaff soliloquises on the word
" honour," describing it as a " mere word," and a " trim reckoning," but as he is
" loath to die before his time " : " 'Tis not due yet ; I would be loath to pay God
before his day," he will have " none of it.   Honour is a mere scutcheon : and so ends
my catechism."   Cf *Extract* 10 from Holinshed.

We return to the Rebel Camp in the second scene.   Addressing Vernon, Worcester tells him that Hotspur must not be told of Henry's unconditional offer of
pardon : " O, no, my nephew must not know, Sir Richard, The liberal and kind offer

of the king." Vernon considers it is better he did know, but Worcester retorts : " Then are we all undone," as the king is not to be trusted, adding that Hotspur may be forgiven on account of his youth and passionate temperament, while on the other hand they would always be under suspicion :

> My nephew's trespass may be well forgot ;
> It hath the excuse of youth and heat of blood,
> .   .   .   .   .   .
> All his offences live upon my head
> And on his father's ; we did train him on,
> And, his corruption being ta'en from us,
> We, as the spring of all, shall pay for all.
> Therefore, good cousin, let not Harry know,
> In any case, the offer of the king.

Vernon falls in with this suggestion : " Deliver what you will ; I 'll say 'tis so." At this point Hotspur and Douglas enter and the former asking " Uncle, what news ? " is told by Worcester that the king will " bid you battle presently," In a rage, Douglas, who is anxious to fight, leaves with the intention of dispatching a challenge, and Worcester then informs Hotspur that the king " called them rebels, traitors," and that he intended to " scourge With haughty arms this hateful name in us," which throws Hotspur into such a rage that he has no option but to fight. Douglas re-enters, and announces that he has dispatched his challenge, and calls them to arms : " Arm, gentlemen ; to arms ! for I have thrown A brave defiance in King Henry's teeth." Worcester next tells Hotspur of the Prince's challenge : " The Prince of Wales stepp'd forth before the king, And, nephew, challenged you to single fight," and Hotspur enquires whether the challenge was issued with contempt : " Tell me, tell me, How show'd his tasking ? seem'd it in contempt ? " but is assured by Vernon that the " challenge was urged " in a most " modest " fashion : " No, by my soul ; I never in my life Did hear a challenge urged more modestly," adding that if the Prince lives he will be a man of whom England will be proud : " but let me tell the world, If he outlive the envy of this day, England did never owe so sweet a hope, So much misconstrued in his wantonness." This is not pleasing to Hotspur, who considers that Vernon is " enamoured with the Prince's follies," but before night he will " embrace him with a soldier's arm, That he shall shrink under my courtesy." A messenger enters with letters, but Hotspur declares he cannot read them now. Another messenger enters with the news that the king's troops are advancing : " My lord, prepare ; the king comes on apace." Counselling all to do their best, and uttering his famous war-cry " Esperance ! Percy ! " Hotspur, amid the blowing of trumpets, leads his men forward to the attack :

> Sound all the lofty trumpets of war,
> And by that music let us all embrace ;
> For, heaven to earth, some of us never shall
> A second time do such a courtesy.

Cf. *Extract* 11 from Holinshed.

The third scene, enacted on the Plain between the Camps, is descriptive of the first part of the Battle of Shrewsbury. In order to delude Douglas, who has sworn to fight with none but the king, several knights appear wearing the king's arms on their surcoats. Two of these, Lord Stafford and Sir Walter Blunt, are attacked and slain by Douglas :

Blunt.	What is thy name, that in the battle thus Thou crossest me ? what honour dost thou seek Upon my head ?
Doug.	Know then, my name is Douglas ; And I do haunt thee in the battle thus, Because some tell me that thou art a king.
Blunt.	They tell thee true.
Doug.	The Lord of Stafford dear to-day hath bought Thy likeness ; for instead of thee, King Harry, This sword hath ended him : so shall it thee, Unless thou yield thee as my prisoner.
Blunt.	I was not born a yielder, thou proud Scot ; And thou shalt find a king that will revenge Lord Stafford's death. *[They fight. Douglas kills Blunt.*

At this moment Hotspur enters, and tells Douglas that if he had fought as bravely at Holmedon as he has done in this battle, he [Hotspur] would never have defeated him. Douglas replies that the day is won as the king is slain : " All's done, all's won ; here breathless lies the king," but Hotspur tells him it is none other than Sir Walter Blunt : " This Douglas ? no : I know this face full well : A gallant knight he was, his name was Blunt ; Semblably furnish'd like the king himself," and Douglas finding himself deceived, swears he will piece by piece, cut his way through the king's wardrobe and kill " all the kings on the battlefield." Falstaff enters and seeing the body of Blunt mutters to himself : " Though I could 'scape shot-free at London, I fear the shot here ; here's no scoring but upon the pate. Soft ! who are you ? Sir Walter Blunt ; there's honour for you ! here's no vanity ! I am as hot as molten lead, and as heavy too : God keep lead out of me ! I need no more weight than mine own bowels." Falstaff has lost the greater part of his force in the fight : " I have led my ragamuffins where they are peppered : there's not three of my hundred and fifty left alive." Being hot and tired he is leaning on his sword, when the Prince dashes up. The Prince has lost his sword in the fight, and asks Falstaff for the loan of his : " What, stand'st thou idle here ? lend me thy sword : Many a nobleman lies stark and stiff." Falstaff begins to boast of the brave deeds he has done, having killed Hotspur : " O Hal, I prithee, give me leave to breathe a while. Turk Gregory never did such deeds in arms as I have done this day. I have paid Percy, I have made him sure," but when the Prince tells him that Percy is still alive, Falstaff refuses to lend the Prince his sword but offers his pistol instead : " Nay, before God, Hal, if Percy be alive, thou get'st not my sword ; but take my pistol, if thou wilt." " Is it in the case ? " asks the prince, to which Falstaff replies : " Ay, Hal ; 'tis hot, 'tis hot ; there's that will sack a city," and putting his hand in Falstaff's pistol-case the prince draws out a bottle of sack, and remarking : " What, is it a time to jest and dally now ? " throws the bottle at Falstaff and hastens away, while Falstaff vows if he meets Percy he will kill him " if he do come in my way, so : if he do not, if I come in his willingly, let him make a carbonado of me," for I like not such " grinning honour " as Blunt hath, " give me life : which if I can save, so " ; but if I cannot save my life, I must inevitably accept the " honour which comes unlooked for," and that's an end to it all. Cf. *Extract* 12 from Holinshed.

The fourth scene, which shows the second part of the battle, is enacted on another part of the battlefield. The prince, who has been wounded in the fight and is bleeding freely, is implored by the king to retire and have his wounds dressed, and bids Lord John of Lancaster to go with the prince, but Lancaster refuses unless he " bleeds too." The prince, however, not only refuses to retire but insists on returning to the fight, and warmly eulogises his younger brother—who leaves with Westmoreland—for his gallantry. As the prince leaves, Douglas enters, and seeing the king, who is clad in royal armour, calls him " counterfeit " :

> Another king ! they grow like Hydra's heads :
> I am the Douglas, fatal to all those
> That wear those colours on them : what art thou,
> That counterfeit'st the person of a king ?

" The king himself ; who, Douglas, grieves at heart So many of his shadows thou hast met And not the very king," replies Henry, and my " two boys Seek Percy and thyself about the field " : adding, that even alone he is prepared to defend himself. " I fear thou art another counterfeit ; And yet, in faith, thou bear'st thee like a king : But mine I am sure thou art, whoe'er thou be, And thus I win thee," declares Douglas, and sets on Henry who is in danger of being slain when the prince dashes up and engaging Douglas, puts him to flight :

> Hold up thy head, vile Scot, or thou art like
> Never to hold it up again ! the spirits
> Of valiant Shirley, Stafford, Blunt, are in my arms :
> It is the Prince of Wales that threatens thee ;
> Who never promiseth but he means to pay.
> *[They fight. Douglas flies.*

The Prince then informs the king that both Sir Nicholas Gawsey and Sir John Clifton call for assistance, and the king implores the prince to " Stay, and breathe a while " : but he refuses to do so, and both forthwith hasten away. Hotspur rides in, and addressing the prince, says : " If I mistake not, thou art Harry Monmouth," " Thou speak'st as if I would deny my name," answers the prince, and adding " Two stars keep not their motion in one sphere ; Nor can one England brook a double reign, Of Harry Percy and the Prince of Wales " ; they fight, for in the words of Hotspur the " hour is come To end the one of us." During the encounter Falstaff appears who urges on the prince : " Well said, Hal ! to it, Hal ! Nay, you shall find no boy's play here, I can tell you," only to be in his turn challenged by Douglas, who dashes in at this moment. Being no match for the latter Falstaff falls to the ground feigning death, and Douglas dashes away again. Meanwhile, the Prince and Hotspur continue their fight, but fortune is against the latter and he falls to the ground mortally wounded :

> O, Harry, thou hast robb'd me of my youth !
> .   .   .   .   .   .
>   O, I could prophesy,
> But that the earthy and cold hand of death
> Lies on my tongue : no, Percy, thou art dust,
> And food for—   *[Dies.*

" For worms, brave Percy : fare thee well, great heart ! . . . this earth that bears thee dead Bears not alive so stout a gentleman . . . Adieu, and take thy praise with thee to heaven ! Thy ignominy sleep with thee in the grave, But not remember'd in thy epitaph." A moment later his eye falls on Falstaff who is lying on the ground as one dead : " What, old acquaintance ! could not all this flesh Keep in a little life ? Poor Jack, farewell ! " lie there by Percy until the battle is over and I will see thee properly embowelled and interned. Immediately the prince has gone, Falstaff comes to life. " Embowell'd ! " he exclaims, " if thou embowel me to-day, I 'll give you leave to powder me and eat me too to-morrow," adding that " The better part of valour is discretion ; in the which better part I have saved my life." Rising to his feet he perceives the body of Hotspur and wishing to take the credit for having killed him, runs his sword through the thigh of the dead man. Hoisting the body on his shoulders he is on the point of bearing it away, when the Prince and his brother appear. " Did you not tell me this fat man was dead ? " asks Lancaster, " I did " ; replies the Prince, " I saw him dead." Throwing the body of Hotspur on the ground, Falstaff declares that he looks forward to some signal honour for killing such a gallant foe as Percy : " There is Percy : if your father will do me any honour, so ; if not, let him kill the next Percy himself. I look to be either earl or duke, I can assure you." " Why," exclaims the Prince, " Percy I killed myself, and saw thee dead." " Didst thou ? " replies Falstaff. " Lord, Lord, how this world is given to lying ! I grant you I was down and out of breath ; and so was he : but we rose both at an instant, and fought a long hour by Shrewsbury clock," where I gave him his death wound. " If I may be believed, so ; if not, let him that should reward valour bear the sin upon their own heads. I 'll take it upon my death, I gave him this wound in the thigh : if the man were alive, and would deny it, 'zounds, I would make him eat a piece of my sword." Lancaster declares " This is the strangest tale that ever he heard," and " This is the strangest fellow, brother John," replies the Prince, who, accustomed to Falstaff's disregard of the truth, declares that " if a lie may do him grace, he will gild it with the happiest terms he has." Immediately a retreat is sounded, and turning to his brother, the Prince remarks : " The trumpet sounds retreat ; the day is ours. Come, brother, let us to the highest of the field, To see what friends are living, who are dead," Falstaff declaring he will follow them to obtain his reward, for :

> He that rewards me, God reward him ! If I do grow great, I'll grow less ; for I'll purge, and leave sack, and live cleanly as a nobleman should do.

Cf. *Extract* 13 from Holinshed.

The final scene of the Play shows us another part of the battlefield. The king's troops have gained the victory, and Worcester and Vernon have been taken prisoners. Turning to Worcester, whom he describes as " ill-spirited " the king reminds him of the " pardon and terms of love " he had offered to all of them, and reproaches him for betraying the trust reposed in him by his kinsman—Hotspur—for had he " like a Christian truly borne Betwixt the two armies true intelligence," many a gallant soldier now dead would have " been alive this hour." Worcester replies he adopted what he considered the best course : " What I have done my safety urged me to ; And I embrace this fortune patiently, Since not to be avoided it falls on me." Henry orders him and Vernon to be beheaded : " Bear Worcester to the death, and Vernon too " : adding " Other offenders we will pause upon." The prince reports that Douglas, seeing the battle going against him had fled and falling down a precipice had been taken prisoner : " The noble Scot, Lord Douglas, when he saw The fortune of the day quite turn'd from him, The noble Percy slain, and all his men Upon the foot of fear, fled with the rest ; And falling down a hill, he was so bruised That the pursuers took him," and asks for permission to dispose of him as he thinks fit : " At my tent the Douglas is ; and I beseech your grace I may dispose of him." This being granted, the prince pardons Douglas, and for his bravery in the field, bids his younger brother to set him free without ransom : " Then, brother John of Lancaster, to you This honourable bounty shall belong : Go to the Douglas, and deliver him Up to his pleasure, ransomless and free : His valour shown upon our crests to-day Hath taught us how to cherish such high deeds Even in the bosom of our adversaries." This is pleasing to Prince John, who considers it as an " high courtesy," and the play ends with the king announcing that Prince John and Westmoreland shall forthwith proceed northwards and attack Northumberland and the Archbishop of York for having taken part in the rebellion :

> You, son John, and my cousin Westmoreland
> Towards York shall bend you with your dearest speed,
> To meet Northumberland and the prelate Scroop,
> Who, as we hear, are busily in arms :

while he and the Prince of Wales will march westward against Glendower and the Earl of March, for

> Rebellion in this land shall lose his sway,
> Meeting the check of such another day :
> And since this business so fair is done,
> Let us not leave till all our own be won.

Cf *Extract* 14 from Holinshed.

Scene : England : Wales.

CHARACTERS, PLACE-NAMES, ETC.

Adam. III. iii. 166.

Dost thou hear, Hal ? thou knowest in the state of innocency Adam fell ; and what should poor Jack Falstaff do in the days of villany ?   [III. iii. 165–167.]

All-hallown. I. ii. 157.

= Hallowmass, or All Saints' Day which is the first of November.

Amamon. II. iv. 336.

In demonology one of the four kings of hell. According to Scot in his *Discovery of Witchcraft* Amamon was a spirit who might be bound at certain hours of the day and night. He was a fit subject, therefore, for Glendower to exercise his magic upon.

Angus. I. i. 73.

George Douglas, the only son of William first Earl of Douglas. His mother, Margaret Stewart, was Countess of Angus in her own right. Taken prisoner at the battle of Holmedon.

Archibald, Earl of Douglas. I. i. 53, 67, 72 ; I. iii. 296 ; II. iii. 27 ; II. iv. 343, 368 ; III. ii. 107, 114, 119, 165 ; IV. i. p.1, 3 ; IV. iii. p.1, 8 ; IV. iv. 22 ; V. i. 116 ; V. ii. p.28, 33, p.42 ; V. iii. p.1, 3, 14, 19 ; V. iv. p.25, 27, 29, 54, 77 ; V. v. 17, 23, 27.

His character is somewhat on a par with that of Hotspur, for he possesses the same arrogant bearing, and is likewise a brave soldier. Reckless, and always eager for the fight he is in favour of encountering the king's forces as soon as they reach the camp near Shrewsbury.

He does not however possess the poetical qualities of Hotspur, his phraseology being of a commonplace nature,

That he is a great soldier is acknowledged by Henry when he is describing the rebel leaders to Prince Henry :

whose high deeds,
Whose hot incursions and great name in arms
Holds from all soldiers chief majority
And military title capital
Through all the kingdoms that acknowledge Christ :
[III. ii. 107–111.]

but one cannot help noticing that Douglas is fully conscious of " his great name in arms," which makes him arrogant and conceited. He boasts that " he will kill all the king's coats, and murder all his wardrobe piece by piece, Until he meets the king."

He is however no match against the prince when they meet in battle, and is forced to fly.

In the last scene of the play we find that he has been taken prisoner by the king's forces, and the prince is asking his father if he can dispose of him at will. The prince's request is granted, and he bids his brother John of Lancaster :

Go to the Douglas, and deliver him
Up to his pleasure, ransomless and free :
His valour shown upon our crests to-day
Hath taught us how to cherish such high deeds
Even in the bosom of our adversaries.   [V. v. 27–31.]

[Archibald, Earl of Douglas was the fourth earl of that name, and a nephew of the second earl who was slain at the battle of Otterburn. Defeated and taken prisoner at the battle of Holmedon Hill on September 24th, 1402. He was induced to join the Percy rebellion by a promise that Berwick and a part of Northumberland should be given to him. Taken prisoner at the battle of Shrewsbury, but was not, as Shakespeare says, set free but remained in captivity until 1408. Defeated and slain at Verneuil in 1424, and buried at Tours. He married the Princess Margaret Stewart, eldest daughter of Robert III King of Scots, by whom he had a son and two daughters : the former, Archibald, became fifth Earl of Douglas.]

Attendants.

Aunt Percy. III. i. 196.

= Lady Percy, and sister to Mortimer. Shakespeare confuses the two Mortimers, Lady Percy being aunt to Edmund Earl of March.

Bangor.   The Archdeacon's House.

The Scene of Act III., Scene i. Marks the progress of the rebellion, an alliance having been formed between Hotspur, Mortimer and Glendower. They meet at Bangor where they divide the kingdom into three parts over which they are to rule after having defeated the king. With the exception of Glendower—whose forces are not ready—they decide to proceed to Shrewsbury.

Barbary.   II. iv. 75.

Little Barbary was a cant name for Wapping. It is here used to mystify the drawer Francis.

Bardolph.   I. ii. 161 ; II. ii. 21, p.48, 50 ; II. iv. p.113, 298, 474, p.481 ; III. iii. p.1, 1, 59, 141, 194 ; IV. ii. p.1, 1.

One of Falstaff's friends who takes part in robbing the travellers at Gadshill. His chief characteristic is his " red nose " of which Falstaff makes jest :

> Do thou amend thy face, and I'll amend my life :
> thou art our admiral, thou bearest the lantern in the
> poop, but 'tis in the nose of thee ; thou art the
> Knight of the Burning Lamp.   [III. iii. 24–27.]

In Act III., Scene iii., he enters in haste and announces the arrival of the Sheriff :

> O, my lord, my lord ! the sheriff with a most
> monstrous watch is at the door.   [II. iv. 481–482.]

and later is sent by the prince with letters to Prince John of Lancaster and the Earl of Westmoreland.

He acts as steward to Falstaff when the latter is marching with his ' ragged contingent ' on the way to Shrewsbury, and is sent by Falstaff into Coventry to procure a bottle of sack :

> Bardolph, get thee before to Coventry ; fill me a
> bottle of sack ;   [IV. ii. 1–2.]

French says : " The poet evidently does not imply that this person's name had any affinity with that of the noble house of Bardolf. It was probably suggested by that of a townsman of Shakespeare's native place, who is known to have been a contemporary. Falstaff says of Bardolph, ' I bought him in Paul's ' ; and in Ben Jonson's *Every Man in his Humour*, the famous swaggerer is called ' Captain Bobadill, a Paul's man,' which is explained in the editor's note ;—' the middle aisle of St. Paul's Cathedral was the common resort of cast captains, sharpers, gulls, and gossips of every description.' "

[Bardolph also appears in the *Second Part of King Henry the Fourth* (q.v.)]

Berkley-castle.   I. iii. 249.

In Gloucestershire where the Duke of York (see *The Tragedy of King Richard the Second*) ordered his men to be mustered. Hotspur alludes to it as the place " where the madcap duke his uncle kept."

Boar's-Head Tavern in Eastcheap, The. The Scene of Act II., Scene iv. Act III., Scene iii.

Act II., Scene iv. After robbing Falstaff and his friends, the Prince and Poins proceed to the Boar's Head Tavern in Eastcheap, where they have a little jest with Francis, one of the drawers. Falstaff and his friends arrive later and pour out a highly-coloured and concocted tale of the robbery at Gadshill. A courtier arrives with the news of the Percy rebellion and another comic scene is enacted between the Prince and Falstaff. Here the comic scene links with the main plot. The sheriff with a carrier enters, and Falstaff is thrust behind the arras where he falls asleep, during which time the matter of the robbery is settled, and the scene concludes with a promise from the prince to procure for Falstaff the charge of a company of foot.

Act III., Scene iii. The last of the tavern scenes and the last scene of the underplot. A lively scene takes place between Falstaff and the hostess of the tavern, who charges him with not paying his debts. The Prince enters and informs Falstaff he has procured for him a charge of foot and tells him to meet him on the morrow at Temple Hall to make the necessary arrangements. The underplot is concluded by the money that was robbed from the pilgrims and traders being repaid.

French says : " The ' Boar's Head Tavern ' of Shakespeare's own time, which really did exist in Eastcheap was destroyed in the Great Fire of 1666, and rebuilt two years afterwards, but taken down in 1831 ; and the sign of the ' Boar's Head,' carved in stone, having the initials of the landlord, or mine host. I. T. and the date 1668, is preserved in the Museum of the Corporation of London, attached to the Library, at Guildhall," while Bell in *The Great Fire of London* in 1666, observes : " Some time in the night the Boar's Head tavern in Eastcheap was consumed—first of many taverns made famous by Elizabethan wits which were lost to London in the Great Fire. Shakespeare and Burbage and Ben Jonson are said to have frequented it on their way over London Bridge to the theatres in Southwark and Bankside, and when returning after the play. Shakespeare has immortalized the house as the scene of the drunken debaucheries of Sir John Falstaff and his noisy dependants, Bardolph and Pistol, when Dame Quickly kept the reckoning, and of Doll Tearsheet's frailties.

Bolingbroke. I. iii. 137.

> But I will lift the down-trod Mortimer
> As high in the air as this unthankful king,
> As this ingrate and canker'd Bolingbroke.
> [I. iii. 135-137.]

= Henry the Fourth, surnamed Bolingbroke from the place of his birth. *Canker'd* = corrupted, malignant.

Bolingbroke. I. iii. 176, 229.

> To put down Richard, that sweet lovely rose,
> And plant this thorn, this canker, Bolingbroke ?
> [I. iii. 175-176.]

= Henry the Fourth. *Canker :* the cankerrose is the dog-rose, the flower of the Cynosbaton.

Bolingbroke. I. iii. 229.

= Henry the Fourth,

Bolingbroke. I. iii. 241.

> Of this vile politician, Bolingbroke. [I. iii. 241.]

= Henry the Fourth. *politician* = used contemptuously ; in Elizabethan times the word " politician " was used in a derogatory sense.

Bolingbroke. I. iii. 246.

> where I first bow'd my knee
> Unto this king of smiles, this Bolingbroke.
> [I. iii. 245-246.]

= Henry the Fourth. Cf. *King Richard the Second*, II. iii. 41-50.

Bolingbroke. III. ii. 49.

> " Where, which is Bolingbroke ? "
> And then I stole all courtesy from heaven.
> [III. ii. 49-50.]

= Henry the Fourth. " An allusion to the story of Prometheus's theft, who stole fire from thence ; and as with this he made a man, so with that, Bolingbroke made a king. As the Gods were supposed jealous in appropriating reason to themselves, the getting fire from thence, which lifted it up in the mind, was called a theft ; and as power in their prerogative, the getting courtesie from thence, by which power is best procured, is called a theft. The thought is exquisitely great and beautiful." *Warburton.*

Bridgenorth. III. ii. 175, 178.

A town in Shropshire on the river Severn, eighteen miles south-east of Shrewsbury. It was the rendezvous of the king's forces previous to the battle of Shrewsbury.

Bristow. I. iii. 271.

> who bears hard
> His brother's death at Bristow, the Lord Scroop.
> [I. iii. 270-271.]

= Bristol. Sir William Scroop, created Earl of Wiltshire by Richard II., whose Lord High Treasurer he was, was executed at Bristol by Bolingbroke.

Burton. III. i. 96.

Methinks my moiety, north from Burton here,
In quantity equals not one of yours :   [III. i. 96–97.]

= Burton-upon-Trent. The river from this point flows north-east and a " huge half-moon " is formed.

Henry IV. was at Burton-upon-Trent when the news was brought to him of Hotspur's advance to Shrewsbury, and on the 16th July the king issued a proclamation that is still preserved.

Butler. II. iii. 69, 74.

Groom to Hotspur.

Cambyses. II. iv. 386.

The reference here is supposed to be to Cambyses, the ranting hero in a tragedy by Thomas Preston, written in 1561, entitled *A Lamentable Tragedy, mixed full of Pleasant Mirth*, containing the life of Cambyses, King of Persia. In allusion to a passage in the play " Cambyses' vein " being cited by Shakespeare it has in consequence become proverbial for rant : " for I must speak in passion, and I will do it in King Cambyses' vein."

Canterbury. I. ii. 126.

there are pilgrims
going to Canterbury with rich offerings,
[I. ii. 125–126.]

The pilgrims were probably making their way to Canterbury to offer gifts at the shrine of Thomas à Becket in the Cathedral there.

Carriers, Two. II. 1. p.1, p.8 ; II. iv. p.504.

In Act II., Scene i., the carriers enter and prepare to set out upon their journey.

In Act II., Scene iv., one of the carriers enters in company with the sheriff, when the latter proceeds to the Boar's-Head Tavern in Eastcheap in search of the thieves.

Chamberlain. II. i. p.53.

A friend of Gadshill's whom the latter meets in the Inn-yard at Rochester. He informs Gadshill that wealthy travellers are on the point of setting-out on their journey :

there's a franklin in the
wild of Kent hath brought three hundred marks
with him in gold : I heard him tell it to one of his
company last night at supper ; a kind of auditor ;
one that hath abundance of charge too, God knows
what. They are up already, and call for eggs and
butter : they will away presently.   [II. i. 54–60.]

and in return for the information is promised " a share in the purchase " :

Give me thy hand : thou shalt have a share in our
purchase, as I am a true man.   [II. i. 92–93.]

At the same time the chamberlain bids Gadshill beware of the hangman.

Charing-cross. II. i. 25.

The junction of Whitehall and the Strand. It derived its name from the stone cross erected as a memorial to Eleanor, queen of Edward I.

" Charing was anciently a village detached from London ; and Charing Cross was erected on the last spot where the body of Eleanor, the queen of Edward I., rested, in the road to Westminster. The cross was pulled down by the populace in 1643, through that intolerant fury against what were called superstitious Edifices what has destroyed so many beautiful monuments of art in this country and in Scotland." *Knight*.

Charles' wain. II. i. 2.

The constellation of Ursa Major, a wagon without a wagoner, an old English name for the constellation of the Great Bear. The name appears to arise out of the verbal association of the star Arcturus with Arturus or Arthur and the legendary association of Arthur and Charlemagne. In Welsh the constellation Great Bear is called the chariot of Arthur.

Clifton. IV. iv. 46, 58.

Sir John Clifton. He was slain at the battle of Shrewsbury fighting for the king ; having been made a banneret on the field. One of his descendants, Sir Gervas Clifton, fought for Henry VI. at the battle of Tewkesbury ; and another, Sir Gervas Clifton, was slain at Bosworth following Richard III. in his last desperate charge.

Colossus. V. i. 123.

A reference to the famous Colossus at Rhodes, a gigantic statute of Apollo, which was 105 feet high, and took twelve years to build at a cost of about £120,000. It was one of the wonders of the ancient world.

Corinthian. II. iv. 12.

A gay fellow ; an allusion to the easy morality ascribed to the Corinthians.

Coventry. IV. ii. 1, 39.

A City of Warwickshire.

Cut's saddle. II. i. 5.

> I prithee, Tom, beat Cut's saddle. [II. i. 5.]

Cut was the name of a horse. *beat Cut's saddle* = to beat the horse's saddle to make it soft.

Dame Partlet the hen. III. iii. 52.

The name of the hen in the story of *Reynard the Fox.* In Chaucer's *Cock and the Fox* the favourite hen is called dame Pertelote.

Daventry. IV. ii. 48.

A town in Northamptonshire, on the way from London to Shrewsbury.

Diana's foresters. I. ii. 25.

= Diana's gamekeepers. One of Diana's attributes was that of being a great huntress.

Dick. II. iv. 8.

A drawer in the Boar's Head Tavern in Eastcheap. Dekker in his *Gull's Horn-Book,* 1609, says : " that to be familiar with drawers, and to know their names, was an accomplishment of gallants some ten or twelve years after Shakespeare wrote this play. " Your first compliment shall be to grow most inwardly acquainted with the drawers ; to learn their names, as Jack, and Will, and Tom."

Dives. III. iii. 32.

> I never see thy face but I think upon hell-fire, and Dives that lived in purple ; for there he is in his robes, burning, burning. [III. iii. 31—33.]

The name given to the rich man in the Parable of the Rich Man and Lazarus. *See St. Luke,* XVI. Cf. Lazarus.

Doncaster. V. i. 42, 58.

> And you did swear that oath at Doncaster,
> That you did nothing purpose 'gainst the state ;
> [V. i. 42—43.]

At Doncaster, Bolingbroke swore that he had come to claim only his rightful possessions. Holinshed says : " At his Bolingbroke's comming vnto Doncaster, the earle of Northumberland, and his sonne, sir Henrie Persie, wardens of the marches against Scotland, with the earle of Westmerland, came vnto him ; where he sware vnto those lords, that he would demand no more, but the lands that were to him descended by inheritance from his father, and in right of his wife."

Douglas' son. I. iii. 261.

= Mordake (q.v.).

Drawers.

Waiters in a tap-room.

Earl of Athol. I. i. 73.

According to French there was at the time of the battle of Holmedon no Earl of Athol. The dignity was resigned to the crown in 1341, and not revived until nearly seventy years after in the person of Walter Stewart, son of King Robert II.

Earl of March. I. iii. 84.

> Against that great magician, damn'd Glendower,
> Whose daughter, as we hear, the Earl of March
> Hath lately married. [I. iii. 83—85.]

Shakespeare has confounded Edmund Earl of March, nephew to Lady Percy and the proper Mortimer of the Play with Sir Edmund Mortimer uncle to the former and brother to

Lady Percy. Steevens says: "Shakespeare has fallen into some contradictions with regard to this Lord Mortimer. Before he makes his personal appearance in the play, he is repeatedly spoken of as Hotspur's brother-in-law. In Act II. Lady Percy expressly calls him her brother Mortimer. And yet when he enters in the third Act, he calls Lady Percy his aunt, which in fact she was, and not his sister. This inconsistence may be accounted for as follows. It appears both from Dugdale's and Sandford's account of the Mortimer family, that there were two of them taken prisoners at different times by Glendower; each of them bearing the name of Edmund: one being Edmund Earl of March, nephew to Lady Percy and the proper Mortimer of the play; the other, Sir Edmund Mortimer, uncle to the former and brother to Lady Percy.

Earl of Westmoreland. I. i. p.1, 31; III. ii. 170; III. iii. 197; IV. i. 88; IV. ii. p.50, 52; IV. iv. 30; V. ii. 29, 32, 44; V. iv. p.1, 8, 15; V. v. p.1, 35.

One of the minor characters of the play who supports King Henry in the suppression of the rebels. At the end of the play he is bidden by the king to accompany his son, John of Lancaster, towards York to encounter Northumberland and the Archbishop of York who are at the head of an armed force:

> You, son John, and my cousin Westmoreland
> Towards York shall bend you with your dearest speed,
> To meet Northumberland and the prelate Scroop,
> Who, as we hear, are busily in arms: [V. v. 35–38.]

This nobleman may be well called, in the usual lists of the characters, one of the 'Friends to the King.' He was the head of that great Northern house of Nevill, which exercised so much sway in this and several succeeding reigns. Gilbert de Nevill came in with the Conqueror, and his grandson, Gilbert de Nevill, married the daughter and heir of Bertram de Bulmer, a powerful Northern baron, by which alliance Brancepeth Castle came to the Nevills. Their daughter, Isabel de Nevill, married Robert Fitz-Maldred, Lord of Raby, and their son Geoffrey took his mother's name, and his great-grandson, Ranulph de Nevill, was summoned to Parliament, 22 Edward I., 1294, as Baron Nevill

of Raby; his son and grandson were distinguished persons in the reigns of Edward III. and Richard II.; and the grandson, Ralph Nevill, fourth baron, is the character of this play. He was born in 1365, succeeded his father, John Nevill, in 1389, was created Earl of Westmoreland in 1397, by Richard II. but was the first to join Bolingbroke's standard and the earl became his most powerful supporter against the rebellious Percies. *French.*

[The Earl of Westmoreland is also a character in the *Second Part of King Henry the Fourth.* (q.v.)]

Eastcheap. I. ii. 130, 156, 191; II. iv. 15, 440.

A Street in London in which was situated the Boar's Head Tavern, of which Dame Quickly was the hostess. Stow says: "This Eastcheap is now a flesh market of butchers there dwelling on both sides of the street: it had sometime also cooks mixed amongst the butchers, and such other as sold victuals ready dressed of all sorts. For of old time, when friends did meet, and were disposed to be merry, they went not to dine and sup in taverns, but to the cooks, where they called for meat what they liked, which they always found ready dressed at a reasonable rate."

Ebrew Jew. II. iv. 181.

> You rogue, they were bound, every man of them;
> or I am a Jew else, an Ebrew Jew. [II. iv. 180–181.]

A Jew by blood and by nature. A Jew in which no faith could be put.

Edmund Mortimer, Earl of March. I. i. 38; I. iii. 80, 84, 92, 93, 110, 119, 130, 135, 144, 156, 219, 220, 222, 225, 281, 295; II. iii. 25, 83; II. iv. 341; III. i. p.1, 3, 146, 264; III. ii. 119, 164; IV. iii. 93; IV. iv. 22, 23; V. v. 19, 40.

Supplies the romantic touch in the play in his amorous dealings with his Welsh wife—Glendower's daughter — who cannot speak English, while he can speak no Welsh.

At the beginning of the play, Mortimer is in command of the Herefordshire men, but is defeated and taken prisoner by Glendower, who has rebelled against Henry.

Mortimer is brother-in-law to Hotspur, and when the latter appears before the king at Windsor to answer for his refusal to surrender the prisoners taken by him at the battle of Holmedon hill, he offers to surrender them conditionally upon Henry ransoming Mortimer.

Henry, being afraid of Mortimer—who was proclaimed by Richard as his successor—denounces him as a traitor. Hotspur takes exception to Mortimer being thus denounced, and describes how bravely the latter fought on the banks of the Severn :

> to prove that true
> Needs no more but one tongue for all those wounds,
> Those mouthed wounds, which valiantly he took,
> When on the gentle Severn's sedgy bank,
> In single opposition, hand to hand,
> He did confound the best part of an hour
> In changing hardiment with great Glendower :
> Three times they breathed and three times did they
>   drink,
> Upon agreement, of swift Severn's flood ;
> Who then, affrighted with their bloody looks,
> Ran fearfully among the trembling reeds,
> And hid his crisp head in the hollow bank
> Bloodstained with these valiant combatants.
>   [I. iii. 95–107.]

Later Mortimer makes peace with Glendower and both join Hotspur in the rebellion against Henry.

In the last act we find Mortimer and Glendower in rebellion in the West, and after the battle of Shrewsbury, Henry and his son march against them.

[Edmund Mortimer was the youngest son of Edmund de Mortimer, third Earl of March. Joined Bolingbroke on his return to England in 1399. On the revolt of Owen Glendower he raised the men of Herefordshire and fighting against the Welsh chieftain was captured. On Henry the Fourth refusing to ransom him, Mortimer joined with Glendower in his desire to either restore Richard to the throne, or in case of Richard's death, to bestow it upon his nephew, Edmund Mortimer son of Roger Mortimer. According to some authorities Mortimer married a daughter of Glendower. Although in sympathy with the Percys, he was not present at the battle of Shrewsbury. He is supposed to have lost his life during the siege of Harlech in 1407.]

England. I. ii. 59 ; II. iv. 14, 51, 131, 305, 409 ; III. i. 45, 74 ; V. i. 54 ; V. iv. 66.

Esperance ! Percy ! V. ii. 97.

The war-cry of Percy. *Esperance* or *Esperanza* was the motto of the Percy family. The present motto is *Esperance en Dieu.*

Europe. III. iii. 46.

Finsbury. III. i. 253.

> And give such sarcenet surety for thy oaths,
> As if thou never walk'dst further than Finsbury.
>   [III. i. 252–253.]

Open walks and fields near Chiswell Street London Wall, and a common resort of the citizens of London.

Foot land-rakers. II. i. 74.

= beggars who travel the country and commit petty thefts.

France. III. ii. 95.

Francis. II. iv. 8, 32, 35, 37, p.38, 40, 42, 44, 47, 52, 54, 56, 58, 63, 65, 66, 67, 74, 78, p.96, 96, p.113.

A drawer in the Boar's Head Tavern in Eastcheap. *See* Dick.

[Francis also appears in the *Second Part of King Henry the Fourth* as Page to Falstaff.]

Gadshill. I. ii. 107, 128, 161 ; II. i. p.32, 53 ; II. ii. p.48 ; II. iv. p.113.

One of Falstaff's highwaymen who receives his name from a place where many robberies have been committed on the road between Canterbury and London.

He acts as a spy upon travellers from Rochester, and in consequence earns the name of " our setter " :

> *Gads.* Stand.
> *Fal.* So I do, against my will.
> *Poins.* O, 'tis our setter : I know his voice.
>   [II. ii. 48–50.]

He is described as a " suspicious-looking character, a braggart and a coward." He assists in
the robbing of the travellers, but takes to his
heels with the others when set upon by the
Prince and Poins.

Gadshill is a character in the *Famous Victories*,
in which he is the person who robs the carrier, is
taken before Judge Gascoigne, and for whose
rescue Prince Hal involves himself in disgrace.
He is called in that play ' The Theefe,' but
Derrick addresses him by his name,—

> ' Whoop, hallo, now Gadshill, knowest thou
> me ? '   *French.*

Gadshill. I. ii. 125 ; IV. iii. 38.

A hill near Rochester, notorious for highway
robbers. A ballad entitled *The Robbery at
Gadshill* was entered in the Stationers' Register
in 1558. In Dekker and Webster's *Westward
Hoe*, 1606, we have : " — Why, how lies she ?
Troth, as the way lies over Gads-hill, very dangerous," and in *The Famous Victories of Henry the
Fifth :* " And I know thee for a taking fellow Upon
Gads-hill in Kent." From a paper by Sir Henry
Ellis, the following extract is taken : " In the
course of that Mychaelmas Terme, I being at
London, many robberyes weare done in the hye
wayes at Gadeshill on the west parte of Rochester, and at Chatham downe on the East
parte of Rochester, by horse theves, with suche
fatt and lustye horses as weare not lyke hackney
horsses, and one of them sometyme wearing a
vizarde greye bearde, (by reason that to the
persons robbed the Theves did use to mynister
an othe that there should bee no hue and crye
made after, and also did gyve a watche worde
for the parties robbed, the better to escape
other of their Theves companye devyded vppon
the hyghe waye,) he was by common report in
the Contry called Justice greye Bearde ; and no
man durst travell that waye without great
companye." And Harper in his *Dover Road*
says : Is this, then, the famous hill where travellers were wont to be robbed ? Is this the place
referred to by that seventeenth-century robber
turned *littérateur*, John Clavell, who, in his
Recantation of an Ill-led Life, speaks so magnilo-
quently of—

> Gad's Hill, and those
> Red tops of mountains, where good people lose
> Their ill kept purses.

Was it here, then, upon this paltry pimple of a
hill that Falstaff and Prince Hal, Poins and the
rest of them, robbed the merchants, the frank-
lins, and the flea-bitten carriers, who, Charles's
Wain being over the chimneys of their inn at
Rochester, set out early in the morning for
London ? Was this the spot where Falstaff
brave amid so many confederates, added insult
to injury of those travellers by calling them
' gorbellied knaves ' and ' caterpillars,' and
where Prince Henry, in his turn, alluded to the
knight as ' fat guts ' ? Yes, this is the place,
but how changed from then. To see Gad's Hill
as it was in those times it would be necessary to
sweep away the row of mean cottages that form
quite a hamlet here, together with Gad's Hill
Place, the hedges and enclosures, and to clothe
the hillsides with dense woodlands, coming close
up to, and overshadowing the highway, which
should be full of ruts and sloughs of mud. Then
we should have some sort of an idea how terrible
the hill could be o' nights when the rogues who
lurked in the shadow of the trees pounced upon
rich travellers, and tricked out in

> vizards, hoods, disguise,
> Masks, muzzles, mufflers, patches on their eyes ;
> Those beards, those heads of hair, and that great wen
> Which is not natural,

relieved them of their gold.

And not only rogues of low estate, but others
of birth and education, pursued this hazardous
industry, so that Shakespeare, when he made
the Prince of Wales and Sir John Falstaff appear
as highwaymen on this scene, was not altogether
drawing upon his imagination. Thus, when the
Danish Ambassador was set upon and plundered
here in 1656, they were not poor illiterates who
sent him a letter the next day in which they took
occasion to assure him that ' the same necessity
that enforc't ye Tartars to breake ye wall of
China compelled them to wait on him at Gad's
Hill.' But travellers did not always tamely
submit to be robbed and cudgelled, as you shall
see in these extracts from Gravesend registers—
' 1586, September 29th. daye, was a thiefe yt
was slayne, buryed ; ' and, again, ' 1590,
Marche, the 17th daie, was a theefe yt was at
Gad'shill wounded to deathe, called Robert
Writs, buried.'

Gaunt, dukedom of Lancaster. V. i. 45.

The seat of Gaunt, dukedom of Lancaster :
To this we swore our aid. [V. i. 45–46.]

See under Doncaster.

Gilliams. II. iii. 68.

= Hotspur's servant ; another form of the name Williams.

Gloucestershire. I. iii. 243.

—what do you call the place ?—
A plague upon it, it is in Gloucestershire ;
[I. iii. 242–243.]

Hotspur means " Berkeley " but being excited cannot recall the name.

Gloucestershire. III. ii. 176.

Good Friday. I. ii. 116.

how agrees the devil and thee about thy soul,
that thou soldest him on Good Friday last for a cup
of Madeira and a cold capon's leg ? [I. ii. 115–117.]

Deighton remarks : " which, as the anniversary of Christ's crucifixion, is specially a day for repentance, and therefore a day on which Falstaff's bargain would be all the more heinous."

Goodman Adam. II. iv. 93.

I am now of all humours that have showed themselves humours since the old days of goodman Adam to the pupil age of this present twelve o'clock at midnight. [II. iv. 92–95.]

= A common term of familiarity.

Great Oneyers. II. i. 76.

= Great ones. A Moneyer. A moneyer is an officer of the Mint, who makes coin, and delivers out the king's money. Moneyers are also taken for bankers, or those that make it their trade to turn and return money.

Gregory. V. iii. 45.

Turk Gregory never did such deeds in arms as I have done this day. [V. iii. 45–46.]

Pope Gregory the Seventh, called Hildebrand. A man of obscure origin ; elected pope in 1073. Deposed by the emperor Henry IV., but Gregory retaliated by excommunicating the emperor and finally compelling him to do penance. On account of his vice and enormity of every description he earned the name of " Turk Gregory." The Turks were always considered to be proverbial for their cruelty.

Hal. I. ii. 1, 13, 69, 82, 94, 95, 105, 113, 137 ; II. ii. 7, 20, 40, 66 ; II. iv. 3, 193, 198, 208, 222, 282, 329, 365, 490 ; III. iii. 102, 137, 146, 165, 176 ; IV. ii. 51, 64 ; V. i. 125 ; V. iii. 50, 53 ; V. iv. 75.

An abbreviation for Henry, Prince of Wales, used by Falstaff and Poins.

Half-moon. II. iv. 28.

" Anon, anon, sir ! Score a pint of bastard
in the Half-moon, " or so. [II. iv. 27–28.]

The name of a room in the Boar's Head Tavern.

Harry Monmouth. V. ii. 50 ; V. iv. 59.

Prince Henry, so-named from the town of Monmouth where he was born.

Henry Bolingbroke. III. i. 64.

Three times hath Henry Bolingbroke made head
Against my power ; thrice from the banks of Wye
And sandy-bottom'd Severn have I sent him
Bootless home and weather-beaten back.
[III. i. 64–67.]

Moorman remarks : " The first occasion was in 1400, when the king waged war in person with Glendower, who, withdrawing to the mountains of the Snowdon district, escaped capture. In the following year war broke out again, and resulted in the victory of Glendower over the Lord Grey of Ruthven, who was captured. The third occasion was in 1402, when, after the Earl of March had been taken prisoner by Glendower, the king himself again entered Wales, but again, as Holinshed says, ' lost his labour.' The word weather-beaten probably refers to the storms which King Henry encountered on this last expedition, and of which Holinshed writes as follows : ' Owen conveied himselfe out of the waie, and (as was thought) through art magike, he caused such foule weather of winds, tempest, raine, snow and haile to be raised, for the annoiance of the kings armie, that the like had not been heard of.' " *Warwick edition.* See *Extract* 5 from Holinshed.

Henry Percy, Earl of Northumberland.
I. i. 79 ; I. iii. p.1, 122 ; II. iv. 342 ; III. ii. 118 ; IV. iii. 67 ; IV. iv. 14 ; V. v. 37.

This character, whom we first met in *King Richard the Second* still displays the characteristics shown in that play, being " half-hearted and timorous," and as contemptible in his actions as Worcester.

Having deserted Richard for Bolingbroke he plots against the latter almost as soon as he ascends the throne as Henry the Fourth, which conduct shows him to be utterly selfish, turning to whichever side seems to be of advantage to himself.

We see but little of Northumberland in this part of *King Henry the Fourth.* He is not present at the battle of Shrewsbury on account of being sick—which is afterwards found to be feigned—he not being willing to run any risk himself but ready to allow others to fight for him, while simulating an intense interest in their fortunes.

The prophetic words of King Richard in the preceding play find their accomplishment in this :

' Northumberland, thou ladder wherewithal
　The mounting Bolingbroke ascends my throne,
　.　.　.　.　.　.　thou shalt think,
　Thou he divide the realm, and give thee half,
　It is too little, helping him to all.'

' The impatient spirit of Henry Percy, and the factious disposition of the Earl of Worcester, younger brother of Northumberland, inflamed the discontent of that nobleman, and the precarious title of Henry tempted him to seek revenge by overturning that throne which he had at first established.' *Hume.* The illness of the earl, the command of his troops devolving on his fiery son, and the defeat of their army, are admirably described in the play.

This powerful noble married first, Margaret Nevill, youngest daughter of Ralph, second Lord Nevill of Raby, by whom he had four sons : 1. Henry Percy, surnamed ' Hotspur ' ; 2. Sir Thomas Percy, and 3. Sir Ralph Percy, Knights ; these two brothers married their father's wards, Elizabeth and Philippa de Strabolgi, daughters and co-heirs of David, last Earl of Athol of that surname ; 4. Alan Percy. The Earl of Northumberland married secondly, Maud Lucy, daughter of Thomas, second Baron Lucy ; she brought Cockermouth Castle to the Percies. There was no issue by this second marriage. *French.*

[The Earl of Northumberland is also a character in the *Second Part of King Henry the Fourth.* (q.v.)]

Henry Percy, surnamed Hotspur.
I. i. 52, 53, 70, 86, 89, 90, 92 ; I. iii. p.1, 24, 71, 113, 254 ; II. iii. p.1, 41, 82, 89, 110 ; II. iv. 101, 102, 105, 109, 335, 368 ; III. i. p.1, 7, 52, 83, 147, 265 ; III. ii. 29, 85, 96, 112, 118, 122, 126, 132, 140, 141, 173, 175 ; III. iii. 204 ; IV. i. p.1, 104, 122 ; IV. ii. 75 ; IV. iii. p.1 ; IV. iv. 13, 19, 24, 36 ; V. i. 87, 116 ; V. ii. 19, 24, p.28, 97 ; V. iii. p.14, 46, 50, 55 ; V. iv. 21, 32, p.59, 61, 63, 67, 85, 87, 110, 122, 145.

Is a " great contrast both to his father and to King Henry," for instead of the " cool and calculating tactfulness " which characterises both Northumberland and the king, we find in Hotspur a quick-tempered, impulsive, and rash character.

He is a typical soldier, somewhat " rough in speech, but at the same time a very heroic figure."

The very soul of honour, and professing contempt of pretentiousness, he thus offends Glendower, when he bids him :

O, while you live, tell truth, and shame the devil !
[III. i. 62.]

Hotspur evidently looks upon the " fine arts with contempt " as he says " nothing would set his teeth on edge So much as mincing poetry," but one notices that when he becomes " excited " his sayings are remarkable for their "imaginative quality," as is exemplified in his speech on 'honour' and his description of the "fight between Glendower and Mortimer."

He enters into the plot against Henry with characteristic eagerness, but his lack of tact and self-restraint make him unfitted to take a leading part in the conspiracy, for he "wishes to fight as soon as he has reached the camp near Shrewsbury, but is restrained by more prudent counsel."

Although one admires Hotspur's courage, he lacks the modesty of the prince, being given to boastful language, and thinks that his success is a foregone conclusion, anticipating with "eager delight" the time when he shall meet "this madcap Prince of Wales," face to face in single combat.

He meets the prince in the battle of Shrewsbury and is mortally wounded, but Hotspur's dying words express no fear of death, but a regret that he has been "robb'd of his youth," and would "better brook the loss of brittle life Than those proud titles the prince had won of him."

After the battle of Shrewsbury, Hotspur's body was given to his kinsman, Thomas Neville, Lord of Furnival who had it interred at Whitchurch, but a few days afterwards it was disinterred and publicly exhibited at Shrewsbury and then beheaded and quartered. His head was sent to York and placed above the gate of that city, and his quarters to London, Bristol, Newcastle-upon-Tyne and Chester. There they remained until November when the king ordered that the head and quarters should be given up to his widow, who finally interred her husband's remains in York Minster.

Extract from *Close Roll, 5 Henry IV., pars. 1.* Concerning the delivery of the head and quarters of Percy:

The King to the mayor and sheriffs of the City of York greeting. Whereas of our special grace we have granted to our kinswoman Elizabeth, who was the wife of Henry de Percy, Chivaler, deceased, the head and the quarters of the same Henry to be buried. We command you that you deliver the aforesaid head, placed by our command above the gate of the aforesaid City, to the same Elizabeth to be buried according to our grant above said. Witness the King at Cirencester the third day of November. By writ of privy seal.

The king to the mayor and sheriffs of the Town of New Castle upon Tyne greeting. Whereas of our special grace we have granted to our kinswoman Elizabeth who was the wife of Henry de Percy, Chivaler, deceased, the head and the quarters of the same Henry to be buried. We command you that you deliver to the same Elizabeth a certain quarter of the same Henry above the gate of the aforesaid City, to the same Elizabeth to be buried according to our grant above said. By the same writ.

Life briefs are directed to the underwritten for the other quarters of the same Henry Percy under the same date, namely,

To the Mayor and Sheriffs of London.

To the Mayor, Sheriffs and Bailiffs of the Town of Bristol.

To the Mayor and Bailiffs of the Town of Chester.

Commenting on the character of Hotspur, Gervinus says: "Never was a more living character delineated in poetry; ballads designed to sing his glory might have borrowed their boldest traits and images from this drama. There is too, scarcely any part more grateful to the actor; Betterton, the cleverest actor of the old English school, hesitated whether he should himself choose Percy, or the favourite of all parts, Falstaff. . . . For Henry Percy is the ideal of all genuine and perfect manliness, and of that active nature which makes the man a man. . . . When he hears of Henry's proud bearing before the battle of Shrewsbury, this jealousy urges him imprudently into the most dangerous actions. Danger has ever an alluring charm for him; when the goad of emulation is added to it, it decides him completely to venture on the unequal fight, and with the most painful impatience he leaves explanatory letters unread, and every earnest appeal to his military talent, to his foresight, and to his honour unheeded. His courage makes him a sophist, just as his quick passion occasionally makes him a statesman—two capacities which lie in direct opposition to his soldierly nature. . . . Accused by the king of having refused the prisoners made at Holmedon, he excuses his refusal of the demand; but when the king gives him the lie, and threatens him, he is at once no longer master of his pride and anger. With his heated imagination, which the mere idea of a great exploit carries beyond the bounds of patience and reflection, he utters presagingly bold schemes of revolt ; and when his spirit is excited into violent passion, the political Worcester suggests his long-matured plans against Henry to the ' quick conceiving discontents' of the hot-blooded youth. This blind passion throws the spotless hero into traitorous connections, it leads the resolute man into league with the undecided and the weak, the warrior and soldier into schemes with artful diplomatists, the man of valour and fidelity into alliance with traitors and cowards, and the man imprudent himself into undertakings imprudently designed. And when candid advisers suspect these plans and his friends, the honest man bears ill-will against the honest counsellor, because he himself does not believe in dishonesty. This passionateness, this want of penetration and knowledge of human nature, prove the ruin of the trustful man ; for the want of self-command, which leads him to immoderate ebullitions and arrogant blame, forms, in Worcester's opinion, the principal blemish in the extreme beauty of his character. Beyond this, there is no ignoble vein in the man," and Hudson : " It is difficult to speak of Hotspur satisfactorily ; not indeed but that the lines of his character are bold and emphatic enough, but rather because they are so much so . . . There is no mistaking him : no character in Shakespeare stands more apart in plenitude of peculiarity ; and stupidity itself cannot so dis-feature him with criticism, but that he will be recognized by any one who has ever been with him. He is as much a monarch in his sphere as the King and Falstaff are in theirs ; only they rule more by power, he by stress : . . . Who that has been with him in the scenes at the Palace and at Bangor can ever forget his bound-ing, sarcastic, overbearing spirit ? . . . and what with Glendower, the poetry is as unrivalled in its kind as the wit and humour in the best scenes at Eastcheap. What a dressing Hotspur gives the silken courtier who came to demand the prisoners ! Still better, however, is the dialogue that presently follows in the same scene ; where Hotspur seems to be under a spell, a fascination of rage and scorn : nothing can check him, he cannot check himself ; because, besides the boundings of a most turbulent and impetuous nature, he has always had his own way, having from his boyhood held the post of

a feudal war-chief. Irascible, headstrong, im-patient, every effort to arrest or divert him only produces a new impatience. . . . Hotspur is a general favourite : whether from something in himself or from the king's treatment of him, he has our good-will from the start ; nor is it without some reluctance that we set the prince above him in our regard. Which may be owing in part to the interest we take, and justly, in his wife ; who, timid, solicitous, affectionate, and playful, is a woman of the true Shakespearian stamp. How delectable is the harmony felt between her prying, inquisitive gentleness and his rough, stormy courage ! for in her gentleness there is much strength, and his bravery is not without gentleness. The scene at Warkworth, where they first appear together, is a choice heart-reflection : combining the beauty of move-ment and of repose, it comes into the surrounding elements like a patch of sunshine in a tempest."

[Hotspur was the eldest son of Sir Henry Percy, first Earl of Northumberland. In 1388 as governor of Berwick came into conflict with the Scots, and at the battle of Otterburn was captured by the Earl of Douglas, who was killed in the battle. Assisted in placing Henry the Fourth on the throne for which services was appointed justiciary of North Wales. In 1402—with his father and the Earl of March—routed the Scottish forces at Holmedon Hill, taking prisoner Archibald Earl of Douglas—the Douglas of the play, and nephew to the Douglas slain at Otterburn—and many other Scottish nobles. Became discontented with Henry, and on the king refusing to ransom Sir Edmund Mortimer—his brother-in-law—a prisoner in the hands of Owen Glendower, revolted. Set free the Earl of Douglas who joined in the rebellion, and at the battle of Shrewsbury on July 21st, 1403, was defeated and killed by an unknown hand, having penetrated the royal line till completely sur-rounded by enemies. He married Elizabeth, eldest daughter and co-heir of Edmund Mortimer, third Earl of March, by the Lady Philippa Plan-tagenet, only child of Lionel of *Antwerp*, third son of Edward III. By his wife, the ' Lady Percy ' in this play, Hotspur left a son and one daughter, Elizabeth Percy, married first to John, Lord Clifford, and secondly to Ralph Nevill, second Earl of Westmoreland. The son of Hotspur, Henry Percy, became second Earl of

Northumberland in 1414 ; he was slain at the first battle of St. Albans, 1455 ; and his eldest son is the ' Earl of Northumberland ' in the *Third Part of King Henry the Sixth.*]

Henry, Prince of Wales, Son to King Henry the Fourth. I. ii. p.1 ; I. iii. 230 ; II. ii. p.1, p.90, 96 ; II. iv. p.1, 10, 139, 397, 410, 414, 425, 439, 477, 478 ; III. ii. p.1, 1 ; III. iii. p.88 ; IV. i. 95, 121, 122 ; IV. ii. p.50 ; IV. iv. 29 ; V. i. p.1, 86, 101 ; V. ii. 46 ; V. iii. p.40 ; V. iv. p.1, 2, 12, 42, 63, 67, 68, 77, p.131 ; V. v. p.1, 39.

Although at the beginning of the play led to believe that Prince Henry is a thoroughly dissolute character, we find in reviewing his actions through its course that nothing could be further from the truth.

It is true that his father speaks of him in disparaging terms, wishing Hotspur were his son instead :

> Yea, there thou makest me sad and makest me sin
> In envy that my Lord Northumberland
> Should be the father to so blest a son,
> A son who is the theme of honour's tongue ;
> Amongst a grove, the very straightest plant ;
> Who is sweet Fortune's minion and her pride :
> Whilst I, by looking on the praise of him,
> See riot and dishonour stain the brow
> Of my young Harry. O that it could be proved
> That some night-tripping fairy had exchanged
> In cradle-clothes our children where they lay,
> And call'd mine Percy, his Plantagenet !   [I. i. 78–89].

but on making the acquaintance of Prince Hal— in company with his fellow-revellers, Sir John Falstaff and Poins—we find that he is but a gay, light-hearted youth, determined to find the highest excitement in life before he is king, but ready, when the time shall come, to assume his regal position worthily, for he says :

> So, when this loose behaviour I throw off
> And pay the debt I never promised,
> By how much better than my word I am,
> By so much shall I falsify men's hopes ;
> And like bright metal on a sullen ground,
> My reformation, glittering o'er my fault,
> Shall show more goodly and attract more eyes
> Than that which hath no foil to set it off.
> I'll so offend, to make offence a skill ;
> Redeeming time when men think least I will.
> [I. ii. 207–216.]

There is an ulterior motive, too, in Prince Henry's association with these common folk, for he knows that to rule wisely, it is necessary

to have an insight into the life of all classes of his subjects, and we find later, when he is king, that his experience has taught him to be considerate and just in all his actions.

He promises his anxious father that he will reform :

> I shall hereafter, my thrice gracious lord,
> Be more myself,   [III. ii. 92–93.]

and just before the battle of Shrewsbury is about to take place, shows his valour by offering to meet Hotspur in single combat, in order to avoid needless bloodshed :

> And so I hear he doth account me too ;
> Yet this before my father's majesty—
> I am content that he shall take the odds
> Of his great name and estimation,
> And will, to save the blood on either side,
> Try fortune with him in a single fight.
> [V. i. 95–100.]

Thus we see that he is considerate, bold, and fearless, and he enters into the battle with all energy, succeeds in isolating Hotspur and eventually killing him.

In summing up Prince Henry's character, we may say that he is Shakespeare's " man of action," and becomes in the next play his " ideal king." Unlike other of the poet's heroes he is intensely practical and human and shows himself eminently suitable for the regal dignity he is to attain.

In the preceding play we have a slight glimpse of the ' Prince Hal ' of this drama, in the anxious enquiry of Bolingbroke, Act V., Scene 3 :

> ' Can no man tell of my unthrifty son ? '

Shakespeare has drawn a lively portrait of this ' mad-cap prince,' who afterwards so nobly redeemed the follies of his youth. The death of his mother, when he was but seven or eight years old, must have left him early without sufficient control, but his grandmother, the Countess of Hereford, sister of Archbishop Arundel, bestowed some pains on his education, and at eleven years of age he was entered a student at Queen's College, Oxford, a fact which is recorded by an inscription on one of the windows :

> In Perpetuam Rei Memoriam :—
> Imperator Britanniæ,
> Triumphator Galliæ,
> Hostium Victor et sui,
> Henricus V.,
> Parvi Hujus Cubiculi,
> Olim magnus incola.
> Wood's *Athenæ Oxoniensis.*

Fuller alludes to the chamber over the gateway as the one used by Henry when a scholar at Oxford.

Shakespeare in his portrait of ' Prince Hal ' has taken the groundwork of his facts chiefly from Holinshed and Stow, with some few hints from the old drama, called *The Famous Victories of Henry the Fifth ;* but these facts and hints have been clothed in the poet's own immortal language with singular felicity and beauty. The Prince of Wales, who was so created the day after his father's coronation, won his spurs at Shrewsbury, where he behaved with great bravery, and was ' hurt in the face by an arrow ' (Holinshed), a wound which the young hero calls in the play ' A shallow scratch,' and refuses to quit the field. *French.*

[Prince Henry is also a character in the *Second Part of King Henry the Fourth* (q.v.)]

Hercules. II. iv. 269.

Herefordshire. I. i. 39.

Highway, The, near Gadshill.

The Scene of Act II., Scene ii. The Gadshill robbery. Falstaff and his friends waylay the travellers and rob them, and are afterwards themselves robbed by the Prince and Poins.

Holmedon. I. i. 55, 65, 70 ; I. iii. 24 ; V. iii. 14.

Hambleton, near Wooler, Northumberland. In 1402 the Scots under the Earl of Douglas invaded England, and on September 14th, of the same year a decisive battle was fought at Holmedon Hill in which the English were successful. See *Extract* 1 from Holinshed.

Humbleton Hill itself is terraced in three successive tiers, and has an elevation of nearly 1000 feet above the sea. . . . It was on the terraces of Humbleton that the Scotch took up their position, and, according to tradition, numbered 10,000. This estimate, however, is probably an exaggeration. The victory was won for the English by the archers, there being little or no fighting at close quarters. North of the hill, in

the Red Riggs, is an old stone pillar known as the Bendor Stone, which was erected to commemorate this archers' victory.

Holy Land. I. i. 48.

> It seems then that the tidings of this broil
> Brake off our business for the Holy Land.
> > [I. i. 47–48.]

= Palestine. It was the intention of Henry IV to go on crusade to the Holy Land to expiate his guilt for the murder of Richard II.

Holy-rood. I. i. 52.

The 14th September. " This festival, called also Holy Cross Day, was instituted on account of the recovery of a large piece of the Cross by the emperor Heraclius, after it had been taken away, on the plundering of Jerusalem by Chosroes, king of Persia, about the year of Christ 615." *Brand.* In Howe's edition of Stow's *Chronicle,* we read : " The 17 of Nov. was begun to be pulled downe the roode of Paules Church, with Mary and John, and all other images in the church, and then the like was done in all the churches in London, and so throughout England, and texts of Scripture were written upon the walls of those churches against images," etc.

Hotspur. I. i. 52, 70 ; II. iv. 102 ; III. i. 7 ; III. ii. 112, 140 ; V. i. 116 ; V. ii. 19.

Holinshed in his History of Scotland says : " This Harry Percy was surnamed, for his *often pricking* [*i.e.* spurring a horse, riding hard], Henry Hotspur, as one that seldom times rested, if there were anie service to be done abroad."

Hybla. I. ii. 43.

A locality in Sicily famous for its bees.

Hydra's heads. V. iv. 25.

A monster with nine heads—of which the middle one was immortal—the offspring of Typhon and Echidna, which ravaged the country of Lerna, near Argos. One of the twelve labours imposed upon Hercules by Eurystheus, was the destruction of this monster. Hercules struck off its heads with his club, but in place of each head cut off, two new ones grew forth, but with the assistance of his servant Iolaus, Hercules burnt off the eight mortal heads and buried the ninth, which was immortal, under a huge rock.

India. III. i. 169.

Jack. I. ii. 100, 115 ; II. ii. 68 ; II. iv. 113, 127, 162, 189, 209, 234, 251, 265, 295, 325, 327, 355, 479 ; III. iii. 97, 101, 139, 187, 200 ; IV. ii. 50, 62 ; V. iv. 103.

An abbreviation for John (Sir John Falstaff).

Jack. II. iv. 11.

> And tell me flatly I am no proud Jack, like Falstaff.
> [II. iv. 11.]

A contemptuous term.

Jack. II. iii. 85.

> How ! the prince is a Jack, a sneak-cup.
> [III. iii. 85.]

= A knave.

Jerusalem. I. i. 102.

> And for this cause a while we must neglect
> Our holy purpose to Jerusalem.   [I. i. 101–102.]

The projected crusade to the Holy Land is consequently postponed.

John of Gaunt. II. ii. 65.

= Gaunt or thin John.

John of Lancaster, son to King Henry the Fourth. I. i. p.1 ; III. i. 8 ; III. ii. 171 ; III. iii. 196, 197 ; IV. i. 88 ; IV. iii. 61 ; IV. iv. 29 ; V. i. p.1 ; V. iv. p.1, 3, 17, 19, p.131, 131, 156 ; V. v. p.1, 25, 35.

Takes no important part in the action of the play, but from the part in which he does appear, we gather that he is a brave man, who served his father well in the battle against the rebels, for we see him on the battle-field eager to do his duty :

> We breathe too long : come, cousin Westmoreland,
> Our duty this way lies ; for God's sake, come.
> [V. iv. 15–16.]

and the king and the Prince of Wales praise him for his gallant deeds :

> *Prince.* By God, thou hast deceived me, Lancaster ;
> I did not think thee lord of such a spirit :
> Before, I loved thee as a brother, John ;
> But now, I do respect thee as my soul.
> *King.* I saw him hold Lord Percy at the point,
> With lustier maintenance than I did look for
> Of such an ungrown warrior.   [V. iv. 17–23.]

Lancaster considers it " high courtesy " when he is bidden by his brother Prince Henry to " go to the Douglas, and deliver him Up to his pleasure, ransomless and free " ; and at the end of the play he is ordered by his father to proceed —with Westmoreland—towards York to meet Northumberland and the Archbishop of York who are in arms against the king :

> You, son John, and my cousin Westmoreland
> Towards York shall bend you with your dearest speed,
> To meet Northumberland and the prelate Scroop,
> Who, as we hear, are busily in arms :   [V. v. 35–38.]

John Plantagenet, third son of Henry the Fourth, born in 1389, is here rightly called as above, since he did not receive any other style until the reign of his brother, who created him ' Duke of Bedford,' under which name he is a character in *King Henry V.* ; but he figures more prominently in the *First Part of King Henry VI.*, as the ' Regent of France.' He was however made by his father Constable of England, Governor of Berwick, Warden of the East Marches towards Scotland, and a K.G.

[Prince John of Lancaster is also a character in the *Second Part of King Henry the Fourth* (q.v.)]

Kate. II. iii. 37, 93, 97, 104, 108, 110, 114, 116, 119 ; III. i. 228, 246, 254.

> How now, Kate ! I must leave you within these two
> hours.   [II. iii. 37–38.]

= Lady Percy. Her real name was Elizabeth. Holinshed gives it as Eleanor. Steevens says : " Shakespeare either mistook the name of Hotspur's wife, (which was not Katharine, but Elizabeth,) or else designedly changed it, out of the remarkable fondness he seems to have had for the familiar appellation of Kate, which he is never weary of repeating, when he has once introduced it ; as in this scene, the scene of

Katharine and Petruchio, and the courtship between King Henry V. and the French Princess."

Kendal Green. II. iv. 221, 230.

Kendal, a town in Westmoreland was famous
for its manufacture of cloths. A green cloth
made first at Kendal was the dress worn by
Robin Hood and his merry men in Sherwood
Forest.

Kent, Wild of. II. i. 55.

> there 's a franklin in the
> wild of Kent hath brought three hundred marks
> with him in gold :   [II. i. 54–56.]

= the Kentish weald.

King Henry the Fourth. I. i. p.1 ; I. iii. p.1 ; III. ii. p.1 ; V. i. p.1 ; V. ii. 43 ; V. iii. p.1, 8 ; I. iv. p.1 ; V. v. p.1.

The Henry Bolingbroke of *Richard the Second*
does not figure in this play as a very prominent
character.   His characteristics show the development of his nature as portrayed in *Richard the
Second ;* he is the same practical man,—diplomatic and dominant in purpose.

Throughout the play it is evident that he feels
the "insecurity of his position," and is conscious
of the unjust methods he used in securing the
crown.

Addressing the nobles at the opening of the
play, he rejoices that peace having at last been
concluded, he can now undertake a pilgrimage
to the Holy Land as a penance for the murder of
Richard, but the news that Mortimer has been
defeated and taken prisoner compels him to
abandon this projected pilgrimage for the
present :

> It seems then that the tidings of this broil
> Brake off our business for the Holy Land. [I. i. 47–48.]

This decision is strengthened on Westmoreland
announcing Hotspur's victory over Douglas at
Holmedon. This victory causes jealousy to
arise in the mind of Henry—particularly as his
own son, Prince Henry, is causing him trouble
by his dissolute habits, and at the same time
he is suspicious of Mortimer who has a prior
claim to the crown, and this jealousy and suspicion leads to the rebellion of the Percys,

In this rebellion the old spirit of Henry is revived, and we find him diplomatic and practical,
fearless and " mighty and to be feared." At
the same time he can be lenient when it suits his
purpose as is evidenced by his offer of unconditional pardon to Hotspur the day previous to
the battle of Shrewsbury :

> The king hath sent to know
> The nature of your griefs, and whereupon
> You conjure from the breast of civil peace
> Such bold hostility, teaching his duteous land
> Audacious cruelty. If that the king
> Have any way your good deserts forgot,
> Which he confesseth to be manifold,
> He bids you name your griefs ; and with all speed
> You shall have your desires with interest,
> And pardon absolute for yourself and these
> Herein misled by your suggestion.   [IV. iii. 41–51.]

Shakespeare does not portray Henry's share
in the battle of Shrewsbury—in which the rebels
are completely routed and Hotspur slain—but
makes Prince Henry the dominant character.

So far we find Henry the same " calm and dignified" man as he appeared in Richard the Second,
but although fortune favours him in the suppression of the rebels, the "dread of retribution"
for his past misdeeds continually haunts him :

> I know not whether God will have it so,
> For some displeasing service I have done,
> That, in his secret doom, out of my blood
> He'll breed revengement and a scourge for me ;
> But thou dost in thy passages of life
> Make me believe that thou art only mark'd
> For the hot vengeance and the rod of heaven,
> To punish my mistreadings.   [III. ii. 4–11.]

and he is conscious that fate is leading him to
his downfall.

Bolingbroke had been seated for three years
on his illgotten throne when the action of this
plays opens ; the first scene recording the recent
battle of Homledon, now Hambleton, near
Wooler, co Northumberland, fought on Holy-
rood day, Sept. 14, 1402 ; and the drama closes
with the victory of Shrewsbury, July 21, 1403.
The former battle was gained for the king by
the Percies, who were arrayed against him in
the latter conflict. Henry IV. behaved with
signal valour at Shrewsbury, killing, it is said,
sixteen, or according to some writers thirty-six,
of the enemy with his own hand, thus performing
the part of a gallant knight as well as of a skilful
leader,

Henry the Fourth's first wife was the great co-heiress, Mary de Bohun, second daughter of Humphrey, the last Earl of Hereford, to whom he was married in 1384. It is said that after he came to the throne he ordered 10,000 masses to be sung for the repose of her soul under the style of 'Queen Mary,' although she never enjoyed that title, as she died in 1394. The children of this marriage were four sons, and two daughters ; of the latter, Blanche became the wife of Lewis II., *Barbatus*, Duke of Bavaria ; and Philippa married Eric X., King of Norway. The sons were, 1. Henry of *Monmouth*, born in the Norman castle there, according to the inscription upon his statue in that town, 'August ix, 1387,' although most writers place his birth a year later. Rapin ascribes it to the year 1386, and Buswell to 1385. One hardly reconciles the date usually given, 1388, for the birth of 'Prince Hal,' for that would only make him eleven years old when he is represented as boasting, that in a tournament—

'He would unhorse the lustiest challenger.'

2. Prince Thomas, born in 1388, afterwards Duke of Clarence, a character in the next play ;
3. 'Prince John of Lancaster' in this play ;
4. Prince Humphrey, the 'Duke of Gloucester' in the *Second Part*.

Henry IV., married secondly, Feb. 7, 1403, the widow of his friend John de Montfort, Duke of Britany ; she was Joan, daughter of Charles *le Mauvais*, King of Navarre, and was crowned Feb. 25, 1403 ; she died in the reign of Henry VI., 1437, and was buried in Canterbury Cathedral, in the splendid tomb of her royal husband, whereon are their life-like effigies. Joan of Navarre had no issue by her second marriage. *French.*

[King Henry the Fourth is also a character in the *Second Part of King Henry the Fourth* (q.v.)]

King's Camp near Shrewsbury.

The Scene of Act V., Scene i. Continues Act IV., Scene iii. Worcester appears in the royal camp with a letter from Hotspur, but it is merely a repetition of Hotspur's speech to Blunt in Act IV., Scene iii. In order to save bloodshed Prince Henry challenges Hotspur to single combat, after which the king offers uncondi-

tional pardon if the rebels will return to their allegiance.

Knight of the Burning Lamp. III. iii. 27.

The 'Knight of the burning lamp' and the 'Knight of the burning pestle' were humorous names invented to ridicule knightly heroes in the days of chivalry.

Lady Mortimer, daughter to Glendower, and wife to Mortimer. II. iv. 110 ; III. i. p.192.

Strangely enough Lady Mortimer can speak no English, and her husband can speak no Welsh. Mortimer says :

> This is the deadly spite that angers me ;
> My wife can speak no English, I no Welsh.
> [III. i. 192–193.]

She has however a great love for her husband and is overcome with grief when she is told that he has to go to the wars, and vows : " she will not part with him ; She'll be a soldier too, she'll to the wars," but Glendower—acting as interpreter—explains to her that the parting will not be for long. Then comes the tender parting with her husband, and she bids him lie down upon the grass, and put his head upon her lap while she softly sings him to sleep :

> *Glend.* She bids you on the wanton rushes lay you down
> And rest your gentle head upon her lap,
> And she will sing the song that pleaseth you,
> And on your eyelids crown the god of sleep,
> Charming your blood with pleasing heaviness,
> Making such difference 'twixt wake and sleep
> As is the difference betwixt day and night
> The hour before the heavenly-harness'd team
> Begins his golden progress in the east.
> [III. i. 213–221.]

[Lady Mortimer was the daughter of Owen Glendower, and according to Shakespeare the wife of Sir Edmund Mortimer. Welsh historians do not, however, bear out this statement.]

Lady Percy, wife to Hotspur, and sister to Mortimer. II. iii. p.37, 110 ; III. i. p.192.

Presents an "attractive figure" in the play. Her nature is closely allied to that of her husband in its "mixture of banter and seriousness," and she also shows the same poetical quality in her speech. She has a great love for her husband and is greatly troubled about him, saying that "he has lost the fresh blood in his cheeks," and talks in his sleep :

> Of sallies and retires, of trenches, tents,
> Of palisadoes, frontiers, parapets,
> Of basilisks, of cannon, culverin,
> Of prisoners' ransom, and of soldiers slain,
> And all the currents of a heady fight. [II. iii. 53–57.]

We can see that beneath his seeming roughness Hotspur has a great affection for his "dear lady," whose tribute to her "heart's dear Harry" is not all paid to his heroism.

[Lady Percy is also a character in the *Second Part of King Henry the Fourth* (q.v.)]

Lazarus. IV. ii. 25.

> slaves as ragged as Lazarus
> in the painted cloth,   [IV. ii. 25–26.]

= The beggar Lazarus represented on a painted canvas. In ancient times a cloth or canvas painted in oils was a cheap substitute for tapestry for hanging the rooms of dwelling-houses, the subjects usually depicted being of a scriptural or allegorical nature.

Leather-jerkin. II. iv. 69.
Crystal-button. II. iv. 69.
Not-pated. II. iv. 70.
Agate-ring. II. iv. 70.
Puke-stocking. II. iv. 70.
Caddis-garter. II. iv. 70.
Spanish-pouch. II. iv. 71.

The Prince is here describing the vintner of the tavern. *Leather-jerkin—Crystal-button* = a a man who wears a leather jacket with glass buttons. They were usually worn by vintners. From Greene's *Quip for an Upstart Courtier*, 1620, we read that "a leather jerkin with crystal-buttons was the habit of a pawn-broker." *Not-pated* = having the hair cut short and round. Steevens quotes from Stowe's *Annals* for the Year 1535, 27th, of Henry the Eighth : "He caused his own head to bee polled, and from thenceforth his beard to bee notted and no more shaven." *Agate-ring* = a ring with a cheap stone in it. *Puke-stocking* = a puke colour, a

colour between russet and black. In *The Order of my Lorde Maior, &c., for their Meetings and Wearing of theyr Apparel throughout the Yeere,* 1586, appears "the maior, &c., are commanded to appeare on Good Fryday in their pewke gownes, and without their chaynes and typetes." *Caddis-garter* = A garter made of worsted material in contradistinction to the silk garter worn by men of fashion. The garters of Shakespeare's time were worn in sight, and consequently were expensive. Steevens quotes from *Warres, or the Peace is Broken :* "—fine piecd silke stockens on their legs, tyed up smoothly with caddis garters—" and in Stow's *Chronicle* we have : "men of mean rank weare garters and shoe-roses of more than five pound price." *Spanish-pouch* = the pouch of Spanish leather usually worn by vintners in which he placed his money.

Lincolnshire. I. ii. 77.

> Yea, or the drone of a Lincolnshire bagpipe   [I. ii. 77.]

= the wail of a Lincolnshire bagpipe. Lincolnshire bagpipes are mentioned in *A Nest of Ninnies,* by Robert Armin, 1608 : "At a Christmas time, when great logs furnish the hall fire : when brawne is in season, and indeed all reveling is regarded : this gallant knight kept open house for all commers, where beefe, beere, and bread was no niggard. Amongst all the pleasures provided, a noyse of minstrells and a Lincolnshire bagpipe was prepared : the minstrells for the great chamber, the bagpipe for the hall ; the minstrells to serve up the knight's meate, and the bagpipe for the common dauncing. *The drone of the bagpipe* is considered to mean the dull croak of a frog, one of the native musicians of that waterish county."

London. I. ii. 127 ; II. i. 15, 42 ; II. ii. 91 ; V. iii. 30.

London. An Apartment of the Prince's.

The Scene of Act I., Scene ii. A great contrast to the preceding scene. It introduces us to Prince Henry (Hal) and Falstaff. There is a plot to rob the Canterbury pilgrims and the London traders at Gadshill and a counterplot by the Prince and Poins to rob Falstaff and his friends of their ill-gotten gain. The lies and subterfuges of Falstaff provide great fun.

London. The Palace.

The Scene of Act I., Scene i. Act I., Scene iii. Act III., Scene ii.

Act I., Scene i. Introduces the chief characters of the Play. Henry declares his intention of going on crusade to the Holy Land. Westmoreland announces that Glendower has raised the standard of rebellion in Wales and has taken Edmund Mortimer prisoner. He also announces the defeat at Holmedon hill by Hotspur of a Scottish force under the Earl of Douglas. Henry demands of Hotspur the prisoners he has captured at Holmedon, but refusing to accede to the king's demand, has summoned Hotspur to appear before a council at Windsor.

Act I., Scene iii. Continues Scene i. At the opening of the scene Worcester is dismissed the king's presence. Hotspur appears and is prepared to surrender the prisoners taken at Holmedon conditionally upon Henry ransoming Edmund Mortimer, a prisoner in the hands of Glendower. Principally from personal motives —Mortimer being the real heir to the crown— Henry refuses this request and dismisses the council. Hotspur's outbursts of passion and the cool and calculating schemes of Worcester provide a great contrast.

Act III., Scene ii. This scene shows us the interview between Henry and the Prince of Wales. The king chides his son for keeping such low company, and the prince asks for forgiveness. The interview ends with a reconciliation between father and son and Henry promises the prince a high place of ' sovereign trust ' in the war. The interview is interrupted by Sir William Blunt who enters with the news that Hotspur and Douglas have joined forces at Shrewsbury. Malone points out that the reference in this scene to the expulsion of King Henry from the Privy Council is an anachronism. The prince had been president of the council, and was removed from the office in consequence of his striking Lord Chief Justice Gascoigne ; but this was some years after the battle of Shrewsbury (1403). *See under* Lord Chief Justice of the

King's Bench in the *Second Part of King Henry the Fourth.*

Long-staff sixpenny strikers. II. i. 74.

Contemptible fellows who carried long staffs and would knock a man down for sixpence. Cf. *The London Prodigal,* 1605 : " Nay, now I have had such a fortunate beginning, I'll not let a six-penny-purse escape me." *Malone.*

Lord Mortimer of Scotland. III. ii. 164.

Lord Mortimer of Scotland hath sent word
That Douglas and the English rebels met
The eleventh of this month at Shrewsbury.
[III. ii. 164–166.]

Steevens says : There was no such person as Lord Mortimer of Scotland ; but there was a Lord March of Scotland, (George Dunbar,) who having quitted his own country in disgust, attached himself so warmly to the English, and did them such signal services in their wars with Scotland, that the Parliament petitioned the King to bestow some reward on him. He fought on the side of Henry in this rebellion, and was the means of saving his life at the battle of Shrewsbury, as is related by Holinshed. This, no doubt, was the lord whom Shakespeare designed to represent in the act of sending friendly intelligence to the King. Our author had a recollection that there was in these wars a Scottish lord on the King's side, who bore the same title with the English family, on the rebel side, (one being the Earl of March in England, the other, Earl of March in Scotland,) but his memory deceived him as to the particular name which was common to both. He took it to be Mortimer instead of March.

Lord of Stafford. V. iii. 7, 13 ; V. iv. 41.

Edmund, fifth Earl of Stafford, who was killed at the battle of Shrewsbury while leading the king's foreward. For his valour in the field he had been made Lord High Constable of England by Henry. He was killed by Douglas who mistook him for the king, being one of several knights who were wearing the king's arms on their surcoats, hence : " The Lord of Stafford dear to-day hath bought Thy likeness."

[Edmund Stafford, Earl of Stafford, was the third son of Hugh Earl of Stafford, and his wife Philippa, daughter of Thomas Beauchamp, the elder Earl of Warwick, and the heir of his brothers Thomas and William, and was after their deaths without issue, the fifth Earl of Stafford and Lord of Tunbridge. He married Anne, daughter of Thomas of Woodstock, Duke of Gloucester, sixth son of Edward III. He was the father of Humphrey Stafford, first Duke of Buckingham, slain at the battle of Northampton fighting for the Lancastrian party in 1460.]

Lord Scroop.   I. iii. 271.

> who bears hard
> His brother's death at Bristow, the Lord Scroop.
> [I. iii. 270–271.]

Shakespeare is mistaken here. Lord Scroop was not brother to the Archbishop of York. Lord Scroop, afterwards the Earl of Wiltshire who was executed at Bristol by Bolingbroke, was the youngest son of Henry le Scroop, first baron of Masham, whilst the Archbishop of York was the second son of Richard, Lord Scroop of Bolton.

Lords.

Lucifer.   II. iv. 337.

Madeira.   I. ii. 116.

A rich wine of the sherry class, produced in Madeira.

Maid Marian.   III. iii. 115.

> and for womanhood, Maid Marian may be the
> deputy's wife of the ward to thee.   [III. iii. 115–116.]

The paramour of Robin Hood in Sherwood Forest. The allusion here is to her as one of the characters in the morris-dance, held generally on May-day, in which she was represented as a woman of dissolute character.

Malt-worms.   II. i. 75.

> Mad mustachio purple-hued malt-worms.   [II. i. 75.]

Drunkards whose faces were red with drinking ale, and whose large moustaches gave them fierce countenances. In *The Life and Death of Jack Straw*, 1503, we have : " You shall purchase the prayers of all the alewives in town, for saving a malt-worm and a customer."

Manningtree ox.   II. iv. 451.

Manningtree : a town in Essex, famous for its fat oxen and its great fairs at which morality plays were performed, and eating and drinking were done on a large scale. In Dekker's *Newes from Hell, brought by the Devil's Carrier* we have : " —you shall have a slave eat more at a meale than ten of the guard ; and drink more in two days, than all Manningtree does at a Whitsun-ale."

Mars.   III. ii. 112.

> Thrice hath this Hotspur, Mars in swathing clothes,
> This infant warrior, in his enterprises
> Discomfited great Douglas.   [III. ii. 112–114.]

Mars was the god of war, and Hotspur is here represented as young Mars. He defeated the Scotch at Nesbit and at Holmedon, but was himself defeated by the Scotch at Otterburn, being taken prisoner, after killing the then Earl of Douglas.

Mars.   IV. i. 116.

> And to the fire-eyed maid of smoky war
> All hot and bleeding will we offer them :
> The mailed Mars shall on his altar sit
> Up to the ears in blood.   [IV. i. 114–117.]

Fire-eyed maid of smoky war = Bellona the Roman goddess of war. *Mailed Mars* = The god of war clad in armour. Both the goddess and the god are represented here as receiving the sacrifice.

May.   IV. i. 101.

Menteith.   I. i. 73.

One of the titles held by Murdach Stewart, Earl of Fife, whose mother, Margaret Graham, was Countess of Menteith in her own right. He was a captive in England for thirteen years, and was reclaimed in 1415 for the Earl of Northumberland.

Mercury. IV. i. 106.

> Rise from the ground like feather'd Mercury,
> [IV. i. 106.]

An allusion to the wings attached to the ankles of the god Mercury suggestive of rapid speed. Mercury was the winged messenger to the gods.

Merlin. III. i. 150.

> I cannot choose : sometime he angers me
> With telling me of the moldwarp and the ant,
> Of the dreamer Merlin and his prophecies.
> [III. i. 148–150.]

An allusion to an old prophecy, that is said to have induced Glendower to rebel against King Henry. Cf. *The Mirrour for Magistrates*, 1559, where Glendower is introduced, speaking of himself :

> And for to set us hereon more agog,
> A prophet came (a vengeaunce take them all !)
> Affirming Henry to be Gogmagog,
> Whom Merlyn doth a *mouldwarp* ever call,
> Accurs'd of God that must be brought in thrall,
> By a wulf, a dragon, and a lyon strong,
> Which shuld devide his kingdome them among.

Holinshed says : " This [the division of the realm between Mortimer, Glendower, and Percy,] was done (as some have sayde) through a foolish credite given to a vaine prophesie, as though King Henry was the *molde-warpe*, cursed of God's own mouth, and they three were the *dragon*, the *lion*, and the *wolfe*, which should divide this realm between them."

Messengers. IV. i. p.13 ; V. ii. p.80, p.90.

In Act IV., Scene i., one of the messengers enters and hands a letter to Hotspur. The letter is from his father the Earl of Northumberland who is unable to join him as he is sick :

> He cannot come, my lord ; he is grievous sick.
> [IV. i. 16.]

In Act V., Scene ii., he again enters with letters, but Hotspur has no time to read them ; after which another messenger enters and informs Hotspur that the king and his forces are approaching :

> My lord, prepare ; the king comes on apace. [V. ii. 90.]

Michaelmas. II. iv. 55.

The festival of St. Michael and All Angels, the 29th of September.

Mistress Quickly, hostess of a tavern in Eastcheap. II. iv. p.283, p.484 ; III. iii. p.52, 92.

Is mainly distinguished by her " density of understanding." She first enters with news for the prince that " there is a nobleman of the court at door would speak with you : he says he comes from your father."

Later she has words with Falstaff, who declares that his pockets have been picked, but she tells him that she does not keep thieves in her house, and defies him, saying that he owes her for the garments he wears, as well as for his board, drink and various sums of money she has lent him from time to time :

> you owe me money, Sir John ;
> and now you pick a quarrel to beguile me of it : I
> bought you a dozen of shirts to your back.
> [III. iii. 66–68.]

and

> You owe money here besides, Sir
> John, for your diet and by-drinkings, and money
> lent you, four and twenty pound. [III. iii. 72–74.]

At this juncture their quarrel is interrupted by the entry of the prince, who—on hearing Falstaff's detailed description of his lost valuables —confesses that it was he (the prince) who rifled Falstaff's pockets. Hearing this, Falstaff forgives the hostess, who then leaves the room.

[Mistress Quickly also appears in the *Second Part of King Henry the Fourth* (q.v.)]

Monsieur Remorse. I. ii. 113.

A nonce name, or a name coined for the occasion. Applied to Falstaff by Poins.

Moor-ditch. I. ii. 79.

A ditch in the neighbourhood of Bishopsgate and Cripplegate proverbial for its muddy, stagnant character. Stow in his *Survey of London* says : " The ditch, which partly now remaineth, and compassed the wall of the city, was begun to be made by the Londoners in the year 1213, the 15th, of King John. This ditch being then made of 200 feet broad, caused no small hindrance to the canons of the Holy Trinity, whose church stood near unto Aldgate ; for that the said ditch passed through their ground from the Tower of London unto Bishopsgate. This ditch, being originally made for the defence of the city, was also long together carefully cleansed and maintained, as need requireth ; but now of late neglected and forced either to a very narrow, and the same a filthy channel, or altogether stopped up for gardens planted, and houses built thereon ; even to the very wall, and in many places upon both ditch and wall houses to be built ; to what danger of the city, I leave to wiser consideration, and can but wish that reformation might be had." And in *Gull's Hornbrook* by Thomas Dekker, we read : " it will be a sorer labour than the cleansing of Augeas' stable, or the scowring of Moor-ditch."

Mordake, Earl of Fife. I. i. 71 ; II. iv. 357 ; IV. iv. 24.

Murdach Stewart, eldest son of Robert, Duke of Albany, Regent of Scotland, who was third son of King Robert II. Shakespeare following Holinshed makes him the son to the governor Douglas. Earl Mordake also held the title of the Earl of Menteith. He was taken prisoner at the battle of Holmedon.

Mordake, Earl of Fife. I. i. 95.

and sends me word,
I shall have none but Mordake Earl of Fife.
[I. i. 94–95.]

Henry was going beyond his right in demanding the prisoners captured at Holmedon. By the law of arms, every man who had taken any captive, and whose redemption did not exceed ten thousand crowns, had him clearly for himself, either to acquit or ransom at his pleasure. Mordake being a prince of the royal blood was the only prisoner Henry could justly claim by his acknowledged military prerogative. Pounouny Castle in Scotland is considered to have been built out of the ransom of Henry Percy when taken prisoner at the battle of Otterbourne by an ancestor of the present Earl of Eglinton. *Malone.*

Mortimer. I. iii. 144.

Trembling even at the name of Mortimer.   [I. iii. 144.]

Johnson and Steevens seem to think that Hotspur meant to describe the King as trembling not with fear, but rage ; but surely they are mistaken. The king had no reason to be enraged at Mortimer, who had been taken prisoner in fighting against his enemy ; but he had much reason to fear the man who had a better title to the crown than himself, which had been proclaimed by Richard II ; and accordingly, when Hotspur is informed of that circumstance, he says :

Nay, then I cannot blame his cousin king
That wish'd him on the barren mountains starv'd.

and in the very next line, Worcester says : " He cannot blame him for trembling at the name of Mortimer, since Richard had proclaimed him next of blood. *Malone.*

Mortimer. I. iii. 156.

did King Richard then
Proclaim my brother Edmund Mortimer
Heir to the crown ?   [I. iii. 155–157.]

Roger Mortimer, Earl of March, who was born in 1371, was declared heir apparent to the crown in the 9th year of King Richard II (1385). But he was killed in Ireland in 1398. The person who was proclaimed by Richard heir apparent to the crown, previous to his last voyage to Ireland, was Edmund Mortimer, (the son of Roger,) who was then but seven years old ; but he was not Percy's wife's brother, but her nephew.

Edmund Mortimer, Earl of March, was the undoubted heir to the crown after the death of Richard, as appears from the following table ; in which the three younger children of King Edward III., are not included, as being immaterial to the subject before us :

King Edward III.

Edward, Prince of Wales.	William of Hatfield died without issue.	Lionel, duke of Clarence.	John of Gaunt, duke of Lancaster.
King Richard II., died without issue.		Philippa, married to Edmund Mortimer, Earl of March.	Henry, duke of Hereford, afterwards King Henry IV.
		Roger Mortimer, Earl of March.	
Edmund Mortimer, Earl of March.		Eleanor died without issue.	Anne, married to Richard, Earl of Cambridge.

Edmund, Earl of March, (the Mortimer of this play,) was married to Anne Stafford, daughter of Edmund, Earl of Stafford. Thomas Walsingham asserts that he married a daughter of Owen Glendower ; but this is a very doubtful point, for the Welsh writers make no mention of it. Sandford says that this Earl of March was confined by the jealous Henry in the castle of Trim in Ireland, and that he died there, after an imprisonment of twenty years, on the 19th of January, 1424. But this is a mistake. There is no proof that he was confined a state-prisoner by King Henry the Fourth, and he was employed in many military services by his son Henry the Fifth. He died at his own castle at Trim in Ireland, at the time mentioned by Sandford, but not in a state of imprisonment.

I learn that Owen Glendower's daughter was married to his antagonist Lord Grey of Ruthven. Holinshed led Shakespeare into the error of supposing her the wife of Edmund Mortimer, Earl of March. This nobleman, who is the Mortimer of the present play, was born in November, 1392, and consequently at the time when this play commences, was little more than ten years old. The Prince of Wales was not fifteen. *Malone.*

Mugs. II. i. 44.

The name by which the ' First Carrier ' is addressed.

Murray. I. i. 74.

Thomas Dunbar, second Earl of Murray, and grandson of Patrick, ninth Earl of Dunbar and Marche, whose wife was Agnes, daughter of Sir Thomas Randolph who at Bannockburn commanded the left wing of the army of his uncle, King Robert Bruce, who created his nephew, Earl of Moray. Taken prisoner at the battle of Holmedon.

Ned. I. ii. 112 ; II. ii. 105 ; II. iv. 1, 20, 22, 28.

= Poins.

Newgate fashion. III. iii. 90.

Yea, two and two, Newgate fashion.   [III. iii. 90.]

Like prisoners on their way to Newgate gaol, fastened two and two together.

Officers.

Owen Glendower. I. i. 40 ; I. iii. 83, 101, 114, 117, 295 ; II. iii. 26 ; II. iv. 340, 341, 369 ; III. i. p.1, 3, 11, 78, 87, p.192 ; IV. i. 124, 131 ; IV. iv. 16 ; V. v. 40.

A Welsh chieftain and ally of Hotspur, who, though he does not show his nationality in his speech, betrays it in his being endowed with a love of poetry and art ; possessing such refinement and high-bearing which is characteristic of his race,—indeed his character conveys to us the beautiful atmosphere and artistic mysticism of medieval Wales.

His character however, is somewhat spoiled by a " complacent conceit," as he ostentatiously regards himself " as not in the roll of common men," for he says :

> at my nativity
> The front of heaven was full of fiery shapes,
> Of burning cressets ; and at my birth
> The frame and huge foundation of the earth
> Shaked like a coward.   [III. i. 13–17.]

to which Hotspur replies :

> Why, so it would have done at the same season, if
> your mother's cat had but kittened, though yourself
> had never been born.   [III. i. 18–20.]

We cannot but notice the humorous side of his attempts to convince Hotspur that he is gifted with supernatural powers, claiming that he can call up spirits from the " vasty deep " which assertion Hotspur ridicules in such a fashion that he makes Glendower wild with fury :

> *Glend.* I can call spirits from the vasty deep.
> *Hot.* Why, so can I, or so can any man ;
>   But will they come when you do call for them ?
> *Glend* Why, I can teach you, cousin, to command
>   The devil.
> *Hot.* And I can teach thee, coz, to shame the devil
>   By telling truth : tell truth, and shame the devil.
>   [III. i. 53–59.]

Glendower's belief in himself, however, has a curious effect upon others, for even the king, when he fails to bring him into subjection, declares that Glendower has the assistance of the supernatural, and calls him " that great magician, damn'd Glendower." See *Extract* 5 from Holinshed.

Commenting on this character, Hudson says : " The best of historical matter for poetical and dramatic uses has seldom been turned to better account that way than in the portrait of Glendower. He is represented, with great art and equal truth, according to the superstitious belief of his time ; a belief in which himself doubtless shared : for, if the winds and tempests came *when* he wished them, it was natural for him to think, as others thought, that they came *because* he wished them. The popular ideas respecting him all belonged to the region of poetry ; and Shakespeare has given them with remarkable exactness, at the same time penetrating and filling them with his own spirit.

Crediting the alleged portents of his nativity, Glendower might well conclude he was " not in the roll of common men " ; and so betake himself to the study and practice of those magic arts which were generally believed in then, and for which he was specially marked by his birth and all the courses of his life. And for the same cause he would naturally become somewhat egotistical, long-winded, and tedious ; presuming that what was interesting to him as relating to himself would be equally so to others for its own sake. So that we need not altogether discredit Hotspur's account of the time spent by him " in reckoning up the several devils' names that were his lacqueys." For, though Hotspur exaggerates here, as usual, yet we see that he has some excuse for his sauciness to Glendower, in that he has been dreadfully bored by him. And there is something ludicrous withal in the Welshman's being so wrapped up in himself as not to perceive the unfitness of talking thus to one so hare-brained and skittish.

Glendower, however, is no ordinary enthusiast. A man of wild and mysterious imaginations, yet he has a practical skill that makes them tell against the King ; his dealing in magic rendering him even more an object of fear than his valour and conduct. And his behaviour in the disputes with Hotspur approves him as much superior in the external qualities of a gentleman as he is more superstitious. Though no suspicion of any thing false or mean can attach to Hotspur, it is characteristic of him to indulge his haughty temper even to the thwarting of his purpose : he will hazard the blowing-up of the conspiracy rather than put a bridle on his impatience ;

which the Welshman, with all his grandeur and earnestness of pretension, is too prudent to do."

[Owen Glendower was the son of Griffith Vaughan who married the daughter of Llewelyn, the last prince of North Wales. Trained in the English court he became a supporter of Richard the Second. His estates being seized by Lord Grey of Ruthin he petitioned Parliament for redress but being refused rebelled against Henry. Defeated and captured Lord Grey and Sir Edmund Mortimer. Joined the Percys' rebellion, but was not present at the battle of Shrewsbury, though according to some historians he committed great ravages in Shropshire. In *English Forests and Forest Trees*, we read : " An oak, called the ' Shelton Oak,' growing near Shrewsbury, was celebrated for Owen Glyndwr having mounted on it to observe the battle of Shrewsbury, fought on the 21st., of June, 1403, between Henry IV. and Harry Percy. The battle had commenced before Glyndwr had arrived, and he ascended the tree to see how the day was likely to go ; finding that Hotspur was beaten, and the force of the king was overpowering, he retired with his 12,000 men to Oswestry." On the accession of Henry the Fifth in 1413 he was included in the general pardon, after which he retired into obscurity and his end is unknown. Holinshed says : " The Welsh rebell Owen Glendower made an end of his wretched life in this tenth yeare [1408–9] of king Henrie his reigne ; being driuen now in his latter time (as we find recorded) to such miserie, that, in manner despairing of all comfort, he fled into desert places and solitarie caues ; where, being destitute of all releefe and succour, dreading to shew his face to anie creature, and finallie lacking meat to susteine nature, for meere hunger and lacke of food, [he] miserable pined awaie and died."]

Paul's. II. iv. 524.

This oily rascal is known as well as Paul's. [II. iv. 524.]

= St. Paul's Cathedral, it being the most conspicuous building in London.

Pegasus. IV. i. 109.

A winged horse said to have sprung from the blood of Medusa when her head was cut off by Perseus.

Peto. I. ii. 161 ; II. ii. 21, p.48 ; II. iv. p.113, 298, 473, 548 ; III. iii. p.88, 198 ; IV. ii. 9.

One of Falstaff's band of robbers, who, like his confederates, is a braggart and a coward.

He tells how Falstaff hacked his sword with a dagger to make believe it was done in the fight, after the robbery at Gadshill. He acts as lieutenant to Falstaff in his 'charge of foot.'

The name of ' Peito ' occurs on the ' Roll of Battel Abbey,' and the family appears to have been seated in the county of Warwick from an early period. In 6 Edward I. Richard de Peito held lands at Drayton, near Stratford-upon-Avon ; and 23 Edward I., 1294, William de Peto, who married Margaret, daughter of Richard Langley, was seated at Wolphamcote, co. Warwick ; and in 1398, a descendant, William de Peto, cousin and heir to Geoffrey de Langley, gave a release of the manor of Milcote, in the same shire, to William Grevill. In the reign of Queen Elizabeth, Sir Humphrey Peyto was of Chesterton, where he is buried with his son and grandson, William and Edward Peyto ; and Sir Edward Peito was governor of Warwick Castle for the earl. It is therefore likely that the poet selected the name from its connection with his native county, and that he intended Peto to take a better rank than Pistol, Bardolph, and Nym ; thus he is classed, in the list of characters of the *Second Part*, in the usual editions, with Poins, as ' Attendants on Prince Henry,' whilst the others are called ' formerly servants to Falstaff,' in *King Henry V.* Peto, in this play, holds the rank of ' lieutenant ' to Falstaff in his ' charge of horse.' *French.*

[Peto also appears in the *Second Part of King Henry the Fourth* (q.v.)]

Pharaoh. II. iv. 472.

> if to be
> fat be to be hated, then Pharaoh's lean kine are to
> be loved. [II. iv. 471–473.]

A reference to Pharaoh's dream. See *Genesis* xli, 2–4.

Phœbus. I. ii. 15.

> and
> not by Phœbus, he, that wandering knight so fair.
> [I. ii. 14–15.]

Apollo the sun-god. Probably an allusion to El Donzel del Febo (Knight of the Sun) the hero of a Spanish romance, translated into English under the title of *The Mirror of Princely Deeds and Knighthood.*

Plantagenet. I. i. 89.

> O that it could be proved
> That some night-tripping fairy had exchanged
> In cradle-clothes our children where they lay,
> And call'd mine Percy, his Plantagenet ! [I. i. 86–89.]

It was a common superstition that among other pranks played by the fairies was stealing babies out of their cots and leaving ugly ones in their place. Brand quotes Willis's *Mount Tabor, or Private Exercises of a Penitent Sinner*, 1639. Under the heading of " Upon an extraordinary accident which befel me in my swaddling cloaths," we read : " When we come to years, we are commonly told of what befell us in our infancie, if the same were more than ordinary. Such an accident (by relation of others) befell me within few daies after my birth, whilst my mother lay in of me, being her second child, when I was taken out of the bed from her side, and by my suddain and fierce crying recovered again, being found sticking between the bed's head and the wall : and if I had not cryed in that manner as I did, our gossips had a conceit that I had been quite carried away by the fairies they know not whither, and some elfe or changeling (as they call it) laid in my room."

Poins. I. ii. p.107, 107 ; II. ii. p.1, 4, 7, 20, 59, p.90, 96, 98 ; II. iv. p.1, 85, p.87, 144, 474.

One of the comic characters, and a friend to Prince Henry and Falstaff. He informs the prince and Falstaff that :

> to-morrow morning, by
> four o'clock, early at Gadshill ! there are pilgrims
> going to Canterbury with rich offerings, and traders
> riding to London with fat purses : [I. ii. 124–127.]

Falstaff suggests that they waylay the travellers, but the prince refuses to accompany them, and when Falstaff has gone Poins suggests playing a trick upon him and his confederates, proposing that after they have robbed the travellers, the prince and himself in disguise, shall rob them. The prince agrees, and they arrange to meet at a certain spot. Their plot succeeds, and Falstaff and his fellow-robbers are put to flight, leaving their booty on the ground.

The prince and Poins then proceed to the Boar's-Head Tavern in Eastcheap, and being in a joyful mood they play a trick on one of the waiters whilst they await the coming of Falstaff, who, on arriving, declares that he cannot overlook his supposed desertion.

French points out : " In the edition of 1623 the ' Actors ' Names' are given at the end of the *Second Part of King Henry the Fourth,* and at the head of the ' Irregular Humourists' is Pointz ; and the name occurs in this *First Part,* spelt ' Pointz, Poynes, and Poines.' As this favourite companion of Prince Hal is evidently of more gentle blood than Gadshill or Bardolph, ' the worst that they can say of me is that I am a second brother,' it is probable that Shakespeare intended him for a cadet of the family of Poyntz, one of high antiquity, found in *Domesday Book,* under Gloucestershire. Nicholas de Poyntz, and his son Hugh de Poyntz, were among the feudal barons in arms against King John ; and Hugh's grandson, Hugh Poyntz, was summoned to Parliament as a baron from 1295 to 1307, and his descendants for three generations were also barons. The family continued to flourish in the county of Gloucester, of which they were sheriffs, from the time of Richard II to that of Elizabeth. Thomas Poyntz was one of the lances at Agincourt in the train of Lord Maltravers.

[Poins also appears in the *Second Part of King Henry the Fourth* (q.v.)]

Pomgarnet. II. iv. 38.

= Pomegranate. A special room in the Boar's Head Tavern. Steevens remarks : " To have windows or loop-holes looking into the rooms beneath them, was anciently a general custom."

Prince of Wales. I. iii. 230.

And that same sword-and-buckler Prince of Wales.
[I. iii. 230.]

A royster or turbulent fellow, that fought in taverns, or raised disorder in the streets, was called a swash-buckler. In this sense *sword-and-buckler* is here used. *Johnson.* Deighton re-

marks : " Henley illustrates the phrase *sword-and-buckler* from Stow. The field, commonly called West Smithfield, was for many years called Ruffian's Hall, by reason it was the usual place of frays and common fighting, during the time that swords and bucklers were in use. When every servingman . . . carried a buckler at his back, which hung by the hilt or pomel of his sword."

Prince of Wales. IV. i. 95.

Where is his son,
The nimble-footed madcap Prince of Wales.
[IV. i. 94–95.]

Stow says : " He (the Prince) was passing swift in running, insomuch that he with two other of his lords, without hounds, bow, or other engine, would take a wild buck, or doe, in a large park."

Prince of Wales. II. iv. 11, 139 ; III. ii. 1 ; IV. i. 121 ; IV. iv. 29 ; V. i. 86, 101 ; V. ii. 46 ; V. iv. 12, 42, 63, 67.

Henry, Prince of Wales (q.v.).

Public Road near Coventry.

The Scene of Act IV., Scene ii. In this scene we see Falstaff with his charge of foot marching towards Coventry. They are overtaken by the Prince and Westmoreland who are highly amused at Falstaff's ragged contingent, but Falstaff declares that they are ' good enough to toss ' and ' food for powder.'

Ralph. II. iv. 39.

A drawer or servant at the Boar's Head Tavern.

Ravenspurgh. I. iii. 248 ; III. ii. 95 ; IV. iii. 77.

Name of the seaport on the Yorkshire coast at which Henry IV—then Bolingbroke—landed on his return from exile in 1399. See *The Tragedy of King Richard the Second,* page 465.

Rebel Camp near Shrewsbury. The Scene of Act IV., Scene i. Act IV., Scene iii. Act V., Scene ii.

Act IV., Scene i. The rebels receive their first set-back by a messenger entering with the news that Northumberland—Hotspur's father—is prevented by sickness from joining them at Shrewsbury. News is brought by Sir Richard Vernon that the Earl of Westmoreland and Prince John with a large army are marching against them, and also that Glendower cannot join them for at least fourteen days.

Act IV., Scene iii. The evening before the battle of Shrewsbury. Hotspur and Douglas are in favour of fighting the same evening, but Worcester and Vernon counsel delay, which advice is adopted consequent upon the arrival of Sir William Blunt from the king with ' gracious offers.' Hotspur promises to send Worcester on the morrow with a reply.

Act V., Scene ii. Worcester and Vernon return to the rebel camp, but Worcester proves false, for instead of imparting to Hotspur the king's offer of pardon, tells him that Henry had denounced them as ' rebels and traitors.' By his treachery, Worcester's object is achieved, and preparations are made to meet the king's troops.

Richard. I. iii. 146, 155, 175, 242 ; III. ii. 94.

= Richard II.

Richard Scroop, Archbishop of York. I. iii. 269, 280 ; II. iii. 21, 25 ; III. ii. 119 ; IV. iv. p.1 ; V. v. 37.

Only appears once in the play, in his palace at York, in company with his friend, Sir Michael.

He bids Sir Michael hasten to deliver some letters which will enable reinforcements to be raised on Hotspur's behalf, whose force is weaker than that of the king.

The Archbishop is anxious that the king shall not gain the victory, for he says :

> And, to prevent the worst, Sir Michael, speed :
> For if Lord Percy thrive not, ere the king
> Dismiss his power, he means to visit us,
> For he hath heard of our confederacy,
> And 'tis but wisdom to make strong against him :
> Therefore make haste.   [IV. iv. 35–40.]

knowing that through being implicated in the plot against Henry, his life would be in danger.

This prelate, Richard le Scrope, was the second son of Richard, Lord Scrope of *Bolton*, who had been chancellor in the reign of Richard II. The archbishop had two brothers, the eldest of whom, Roger, became second Lord Scrope of Bolton ; and his youngest brother was Sir Stephen le Scrope of Bentley and Castlecombe. Nearly all historians and the commentators of Shakespeare have made the mistake, fallen into by the poet, in calling the archbishop a brother of the Earl of Wiltshire, who was a Scrope of Masham, as shown in the memoir of Sir Stephen Scrope in *Richard II.* The name of the Earl of Wiltshire was William le Scrope, who had only one brother, Sir Stephen Scrope, the loyal character in *Richard II.*

[The Archbishop of York is also a character in the *Second Part of King Henry the Fourth* (q.v.)]

Richard's time. V. i. 35.

> For you my staff of office did I break
> In Richard's time.   [V. i. 34–35.]

Worcester was Lord High Steward to King Richard. On his brother—the Earl of Northumberland—being proclaimed a traitor, Worcester broke his staff,—the token of his office—and proceeded to Ravenspurgh to join Bolingbroke. Cf. *King Richard the Second*, II. iii. 26–28 : " he hath forsook the court, Broken his staff of office and dispersed The household of the king." Holinshed says : " Sir Thomas Persie, earle of Worcester, lord steward of the kings house, either being so commanded by the king, or else vpon displeasure (as some write) for that the king had proclaimed his brother the earle of Northumberland, traitor, brake his white staffe, (which is the representing signe and token of his office,) and without delaie went to duke Henrie."

Rivo. II. iv. 111.

The derivation of the word is uncertain. Probably it was a cant word used in English taverns in the time of Shakespeare.

Robin Ostler. II. i. 10.

" In Munday, Drayton, Wilson and Hathaway,

The Life of Sir John Oldcastle, the ostler is summoned by a carrier : ' Ho ! John Hostler.' " *Arden edition.*

Rochester. I. ii. 129.

A City of Kent on the river Medway.

Rochester.   An Inn Yard.

The Scene of Act II., Scene i. The scene is an Elizabethan tavern and the time four o'clock a.m. The carriers enter and prepare to set out for Canterbury. Gadshill obtains information from one of his friends at the tavern the amount of money the travellers carry.

Saint Alban's. IV. ii. 47.

Saint Albans lies on the main road from London to Shrewsbury.

Saint Nicholas' clerks.   II. i. 61, 64.

Sirrah, if they meet not with Saint Nicholas' clerks,
I'll give thee this neck.   [II. i. 61–62.]

Nicholas, or Old Nick, is a cant phrase for the devil, hence highwaymen and robbers were referred to as " Saint Nicholas' clerks." In Rowley's *Match at Midnight*, 1633, we have : " I think yonder comes prancing down the hills from Kingston, a couple of St. Nicholas's clerks." and in *A Christian Turn'd Turk*, 1612 : " —We are prevented ;—St. Nicholas's clerks are stepp'd up before us."

Salamander.   III. iii. 47.

A reptile allied to the newt, considered in the middle ages as an animal that lived in fire without being burnt.

Scotland.   I. iii. 262, 265 ; III. i. 45 ; IV. i. 85.

Scotland.   I. iii. 280.

And then the power of Scotland and of York,
To join with Mortimer, ha ?   [I. iii. 280–281.]

= The forces under Archibald, Earl of Douglas.

Scotland.   III. ii. 264.

Lord Mortimer of Scotland hath sent word
That Douglas and the English rebels met
The eleventh of this month at Shrewsbury.
                                   [III. ii. 164–166.]
See Lord Mortimer of Scotland.

Scroop.   IV. iv. 3.

Lord William Scroop, Earl of Wiltshire, who was executed at Bristol by Bolingbroke. *See* Lord Scroop.

Servants.   II. iii. p.67.

Severn.   III. i. 66.

Three times hath Henry Bolingbroke made head
Against my power ; thrice from the banks of Wye
And sandy-bottom'd Severn have I sent him
Bootless home and weather-beaten back.
                                   [III. i. 64–67.]
See Henry Bolingbroke.

Severn.   III. i. 74, 76.

England, from Trent and Severn hitherto,
By south and east is to my part assigned :
                                   [III. i. 74–5.]
The river Severn was the proposed boundary between the territories of Glendower and Mortimer under the indentures tripartite made at Bangor.

Severn's flood.   I. iii. 103

Severn's sedgy bank.   I. iii. 98.

It was on the banks of the river Severn that Glendower and Mortimer fought hand to hand, the latter being taken prisoner.

Sheriff.   II. iv. p.504.

In company with one of the robbed carriers, goes to the Boar's-Head Tavern in Eastcheap and demands admittance in order to search the house for the thieves.

Upon being admitted, the prince asks :

> Now, master sheriff, what is your will with me ?
>
> [II. iv. 504.]

to which the sheriff replies :

> First, pardon me, my lord. A hue and cry
> Hath follow'd certain men unto this house.
>
> [II. iv. 505–506.]

and that " One of them is well known, . . . A gross fat man," adding " There are two gentlemen Have in this robbery lost three hundred marks." The prince, knowing to whom he refers tells him that the man they seek is not there, but assures him that he will be answerable for his appearance on the morrow. The sheriff then bids the prince " good-night " and departs.

Shirley. V. iv. 41.

Sir Hugh Shirlie, Master of the Hawks to Henry IV. He was slain at the battle of Shrewsbury. See *Extract* 14 from Holinshed.

Shrewsbury. III. i. 86 ; III. ii. 166 ; IV. ii. 54 ; IV. iv. 10.

The County Town of Shropshire. On Hayteley Field, about two miles north of this town, Henry the Fourth defeated, on the 21st of July, 1403, Hotspur and the Earl of Douglas, the former being killed. The two armies were unequal in numbers. Hotspur had some 14,000 men including a large force of Cheshire bowmen, while the king's army numbered about 40,000 men. The battle lasted about three hours and was fought with fierceness, the slaughter being very great ; the loss on Hotspur's side being estimated at 5,000, including many knights and gentlemen of Cheshire.

Three years after the battle Henry gave permission to Roger Ive, the rector of Fitz, 1399, and of Albrighton Hussey (close to the battlefield) from 1398 to 1447, to erect a Church on the site of the grave-pits where the slain were buried as a memorial of the victory, and where masses might be said for the king and for the souls of those who were slain in the battle and there buried. There is, however, no record of who were buried on the field. Over the east window in a niche, surmounted by a Gothic canopy, in which stands a crowned statue of

Henry IV. He wears a jupon, and his right hand holds a dagger, and there has probably been a sword at the left.

Shrewsbury, Battle of. Plain between the Camps.

The Scene of Act V., Scene iii. The first part of the battle of Shrewsbury. Lord Stafford and Sir William Blunt—who appear wearing the royal arms on their surcoats, are mistaken for the king—and are both killed by Douglas.

Shrewsbury, Battle of. Another Part of the Field. The Scene of Act V., Scene iv. Act V., Scene v.

Act V., Scene iv. Continues the battle of Shrewsbury. The Prince after heavy fighting is wounded but refuses to retire to have his wounds dressed. The prince saves his father—who encounters Douglas—from being killed, and afterwards fighting Hotspur, kills him. Falstaff feigns death, but ' coming to life ' swears he has killed Percy whom he finds lying dead beside him.

Courtenay remarks : " The incidents of the battle of Shrewsbury are in part warranted by the Chronicle, in part imaginary. Among the latter is the slaying of Hotspur by the prince himself." Malone says : " Shakespeare has chosen to make Hotspur fall by the hand of the Prince of Wales : but there is, I believe, no authority for the fact. According to Holinshed the king slew that day with his own hand six and thirty persons of his enemies. The other [*i.e.* troops] of his party, encouraged by his doings, fought valiantly, and slew the Lord Percy, called Henry Hotspur. Speed says Percy was killed by an unknown hand.

Act V., Scene V. The king has gained the victory. Worcester and Vernon are sentenced to be beheaded. Douglas—for his bravery in the field—is set free by the Prince, but the final speech of the king ' Let us not leave till all our own be won ' remind us that the rebellion is not fully crushed, and consequently we look forward to the *Second Part of King Henry the Fourth*, for in reality the two parts form one complete play.

For accounts of the Battle *see inter alia* " Battle of Shrewsbury : Battlefield Church and College, together with some account of the Proceedings at the commemoration of the 500th., Anniversary, July, 1903." Brooke's " Visits to Fields of Battle in England, of the fifteenth century," 1857. Barrett's " Battles and Battlefields in England," 1896. " A Collection of the Chronicles and Ancient Histories of Great Britain, now called England. By John de Wavrin. [1399–1422.] *Chronicles and Memorials of Great Britain and Ireland during the Middle Ages.*" Ramsay's " Lancaster and York : a century of English History, (A.D. 1399–1485)," 1892. Gairdner's " Houses of Lancaster and York with the conquest and loss of France," 1927. Ingulph's " Chronicle of the Abbey of Croyland." [Bohn's edition.] 1908.

Shrewsbury clock. V. iv. 149.

but we rose both at an
instant, and fought a long hour by Shrewsbury clock.
[V. iv. 148–149.]

Cf. Beaumont and Fletcher, *The Noble Gentleman*, v. 1 : " Two . . . stars were seen to fight a long hour by the clock." *Arden edition.* Wordsworth quotes " Sh. Key,' " This mention of the church clock by its name not only gives the humorous effect of pretended exactness to Sir John's account of his exploit, but it serves as a reminder of the site of the scene represented and the celebrated event enacted—the battle of Shrewsbury."

Sir John Bracy. II. iv. 333.

This name is not mentioned by Holinshed or any other historian of the period, but there was a family of this name in the county of Worcester from the time of King John.

Sir John Falstaff. I. ii. p.1, 118, 148, 161 ; II. i. 68 ; II. ii. 1, p.4, 105 ; II. iv. 11, 29, 82, 87, 109, p.113, 256, 302, 325, 424, 428, 462, 474, 475, 476, 477, 484, 526 ; III. iii. p.1, 12, 21, 23, 28, 54, 65, 66, 72, p.88, 127, 142, 166 ; IV. ii. p.1, 55, 69, 78 ; V. i. p.1 ; V. iii. p.29 ; V. iv. p.75, 140.

Is probably Shakespeare's greatest comic character, and also the most " humorous creation in the whole field of Literature." His character is so complex that he can be " a knave without malice, a liar without deceit, and a knight, a gentleman, and a soldier without dignity, decency or honour."

He takes nothing seriously as he lives in an atmosphere of humour, ridicule, and sack, and adopts the " Epicurean Philosophy " taking no thought for the morrow.

He finds material for his art of humour in everything around him, in every situation and even in himself, and not only " takes a delight in his ease and sack, but in the world of humour, and incongruous make-believe which he has formed for himself and his friends."

The ring-leader of his merry band, Falstaff " loves to pretend that he is an innocent man among villains," for he tells the prince in his first appearance in the play :

Thou hast done much harm
upon me, Hal; God forgive thee for it ! Before I
knew thee, Hal, I knew nothing ; and now am I, if
a man should speak truly, little better than one of the
wicked. I must give over this life, and I will give
it over: by the Lord, an I do not, I am a villain :
I'll be damned for never a king's son in Christendom.
[I. ii. 93–99.]

and " forgives Mistress Quickly the hostess of the tavern after he has wronged her : "

Hostess, I forgive thee : [III. iii. 172.]

He does not take either life or his own doings very seriously, in fact it would seem impossible to make Falstaff serious at all, and his versatility is apparent when Prince Hal remarks that he sees in Sir John a " good amendment of life ; from praying to purse-taking."

Falstaff cannot be " called a liar in the ordinary sense of the term," as his lies are really gross-exaggerations, and he has no " intention of deceiving, when he increases two men in buckram suits to eleven," and pretends to have fought with Hotspur for an hour by Shrewsbury Clock.

It is these exaggerations which supply the humorous make-believe which is so delightful.

Falstaff is also in " reality no more a coward than a liar, and, although he runs away when set upon by the prince and Poins, and shams death to avoid being killed by Douglas, he shows no fear on the battlefield, and is quite ready for death, though he will prevent it if he can : "

> Well, if Percy be alive, I'll pierce him. If he do come in my way, so : if he do not, if I come in his willingly, let him make a carbonado of me. I like not such grinning honour as Sir Walter hath : give me life : which if I can save, so ; if not, honour comes unlooked for, and there's an end. [V. iii. 55–60.]

Falstaff is an incongruous character, but the world in which he moves is similar, and thus his actions in the play are not out of place. We must not judge his morals harshly as he has created for himself an atmosphere in which they have no bearing.

[Falstaff also appears in the *Second Part of King Henry the Fourth* (q.v.)]

Sir John Paunch. II. ii. 64.

A nonce-name used for the fat Sir John Falstaff by Prince Henry.

Sir John Sack and Sugar. I. ii. 113.

Speaking of the manners of the English people, Hentzner says : " they put a great deal of sugar in their drink."

Much inquiry has been made about Falstaff's sack, and great surprise has been expressed that he should have mixed sugar with it. As they are here mentioned for the first time in this play, it may not be improper to observe, that it is probable that Falstaff's wine was Sherry, a Spanish wine, originally made at Xeres. He frequently himself calls it *Sherris-sack*. Nor will his mixing sugar with sack appear extraordinary, when it is known that it was a very common practice in our author's time to put sugar into all wines.

" Clownes and vulgar men (says Fynes Moryson) only use large drinking of beere or ale,—but gentlemen garrawse only in wine, with which they mix sugar, which I never observed in any other place or kingdom to be used for that purpose. And because the taste of the English is thus delighted with sweetness, the wines in taverns (for I speak not of merchantes' or gentlemen's cellers) are commonly mixed at the filling thereof, to make them pleasant."

Sir Michael, a friend to the Archbishop of York. IV. iv. p.1, 1, 8, 13, 35, 41.

Only appears in one scene of the play in company with his friend the Archbishop of York— in the latter's palace at York. The archbishop bids him hasten to deliver some letters which are to raise reinforcements for Hotspur, as he fears that " the power of Percy is too weak To wage an instant trial with the king." Sir Michael, however, assures the archbishop that " he need not fear " and goes on to name the various great nobles who are supporting them in their cause, adding, " Doubt not, my lord, they shall be well opposed," to which the archbishop answers : " I hope no less, yet needful 'tis to fear " ; and forthwith bids Sir Michael proceed with all possible speed on his errand.

[Nothing is known of this character, but he is considered to have been Chaplain to the Archbishop of York. In the time of Shakespeare, priests were often given the courtesy title of ' Sir.']

Sir Nicholas Gawsey. V. iv. 45, 58.

Sir Nicholas Goushill of Hoveringham, Nottinghamshire. He was slain at the battle of Shrewsbury. He was father of Sir Robert Goushill, knight, also killed in the field, who was the fourth husband of the Lady Elizabeth Fitzalan, great-great-granddaughter of Edward the First, and widow of the " Duke of Norfolk " in *King Richard II*. See *Extract* 14 from Holinshed.

Sir Richard Vernon. IV. i. p.86, 86 ; IV. iii. p.1, 20 ; IV. iv. 24 ; V. i. p.9 ; V. ii. p.1, 1 ; V. v. p.1, 14.

Cousin and ally to Percy.

Although he takes but little part in the play, he shows himself to be an " example of honesty, manly-bearing and generosity."

He is more prudent than Hotspur, and by his counsel succeeds in overcoming the latter's rash wish to fight with the king's forces without delay :

> *Hot.* We'll fight with him to-night.
> . . . . . .
> *Ver.* Do not, my lord.   [IV. iii. 1–6.]

Accompanied by Worcester he visits the king's

camp, and Henry offers them and their friends unconditional pardon if they will return to their allegiance.

This generous offer of the king's is, on the suggestion of Worcester—to which Vernon ultimately agrees—withheld from Hotspur :

Wor. O, no, my nephew must not know, Sir Richard,
     The liberal and kind offer of the king.
Ver. 'Twere best he did.
Wor.   Then are we all undone.
    It is not possible, it cannot be,
    The king should keep his word in loving us ;
    He will suspect us still, and find a time
    To punish this offence in other faults :

    .   .   .   .

    Therefore, good cousin, let not Harry know,
    In any case, the offer of the king.
Ver. Deliver what you will ; I'll say 'tis so.
                         [V. ii. 1–26.]

and this step of being a party to Worcester's treacherous act, causes Vernon to stake his all on the losing side, and proves to be the cause of his subsequent death.

Hudson says : " Vernon, with his well-poised discretion in war-council and his ungrudging admiration of the Prince, makes a happy foil to Hotspur, whose intemperate daring in conduct, and whose uneasiness at hearing Prince Henry's praises spoken, would something detract from his manhood, but that no suspicion of dishonour can fasten upon him."

[Sir Richard Vernon evidently belonged to a very ancient family although little is known of him. He joined in the rebellion against Henry and being captured at the battle of Shrewsbury was beheaded at the High Cross, Shrewsbury. Sir Richard Vernon married Elizabeth, daughter of Sir Piers Malbank, and left a son, Sir Richard Vernon, whose only daughter and heir, Johanna, married Sir Richard Foulshurst, knight.]

Sir Walter Blunt. I. i. p.1, 63, 69 ; I. iii. p.1 ; III. ii. p.162, 162 ; IV. iii. p.30, 32, 107 ; IV. iv. 30 ; V. i. p.1 ; V. iii. p.1, 20, 32, 58 ; V. iv. 41.

A noble and trustworthy man and a gallant follower of King Henry.

He is sent by the king to the rebel camp with " gracious offers," and tells Hotspur that the king wishes to know the nature of his grievances, promising a " pardon absolute " if he will return to his allegiance :

              The king hath sent to know
    The nature of your griefs, and whereupon
    You conjure from the breast of civil peace
    Such bold hostility, teaching his duteous land
    Audacious cruelty. If that the king
    Have any way your good deserts forgot,
    Which he confesseth to be manifold,
    He bids you name your griefs ; and with all speed
    You shall have your desires with interest,
    And pardon absolute for yourself and these
    Herein misled by your suggestion.   [IV. iii. 41–51.]

Hotspur tells Blunt of the king's past misdeeds, and that his refusal to ransom Mortimer had forced him to rebel. When however, Blunt asks whether he " shall return this answer to the king," Hotspur says he will consider the king's offer, and answer it on the morrow.

In the battle which follows, Blunt encounters Douglas, and the latter mistaking him for the king, demands him to surrender :

    The Lord of Stafford dear to-day hath bought
    Thy likeness ; for instead of thee, King Harry,
    This sword hath ended him : so shall it thee,
    Unless thou yield thee as my prisoner. [V. iii. 7–10.]

but the brave Blunt answers :

    I was not born a yielder, thou proud Scot :
    And thou shalt find a king that will revenge
    Lord Stafford's death.   [V. iii. 11–12.]

and engaging in combat is slain.

This gallant knight, standard-bearer to Henry the Fourth, fell on the battle-field of Shrewsbury, mistaken for his royal master, being—

    ' Semblably furnish'd like the king himself.'

He was one of the ancient family of Blount of Sodington, which came to his father, Sir Walter Blount, by marrying Joan, daughter and sole heir of Sir William de Sodington, his first wife. By his second wife, Eleanor, daughter and heir of Sir John Beauchamp, he was father of the character in this play. Sir Walter Blount's last male descendant, Sir Harry Pope Blount, Baronet, died in 1757, without issue, when the family estates passed to his niece Katherine Freeman, who married the Hon. Charles Yorke, father of Philip, third Earl of Hardwicke. The knight in this play was one of the executors to the will of John of *Gaunt*, who left him a bequest ; ' a Mons' Waut ' Blount, Mons' Chambleyn, cent marcs.' *French*.

Sunday-citizens. III. i. 257.

= Citizens dressed in their finery on Sundays. Trimmings of velvet were fashionable in the time of Shakespeare.

Sutton Co'fil'. IV. ii. 3.

> Bardolph, get thee before to Coventry ; fill me a
> bottle of sack : our soldiers shall march through ;
> we'll to Sutton Co'fil' to-night.   [IV. ii. 1–3.]

A contraction of Sutton Coldfield, a small town north-west of Coventry. " The town is marked " Sutton Cofeild " in the map of Hemlingford Hundred in Dugdale's *Warwickshire.* The borough is named in its Charter of Incorporation (20 Henry VIII.) " Sutton Coldefeld . . . otherwise called Sutton Colvyle . . . otherwise called Sutton Coldefylde," and in a subsequent Charter (16 Charles II.), " St. Coleville . . . otherwise Sutton in Colefield." *Arden Edition.*

Temple hall. III. iii. 201.

> Jack, meet me to-morrow in
> the Temple hall at two o'clock in the afternoon.
>   [III. iii. 200–201.]

The Hall of the Middle Temple was built in 1572. It was in this Hall that the *Twelfth Night* was acted on the 2nd of February, 1601.

Termagant. V. iv. 114.

See Hamlet pages 233-234.

Thieves. II. ii. p.95.

Falstaff, Gadshill, Bardolph and Peto, who set upon the travellers and rob and bind them. They are, however, put to flight on the appearance of Prince Henry and Poins, and leave their booty behind them.

Thomas Percy, Earl of Worcester. I. i. 96 ; I. iii. p.1, 15, p.130 ; II. iv. 358 ; III. i. p.1, 5, 84 ; IV. i. p.1, 125 ; IV. iii. p.1, 21 ; IV. iv. 25 ; V. i. p.9, 9, 103 ; V. ii. p.1 ; V. v. p.1, 2, 14.

Uncle to Henry Percy, and the instigator of the rebellion against Henry the Fourth.

Westmoreland informs the king that this is his view, saying :

> This is his uncle's teaching : this is Worcester,
> Malevolent to you in all aspects ;
> Which makes him prune himself, and bristle up
> The crest of youth against your dignity.
>   [I. i. 96–99.]

and later when we find Worcester in conversation with Percy it is apparent that the former is the leader of the conspiracy. He advises Hotspur :

> Then once more to your Scottish prisoners.
> Deliver them up without their ransom straight,
> And make the Douglas' son your only mean
> For powers in Scotland ; which, for divers reasons
> Which I shall send you written, be assured,
> Will easily be granted.   [I. iii. 259–264.]

and arranges an ingenious scheme with Northumberland against the king.

When he appears before the king on the eve of the battle of Shrewsbury he says that :

> For mine own part, I could be well content
> To entertain the lag-end of my life
> With quiet hours ; for, I protest,
> I have not sought the day of this dislike.
>   [V. i. 23–26.]

and on the king enquiring how the rebellion came about had he not sought it, replies that when he (Bolingbroke) came to England to oppose Richard he declared he had only come to claim his rightful possessions and not the crown.

In reply to this the king generously offers to forgive the rebels if they will abandon their project, but Worcester, prompted by cowardice refuses to accept Henry's offer, and the sentence of death passed on him later is a just reward for his treachery.

[Sir Thomas Percy, Earl of Worcester, son of Sir Henry Percy, third baron Percy, and younger brother of Henry Percy, Earl of Northumberland. Took part in the French campaigns 1369–73, and in John of Gaunt's Spanish enterprise in 1386. Steward of Richard the Second's household 1394, and was created Earl of Worcester and Lord High Admiral of England by Richard in 1397. When his brother—the Earl of Northumberland—was proclaimed a traitor he deserted Richard for Bolingbroke, and from being one of the warmest supporters of the new king Worcester became one of his most bitter enemies, being termed by Holinshed as " the procurer and setter-forth of all the mischief." In

1403 joined in the rebellion against Henry, and, being captured at the battle of Shrewsbury was executed two days later at the High Cross, Shrewsbury. His head was placed on London Bridge and his body is believed to have been buried in the Holy Trinity chapel of St. Mary's, Shrewsbury.]

Titan.　II. iv. 120, 121.

> Didst thou never see Titan kiss a dish of butter ?
> [II. iv. 120.]

= the sun. The Prince is here comparing Falstaff melting in the heat as butter is melted by the sun.

Tom.　II. i. 5.

An Ostler.

Tom.　II. iv. 8.

A drawer in the Boar's Head Tavern in East-cheap. *See* Dick.

Travellers.　II. ii. p.76.

According to Gadshill " some eight or ten in number " who are set upon, bound and robbed by Falstaff and the other thieves, on the highway near Gadshill.

Trent.　III. i. 74.

> England, from Trent and Severn hitherto,
> By south and east is to my part assign'd :
> [III. i. 74–75.]

The river Trent was the proposed boundary between the territories of Mortimer and Percy, under the indentures tripartite made at Bangor.

Trent.　III. i. 79.

> and, dear coz, to you
> The remnant northward, lying off from Trent.
> [III. i. 78–79.]

Under the agreement made at Bangor all the territory north of the Trent to the Scottish border was assigned to the Percys.

Trent.　III. i. 102.

> And here the smug and silver Trent shall run
> In a new channel, fair and evenly ;
> [III. i. 102–103.]

From Burton-upon-Trent the river Trent takes a north-easterly course, and a " huge half-moon " is formed. Hotspur proposed cutting a channel so that it would run straight and add additional territory to his portion.

Trent.　III. i. 136.

> Come, you shall have Trent turn'd.　[III. i. 136.]

As Hotspur is intractable, Glendower consents to Hotspur diverting the river as he wishes.

Trojans.　II. i. 69.

A cant term for robbers.

Turk Gregory.　V. iii. 45.

See Gregory.

Vintner.　II. iv. p.80.

Presumably the husband of Dame Quickly, the hostess of the Boar's-Head Tavern in East-cheap. He enters and announces to the prince the arrival of Falstaff and his friends :

> My lord, old Sir John, with half-a-dozen more, are
> at the door : shall I let them in ?　[II. iv. 82–83.]

Wales.　II. iv. 336.

> That same mad fellow of the north, Percy
> and he of Wales, that gave Amamon the bastin-
> ado,　[II. iv. 335–337.]

= Glendower.

Wales.　III. i. 76.

> All westward, Wales beyond the Severn shore,
> And all the fertile land within that bound,
> To Owen Glendower :　[III. i. 76–78.]

The territory assigned to Glendower under the agreement made at Bangor.

Wales.　I. i. 37 ; III. i. 45 ; IV. iii. 95 ; V. v. 39.

Warkworth Castle.

The Scene of Act II., Scene iii. The ancient seat of the Percys in Northumberland. Percy receives a letter written by an unknown lord warning him that the course he is pursuing is dangerous. Gives an insight into Hotspur's domestic life, and although there is much sympathy between him and his wife he refuses to take her into his confidence.

Warwickshire. IV. ii. 52.

Windsor. I. i. 104.

Percy was summoned to Windsor by Henry to answer for his refusal in surrending the prisoners taken at the battle of Holmedon.

Wye. III. i. 65.

Three times hath Henry Bolingbroke made head
Against my power ; thrice from the banks of Wye
And sandy-bottom'd Severn have I sent him
Bootless home and weather-beaten back,
[III. i. 64–67.]

See Henry Bolingbroke.

Yedward. I. ii. 134.

A dialectal form of Edward—Poins' christian name—probably Kentish.

York. I. iii. 245.

The reference is to Edmund, Duke of York, fifth son of Edward III., and uncle to Henry IV. He was Regent of England during Richard II's absence in Ireland in 1399 and opposed Bolingbroke on his landing at Ravenspurgh.

York. I. iii. 280.

And then the power of Scotland and of York,
To join with Mortimer, ha ?   [I. iii. 280–281.]

= the Archbishop of York.

York. V. v. 36.

You, son John, and my cousin Westmoreland
Towards York shall bend you with your dearest speed,
[V. v. 35–36.]

= City of York.

York. The Archbishop's Palace.

The Scene of Act IV., Scene iv. The Archbishop of York—one of the conspirators—has misgivings as to the success of the rebellion. He therefore writes letters which he hands to Sir Michael—probably his chaplain—with instructions for them to be delivered without delay.

APPENDIX I.

1. Owen Glendouer, according to his accustomed manner, robbing and spoiling within the English borders, caused all the forces of the shire of Hereford to assemble togither against them, vnder the conduct of Edmund Mortimer, earle of March.[2] But, comming to trie the matter by battell, whether by treason or otherwise, so it fortuned, that the English power was discomfited, the earle taken prisoner, and aboue a thousand of his people slaine in the place. The shameful villanie vsed by the Welshwomen towards the dead carcasses, was such as honest eares would be ashamed to heare, and continent toongs to speake thereof. The dead bodies might not be buried, without great summes of monie for libertie to conueie them awaie.

[A Scottish army having been defeated on June 22, 1402,[3] while returning from a border foray,] Archembald, earle Dowglas, sore displeased in his mind for this ouerthrow, procured a commission to inuade England, and that to his cost, as ye may likewise read in the Scottish histories. For, at a place called Homildon, they were so fiercelie assailed by the Englishmen, vuder the leading of the lord Persie, surnamed Henrie Hotspur, and George earle of March,[4] that with violence of the English shot they were quite vanquished and put to flight, on the Rood daie in haruest, with a great slaughter made by the Englishmen. . . . There were slaine . . . three and twentie knights, besides ten thousand of the commons ; and of prisoners among other were these : Mordacke earle of Fife, son to the gouernour, Archembald earle Dowglas, (which in the fight lost one of his eies,) Thomas erle of Murrey, George earle of Angus, and (as some writers haue) the earles of Atholl & Menteith ; with fiue hundred other of meaner degrees.

2. Henrie, earle of Northumberland, with his brother Thomas, earle of Worcester, and his sonne the lord Henrie Persie, surnamed Hotspur, which were to king Henrie, in the beginning of his reigne, both faithfull freends, and earnest aiders, began now to enuie his wealth and felicitie ; and especiallie they were greeued, bicause the king demanded of the earle and his sonne such Scotish prisoners as were taken at Homeldon and Nesbit : for, of all the captiues which were taken in the conflicts foughten in those two places, there was deliuered to the kings possession onelie Mordake earl of Fife, the duke of Albanies sonne ; though the king did diuers and sundrie times require deliuerance of the residue, and that with with great threatnings : wherewith the Persies being sore offended, (for that they claimed them as their owne proper prisoners, and their peculiar preies,) by the counsell of the lord Thomas Persie, earle of Worcester, whose studie was euer (as some write) to procure malice, and set things in a broile, came to the king vnto Windsore, (vpon a purpose to prooue him,) and there required of him, that either by ransome or otherwise, he would cause to be deliuered out of prison Edmund Mortimer earle of March, their cousine germane,[4] whom (as they reported) Owen Glendower kept in filthie prison, shakled with irons ; onelie for that he tooke his part, and was to him faithfull and true.

The king began not a little to muse at this request, and not without cause : for in deed it touched him somewhat neere, sith this Edmund was sonne to Roger earle of March, sonne to the ladie Philip, daughter of Lionell duke of Clarence, the third sonne of king Edward the third ; which Edmund, at king Richards going into Ireland, was proclaimed heire apparant to the crowne and realme ; whose aunt, called Elianor, the lord Henrie Persie had married ; and therefore king Henrie could not well beare, that anie man should be earnest about the aduancement of that linage. The king, when he had studied on the matter, made answer, that the earle of March was not taken prisoner for his cause, nor in his seruice, but willinglie suffered himselfe to be taken, bicause he would not withstand the attempts of Owen Glendouer, and his complices ; & therefore he would neither ransome him, nor releeue him.

---

1. Shakespeare's Holinshed, by W. G. Boswell-Stone.

2. In 1402, Edmund Mortimer, fifth Earl of March, being a minor, was Henry's ward.—Glendower's prisoner was Sir Edmund Mortimer, brother to Roger Mortimer, fourth Earl of March, and uncle to the fifth Earl.

3. They were defeated at Nisbet, Roxburghshire.   4. Shakspere's "Lord Mortimer of Scotland."

4. Henry IV. and Hotspur were cousins, Henry's grandfather, Henry Plantagenet Duke of Lancaster, being brother german to Mary, Hotspur's grandmother.

The Persies with this answer and fraudulent excuse were not a little fumed, insomuch that Henrie Hotspur said openlie : " Behold, the heire of the relme is robbed of his right, and yet the robber with his owne will not redeeme him ! " So in this furie the Persies departed, minding nothing more than to depose king Henrie from the high type of his roialtie, and to place in his seat their cousine Edmund earle of March, whom they did not onelie deliuer out of captiuitie, but also (to the high displeasure of king Henrie) entered in league with the foresaid Owen Glendouer. . . .

King Henrie, not knowing of this new confederacie, and nothing lesse minding than that which after happened, gathered a great armie to go againe into Wales ; whereof the earle of Northumberland and his sonne were aduertised by the earle of Worcester, and with all diligence raised all the power they could make, and sent to the Scots, which before were taken prisoners at Homeldon, for aid of men : promising to the earle of Dowglas the towne of Berwike, and a part of Northumberland, and, to other Scotish lords, great lordships and seigniories, if they obteined the vpper hand. The Scots, in hope of gaine, and desirous to be reuenged of their old greefes, came to the earle with a great companie well appointed.

The Persies, to make their part seeme good, deuised certeine articles, by the aduise of Richard Scroope, archbishop of Yorke, brother to the lord Scroope, whome king Henrie had caused to be beheaded at Bristow.

Edmund Mortimer, earle of March, prisoner with Owen Glendouer, whether for irkesomnesse of cruell captiuitie, or feare of death, or for what other cause, it is vncerteine, agreed to take part with Owen against the king of England ; and tooke to wife the daughter of the said Owen.

The king was not hastie to purchase the deliuerance of the earle March, bicause his title to the crowne was well inough knowen, and therefore suffered him to remaine in miserable prison ; wishing both the said earle, and all other of his linage, out of this life, with God and his saincts in heauen, so they had beene out of the waie, for then all had beene well inough as he thought.

3. These articles being shewed to diuerse noblemen, and other states of the realme, mooued them to fauour their purpose, in so much that manie of them did not onlie promise to the Persies aid and succour by words, but also by their writings and seales confirmed the same. Howbeit, when the matter came to triall, the most part of the confederates abandoned them, and at the daie of the conflict left them alone.

4. Thus, after that the conspirators had discouered themselues, the lord Henrie Persie, desirous to proceed in the enterprise, vpon trust to be assisted by Owen Glendouer, the earle of March [*i.e.* Sir Edmund Mortimer], & other, assembled an armie of men of armes and archers foorth of Cheshire and Wales.

His vncle Thomas Persie, earle of Worcester, that had the gouernement of the Prince of Wales, who as then laie at London, in secret manner conueied himselfe out of the princes house ; and comming to Stafford (where he met his nephue) they increased their power by all waies and meanes they could deuise.

5. Strange wonders happened (as men reported) at the natiuitie of this man, for, the same night he was borne, all his fathers horsses in the stable were found to stand in bloud vp to the bellies.

In the moneth of March [1402] appeared a blasing starre, first betweene the east part of the firmament and the north, flashing foorth fire and flames about it, and, lastlie, shooting foorth fierie beams towards the north ; foreshewing (as was thought) the great effusion of bloud that followed, about the parts of Wales and Northumberland. For much about the same time, Owen Glendouer (with his Welshmen) fought with the lord Greie of Ruthen, comming foorth to defend his possessions, which the said Owen wasted and destroied ; and, as the fortune of that daies worke fell out, the lord Greie was taken prisoner, and manie of his men were slaine. This hap lifted the Welshmen into high pride, and increased meruelouslie their wicked and presumptuous attempts.

About mid of August [1402], the king, to chastise the presumptuous attempts of the Welshmen, went with a great power of men into Wales, to pursue the capteine of the Welsh rebels, Owen Glendouer ; but in effect he lost his labor, for Owen coueied himselfe out of the waie into his knowen lurking places, and (as was thought) through art magike, he caused such foule weather of winds, tempest, raine, snow, and haile to be raised, for the annoiance of the kings armie, that the like had not beene heard of : in such sort, that the king was constreined to returne home, hauing caused his people yet to spoile and burne first a great part of the countrie.

[Henry] tooke his iournie [1405] directlie into Wales, where he found fortune nothing fauourable vnto him, for all his attempts had euill successe ; in somuch that, losing fiftie of his cariages through abundance of raine and waters, he returned.

[According to Holinshed, Northumberland, Hotspur and Glendower,] by their deputies, in the house of the archdeacon of Bangor, diuided the realme amongst them ; causing a tripartite indenture to be made and sealed with their seales, by the couenants, whereof, all England from Seuerne and Trent, south and eastward, was assigned to the earle of March : all Wales & the lands beyond Seuerne westward, were appointed to Owen Glendouer : and all the remnant from Trent northwards, to the lord Persie.

This was doone (as some haue said) through a foolish credit giuen to a vaine prophesie, as though king Henrie was *the moldwarpe,* curssed of Gods owne mouth, and they three were the *dragon,* the *lion,* and the woolfe, which should diuide this realme betweene them.

6.   Lord Henrie, prince of Wales, eldest sonne to king Henrie, got knowledge that certeine of his fathers seruants were busie to giue informations against him, whereby discord might arise betwixt him and his father : for they put into the kings head, not onelie what euill rule (according to the course of youth) the prince kept to the offense of manie, but also what great resort of people came to his house ; so that the court was nothing furnished with such a traine as dailie followed the prince.   These tales brought no small suspicion into the kings head, least his sonne would presume to vsurpe the crowne, he being yet aliue ; through which suspicious gelousie, it was perceiued that he fauoured not his sonne, as in times past he had doone.

The prince (sore offended with such persons as, by slanderous reports, southy not onelie to spot his good name abrode in the realme, but to sowe discord also betwixt him and his father) wrote his letters into euerie part of the realme, to reproue all such slanderous deuises of those that sought his discredit.   And to cleare himselfe the better, (that the world might vnderstand what wrong he had to be slandered in such wise,) about the feast of Peter and Paule, to wit, the nine and twentith daie of June, he came to the court with such a number of noble men and other his freends that wished him well, as the like traine had beene sildome seene repairing to the court at any one time in those daies.

Thus were the father and the sonne reconciled, betwixt whom the said *pickthanks* had sowne diuision, insomuch that the sonne, vpon a vehement conceit of vnkindnesse sproong in the father, was in the waie to be worne out of fauour.   Which was the more likelie to come to passe, by their informations that priuilie charged him with riot and other vnciuill demeanor vnseemelie for a prince.   Indeed he was youthfullie giuen, growne to audacitie, and had chosen him companions agreeable to his age ; with whome he spent the time in such recreations, exercises, and delights as he fansied.   But yet (it should seeme by the report of some writers) that his behauiour was not offensiue or at least tending to the damage of anie bodie ; sith he had a care to auoid dooing of wrong, and to tedder his affections within the tract of vertue ; whereby he opened vnto himselfe a redie passage of good liking among the prudent sort, and was beloued of such as could discerne his disposition, which was in no degree so excessive, as that he deserued in such vehement maner to be suspected.

The king after expelled him out of his priuie councell, banisht him the court, and made the duke of Clarence (his yoonger brother) president of councell in his steed.

King Henrie, aduertised of the proceedings of the Persies, foorthwith gathered about him such power as he might make, and, being earnestlie called vpon by the Scot, the earle of March, to make hast and giue battell to his enimies, before their power by delaieng of time should still too much increase, he passed forward with such speed, that he was in sight of his enimies, lieng in campe neere to Shrewesburie, before they were in doubt of anie such thing ; for the Persies thought that he would haue staied at Burton vpon Trent, till his councell had come thither to him to giue their aduise what he were best to doo.   But herein the enimie was deceiued of his expectation, sith the king had great regard of expedition and making speed for the safetie of his owne person ; wherevnto the earle of March incited him, considering that in delaie is danger, & losse in lingering.

7.   The earle of Northumberland himselfe was not with them, but, being sicke, had promised vpon his amendement to repaire vnto them (as some write) with all conuenient speed.

8.   Vnderstanding that the duke of Glocester, and manie other noblemen would see the muster of his men, vsed all diligence, and spared for no costs, to haue the most choisest and pikedst fellowes that might be gotten ; not following the euill example of others in times past, which receiued tag and rag to fill vp their numbers, whom they hired for small wages, and reserued the residue to their pursses.

9.   The next daie in the morning earlie, being the euen of Marie Magdalene, they set their battels in order on both sides, and now, whilest the warriors looked when the token of battell should be giuen, the abbat of Shrewesburie, and one of the clearks of the priuie seale, were sent from the king vnto the Persies, to offer them pardon, if they would come to any reasonable agree-

ment. By their persuasions, the lord Henrie Persie began to giue eare vnto the kings offers, & so sent with them his vncle the earle of Worcester, to declare vnto the king the causes of those troubles, and to require some effectuall reformation in the same.

Now when the two armies were incamped, the one against the other, the earle of Worcester and the lord Persie with their complices sent the articles (whereof I spake before), by Thomas Caiton, and Roger Saluain, esquiers, to king Henrie, vnder their hands and seales ; which articles in effect charged him with manifest periurie, in that (contrarie to his oth receiued vpon the euangelists at Doncaster, when he first entred the realme after his exile) he had taken vpon him the crowne and roiall dignitie, imprisoned king Richard, caused him to resigne his title, and finallie to be murthered. Diuerse other matters they laid to his charge, as leuieng of taxes and tallages, contrarie to his promise, infringing of lawes & customes of the realme, and suffering the earle of March to remaine in prison, without trauelling to haue him deliuered. All which things they, as procurors & protectors of the common-wealth, tooke vpon them to prooue against him, as they protested vnto the whole world.

10. King Henrie, after he had read their articles, with the defiance which they annexed to the same, answered the esquiers, that he was readie with dint of sword and fierce battell to prooue their quarrell false, and nothing else than a forged matter ; not doubting, but that God would aid and assist him in his righteous cause, against the disloiall and false forsworne traitors.

11. It was reported for a truth, that now when the king had condescended vnto all that was resonable at his hands to be required, and seemed to humble himselfe more than was meet for his estate, the earle of Worcester (vpon his returne to his nephue) made relation cleane contrarie to that the king had said, in such sort that he set his nephues hart more in displeasure towards the king, than euer it was before ; driuing him by that meanes to fight whether he would or not ; . . . then suddenlie blew the trumpets, the kings part crieng, " S. George ! vpon them ! " the aduersaries cried, " *Esperance ! Persie !* " and so the two armies furiouslie ioined. The archers on both sides shot for the best game, laieng on such load with arrowes, that manie died, and were driuen downe that never rose againe.

12. The Scots (as some write), which had the fore ward on the Persies side, intending to be reuenged of their old displeasures doone to them by the English nation, set so fiercelie on the kings fore ward, led by the earle of Stafford, that they made the same draw backe, and had almost broken their aduersaries arraie. The Welshmen also, which before had laine lurking in the woods, mounteines, and marishes, hearing of this battell toward, came to the aid of the Persies, and refreshed the wearied people with new succours. The king perceiuing that his men were thus put to distresse, what with the violent impression of the Scots, and the tempestuous stormes of arrowes, that his aduersaries discharged freely against him and his people,—it was no need to will him to stirre : for suddenlie, with his fresh battell, he approached and relieued his men ; so that the battell began more fierce than before. Here the lord Henrie Persie, and the earle Dowglas, a right stout and hardie capteine, not regarding the shot of the kings battell, nor the close order of the ranks, pressing forward togither, bent their whole forces towards the kings person ; comming vpon him with speares and swords so fiercelie, that the earle of March, the Scot, perceiuing their purpose, withdrew the king from that side of the field (as some write) for his great benefit and safegard (as it appeared) ; for they gaue such a violent onset vpon them that stood about the kings standard, that, slaieng his standard-bearer sir Walter Blunt, and ouerthrowing the standard, they made slaughter of all those that stood about it ; as the earle of Stafford, that daie made by the king constable of the realme, and diuerse other.

13. The prince that daie holpe his father like a lustie yoong gentleman ; for although he was hurt in the face with an arrow, so that diuerse noble men, that were about him, would haue conueied him foorth of the field, yet he would not suffer them so to doo, least his departure from amongst his men might happilie haue stricken some feare into their harts : and so, without regard of his hurt, he continued with his men, & neuer ceassed either to fight where the battell was most hot, or to incourage his men when it seemed most need. This battell lasted three long houres, with indifferent fortune on both parts, till at length, the kind, crieng, " saint George ! victorie ! " brake the arraie of his enimies ; and aduentured so farre, that (as some write) the earle Dowglas strake him downe, & at that instant slue sir Walter Blunt, and three other, apparelled in the kings sute and clothing, saieng : " I maruell to see so many kings thus suddenlie arise one in the necke " of an other." The king, in deed, was raised, & did that daie manie a noble feat of armes, for, as it is written, he slue that daie with his owne hands six and thirtie persons of his enimies. The other on his part, incouraged by his dooings, fought valiantlie, and slue the lord Persie, called sir Henrie Hotspurre.

14. There was also taken the earle of Worcester, the procuror and setter foorth of all this mischeefe, sir Richard Vernon, and . . . diuerse other. There were slaine vpon the kings part, beside the earle of Stafford, . . . sir Hugh Shorlie, sir Iohn Clifton, . . . sir Robert Gausell, sir Walter Blunt, . . . There died in all vpon the kings side sixteene hundred, and foure thousand were greeuouslie wounded. On the contrarie side were slaine, besides the lord Persie, the most part of the knights and esquiers of the countie of Chester, to the number of two hundred, besides yeomen and footmen : in all there died of those that fought on the Persies side, about fiue thousand. This battell was fought on Marie Magdalene euen, being saturdaie. Upon the mondaie folowing, the earle of Worcester, . . . and sir Richard Vernon . . . were condemned and beheaded. The earles head was sent to London, there to be set on the bridge.

To conclude, the kings enimies were vanquished, and put to flight ; in which flight, the earle of Dowglas, for hast, falling from the crag of an hie mounteine, brake one of his cullions, and was taken, and for his valiantnesse, of the king frankelie and freelie deliuered.

APPENDIX II.

EXTRACTS FROM *The Famous Victories of Henry the Fifth, conteining the Honorable Battell of Agincourt,* THAT ILLUSTRATE THE COMIC SCENES IN THE *First Part of King Henry the Fourth.*[1]

1. THE HIGHWAY ROBBERY SCENE.

Enter the yoong Prince, Ned, and Tom.

Hen.	Come away Ned and Tom.
Both.	Here my Lord.
Hen. V.	Come away my Lads:
	Tell me sirs, how much gold haue you got ?
Ned.	Faith my Lord, I haue got fiue hundred pound.
Hen. V.	But tell me, Tom, how much hast thou got ?
Tom.	Faith my Lord, some foure hundred pound.
Hen. V.	Foure hundred pounds, brauely spoken Lads.
	But tell me sirs, thinke you not that it was a villainous
	part of me to rob my fathers Receuers ?
Ned.	Why no my Lord, it was a tricke of youth.
Hen. V.	Faith Ned, thou sayest true.
	But tell me sirs, whereabouts are we ?
Tom.	My Lord, we are now about a mile off *London*.
Hen. V.	But sirs, I maruell that sir Iohn Old-Castle
	Comes not away : Sounds see where he comes.

Enters Iockey.

	How now Iockey, what newes with thée ?
Iockey.	Faith my Lord, such newes as passeth,
	For the Towne of Detfort is risen,
	With hue and crie after your man,
	Which parted from vs the last night,
	And has set vpon, and hath robd a poore Carrier.
Hen. V.	Sownes, the vilaine that was wont to spie
	Out our booties.

1. Shakespeare's Library, edited by Hazlitt,

Iock.	I my Lord, euen the very same.
Hen. V.	Now baseminded rascal to rob a poore carrier,
	Wel it skils not, ile saue the base vilaines life :
	I, I may : but tel me Iockey, wherabout be the Receiuers ?
Iock.	Faith my Lord, they are hard by,
	But the best is, we are a horse backe and they be a foote,
	So we may escape them.
Hen. V.	Wel, I the vilaines come, let me alone with them.
	But tel me Iockey, how much gots thou from the knaues ?
	For I am sure I got something, for one of the vilaines
	So belamd me about the shoulders,
	As I shal féele it this moneth.
Iock	Faith my Lord, I haue got a hundred pound.
Hen V.	A hundred pound, now bravely spoken Iockey :
	But come sirs, laie al your money before me,
	Now by heauen here is a braue shewe :
	But as I am true Gentleman, I wil haue the halfe
	Of this spent to night, but sirs take vp your bags,
	Here comes the Receiuers, let me alone.

Enters two Receiuers.

One.	Alas good fellow, what shal we do ?
	I dare neuer go home to the Court, for I shall be hangd.
	But looke, here is the yong Prince, what shal we doo ?
Hen. V.	How now you vilaines, what are you ?
One Recei.	Speake you to him.
Other.	No I pray, speake you to him.
Hen. V.	Why how now you rascals, why speak you not ?
One.	Forsooth we be. Pray speake you to him.
Hen. V.	Sowns, vilains speak, or il cut off your heads.
Other.	Forsooth he can tel the tale better than I.
One.	Forsooth we be your fathers Receiuers.
Hen. V.	Are you my fathers Receiuers ?
	Then I hope ye haue brought me some money.
One.	Money, Alas sir wee be robd.
Hen. V.	Robd, how many were there of them ?
One.	Marry sir, there were foure of them :
	And one of them had sir Iohn Old-Castles bay Hobbie,
	And your blacke Nag.
Hen. V.	Gogs wounds how like you this Iockey ?
	Blood you vilaines : my father robd of his money abroad,
	And we robd in our stables.
	But tell me, how many were there of them ?
One Recei.	If it please you, there were foure of them,
	And there was one about the bignesse of you :
	But I am sure I so belambd him about the shoulders,
	That he wil féele it this month.
Hen. V.	Gogs wound you lamd them faierly,
	So that they haue carried away your money.
	But come sirs, what shall we do with the vilaines ?
Both Recei.	I beséech your grace, be good to vs.
Ned.	I pray you my Lord forgiue them this once.
	Well stand vp and get you gone,
	And looke that you speake not a word of it,
	For if there be, sownes ile hang you and all your kin.
	[*Exit Purseuant.*
Hen. V.	Now sirs, how like you this ?
	Was not this brauely done ?
	For now the vilaines dare not speake a word of it,
	I haue so feared them with words.
	Now whither shall we goe ?
All.	Why my Lord, you know our old hostes at Feuersham.

Hen. V.	Our hostes at Feuersham, blood what shal we do there ?
	We haue a thousand pound about vs,
	And we shall go to a pettie Ale-house.
	No, no : you know the olde Tauerne in Eastcheape,
	There is good wine : besides, there is a prettie wench
	That can talke well, for I delight as much in their tongies,
	As any part about them.
All.	We are readie to waite vpon your grace.
Hen. V.	Gogs wounds wait, we will go altogither,
	We are all fellowes, I tell you sirs, and the King
	My father were dead, we would be all Kings,
	Therefore come away.
Ned.	Gogs wounds, brauely spoken Harry.

2. THE TAVERN SCENE.

Enter Dericke and Iohn Cobler.

Der.	Sownds maisters, heres adoo,
	When Princes must go to prison :
	Why Iohn, didst euer sée the like ?
Iohn.	O Dericke, trust me, I neuer saw the like.
Der.	Why Iohn thou maist sée what princes be in choller,
	A Iudge a boxe on the eare, Ile tel thée Iohn, O Iohn,
	I would not haue done it for twentie shillings.
Iohn.	No nor I, there had bene no way but one for vs,
	We should haue been hangde.
Der.	Faith Iohn, Ile tel thée what, thou shalt be my Lord
	chiefe Iustice, and thou shalt sit in the chaire,
	And ile be the yong Prince, and hit thée a box on the eare,
	And then thou shalt say, to teach you what prerogatiues
	meane, I commit you to the Fléete.
Iohn.	Come on, Ile be your Iudge,
	But thou shalt not hid me hard.
Der.	No, no.
Iohn.	What hath he done ?
Der.	Marry he hath robd Dericke.
Iohn.	Why then I cannot let him goe.
Der.	I must néeds haue my man.
Iohn.	You shall not haue him.
Der.	Shall I not haue my man, say no and you dare :
	How say you, shall I not haue my man ?
Iohn.	No marry shall you not.
Der.	Shall I not Iohn ?
Iohn.	No Dericke.
Der.	Why then take you that till more come,
	Sownes, shall I not haue him ?
Iohn.	Well I am content to take this at your hand,
	But I pray you who am I ?
Der.	Who art thou, Sownds, doost not know thy selfe ?
Iohn.	No.
Der.	Now away simple fellow,
	Why man, thou art Iohn the Cobler.
Iohn.	No, I am my Lord chiefe Iustice of England.
Der.	Oh Iohn, Masse thou saist true, thou art indéed.
Iohn.	Why then to teach you what prerogatiues mean I commit
	you to the Fléete.
Der.	Wel I wil go, but yfaith you gray beard knaue, Ile course you.
	[*Exit. And straight enters again.*
	Oh Iohn, Come, come out of thy chaire, why what a clown
	weart thou, to let me hit thée a box on the eare, and now
	thou seest they will not take me to the Fléete, I thinke
	that thou art one of these Worenday Clownes.
Iohn.	But I maruell what will become of thée ?

3. JUSTICE WHEN THE PRINCE IS KING.

Hen. V.	But Ned, so soone as I am King, the first thing I wil do, shal be to put my Lord chief Iustice out of office. And thou shalt be my Lord chiefe Iustice of England.
Ned.	Shall I be Lord chiefe Iustice ? By gogs wounds Ile be the brauest Lord chiefe Iustice That euer was in England.
Hen. V.	Then Ned, Ile turne all these prisons into Fence Schooles, and I will endue thée with them, with landes to maintaine them withall : then I wil haue a bout with my Lord chiefe Iustice, thou shalt hang none but picke purses, and horse stealers, and such base minded villaines, but that fellow that wil stand by the highway side couragiously with his sword and buckler and take a purse, that fellow giue him commendations, beside that, send him to me, and I will giue him an anuall pension out of my Exchequer, to maintaine him all the dayes of his life.
Ioh.	Nobly spoken Harry, we shall neuer haue a mery world til the old king be dead.
Ned.	But whither are ye going now ?
Hen. V.	To the Court, for I heare say, my father lies verie sicke.
Tom.	But I doubt he wil not die.
Hen. V.	Yet will I goe thither, for the breath shal be no sooner out of his mouth, but I wil clap the Crowne on my head.

4. THE INTERVIEW BETWEEN THE PRINCE AND HIS FATHER.

Enters the Prince with a dagger in his hand.

Hen. IV.	Come my sonne, come on a God's name, I know wherefore thy comming is, Oh my sonne, my sonne, what cause hath euer bene, That thou shouldst forsake me, and follow this vilde and Reprobate company, which abuseth youth so manifestly : Oh my sonne, thou knowest that these thy doings Wil end thy fathers dayes. *He weeps.* I so, so, my sonne, thou fearest not to approach the presence of thy sick father, in that disguised sort, I tel thée my sonne, that there is neuer a néedle in thy cloke, but it is a prick to my heart, & neuer an ilat-hole, but it is a hole to my soule ; and wherefore thou bringest that dagger in thy hande I know not, but by coniecture. *He weeps.*
Hen. V.	My conscience accuseth me, most soueraign Lord, and welbeloued father, to answere first to the last point, That is, whereas you coniecture that this hand and this dagger shall be armde against your life : no, know my beloued father, far be the thoughts of your sonne, sonne said I, an vnworthie sonne for so good a father : but farre be the thoughts of any such pretended mischiefe : and I most humble render it to your Maiesties hand, and liue my Lord and soueraigne for euer : and with your dagger arme show like vengeance vpon the bodie of your sonne, I was about say and dare not, ah woe is me therefore, that your wilde slaue, tis not the Crowne that I come for, sweet father, because I am vnworthie, and those wilde & reprobate company I abandon, & vtterly abolish their company for euer. Pardon sweete father, pardon : the least thing and most desire : and this ruffianly cloake, I here teare from my backe, and sacrifice it to

Hen. V.	the diuel, which is maister of al mischiefe : Pardon me,
(contd.)	swéet father, pardō me : good my Lord of Exeter, speak for
	me : pardon me, pardō good father, not a word : ah he wil
	not speak one word : A Harry, now thrice vnhappie Harry.
	But what shal I do ? I wil go take me into some solitarie
	place, and there lament my sinfull life, and when I haue
	done, I wil lay me downe and die. [*Exit.*
Hen. IV	Call him againe, call my sonne againe.
Hen. V	And doth my father call me againe ? now Harry,
	Happie be the time that thy father calleth thée againe.
Hen. IV.	Stand vp my son, and do not think thy father,
	But at the request of thée my sonne, I wil pardon thée,
	And God blesse thée, and make thée his seruant.
Hen. V.	Thanks good my Lord, & no doubt but this day,
	Euen this day, I am borne new againe.
Hen. IV.	Come my son and Lords, take me by the hands. [*Exeunt omnes.*

Second Part of King Henry the Fourth

Written. 1598–1599. Mention is made of *King Henry the Fourth* by Meres in his *Palladis Tamia, Wit's Treasury* in 1598, but the reference is considered to be to the *First Part of King Henry the Fourth*. From this inference it is assumed that the *Second Part* was not written earlier than 1598.

Ben Jonson in his *Every Man out of His Humour*, published in 1599, alludes to Justice Silence, one of the characters in the *Second Part of King Henry the Fourth*, this evidence fixing the date of composition not later than 1599.

A Passage in the Epilogue of the Play, " and make you merry with fair Katharine of France ": refers to King Henry the Fifth, and as the play of that name was known to have been written in the year 1599, this passage is in agreement with the later date of composition, *i.e.* 1599.

Published. Entered in the Stationers' Register under date 23rd of August, 1600, and bears the following title : " THE | Second part of Henrie | the fourth, continuing to his death, | *and coronation of Henrie* | the fift. | With the humours of sir Iohn Fal- | *staffe, and swaggering* | Pistoll. | *As it hath been sundrie times publikely* | acted by the right honourable, the Lord | Chamberlaine his seruants. | *Written by William Shakespeare.* | LONDON | Printed by V. S. for Andrew Wise, and | William Aspley. | 1600."

Source of the Plot. As in the case of the *First Part of King Henry the Fourth*, the materials for the plot are mainly taken from Holinshed's *Chronicles*,[1] and the old play *The Famous Victories of Henry V., containing the honourable battle of Agincourt*.[2]

Outline of the Play. The *Second Part of King Henry the Fourth* continues the story of the First Part, but is more pathetic and less humorous in character.

The action dates from the battle of Shrewsbury on the 21st July, 1403, in which battle Hotspur is killed, to the death of King Henry the Fourth and the accession of King Henry the Fifth.

The play opens with an Induction in which the Goddess of Rumour, " painted full of tongues," appears before the castle of Warkworth, and bids all :

Open your ears ; for which of you will stop
The vent of hearing when loud Rumour speaks ?
I, from the orient to the drooping west,
Making the wind my post-horse, still unfold
The acts commenced on this ball of earth :
Upon my tongues continual slanders ride,
The which in every language I pronounce,
Stuffing the ears of men with false reports,

1. *See* Appendix I.   2. *See* Appendix II.

for

> Rumour is a pipe
> Blown by surmises, jealousies, conjectures,
> And of so easy and so plain a stop
> That the blunt monster with uncounted heads,
> The still-discordant wavering multitude,
> Can play upon it.

She tells of King Henry's victory over Hotspur :

> Why is Rumour here ?
> I run before King Harry's victory ;
> Who in a bloody field by Shrewsbury
> Hath beaten down young Hotspur and his troops,
> Quenching the flame of bold rebellion
> Even with the rebels' blood.

But, she continues, why speak the truth ? for her first office is to spread false news, indeed through all the " peasant towns " from the battle-field of Shrewsbury to the castle of Warkworth, where Northumberland is lying " crafty-sick," she has proclaimed that Hotspur has defeated the royal forces :

> But what mean I
> To speak so true at first ? my office is
> To noise abroad that Harry Monmouth fell
> Under the wrath of noble Hotspur's sword,
> And that the king before the Douglas' rage
> Stoop'd his anointed head as low as death.
> This have I rumour'd through the peasant towns
> Between that royal field of Shrewsbury
> And this worm-eaten hold of ragged stone,
> Where Hotspur's father, old Northumberland,
> Lies crafty-sick : the posts come tiring on,
> And not a man of them brings other news
> Than they have learn'd of me : from Rumour's tongues
> They bring smooth comforts false, worse than true wrongs.

We are still before Warkworth Castle when the First Act opens. Having spread her direful tidings, Rumour withdraws from the scene, as Lord Bardolph rides in haste to the gates of the fortress, eager to impart to the Earl—who is anxiously waiting news of the battle—tidings of a " glorious victory." " Who keeps the gate here, ho ! " demands Bardolph, and on the Porter opening the gate and asking : " What shall I say you are ? " Bardolph answers : " Tell thou the earl That the Lord Bardolph doth attend him here." " His lordship is walk'd forth into the orchard : Please it your honour, knock but at the gate, And he himself will answer," replies the Porter. Presently Northumberland appears, and addressing Bardolph :

> What news, Lord Bardolph ? every minute now
> Should be the father of some stratagem :
> The times are wild ; contention, like a horse
> Full of high feeding, madly hath broke loose
> And beard down all before him.

to which Bardolph replies :

> As good as heart can wish :
> The king is almost wounded to the death ;
> And, in the fortune of my lord your son,
> Prince Harry slain outright ; and both the Blunts
> Kill'd by the hand of Douglas ; young Prince John
> And Westmoreland and Stafford fled the field ;
> And Harry Monmouth's brawn, the bulk Sir John,
> Is prisoner to your son : O, such a day,
> So fought, so follow'd and so fairly won,
> Came not till now to dignify the times,
> Since Cæsar's fortunes !

But Northumberland, who is sceptical, asks : " How is this derived ?   Saw you the field ?   came you from Shrewsbury ? " and Bardolph admits that he has had the news from a gentleman who had come from the battle-field, " A gentleman well bred and of good name." Almost immediately, Travers—one of Northumberland's retainers—appears, and confirms the news :

> *North.*   Now, Travers, what good tidings comes with you ?
> *Tra.*   My lord, Sir John Umfrevile turn'd me back
>   With joyful tidings ; and, being better horsed
>   Out-rode me,

but at the same time he has heard contradictory reports from a royal messenger :

> After him came spurring hard
> A gentleman, almost forspent with speed,
> That stopp'd by me to breathe his bloodied horse.
> He ask'd the way to Chester ; and of him
> I did demand what news from Shrewsbury :
> He told me that rebellion had bad luck,
> And that young Harry Percy's spur was cold,

after which, " bending forward " he " gave his able horse the head " and striking his spurs " Against the panting sides of his poor jade Up to the rowel-head," dashed away at a furious speed.   " Ha !   Again " :   exclaims Northumberland, " Said he young Harry Percy's spur was cold ? "   This causes Lord Bardolph to remark that if Hotspur has not won the day he is prepared to surrender his barony for a " silken point."   " Why should that gentleman that rode by Travers, give them such instances of loss ? " queries Northumberland and Bardolph describes him as " some hilding fellow that had stolen the horse he rode on, and   .   .   .   spoke at a venture." As they are in conversation, a third horseman spurs across the plain.   It is Morton— another of Northumberland's retainers—who has ridden in hot-haste from the battle-field.   A glance at his face tells Northumberland that he is the bearer of ill tidings :

> Yea, this man's brow, like to a title-leaf,
> Foretells the nature of a tragic volume :
>
>   .   .   .   .   .
>
> Say, Morton, didst thou come from Shrewsbury ?
>
>   .   .   .   .   .
>
>   How doth my son and brother ?
> Thou tremblest ; and the whiteness in thy cheek
> Is apter than thy tongue to tell thy errand.

" I ran from Shrewsbury, my noble lord :   where hateful death put on his ugliest mask to fright our party,   .   .   .   Douglas is living, and your brother, yet ; But, for my lord your son,—" began Morton, " Why, he is dead.   See what a ready tongue suspicion hath !   .   .   .   I see a strange confession in thine eye :   Yet, for all this, say not that Percy's dead.   Thou shakest thy head, and hold'st it fear or sin To speak a truth.   If he be slain, say so " ; ejaculates Northumberland, to which Bardolph adds :   " I cannot think, my lord, your son is dead."   But Morton can but answer that the terrible news is only too true—that Hotspur is dead, slain by Prince Henry, Worcester and " that furious Scot, the bloody Douglas "—who, " Had three times slain the appearance of the king "—taken prisoner, the army utterly routed, and further, that a powerful force under Prince John of Lancaster and the Earl of Westmoreland has been despatched by the king against Northumberland and the Archbishop of York.   " This is the news at full," adds the fatigued Morton.   Stunned by the heavy tidings, Northumberland, as he paces up and down, exclaims that he will " have time enough to mourn," declaring that if he had been well " the news would have made him sick," but " being sick " the news has " in some measure made him well," and although " weaken'd with grief," he must now exchange his " crutch " for " a scaly gauntlet with joints of steel."   Northumberland is reminded by Morton that many lives depend upon him : " The lives of all your loving complices Lean on your health " ; and further, that the Archbishop will prove a powerful ally : " 'Tis more than time : and, my most noble lord, I hear for certain, and do speak the truth, The gentle Archbishop of York is up With well-appointed powers " : adding, that as the Archbishop, being " sincere and holy in his thoughts," had turned " insurrection to religion,"—and had gathered around him a large force in conse- quence—the rebellion, hallowed as it is " with the blood Of fair King Richard, scraped from Pomfret stones " ; would ultimately succeed.   Encouraged by these words, Northumberland invites them into his castle, to confer together

> The aptest way for safety and revenge :
> Get posts and letters, and make friends with speed :
> Never so few, and never yet more need.

The second scene is a Street in London.   Falstaff enters, accompanied by a boy as his page—a gift from the prince—bearing his sword and buckler.   The boy is Falstaff's *general factotum*.   Having inquired of the boy as to the answer he brings from the doctor, Falstaff remarks : " Men of all sorts take a pride to gird at me " : and " What said Master Dumbleton about the satin for my short cloak and my slops ? " asks Falstaff, to which the page replies that his tailor had demanded " better assurance than Bardolph : he would not take his band and yours ; he liked not the security."   " Let him be damned, like the glutton ! pray God his tongue be hotter ! A whoreson Achitophel ! a rascally yea-forsooth knave ! " but " where 's Bardolph ? " to which the page answers " He 's gone to Smithfield to buy your worship a horse."

At this point the Lord Chief Justice—who had committed the Prince of Wales for contempt of court—enters, accompanied by a servant.   The page warns Falstaff of the Chief Justice's approach : " Sir, here comes the nobleman that committed the prince for striking him about Bardolph."   Falstaff pretends not to see the Chief Justice, but is recognised by the latter's servant, and on the Chief Justice asking : " He that was in question for the robbery ? " the servant replies : " He, my lord " ; adding, that he " hath since done good service at Shrewsbury ; and, as I hear, is now going with some charge to the Lord John of Lancaster."   Falstaff had, before the battle of Shrewsbury been sent for by the Chief Justice in connection with the robbery at Gadshill, but had managed to keep out of the way, and knowing that Falstaff was presently to accompany Lord John of Lancaster to York, the Judge tells his servant to call him, as he wishes to have a few words with him before departing. " Sir John Falstaff," cries the servant, and Falstaff pretending to be deaf, whispers to the page : " Boy, tell him I am deaf," to which the Judge observes : I am sure he is, to the hearing of any thing good."   Telling his servant " Go, pluck him by the elbow ; I must speak with him," Falstaff rebukes the servant for begging :

> What ! a young knave, and begging ! Is there not
> wars ? is there not employment ? doth not the king
> lack subjects ? do not the rebels need soldiers ?
> Though it be a shame to be on any side but one, it
> is worse shame to beg than to be on the worst side,
> were it worse than the name of rebellion can tell
> how to make it.

but when the servant tells Falstaff " You mistake me, sir," an argument ensues between them.   The Chief Justice, however, insists on speaking with Falstaff : " Sir John Falstaff, a word with you," and finding himself cornered, Falstaff, with the intention of evading awkward questions, greets the judge with a fluency of speech. " Sir John, I sent for you before your expedition to Shrewsbury," says the Judge, and Falstaff replies : " An 't please your lordship, I hear his majesty is returned with some discomfort from Wales, . . . fallen into a whoreson apoplexy . . . a kind of lethargy, brought on by study and perturbation of the brain : I have read the cause of its effects in Galen : it is a kind of deafness," to which the Chief Justice very cogently and coldly remarks : " I think you are fallen into the disease." His evasions, however, prove utterly futile, for the Lord Chief Justice tells him " the truth is, Sir John, you live in great infamy," for " You have misled the youthful prince," to which Falstaff retorts " The young prince hath misled me : " But, adds the Judge : " I am loath to gall a new-healed wound " : and Falstaff's services at the battle of Shrewsbury had " gilded over his night's exploit on Gadshill," and he could only " thank the unquiet time " that the matter had been overlooked.

On Falstaff referring to himself as a young man, the Chief Justice smilingly asks : " Do you set down your name in the scroll of youth, that are written down old with all the characters of age ? Have you not a moist eye ? a dry hand ? a yellow cheek ? a white beard ? a decreasing leg ? an increasing belly ? is not your voice broken ? your wind short ? your chin double ? your wit single ? and every part about you blasted with antiquity ? and will you yet call yourself young ? Fie, fie, fie, Sir John ! " and the wily knight replies : " My lord, I was born about three of the clock in the afternoon, with a white head and something a round belly. For my voice, I have lost it with halloing and singing of anthems. To approve my youth further, I will not : the truth is, I am only old in judgement and understanding ; and he that will caper with me for a thousand marks, let him lend me the money, and have at him. For the box of the ear that the prince gave you, he gave it like a rude prince, and you took it like a sensible lord. I have checked him for it, and the young lion repents ; marry, not in ashes and sackcloth, but in new silk and old sack."

Expressing a hope that God would send the prince a better companion than Falstaff, the Chief Justice remarks : " I hear you are going with Lord John of Lancaster against the Archbishop and the Earl of Northumberland," and Falstaff remarks he wishes that his " name was not so terrible to the enemy as it is : I were better to be eaten to death with a rust than to be scoured to nothing with perpetual motion." After the Judge has wished the expedition every success : " Well, be honest, be honest ; and God bless your expedition ! " the fat knight suavily asks him for the loan of a thousand pounds to buy equipment for the campaign. " Not a penny, not a penny ; you are too impatient to bear crosses. Fare you well : commend me to my cousin Westmoreland," replies the Chief Justice, and departs forthwith. The Judge gone, Falstaff inquires as to the amount of money he possesses, and the page answering that he has only " Seven groats and two pence," Falstaff remarks : " there is no remedy against this consumption of the purse : borrowing only lingers and lingers it out, but the disease is incurable," and forthwith despatches his page with four letters : " this letter to my Lord of Lancaster ; this to the prince ; this to the Earl of Westmoreland ; and this to old Mistress Ursula, whom I have weekly sworn to marry since I perceived the first white hair on my chin." The page having gone, the scene closes with Falstaff complaining that the gout " plays the rogue with his great toe," but " 'Tis no matter if I do halt ; I 'll make the wars an excuse to get a big pension," for " A good wit will make use of any thing," even to making a profit out of diseases.

The Archbishop's palace at York supplies the next scene, where we find the prelate in consultation with the Lords Hastings, Mowbray and Bardolph as to the prospects of their enterprise.   It opens with the archbishop reminding them that they are already aware of their cause and know their means, and invites them to speak plainly their opinion as to their prospects.   Mowbray replies that he is quite satisfied as to the reason they have taken up arms, but he would be more satisfied if their power was much larger.   Hastings exclaims that they have but twenty-five thousand men at their command :

> Our present musters grow upon the file
> To five and twenty thousand men of choice ;
> And our supplies live largely in the hope
> Of great Northumberland, whose bosom burns
> With an incensed fire of injuries.

Then the point to be considered—observes Lord Bardolph, who counsels caution—is, whether such a small force can be successful without the aid of Northumberland :

> The question then, Lord Hastings, standeth thus ;
> Whether our present five and twenty thousand
> May hold up head without Northumberland ?

to which Hastings replies : " With him, we may."   To this Lord Bardolph enjoins that without Northumberland's aid their chances of success are very remote :

> Yea, marry, there 's the point :
> But if without him we be thought too feeble,
> My judgement is, we should not step too far
> Till we had his assistance by the hand ;
> For in a theme so bloody-faced as this
> Conjecture, expectation, and surmise
> Of aids incertain should not be admitted ;

and with this the archbishop agrees :   " 'Tis very true, Lord Bardolph ; for indeed It was young Hotspur's case at Shrewsbury."   This causes Lord Bardolph to add that as they had in hand a bold and warlike enterprise " Which is almost to pluck a kingdom down And set another up," they must proceed very cautiously, otherwise they would court disaster, and reminds them that an architect before he commences to build, first draws a plan, and afterwards counts the cost of the projected erection :

> When we mean to build,
> We first survey the plot, then draw the model ;
> And when we see the figure of the house,
> Then must we rate the cost of the erection ;
> Which if we find outweighs ability,
> What do we then but draw anew the model
> In fewer offices, or at least desist
> To build at all ?

therefore they should consider the matter very carefully, and satisfy themselves that their power was strong enough to carry them through, otherwise they would be " Like one that draws the model of a house Beyond his power to build it ; who, half through, Gives o'er and leaves his part-erected cost A naked subject to the weeping clouds, And waste for churlish winter's tyranny."   Lord Hastings, on the other hand is more sanguine of success, for " we are a body strong enough, Even as we are, to equal with the king."   " What, is the king but five and twenty thousand ? " queries Lord Bardolph, and Hastings replies " To us no more ; nay, not so much, Lord Bardolph," for his forces are divided, one part against the French who have landed a large army in Wales, and another against Glendower, in consequence of which they have only to count on meeting a third of the royal forces : " one power against the French, And one against Glendower ; perforce a third Must take us up : so is the infirm king In thee divided."   But Lord Bardolph is not satisfied, and asks who is in command of the forces sent against them, and Hastings replies the Duke of Lancaster and Westmoreland, while the king and the prince are in command of the force sent against Glendower and the Welsh, but as to who is in charge of the army against the French " I have no certain notice." On hearing this the archbishop decides for prompt action : " Let us on, And publish the occasion of our arms," for the " commonwealth is sick of their own choice " ; in accepting Bolingbroke in the place of Richard. To this they all agree, and decide to hasten away and assemble their forces :

> *Mowb.* Shall we go draw our numbers, and set on ?

to which Hastings replies :

> We are time's subjects, and time bids be gone.

We are in a London Street at the opening of the second Act. It opens with Mistress Quickly inquiring of Fang and Snare—two Sheriff's officers—if they have entered the action against Falstaff for the recovery of the money he owes her. Being assured by Fang that " It is entered," she warns them to beware of Falstaff as he " cares not what mischief he does, if his weapon be out : he will foin like any devil ; he will spare neither man, woman, or child." Promising to be " at their elbow," if assistance should be required, she enjoins upon them to " hold him sure : . . . let him not scape," for " A hundred mark is a long one for a poor lone woman to bear : and I have borne, and borne, and borne ; and have been fubbed off, and fubbed off, and fubbed off, from this day to that day, that it is a shame to be thought on. There is no honesty in such dealing ; unless a woman should be made an ass and a beast, to bear every knave's wrong. Yonder he comes ; and that arrant malmsey-nose knave, Bardolph, with him." On Falstaff appearing in company with his page and Bardolph, he enquires : " How now ! whose mare's dead ? what 's the matter ? " and is at once arrested by Fang : " Sir John, I arrest you at the suit of Mistress Quickly."

Falstaff calls upon Bardolph to draw his sword and strike the officer, and throw the hostess into the ditch : " Away, varlets ! Draw, Bardolph : cut me off the villain's head : throw the quean in the channel," to which Mistress Quickly replies : " Throw me in the channel ! I 'll throw thee in the channel. Wilt thou ? wilt thou ? thou bastardly rogue ! Murder, murder ! Ah, thou honey-suckle villain ! wilt thou kill God's officers and the king's ? Ah, thou honey-seed rogue ! thou art a honey-seed, a man-queller, and a woman-queller." During the scuffle Fang appeals for assistance : " A rescue ! a rescue ! " " Good people, bring a rescue or two," shouts the hostess, only to be pushed on one side by Falstaff's page, with the remark : " Away, you scullion ! you rampallian ! you fustilarian ! "

At this point the Lord Chief Justice appears and orders them to keep the peace. Telling Falstaff that he ought to " have been on his way to York and not brawling here," he demands to know the reason for his arrest. " O my most worshipful lord, an' please your grace, I am a poor widow of Eastcheap, and he is arrested at my suit," answers Mistress Quickly. " Forwhat sum ? " asks the Chief Justice, to which the hostess replies : " It is more than for some, my lord, it is for all, all I have. He hath eaten me out of house and home." Being told by the Judge that he ought to be ashamed of himself, Falstaff inquires the gross amount he owes her, only to be told that he owes her marriage as well as money : " Marry, if thou wert an honest man, thyself and the money too. Thou didst swear to me upon a parcel-gilt goblet, sitting in my Dolphin-chamber, at the round table, by a sea-coal fire, upon Wednesday in Wheeson week, when the prince broke thy head for liking his father to a singing-man of Windsor, thou didst swear to me then, as I was washing thy wound, to marry me and make me my lady thy wife. Canst thou deny it ? . . . And didst thou not kiss me and bid me fetch thee thirty shillings ? I put thee now to thy book-oath : deny it, if thou canst." "My lord, this is a poor mad soul ; and she says up and down the town that her eldest son is like you : she hath been in good case, and the truth is, poverty hath distracted her," is Falstaff's remark to the Judge, but the Chief Justice tells him that he is "well acquainted with his manner of wrenching the true cause the false way," but neither his "confident brow" nor his "impudent sauciness" will alter his opinion, for he "had practised upon the easy-yielding spirit of this woman, and made her serve his uses both in purse and in person," and orders him to "Pay her the debt you owe her, and unpay the villainy you have done her : the one you may do with sterling money, and the other with current repentance." To this Falstaff replies that he will not let this reprimand go unanswered : "You call honourable boldness impudent sauciness : if a man will make courtesy and say nothing, he is virtuous ; no, my lord, my humble duty remembered, I will not be your suitor. I say to you, I do desire deliverance from these officers, being upon hasty employment in the king's affairs."

At this point a gentleman of the court—Gower—enters and reports that the king and the Prince of Wales are at hand, at the same time handing the Chief Justice a letter. While the judge is perusing the letter, Falstaff prevails upon the hostess, not only to withdraw her action, but also to lend him ten pounds : "Let it be ten pound, if thou canst. Come, an 'twere not for thy humours, there 's not a better wench in England. Go, wash thy face, and draw the action. Come, thou must not be in this humour with me ; dost not know me ? come, come, I know thou wast set on to this," after which she actually invites Falstaff to supper at the Boar's Head tavern, when "You 'll pay me all together" adding "Will you have Doll Tearsheet meet you at supper ?" "No more words ; let 's have her," is Falstaff's reply. As Dame Quickly hurries away, Falstaff turns to the Chief Justice : "What 's the news, my lord ?" but as the judge pretends not to hear him, Falstaff turns to Gower, and inquires : "Where lay the king to-night ?" "At Basingstoke, my lord," is Gower's reply. "I hope, my lord, all 's well : what is the news, my lord ?" Falstaff asks again, but still the judge pays no heed. Turning to Gower, the Chief Justice inquires whether the king is returning with all his forces, to which Gower replies : "No ; fifteen hundred foot, five hundred horse, Are march'd up to my Lord of Lancaster, Against Northumberland and the Archbishop." "Come, go along with me, good Master Gower, You shall have letters of me presently," adds the judge, and as he and Gower are on the point of leaving, Falstaff invites the latter to dine with him at the Boar's Head tavern. Gower thanks Falstaff for the invitation which he is unable to accept as he has to wait on the Chief Justice, who, turning to Falstaff tells him : "Sir John, you loiter here too long, seeing you are to take soldiers up in counties as you go," and on Falstaff repeating the invitation to Gower, the judge sharply rebukes him with the words : "What foolish master taught you these manners, Sir John ?" "Master Gower, if they become me not, he was a fool that taught them me. This is the right fencing grace, my lord ; tap for tap, and so part fair," answers Falstaff, only to receive from the judge the caustic remark : "Now the Lord lighten thee ! thou art a great fool."

The next scene is enacted in another Street in London, where we meet the prince and Poins, the former acknowledging himself to be "exceeding weary," and desiring —although it makes him blush—a drink of "small beer," which he considers not very fitting for a prince. Being so familiar with Poins—which he declares is a disgrace to him—the prince proceeds to enumerate the articles in his wardrobe, but Poins tells him that he should not talk so idly, particularly as his father is lying ill, to which the prince retorts that although his " heart bleeds inwardly that his father is so sick," the fact of " keeping such vile company as his hath in reason taken from him all ostentation of sorrow." At this point Bardolph enters, accompanied by Falstaff's page, and the prince makes comments on the fantastic livery the page is wearing, averring that when he gave him to Falstaff he was a Christian. The page then alludes to Bardolph's red nose, and Bardolph angrily retorts " Away, you whoreson upright rabbit, away ! " to which the page replies : " Away, you rascally Althæa's dream, away ! " " Instruct us, boy ; what dream, boy ? " enjoins the prince, and the page goes on to confound Althæa's fire-brand, which was real, with Hecuba, who dreamed she was delivered of a fire-brand which was to be the cause of the destruction of Troy. The prince considers his " interpretation " is worth a crown, but gives him sixpence to " preserve him." The prince next inquires about Falstaff, and Bardolph replies that having heard of the prince's coming to town, Sir John has entrusted him with a letter, which he hands to the prince. The letter which is read aloud by Poins—who makes comments upon it as he reads it—ran :

" Sir John Falstaff, knight, to the son of the king, nearest his father, Harry Prince of Wales, greeting." [" Why, this is a certificate," observes Poins. " Peace ! " requests the prince.] " I will imitate the honourable Romans in brevity " : [" He sure means brevity in breath, short-winded," is Poins' comment.] " I commend me to thee, I commend thee, and I leave thee. Be not too familiar with Poins ; for he misuses thy favours so much, that he swears thou art to marry his sister Nell. Repent at idle times as thou mayest ; and so, farewell.
" Thine, by yea and no, which is as much as to say, as thou
usest him, JACK FALSTAFF with my familiars, JOHN with
my brothers and sisters, and SIR JOHN with all Europe."

" My lord, I 'll steep this letter in sack, and make him eat it," enjoins Poins. " Must I marry your sister ? " asks the prince, and Poins replies : " God send the wench no worse fortune ! But I never said so," to which the prince adds : " Well, thus we play the fools with the time ; and the spirits of the wise sit in the clouds and mock us." Being told by Bardolph that Falstaff is supping at the " old place in East-cheap," to which the page adds, with " Ephesians, my lord, of the old church," and with Mistress Quickly and Mistress Doll Tearsheet, the prince decides to pay them a surprise visit, and Bardolph and the page having gone, Poins procures a couple of " leathern jerkins and aprons," with which they purpose disguising themselves in order to appear in the capacity of " drawers " at Falstaff's table, the prince humorously exclaiming that even the great god Jove assumed disguises :

From a god to a bull ? a heavy descension ! it
was Jove's case. From a prince to a prentice ? a
low transformation ! that shall be mine ; for in
every thing the purpose must weigh with the folly.
Follow me, Ned.

We are transferred to Warkworth Castle in the next scene, where we find North-umberland in conversation with his wife and widowed daughter-in-law, Lady Percy. It opens with Northumberland entreating his wife and daughter-in-law not to oppose the stern course he intends to pursue :

I pray thee, loving wife, and gentle daughter,
Give even way unto my rough affairs :

averring that, his " honour is in pawn." Then " I will speak no more : Do what you will ; your wisdom be your guide," replies his wife.   His daughter-in-law then tries to persuade him not to " go to these wars ! " and reminds him that he has already " broken his word," and that at the time " When he was more endear'd to it than now ; When his own Percy, when her heart's dear Harry, Threw many a northward look to see his father Bring up his powers ; but he did long in vain," and asks him " Who then persuaded him to stay at home," and goes on to compare her late husband—Hotspur—as the " mark and glass, copy and book, That fashion'd others," adding that if he had had the support at the battle of Shrewsbury which was promised him, he would not have been defeated :

> Had my sweet Harry had but half their numbers,
> To-day might I, hanging on Hotspur's neck,
> Have talk'd of Monmouth's grave.

Northumberland bids her " Beshrew her heart " : " Fair daughter, you do draw my spirits from me With new lamenting ancient oversights," adding that he must " go and meet with danger " otherwise " it will seek him out in another place And find him worse provided."   His wife entreats him to " fly to Scotland," until a sufficient army can be mobilised to meet his needs, in which she is supported by Lady Percy, and Northumberland decides to take their advice :

> I will resolve for Scotland : there am I,
> Till time and vantage crave my company.

In the next scene we are at the Boar's Head Tavern in Eastcheap.   Two drawers enter, and proceed to prepare the supper : *First Draw.*   " What the devil hast thou brought there ? apple-johns ? thou knowest Sir John cannot endure an apple-john." *Sec. Draw.*   " Mass, thou sayest true.   The prince once set a dish of apple-johns before him, and told him there were five more Sir Johns ; and, putting off his hat, said, ' I will now take my leave of these six dry, round, old, withered knights." One of the drawers mentions that music is to animate the feast, while the other adds that the prince and Poins are to disguise themselves and take their places as servers, but Falstaff is not to know it, hence there will be " rare sport."

Mistress Quickly and Doll Tearsheet enter, and addressing the latter, Mistress Quickly, endeavouring to assume an air of gentility, causes great amusement by her misapplication of language : " I' faith, sweatheart, methinks now you are in an excellent good temperality : your pulsidge beats as extraordinarily as heart would desire ; and your colour, I warrant you, is as red as any rose, in good truth, la ! But, i' faith, you have drunk too much canaries ; and that 's a marvellous searching wine, and it perfumes the blood ere one can say ' What 's this ? '   How do you now ? " Almost immediately, Falstaff appears, singing—at the same time calling for sack— " When Arthur first in court "—Empty the jordan. [*Exit First Drawer*]—[*Singing*] " And was a worthy king," " How now, Mistress Doll ! "   High words ensue between him and Doll, the latter describing Falstaff as a " muddy rascal " and a " muddy conger," telling him to go and hang himself.   To prevent a quarrel between them Mistress Quickly intervenes : " By my troth, this is the old fashion ; you two never meet but you fall to some discord : you are both, i' good truth, as rheumatic as two dry toasts ; you cannot one bear with another's confirmities."   Eventually they agree to be friends as it is doubtful whether they will meet again, as Falstaff is to accompany Lord John of Lancaster to York : " Come, I 'll be friends with thee, Jack ; thou art going to the wars ; and whether I shall ever see thee again or no, there is nobody cares."   The first drawer re-enters, and announces that Pistol— Falstaff's lieutenant—wishes to see him.   Doll Tearsheet objects, and denounces

Pistol as a " swaggering rascal," and the " foul-mouthedst rogue in England," which makes the hostess declare she will not allow him to enter her house : " If he swagger, let him not come here : no, by my faith ; I must live among my neighbours ; I 'll no swaggerers : I am in good name and fame with the very best : shut the door ; there comes no swaggerers here : I have not lived all this while, to have swaggerers now ; shut the door, I pray you." But Falstaff protests and assures Mistress Quickly that Pistol—whom he calls his ' ancient '—is no swaggerer. " Pray ye, pacify yourself, Sir John : there comes no swaggerers here," enjoins the hostess, adding that on " Wednesday last Master Tisick, the debuty " told her to receive in her house only " those that are civil " for she was an " honest woman, and well thought on ; therefore take heed what guests you receive : receive," said he, " no swaggering companions." Falstaff again avers that Pistol is no swaggerer, but a " tame cheater, i' faith, you may stroke him as gently as a puppy greyhound," and turns to the drawer with the remark : " Call him up, drawer." Pistol enters, accompanied by Bardolph and the page, while the two women protest against his admittance. A lively passage follows in which Doll Tearsheet denounces Pistol as a " scurvy companion . . . a base, rascally, cheating, lack-linen mate ! . . . a mouldy rogue, . . . a cut-purse rascal ! . . . a bottle-ale rascal ! . . . a basket-hilt stale juggler, . . . an abominable damned cheater, who ought to be ashamed to be called ' captain,' and one who lives upon mouldy stewed prunes and dried cakes," at the same time threatening to " thrust her knife into his mouldy chaps." Pistol calls for a drink and lays down his sword with the remark : " Give me some sack : and, sweetheart, lie thou there," but Doll Tearsheet is not to be quietened and calls for Pistol's exclusion : " For God's sake, thrust him down stairs," for she " cannot endure such a fustian rascal," which remark makes Pistol so angry that he draws his sword. Falstaff declares he will have no brawling, and drawing his sword chases Pistol out of the room, which causes such a tumult that the hostess declares she is prepared to " forswear keeping house, afore I 'll be in these tirrits and frights." Assuring themselves that Falstaff has not been hurt in the fraças, Bardolph re-enters and reports that Pistol—who is drunk—has been wounded in the shoulder. Falstaff describes him as a " rascal ! to brave him ! " while Doll declares that Falstaff is as " valorous as Hector of Troy, worth five of Agamemnon, and ten times better than the Nine Worthies." Proud of the part he has played, for the " rogue fled from him like quicksilver," Falstaff invites Doll Tearsheet to sit upon his knee while they listen to " Sneak's string-band." At this point the prince and Poins enter, disguised as waiters, and listen to the conversation between Doll and Falstaff, the latter describing Poins as a " baboon " who's " wits are as thick as Tewkesbury mustard," asserting that the " Prince himself is such another," for they are so similar in size that the " weight of a hair will turn the scales between their avoirdupois," remarks that so annoy the prince and Poins, that the latter suggests giving him a good thrashing. Both the prince and Poins are highly amused as Falstaff kisses and dallies with Doll, who declares—when Falstaff tells her he is an old man—that she loves him more " than I love e'er a scurvy young boy of them all," and Falstaff is so flattered that he promises to buy her a new dress : " What stuff wilt have a kirtle of ? I shall receive money o' Thursday," but Doll tells him she will not " dress handsome " until he returns from the war. On Falstaff calling for some sack, the prince and Poins draw near with the words " Anon, anon, sir," and are immediately recognised. The prince demands to know the meaning of " speaking so vilely about him " before this " honest, virtuous, civil gentlewoman ! " to which Falstaff replies that he " dispraised him before the wicked, that the wicked might not fall in love with him ; in which doing, he had done the part of a careful friend and a true subject, and his father ought to give him thanks for it.   No abuse, Hal : none, Ned, none : no, faith, boys, none."   The conversation is interrupted by a loud knocking at the door, and Peto enters and informs the prince that " The king your father is at Westminster," as there is stirring news from the north, and that as he journeyed hither " he met and overtook a dozen captains, Bare-headed, sweating, knocking at the taverns, And asking every one for Sir John Falstaff."   Calling for his sword and cloak, the prince declares that it is a time for action and not for drunken revelry, and hurriedly takes his departure, accompanied by Poins, Peto and Bardolph :

> By heavens, Poins, I feel me much to blame,
> So idly to profane the precious time ;
> When tempest of commotion, like the south
> Borne with black vapour, doth begin to melt,
> And drop upon our bare unarmed heads.
> Give me my sword and cloak.   Falstaff, good night.

Immediately they are gone more knocking is heard at the door, and Bardolph re-enters and tells Falstaff that a dozen captains are at the door waiting to accompany him to court.   Leaving his page to pay the musicians, Falstaff bids the hostess and Doll Tearsheet farewell : " Farewell, hostess ; farewell, Doll.   You see, my good wenches, how men of merit are sought after : the undeserver may sleep, when the man of action is called on.   Farewell, good wenches " : and departs in company with Bardolph, while Dame Quickly extols his excellency of character : " Well, fare thee well : I have known thee these twenty nine years, come peascod-time ; but an honester and truer-hearted man,—well, fare thee well," and Doll Tearsheet gives vent to tears.   " O, run, Doll, run ; run, good Doll : come.   [*She comes blubbered.*] Yea, will you come, Doll ! "

The third Act opens in the palace at Westminster.   It is one o'clock a.m., and the king, unable to sleep, enters in his nightgown, and bids a page call the Earls of Surrey and of Warwick, who are to " o'er-read—and well consider—the letters which he sends them " :

> Go call the Earls of Surrey and of Warwick ;
> But, ere they come, bid them o'er-read these letters,
> And well consider of them : make good speed.

The page gone, the king, who is suffering from melancholia, and fearing retribution for the indirect way in which he has gained the crown, soliloquises on sleep—" Nature's soft nurse "—which is denied him, while those who " liest in smoky cribs " and the " wet seaboy on the boisterous ocean " can indulge in peaceful repose.   This soliloquy is considered to be one of the finest passages in the play, ending as it does with the well-known and often-quoted line : " Uneasy lies the head that wears a crown " :

> How many thousand of my poorest subjects
> Are at this hour asleep !   O sleep, O gentle sleep,
> Nature's soft nurse, how have I frighted thee,
> That thou no more wilt weigh my eyelids down,
> And steep my senses in forgetfulness ?
> Why rather, sleep, liest thou in smoky cribs,
> Upon uneasy pallets stretching thee,
> And hush'd with buzzing night-flies to thy slumber,
> Than in the perfumed chambers of the great,
> Under the canopies of costly state,
> And lull'd with sound of sweetest melody ?
> O thou dull god, why liest thou with the vile
> In loathsome beds, and leavest the kingly couch
> A watch-case or a common 'larum-bell ?

> Wilt thou upon the high and giddy mast
> Seal up the ship-boy's eyes, and rock his brains
> In cradle of the rude imperious surge,
> And in the visitation of the winds,
> Who take the ruffian billows by the top,
> Curling their monstrous heads, and hanging them
> With deafening clamour in the slippery clouds,
> That, with the hurly, death itself awakes ?
> Canst thou, O partial sleep, give thy repose
> To the wet sea-boy in an hour so rude ;
> And in the calmest and most stillest night,
> With all appliances and means to boot,
> Deny it to a king ?   Then happy low, lie down !
> Uneasy lies the head that wears a crown.

The Earls of Surrey and of Warwick enter, and after ascertaining that they have read the letters he has sent them, the king tells them that they will see from those letters how " Foul the body of the kingdom is ; what rank diseases grow, And with what danger, near the heart of it," but Warwick considers that with " good advice and little medicine " the trouble will soon be " cool'd."   But Henry—who was wont to " read the book of fate " :

> O God ! that one might read the book of fate,
> And see the revolution of the times
> Make mountains level, and the continent,
> Weary of solid firmness, melt itself
> Into the sea ! and, other times, to see
> The beachy girdle of the ocean
> Too wide for Neptune's hips ; how chances mock,
> And changes fill the cup of alteration
> With divers liquors !   O, if this were seen,
> The happiest youth, viewing his progress through,
> What perils past, what crosses to ensue,
> Would shut the book, and sit him down and die,

remembers the prophecy of King Richard, that Northumberland—the ladder by which he (Henry) had ascended the throne—would prove a fatal enemy to him, and reminds them that it is only " eight years since This Percy was the man nearest his soul," and now he is in rebellion ; and then turning to Warwick, says :

> But which of you was by—
> You, cousin Nevil, as I may remember—[*To Warwick.*
> When Richard, with his eye brimful of tears,
> Then check'd and rated by Northumberland,
> Did speak these words, now proved a prophecy ?
> " Northumberland, thou ladder by the which
> My cousin Bolingbroke ascends my throne " ;
> Though then, God knows, I had no such intent,
> But that necessity so bow'd the state,
> That I and greatness were compell'd to kiss :
> ' The time shall come,' thus did he follow it,
> ' The time will come, that foul sin, gathering head,
> Shall break into corruption ' : so went on,
> Foretelling this same time's condition,
> And the division of our amity.

The lords try to cheer him, Warwick exclaiming—when Henry tells them that the forces under the command of the archbishop and Northumberland are fifty thousand strong—that like " Rumour that doubles " and the " voice that echoes " the number has been greatly overestimated.   Advising the king to go to bed : " Your majesty hath been this fortnight ill ; And these unseason'd hours perforce must add Unto your sickness," they assure Henry that the royal forces sent against the archbishop and Northumberland will prove victorious, and, to comfort the king further, tell him

that news has been received that Glendower is dead. " I will take your counsel " :
is the king's answer, and taking leave of the two lords, repeats his intentions that
when the strife at home is concluded, he will pay a visit to the Holy Land :

> And were these inward wars once out of hand,
> We would, dear lords, unto the Holy Land.

We are before Justice Shallow's house in Gloucestershire in the second scene.
Shallow, a Justice of the Peace, and Silence, another Justice and cousin to Shallow,
enter, and Shallow, who is a very self-important and talkative person, welcomes his
relative in a very pompous manner, making searching inquiries as to the health of
the wife and daughter of Silence, and then proceeds to speak of his schoolboy days,
when Falstaff—now Sir John—was a boy and page to Thomas Mowbray, Duke of
Norfolk. Bardolph and " one with him " enter, and Bardolph inquires for Justice
Shallow, whereupon Shallow very ostentatiously introduces himself : " I am Robert
Shallow, sir ; a poor esquire of this county, and one of the king's justices of the
peace." Bardolph delivers Falstaff's compliments. They are indulging in witticisms when Falstaff enters, and is greeted by Shallow : " Give me your good hand,
give me your worship's good hand : by my troth, you like well and bear your years
very well : welcome, good Sir John." " I am glad to see you well, good Master
Robert Shallow " replies Falstaff, and then referring to Silence, says : " Master
Surecard, as I think ? " " No, Sir John, rejoins Shallow, " It is my cousin Silence,
in commission with me," to which Falstaff observes : " Good Master Silence, it well
befits you should be of the peace." Falstaff then inquires whether Shallow has
" provided him with half a dozen sufficient men ? " Requesting Falstaff to take a
seat, Shallow produces the roll, and summons the six recruits one by one for Falstaff's
inspection. They are rustics of a grotesque type, and Falstaff makes great fun of
their names, appearances, and their answers. The first to appear is Ralph Mouldy.
" Is thy name Mouldy ? " asks Falstaff. " Yea, an 't please you," is Mouldy's
reply. " 'Tis the more time thou wert used," is Falstaff's retort. " Ha ha, ha !
most excellent, i' faith ; things that are mouldy lack use : very singular good ! in
faith, well said, Sir John ; very well said." " Prick him," says Falstaff. " There
are other men fitter to go out than I," replies Mouldy, " I was pricked well enough
before, an you could have let me alone : my old dame will be undone now, for one to
do her husbandry and her drudgery." " Peace, fellow, peace " ; demands Shallow,
" stand aside : know you where you are ? " The second to appear is Simon Shadow.
" Shadow, whose son art thou ? " asks Falstaff. " My mother's son, sir," replies
Shadow. " Thy mother's son ! like enough, and thy father's shadow, prick him,
he will serve for summer, for we have a number of shadows to fill up the muster-
book." The next is Thomas Wart. " Is thy name Wart ? " " Yea, sir," replies
Wart. " Thou art a very ragged wart," is Falstaff's comment. " Shall I prick
him, Sir John ? " asks Shallow, but Falstaff considers he is not worth troubling about
as " his apparel is built upon his back, and his whole frame stands upon pins. " Ha,
ha, ha ! you can do it, sir ; you can do it : I commend you well," is Shallow's
comment. Francis Feeble is the next recruit. " What trade art thou, Feeble ?
is the question. " A woman's tailor, sir." " Shall I prick him," asks Shallow, to
which Falstaff makes answer : " You may : but if he had been a man's tailor, he
'ld ha' pricked you. Wilt thou make as many holes in an enemy's battle as thou
hast done in a woman's petticoat ? " " I will do my good will, sir : you can have
no more," says Feeble, to which Falstaff replies " Well said, good woman's tailor !
well said, courageous Feeble ! thou wilt be as valiant as the wrathful dove or most
magnanimous mouse. Prick the woman's tailor : well, Master Shallow ; deep,

Master Shallow." " I would Wart might have gone, sir," adds Feeble, to which Falstaff remarks : " I would thou wert a man's tailor, that thou mightst mend him and make him fit to go. I cannot put him to a private soldier, that is the leader of so many thousands : let that suffice, most forcible Feeble," and who is the next ? " Peter Bullcalf o' the green." On Bullcalf appearing Falstaff remarks : " Fore God, a likely fellow ! Come, prick me Bullcalf till he roar again." But Bullcalf considers he ought to be excused as he is troubled with a " whoreson cold, sir, a cough, sir, which I caught with ringing in the king's affairs upon his coronation-day, sir," but Falstaff tells him he shall go to the wars in a gown to keep him warm, " we will have away thy cold ; and I will take such order that thy friends shall ring for thee." " Is here all ? " asks Falstaff. " There is two more called than your number, you must have but four here, sir," remarks Shallow, so " I pray you, go in with me to dinner." While Falstaff is dining, two of the recruits—Bullcalf and Mouldy— bribe Bardolph to excuse them from service, but the others being unable to pay are compelled to serve in Falstaff's company. To Bardolph, Bullcalf says : " Good master corporale Bardolph, stand my friend ; and here 's four Harry ten shillings in French crowns for you," to which Bardolph replies : " Go to ; stand aside." " And, good master corporal captain, for my old dame's sake, stand my friend : she has nobody to do anything about her when I am gone ; and she is old, and cannot help herself : you shall have forty, sir," says Mouldy, only to receive the same answer as Bullcalf. But Feeble, for his part is ready to go. " By my troth, I care not ; a man can die but once : . . . and let it go which way it will, he that dies this year is quit for the next," to which Bardolph makes answer : " Well said ; thou 'rt a good fellow." On Falstaff and the two Justices re-appearing, Bardolph whispers to Falstaff : " I have three pound to free Mouldy and Bullcalf," therefore, to Shallow's surprise, Falstaff rejects the two most serviceable recruits. Addressing Mouldy and Bullcalf, Falstaff says : " Mouldy and Bullcalf : for you, Mouldy, stay at home till you are past service : and for your part, Bullcalf, grow till you come unto it : I will none of you," but Shallow tells him he " wrongs himself as they are his likeliest men," and Falstaff asks Shallow if he wants to instruct him how to choose a man, adding, that he prefers " spare men . . . with spirit," who " present no mark to the enemy," to those " big of limb and tall of stature." Com- manding Bardolph to provide the men with soldiers' coats, Falstaff bids them farewell, promising on his return again to accept the hospitality of Justice Shallow.

The fourth Act opens in Gaultree Forest in Yorkshire, where the forces of the archbishop, Mowbray and Hastings are assembled. After inquiring the name of the Forest, the archbishop suggests that " discoverers be sent forth to know the numbers of their enemies." A scout is therefore sent out to ascertain the strength of the king's troops. In the meantime the archbishop reports that he has received " New-dated letters from Northumberland," stating that he has been unable to levy troops, in consequence of which he has retired to Scotland :

> My friends and brethren in these great affairs,
> I must acquaint you that I have received
> New-dated letters from Northumberland ;
> Their cold intent, tenour and substance, thus ;
> Here doth he wish his person, with such powers
> As might hold sortance with his quality,
> The which he could not levy ; whereupon
> He is retired, to ripe his growing fortunes,
> To Scotland : and concludes in hearty prayers
> That your attempts may overlive the hazard
> And fearful meeting of their opposite,

to which Mowbray enjoins that the " hopes " they had in Northumberland, had
" touched ground And dashed themselves to pieces."

The scout returns with the news that the king's forces are scarcely a mile to the
west of the forest, and " by the ground they hide " he estimates them to number
about thirty thousand, and Mowbray, who mentions that was the number they judged
the king's forces to be, suggests that they press forward and meet them face to face
on the field.   The scout has scarcely delivered his message, when the Earl of Westmoreland appears with greetings from Prince John : " Health and fair greeting from
our general, The prince, Lord John and Duke of Lancaster," and being asked what
brings him hither, Westmoreland inquires of the archbishop why he has placed
himself at the head of this insurrection, seeing that his See is by " civil peace
maintain'd," and " Whose learning and good letters peace hath tutor'd, Whose
white investments figure innocence, The dove and very blessed spirit of peace."   To
this the archbishop replies that he does not profess to be a physician, nor does his
presence at the head of a " Troop of military men " necessarily imply that he is an
enemy of peace, but to speak plainly he has " weigh'd in equal balance What wrongs
their arms will do, what wrongs they suffer," and has " found their griefs heavier
than their offences," in consequence of which they were compelled to take up arms
to secure their just rights.   " When ever yet was your appeal denied ? " inquires
Westmoreland, and the archbishop replies that it is with the general misgovernment
of the realm, and the execution of his brother that he makes his " quarrel in
particular," and Westmoreland retorts by telling him that it is no concern of his.
" Why not to him in part, and to us all That feel the bruises of the days before, And
suffer the condition of these times To lay a heavy and unequal hand Upon our
honours ? " enjoins Mowbray, and Westmoreland reminds him that he has been
restored to all the " Duke of Norfolk's signories, Your noble and right well remember'd
father's."   After the parley has proceeded for some time, in which Westmoreland
tells Mowbray that he is too confident of defeating the king and compelling him to
concede all their demands, he points out that the king's offer " comes from mercy,
not from fear " : as the royal army outnumber, and are " more perfect in the use of
arms " than the forces under the command of the archbishop.   Hastings then
inquires whether Prince John has full powers granted to him by his father the king
to come to an agreement, and Westmoreland replying in the affirmative, the archbishop hands to him a schedule setting forth their " general grievances " which
Westmoreland undertakes to submit to Prince John, and forthwith departs.   Immediately he has gone, Mowbray exclaims he has a presentiment that the terms offered
by Prince John will not stand :

> There is a thing within my bosom tells me
> That no conditions of our peace can stand,

an opinion with which Hastings does not agree :

> Fear you not that : if we can make our peace
> Upon such large terms and so absolute
> As our conditions shall consist upon,
> Our peace shall stand as firm as rocky mountains.

But if terms of peace were concluded they would always be subject to suspicion,
enjoins Mowbray, an opinion the archbishop does not share, because the king, on
account of his illness, would be only too glad to see peace restored in the realm, and
therefore suggests a treaty, in which he is supported by Mowbray.   Presently Westmoreland re-appears and announces that Prince John will meet and consult with

them midway between their respective forces, and they forthwith depart to partake in this all-important parley :

> *West.*   The prince is here at hand : pleaseth your lordship
> To meet his grace just distance 'tween our armies.
> *Mowb.*   Your grace of York, in God's name, then, set forward.
> *Arch.*   Before, and greet his grace : my lord, we come.

The next scene shows us another part of the Forest where Mowbray, with the archbishop, Hastings and others enter from one side, and Prince John of Lancaster and Westmoreland, officers and others from the other side. The prince with an ostentatious show of civility and politeness welcomes his opponents :

> You are well encounter'd here, my cousin Mowbray :
> Good day to you, gentle lord archbishop ;
> And so to you, Lord Hastings, and to all.

and then addressing the archbishop tells him it would look better of him if he assembled his flock and expounded to them the " holy text " than being in armour, and " Cheering a rout of rebels with his drum, Turning the word to sword and life to death," for a man in his exalted position who possesses his sovereign's confidence, should not abuse the king's favour, having under the " counterfeited zeal of God," taken up arms against the " peace of heaven and the king."

> My Lord of York, it better show'd with you
> When that your flock, assembled by the bell,
> Encircled you to hear with reverence
> Your exposition on the holy text,
> Than now to see you here an iron man,
> Cheering a rout of rebels with your drum,
> Turning the word to sword and life to death.
> That man that sits within a monarch's heart
> And ripens in the sunshine of his favour,
> Would he abuse the countenance of the king,
>
> .   .   .   .   .   .
>   You have ta'en up,
> Under the counterfeited zeal of God,
> The subjects of his substitute, my father,
> And both against the peace of heaven and him
> Have here up-swarm'd them.

To this the archbishop replies that they have not taken up arms against the king, but merely to obtain their " just and right desires," to which Mowbray adds that if their grievances are not remedied they will fight to the last man. Hastings enjoins that if they are defeated others will take their places and so " success of mischief shall be born, And heir from heir shall hold this quarrel up, Whiles England shall have generation." Lancaster considers Hastings is " too shallow, much too shallow," to speak of what will happen in the future, and being asked by Westmoreland whether he approves of the articles in the schedule submitted by the rebels, the prince undertakes that all their grievances shall be redressed : " I like them all, and do allow them well ; And swear here, by the honour of my blood, My father's purposes have been mistook ; And some about him have too lavishly Wrested his meaning and authority. My lord, these griefs shall be with speed redress'd ; Upon my soul, they shall," an assurance which the archbishop accepts : " I take your princely word for these redresses," to which Prince John adds : " I give it you, and will maintain my word : And thereupon I drink unto your grace." Terms of peace having been concluded, Hastings forthwith pays and disbands his army : " Go, captain, and deliver to the army This news of peace : let them have pay, and part : I know it will well please them. Hie thee, captain," and the captain forthwith departs. While they are " toasting " the cheers of the forces are heard welcoming news of peace :

> *Lan.* The word of peace is render'd : hark, how they
> shout !
> *Mowb.* This had been cheerful after victory.
> *Arch.* A peace is of the nature of a conquest ;
> For then both parties nobly are subdued,
> And neither party loser.

The prince then gives orders for the royal forces to be disbanded, and Westmoreland departs to put the order into execution : " Go, my lord, And let our army be discharged too." Westmoreland having gone, Prince John cunningly suggests that their respective armies shall march past, in order that each can observe what opposition they would have had to encounter had there been a recourse to arms, a suggestion with which the archbishop concurs. A moment later, Westmoreland re-enters, with the news that the leaders of the royal forces, having had direct orders from the prince to keep their positions, refuse to be disbanded without the prince's direct command, to which the latter observes : " They know their duties." Learning from Hastings—who now re-enters—that the rebel army has rapidly dispersed : " My lord, our army is dispersed already : Like youthful steers unyoked, they take their courses East, west, north, south ; or, like a school broke up, Each hurries toward his home and sporting-place," the prince orders their leaders' arrest on the charge of high treason :

> Good tidings, my Lord Hastings ; for the which
> I do arrest thee, traitor, of high treason :
> And you, lord Archbishop, and you, Lord Mowbray,
> Of capital treason I attach you both.

" Is this proceeding just and honourable ? " asks Mowbray, to which Westmoreland retorts : " Is your assembly so ? " " Will you thus break your faith ? " demands the archbishop, only to receive the dishonourable reply : " I pawn'd thee none : I promised you redress of these same grievances Whereof you did complain ; which, by mine honour, I will perform with a most Christian care." Telling them to prepare themselves for the punishment " Meet for rebellion and such acts as theirs," the prince orders the drums to be sounded for the pursuit of the rebel forces, and exclaiming " God, and not we, hath safely fought to-day," with the name of the Almighty on his lips commits an act of treachery by ordering the execution of the rebel leaders :

> Some guard these traitors to the block of death,
> Treason's true bed and yielder up of breath.

We are in another part of the Forest in scene three. Falstaff, who has joined in the pursuit of the disbanded rebel forces, meets Sir John Colville of the dale, whose name and place he ridicules :

> *Fal.* What 's your name, sir ? of what condition are you,
> and of what place, I pray ?
> *Col.* I am a knight, sir ; and my name is Colevile of the
> dale.
> *Fal.* Well, then, Colevile is your name, a knight is your
> degree, and your place the dale : Colevile shall be
> still your name, a traitor your degree, and the
> dungeon your place, a place deep enough ; so shall
> you be still Colevile of the dale.

Falstaff demands his surrender : " Do ye yield, sir ? or shall I sweat for you ? If I do sweat, they are the drops of thy lovers, and they weep for thy death : therefore rouse up fear and trembling, and do observance to my mercy," to which Colville replies : " I think you are Sir John Falstaff, and in that thought yield me," and Falstaff observes that he has a " whole school of tongues " and they all speak no other word than his own name. Prince John enters, and ordering the trumpet to sound " cease pursuit," chastises Falstaff for disobeying orders : " Now, Falstaff, where have you been all this while ? When every thing is ended, then you come : These tardy tricks of yours will, on my life, One time or other break some gallows' back," and Falstaff begins to brag of having captured in his " pure and immaculate valour, . . . a most furious knight and valorous enemy," and requests the prince that the deed be recorded, or he will have a ballad specially composed with his own " picture on the top on 't, Colevile kissing his foot." After telling Colville that he is a " famous rebel," to which Falstaff ejaculates " And a famous true subject took him," the prince orders Colville to be sent to York to be executed : " Send Colevile with his confederates To York, to present execution " : after which the news of their triumph is dispatched to the king : " And now dispatch we toward the court, my lords : I hear the king my father is sore sick : Our news shall go before us to his majesty, Which, cousin, you shall bear to comfort him ; And we with sober speed will follow you." After Falstaff has asked and been granted permission to leave :

> *Fal.*   My lord, I beseech you, give me leave to go
>   Through Gloucestershire : and, when you come to court,
>   Stand my good lord, pray, in your good report.
> *Lan.*   Fare you well, Falstaff : I, in my condition,
>   Shall better speak of you than you deserve,

all depart with the exception of Sir John, who muses on the serious mindedness of the prince : " Good faith, this same young sober-blooded boy doth not love me ; nor a man cannot make him laugh ; but that 's no marvel, he drinks no wine," asserting that none of these " demure boys " ever prove their worth, for as they drink only " thin drink " which so " over-cools their blood," and eat such an amount of fish, that they " fall into a kind of male green-sickness," and proceeds to comment on the excellency of sherry, how it enters the brain, and dries up all the " foolish and dull and crudy vapours which environ it ; makes it apprehensive, quick, forgetive, full of nimble, fiery and delectable shapes ; which, delivered o'er to the voice, the tongue, which is the birth, becomes excellent wit," how it " warms the blood " and " illuminates the face," and finally it passes to the heart, " who, great and puffed up with this retinue, doth any deed of courage ; and this valour comes of sherris." Bardolph enters, and informs Falstaff that the " army is discharged all and gone," and remarking " Let them go," Falstaff departs intending to pay a visit to Justice Shallow—whom he declares he has already between his finger and his thumb—on his way through Gloucestershire, and invites Bardolph to accompany him, which invitation Bardolph accepts.

The fourth scene opens in the Jerusalem chamber at Westminster, where we find Henry announcing to the lords assembled that should " God give successful end to this debate that bleedeth at our doors," he will go on a crusade to the Holy Land. The king then inquires for two of his sons, Prince Henry and Thomas Duke of Clarence. The former is hunting at Windsor, but the latter being present, the king entreats him to foster the company of the Prince of Wales, for although " thou dost neglect him, Thomas ; Thou hast a better place in his affection Than all thy brothers : cherish it, my boy, And noble offices thou mayst effect Of meditation, after I am

dead, Between his greatness and thy other brethren : Therefore omit him not."
Being of a gracious turn of mind he hath a " tear for pity, and a hand Open as day
for melting charity " : yet when roused he is as hard as flint, " As humorous as
winter, and as sudden As flaws congealed in the spring of day." Observe him well
and " Chide him for faults, and do it reverently," and when he is in an angry frame
of mind give him time and scope Till that his passions exhaust themselves. " Learn
this, Thomas, And thou shalt prove a shelter to thy friends, A hoop of gold to bind
thy brothers in," and Clarence faithfully promises to " observe his brother with all
care and love." He then tells his father that Prince Henry is dining in London with
" Poins, and other his continual followers," which makes the king regret that his
heir should frequent such inordinate company. But Warwick tells Henry that the
prince " but studies his companions Like a strange tongue, wherein to gain the
language," and will in the " perfectness of time Cast off all these undesirable followers ;
and their memory Shall as a pattern or a measure live, By which his grace must mete
the lives of others, Turning past evils to advantages," to which the king makes the
cogent comment : " 'Tis seldom when the bee doth leave her comb In the dead
carrion."

Westmoreland now appears and announces Prince John's bloodless victory over
the rebel forces, and the arrest and execution of the rebel leaders : " Mowbray, the
Bishop Scroop, Hastings and all Are brought to the correction of your law ; There
is not now a rebel's sword unsheathed, But Peace puts forth her olive every where."
This welcome news is followed by the entry of Harcourt who announces that
Northumberland and Lord Bardolph with their Scotch allies have been defeated by
the sheriff of Yorkshire. But the king, who is feeling faint calls for assistance :
" And now my sight fails, and my brain is giddy : O me ! come near me ; now I am
much ill," and his two sons, with Westmoreland and Warwick rush to his assistance.
On his showing signs of recovery, Warwick requests those present to " Speak lower,
princes, for the king recovers," and at Henry's request they tenderly bear him away
into an adjoining chamber :

> I pray you, take me up, and bear me hence
> Into some other chamber : softly, pray.

The final scene of this Act shows us the royal sick-room. The king, lying on a
bed, requests that " there be no noise made " unless it is sweet music to cheer up his
" weary spirit." Warwick therefore calls for the musicians to play softly in the
adjoining room, and the king requests that his crown be placed on his pillow, while
Clarence makes comments on his changed appearance. Prince Henry enters and
inquires for the king, and being told he is " exceedingly ill " suggests that his father
be informed of the good news from the north, and being told that it was the joyful
tidings that brought on the present attack, exclaims : " If he be sick with joy, he 'll
recover without physic." " Not so much noise, my lords : sweet prince, speak low :
The king your father is disposed to sleep," exclaims Warwick, while Clarence suggests
withdrawing to the next room, but the Prince of Wales decides to remain at the royal
bedside : " No ; I will sit and watch here by the king." After they have left, the
prince's eyes light upon the crown : " Why doth the crown lie there upon his pillow,
Being so troublesome a bedfellow ? O polish'd perturbation ! golden care ! That
keep'st the ports of slumber open wide To many a watchful night ! " Taking the
crown in his hands and with the words : " sleep with it now ! Yet not so sound and
half so deeply sweet As he whose brow with homely biggen bound Snores out the
watch of night. O majesty ! When thou dost pinch thy bearer, thou dost sit Like
a rich armour worn in heat of day, That scalds with safety," he lays it down again.

As he does so he notices that a " downy feather " lies close to the king's lips. Bending over his father, he perceives that the feather " stirs not," and concludes the king has passed away. Dropping on his knees by the bedside, the prince exclaims : " My gracious lord ! my father ! This sleep is sound indeed ; this is a sleep, That from this golden rigol hath divorced So many English kings." Taking the crown again from the pillow and holding it above his head, he proceeds : " Thy due from me Is tears and heavy sorrows of the blood, Which nature, love, and filial tenderness, Shall, O dear father, pay thee plenteously : My due from thee is this imperial crown," and placing the diadem upon his head, remarks : " Lo, here it sits, Which God shall guard : and put the world's whole strength Into one giant arm, it shall not force This lineal honour from me : this from thee Will I to mine leave, as 'tis left to me," and then casting a hasty glance at the king withdraws silently from the room. Imme- diately he has gone the king arouses from his slumber, and seeing no one in the room, calls out : " Warwick ! Gloucester ! Clarence ! " As they hasten to his bedside the king inquires : " Why did you leave me here alone, my lords ? " to which Clarence answers that they left the Prince of Wales to watch over him. " The Prince of Wales ! exclaims the king, " Where is he ? let me see him " : and then noticing that the crown is missing calls out : " Where is the crown ? who took it from my pillow ? " to which Warwick replies : " When we withdrew, my liege, we left it here." " The prince hath ta'en it hence " : continues the king, " go, seek him out. Is he so hasty that he doth suppose My sleep my death ? Find him, my Lord of Warwick ; chide him hither," and Warwick leaves the room in search of the prince. The prince is found in an adjoining room overcome with grief at the supposed death of his father : " My lord, I found the prince in the next room, Washing with kindly tears his gentle cheeks, With such a deep demeanour in great sorrow, That tyranny, which never quaff'd but blood, Would, by beholding him, have wash'd his knife With gentle eye-drops," exclaims Warwick, and the prince being told the king is still alive hastens to his bedside. Wishing to be alone with his son, the king dismisses the others. " I never thought to hear you speak again," is the prince's remark after they have left, but his father tells him that the wish was father to the thought, for " I stay too long for thee, I weary thee. Dost thou so hunger for mine empty chair That thou wilt needs invest thee with my honours Before thy hour is ripe ? O foolish youth ! Thou seek'st the greatness that will overwhelm thee." With bitter- ness Henry adds that he foresees he will soon be forgotten, and that under his son's régime England " will be a wilderness again, Peopled with wolves, thy old inhabitants ! The prince, overcome with emotion asks pardon of his father [IV. v. 138–176] and handing back the crown, remarks : " There is your crown ; And He that wears the crown immortally Long guard it yours ! " The king is greatly pleased at his son's words, and requesting the prince to sit by his bed while he gives him the " very latest counsel That ever I shall breathe," charges him to keep giddy minds busy with foreign wars, and prays that God will forgive his usurpation of the crown, and " grant it may with thee in true peace live ! " " My gracious liege," answers the prince, " You won it, wore it, kept it, gave it me ; Then plain and right must my possession be : Which I with more than with a common pain 'Gainst all the world will rightfully maintain." This conversation between the king and his eldest son is interrupted by the entry of Prince John. " Health, peace, and happiness to my royal father," exclaims the prince, but the king, whose life is slowly ebbing, can only feebly answer : " Thou bring'st me happiness and peace, son John ; But health, alack, with youthful wings is flown From this bare wither'd trunk " : for all my " worldly business " is drawing to a close. Calling for Warwick, the king asks him whether there is any particular name for the chamber in which he first swooned, and being told it is called

" Jerusalem," exclaims that the prophecy shall be fulfilled, and that " In that Jerusalem shall Harry die " :

> Laud be to God ! even there my life must end.
> It hath been prophesied to me many years,
> I should not die but in Jerusalem ;
> Which vainly I supposed the Holy Land :
> But bear me to that chamber ; there I 'll lie ;
> In that Jerusalem shall Harry die.

With reverent and filial obedience the nobles carry the king into the " Jerusalem " chamber, and a few hours later the troubled spirit of Henry passed beyond the veil, and so Prince Hal ascended the throne as King Henry the Fifth.

The fifth Act opens in the house of Justice Shallow in Gloucestershire.   Falstaff —accompanied by his page and Bardolph—is, according to promise, revisiting Shallow on his way back from the wars.   The visit is intended to be a very short one as Falstaff is anxious to get back to London, but his host tells him he will not excuse him : " I will not excuse you ; you shall not be excused ; excuses shall not be admitted ; there is no excuse shall serve ; you shall not be excused."   Shallow then calls his servant Davy, and gives him orders to prepare food for the guests : " Some pigeons, Davy, a couple of short-legged hens, a joint of mutton, and any pretty tiny kickshaws, tell William cook."   " Doth the man of war stay all night, sir," asks Davy, to which Shallow answers : " Yea, Davy, I will use him well : a friend i' the court is better than a penny in purse.   Use his men well, Davy ; for they are arrant knaves, and will backbite."   " No worse than they are backbitten, sir ; for they have marvellous foul linen," retorts Davy, but Shallow, who considers Davy very witty, orders him to get about his business.   Inquiring for Falstaff Shallow tells them to remove his boots, and then welcomes Bardolph and " my tall fellow " [the page]. Giving Bardolph and the page instructions to attend to their horses, Falstaff muses to himself that " If he were sawed into quantities, he would make four dozen of such bearded hermits' staves as Master Shallow," and proceeds to ridicule the servants in their apeing of their master's mannerisms : " It is a wonderful thing to see the semblable coherence of his men's spirits and his : they, by observing of him, do bear themselves like foolish justices ; he, by conversing with them, is turned into a justice-like serving-man : their spirits are so married in conjunction with the participation of society that they flock together in consent, like so many wild-geese," and declares he will from his visit, invent sufficient comic matter out of Shallow, that will keep Prince Harry in " continual laughter " until " his face be like a wet cloak laid up ! "

The next scene is enacted in the palace at Westminster.   It opens with the Lord Chief Justice inquiring : " How doth the king ? " to which Warwick replies : " Exceeding well ; his cares are now all ended."   " I hope, not dead," is the Chief Justice's next question, only to receive the answer : " He 's walk'd the way of nature ; And to our purposes he lives no more."   " I would his majesty had call'd me with him," adds the Chief Justice, because the " service which I had rendered the late king leaves me open to all injuries," a statement in which Warwick acquiesces : " Indeed I think the young king loves you not."   On the entry of Lancaster, Clarence, Gloucester, Westmoreland and others, Warwick regrets that the worst of the late king's sons should succeed to the throne, to which the Chief Justice enjoins : " O God, I fear all will be overturn'd ! "   Gloucester expresses sympathy with the Chief Justice in having lost a friend in the person of the late king, while Clarence suggests that he gain the favour of Falstaff " who swims against your stream of quality."

But the Chief Justice merely replies that he has done what he considers his duty, and if " truth and upright innocency is denied him he will follow his dead master, and tell him who hath sent him after him."

At this point the new king enters and remarks : " This new and gorgeous garment, majesty, sits not so easy on me as you think," and then turning to his brothers, observes : " Brothers, you mix your sadness with some fear : This is the English, not the Turkish court ; Not Amurath an Amurath succeeds, But Harry Harry." After imploring their aid he asks why " they look so strangely on him : You are, I think, assured I love you not," to which the Chief Justice replies : " That his majesty hath no just cause to hate him," and the new king then reminds him that he once committed him to prison, an indignity which is not soon forgotten :

> How might a prince of my great hopes forget
> So great indignities you laid upon me ?
> What ! rate, rebuke, and roughly send to prison
> The immediate heir of England ? Was this easy ?
> May this be wash'd in Lethe, and forgotten ?

and the Chief Justice in very quiet and dignified language reminds the new king that he had to execute the laws with impartial justice, and asks him whether he would like to see his " decrees set at nought," and " Justice plucked down from his awful bench, To trip the course of law and blunt the sword That guards the peace and safety of his person." Henry is so struck with the Lord Chief Justice's speech [V. ii. 73–101] that he confers upon him the same office he had held under Henry the Fourth, and bids him continue to be the same " bold, just, and impartial judge," at the same time beseeching his aid and advice [V. ii. 102–145]. After declaring his willingness to devote all his energies—with the aid of his Parliament—to the good government of the realm, the scene closes with the king invoking the aid of God in all his good intentions, so that :

> No prince nor peer shall have just cause to say,
> God shorten Harry's happy life one day !

In the next scene we behold Falstaff and his friends in Justice Shallow's orchard. They are in merry mood, having feasted well and drunk liberally of sack. Shallow is very anxious for his guests to view his orchard of which he is very proud, and conducts them to an arbour in the orchard where dessert is provided in the shape of " last year's pippin of Shallow's own grafting, with a dish of caraways, and so forth." As they sit within the arbour drinking merrily, Silence breaks out in song :

> Do nothing but eat and make good cheer,
> And praise God for the merry year ;
> When flesh is cheap and females dear,
> And lusty lads roam here and there
>   So merrily,
> And ever among so merrily.

" There 's a merry heart ! Good Master Silence, I 'll give you a health for that anon," observes Falstaff. Davy leaves for the purpose of fetching wine and Silence again breaks out in song :

> Be merry, be merry, my wife has all ;
> For women are shrews, both short and tall :
> 'Tis merry in hall when beards wag all,
>   And welcome merry Shrove-tide.
> Be merry, be merry.

" I did not think Master Silence had been a man of this mettle," observes Falstaff, to which Silence retorts : " Who, I ? I have been merry twice and once ere now."

Davy now re-enters bringing with him a " dish of leather-coats," and Bardolph calls for a cup of wine. This causes Silence to break out into song once more :

A cup of wine that 's brisk and fine,
And drink unto the leman mine ;
    And a merry heart lives long-a.
Fill the cup, and let it come ;
I 'll pledge you a mile to the bottom.

As the merriment proceeds, a loud knocking is heard, and Davy hurries away to answer the call, and returning presently, announces that " Pistol has come from the court with news." " From the court," observes Falstaff, " let him come in," and on the entrance of Pistol, Falstaff remarks : " What wind blew you hither, Pistol ? " " Not the ill wind which blows no man to good. Sweet knight, thou art now one of the greatest men in this realm," is Pistol's reply, to which Silence enjoins : " By 'r lady, I think a' be, but goodman Puff of Barson." " Puff ! " retorts Pistol, " Puff in thy teeth, most recreant coward base," and then turning to Falstaff says : " Sir John, I am thy Pistol and thy friend, And helter-skelter have I rode to thee, And tidings do I bring and lucky joys And golden times and happy news of price," adding, that King Henry the Fourth is dead, and that Prince Hal has ascended the throne as King Henry the Fifth. Falstaff is inclined to disbelieve the news at first, but being assured by Pistol that the old king is dead " as nail in door : the things I speak are just," Falstaff orders his horse to be saddled, and turning to Shallow, says : " Master Robert Shallow, choose what office thou wilt in the land, 'tis thine," while he promises Pistol to " double-charge him with dignities." " O joyful day ! I would not take knighthood for my fortune," observes Bardolph. " Carry Master Silence to bed. Master Shallow, my Lord Shallow,—be what thou wilt ; I am fortune's steward," excitedly exclaims Falstaff, " get on thy boots : we 'll ride all night. O sweet Pistol ! Away, Bardolph ! Come, Pistol, utter more to me ; and withal devise something to do thyself good. Boot, boot, Master Shallow ! I know the young king is sick for me," and shouting in an ecstasy of joy the " laws of England are at my commandment. Blessed are they that have been my friends ; and woe to my lord chief justice," leaves for London forthwith.

A London Street supplies the next scene. Mistress Quickly and Doll Tearsheet are arrested by Beadles, who threaten to give Doll a severe whipping for causing disturbances in which several men have lost their lives : " The constables have delivered her over to me " ; remarks the first Beadle, " and she shall have whipping-cheer enough, I warrant her : there hath been a man or two lately killed about her." The women cause a great deal of commotion, and Doll calls the Beadle foul and coarse names as : " nut-hook, nut-hook, . . . thou damned tripe-visaged rascal, . . . thou paper-faced villain, . . . you blue-bottle rogue, you filthy famished correctioner," and uses other similar epithets.

The final scene of this Act is a public place near Westminster Abbey. It is the day fixed for the coronation of the new king. The trumpets sound heralding the approach of the coronation procession, and two grooms enter and strew the ground with rushes. Falstaff, Shallow, Pistol, Bardolph and page now appear. Falstaff pushes himself to the front, and requests Shallow to stand beside him, remarking : " I will make the king do you grace : I will leer upon him as a' comes by ; and do but mark the countenance that he will give me." Turning to Pistol he says : " Come here, Pistol ; stand beside me," wishing there had been time to have bought new liveries in which case he would have spent the thousand pounds he borrowed of him. As they wait, Pistol tells Falstaff that Doll Tearsheet has been committed to prison :

" My knight, I will inflame thy noble liver, And make thee rage. Thy Doll, and Helen of thy noble thoughts, Is in base durance and contagious prison " ; but Falstaff replies : " I will deliver her." There are shouts, and Heralds announce the approach of the king, and the new monarch and his train, accompanied by the Lord Chief Justice enter. " God save thy grace, King Hal ! my royal Hal ! " shouts Falstaff, to which Pistol adds : " The heavens thee guard and keep, most royal imp of fame ! " " God save thee, my sweet boy ! " again shouts Falstaff. " My lord chief justice, speak to that vain man," is the king's command. " Have you your wits ? know you what 'tis you speak ? " chides the justice, but Falstaff pays no heed to his rebukes, and pushing his way to the king, says : " My king ! my Jove ! I speak to thee, my heart ! " The king halts, and addressing Falstaff in distinct and cold words tells him " I know thee not, old man : fall to thy prayers ; How ill white hairs become a fool and jester ! " adding " For God doth know, so shall the world perceive, That I have turn'd away my former self ; So will I those that kept me company," who will have to keep " ten miles away from my person " until they " reform themselves." Giving orders for the procession to proceed, King Henry passes on. Falstaff, on whose face there is sadness, tells Shallow not to " grieve " for the king only disowned him under a pretence, and will " send for him in private," and invites Pistol and Bardolph to dine with him : " Fear no colours : go with me to dinner : come, Lieutenant Pistol ; come, Bardolph : I shall be sent for soon at night." But even this hope is short-lived, for Prince John and the Lord Chief Justice, accompanied by officers, appear, and orders are given for the arrest of Falstaff and his companions :

> Go, carry Sir John Falstaff to the Fleet :
> Take all his company along with him.

" My lord, my lord,"—stammers Falstaff, but the Chief Justice curtly replies : " I cannot now speak : I will hear you soon. Take them away," while Pistol mutters the philosophic Latin phrase : " Si fortuna me tormenta, spero contenta."

The scene is brought to a close by Prince John announcing that Henry has summoned Parliament, for he has a suspicion that before the year expires there will be war between England and France :

> I will lay odds that, ere this year expire,
> We bear our civil swords and native fire
> As far as France : I heard a bird so sing,
> Whose music, to my thinking, pleased the king.
> Come, will you hence.

The Play closes with an Epilogue spoken by a dancer, who after saluting the audience with a curtsy, expresses a hope that " their patience has not been tried at such a displeasing play," in which case he craves pardon : " First my fear ; then my curtsy ; last my speech. My fear is, your displeasure ; my curtsy, my duty ; and my speech, to beg your pardons." If however his " tongue cannot acquit him " he will try to win favour by dancing, but a " good conscience will make any possible satisfaction, and so would I," for " All the gentlewomen here have forgiven me : if the gentlemen will not, then the gentlemen do not agree with the gentlewomen, which was never seen before in such an assembly." He then promises to continue the story " If you be not too much cloyed with fat meat," with " Sir John in it, and make you merry with fair Katharine of France : where, for any thing I know, Falstaff shall die of a sweat, unless already a' be killed with your hard opinions." But the dancer's " tongue is weary " and his " legs too," so bidding all good-night, he kneels down and prays for the queen, as the curtain slowly falls upon the scene.

Scene : England

CHARACTERS, PLACE-NAMES, ETC.

Achitophel. I. ii. 34.

> A whoreson Achitophel ! a rascally
> yea-forsooth knave !   [I. ii. 34–35.]

Achitophel or Ahithophel was a Gilonite who deserted David for Absalom, hence a treacherous friend. He was David's counsellor, whose advice was deemed infallible. " And the counsel of Ahithophel, which he counselled in those days, was if a man had enquired at the oracle of God : so was all the counsel of Ahithophel both with David and with Absalom."—2 *Samuel* xvi. 23. Being Bathsheba's grandfather he became alienated by David's conduct, and sought to slay him, but being thwarted committed suicide.

Africa. V. iii. 99.

> I speak of Africa and golden joys.   [V. iii. 99.]

An allusion to the fabled wealth of Africa.

Agamemnon. II. iv. 216.

King of Mycenæ and leader of the Grecian expedition against Troy.

Alecto's snake. V. v. 37.

One of the three Greek goddesses of vengeance, represented as having her head covered with serpents.

Althæa's dream. II. ii. 82, 84.

The page's mistake. It was Hecuba, queen of Troy who dreamed that she was delivered of a brand that was to consume the city of Troy.

Althæa was the daughter of Thestius, and wife of Œneus, king of Calydon, and mother of Meleager. When the latter was born, the Fates placed a log of wood on the fire and said that Meleager would live just as long as it was preserved. The mother contrived to keep the log unconsumed for many years, but when Meleager killed Althæa's two brothers, to revenge their death, angrily threw the log into the fire where it was quickly consumed, Meleager expiring at the same time.

Amurath. V. ii. 48.

> This is the English, not the Turkish court ;
> Not Amurath an Amurath succeeds,
> But Harry Harry.   [V. ii. 47–49.]

Amurath the Third, sixth sultan of the Turks (1574–1595). His first act on ascending the throne was to invite all his brothers to a banquet and strangle them.

Ancient Pistol. II. iv. 68, 110.

= Ensign Pistol. Falstaff was captain, Peto lieutenant and Pistol ensign or ancient. ' Ancient ' is a corruption of ' ensign.'

Arthur. II. iv. 33.

> " When Arthur first in court."   [II. iv. 33.]

From an old ballad (Sir Launcelot du Lake) printed in Percy's *Reliques of English Poetry*. A stanza is repeated by the Fool in *King Lear* I. iv. 192–195.

Arthur's show. III. ii. 276.

Probably an interlude or masque, which actually existed, and was very popular in Shakespeare's age. It seems to have been compiled from Malory's *Morte d'Arthur, or the History of King Arthur*. Malone.

Cowl says : " An exhibition of archery by a society called ' The Auncient Order, Society, and Unitie laudable of Prince Arthure and his Knightly Armory of the Round Table.' The society consisted of fifty-eight members who took the names of knights in the *Morte Arthur*, and its meeting place was Mile-end Green."

Asia. II. iv. 161.

> And hollow pamper'd jades of Asia.
> Which cannot go but thirty mile a day,
> [II. iv. 161–162.]

These lines are in part a quotation out of an old absurd fustian play, entitled *Tamburlaine's Conquests ; or, The Scythian Shepherds*, 1590, by C. Marlow. The lines are addressed by Tamburlaine to the captive princes who draw his chariot :

> Holla, you pamper'd jades of Asia,
> What ! can you draw but twenty miles a day ?

Atropos. II. iv. 195.

One of the three Greek goddesses of vengeance, who severs the thread of human existence.

Attendants.

Bardolph. I. ii. 31, 47, 54 ; II. i. 38, p.41, 44, 52 ; II. ii. 65, p.66, 70, 93, 155 ; II. iv. 18, p.109, 150, 188, p.208, 322, 325, p.362 ; III. ii. p.55, 216, 266, 285, 294 ; IV. iii. p.126, 126 ; V. i. p.1, 54, 56, 60 ; V. iii. p.1, 25, 30, 54, 57, 62, 121, 130 ; V. v. p.5, 90.

One of Falstaff's companions. Mistress Quickly has evidently not a very good opinion of him for she refers to him as an " arrant malmsey-nose knave."

He accompanies Sir John on all occasions, and generally acts as messenger for him.

[According to Halliwell-Phillipps, ' the names of Bardoulf and Pistail are found in the muster-roll of artillerymen serving under Humphrey Fitz-Allan, Earl of Arundel, at the siege of St. Laurens des Mortiers, November 11, 1435.' French, however, says that this nobleman was only seven years old in 1435. *Irving edition.*]

[Bardolph also appears in *The Life of King Henry the Fifth*. (q.v.)]

Barson. V. iii. 88.

A corruption of Barston, a village in Warwickshire.

Bartholomew boar-pig. II. iv. 226.

Refers to the sale of pigs at St. Bartholomew's fair. These pigs were roasted and sold piping hot. " Bartholomew Faire begins on the twenty-fourth day of August, and is then of so vast an extent, that it is contained in no less than four several parishes, namely Christ Church, Great and Little St. Bartholomew, and St. Sepulchres. Hither resort people of all sorts and conditions. Christ Church cloisters are now hung full of pictures. It is remarkable and worth your observation to beholde and heare the strange sights and confused noise in the faire. Here, a knave in a fooles coate, with a trumpet sounding, or on a drumme beating, invites you to see his puppets ; there, a rogue like a wild woodman, or in an antick shape like an Incubus, desires your company to view his motion : on the other side, hocus pocus, with three yards of tape, or ribbin, in's hand, showing his art of legerdemaine, to the admiration and astonishment of a company of cockoloaches." And Sir John Bramston, in his *Autobiography*, 1688, refers to the annual custom by which the Lord Mayor proclaimed St. Bartholomew Fair on that Saint's Eve, and riding past Newgate was accustomed to receive from the keeper or governor a cup of sack. In *Wit and Drollery*, 1682, we have :

> Now London Mayor, in Saddle new :
> Rides into fair of Bartholomew :
> He twirles his Chain, and looketh big,
> As he would fright the head of Pig :
> Which gaping lies on greasy stall—

Basingstoke. II. i. 165.

A town in Hampshire.

Beadles. V. iv. p.1.

Inferior officers who could arrest persons, and punish petty offences.

Besonian. V. iii. 112.

= a worthless fellow ; a soldier of low military rank.

Blunt. IV. iii. p.24, 74.

Only appears on one occasion, during the expedition against Northumberland, Scroop and the other rebels.

[Blunt, who is a *persona muta* in the play, is probably Sir John Blunt, a son of Sir Walter Blunt in the *First Part* . . . In 1412 being besieged in a fortress in Guienne by the Lord of Helie one of the marshals of France with a large army, Blunt, with a few hundred men defeated the assailants and captured the marshal. Blunt served at Harfleur with Henry V., in 1415, was made a K.G. in 1417, and died in 1418.]

Blunts. I. i. 16.

> and both the Blunts
> Kill'd by the hand of Douglas ;   [I. i. 16-17.]

In the *First Part of King Henry the Fourth*, Act V., Scene iii., one of the Blunts (Sir Walter Blunt) is killed by Douglas.

Bolingbroke. I. i. 208 ; I. iii. 92.

Henry Bolingbroke, Duke of Hereford, afterwards King Henry the Fourth.

Bolingbroke. I. iii. 105.

> Thou, that threw'st dust upon his goodly head
> When through proud London he came sighing on
> After the admired heels of Bolingbroke,
>   [I. iii. 103-105.]

" when at the heels of the admired Bolingbroke he rode in such plight through London, then rejoicing at his downfall." *Deighton.*

Bolingbroke. III. i. 71.

> Northumberland, thou ladder by the which
> My cousin Bolingbroke ascends my throne :
>   [II. i. 70-71.]

See *The Tragedy of King Richard the Second*, V. i. 55-70.

Bourdeaux. II. iv. 63.

> there 's a whole merchant's venture of
> Bourdeaux stuff in him.   [II. iv. 62-63.]

= a whole consignment of wines from Bourdeaux.

Boy. II. i. p.1.

Fang, the Sheriff's officer's boy.

Bullcalf. III. ii. p.1, 168, 169, 171, 240, 244, 245, 247.

One of the six " recruits " brought before Falstaff to be his bodyguard.

Bullcalf is one of the two who bribe Bardolph to excuse them from service.

> Good master corporate Bardolph, stand my friend ;
> and here 's four Harry ten shillings in French crowns
> for you. In very truth, sir, I had as lieve be hanged,
> sir, as go : and yet, for mine own part, sir, I do not
> care ; but rather, because I am unwilling, and, for
> mine own part, have a desire to stay with my friends
> else, sir, I did not care, for mine own part, so much.
>   [III. ii. 216-222.]

Cæsars. II. iv. 163.

Cain. I. i. 157.

An allusion to Cain who murdered his brother Abel.

Calipolis. II. iv. 175.

> Then feed, and be fat, my fair Calipolis.
>   [II. iv. 175.]

An allusion to the wife of Muley Mahamet in *The Battle of Alcazar*, a drama by George Peele, 1582. During a famine her husband presents her with a bit of meat stolen from a lioness with the words : " Feed then, and faint not, fair *Calypolis*."

Cannibals. II. iv. 163.

Pistol's blunder for Hannibal.

Captain Pistol. II. iv. 135.

> *Host.* No, good Captain Pistol ; not here, sweet captain.
> *Dol.* Captain ! thou abominable damned cheater, art thou
> not ashamed to be called captain ? [II. iv. 135-137.]

Malone says : " Pistol's character seems to have been a common one on the stage in the time of Shakspeare." In *A Woman's a Weather-*

cock, by N. Field, 1612, there is a personage of the same stamp, who is thus described :

> Thou unspeakable rascal, thou a soldier !
> That with thy slops and cat-a-mountain face,
> Thy blather chaps, and thy robustious words,
> Fright'st the poor whore, and terribly doth exact
> A weekly subsidy, twelve pence a piece,
> Whereon thou livest : and on my conscience,
> Thou snap'st besides with cheats and cut-purses.

Cerberus. II. iv. 165.

In Mythology a dog with fifty heads which guarded the entrance to hell.

Chester. I. i. 39.

Clement Perkes o' the hill. V. i. 37.

Probably suggested by a name common in Warwickshire. " Edward Perkes " occurs among the baptisms registered at Stratford-upon-Avon, 1603, born at Shottery, Ann Hathaway's own hamlet : and the family of Perkes was connected with that of Shakespeare.

Clement's Inn. III. ii. 14, 204, 275, 303.

An Inn of Court at the entrance to Wych Street. It was originally intended for the use of patients who came to use the so-called miraculous waters of St. Clement's Well.

Corporal Bardolph. II. iv. 150.

Bardolph, one of Falstaff's companions. He helps to eject Pistol from the Boar's Head Tavern.

Cotswold. III. ii. 21.

= The Cotswold Hills in Gloucestershire. " The games at Cotswold were, in the time of our author, very famous. Of these I have seen accounts in several old pamphlets ; and Shallow, by distinguishing Will Squele as a Cotswold man, meant to have him understood as one who was well versed in manly exercises, and consequently of a daring spirit, and an athletic constitution." *Steevens.*

Coventry. IV. i. 135.

> He ne'er had borne it out of Coventry : [IV. i. 135.]

" he would never have escaped from Coventry (where the lists were held) with his life." *Deighton.*

Dancer, Speaker of the Epilogue. Epilogue p.1.

Who, after making the usual apologies and expressing the hope that the play has met with the approval of the audience, informs them that the play shall be continued " with Sir John in it, and make you merry with fair Katharine of France."

Davy, Servant to Shallow. V. i. 2, 6, p.7, 8, 9, 15, 25, 29, 31, 35, 38, 52 ; V. iii. p.1, 8, 9, 10, 25, p.41, 42, 60, p.79.

On being told to prepare food for Falstaff and his men, Davy makes some ado, but is ordered by Shallow to go about his business.

He informs the others when in Shallow's garden of the arrival of Pistol with news from London.

Doll. II. iv. 45, 223, 229, 257, 366, 382, 383 ; V. v. 33, 38.

= Doll Tearsheet (q.v.).

Doll Tearsheet. II. i. 160 ; II. ii. 146, 161 ; II. iv. 11, p.22, 35, 41, 45, 119, 124, 149, 223, 229, 257, 366, 378, 380, 382, 383 ; V. iv. p.1.

First appears at the Boar's Head Tavern with Mistress Quickly and indulges in a series of witty .remarks with Falstaff.

Her character is finely drawn, and we see, that in spite of her morals, she has a sense of dignity, for although she likes Falstaff a great deal, he is not allowed to treat her too lightly, neither will she stand the insults of Pistol, whom she upbraids in no uncertain words.

We last see her being arrested by beadles for being the cause of many quarrels among men, and Doll in her anger hurls abuse at the men as they haul her to prison.

Dolphin-chamber. II. i. 84.

The name of a room in the tavern. In the time of Shakespeare it was customary to give particular names to dining-rooms in inns and taverns.

Double. III. ii. 41, 53.

An acquaintance of Justice Shallow's. Double was an archer and could ' draw a good bow.'

Douglas. I. i. 17, 77, 82.

= Archibald, Earl of Douglas. See the *First Part of King Henry the Fourth.*

Douglas. I. i. 127.

> and that furious Scot,
> The bloody Douglas, whose well-labouring sword
> Had three times slain the appearance of the king,
> [I. i. 126–12.]

Archibald, Earl of Douglas. Cf. *First Part of Henry the Fourth*, V. iii. 25–28 :

> *Hot.* The king hath many marching in his coats.
> *Doug.* Now, by my sword, I will kill all his coats ;
> I 'll murder all his wardrobe, piece by piece,
> Until I meet the king.

Douglas' rage. Induction 31.

> And that the king before the Douglas' rage
> Stoop 'd his anointed head as low as death.
> [Induction 31–32.]

Douglas had killed several knights who were wearing a dress similar to that of the king.

Drawers. II. iv. p.1, p.68.

Waiters at the Boar's Head Tavern.

Duke of Norfolk's signories. IV. i. 111.

> were you not restored
> To all the Duke of Norfolk's signories,
> [IV. i. 110–111.]

" The rights and possessions belonging to his title as Duke of Norfolk." *Deighton.*

Earl of Hereford. IV. i. 131.

> The Earl of Hereford was reputed then
> In England the most valiant gentleman :
> [IV. i. 131–132.]

= Bolingbroke, who was Duke of Hereford.

Earl of Northumberland. Induction 36 ; I. i. p.7, 152 ; I. ii. 201 ; I. ii. 13, 17 ; II. i. 171 ; II. iii. p.1 ; III. i. 44, 58, 68, 70, 89, 95 ; IV. i. 8 ; IV. iv. 97.

The unscrupulous leader of the rebels against Henry the Fourth has nothing admirable in his character.

He appears in the first scene, and learns of the defeat of his forces, which news causes him to be very grieved, and in a passionate outburst talks of all that he will do in revenge, but later we find that he decides to go to Scotland, and avoid the danger of the second rebellion, leaving others to carry it out. Thus the meanness and selfishness of his character are shown.

He helped Bolingbroke to get the throne, and now wants to take it from him, and adopts the lowest methods of achieving his object, using his followers as pawns to work for him while he stays in the background, ready to step forward and receive the spoils.

Commenting on this character, Hudson says : " Northumberland makes good his character as found in history. Evermore talking big and doing nothing ; full of verbal tempest and practical impotence ; and still ruining his friends, and at last himself, between " I would " and " I dare not " ; he lives without our respect, and dies unpitied of us ; while his daughter-in-law's remembrance of her noble husband kindles a sharp resentment of his mean-spirited backwardness, and a hearty scorn of his blustering verbiage."

[Sir Henry Percy, son of Henry Lord Percy and Mary his wife, sister of Henry Duke of Lancaster. Created first Earl of Northumberland at the coronation of King Richard the Second in 1377, but becoming alienated to Richard joined Henry of Lancaster ; revolted against Henry, but after the battle of Shrewsbury submitted and was pardoned ; conspired with Owen Glendower and Sir Edmund Mortimer and was declared a traitor. In company with Lords Bardolph and Mowbray, and Archbishop Scroop he took up arms in 1405. Mowbray and the Archbishop paid for their precipitancy with their heads, and Northumberland thereupon fled to Scotland, whence, through fear of treachery, he and Bardolph afterwards betook themselves to Wales. In 1408 he made another rebellious inroad into Yorkshire, and at Bramham Moor, near Tadcaster on the 18th of February of that year was encountered by Thomas Rokeby, Sheriff of Yorkshire, the earl being defeated and slain.]

Earl of Surrey. III. i. 1, p.32.

One of the nobles of the king's party, who appears with the Earl of Warwick when the king is troubled and unable to sleep for the cares of state, and the fear of further insurrection by Northumberland.

[Thomas, Earl of Arundel and Surrey, born 1381. Created by Henry IV., one of the first knights of the Bath ; procured the execution of Archbishop Scroop and Lord Mowbray in 1405 and was made Lord Treasurer and Warden of the Cinque Ports by Henry V., 1413, and two years later took part in the siege of Harfleur. He died in 1415 of dysentery.]

Earl of Warwick. III. i. 1, p.32 ; IV. iv. p.1 ; V. v. p.1, 47, 62, p.80, 231, p.232 ; V. ii. p.1, 20.

A noble of the king's party, who, with the Earl of Surrey is summoned to the king's chamber to talk over the affairs of state.

On being asked his opinion as to the state of the country he remarks :

> It is but as a body yet distemper'd ;
> Which to his former strength may be restored
> With good advice and little medicine :
> My Lord Northumberland will soon be cool'd.
>   [III. i. 41–44.]

He endeavours to ease the king's mind by telling him that the rumours current as to the strength of the rebels are grossly exaggerated.

At another point Warwick defends Prince Henry in his choice of companions, reminding the king that he does so to gain experience :

> The prince but studies his companions
> Like a strange tongue, wherein, to gain the language,
> 'Tis needful that the most immodest word
> Be look'd upon and learn'd ; which once attained,
> Your highness knows, comes to no further use
> But to be known and hated. So, like gross terms,
> The prince will in the perfectness of time
> Cast off his followers ; and their memory
> Shall as a pattern or a measure live,
> By which his grace must mete the lives of others,
> Turning past evils to advantages.   [IV. iv. 68–78.]

Shakespeare is under a mistake as to the identity of this character, when he makes the king address him, in Act III., Scene i :

> ' You, cousin Nevil, as I may remember ' ;—

but the title at the time was held by Richard Beauchamp, fifth Earl of Warwick of his name. His youngest daughter, Anne Beauchamp, married Richard Nevill, the famous ' king-maker,' who became Earl of Warwick, but not until the reign of Henry VI., and hence the mistake of the poet as to surname. The illustrious Warwick of this play, born in 1381, descended from Hugh de Beauchamp, who had large grants from the Conqueror, and received his name from his sponsors, King Richard II., and Richard Scrope, Archbishop of York. Like his ancestors, he was a famous warrior ; he behaved with great valour against Glendower, whose person he nearly captured, taking his standard ; and at Shrewsbury, ' he notably and manly behaved himself to his great laud and worship.' In 9 Henry IV. he made a pilgrimage to the Holy Land, and during his progress displayed the highest accomplishments of chivalry at different tournaments, wherein he had no superior for courtesy and valour. Southey alludes to his fame in his poem, *Joan of Arc,*—

> ' Warwick, he whose wide renown,
> Greece knew, and Antioch, and the holy soil
> Of Palestine, since there in arms he went
> On gallant pilgrimage.

In the last year of Henry IV. he was sent to Scotland to treat of peace with the Regent Albany. At the coronation of Henry V., with which this play concludes, April 9, 1413, the Earl of Warwick acted as Lord High Steward of England. *French.*

[Warwick is also a character in the *Life of King Henry the Fifth.* (q.v.)]

Earl of Westmoreland. I. i. 18, 135 ; I. ii. 224, 237 ; I. iii. 82 ; IV. i. p.26, 26, 29, 59, 168, 224, p.225 ; IV. ii. p.1, 32, 72, p.98 ; IV. iii. p.24, 25, p.70 ; IV. iv. p.80, 80, 91 ; V. ii. p.14.

A noble of the king's party, who first appears in the fourth act of the play, before the rebel leaders in a forest in Yorkshire as a messenger from the king.

It is his duty to endeavour to persuade the rebels to disband their forces, but to this they will not agree, and having told Westmoreland of their grievances he leaves them and returns to Prince John, who is in command of the royal forces.

A little later he re-appears with the news that the prince will meet the rebel leaders between their respective camps to discuss terms of peace.

Later Westmoreland appears at Westminster to inform the king of the happenings in Yorkshire.

This nobleman, the Ralph Nevill of the *First Part*, is an important character in this play, . . . He was amply rewarded for his great services by Henry IV., who gave him the county of Richmond for life, made him Earl Marshal, Governor of Carlisle, Warden of the West Marches towards Scotland, Governor of Roxburgh Castle, and a K.G.

By his two wives he had twenty-two children ; many of the sons were eminent characters in history, whilst the marriages of his daughters increased the influence of the Nevills. His first wife was Margaret Stafford, daughter of Hugh, second Earl of Stafford, K.G., by whom he had two sons and seven daughters ; the eldest son, John Lord Nevill, died before his father, leaving a son, Ralph, who succeeded his grandfather as second 'Earl of Westmoreland,' under which title he is a character in the *Third Part of King Henry VI.*

The earl's second wife was the Lady Joan Beaufort, only daughter of John of *Gaunt* and Catherine Swynford ; the issue of this marriage were eight sons and five daughters. Of the former,—1. Richard Nevill is the ' Earl of Salisbury ' in the *Second Part of King Henry VI.* ; 2. William Nevill became Lord Fauconberg, and a K.G. ; 3. George Nevill became Lord Latimer ; 4. Edward Nevill was summoned to Parliament, *jure uxoris*, as Baron Bergavenny ; 5. Robert Nevill was Bishop of Durham ; 6, 7, 8. Cuthbert, Henry, and Thomas, died without issue. Of the daughters, the youngest Cicely Nevill, called the ' Rose of Raby,' by her marriage with Richard Plantagenet, the ' Duke of York ' in *King Henry VI.*, was mother of two kings, Edward IV. and Richard III. *French.*

[Westmoreland is also a character in *The Life of King Henry the Fifth.* (q.v.)]

Eastcheap. II. i. 67 ; II. ii. 142.

See *First Part of King Henry the Fourth*, page 516.

Edward. IV. iv. 128.

> The river hath thrice flow'd, no ebb between
> And the old folk, time's doting chronicles,
> Say it did so a little time before
> That our great-grandsire, Edward, sick'd and died.
> [IV. iv. 125–128.]

The prodigies that preceded the king's death are recorded by Holinshed : " In this year (1412), and upon the 12th day of October, were three floods in the Thames, the one following upon the other, and no ebbing between, which thing no man living could remember the like to be seen." Similar portents are said to have preceded the death of King Edward the Third.

Ellen. III. ii. 7.

Daughter of Justice Silence, and god-daughter of Justice Shallow.

England. II. i. 146, 20 ; II. iv. 71 ; IV. i. 132 ; IV. ii. 49 ; IV. v. 128, 129 ; V. ii. 71 ; V. iii. 134.

Ephesians. II. ii. 144.

> Ephesians, my lord, of the old church. [II. ii. 144.]

Ephesians = At the period a cant term for a boon-companion. *Old Church* = companions of the old sort.

Epilogue. **Spoken by a Dancer.**

The closing of the play in which a dancer speaks to the audience, craving their pardon if they have been bored, and promising to continue the story, and make them merry with Fair Katharine of France.

Erebus. II. iv. 154.

See Pluto's damned lake.

Europe. II. ii. 128 ; IV. iii. 22.

Fang, Sheriff's officer. II. i. p.1, 1, 23, 39.

An officer commissioned with Snare to arrest Falstaff at the suit of Mistress Quickly who alleges that the fat knight owes her " a hundred mark."

Feeble. III. ii. p.1, 147, 149, 158, 165, 167, 244, 263.

One of the rustics picked out to be in Falstaff's bodyguard.

Fleet. V. v. 92.

An ancient prison in London standing on the eastern side of the Fleet river from which it derived its name. It was destroyed in the Great Fire and rebuilt, but demolished in 1846.

France. V. v. 108.

> I will lay odds, that, ere this year expire,
> We bear our civil swords and native fire
> As far as France : I heard a bird so sing,
> Whose music, to my thinking, pleased the king.
> [V. v. 106–109.]

An allusion to an old adage, that a bird from its vantage-point in the air spied out all secret things and imparted them to such as could understand. The phrase occurs in the ancient Ballad of *The Rising in the North :*

> I heare a bird sing in mine eare,
> That I must either fight or flee.

According to the Koran, Solomon was informed by a lapwing of all the doings of the Queen of Sheba. Mahomet was informed by a dove which whispered in his ear.

In *Princess Chery* the Little Green Bird could reveal every secret and impart information of events, past, present, or to come.

Literature abounds with allusions of the spying habits of birds. " None sees me but the bird that flieth by " is a well-known Greek proverb, and in the *Nibelungen Lied* we have : " No one hears us but God and the forest bird."

Cf. Webster and Rowley : *A Cure for a Cuckold*, V. i. : " I heard A bird sing lately, you are the only cause Works the division," and Chapman : *The Widow's Tears*, I. i. : " I have a little bird in a cage here that Sings me better comfort."

Francis. II. iv. 275, 345.

The name by which Falstaff addresses Prince Hal when the latter assumes the disguise of a waiter at the Boar's Head Tavern in Eastcheap.

Francis Pickbone. III. ii. 20.

A former acquaintance of Justice Shallow's at Clement's Inn.

Furies' lap. V. iii. 105.

Gadshill. I. ii. 146 ; II. iv. 300.

See *First Part of King Henry the Fourth*, page 518.

Galen. I. ii. 115.

An allusion to a celebrated Greek physician named Claudius Galenus of Pergamos. He went to Rome, where he gained great renown in the medical profession, and undertook scientific journeys through Greece and Asia. He was a great writer, being author of some 300 volumes, and his writings, which left no branch of medicine untouched, formed for many centuries the chief text-books for physicians and doctors.

Galloway nags. II. iv. 186.

= common hacknies. A small breed of horses called Galway Nagges from Galloway in Scotland.

Gaultree Forest. IV. i. 2.

An extensive forest, called the Forest of Gaultries, once existed in the centre of Yorkshire, and came up close to the walls of York. Portions of it yet remain, but enclosed, and out of the jurisdiction of the crown. It was formerly a favourite hunting-ground of the clergy ; and the following quaint story is as quaintly told of one of the Bishops of Durham while out hunting there : " Sir Anthon Bek, Busshop of Dureme in the tyme of King Eduarde, the son of King Henry, was the maist prowd and masterfull busshopp in all England, and it was comonly said that he was the prowdest lord in Christienty. It chaunced that among other lewd persons, this Sir Anthon entertained at his court one Hugh de Pountchardon, that for his evill deeds and manifold robberies had been driven out of the Inglische Courte, and had come from the southe to seek a little bread and to live by stalynge. And to this Hughe, whom also he imployed to good purpose in the warr in Scotland, the busshop gave the lande of Thikley, since of him caullid Thikley-Puntchardon, and also made him his chiefe huntsman. And after, this blake Hugh dyed afore the busshop, and efter that the busshop chasid the wild hart in Galtres forest, and sodainly ther met with him Hugh de Pontchardin that was afore deid, on a wythe [white] horse ; and the said Hugh loked earnestly on the busshop, and the busshop said unto him, ' Hughe, what maketh thee here ? ' and he spake never word, but lifte up his cloke, and then he shewed Sir Anton his ribbes set with bones, and nothing more ; and none other of the varlets saw him, but the busshop only ; and ye said Hugh went his way, and Sir Anton toke corage, and cheered the dogges, and shortly efter he was made Patriarque of Hierusalem, and he saw nothing no moe : and this Hugh is him that the silly people in Galtres doe call Le Gros Veneur, and he was seen twice efter that by simple folk, afore yat the forest was felled in the tyme of Henry, father of Henry yat now ys."

George Barnes. III. ii. 20.

Barnes was a former acquaintance of Justice Shallow's at Clement's Inn.

Glendower. I. iii. 72.

> For his divisions, as the times do brawl,
> Are in three heads : one power against the French,
> And one against Glendower ;   [I. iii. 70–72.]

During the rebellion of Northumberland and the Archbishop, a French army of twelve thousand men under Marshal Montmerancie landed at Milford Haven for the aid of Glendower. Cf. *Extract* 2 from Holinshed.

Glendower. III. i. 103.

> I have received
> A certain instance that Glendower is dead.
>   [III. i. 102–103.]

Glendower did not die until after Henry the Fourth. Shakespeare was misled by Holinshed who places Glendower's death in the tenth year of Henry's reign. See *Extract* 4 from Holinshed.

Gloucestershire. IV. iii. 81, 128.

Gloucestershire.   Before Justice Shallow's house.

The Scene of Act III., Scene ii. Shallow welcomes Falstaff and Bardolph. Shallow presents some recruits to Falstaff, who interviews them. Shallow invites Falstaff to dinner, who later, having commanded Bardolph to equip the recruits with soldiers' coats, takes leave of Justice Shallow, promising to accept the latter's hospitality again.

Gloucestershire.   Shallow's house.

The Scene of Act V., Scene i. Falstaff and his friends have called on Shallow, who insists—in spite of their protests—that they accept his hospitality, and orders them to make themselves comfortable.

Gloucestershire.   Shallow's orchard.

The Scene of Act V., Scene iii. Justice Shallow is entertaining Falstaff and his friends in his orchard. Pistol enters with the news that Henry the Fourth has passed away, and that Prince Hal has succeeded to the crown. On hearing this Falstaff announces his intention to depart for London forthwith.

Gower. II. i. p.131, 131, 174, 177, 182, 185.

Appears with a message for the Lord Chief Justice from the king, relative to the progress of the preparations to meet the rebellious nobles.

[The person intended may, French thinks, be Thomas Gower, son of Sir Thomas Gower, of Stitenham, Yorkshire. He was one of the commissioners of assay in the North Riding of Yorkshire under Henry IV., and afterwards served with Henry V., of France, where he was made governor of Mans. *Irving edition.*]

Gray's Inn. III. ii. 33.

One of the London Inns of Court situated in Holborn. It was once the head of the Inns, but now is the fourth in importance and size. It derived its name from the family of Gray of Wilton, whose residence it originally was.

Grooms. V. v. p.1.

When trumpets herald the approach of the coronation procession of King Henry the Fifth, the grooms enter and strew the ground with rushes.

It was customary at ceremonial entertainments, to strew the floor with rushes. Steevens observes : " Chambers, and indeed all apartments usually inhabited, were formerly strewed in this manner. As our ancestors rarely washed their floors, disguises of uncleanliness became necessary things. In the present instance, however, the rushes are supposed to be scattered on the pavement of a street, or on a platform." Cf. *Cymbeline*, II. ii. 12–14.

Hal. II. iv. 306, 309, 316.

Henry, Prince of Wales, afterwards King Henry the Fifth. (q.v.)

Hal. V. v. 41.

> God save thy grace, King Hal! my royal Hal!
> [V. v. 41.]

= King Henry the Fifth.

Harcourt. IV. iv. p.93.

Appears before the king at Westminster, and informs him that the rebels have been defeated in Yorkshire.

[Perhaps Sir Thomas Harcourt of Stanton, Oxfordshire, who was Sheriff of Berkshire, 9 Henry IV., 1407. He died in 1417.]

Harry. II. iii. 12, 43.

= Henry Percy, surnamed Hotspur.

Harry. IV. v. 240 ; V. ii. 14, 49, 59 ; V. iii. 113, 114.

= King Henry the Fourth.

Harry. II. i. 132 ; II. ii. 115 ; IV. v. 89, 92, 130, 181, 212 ; V. ii. 15.

= Henry, Prince of Wales, afterwards King Henry the Fifth. (q.v.)

Harry. V. ii. 49, 60, 145 ; V. iii. 114, 116.

= King Henry the Fifth.

Harry Monmouth. Induction 29 ; I. i. 109 ; I. iii. 83.

= Henry, Prince of Wales, afterwards King Henry the Fifth, so-called from the place of his birth.

Harry Monmouth's brawn. I. i. 19.

= Sir John Falstaff, so-called on account of being a clumsy and heavy man.

Harry Percy's spur. I. i. 42, 49.

> He told me that rebellion had bad luck,
> And that young Harry Percy's spur was cold.
> [I. i. 41–42.]

= That Hotspur was cold in death.

Harry ten shillings. III. ii. 217.

> and here 's four Harry ten shillings in French crowns
> for you. [III. ii. 217–218.]

An anachronism. There were no coins of ten shillings value in the reign of Henry the Fourth. Shakespeare's Harry ten shillings were those of Henry the Seventh. Cowl says : " At the date of the play the Harry ten shillings or demi-sovereign of Henry VII., originally worth eleven shillings and threepence, was current at five shillings, and the French crown, formerly worth six shillings, was current at four shillings. Four Harry ten shillings were therefore equivalent to five French crowns or one pound."

Hector of Troy. II. iv. 215.

> i' faith, I
> love thee : thou art as valorous as Hector of Troy,
> [II. iv. 214–215.]

Hector was the son of Priam and Hecuba, and the chief hero among the Trojans in their defence of Troy against the Greeks.

Helen. V. v. 33.

> Thy Doll, and Helen of thy noble thoughts.
> [V. v. 33.]

An allusion to Helen of Troy. Deighton remarks : " She who is to you what Helen was to the Greeks of old, the type of beauty and the worthy theme of love." Cf. Beaumont and Fletcher, II. ii. : " Welcome to Troy ! Come, thou shall kiss my Helen, And court her in a dance."

Helicons. V. iii. 103.

A range of mountains in Bœotia, in Greece sacred to Apollo and the Muses. Pistol supposes the Helicons to refer to certain redoubtable personages.

Henry Bolingbroke. IV. i. 117, 124, 129.

Henry Bolingbroke, Duke of Hereford, afterwards King Henry the Fourth.

Henry, Prince of Wales, afterwards King Henry V. I. i. 16 ; I. ii. 199, 236 ; II. i. 132 ; II. ii. p.1, 115 ; II. iv. p.229 ; IV. iii. 117 ; IV. v. p.8, 53 ; IV. v. p.89, 89, 92, 130, 181, 212 ; V. i. 79 ; V. ii. 15, p.43, 49, 60, 145 ; V. iii. 113, 116 ; V. v. p.41.

A great change makes itself apparent in the character of Prince Henry during the course of this part of the play.

When we first met him we found him a gay, irresponsible young man, eager to find entertainment in the company of Sir John Falstaff and his cronies, but now he seems to grow up and becomes more like his father in his strength of purpose, and his general outlook on life.

We were given a hint that he was not really the light-hearted, care-free man he appeared to be on the surface in the *First Part of King Henry the Fourth*, for there he says that when the time comes he will be ready to take the responsibility of government, and as this part proceeds we see a gradual change coming over him and he finally appears to us as a man fully qualified to govern the realm.

He gives up the company of Falstaff and the others ; only appearing in the company of the knight in one scene, and at the end of the play in the scene where the coronation procession takes place, Falstaff is ignored, the young king saying to him when greeted in the old familiar way, " I know thee not, old man."

" I am exceeding weary," says Prince Henry, on his first appearance in this part. What a change from his demeanour in the *First Part* of the play. The knowledge of his approaching responsibilities seems to weigh heavily upon him, and this tone deepens until the time when the old king falls ill, when the Prince becomes

thoroughly stabilised in his characteristics for he knows that the cares of state will fall upon his shoulders very soon.

That he has overcome his early loose habits which were the source of such anxiety to his father is shown when the old king on his deathbed gives him his last counsel, telling him how difficult it has been to hold the crown, and expressing the opinion that it will " descend with better quiet " on his head, while at the same time he must be very careful to " busy giddy minds with foreign quarrels " in order to retain his position against traitorous ' friends.'

The new king does not find his position a tranquil one from the beginning, for he says on being addressed as " your majesty " for the first time, that

> This new and gorgeous garment, majesty,
> Sits not so easy on me as you think. [V. ii. 44–45.]

and addressing his brothers, assures them

> I 'll be your father and your brother too ;
> Let me but bear you love, I 'll bear your cares :
>   [V. ii. 57–58.]

showing that he is determined to rule the country justly if given their allegiance and their help.

French remarks : " Stow mentions his robbing his father's receivers of rents, and he was arrested by John Hornesby, Mayor of Coventry, and placed in gaol for a riot. The prince had near that town the manor of Cheylesmore, which was the scene of frequent disturbances. His great poverty has been alleged as the cause of his excesses. The taking away of the crown by the prince, who imagines that his father is dead, is from Holinshed. The early chroniclers lead us to believe that Prince Henry and his father were not on cordial terms, and that the king's mournful reproach in the play, Act IV., Scene iv., was but too well deserved ;

> ' Thy life did manifest thou lovedst me not,
> And thou wilt have me die assured of it.'

[Prince Henry—as King Henry the Fifth—is also a character in *The Life of King Henry the Fifth*. (q.v.)]

Henry the Fifth. V. ii. p.43 ; V. v. p.41.

Hereford. IV. i. 138.

= Henry Bolingbroke, who was Duke of Hereford.

Hinckley. V. i. 24.

A market town in Leicestershire.

Hiren. II. iv. 156, 171.

An allusion to Hiren, a strumpet in a play by George Peele entitled *The Turkish Mahomet, and Hiren the Fair Greek.* The word is a corruption of the Greek Irene, and is used to designate a swaggerer.

Holy Land. III. i. 109 ; IV. v. 210, 238.

> And were these inward wars once out of hand,
> We would, dear lords, unto the Holy Land.
> [III. i. 108–109.]

" Henry IV always cherished the idea of going on a pilgrimage to the Holy Land to atone for the blood of the murdered Richard." *Winstanley.*

Johnson says : " This journey to the Holy Land, of which the king very frequently revives the mention, had two motives, religion and piety. He durst not wear the ill-gotten crown without expiation, but in the act of expiation he contrives to make his wickedness successful."

Hotspur. Induction 25.

= Henry Percy, son of Henry, Earl of Northumberland. See *First Part of King Henry the Fourth,* page 520.

Hotspur. I. iii. 26.

> for indeed
> It was young Hotspur's case at Shrewsbury.
> [I. iii. 25–26.]

" this trusting to probabilities was what caused Hotspur's downfall at Shrewsbury." *Deighton.*

Hotspur Coldspur. I. i. 50.

> Said he young Harry Percy's spur was cold ?
> Of Hotspur Coldspur ?   [I. i. 49–50.]

" did he say that from being Hotspur my son had become Coldspur ? " *Deighton.*

Hotspur's loss. I. i. 121.

> all the rest
> Turn'd on themselves, like dull and heavy lead :
> And as the thing that 's heavy in itself,
> Upon enforcement flies with greatest speed,
> So did our men, heavy in Hotspur's loss,
> [I. i. 117–121.]

Winstanley says : " Hotspur's high-tempered courage seems to steel the hearts of all the rest ; but, his courage being ' abated ' or tamed by death, the rest become no better than lead, dull and heavy, with an edge easily turned. Moreover, they are so heavy that, the impetus of flight being once given them by their fear, they fly with the greater speed."

Hotspur's name. II. iii. 37.

> to abide a field
> Where nothing but the sound of Hotspur's name
> Did seem defensible :   [II. iii. 36–38.]

Winstanley says : " Lady Percy means that only Hotspur's name made the battle of Shrewsbury seem possible at all, since the odds were so heavily against the rebels."

Hotspur's neck. II. iii. 44.

See Monmouth's grave.

Hotspur's sword. Induction 30.

Hydra. IV. ii. 38.

See *First Part of King Henry the Fourth,* page 524.

Jack. II. iv. 65, 198, 204, 372.

= Sir John Falstaff (q.v.).

Jane Nightwork. III. ii. 193.

A personal name. Mother to Robin Nightwork. Cowl says : " For the implication in the name, cf. Middleton : *A Mad World, my Masters,* I. ii., " She may make night-work on 't . . . He-cats and courtesans stroll most i' th' night."

Japhet. II. ii. 113.

> Nay, they will be kin to us, or they will fetch it
> from Japhet.   [II. ii. 112–113.]

Cowl says : " Christian in *Pilgrim's Progress,* says, ' I came of the race of Japhet.' " Divines and early ethnologists traced the descent of the peoples of European stock from Japhet.

Jerusalem. IV. v. 234, 237, 240.

> *King.* Doth any name particular belong
> Unto the lodging where I first did swoon ?
> *War.* 'Tis call'd Jerusalem, my noble lord.
> [IV. v. 232–234.]

The Jerusalem Chamber was built by Abbot Littlington as a guest-chamber for the Abbot's house. It was in this chamber that Henry the Fourth died of apoplexy, March 20, 1413. See *Extract* 13 from Holinshed.

Job. I. ii. 124.

> I am as poor as Job, my lord, but not so patient.
> [I. ii. 124.]

= A type of poverty and of patience.

John. V. iii. 102.

'Little John,' Lieutenant to Robin Hood.

John a Gaunt. II. ii. 45 ; III. ii. 315, 319.

Winstanley says : " John of Gaunt was always a favourite character with the Elizabethans, both because of his own valour and because the Tudor claim to the crown was derived through him."

John Doit of Staffordshire. III. ii. 19.

Evidently a former acquaintance of Justice Shallow's at Clement's Inn.

Jove. V. v. 47.

= My Lord.

Jove's case. II. ii. 169.

An allusion to Jupiter who transformed himself into a bull.

Katharine of France. Epilogue 28.

The French princess who married King Henry the Fifth.

Keech. II. i. 90.

> Did not goodwife Keech, the butcher's
> wife, come in then and call me gossip Quickly ?
> [II. i. 90–91.]

= my gossip Keech. The word means a lump of congealed fat. In *King Henry the Eighth*, I. i. 55, it is applied to Cardinal Wolsey, the butcher's son. Steevens says : " A *Keech* is the fat of an ox rolled up by the butcher into a round lump."

King Cophetua. V. iii. 101.

An imaginary king of Africa. Sitting one day at his palace window he saw a beggar maid pass, and fell in love with her and married her. Cf. *Love's Labour's Lost*, IV., i., " The magnanimous and most illustrate king Cophetua set eye upon the pernicious and indubitate beggar Zenelophon."

King Henry the Fourth. Induction 23 ; II. i. 132 ; III. i. p.1 ; IV. iv. p.1 ; IV. v. p.1, 240 ; V. ii. 14, 49, 59 ; V. iii. 113, 114.

When we first meet with the king in this part of the play we find him in a very melancholy and depressed state. He is unable to sleep, and his soliloquy ending with the words " Uneasy lies the head that wears a crown " shows how the cares of state have affected him. He remembers Richard's words that " Northumberland the ladder by the which my cousin Bolingbroke ascends the throne " should ultimately be the cause of his downfall, and broods over the future, but on being reassured by his nobles that the rebels are not so strong as has been reported, the king is now at ease, and reiterates his vow to make a pilgrimage to the Holy Land, as soon as the affairs at home are settled. His spirit, however, is well-nigh broken by the frequent insurrections against him, and he is, right up to the time of his death, depressed and anxious.

On being told of the rout of Northumberland in Yorkshire, the news, good as it is, causes him to swoon, after having exclaimed : " Will fortune never come with both hands full ? " showing how his worries have deadened his sense of success and make him feel that even good news is not enough.

The Duke of Clarence has noticed for some time what effect the worries of the state have had upon the king, for he exclaims, when Warwick tells him that Henry's fainting attack is but transitory :

> No, no, he cannot long hold out these pangs :
> The incessant care and labour of his mind
> Hath wrought the mure, that should confine it in,
> So thin that life looks through and will break out.
>
> [IV. iv. 117–120.]

Prince Henry is tempted to try on the crown which is lying on his father's pillow, and takes it away into another room, when the king, awakening to find it gone, calls for Warwick and his sons, and on being told that Prince Henry has taken the crown, sends for him and upbraids him. Being touched, however, by the Prince's genuine remorse at having been so hasty he forgives him, and his mind is set at rest knowing his son is all that he could wish him to be and will rule in the same determined way as he himself has done.

The characteristic which strikes one most of all in King Henry is his fixity of purpose ; he set out to get the crown ; succeeded ; and then by sheer determination held it, although its possession did not give him the happiness and peace for which he had hoped, and finally his comfort on his death-bed is the assurance that his son will continue in the way he has set for him.

Commenting on the character of King Henry the Fourth, Hudson says : " So that, taking the whole delineation together, we have at full length and done to the life, the portrait of a man in act prompt, bold, decisive, in thought sly, subtle, far-reaching ; a character hard and cold indeed to the feelings, but written all over with success ; which has no impulsive gushes or starts, but all is study, forecast, and calm suiting of means to preappointed ends. And this perfect self-command is in great part the secret of his strange power over others, making them almost as pliant to his purposes as are the cords and muscles of his own body ; so that, as the event proves, he grows great by their feeding, till he can compass food enough without their help, and, if they go to hindering him, can eat them up. For so it turned out with the Percys ; strong sinews indeed with him for a head ; while, against him, their very strength served but to work their own overthrow. . . .

But, though policy was the leading trait of this able man, nevertheless it was not so prominent but that other and better traits were strongly visible. And even in his policy there was much of the breadth and largeness which distinguish the statesman from the politician. Besides, he was a man of prodigious spirit and courage, had a real eye to the interests of his country as well as of his family, and in his wars he was humane much beyond the custom of his time. And in the last scene of the Poet's delineation of him, where he says to the Prince,—

> ' Come hither, Harry ; sit thou by my bed,
> And hear, I think, the very latest counsel
> That ever I shall breathe ' ;

though we have indeed his subtle policy working out like a ruling passion strong in death, still its workings are suffused with gushes of right feeling, enough to show that he was not all politician ; that beneath his close-knit prudence there was a soul of moral sense, a kernel of religion. Nor must I omit how the Poet, following the leadings both of nature and history, makes him to be plagued by foes springing up in his own bosom in proportion as he ceases to be worried by external enemies ; the crown beginning to scald his brows as soon as he has crushed those who would pluck it from him."

The aspiring Bolingbroke and active general of the two preceding plays is in this drama represented in failing health and broken spirits, subject to epileptic attacks, of which the poet speaks,—

> ' these fits
> Are with his highness very ordinary ' ;

and his latter years are said to have been haunted by remorse for the ' indirect crook'd ways ' by which he obtained the crown. He was praying, ' as was his wont of late,' before the shrine of St. Edward the Confessor, in Westminster Abbey, March 20, 1413, when he was seized with his last fit, and it was supposed at first that he was dead, but being carried into the Jerusalem Chamber, and laid before a fire, he revived sufficiently to give his parting advice to his successor ; his asking the name of the apartment in which he was dying is from history. In this most interesting room, the Jerusalem Chamber, is still preserved the fine original portrait of Richard the Second, upon which his rival must have often looked in his visits to the

Abbey. English writers, as Walsingham and Hardyng, and the French historian, Mezeray, state that Henry IV. died of a dreadful leprous disease, affecting the lower part of his face. *French.*

King Richard. I. i. 205.

> And doth enlarge his rising with the blood
> Of fair King Richard, scraped from Pomfret stones.
> [I. i. 204–205.]

King Richard the Second. *See* Pomfret stones.

Lady Northumberland. II. iii. p.1.

Appears with Lady Percy and Northumberland before Warwick Castle, and entreats her husband to fly to Scotland and seek refuge there until the time is more propitious and the rebellion is more established :

> O, fly to Scotland,
> Till that the nobles and the armed commons
> Have of their puissance made a little taste.
> [II. iii. 50–52.]

[Lady Northumberland was the widow of Gilbert de Umphreville, Earl of Angus, when she was married to the earl. She was not the mother of Hotspur, being the Earl of Northumberland's second wife.]

Lady Percy. II. iii. p.1.

Daughter-in-law to the Earl of Northumberland, widow of Hotspur, who was killed at the battle of Shrewsbury.

She deeply mourns the loss of her husband, and upbraids Northumberland for not having gone to his assistance in the rebellion.

Her love for her husband was very great. She refers to him as " my heart's dear Harry " and speaks of him in the highest terms, and her grief at his death is doubled because she feels that his defeat was due to lack of support by Northumberland.

[Lady Percy was born in 1371, and was named for her grandmother, Elizabeth de Burgh, wife of Lionel of Clarence. Her father was Edmund Mortimer, third Earl of March, and her mother Philippa Plantagenet, granddaughter of Edward III. After the death of her husband Lady Percy was arrested at the order of Henry IV.,

and brought before him to be questioned. Of her subsequent history there is no record of any importance. *Irving edition.*]

Lethe. V. ii. 72.

> May this be wash'd in Lethe, and forgotten ?
> [V. ii. 72.]

A river of Hell, of which the souls of the departed are obliged to drink in order to forget everything that had occurred in their past lives. Cf. Milton : *Paradise Lost*, I. 582–586 :

> Far off from these, a slow and silent stream,
> Lethe, the river of oblivion, rolls
> Her watery labyrinth, whereof who drinks
> Forthwith his former state and being forgets—
> Forgets both joy and grief, pleasure and pain.

London. I. iii. 104.

See Bolingbroke, I. iii. 105.

London. V. iii. 58.

> I 'll drink to Master Bardolph, and to
> all the cavaleros about London.   [V. iii. 57–58.]

Johnson remarks : " This was the term [cavaleros] by which an airy splendid irregular fellow was distinguished. The soldiers of King Charles were called Cavaliers, from the gayety which they affected in opposition to the sour faction of the parliament."

London. II. iv. 138, 163, 286 ; IV. iv. 51 ; V. iii. 59.

London. A Street.

The Scene of Act I., Scene ii. Act II., Scene i. Act V., Scene iv.

In Act I., Scene ii. we find Falstaff in conversation with his page-boy. They are interrupted by the arrival of the Lord Chief Justice. Falstaff pretends not to see the chief justice, and does all he can to evade a conversation. The Chief Justice however is determined to speak with Falstaff, and tells him that were it not for the services he had rendered at the battle of Shrewsbury he would suffer for his many misdeeds.

In Act II., Scene i. Mistress Quickly is endeavouring to effect the arrest of Falstaff for the recovery of the money he owes her. Fang—a sheriff's officer—enters and arrests Falstaff. A scuffle ensues during which the Lord Chief Justice appears, who, on learning the cause of Falstaff's arrest severely reproves him. Gower enters with news for the Chief Justice, and hands him a letter, and whilst the latter is perusing it, Falstaff prevails upon the hostess to withdraw her action. The Chief Justice turns a deaf ear to Falstaff's enquiry for news, and sternly rebukes him for his ill-manners.

In Act V., Scene iv., Mistress Quickly and Doll Tearsheet are arrested by beadles. They cause a great commotion and call the beadles many foul names.

London.   Another Street.

The Scene of Act II., Scene ii. The Prince and Poins are in conversation, when Bardolph enters with Falstaff's page. They engage in a series of witticisms, and the prince making inquiries about Falstaff, Bardolph hands him a letter from the latter, which Poins reads aloud. Being told that Falstaff is supping at the Boar's Head Tavern in Eastcheap, the prince and Poins decide to pay a surprise visit in the guise of waiters.

London.   The Boar's-head Tavern in Eastcheap.

The Scene of Act II., Scene iv. Describes Falstaff's supper with Mistress Quickly and Doll Tearsheet, at which the Prince and Poins appear in the guise of waiters. Their revelry is interrupted by the appearance of Peto who tells the prince that the king is waiting for him, and the prince leaves forthwith. Bardolph enters and informs Falstaff that he is required at court, and the latter bids farewell to his friends and departs.

Lord Bardolph. I. i. p.1, 3, 7 ; I. iii. p.1, 25, 69 ; IV. iv. 97.

Appears at the beginning of the play and informs Northumberland that the battle of Shrewsbury has been entirely successful. This news is denied by Travers, and the denial is confirmed by Morton.

At the conference of the rebel leaders in the Archbishop's palace, Lord Bardolph suggests that action be deferred until the assistance of the Earl of Northumberland is assured :

> My judgement is, we should not step too far
> Till we had his assistance by the hand ; [I. iii. 20-21.]

his reason being that he is anxious for their position to be made secure, but he eventually agrees to the opinions of the others that immediate action be taken.

Commenting on this character, Hudson says : " Lord Bardolph is shrewd and sensible, of a firm practical understanding, and prudent forecast ; and none the less brave, that his cool judgment puts him upon looking carefully before he leaps."

Thomas Bardolph, fifth baron ; summoned to Parliament from 1390 to 1404. His ancestor, Doun Bardolf, married Beatrice, eldest daughter and co-heir of Reginald de Warren (grandson of the Earl of Warrenne who married the Conqueror's youngest daughter Gundred), feudal lord of Wirmegay, co. Norfolk. Doun Bardolf's grandson, Hugh Bardolf, who served in the French and Scottish wars of Edward I., was summoned to Parliament from 1299 to 1302, as Baron Bardolf of Wirmegay, and his great grandson, William, was summoned as fourth baron from 1376 to 1385. His son, the character in this play, joining in the archbishop's insurrection against Henry IV., was defeated at Bramham Moor, where ' he was taken but sore wounded, so that he shortly after died of his hurts.' By his wife, Avice, daughter of Ralph, Lord Cromwell, he had two daughters, his co-heirs ; 1. Anne Bardolf, who married first Sir William Clifford, Knt. ; and secondly Sir Reginald Cobham, the third Lord Cobham of Sterborough ; 2. Joan Bardolf, who married Sir William Phelip, K.G., who is sometimes called Lord Bardolf ; he was one of the heroes of Agincourt ; his only child, Elizabeth Phelip, married John Viscount Beaumont, K.G., ancestor of the present Lord Beaumont. *French.*

Lord Chief Justice of the King's Bench.
I. ii. p.53 ; II. i. 59 ; V. ii. p.1, 1 ; V. iii. 136 ; V. v. p.41, 45, p.92.

Represented as a high-minded and noble official, who carries out his duties without fear or favour, and yet is most likeable and liked by those with whom he comes in contact.

We first meet him in a street in London, when we hear that he had committed Prince Henry for contempt of court, which incident gives us an idea of the fearlessness with which he administers justice.

He approaches Falstaff to speak to him with reference to the robbery at Gadshill in which Sir John was implicated, but the knight evades his questions and a series of witty remarks pass between them, at the end of which the Chief Justice, being a man, as well as a judge, over-looks the case, and wishes Falstaff's expedition against the rebels every success.

We meet the Chief Justice again in another street in London, when Falstaff is about to be arrested by an officer at the suit of Mistress Quickly to whom he owes a sum of money, and once more a scene takes place between the two, the justice remarking to Falstaff :

> I am well acquainted with
> your manner of wrenching the true cause the false
> way. [II. i. 107–109.]

When the Chief Justice next appears he meets the young king—Henry V.—and on hearing the king's remarks on his former action in commit-ting him, the Chief Justice in a very fine speech [Act V., Scene ii.] defends himself, and shows us in how honourable a way he does his duty, his explanation pleasing the young king who says :

> You are right, justice, and you weigh this well ;
> Therefore still bear the balance and the sword :
> And I do wish your honours may increase,
> Till you do live to see a son of mine
> Offend you, and obey you, as I did.
> So shall I live to speak my father's words :
> " Happy am I, that have a man so bold,
> That dares do justice on my proper son ;
> And not less happy, having such a son,
> That would deliver up his greatness so
> Into the hands of justice." [V. ii. 102–112.]

Cf. The Famous Victories of Henry the Fifth :

> *Enters Lord chiefe Iustice of England.*
>
> *Exe.* Here is the King my Lord.
> *Iust.* God preserue your Maiestie.
> *Hen. V.* Why how now my lord, what is the matter ?
> *Iust.* I would it were vnknowne to your Maiestie.
> *Hen. V.* Why what aile you ?
> *Iust.* Your Maiestie knoweth my griefe well.
> *Hen. V.* Oh my Lord, your remember you sent me to the Fléete, did you not ?
> *Iust.* I trust your grace haue forgotten that.

> *Hen. V.* I truly my Lord, and for reuengement,
> I haue chosen you to be my Protector ouer my Realme
> Vntil it shall please God to giue me spéedie returne
> Out to France.
> *Iust.* And if it please your Maiestie, I am far vnorthie
> Of so high a dignitie.
> *Hen. V.* Tut my Lord, you are not vnworthie,
> Because I thinke you worthie
> For you that would not spare me,
> I thinke wil not spare another,
> It must néeds be so, and therefore come,
> Let vs be gone, and get our men in a readinesse.

Commenting on the character of the Chief Justice, Hudson says : " The Chief Justice, besides the noble figure he makes at the close, is, with capital dramatic effort, brought forward several times in passages at arms with Falstaff ; where his good-natured wisdom, as discovered in his suppressed enjoyment of the fat old sinner's wit, just serves to sweeten without at all diluting the reverence that waits upon his office and character."

" This was Sir William Gascoigne, born at Gawthorp, in the parish of Harewood, near Leeds, about 1350. He was appointed Chief Justice, Nov., 15, 1400. The story of Prince Henry's insolence, and his commitment to prison by the Chief Justice, rests on the authority of Sir Thomas Elyot (see below). On Henry V.'s accession Gascoigne was removed from the office of Chief Justice. The appointment of his suc-cessor, Sir William Hankford, is dated March 29, 1413. Sir William Gascoigne is buried in the parish church of Harewood, and the mutilated inscription on his monument states that he died on Sunday, the 17th of December. The year has been torn off, but it was doubtless 1419, for his will is dated December 15, 1419, and probate of it was granted at York on the 23rd of the same month." *Irving edition.*

" The retaining of Gascoigne in office has been commonly set down as a breach of history, justifiable, perhaps, dramatically, but untrue in point of fact, he having died before the King. It has been found, however, that among the persons summoned to the first Parliament of Henry V., was ' Sir William Gascoigne, Knight, Chief Justice of our Lord the King.' A royal warrant has also come to light, dated November 28, 1414, granting to ' our dear and well-beloved William Gascoigne, Knt., an allowance, during the term of his natural life, of four bucks and four does every year out of our forest of Ponti-

'ract.' And Mr. Tyler has put the matter beyond question by discovering his last will and testament, which was made December 15, 1419. From all which Lord Campbell, in his *Lives of the Chief Justices*, concludes it certain that he did survive Henry IV., who died March 20, 1413, and was reappointed to the King's Bench by Henry V. So that we can take the Poet's lesson of magnanimity without any abatement on the score of history." *Windsor edition*.

The story of Prince Henry's committal by Chief Justice Gascoigne is told by Sir Thomas Elyot, Knight in *The Boke named the Governour :* " The moste renomed prince, kynge Henry the fifte, late kynge of Englande, durynge the life of his father was noted to be fierce and of wanton courage. It hapned that one of his seruantes whom he well fauored, for felony by hym committed, was arrayned at the kynges benche ; wherof he being aduertised, and incensed by light persones aboute hym, in furious rage came hastily to the barre, where his seruant stode as a prisoner, and commaunded hym to be ungyued and sette at libertie, where at all men ' were abasshed, reserued the chiefe iustice, who humbly exhorted the prince to be contented that his seruant mought be ordred accordyng to the auncient lawes of this realme, or if he wolde haue hym saued from the rigour of the lawes, that he shuld optaine, if he moughte, of the kynge, his father, his gracious pardone ; wherby no lawe or iustice shulde be derogate. With whiche answere the prince nothynge appeased, but rather more inflamed, endeuored hym selfe to take away his seruant. The iuge consideringe the perilous example and inconuenience that moughte therby ensue, with a valiant spirite and courage commaunded the prince upon his alegeance to leue the prisoner and departe his waye. With which commandment the prince, being set all in a fury, all chafed, and in a terrible maner, came up to the place of iugement—men thinkyng that he wolde haue slayne the iuge, or haue done to hym some damage ; but the iuge sittyng styll, without mouynge, declarynge the maiestie of the kynges place of iugement, and with an assured and bolde countenance, hadde to the prince these words folowyng : ' Sir, remember your selfe ; I kepe here the place of the king, your soueraigne lorde and father, to whom ye owe double obedience, wherfore,

eftsones in his name, I charge you desiste of your wilfulnes and unlaufull entreprise, and from hensforth gyue good example to those whiche hereafter shall be your propre subiectes. And nowe for your contempt and disobedience, go you to the prisone of the kynges benche, where unto I committee you ; and remayne ye there prisoner untill the pleasure of the kyng, your father, be further knowen. With which wordes being abasshed, and also wondrynge at the meruailous grauitie of that worshipful Justice, the noble prince, layinge his waipon aparte, doinge reuerence, departed and wente to the kynges benche as he was commaunded. Whereat his seruants disdainying, came and shewed to the kynge all the hole affaire. Wherat he a whiles studienge, after as a man all rauisshed with gladness, holdyng his eien and handes up towarde heuen, abrayded, sayinge with a loude voice, O mercifull god, howe moche am I, aboue all other men, bounde to your infinite goodnes ; specially for that ye have gyuen me a iuge, who feareth nat to ministre iustice, and also a sonne who can suffre semblably and obey iustice ? "

See also Appendix III.

Lord Hastings. I. iii. p.1, 15 ; IV. i. p.1 ; IV. ii. p.1, 3, 50, 95, p.102, 106 ; IV. iv. 84.

A leader of the rebel forces. At a conference in the Archbishop's palace at York, Hastings informs the other nobles that the forces under their command number twenty-five thousand, and to be sure of success the assistance of the Earl of Northumberland is necessary. On discussing the situation, however, they conclude that only a third of the royal forces will be sent against them and the rebels therefore decide on immediate action.

Hastings takes part in the parley between the opposing leaders and is arrested with the other rebels, after he has brought the news that their army has dispersed.

[The person meant is Sir Ralph Hastings, who was never ' Lord Hastings,' though that is the name by which the chroniclers speak of him. He was the eldest son of Sir Ralph Hastings, Knight, by his second wife, Maud, daughter of Sir Robert de Sutton, of Sutton, co. York. . . . He was beheaded at Durham in June, 1405.]

Lord Mowbray. I. iii. p.1 ; IV. i. p.1, 103, 130, 149 ; IV. ii. p.1, 1, 78, 108 ; IV. iv. 84.

One of the leaders of the rebels against King Henry the Fourth.

We first meet him in this part of the play in the Archbishop of York's palace at York, where he is discussing with the other leaders their chances of success in their second attempt at rebellion.

They eventually decide on immediate action, and we next find Mowbray with his fellow rebels in Gaultree Forest, where they are preparing to meet the king's forces.

A parley is arranged between the opposing leaders and terms of peace settled, but Prince John commits an act of treachery by arresting Mowbray and the other leaders on a charge of high treason, as soon as their forces are disbanded.

This noble, Thomas Mowbray, eldest son of the Duke of Norfolk in *King Richard II.*, was only fourteen years old at his father's death, and never enjoyed his superior title, but held the ancient dignity of his family, and was seventh Baron Mowbray, although Holinshed, followed by Hume, calls him Earl of Nottingham, a title never held by him, but which was revived in his brother. He was also known as 'lord marshall,' and as such Shakespeare correctly makes the archbishop address him,—

'And first, lord marshal, what say you to it ?'

Lord Mowbray was beheaded at York, after the dispersion of the confederate forces. Having no issue by his wife, Constance Holland, daughter of John Duke of Exeter, he was succeeded by his brother, John Mowbray, as eighth Lord Mowbray, who was restored to his father's forfeited title as 'Duke of Norfolk'; and his grandson, John Mowbray, is the character under that style in the *Third Part of King Henry VI.* The forfeited estates of the Earl of Northumberland, the lord marshall, and Lord Bardolph, in this play, were bestowed by Henry IV. on his Queen Joanna, August 10, 1405. *French.*

Lords.

Lubber's-head. II. i. 27.

Mrs. Quickly's blunder for Libbard's-head. It was a sign adopted by silkmen.

Lucifer's privy-kitchen. II. iv. 326.

Cowl refers to : " the description of Lucifer's kitchen in the Pardoner's account of how he delivered Margery Corson from Hell in J. Heywood's *The Four P.P.*

> straight unto the master-cook
> I was had into the kitchen,
> For Margery's office was therein,
>
> .　 .　 .　 .　 .　 .　 .　 .
>
> For many a spit here hath she turned,
> And many a good spit hath she burned."

Lumbert Street. II. i. 27.

Lombard Street, London, a street where the Lombard merchants established themselves in the middle ages.

Martlemas. II. ii. 97.

A corruption of Martinmas, the feast of St. Martin, the 11th of November.

Master Dumbe. II. iv. 86.

See Tisick, the debuty.

Master Dumbleton. I. ii. 28.

> What said Master Dumbleton about the satin for my short cloak and my slops ?　　　　[I. ii. 28–29.]

Evidently Falstaff's tailor. Dumbleton is the name of a village in Gloucestershire.

Master Smooth. II. i. 28.

The silkman mentioned by Hostess Quickly.

Master Surecard. III. ii. 87.

A term for a boon companion.

Men. II. i. p.59.

Officers who accompany the Lord Chief Justice.

Messenger. IV. i. p.19.

Informs the rebel leaders of the approach of the king's forces, thirty thousand strong.

Mile-end Green. III. ii. 274.

A drill ground where London citizens were trained and exercised. It appears, however, that the pupils of this military school were but slightly thought of, for in Barnabie Riche's *Souldiers Wishe, to Britons Welfare, or Captaine Skill and Captain Pill*, 1604, we have the following : " *Skill.* God blesse me, my countrey, and frendes, from his direction that hath no better experience than what hee hath atteyned unto at the fetching home of a Maye-pole, at a Midsomer sighte, or from a *trayning at Mile-end greene.* Steevens.

Mistress Doll. II. iv. 35, 149.

= Doll Tearsheet (q.v.).

Mistress Dorothy. II. iv. 119, 124.

Doll Tearsheet (q.v.).

Mistress Quickly. II. i. p.1, 42, 91 ; II. ii. 146 ; II. iv. p.22, 86, 88 ; V. iv. p.1.

The hostess of the Boar's Head Tavern, frequented by Falstaff and his friends, is a character whom Shakespeare has carefully drawn, and we have in her a picture of the average type of a London hostess in the time of the dramatist.

Her character possesses a humorous trait, and the way in which she misuses long words is a noticeable feature.

Falstaff makes love to her, promising to make her his wife, but it is only to get money from her, knowing she is so susceptible to flattery.

Hudson says of this character : " We have had several glimpses of Mrs. Quickly, the Hostess of Eastcheap. She is well worth a steady looking at. One of the most characteristic passages in the play is her account of Falstaff's engagement to her ; which has been aptly commented on by Coleridge as showing how her mind runs altogether in the rut of actual events. She can think of things only in the precise order of their occurrence, having no power to select such as touch her purpose, and to detach them from the circumstantial irrelevancies with which they are consorted in her memory.

In keeping with this mental peculiarity, her character savours strongly of her whereabout in life ; she is plentifully trimmed with vices and vulgarities, and these all taste rankly of her place and calling, thus showing that she has as much of moral as of mental passiveness. Notwithstanding, she always has an odour of womanhood about her, even her worst features being such as none but a woman could have. Nor is her character, with all its ludicrous and censurable qualities, unrelieved, as we have seen, by traits of generosity that relish equally of her sex. It is even doubtful whether she would have entertained Sir John's proposals of marriage so favourably, but that at the time of making them he was in a condition to need her kindness. Her woman's heart could not stint itself from the plump old sinner when he had wounds to be dressed and pains to be soothed. And who but a woman could speak such words of fluttering eagerness as she speaks in urging on his arrest : ' Do your offices, do your offices, Master Fang and Master Snare ; do me, do me, do me your offices ' ; where her heart seems palpitating with an anxious hope that her present action may make another occasion for her kind ministrations ? Sometimes, indeed, she gets wrought up to a pretty high pitch of temper, but she cannot hold herself there ; and between her turns of anger and her returns to sweetness there is room for more of womanly feeling than I shall venture to describe. And there is still more of the woman in the cunning simplicity—or is it simpleness ?—with which she manages to keep her good opinion of Sir John ; as when, on being told that at his death ' he cried out of women, and said they were devils incarnate,' she replies, ' A never could abide carnation ; 't was a colour he never liked ' ; as if she could find no sense in his words but what would stand smooth with her interest and her affection.

It is curious to observe how Mrs. Quickly dwells on the confines of virtue and shame, and sometimes plays over the borders, ever clinging to the reputation, and perhaps to the consciousness, of the one, without foreclosing the invitations of the other. For it is very evident that even in her worst doings she hides from herself their ill-favour under a fair name ; as people often paint the cheeks of their vices, and then look them sweetly in the face, though they cannot but know the paint is all that keeps them from being unsightly and loathsome. In her case, however, this may spring, in part, from a simplicity not unlike that which sometimes causes little children to shut their eyes at what affrights them, and then think themselves safe. And yet she shows considerable knowledge of the world ; is not without shrewdness in her way ; but, in truth, the world her soul lives in, and grows intelligent of, is itself a discipline of moral obtuseness ; and this is one reason why she loves it. On the whole, therefore, Mrs. Quickly must be set down as a naughty woman ; The Poet clearly meant her so ; and, in mixing so much of good with the general preponderance of bad in her composition, he has shown a rare spirit of wisdom, such as may well remind us that ' both good men and bad men are apt to be less so than they seem.' "

[Mistress Quickly also appears in *The Life of King Henry the Fifth.* (q.v.)]

Mistress Ursula. I. ii. 238.

= Mistress Quickly whom " I have weekly sworn to marry since I perceived the first white hair on my chin."

Monmouth's grave. II. iii. 44.

> To-day might I, hanging on Hotspur's neck,
> Have talk'd of Monmouth's grave. [II. iii. 44–45.]

= the death of Henry, Prince of Wales.

Morton. I. i. p.60, 64, 87.

A servant to Northumberland, who confirms Travers' statement that the rebel army has been defeated at Shrewsbury.

He enters with the words :

> I ran from Shrewsbury, my noble lord ;
> Where hateful death put on his ugliest mask
> To fright our party. [I. i. 65–67.]

and Northumberland inquires if his son Hotspur is safe only to see in Morton's face the news of his death. Morton says :

> I am sorry I should force you to believe
> That which I would to God I had not seen ;
> But these mine eyes saw him in bloody state,
> Rendering faint quittance, wearied and outbreathed,
> To Harry Monmouth ; whose swift wrath beat down
> The never-daunted Percy to the earth,
> From whence with life he never more sprung up.
> [I. i. 105–111.]

He informs Northumberland that the Archbishop of York is raising a force against the king, and Northumberland agrees to throw in his lot with Scroop.

Mouldy. III. ii. p.1, 99, 101, 105, 117, 240, 244, 245.

One of the rustics brought forward to serve in Falstaff's bodyguard. He is selected, but afterwards bribes Bardolph to excuse him :

> And, good master corporal captain, for my old dame's sake, stand my friend : she has nobody to do anything about her when I am gone ; and she is old, and cannot help herself : you shall have forty, sir. [III. ii. 224–228.]

Music. II. iv. p.221.

= Musicians. Sneak's band.

Ned. II. ii. 133, 152, 172 ; II. iv. 311, 316.

= Poins.

Nell. II. ii. 123.

= Poins' sister.

Neptune's hip. III. i. 51.

> to see
> The beachy girdle of the ocean
> Too wide for Neptune's hips ; [III. i. 49–51.]

" see how the ocean retreats, leaving a beach wider than is needed as its boundary." *Deighton.*

Nevil. III. i. 66.

> You, couson Nevil, as I may remember—
> [III. i. 66.]

Shakespeare has mistaken the name of the present nobleman. The earldom of Warwick was, at this time, in the family of Beauchamp, and did not come into that of the Nevils till many years after, in the latter end of the reign of King Henry VI., when it descended to Anne Beauchamp, (the daughter of the earl here introduced), who was married to Richard Nevil, Earl of Salisbury. *Steevens.*

Anne Beauchamp was the wife of that Richard Nevil, (in her right), Earl of Warwick, and son to Richard Earl of Salisbury, who makes so conspicuous a figure in our author's *Second* and *Third Parts of King Henry VI.* He succeeded to the latter title on his father's death, in 1460, but is never distinguished by it.

See under Earl of Warwick.

Nightwork. III. ii. 204.

Nine Worthies. II. iv. 217.

and ten times better than
the Nine Worthies :   [II. iv. 216–217.]

Falstaff is ten times better than the Nine Worthies. The Nine Worthies of History were Hector, Alexander the Great, Julius Cæsar (three pagans) ; Joshua, David, Judas Maccabæus (three Jews) ; and Arthur, Charlemagne and Godfrey of Bouillon (three Christians).

Officers. IV. ii. p.1 ; V. v. p.92.

Oldcastle. Epilogue 31.

for
Oldcastle died a martyr, and this is not the man.
[Epilogue 30–31.]

Sir John Oldcastle, Lord Cobham. In the original draft Sir John Falstaff was called Sir John Oldcastle, but exception being taken to the character of Oldcastle being travestied after his death by the anti-Lollard party, the name was changed. Oldcastle was the famous Lollard leader and was burned to death as a heretic in 1417. Winstanley remarks : " The Epilogue was probably appended specially in order to make this retractation."

Oxford. III. ii. 10.

= Oxford University.

Page. III. i. p.1.

The boy who attends upon Henry IV., when the king, unable to sleep enters in his night-gown at one o'clock a.m. He bids the page to summon the Earls of Surrey and of Warwick :

Go call the Earls of Surrey and of Warwick ;
But, ere they come, bid them o'er-read these letters,
And well consider of them : make good speed.
[III. i. 1–3.]

Page to Falstaff. I. ii. p.1 ; II. i. p.4 ; II. ii. p.66 ; II. iv. p.109 ; V. i. 1 ; V. iii. p.1 ; V. v. p.5.

Accompanies his master in practically all the scenes in which the latter appears.

He was given to Falstaff by Prince Henry, who on seeing him, remarks :

And the boy that I gave Falstaff : a' had him
from me Christian ; and look, if the fat villain have
not transformed him ape.   [II. ii. 66–68.]

[The Page—as Boy—also appears in *The Life of King Henry the Fifth.* (q.v.)]

Paul's. I. ii. 50.

= St. Paul's Cathedral, London. Nares in his *Glossary of Words, Phrases and Allusions* says : " The body of old St. Paul's church in London was a constant place of resort for business and amusement. Advertisements were fixed up there, bargains made, servants hired, politics discussed, etc., etc." Cf. Nashe's *Fearful and lamentable Effects of Two dangerous Comets :* " *Paule's* church is in wonderfull perill thys yeare without the help of our conscionable brethren, for that day it hath not eyther broker, *maisterless serving-man,* or pennilesse companion, in the middle of it, the usurers of London have sworne to bestow a newe steeple upon it," and Lodge in his *Wit's Miserie, and the World's Madnesse,* 1596, the devil is described thus : " In *Powls* hee walketh like a gallant courtier, where if he meet some rich chuffes worth the gulling, at every word he speaketh, he maketh a mouse an elephant, and telleth them of wonders, done in Spaine by his ancestors."

Peesel. II. iv. 158.

Mistress Quickly's perversion of Pistol.

Percy. II. iii. 4 ; III. i. 61.

= the Earl of Northumberland (q.v.).

Percy. I. i. 93 ; II. iii. 12.

= Henry Percy, surnamed Hotspur.

Peto. II. iv. p.346, 346.

Peto's only appearance in this part is when he meets Prince Henry at the Boar's Head Tavern

and informs him that his father is at Westminster :

> The king your father is at Westminster ;
> And there are twenty weak and wearied posts
> Come from the north : and, as I came along,
> I met and overtook a dozen captains,
> Bare-headed, sweating, knocking at the taverns,
> And asking every one for Sir John Falstaff.
> [II. iv. 347–352.]

Pie-corner. II. i. 25.

Near Giltspur Street, afterwards famous as
the point at which the Great Fire ended.

Pistol. II. iv. 68, p.109, 110, 133, 134, 135, 181 ; V. iii. 79, p.82, 82, 84, 92, 105, 117, 123, 130, 131 ; V. iv. 18 ; V. v. p.5, 10, 38, 90.

One of Falstaff's companions, a most amusing
character. He is very fond of quoting snatches
from various plays, showing the effect the plays
of the time had on their hearers.

In this play we are first introduced to this
famous ' tamecheater' and swaggering bully,
' with a killing tongue and a quiet sword,' one of
the class described by Ben Jonson, in *Captain
Bobadil* (*Every Man in his Humour*), followed by
Congreve in his *Bluff* (*Old Bachelor*), and later
still by Sir Walter Scott in his Alsatian swash-
buckler, in the *Fortunes of Nigel*, Captain Cole-
pepper. A similar character, a compound of
buffoon and bully, called ' Piston,' is introduced
in a play entitled *Solimen and Perseda* which
was printed in 1599, a date somewhat later than
that usually ascribed to this *Second Part* by
Malone, Chalmers, and Drake.

Mr. J. O. Halliwell-Phillipps tells us,—' the
names of Bardoulf and Pistail are found in the
muster-roll of artillerymen serving under Humphrey Fitz-allan, Earl of Arundel, at the siege of
St. Laurens des Mortiers, Nov. 11, 1435.' But
that nobleman was only seven years old at this
date, succeeding in 1434 his father, John Fitz-
Alan, thirteenth earl, K.G., who was also Duke
of Touraine, and had served much in France
under the great Talbot. *French.*

[Pistol also appears in *The Life of King Henry
the Fifth.* (q.v.)]

Pluto's damned lake. II. iv. 153.

> I 'll see her damned first ; to Pluto's damned lake,
> by this hand, to the infernal deep, with Erebus and
> tortures vile also.   [II. iv. 153–155.]

These words, I believe, were intended to allude
to he following passage in an old play called the
Battel of Alcazar, 1594, from which Pistol afterwards quotes a line :

> You dastards of the night and Erebus,
> Fiends, fairies, hags, that fight in beds of steel,
> Range through this army with your iron whips ;—
> Descend and take to thy *tormenting hell*
> The mangled body of that traitor king.—
> Then let the earth discover to his ghost
> Such *tortures* as usurpers feel below.—
> *Damn'd* let him be, *damn'd* and condemn'd to bear
> All torments, *tortures*, pains and plagues of hell.

Malone.

Poins. II. ii. p.1, 31, 122 ; II. iv. 15, p.229, 234, 278, 353 ; IV. iv. 53.

A companion of Prince Henry's. He and the
prince disguise themselves as drawers and wait
upon Falstaff at the Boar's Head Tavern in order
to amuse themselves at his expense.

Pomfret stones. I. i. 205.

Pomfret (Pontefract) castle in Yorkshire,
which Shakespeare describes as being the place
of the murder of King Richard the Second. At
the battle of Agincourt, Henry the Fifth, afraid
of losing the battle, refers to it :

> Not to-day, O Lord !
> O ! not to-day, think not upon the fault
> My father made in compassing the crown.
> I Richard's body have interred new,
> And on it have bestow'd more contrite tears
> Than from it issued forced drops of blood.
> Five hundred poor I have in yearly pay,
> Who twice a day their wither'd hands hold up
> Toward heaven, to pardon blood ; and I have built
> Two chantries, where the sad and solemn priests
> Sing still for Richard's soul. More will I do ;
> *King Henry the Fifth.* IV. i. 298–308.]

Cowl quotes : " Some suppose that the archbishop exhibited drops of King Richard's blood
as a hallowed relic."

Porter. I. i. p.2.

The man in charge of the gate of Warkworth
castle, the seat of the Earl of Northumberland.

Priam's curtain. I. i. 72, 74.

> Drew Priam's curtain in the dead of night,
> And would have told him half his Troy was burnt ;
> But Priam found the fire ere he his tongue,
> [I. i. 72–74.]

Deighton says : " but Priam became aware of the fire before the messenger could bring himself to deliver his message " ; *to find one's tongue :* " is a common phrase for bringing oneself to speak after continuing silent, as though the person suddenly became aware that he had a tongue and some cause to use that organ." Cf. Kyd : *Spanish Tragedy*, III., " like old Priam of Troy, Crying the houfe is on fire, the houfe is on fire."

Prince Harry. I. i. 16 ; I. ii. 199 ; IV. iii. 117 ; V. i. 79.

= Henry, Prince of Wales, afterwards King Henry the Fifth (q.v.).

Prince Humphrey of Gloucester. IV. iv. p.1, 12 ; IV. v. p.1, 47 ; V. ii. p.14.

Fourth and youngest son of King Henry the Fourth. He was made a K.G. by his father. Takes no part in the development of this play, being introduced towards the end, but takes an active part in the two next reigns, and is a character in the three following plays : *King Henry V* and the *First and Second Parts of King Henry VI.*

Prince John of Lancaster. I. i. 17, 134 ; I. ii. p.61, 200, 236 ; I. iii. 82 ; II. i. 170 ; IV. i. 28, 162 ; IV. ii. p.1, 30 ; IV. iii. p.24 ; IV. iv. 83 ; IV. v. p.225, 225, 227 ; V. ii. p.14 ; V. v. p.92.

Prince John, Henry the Fourth's' third son is in command of the royal troops sent to meet the rebels in Yorkshire.

He, with other nobles, interviews the rebel leaders at a place midway between the camps and the rebels agree to disband on being promised redress for their grievances.

The prince now commits an unpardonable and treacherous act, for learning that the rebel army is already disbanded, forthwith orders the arrest of the leaders—Hastings, the Archbishop Scroop and Mowbray—on a charge of high treason.

This act does not reflect at all honourably on the prince however wrong the rebellion may have been, at the same time it shows his crafty disposition.

Prince John does not appear frequently and his actions do not further the plot, but we are prepared for scenes abroad in the next play when at the conclusion of this he says :

> I will lay odds that, ere this year expire,
> We bear our civil swords and native fire
> As far as France : I heard a bird so sing,
> Whose music, to my thinking, pleased the king,
> Come, will you hence ? [V. v. 106–110.]

[Prince John of Lancaster—as the Duke of Bedford—is also a character in *The Life of King Henry the Fifth.* (q.v.)]

Prodigal. II. i. 142.

An allusion to the parable of the prodigal son.

Public place near Westminster Abbey.

The Scene of Act V., Scene v. Shows the coronation procession on its way to Westminster Abbey. Falstaff and his friends eagerly await the king's coming. On his approach they endeavour to speak with Henry, but the latter refuses to acknowledge them. Later Falstaff and his companions are arrested and committed to the Fleet, and the scene closes with Prince John announcing that the king has summoned a parliament as he fears a war with France.

[Johnson remarks : I do not see why Falstaff is carried to the Fleet. We have never lost sight of him since his dismission by the king ; he has committed no new fault, and therefore incurred no punishment ; but the different agitations of fear, anger, and surprise in him and his company, made a good scene to the eye ; and our author, who wanted them no longer on the stage, was glad to find this method of sweeping them away."]

Puff of Barson. V. iii. 88, 90, 91.

An exclamation of contempt.

Richard. I. iii. 98, 101 ; III. i. 58, 64, 67, 88 ; IV. i. 58.

= King Richard the Second.

Robin Hood. V. iii. 102.

> And Robin Hood, Scarlet, and John. [V. iii. 102.]

This unconnected extract is taken from a

stanza in the old ballad of *Robin Hood and the Pindar of Wakefield*. Robin Hood was the famous outlaw.

Robin Nightwork.   III. ii. 203.

Romans.   II. ii. 118.

> " I will imitate the honourable
> Romans in brevity " :   [II. ii. 117–118.]

Probably refers to Julius Cæsar, whose *veni, vidi vici* is evidently alluded to at the beginning of Falstaff's letter. In IV. iii. 42, Falstaff makes use of the very words of Cæsar.

Rome.   IV. iii. 41.

> with the hook-nosed fellow of Rome,   [IV. iii. 41.]

= Julius Cæsar.

Rumour the Presenter.   Induction p.1, 2, 11, 15, 22, 39.

An allegorical personage, attired in a costume, " painted full of tongues " who speaks a Prologue or Induction to the Play. *See under* Warkworth. Before the Castle.

Saint Alban's.   II. ii. 163.

In Herefordshire.

Saint George's Field.   III. ii. 190.

> O, Sir John, do you remember since we lay all night
> in the windmill in Saint George's field ?
>   [III. ii. 189–190.]

An open space on the Surrey side of the Thames lying between Southwark and Lambeth, and so-called from the adjoining church of St. George the Martyr in Southwark. The windmill was a place of notoriety.

Samingo.   V. iii. 74.

> Do me right,
> And dub me knight :
> Samingo.   [V. iii. 72–74.]

A fragment of an old drinking song. In Nashe's *Summer's last Will and Testament*, 1600, Bacchus sings the following catch :

> Monsieur Mingo for quaffing doth surpass
> In cup, in can, or glass ;
> God Bacchus, do me right,
> And dub me knight,
>   Domingo.

Sampson Stockfish.   III. ii. 32.

A fruiterer, with whom Justice Shallow, in his student days, fought behind Gray's Inn.

Saturn.   II. iv. 258.

> Saturn and Venus this year in conjunction !
>   [II. iv. 258.]

A prodigy. According to astrologers Saturn and Venus are never conjoined.

Scarlet.   V. iii. 102.

One of the companions of Robin Hood.

Scotland.   II. iii. 50, 67 ; IV. i. 14.

In Act II. Northumberland is entreated by his wife and daughter-in-law—Lady Percy—to seek refuge in Scotland until the strife is over.

In Act IV. the Archbishop of York reports that he has received letters from Northumberland, that owing to being unable to levy troops he has " retired to Scotland."

Scroop, Archbishop of York.   I. i. 189, 200 ; I. ii. 201 ; I. iii. p.1 ; II. i. 171 ; II. iii. 65 ; III. i. 95 ; IV. i. p.1, 41, 227 ; IV. ii. p.1, 2, 4, 108 ; IV. iv. 84.

Although one of the leaders of the rebel forces against King Henry the Fourth, Scroop was not at heart such a rogue as Northumberland.

He was actuated to take part in the rebellion more from a mistaken sense of national injury, rather than for lust of power. He thinks that a wrong has been done to the people and sets out to correct it, having first weighed the facts of the case, and from this he does not waver.

On meeting the Earl of Westmoreland in Gaultree forest in Yorkshire, and being asked why he has taken up arms, replies :

> I have in equal balance justly weigh'd
> What wrongs our arms may do, what wrongs we suffer,
> And find our griefs heavier than our offences.
>   [IV. i. 67–69.]

and hands a document to Westmoreland setting forth their grievances.

The emissary having departed Scroop expresses the opinion that the affair will be settled by the king, whom he thinks has had so much trouble in the country that he will do anything to secure peace.

In another part of the forest, the Archbishop and other rebel leaders meet Prince John and his officers. The prince promises redress of their grievances, and the rebel army is given orders to disband, on which being done, Scroop and the others are arrested and their execution ordered.

Commenting on this character, Hudson says : " The Archbishop, so forthright and strong-thoughted, bold, enterprising, and resolute in action, in speech grave, moral, and sententious, forms, all together, a noble portrait."

[Richard le Scrope, Archbishop of York, son of Richard Lord Scrope of Bolton ; elected Archbishop of York, 1398 ; supported the revolution of 1399 ; took up arms at York in concert with Northumberland and Bardolph, who raised the standard of rebellion beyond the Tyne ; induced by treachery to surrender to Westmoreland at Shipton Moor ; condemned and executed at York ; popularly known in the North as ' Saint Richard Scrope.' Hume says : " On the refusal of Sir William Gascoigne to condemn him, a more compliant judge was found in Sir William Fulthorp, who without even a form of trial passed sentence of death upon him, " the first instance of capital punishment inflicted on a bishop." The pious archbishop requested the executioner to dispatch him with five blows of his sword, in allusion to the " five wounds of his Saviour," which the prelate bore on his banner.]

" Semper idem," for " obsque hoc nihil est." V. v. 28.

= " Ever the same " for " without this there is nothing."

Warburton says : " The sentence alluded to is, " 'Tis all in all, and all in every part," and so doubtless it should be read. 'Tis a common way of expressing one's approbation of a right measure to say, " 'tis all in all." To which this phantastic character adds, with some humour, and *all in every part ;* which, both together, make up the philosophic sentence, and compleat the absurdity of Pistol's phraseology."

Servant to the Chief Justice, A. I. ii. p.53.

When the Lord Justice sees Sir John Falstaff

in a street in London, he tells his attendant he wishes to speak to the knight, and an amusing passage of words occurs between Sir John and the attendant, the former pretending to be deaf.

Servants. III. ii. p.1.

Shadow. III. ii. p.1, 122, 125, 127, 244, 260.

Selected as one of Falstaff's bodyguard from among the six rustics presented to him.

Shallow. III. ii. p.1, 4, 8, 15, 16, 56, 57, 86, 160, 188, 191, 195, 198, 201, 209, p.237, 252, 255, 282, 291, 296 ; IV. iii. 129 ; V. i. p.1, 3, 59, 63, 71, 73, 78, 87 ; V. iii. p.1, 121, 127, 128, 132 ; V. v. p.5, 5, 74, 77.

A country justice who is of a very self-important nature, and grandiloquent in his ways.

He is a friend of Falstaff's, and the latter meets him at his house, having come to know if Shallow has found the body of men he promised to provide for him.

He once more entertains Falstaff and his men after the expedition to Yorkshire, and we meet them with Justice Silence in the garden, who entertains them with snatches of song. It is here that they learn of the death of Henry IV., and Falstaff tells Shallow he can choose whatever office he likes in the land and it shall be his.

When the coronation procession of the new king is due to pass by, Shallow and Falstaff take up their positions, and Falstaff brags about how the king will recognise them. Falstaff is ignored, and he turns to Shallow reminding him of the thousand pounds he (Falstaff) owes him, at the same time hinting that he will be able to get him a good position yet.

Shallow is not satisfied with these promises, and wants half of his money back :

> *Fal.*   fear not
> your advancement ; I will be the man yet that shall
> make you great.
> *Shal.* I cannot well perceive how, unless you should give
> me your doublet, and stuff me out with straw. I
> beseech you, good Sir John, let me have five
> hundred of my thousand.   [V. v. 79-85.]

Commenting on the character of Shallow, Hudson says : " Aside from the humour of the characters themselves, there is great humour of art in the bringing-together of Falstaff and Shallow. Whose risibilities are not quietly shaken up to the centre, as he studies the contrast between them, and the sources of their interest in each other ? Shallow is vastly proud of his acquaintance with Sir John, and runs over with consequentiality as he reflects upon it. Sir John understands this perfectly, and is drawn to him quite as much for the pleasure of making a butt of him as in the hope of currying a road to his purse.

One of the most potent spots in Justice Shallow is the exulting self-complacency with which he remembers his youthful essays in profligacy ; wherein, though without suspecting it, he was the sport and byword of his companions ; he having shown in them the same boobyish alacrity as he now shows in prating about them. His reminiscences 'in this line are superlatively diverting, partly, perhaps, as reminding us of a perpetual sort of people, not unfrequently met with in the intercourse of life.

Another choice spot in Shallow is a huge love or habit of talking on when he has nothing to say ; as though his tongue were hugging and kissing his words. Thus, when Sir John asks to be excused from staying with him over night : ' I will not excuse you ; you shall not be excused ; excuses shall not be admitted ; there is no excuse shall serve ; you shall not be excused.' And he lingers upon his words and keeps rolling them over in his mouth with a still keener relish in the garden after supper. This fond caressing of his phrases springs not merely from sterility of thought, but partly also from that vivid self-appreciation which causes him to dwell with such rapture on the spirited sallies of his youth."

French says : " This worshipful gentleman may almost be treated as an historical personage, as it is quite certain that Shakespeare, under the guise of ' Robert Shallow esquire, in the county of Gloster, justice of peace, and coram,' has immortalized his early persecutor, Sir Thomas Lucy, Knight, whose seat, Charlecote, co. Warwick, is distant a few miles from Stratford-upon-Avon."

Sheriff of Yorkshire. IV. iv. 99.

The Earl N rthumberland and the Lord Bardolph,
With a great power of English and of Scots,
Are by the sheriff of Yorkshire overthrown :
[IV. iv. 97–99.]

Sir Thomas Rokeby, descended from an old family, long seated at Rokeby, co. York, a place rendered familiar by Sir Walter Scott's poem of the same name. Cf. *Extract* 9 from Holinshed.

Shrewsbury. Induction 24, 34 ; I. i. 12, 24, 40, 64, 65 ; I. ii. 60, 100, 145 ; I. iii. 26.

The Battle and Battlefield of Shrewsbury. See *First Part of King Henry the Fourth*, page 539

Shrove-tide. V. iii. 35.

And welcome merry Shrove-tide. [V. iii. 35.]

A season of sport and feasting.

" Si fortuna me tormenta, spero contento." V. v. 97.
" Si fortune me tormente, sperato me contento." II. iv. 177.

= " If fortune plagues me, hope contents me." Malone says : " Sir Thomas Hanmer reads : ' Si fortuna me tormenta, il sperare me contenta,' which is undoubtedly the true reading ; but perhaps it was intended that Pistol should corrupt it." *Johnson.* Pistol is only a copy of Hannibal Gonsaga, who vaunted on yielding himself a prisoner, as you may read in an old collection of tales, called *Wits, Fits, and Fancies.* And Sir Richard Hawkins, in his *Voyage to the South-Sea,* 1593, throws out the same gingling distich on the loss of his pinnance." *Farmer.*

Silence. III. ii. p.1, 3, 88, 90, 206, p.237, 283 ; V. iii. p.1, 4, 23, 37, 48, 51, 127.

A country justice in partnership with Shallow He entertains Shallow, Falstaff and the others with songs while they are in Shallow's garden.

Commenting on this character, Hudson says : " One would suppose the force of feebleness had done its best in Shallow, yet it is made to do several degrees better in his cousin, Justice

Silence. The tautology of the one has its counterpart in the taciturnity of the other. And Shallow's habit in this may have grown, in part, from talking to his cousin, and getting no replies ; for Silence has scarce life enough to answer, unless it be to echo the question. The only faculty he seems to have is memory, and he has not force enough of his own to set even this in motion ; nothing but excess of wine can make it stir. So that his taciturnity is but the proper outside of his essential vacuity, and springs from sheer dearth of soul. He is indeed a stupendous platitude of a man ! The character is poetical by a sort of inversion ; as extreme ugliness sometimes has the effect of beauty, and fascinates the eye.

Shakespeare evinces a peculiar delight sometimes in weaving poetical conceptions round the leanest subjects ; and we have no finer instance of this than where Silence, his native sterility of brain being overcome by the working of sack on his memory, keeps pouring forth snatches from old ballads. How delicately comical the volubility with which he trundles off the fag-ends of popular ditties, when ' in the sweet of the night ' his heart has grown rich with the exhilaration of wine ! Who can ever forget the exquisite humour of the contrast between Silence dry and Silence drunk ?

In this vocal flow of Silence we catch the right spirit and style of old English mirth. For he must have passed his life in an atmosphere of song, since it was only by dint of long custom and endless repetition that so passive a memory as his could have got stored with such matter. And the snatches he sings are fragments of old minstrelsy ' that had long been heard in the squire's hall and the yeoman's chimney-corner,' where friends and neighbours were wont to ' sing aloud old songs, the precious music of the heart.' "

Sir Dagonet. III. ii. 275.

King Arthur's Fool and a Knight of the Round Table. " And upon a day Sir Dagonet, King Arthur's fool, came into Cornwall, with two squires with him, . . . For they would not for no good that Sir Dagonet were hurt, for king Arthur loved him passing well, and made him knight with his own hands. And at every tournament he began to make king Arthur to laugh." Malory : *Morte d'Arthur.* Tennyson says that he was made a mock-knight by Gawain :

> Dagonet, the fool, whom Gawain in his mood
> Had made mock-knight of Arthur's Table
> Round
> At Camelot.

Sir John Colville. [Colevile]. IV. iii. p.1, 3, 5, 6, 9, 38, 48, 60, 62, 72.

Colevile is one of the rebel army who is met in Gaultree Forest by Falstaff and arrested by him.

Falstaff makes much ado of his capture, and cannot refrain from making humorous remarks about his captive's name. Being told his name is " Colevile of the dale " the fat knight remarks :

> Well, then, Colevile is your name, a knight is your degree, and your place the dale : Colevile shall be still your name, a traitor your degree, and the dungeon your place, a place deep enough ; so shall you be still Colevile of the dale." [IV. iii. 5–9.]

Prince John enters and orders Colevile to be taken to York to be executed forthwith.

French observes : " In the play, Act IV., Scene iii., Prince John of Lancaster gives a direction respecting this trophy of the ' pure and immaculate valour ' of Falstaff,—

> Send Colevile, with his confederates,
> To York, to present execution."

Hume says that his life was spared ; if so, no doubt he was the same ' Sir John Colvyl, Knight,' who was one of the retinue of Henry V. in his expedition to France, 1415, and to whom, as security for payment of ' his wages,' the king pawned ' a large fleur-de-lys garnished with one great balays, and one other balays, one ruby, three great sapphires, and ten great pearls.' " Sir N. H. Nicholas. The prisoner to Falstaff is perhaps the same Sir John Colvill who was Governor of Wisbeach Castle in 1416, and whose grandfather of the same name served with Edward III., in his French wars,"

In a writ of 13 Henry IV., dated June 12, 1412, occurs the name of ' Johannis Colvyle, Chivaler ' ; and in 2 Henry V. he appears in three writs, dated June 26, 1414, joined with another person as envoys to John Duke of Bretagne, wherein they are styled,—' nos chiers and foiaulx John de Colvyle Chivaler, & Mestre Richard Hals Licentiæ as Loys.' Rymer's *Fœdera.*

Sir John Falstaff. I. i. 19 ; I. ii. p.1, 57, 63, 69, 90, 99, 134, 182 ; II. i. 8, p.41, 42, 62, 77, 107, 150, 179, 180, 184 ; II. ii. 43, 58, 66, 104, 113, 126, 127, 128, 164 ; II. iv. 2, 17, 32, p.33, 79, 82, 109, 113, 198, 204, 352, 358 ; III. ii. 25, 27, 29, 54, 61, p.82, 82, 85, 88, 103, 110, 121, 133, 142, 189, 207, 212, p.237, 242, 249, 287 ; IV. iii. p.1, 10, 16, 26, 83 ; V. i. p.1, 10, 19, 52, 58, 86 ; V. ii. 33 ; V. iii. p.1, 8, 13, 83, 92, 115 ; V. iv. 12 ; V. v. p.5, 75, 84, 88, 92 ; Epilogue 27, 29.

As in the *First Part of King Henry the Fourth* Falstaff dominates the scenes in which he appears, and to the end of the play he is continually making humour out of all his experiences, and treating everyone and everything with his characteristic buffoonery.

On his first appearance in this part of the play he meets the Lord Chief Justice who has something to say to him about the robbery committed at Gadshill. Falstaff is aware of this, and so pretends to be deaf, and in reply to all the Chief Justice's questions makes some foolish remark not bearing on the subject referred to. This ruse succeeds and Falstaff thus gets out of a difficult position by his wit. Then the impudence of Sir John is shown by the fact that no sooner has he got out of this difficulty and received the good wishes of the Justice than he asks for the loan of a thousand pounds.

We meet Falstaff next when about to be arrested by officers at the suit of Mistress Quickly to whom he owes a " hundred mark," when the Chief Justice enters and on upbraiding Sir John is met by the latter's witty remark, who, by this means once more avoids a difficult situation, and finally persuades Mistress Quickly to provide entertainment for him and his companions at the Boar's Head Tavern.

At the home of Justice Shallow, Falstaff reviews men picked out to serve as soldiers under him, and this scene brings out the humour of the fat knight in a new way. He makes fun of the men's names and their appearances, and does so in a very entertaining manner. This trait is brought out once more when Sir John meets Sir John Colevile, one of the rebel knights. He arrests him, and then proceeds to pun on his

name, afterwards bragging to Prince John of his prowess in capturing such a " furious knight and valorous enemy."

Falstaff can make humour out of any situation, however serious it may really be, for he lives in an atmosphere of fun, and is always a philosopher, for on his last appearance in this play when he is ignored by the new king, and ordered to be cast into prison by the Lord Chief Justice, Falstaff is not so completely crushed as we might have expected him to be ; for he turns to Shallow with the remark :

Master Shallow, I owe you a thousand pound.
[V. v. 74.]

Commenting on the character of Falstaff, Hudson says : " Falstaff's character is more complex than can well be digested into the forms of logical statement ; which makes him a rather impracticable subject for analysis. He has so much, or is so much, that one cannot easily tell what he is. Diverse and even opposite qualities meet in him ; yet they poise so evenly, blend so happily, and work together so smoothly, that no generalities can set him off ; if we undertake to grasp him in a formal conclusion, the best part of him still escapes between the fingers ; so that the only way to give an idea of him is to take the man himself along and show him ; and who shall do this with ' plump Jack ? ' One of the wittiest of men, yet he is not a wit ; one of the most sensual of men, still he cannot with strict justice be called a sensualist ; he has a strong sense of danger and a lively regard to his own safety, a peculiar vein indeed of cowardice, or something very like it, yet he is not a coward ; he lies and brags prodigiously, still he is not a liar nor a braggart. Any such general descriptions applied to him can serve no end but to make us think we understand him when we do not.

If I were to fix upon any one thing as specially characteristic of Falstaff, I should say it is an amazing fund of good sense. His stock of this, to be sure, is pretty much all enlisted in the service of sensuality, yet nowise so but that the servant still overpeers and outshines the master. Then too his thinking has such agility, and is at the same time so pertinent, as to do the work of the most prompt and popping wit ; yet in such sort as to give the impression of something much larger and stronger than wit. For mere wit, be it ever so good, requires to be sparingly used, and the more it tickles the sooner it tires ; like salt, it is grateful as a seasoning, but will not do as food. Hence it is that great wits, unless they have great judgment too, are so apt to be great bores. But no one ever wearies of Falstaff's talk, who has the proper sense for it ; his speech being like pure fresh water, which always tastes good because it is tasteless. The wit of other men seems to be some special faculty or mode of thought, and lies in a quick seizing of remote and fanciful affinities ; in Falstaff it lies not in any one thing more than another, for which cause it cannot be defined : and I know not how to describe it but as that roundness and evenness of mind which we call good sense, so quickened and pointed indeed as to produce the effect of wit, yet without hindrance to its own proper effect. To use a snug idiomatic phrase, what Falstaff says always *fits all round*.

And Falstaff is well aware of his power in this respect. He is vastly proud of it too ; yet his pride never shows itself in an offensive shape, his good sense having a certain instinctive delicacy that keeps him from every thing like that. In this proud consciousness of his re- sources he is always at ease ; hence in part the ineffable charm of his conversation. Never at a loss, and never apprehensive that he shall be at a loss, he therefore never exerts himself nor takes any concern for the result ; so that nothing is strained or far-fetched : relying calmly on his strength, he invites the toughest trials, as knowing that his powers will bring him off without any using of the whip or the spur, and by merely giving the rein to their natural brisk- ness and celerity. Hence it is also that he so often lets go all regard to prudence of speech, and thrusts himself into tight places and pre- dicaments : he thus makes or seeks occasions to exercise his fertility and alertness of thought, being well assured that he shall still come off uncornered, and that the greater his seeming perplexity, the greater will be his triumph. Which explains the purpose of his incompre- hensible lies : he tells them, surely, not expecting them to be believed, but partly for the pleasure he takes in the excited play of his faculties, partly for the surprise he causes by his still more incomprehensible feats of dodging. . . .

I must not leave Sir John without remarking how he is a sort of public brain from which shoot forth nerves of communication through all the limbs and members of the commonwealth. The most broadly-representative, perhaps, of all ideal characters, his conversations are as diversi- fied as his capabilities ; so that through him the vision is let forth into a long-drawn yet clear perspective of old English life and manners. What a circle of vices and obscurities and nobili- ties are sucked into his train ! how various in size and quality the orbs that revolve around him and shine by his light ! from the immediate heir of England and the righteous Lord Chief Justice to poor Robin Ostler who died of one idea, having ' never joy'd since the price of oats rose.' He is indeed a multitudinous man ; and can spin fun enough out of his marvellous brain to make all the world ' laugh and grow fat.' "

Sir Johns. II. iv. 6.

The prince once set a dish of apple-johns before him, and told him there were five more Sir Johns ; [II. iv. 4–6.]

apple-john = a winter apple which grew withered from keeping. Falstaff had already said of himself I am withered like an old apple- John.

Sir John Umfrevile. I. i. 34.

Mentioned by Travers as bringing tidings of the Battle of Shrewsbury. " My lord, Sir John Umfrevile turn'd me back With joyful tidings."

The families of Percy and Umfrevile were con- nected by marriage ; Robert Umphrevill, only son of the earl's second countess by her first husband married Margaret, daughter of Henry, Lord Percy.

Sisters Three. II. iv. 195.

Untwine the Sisters Three ! [II. iv. 195.]

An allusion to the Fates, Clotho, Lachesis and Atropos.

Skogan. III. ii. 30.

There appears to have been two celebrated Skogans. Henry Skogan, a poet, contemporary with Chaucer, who lived in the reign of Richard the Second and Henry the Fourth. Ben Jonson speaks of him as "a fine gentleman and master of arts." The other named John Skogan was the favourite jester of Edward the Fourth.

Smithfield. I. ii. 48, 51.

An open space in London, long famous for its market. It was to Smithfield that Bardolph went to buy Falstaff a horse.

Snare, Sheriff's Officer. II. i. p.1, 5, 6, 9, 24, 40.

An officer, who with Fang, is commissioned to arrest Falstaff at the suit of Mistress Quickly for the money he owes her.

Sneak's noise. II. iv. 11, 21.

and
> see if thou canst find out Sneak's noise ;
> [II. iv. 10–11.]

Sneak was a street minstrel. It was customary at this period to hire musicians to entertain guests in inns and taverns.

Song.

> Do me right,
> And dub me knight ;
> Samingo.　　　　[V. iii. 72–74.]

See Samingo.

Song.

> Do nothing but eat and make good cheer,
> And praise God for the merry year ;
> When flesh is cheap and females dear,
> And lusty lads roam here and there
> 　　So merrily,
> And ever among so merrily.　　[V. iii. 17–22.]
>
> Be merry, be merry, my wife has all ;
> For women are shrews, both short and tall :
> 'Tis merry in hall when beards wag all,
> 　And welcome merry Shrove-tide.
> Be merry, be merry.　　[V. iii. 32–36.]
>
> A cup of wine that 's brisk and fine,
> And drink unto the leman mine ;
> 　And a merry heart lives long-a.　　[V. iii. 45–47.]
>
> Fill the cup, and let it come ;
> I 'll pledge you a mile to the bottom.　　[V. iii. 52–53.]

No traces have been found of these old songs sung by Silence.

Song.

> When Arthur first in court—　. 　.　.
> 　.　.　.　.　.　.　. And
> was a worthy king.　　[II. iv. 33–35.]

See under Arthur.

Stafford. I. i. 18.

= Edmund, Earl of Stafford. He was killed at the battle of Shrewsbury, where he led the king's "vaward."

Stamford. III. ii. 39.

= Stamford St. Martin ; or, Stamford Baron Parish in Northamptonshire. "This place was anciently called 'Stamford south of the Welland,' or, 'Stamford beyond the Bridge,' but obtained the name of Stamford St. Martin from the patron saint of the Parish. It received the name of Stamford Baron about the middle of the 15th century when the suffix was added, probably on account of 'its being part of those lands which the Abbot of Peterborough held *per baroniam ;*' or which is still more probable, from the strong castle or baronial mansion which, according to Marianus, was built here, on the site now called the 'Nuns' Farm,' by Edward the elder, who also fortified the southern bank of the river to prevent the inroads of the Danes, who frequently occupied its northern side." Whellan's *Northamptonshire.*

Tewkesbury mustard. II. iv. 236.

A town in Gloucestershire, formerly noted for mustard-balls made there.

Thomas, Duke of Clarence. IV. iv. p.1, 16, 19, 21, 41, 50 ; IV. v. p.1, 8, 47 ; V. ii. p.14.

Second son to King Henry the Fourth, only appearing on three occasions, and taking no important part in the action of the play. The Prince of Wales holds a greater affection for Thomas than for his other brothers, and the king, knowing this, pleads with Thomas to use his influence in keeping the prince and his brothers together, saying finally after a speech of admonition :

> Learn this,
> Thomas,
> And thou shalt prove a shelter to thy friends,
> A hoop of gold to bind thy brothers in.
> [IV. iv. 41–43.]

This prince and his brother John of Lancaster, were frequently engaged, according to the chroniclers, in uproars in the city. Stow mentions a riot on St. John's Eve, 1410, in Eastcheap, wherein both these princes were foremost and violent actors. Shakespeare does not include them in the disorderly proceedings of their elder brother ; and Falstaff speaks of Prince John as " a sober-blooded boy,' for which he quite accounts,—' he drinks no wine ' Thomas Plantagenet, born in 1388, was created July 9, 1411, by his father, Earl of Albemarle and Duke of Clarence. As this prince does not figure in the succeeding plays, though he is addressed by his brother as if present at the meeting of the kings at Troyes, *King Henry V.*, Act V., Scene ii., a few words are needful in this place. He was chosen President of his father's Council when Prince Hal was in disgrace, and had been made a K.G. about the year 1400. He was sometime Lord Lieutenant of Ireland, Captain of Calais, and Lieutenant-General of France and Normandy. He was a distinguished commander, and was killed at the battle of Beaugé in Anjou, March 23, 1421. The spear with which the Duke of Clarence was unhorsed by Sir John Swinton was presented by that knight's descendant to Sir Walter Scott. The Duke of Clarence married Margaret Holland, second daughter of Thomas, second Earl of Kent, but had no issue by her. *French.*

Thomas Mowbray, Duke of Norfolk. III. ii. 26.

> Then
> was Jack Falstaff, now Sir John, a boy, and page to
> Thomas Mowbray, Duke of Norfolk.   [III. ii. 24–26.]

Halliwell has ascertained that Sir John Oldcastle, " the good Lord Cobham," was, in his youth, page to Thomas Mowbray, Duke of Norfolk ; and he justly argues that Oldcastle was the original name of Falstaff. *Hudson.*

Tilt-yard. III. ii. 317.

Where tournaments or tilting were held. It was in Westminster.

Tisick, the debuty. II. iv. 84.

> Master Tisick, the debuty, . . . Master Dumbe
> our Minister.

The names are ludicrously intended to denote that the deputy was *pursy* and *short winded :* the minister one of those who did not preach sermons of his own composition, but only read the homilies set forth by authority - such clergymen being termed by the puritans, in a phrase borrowed from the prophet, *dumb dogs :* it was an opprobrious name which continued as late as the reign of Charles II., when the presbyterian ministers who were restored by the king, and did not dare to preach ' to the times ' ; *i.e.* to introduce politicks into their sermons, were called dumb dogs that could not bark. *Malone.*

Travers. I. i. 28, p.30, 33, 55.

Servant to Northumberland, who enters with news of the rebel defeat at Shrewsbury.

Northumberland inquires the nature of his tidings, only to be told that :

> After him came spurring hard
> A gentleman, almost forespent with speed,
> That stopp'd by me to breathe his bloodied horse.
> He ask'd the way to Chester ; and of him
> I did demand what news from Shrewsbury :
> He told me that rebellion had bad luck,
> And that young Harry Percy's spur was cold.
> [I. i. 36–42.]

Trigon. II. iv. 260.

> And, look, whether the fiery Trigon, his man, be
> not lisping to his master's old tables, his note-book,
> his counsel-keeper.   [II. iv. 260–262.]

fiery Trigon = An allusion to the astrological division of the twelve signs of the Zodiac into four trigons or triplicities ; representing three fiery, three airy, three watery and three earthy signs :

> *Fiery :* Aries, Leo, Sagittarius.
> *Airy :* Gemini, Libra, Aquarius.
> *Watery :* Cancer, Scorpio, Pisces.
> *Earthy :* Taurus, Virgo, Capricorn.

Trojan Greeks. II. iv. 164.

One of Pistol's drunken expressions.

Troy. I. i. 73.

A City of Asia Minor. It was taken and destroyed by the Greeks after a ten years' siege.
The story is told by Homer.

Turnbull Street. III. ii. 300.

A notorious neighbourhood in Clerkenwell.
In an old comedy entitled *Ram-Alley, or Merry
Tricks*, this street is mentioned : " You swaggering, cheating, *Turnbull-street* rogue." And
in *Scornful Lady*, by Beaumont and Fletcher we
have : " Here has been such a hurry, such a din,
such dismal drinking, swearing, etc., we have all
lived in a perpetual *Turnbull-street.*"

Venus. II. iv. 258.

> Saturn and Venus this year in conjunction.
> [II. iv. 258.]

See Saturn.

Vice's dagger. III. ii. 314.

The buffoon of the old Morality Plays.
Hanmer says : " Vice was the name given to a
droll figure, heretofore much shown upon our
stage, and brought in to play the fool and make
sport for the populace. His dress was always
a long jerkin, a fool's cap with ass's ears, and a
thin wooden dagger, such as is still retained in
the modern figures of Harlequin and Scara-
mouch."

Wales. I. ii. 102 ; II. i. 172 ; II. iv. 287.

Warkworth. Before the Castle.

The Scene of the Induction. Act I., Scene i.
Act II., Scene iii.

Induction. This speech of Rumour is not in-
elegant or unpoetical, but it is wholly useless,
since we are told nothing which the first scene
does not clearly and naturally discover. The
only end of such prologues is to inform the
audience of some facts previous to the action,
of which they can have no knowledge from the
persons of the drama. *Johnson.*

Painted full of tongues. This, Shakespeare
probably drew from Holinshed's *Description of
a Pageant*, exhibited in the court of Henry VIII.,
with common cost and magnificence : ' Then
entered a person called *Report*, apparelled in
crimson sattin, *full of toongs*, or chronicles.' *T.
Warton.*

Stephen Hawes, in his *Pastime of Pleasure*
exhibited Rumour in the same manner :

> A goodly lady, envyroned about
> With *tongues* of fire.—

In Act I., Scene i., Lord Bardolph arrives at
Warkworth Castle with false news of victory
from Shrewsbury. Travers confirms the news,
but adds, that he has heard contradictory reports. Their conversation is cut short by the
arrival of Morton bearing tidings of Hotspur's
defeat and death.

In Act II., Scene iii., Northumberland's wife
and daughter-in-law beg of him to fly to Scotland until the strife is concluded. At first the
earl feebly protests, saying that he is bound by
honour to remain. Seeing his indecision they
redouble their efforts and Northumberland
ultimately decides to take their advice.
[" This scene between Northumberland, his
wife, and daughter-in-law," says Courtenay, " is
Shakespeare's creature, and of fair proportions.
But the earl did not determine, as Shakespeare
relates, to return into Scotland ; he gave way
to the solicitations of the females of his family,
and, instead of joining the rebel force, betook
himself to Wales. The reasoning of Lady Percy,
plausible though fallacious, might well have
prevailed with one of stouter heart."]

Wart. III. ii. p.1, 136, 139, 161, 255, 265,
267, 271.

One of six chosen as Falstaff's bodyguard,
but he is rejected by the fat knight.

Westminster. II. iv. 347.

Westminster. The Jerusalem Chamber.

The Scene of Act IV., Scene iv. Henry the
Fourth is present with his lords, and having
announced his intention to go on a crusade to

the Holy Land should the issue of the rebellion be successful, inquires for his two sons. The king expresses his regret on hearing that Prince Henry still adheres to his base companions. The king is cheered by Westmoreland announcing Prince John's bloodless victory over the rebels, and the arrest and execution of the rebel leaders. [" Nothing seems clear," says Courtenay, " but that the archbishop, Mowbray, and the others, fell into the hands of the king without any action being fought, and that they were put to death ; not, however, as Shakespeare says, by the authority of Prince John, but by that of one of the king's judges. The Chief Justice Gascoyne, it is said, refused to condemn a bishop ; but one Fulthorpe, or Fulford, was made a judge for the occasion, and condemned Scrope, who was beheaded without a trial, protesting loudly that he had intended no evil against the king. His admirers have not failed to describe the miracles which followed his death."] Henry is suddenly taken ill, and his courtiers bear him away to an adjoining room.

Westminster. Another Chamber.

The Scene of Act IV., Scene v. Shows the royal sick-room. Prince Henry enters. Seeing the crown on the king's pillow, and thinking his father is dead, picks up the crown and forthwith leaves the room. [This story, that the king during his last sickness caused the crown to be brought and set on a pillow at his bed's head is from Holinshed, who avowedly took it from Hall.] The king awakes, notes the absence of his crown, and finding that the prince has taken it, sends for him. The prince is over-joyed on seeing his father alive, and handing back the crown craves his father's pardon. The scene closes with the king enquiring the name of the chamber in which he first " swooned " and being told it is called " Jerusalem " recalls the prophecy that he " should depart this life in Jerusalem."

Westminster. The Palace.

The Scene of Act III., Scene i. Act V., Scene ii.

Act III., Scene i. The king sends for the Earls of Surrey and of Warwick who are to read and express their opinions on certain letters which he sends them. When they appear the king tells them that he has a presentiment of coming danger. The lords endeavour to cheer him, declaring that the royal army will prove victorious. This scene contains the king's soliloquy on sleep, considered to be one of the finest passages in the play. The mention of Glendower's death in line 103 is inaccurate as this personage lived till 1415.

Act V., Scene ii. The Chief Justice makes inquiries about the king and is told that he lives no more. The lords are expressing their regret that such an undeserving son as Prince Hal should succeed to the throne, when the latter enters and declares that it is his intention to reform and devote all his energies to the proper government of his realm and people.

Wheeson week. II. i. 86.

Mrs. Quickly's mistake for Whitsun week.

William. III. ii. 9.

A cousin of Justice Shallow's.

William. V. i. 9, 15, 22, 27.

Justice Shallow's cook.

William Visor of Woncot. V. i. 36, 39.

" Woncot has been usually identified with Wilnecote, a village near Stratford. . . . Madden, however, identifies ' Woncot ' with ' Woodmancote ' the name of a village in Gloucestershire, which is still pronounced as ' Woncot.' Madden mentions that a family of Visor or Vizard has been associated with Woodmancote since the sixteenth century, and that a house on the adjoining Stinchcome Hill (now as ·then locally known as ' The Hill ') was then occupied by the family of Perkes." *Arden edition.*

Will Squele.   III. ii. 21.

A former acquaintance of Justice Shallow's at Clement's Inn.

Windsor.   II. i. 87 ; IV. iv. 14, 50.

Woncot.   V. i. 37.

See William Visor of Woncot.

Worcester.   I. i. 125.

Thomas Percy, Earl of Worcester, brother to the Earl of Northumberland. He was captured at the battle of Shrewsbury, and beheaded. See *First Part of King Henry the Fourth*, page 543.

York.   I. ii. 62 ; II. i. 64 ; IV. iii. 73.

= City of York.

York.   The Archbishop's Palace.

The Scene of Act I., Scene iii. With Lords Hastings, Mowbray, and Bardolph, the Archbishop discusses their prospects. They decide that without Northumberland's aid their chances of victory are very doubtful. Lord Hastings informs them that the king's power is divided. On hearing this the Archbishop decides on prompt action.

[During this rebellion of Northumberland and the Archbishop, a French army landed at Milford Haven in Wales, for the aid of Owen Glendower. See *Extract* 2 from Holinshed.]

Yorkshire.   Gaultree Forest.

The Scene of Act IV., Scene i. Here the Archbishop's troops are mustered. A messenger enters with the news that the king's forces are near at hand. Later the Earl of Westmoreland —an embassy from Prince John—enters, and bids them disband and so avert bloodshed. The Archbishop will not come to terms but sends a list of their grievances to the prince. Westmore-

land re-appears and announces that Prince John will confer with them half-way between their forces, and they forthwith depart for the interview. [The renewal of the rebellion took place in 1405, two years after the Battle of Shrewsbury.]

Yorkshire.   Another part of Gaultree Forest.

The Scene of Act IV., Scenes ii and iii.

In Act IV., Scene ii., Prince John receives the rebel leaders, and promises to redress their grievances. [According to Holinshed it was the Earl of Westmoreland and not Prince John who made this solemn promise. See *Extracts* 5 and 6.] Hastings gives orders for the rebel forces to be disbanded. The prince then gives orders for the royal forces to disband, but they refuse to accept any orders except from the prince himself. Prince John then treacherously orders the arrest of the rebel leaders, and the pursuit of the rebel army. [Stubbs says : " On the 1st of March, 1405, a dispute about precedence took place in council between the earl of Warwick and the earl-marshal, the son of the king's old adversary Norfolk ; it was decided in favour of Warwick, and Mowbray left the court in anger. Whilst this was going on in the south, Northumberland and Westmoreland were preparing for war in the north. Possibly the attitude of Northumberland may have been connected with the Mortimer plot, and Mowbray was certainly cognisant of both . . . the lord Bardolf, who has opposed the king strongly in the recent councils, had joined Northumberland, and Sir William Clifford had associated himself with them. Unfortunately for himself and all concerned, the archbishop of York, Richard le Scrope, placed himself on the same side. These leaders drew up and circulated a formal indictment against the king, whom they described as Henry of Derby. Ten articles were published by the archbishop ; Henry was a usurper and a traitor to king and church ; he was a perjuror who on a false plea had raised the nation against Richard ; . . . he had connived at Richard's murder ; etc. . . . As soon as it was known that the lords were in arms Henry hastened to the north, and having reached Derby on the

28th of May, summoned his forces to meet at Pomfret. The contest was quickly decided. The earl of Westmoreland, John of Lancaster, and Thomas Beaufort, at the head of the king's forces, encountered the rebels at Shipton moor and offered a parley. The archbishop there met the earl of Westmoreland, who promised to lay before the king the articles demanded. The friendly attitude of the leaders misled the insurgent forces ; they dispersed, leaving Scrope and Mowbray at the mercy of their enemies and they were immediately arrested, . . . and on the 8th of June the archbishop and the earl-marshal were beheaded. That done, the king followed the earl of Northumberland and Bardolf to the north. They fled to Scotland, and Henry, having seized the castles of the Percies, returned to the task of defence against the Welsh,"]

In Act IV., Scene iii., Falstaff, who is in pursuit of the rebels, encounters Sir John Colevile and demands his surrender. [Courtenay remarks : " I know not how Shakspeare got hold of the fact of Coleville being made prisoner after the dispersion of the rebel force." According to Holinshed, Coleville was convicted and beheaded. See *Extract* 7.] Prince John enters and upbraids Falstaff for disobeying orders. Colevile and his confederates are then sent to York for execution. Falstaff hearing that the royal army is disbanded leaves, intending on his way home to visit Justice Shallow again.

APPENDIX I.

EXTRACTS FROM HOLINSHED[1] THAT ILLUSTRATE THE *Second Part of King Henry the Fourth.*

1. The earle of Northumberland was now marching forward with great power, which he had got thither, either to aid his sonne and brother (as was thought) or at the least towards the king, to procure a peace ; but the earle of Westmerland, and sir Robert Waterton, knight, had got an armie on foot, and meant to meet him. The earle of Northumberland, taking neither of them to be his freend, turned suddenlie backe, and withdrew himselfe into Warkewoorth castell.

2. [About this time] the French king had appointed one of the marshals of France, called Montmerancie, and the master of his crosbowes, with twelue thousand men, to saile into Wales to aid Owen Glendouer. They tooke shipping at Brest, and, hauing the wind prosperous, landed at Milford hauen, with an hundred and fourtie ships, as *Thomas Walsingham* saith ; though *Enguerant de Monstrellet* maketh mention but of an hundred and twentie.
    [Failing to capture Haverfordwest,] they departed towards the towne of Denbigh, where they found Owen Glendouer abiding for their comming, with ten thousand of his Welshmen. Here were the Frenchmen ioifullie receiued of the Welsh rebels, and so, when all things were prepared, they passed by Glamorganshire towards Worcester, and there burnt the suburbes : but, hearing of the kings approch, they suddenlie returned towards Wales.

3. [Northumberland] hearing that his counsell was bewraied, and his confederats brought to confusion, through too much hast of the archbishop of Yorke, with three hundred horsse got him to Berwike. The king comming forward quickelie, wan the castell of Warkewoorth. Where-vpon the earle of Northumberland, not thinking himselfe in suertie at Berwike, fled with the lord Berdolfe into Scotland, where they were receiued of sir Dauid Fleming.

4. The Welsh rebell Owen Glendouer made an end of his wretched life in this tenth yeare [1408–9] of king Henrie his reigne ; being driuen now in his latter time (as we find recorded) to such miserie, that, in manner despairing of all comfort, he fled into desert places and solitarie caues ; where, being destitute of all releefe and succour, dreading to shew his face to anie creature, and finallie lacking meat to susteine nature, for meere hunger and lacke of food, [he] miserablie pined awaie and died.

1. Shakespeare's Holinshed, by W. G. Boswell-Stone.

5. But at the same time, to his further disquieting, there was a conspiracie put in practise against him at home by the earle of Northumberland, who had conspired with Richard Scroope, archbishop of Yorke, Thomas Mowbraie, earle marshall, sonne to Thomas duke of Norfolke, (who for the quarrell betwixt him and king Henrie had beene banished, as ye haue heard,) the lords Hastings, Fauconbridge, Berdolfe, and diuerse others. It was appointed that they should meet altogither with their whole power, vpon Yorkeswold, at a daie assigned, and that the earle of Northumberland should be cheefteine ; promising to bring with him a great number of Scots. The archbishop, accompanied with the earle marshall, deuised certeine articles of such matters, as it was supposed that not onelie the commonaltie of the Realme, but also the nobilitie found themselues greeued with : which articles they shewed first vnto such of their adherents as were neere about them, & after sent them abroad to their freends further off ; assuring them that, for redresse of such oppressions, they would shed the *last* drop of blood in their bodies, if need were.

The archbishop, not meaning to staie after he saw himselfe accompanied with a great number of men, that came flocking to Yorke to take his part in this quarrell, foorthwith discouered his enterprise ; causing the articles aforesaid to be set vp in the publike streets of the citie of Yorke, and vpon the gates of the monasteries, that ech man might vnderstand the cause that mooued him to rise in armes against the king : the reforming whereof did not yet apperteine vnto him. Herevpon, knights, esquiers, gentlemen, yeomen, and other of the commons, as well of the citie townes and countries about, being allured either for desire of change, or else for desire to see a reformation in such things as were mentioned in the articles, assembled togither in great numbers ; and the archbishop, comming foorth amongst them clad in armor, incouraged, exhorted, and (by all meanes he could) pricked them foorth to take the enterprise in hand, and manfullie to continue in their begun purpose ; promising forgiuenesse of sinnes to all them, whose hap it was to die in the quarrell : and thus not onelie all the citizens of Yorke, but all other in the countries about, that were able to beare weapon, came to the archbishop, and the earle marshall. In deed, the respect that men had to the archbishop caused them to like the better of the cause, since the grauitie of his age, his integritie of life, and incomparable learning, with the reuerend aspect of his amiable personage, mooued all men to haue him in no small estimation.

The king, aduertised of these matters, meaning to preuent them, left his iournie into Wales, and marched with all speed towards the north parts. Also Rafe Neuill, earle of Westmerland, that was not farre off, togither with the lord Iohn of Lancaster the kings sonne, being informed of this rebellious attempt, assembled togither such power as they might make, and, togither with those which were appointed to attend on the said lord Iohn to defend the borders against the Scots, (as the lord Henrie Fitzhugh, the lord Rafe Eeuers, the lord Robert Umfreuill, & others,) made forward against the rebels ; and, comming into a plaine within the forest of Galtree, caused their standards to be pitched downe in like sort as the archbishop had pitched his, ouer against them, being farre stronger in number of people than the other ; for (as some write) there were of the rebels at the least twentie thousand men.

When the earle of Westmerland perceiued the force of the aduersaries, and that they laie still and attempted not to come forward vpon him, he subtillie deuised how to quaile their purpose ; and foorthwith dispatched messengers vnto the archbishop to vnderstand the cause as it were of that great assemble, and for what cause (contrarie to the kings peace) they came so in a[r]mour. The archbishop answered, that he tooke nothing in hand *against* the kings *peace*, but that whatsoeuer he did, tended rather to aduance the peace and quiet of the common-wealth, than otherwise ; and where he and his companie were in armes, it was for feare of the king, to whom he could haue no free accesse, by reason of such a multitude of flatterers as were about him ; and therefore he mainteined that his purpose to be good & profitable, as well for the king himselfe, as for the realme, if men were willing to vnderstand a truth : & herewith he shewed foorth a scroll, in which the articles were written wherof before ye haue heard.

The messengers, returning to the earle of Westmerland, shewed him what they had heard & brought from the archbishop. When he had read the articles, he shewed in word and countenance outwardly that he *liked* of the archbishops holie and vertuous intent and purpose ; promising that he and his would prosecute the same in assisting the archbishop, who, reioising hereat, gaue credit to the earle, and persuaded the earle marshall (against his will as it were) to go with him to a place appointed for them to commune togither. Here, when they were met with like number on either part, the articles were read ouer, and, without anie more adoo, the earle of Westmerland, and those that were with him agreed to doo their best, to see that a reformation might be had, according to the same.

The earle of Westmerland, vsing more policie than the rest : " Well " (said he) " then our " trauell is come to the wished end ; and where our people haue beene long in armour, let them " depart home to their woonted trades and occupations : in the meane time *let us drinke togither* " in signe of agreement ; that the people on both sides maie see it, and know that it is true, that " we be light at a point." They had no sooner shaken hands togither, but that a knight was sent streight waies from the archbishop, to bring word to the people that there was peace concluded ; commanding ech man to laie aside his armes, and to resort home to their houses. The people, beholding such tokens of peace, as shaking of hands, and drinking togither of the lords in louing manner, they being alreadie wearied with the vnaccustomed trauell of warre, brake vp their field and returned homewards ; but, in the meane time, whilest the people of the archbishops side withdrew awaie, the number of the contrarie part increased, according to order giuen by the earle of Westmerland ; and yet the archbishop perceiued not that he was deceiued, vntill the earle of Westmerland arrested both him and the earle marshall, with diuerse other. Thus saith *Walsingham.*

6. But others write somwhat otherwise of this matter ; affirming that the earle of Westmerland, in deed, and the lord Rafe Eeuers, procured the archbishop and the earle marshall, to come to a communication with them, vpon a ground *iust* in the midwaie betwixt both the *armies ;* where the earle of Westmerland in talke declared to them how perilous an enterprise they had taken in hand, so to raise the people, and to mooue warre against the king ; aduising them therefore to submit themselues without further delaie vnto the kings mercie, and his sonne the lord Iohn, who was present there in the field with banners spred, redie to trie the matter by dint of sword, if they refused this counsell : and therefore he willed them to remember themselues well ; &, if they would not yeeld and craue the kings pardon, he bad them doo their best to defend themselues.

Herevpon as well the archbishop as the earle marshall submitted themselues vnto the king, and to his sonne the lord Iohn that was there present, and returned not to their armie. Wherevpon their troops scaled and fled their waies ; but, being pursued, manie were taken, manie slaine, and manie spoiled of that that they had about them, & so permitted to go their waies. Howsoeuer the matter was handled, true it is that the archbishop, and the earle marshall were brought to Pomfret to the king, who in this meane while was aduanced thither with his power ; and from thence he went to Yorke, whither the prisoners were also brought, and there beheaded the morrow after Whitsundaie [June 8, 1405] in a place without the citie : that is to vnderstand, the archbishop himselfe, the earle marshall, sir Iohn Lampleie, and sir William Plumpton. Unto all which persons, though indemnitie were promised, yet was the same to none of them at anie hand performed.

7. At his [Henry's] comming to Durham, the lord Hastings, the lord Fauconbridge, sir Iohn Colleuill of the Dale, and sir Iohn Griffith, being conuicted of the conspiracie, were there beheaded.

8. He [Henry] held his Christmas this yeare at Eltham, being sore vexed with sicknesse, so that it was thought sometime, that he had beene dead : notwithstanding it pleased God that he somwhat recouered his strength againe, and so passed that Christmasse with as much ioy as he might.

9. The earle of Northumberland, and the lord Bardolfe, after they had beene in Wales, in France, and Flanders, to purchase aid against king Henrie, were returned backe into Scotland, and had remained there now for the space of a whole yeare : and, as their euill fortune would, whilest the king held a councell of the nobilitie at London, the said earle of Northumberland and lord Bardolfe, in a dismall houre, *with a great power of Scots,* returned into England ; recouering diuerse of the earls castels and seigniories, for the people in great numbers resorted vnto them. Heerevpon, incouraged with hope of good successe, they entred into Yorkshire, & there began to destroie the countrie. At their comming to Threske, they published a proclamation, signifieng that they were come in comfort of the English nation, as to releeue the common-wealth ; willing all such as loued the libertie of their countrie, to repaire vnto them, with their armor on their backes, and in defensible wise to assist them.

The king, aduertised hereof, caused a great armie to be assembled, and came forward with the same towards his enimies ; but, yer the king came to Notingham, sir Thomas, or (as other copies haue) Rafe Rokesbie, shiriffe of Yorkshire, assembled the forces of the countrie to resist the earle and his power ; comming to Grimbaut brigs, beside Knaresbourgh, there to stop them the passage ; but they, returning aside, got to Weatherbie, and so to Tadcaster, and finallie came forward vnto Bramham more, neere to Haizelwood, where they chose their ground meet to fight vpon. The shiriffe was as readie to giue battell as the earle to receiue it, and so, with a standard of S. George spred, set fiercelie vpon the earle, who, vnder a standard of his owne armes, incountred his aduersaries with great manhood. There was a sore incounter and cruell conflict betwixt the parties, but in the end the victorie fell to the shiriffe. The lord Bardolfe was taken, but sore wounded, so that he shortlie after died of the hurts. As for the earle of Northumberland, he was slaine outright : . . . This battell was fought the nineteenth day of Februarie [1408].

10. In this yeare [1411], and vpon the twelfth day of October, were three flouds in the Thames, the one following vpon the other, & *no ebbing betweene :* which thing no man then liuing could remember the like to be seene.

11. During this his [Henry IV.'s] last sicknesse, he caused his crowne (as some write) to be set on a pillow at his beds head ; and suddenlie his pangs so sore troubled him, that he laie as though all his vitall spirits had beene from him departed. Such as were about him, thinking verelie that he had beene departed, couered his face with a linnen cloth.

The prince, his sonne, being hereof aduertised, entered into the chamber, tooke awaie the crowne, and departed. The father, being suddenlie reuiued out of that trance, quicklie perceiued the lacke of his crowne ; and, hauing knowledge that the prince his sonne had taken it awaie, caused him to come before his presence, requiring of him what he meant so to misuse himselfe. The prince, with a good audacitie, answered : " Sir, to mine and all mens iudgements you seemed " dead in this world ; wherefore I, as your next heire apparant, tooke that as mine owne, and not as " yours." " Well, faire sonne " (said the king with a great sigh), " what right I had to it, God knoweth." " Well " (said the prince), " if you die king, I will haue the garland, and trust to " keepe it with the sword against all mine enimies, as you haue doone." Then said the king, " I commit all to God, and remember you to doo well." With that he turned himselfe in his bed, and shortlie after departed to God in a chamber of the abbats of Westminster called Ierusalem, the twentith daie of March, in the yeare 1413, and in the yeare of his age 46 : when he had reigned thirteene yeares, fiue moneths, and od daies, in great perplexitie and little pleasure. . . .

12. In this fourteenth and last yeare of king Henries reigne, a councell was holden in the white friers in London ; at the which, among other things, order was taken for ships and gallies to be builded and made readie, and all other things necessarie to be prouided for a voiage which he meant to make into the holie land, there to recouer the citie of Ierusalem from the Infidels. . . .

13. We find, that he was taken with his last sickenesse, while he was making his praiers at saint Edwards shrine, there as it were to take his leaue, and so to proceed foorth on his iournie : he was so suddenlie and greeuouslie taken, that such as were about him, feared lest he would haue died presentlie ; wherfore to releeue him (if it were possible) they bare him into a .chamber that was next at hand, belonging to the abbat of Westminster, where they laid him on a pallet before the fire, and vsed all remedies to reuiue him. At length, he recouered his speech, and, vnderstanding and perceiuing himselfe in a strange place which he knew not, he willed to know if the chamber had anie particular name ; wherevnto answer was made, that it was called Ierusalem. Then said the king : " Lauds be giuen to the father of heauen, for now I know that I shall die " heere in this chamber ; according to the prophesie of me declared, that I should depart this " life in Ierusalem."

14. [After his coronation Henry V. is said to have dismissed his unworthy associates,] and in their places he chose men of grauitie, wit, and high policie, by whose wise counsell he might at all times rule to his honour and dignitie ; calling to mind how once, to hie offense of the king his father, he had with his fist striken the cheefe iustice for sending one of his minions (vpon desert) to prison : when the iustice stoutlie commanded himselfe also streict to ward, & he (then prince) obeied.

15. He was crowned the ninth of Aprill, being Passion sundaie, which was a sore, ruggie, and tempestuous day, with wind, snow, and sleet ; that men greatlie maruelled thereat, making diuerse interpretations what the same might signifie. But this king euen at first appointing with himselfe, to shew that in his person princelie honors should change publike manners, he determined to put on him the shape of a new man. For whereas before he had made himselfe a companion vnto misrulie mates of dissolute order and life, he now banished them all from his presence (but not vnrewarded, or else vnpreferred) ; inhibiting them vpon a great paine, not once to approch, lodge, or soiourne within *ten miles* of his court or presence : . . .

16. This king was of a meane stature, well proportioned, and formallie compact ; quicke and liuelie, and of a stout courage. In his latter daies he shewed himselfe so gentle, that he gat more loue amongst the nobles and people of this realme, than he had purchased malice and euill will in the beginning.

But yet to speake a truth, by his proceedings, after he had atteined to the crowne, what with such taxes, tallages, subsidies, and exactions as he was constreined to charge the people with ; and what by punishing such as, mooued with disdeine to see him vsurpe the crowne (contrarie to the oth taken at his entring into this land, vpon his returne from exile), did at sundrie times rebell against him ; he wan himselfe more hatred, than in all his life time (if it had beene longer by manie yeares than it was) had beene possible for him to haue weeded out & remooued.

APPENDIX II.

Extracts from *The Famous Victories of Henry the Fifth, conteining the Honorable Battell of Agincourt*, utilised by Shakespeare in the *Second Part of King Henry the Fourth*.[1]

1. THE RECRUITING SCENE.

Enter a Captaine, Iohn Cobler and his wife.

Cap.	Come, come, there's no remedie,
	Thou must néeds serue the King.
Iohn.	Good maister Captaine let me go,
	I am not able to go so farre.
Wife.	I pray you good maister Captaine,
	Be good to my husband.
Cap.	Why I am sure he is not too good to serue ye king?
Iohn.	Alasse no : but a great deale too bad,
	Therefore I pray you let me go.
Cap.	No, no, thou shalt go.
Iohn.	Oh sir, I haue a great many shooes at home to
	Cobble.
Wife.	I pray you let him go home againe.
Cap.	Tush, I care not, thou shalt go.
Iohn.	Oh wife, and you had béen a louing wife to me,
	This had not bene, for I haue said many times,
	That I would go away, and now I must go
	Against my will. *He weepeth.*

2. THE CROWN SCENE.

Enter the King with his lords.

Hen. IV. Come, my Lords, I see it bootes me not to take any phisick,
for all the Phisitians in the world cannot cure me, no not one.
But good my Lords, remember my last wil and Testament concerning my sonne, for truly my Lordes, I doo not thinke but he wil
proue as valiant and victorious a King, as euer raigned in
England.

Both. Let heauen and earth be witnesse betwéene us, if we accomplish
not thy wil to the vttermost.

Hen. IV. I giue you most vnfained thanks, good my lords,
Draw the Curtaines and depart my chamber a while,
And cause some Musicke to rocke me a sléepe.
He sleepeth. Exeunt Lords.

Enter the Prince.

Hen. V. Ah Harry, thrice vnhappie that hath neglect so long
from visiting of thy sicke father, I wil goe, nay but
why doo I not go to the Chamber of my sick father, to
comfort the melancholy soule of his bodie, his soule said
I, here is his bodie indéed, but his soule is, whereas it
néeds no bodie. Now thrice accursed Harry, that hath offended thy father so much, and could not I craue pardon for
all. Oh my dying father, curst be the day wherin I was borne,
and accursed be the houre wherin I was begotten, but what shal I do?
if wéeping teares which come too late, may suffice the negligence
neglected to some, I wil wéepe day and night vntil the fountaine be
drie with wéeping. *Exit.*

1. Shakespeare's Library, edited by Hazlitt.

Enter Lord of Exeter and Oxford.

Exe.	Come easily my Lord, for waking of the King.
Hen. IV.	Now my Lords.
Oxf.	How doth your Grace féele your selfe.
Hen. IV.	Somewhat better after my sléepe,
	But good my Lords take off my Crowne,
	Remoue my chaire a litle backe, and set me right.
Ambo.	And please your grace, the crown is take away.
Hen. IV.	The Crowne taken away,
	Good my lord of Oxford, go sée who hath done this déed :
	No doubt tis some vilde traitor that hath done it,
	To depriue my sonne, they that would do it now,
	Would séeke to scrape and scrawle for it after my death.

Enter Lord of Oxford with the Prince.

Oxf.	Here and please your Grace,
	Is my Lord the yong Prince with the Crowne.
Hen. IV.	Why how now my sonne ?
	I had thought the last time I had you in schooling,
	I had giuen you a lesson for all,
	And do you now begin againe ?
	Why tel me my sonne,
	Doest thou thinke the time so long,
	That thou wouldest haue it before the
	Breath be out of my mouth ?
Hen. V.	Most soueraign Lord and welbeloved father,
	I came into your Chamber to comfort the melancholy
	Soule of your bodie, and finding you at that time
	Past all recouery, and dead to my thinking,
	God is my witnesse : and what should I doo,
	But with wéeping tears lament ye death of you my father,
	And after that, séeing the Crowne, I tooke it :
	And tel me my father, who might better take it then I,
	After your death ? but séeing you liue,
	I most humbly render it into your Maiesties hands,
	And the happiest man aliue, that my father liue,
	And liue my Lord and Father, for euer.
Hen. IV.	Stand vp my sonne,
	Thine answere hath sounded wel in mine eares,
	For I must néed confesse that I was in a very sound sléep,
	And altogither vnmindful of thy comming :
	But come neare my sonne,
	And let me put thée in possession whilst I liue,
	That none depriue thée of it after my death.
Hen. V.	Well may I take it at your maiesties hands,
	But it shal neuer touch my head, so long as my father liues.
	He taketh the Crowne.
Hen. IV.	God giue thée ioy my sonne,
	God blesse thée, and make thée his seruant,
	And send thée a prosperous raigne.
	For God knowes my sonne, how hardly I came by it,
	And how hardly I haue maintained it.
Hen. V.	Howsoeuer you came by it, I know not,
	And now I haue it from you, and from you I wil kéepe it :
	And he that séekes to take the Crowne from my head,
	Let him looke that his armour be thicker then mine,
	Or I will pearce him to the heart,
	Were it harder than brasse or bollion.
Hen. IV.	Nobly spoken, and like a King.
	Now trust me my Lords, I feare not but my sonne
	Will be as warlike and victorious a Prince,
	As euer raigned in England.

L. Ambo.	His former life shewes no lesse.
Hen. IV.	Wel my lords I know not whether it be for sléep,
	Or drawing neare of drowsie summer of death,
	But I am verie much giuen to sléepe,
	Therefore good my Lords and my sonne,
	Draw the Curtaines, depart my chamber,
	And cause some Musicke to rocke me a sléepe.

[Exeunt omnes. The King dieth.

3. KING HENRY THE FIFTH BANISHES HIS MISLEADERS.

Enter Knightes raunging.

Tom.	Gogs wounds the King is dead.
Iock.	Dead, then gogs blood, we shall be all kings.
Ned.	Gogs wounds, I shall be Lord chiefe Iustice Of England.
Tom.	Why how, are you broken out of prison ?
Ned.	Gogs wounds, how the villaine stinkes.
Iock.	Why what wil become of thée now ?
	Fye vpon him, how the rascall stinkes.
Theefe.	Marry I wil go and serue my maister againe.
Tom.	Gogs blood, doost think that he wil haue any such
	Scab'd knaue as thou art ? what man he is a king now.
Ned.	Hold thée, heres a couple of Angels for thée,
	And get thée gone, for the King wil not be long
	Before he come this way :
	And hereafter I wil tel the king of thée. *[Exit Theefe.*
Iock.	Oh how it did me good, to sée the king
	When he was crowned :
	Me thought his seate was like the figure of heauen,
	And his person like vnto a God.
Ned.	But who would haue thought,
	That the king would haue changde his countenance so ?
Iock.	Did you not sée with what grace
	He sent his embassage into France ? to tel the French king
	That Harry of England hath sent for the Crowne,
	And Harry of England wil haue it.
Tom.	But twas but a litle to make the people beléeue,
	That he was sorie for his fathers death. *The Trumpet sounds.*
Ned.	Gogs wounds, the king comes,
	Let all stand aside.

Enter the King with the Archbishop, and the Lord of Oxford.

Iock.	How do you my Lord ?
Ned.	How now Harry ?
	Tut my Lord, put away these dumpes,
	You are a king, and all the realme is yours :
	What man, do you not remember the old sayings, .
	You know I must be Lord chiefe Iustice of England,
	Trust me my lord, me thinks you are very much changed,
	And tis but with a litle sorrowing, to make folkes beléeue
	The death of your father gréeues you,
	And tis nothing so.
Hen. V.	I prethée Ned, mend thy manners,
	And be more modester in thy tearmes,
	For my vnfeined gréefe is not to be ruled by thy flattering
	And dissembling talke, thou saist I am changed,
	So I am indeed, and so must thou be, and that quickly,
	Or else I must cause thée to be chaunged.
Iock.	Gogs wounds, how like you this ?
	Sownds tis not so swéete as Musicke.
Tom.	I trust we haue not offended your grace no way.

Hen. V.   Ah Tom, your former life gréeues me,
And makes me to abandō & abolish your company fot euer
And therfore not vpō pain of death to approch my presence
By ten miles apace, then if I heare wel of you,
It may be I wil do somewhat for you,
Otherwise looke for no more fauour at my hands,
Then at any other mans : And therefore be gone,
We haue no other matters to talke on.   [*Exeunt Knights.*
Now my good Lord Archbishop of Canterbury ?
What say you to our Embassage into France ?

APPENDIX III.

EXTRACT FROM *The Annales, or Generall Chronicle of England, begun first by maifter Iohn Stow, and after him continued and augmented by Edmond Howes, gentleman,* utilised by Shakespeare in the *Second Part of King Henry the Fourth.*

The renowned Prince king Henry the fift, during the life of his father, was noted to be fierce, and of wanton courage. It hapned that one of his feruants, whom he fauored was for felony by him committed, arraigned at the kings bench, whereof the Prince being aduertised, and incenfed by light perfons about him in furious rage came haftily to the bar where his feruant ftood as prifoner, & comanded him to be vngiued and fet at libertie, whereat all men were abafhed, referued the chiefe Juftice, who humbly exhorted the Prince to be ordered according to the ancient lawes of the Realme, or if he would haue him faued from the rigor of the lawes, that he fhould obtaine if he might of the k. his father, his gracious pardon, whereby no law or iuftice fhould be derogate. With the which anfwere the prince nothing appeafed but rather more inflamed in-deuoured himfelfe to take away his feruant. The Judge, considering the perillous example and inconueniencie that night thereby enfue, with a valiant fpirit & courage commaunded the prince vpon his allegeance to leaue the prifoner, and to departe his way : with which commandment, the Prince being fet all in a furie, all chafed, & in a terrible manner came vp to the place of iudgment, men thinking that hee would haue flaine the Judge, or haue done to him fome domage, but the Judge fitting ftill without moouing, declaring the maieftie of the kings place of iudgement, and with an affured bold countenance, hadde to the prince thefe words following : Sir, remember your felfe, I keepe here the place of the king your foueraigne lord and father, to whom you owe double obeifance, wherefore eftfoones in his name I charge you defift off your wilfulnes and unlawfull enterprife, and from hencefoorth giue good example to thofe which after fhall bee your proper fubiects : and nowe for your contempt and difobedience, goe you to the prifon of the kings bench whereunto I commit you, and remaine you there prifoner untill the pleafure of the king your father be further knowne. With which words, being abafhed, and alfo wondering at the maruellous grauitie of that worshipfull Juftice, the Prince laying his weapon aparte doing reuerence, departed & went to the kings bench as he was commanded. Whereat his feruants difdaining, came and fhewed to the king all the whole affaire. Whereat he a while ftudying, after, as a man all rauifhed with gladnes, holding his hands and eies towards heauen, abraid with a lowde voice : O merciful God how much am I bounde to thy infinite goodnes, efpecially for that thou haft giuen me a Judge, who feareth not to minifter iuftice, and alfo a fonne, who can fuffer femblably and obey iuftice.

The Life of King Henry the Fifth

Written. The date of the composition of *The Life of King Henry the Fifth is* generally considered to be 1599, this date being determined by two passages in the play. In the Chorus prefixed to the first Act, an allusion is made to " this wooden O," *i.e.* the Globe Theatre :

> or may we cram
> Within this wooden O the very casques
> That did affright the air at Agincourt ?

The Globe Theatre, which was built of wood, was opened in June, 1599. By some it is considered that *Henry the Fifth* was first performed at the opening of this theatre. Again, in the *Chorus* prefixed to Act V we read :

> The mayor and all his brethren in best sort,
> Like to the senators of the antique Rome,
> With the plebeians swarming at their heels,
> Go forth and fetch their conquering Cæsar in :
> As, by a lower, but by loving likelihood,
> Were now the general of our gracious empress,
> As in good time he may, from Ireland coming,
> Bringing rebellion broached on his sword,
> How many would the peaceful city quit
> To welcome him ! much more, and much more
>   cause,
> Did they this Harry.

This refers to the Earl of Essex who left London for Ireland on the 27th March, 1599, to suppress the Tyrone rebellion. Essex's campaign was a failure and he returned to London hurriedly, arriving at Court on the 28th September of the same year.

The play is not mentioned by Francis Meres in his *Palladis Tamia ; or, Wit's Treasury*, published in the year 1598. From this it is inferred that the play could not have been written earlier than the year 1599.

Published. Published in an imperfect form in the year 1600, under the following title : " The | Cronicle | History of Henry the fift, | with his battell fought at *Agin Court* in | France. Togither with *Auntient | Pistoll. As it hath been sundry times playd by the Right honorable | the Lord Chamberlaine his seruants.* | LONDON | Printed by *Thomas Creede*, for Tho. Milling- | ton, and Iohn Bushy. And are to be | sold at his house in Carter Lane, next | the Powle head. 1600 | .

From the following entry in the Register of the Stationers' Hall, it appears that the application for a license to print the play was in the first instance withheld :

[1600]   4 Augusti.
As you like yt | a booke
Henry the ffift | a booke
Every man in his humour | a booke   to be staied.
The commedie of muche A adoo about
    nothing a booke |

This ban was however removed, as under date 14th of August of the same year we find :

[1600]   14 Augusti.

Thomas   Entred for his copyes by direction of master white warden vnder
Pavyer.— his hand wryting. These Copyes followinge beinge thinges for-
          merlye printed and sett over to the sayd Thomas Pavyer
                    viz. . . .
          The historye of Henry the Vth with the battell of Agencourt.
                                                                    vid.

The first authorised copy appeared in the Folio of 1623 under the title " The Life of Henry Fift."

In the *Epilogue* to the *Second Part of King Henry the Fourth,* our author promises to " continue the story, with Sir John in it, and make you merry with fair Katharine of France."   This promise however is not carried out as Falstaff does not once appear throughout the play.

The Play covers a period of seven years, from the accession of King Henry the Fifth in 1413, to his betrothal to Katharine of Valois on the 21st May, 1420.

Each Act is preceded by a *Prologue* or *Chorus,* whilst the play closes with an *Epilogue* or *Chorus* which is a general comment on the whole.

Source of the Plot.   The materials for the plot are mainly taken from Holinshed's *Chronicles,*[1] and the old play *The Famous Victories of Henry V., containing the honourable battle of Agincourt.*[2]

Outline of the Play.   In the opening of the *Prologue* or *Chorus* to Act I., the poet invokes divine inspiration to enable him to raise the " swelling scene " to the highest regions of grandeur, and apologises for attempting to enclose within the walls of a theatre " The vasty fields of France," and the " very casques That did affright the air at Agincourt," and makes an eloquent appeal to his audience to " Piece out the imperfections with their thoughts," and as " we talk of horses," to imagine that they see an " imaginary power, . . .   Printing their proud hoofs i' the receiving earth," and " jumping o'er times, Turning the accomplishment of many years Into an hour-glass," and finally craves their humble patience " Gently to hear " and " kindly to judge."

The first Act opens in an Antechamber of the King's Palace in London.   The Archbishop of Canterbury and the Bishop of Ely enter, and discuss a Bill, introduced into Parliament " in the eleventh year of the reign of Henry IV., and re-introduced on the 30th April, 1414, in the second year of the reign of Henry V.," which, if passed into law, would deprive the Church of a great portion of its wealth :

Cant.   If it pass against us,
          We lose the better half of our possession ;
          For all the temporal lands which men devout
          By testament have given to the church
          Would they strip from us ;

Ely observes that the Bill " drinks very deep," while Canterbury considers it " drinks the cup and all," and on Ely asking the best way to prevent it being placed on the Statute book, Canterbury proceeds to comment upon the change in the king's character since his accession, describing him as a " king full of grace and fair regard " ; and a " true lover of the holy church," enjoins Ely, for no sooner had his father passed

1. *See* Appendix I.   2. *See* Appendix II.

away than his wildness became mortified as if some angel had descended from heaven and " whipp'd the offending Adam out of him, Leaving his body as a paradise, To envelop and contain celestial spirits." " We are blessed in the change," remarks Ely, adding, that as the " strawberry grows beneath the nettle, And wholesome berries thrive and ripen best Neighbour'd by fruit of baser quality " ; so the king's " contemplation " which was " obscur'd Under the veil of wildness " will now develop in the right direction. Ely then enquires if the king is inclined towards the bill, to which the Archbishop replies that his majesty " seems indifferent, Or rather swaying more upon our part " than on the part of the introducers of the bill, adding, that in order to obtain the goodwill of the king, he had offered on behalf of the Church, to give a " greater sum than ever the clergy had previously offered " to prosecute war with France. Upon Ely asking how the king " received this offer," Canterbury replies " With good acceptance, . . . Save that there was not time enough to hear," as the king seemed more interested to have explained to him the " severals and unhidden passages " as to his " true titles to some certain dukedoms And generally to the crown and seat of France." " What was the impediment that broke this off ? " enquires Ely, and Canterbury answers that the French Ambassador had arrived and craved audience of his majesty, which audience had been fixed for four o'clock. To this important Council the two prelates had been summoned to give their opinion as to Henry's claim to the French crown, although they can " with a ready guess declare Before the Frenchman speak of a word of it," what the result will be. Cf. *Extract* 1 from Holinshed.

We are in the Presence Chamber in the next scene. The king, with his courtiers, enters, and enquires for the Archbishop of Canterbury, and being told he is " not here in presence " bids Exeter to send for him. In the meantime Westmoreland enquires if the French ambassador shall be admitted. " Not yet, my cousin," replies Henry, " before we hear him," there are " some things of weight That task our thoughts, concerning us and France." The Archbishop, accompanied by the Bishop of Ely, now appears, and greeting the king : " God and his angels guard your sacred throne," Henry enquires of him whether the Salique Law excludes him (Henry) from making a claim to the French crown :

> My learned lord, we pray you to proceed,
> And justly and religiously unfold
> Why the law Salique that they have in France
> Or should, or should not, bar us in our claim,

charging him in the name of God to consider well his answer, as it involves great responsibility. The archbishop then delivers a long disquisition on the ancient law, [I. ii. 32–95] which, according to the French excludes females, or descendants on the female side, from succeeding to the French crown. The archbishop, however, points out that the Law Salique originated in Germany, in the country between the " floods of Sala and of Elbe," and therefore does not apply to France, in consequence of which, Henry—as a descendant of Edward II., who married Isabella of France—has undoubtedly a clear title to the French crown. " May I with right and conscience make this claim ? " demands Henry, and the archbishop urges him to stand for his just claim : " Gracious lord, Stand for your own ; unwind your bloody flag ; For in the book of Numbers it is writ : ' When the man dies, let the inheritance Descend unto the daughter ' " and at the same time reminds the king of the war-like spirit exhibited, and the glorious deeds performed by his ancestors on French soil, in the which he is supported by the Bishop of Ely, and the Lords Exeter and Westmoreland. Canterbury then repeats the offer of the Church to provide a larger sum of money than has ever been granted before, and Henry reminds them of the danger of a Scottish invasion during the army's absence in France, but the archbishop considers that the lords of the marches are strong enough to defend the border against invaders, adding that the Scots had occasion to remember how their king was captured at the battle of Neville's Cross in 1346 by Edward III's queen, during the time that king Edward was absent in France, to which Westmoreland replies by quoting the old adage : " If that you will France win, Then with Scotland first begin : ". After some little argument has passed between Exeter and Canterbury in which each tries to prove his point, the latter suggests that the king shall proceed to France with " one quarter " of his forces with which you " shall make all Gallia shake," leaving " three-fourths " at home to defend the border against any possible invasion from the north :

> Therefore to France, my liege.
> Divide your happy England into four ;
> Whereof take you one quarter into France,
> And you withal shall make all Gallia shake.
> If we, with thrice such powers left at home,
> Cannot defend our own doors from the dog,
> Let us be worried and our nation lose
> The name of hardiness and policy.

This suggestion so convinces Henry, that he orders the French Ambassadors to be admitted, declaring that he is " well resolv'd " to invade France, and with the help of God establish by force of arms his right to the French crown.

The ambassadors being admitted, the king announces that " he is well prepar'd to know the pleasure Of our fair cousin Dauphin ; for we hear Your greeting is from him, not from the king," and the ambassadors, having asked, and obtained the king's permission to speak " with uncurbed plainness " inform Henry that his claim to " certain French dukedoms " is rejected, and that the Dauphin wishing to hear " no more of him, nor of his claim," has sent him " This tun of treasure," at the same time bidding him " to be advis'd " as he " savours too much of his youth," there being nothing in France that can be won by a " nimble galliard." " What treasure, uncle ? " asks the king, and Exeter replies : " Tennis-balls, my liege." On receiving this reply, Henry resents the insult with fiery scorn, and turning to the ambassadors thanks the Dauphin for his " present," and themselves for " their pains in delivering it," adding that " When we have match'd our rackets to these balls, We will in France, by God's grace, play a set Shall strike his father's crown into the hazard." With grim determination Henry exclaims that he will " dazzle all the eyes of France," when he " keeps his state " as the monarch of that country, and instructs the ambassadors to tell the " pleasant prince " that his mock " Hath turn'd his tennis-balls to gun-stones," which will wring tears from " many a thousands widows for their dear husbands " and from " Mothers for their sons," while others yet ungotten and unborn shall have cause to curse the Dauphin's haughty scorn. " This was a merry message," is Exeter's comment after the ambassadors have departed. " We will make the sender blush for it," replies Henry, and giving orders to his nobles to make preparations for the invasion of France with all possible speed, leaves the chamber amid a flourish of trumpets, threatening to " chide this Dauphin at his father's door " :

> Therefore let every man now task his thought,
> That this fair action may on foot be brought.

Cf. *Extract* 2 from Holinshed.

The *Prologue* or *Chorus* preceding Act II describes the preparations made for the invasion of France, the enthusiasm throughout the country over the war :

> Now all the youth of England are on fire,
> And silken dalliance in the wardrobe lies ;
> Now thrive the armourers, and honour's thought
> Reigns solely in the breast of every man :

and the change of scene from London to Southampton. The crossing-over to France is, however, delayed, as a plot to assassinate the king is discovered, the leaders of which are the Earl of Cambridge, Lord Scroop, and Sir Thomas Grey who have been bribed by France to carry out the deed. Cf. *Extract* 3 from Holinshed.

The first scene of Act II. opens in a London street. Corporal Nym and Lieutenant Bardolph—who are to proceed with the army to France—enter, and after greeting one another, comment upon the coming campaign, Nym declaring that he " dare not fight," but he will " hold up his sword and wink," which is very " simple," Bardolph adding that they will go to France as " three sworn brothers " and share in each other's fortunes, to which Nym adds that he " will live so long as he may, that 's the certain of it ; and when he cannot live any longer, he will do as he may : that is his rest, that is the rendezvous of it." Bardolph then enquires if it is true that Pistol is married to Mistress Quickly, just as the newly-married couple enter, and a quarrel ensues between Nym—to whom Mistress Quickly was once " troth-plight "— and Pistol. They call each other foul names, and prepare to fight, but Bardolph interferes, and threatens to kill the first to strike a blow :

> Hear me, hear me what I say : he that strikes
> the first stroke, I 'll run him up to the hilts, as I
> am a soldier.

" I will cut thy throat, one time or other, in fair terms ; that is the humour of it," exclaims Nym, and Pistol tells him to mind his own business, and get along with his flirting with Doll Tearsheet, and not interfere with his wife :

> O hound of Crete, think'st thou my spouse to get ?
> No ; to the spital go,
> And from the powdering-tub of infamy
> Fetch forth the lazar kite of Cressid's kind,
> Doll Tearsheet she by name, and her espouse :
> I have, and I will hold, the quondam Quickly
> For the only she ; and—pauca, there 's enough.
> Go to.

A boy enters and summons " Mine host Pistol " and his wife to his master—Falstaff— who has been suddenly taken ill, and then turning to Bardolph, says : " Good Bardolph, put thy face between his sheets and do the office of a warming-pan. Faith, he 's very ill." " Away, you rogue," shouts Bardolph. " The king has killed his heart," is the hostess' comment, as she departs in company with the boy, after requesting her husband to come home presently. The hostess gone, Pistol and Nym renew their quarrel and again draw their swords, but eventually they become reconciled, for when Nym demands " eight shillings which he has won " from Pistol " at betting," the latter promises to pay the former a " noble " and " liquor likewise." Mistress Quickly hurriedly re-enters, and bids them all come quickly as their old companion—Sir John Falstaff—is dying, " shaked of a burning quotidian tertian, that it is most lamentable to behold," due as Nym remarks, to the king, who " hath run bad humours on the knight," a statement with which Pistol agrees, since Falstaff's " heart is fracted and corroborate." The scene closes with Pistol inviting his companions to go with him and sympathise with Falstaff as they all must live peacefully together like young lambs.

The Council-Chamber at Southampton supplies the next scene. It opens with the Duke of Bedford remarking that the king is " bold to put trust " in men whose plot for his assassination has been discovered, but Exeter replies that they will be " apprehended by and by," although they are not now aware that their conspiracy is known to the king. Amid a flourish of trumpets, Henry—with courtiers, including the three conspirators—enters. He remarks that as the " wind sits fair " they will " aboard " and cross the narrow sea and cut " their passage through the force of France." When asked their opinion on the matter Scroop answers that if " each man does his best " there is no doubt of victory, while Cambridge tells Henry that " Never was monarch better fear'd and lov'd Than is your majesty " : in which he is supported by Grey : " True : those that were your father's enemies Have steep'd their galls in honey, and do serve you With hearts create of duty and of zeal."

Henry next gives orders for a man imprisoned on the previous day for " railing against the king's person " while under the influence of drink, to be released :

> Uncle of Exeter,
> Enlarge the man committed yesterday
> That rail'd against our person : we consider
> It was excess of wine that set him on ;
> And on his more advice we pardon him.

The three traitors, however, urge the king to punish the man for this insult, lest his bad example be emulated by others, but Henry replies that he will exercise clemency in the case of minor offences and reserve severity for " capital crimes, chew'd, swallow'd and digested." " And now to our French causes," continues Henry, and inquires who were the late commissioners to France, and the three conspirators claim this honour :

> *Cam.*   I one, my lord :
> Your highness bade me ask for it to-day
> *Scroop.* So did you me, my liege.
> *Grey.*   And I, my royal sovereign.

The king thereupon hands each of them a scroll, containing information that their plot has been discovered, which he requests them to read :

> Then, Richard Earl of Cambridge, there is yours ;
> There yours, Lord Scroop of Masham ; and, sir knight,
> Grey of Northumberland, this same is yours :
> Read them ; and know, I know your worthiness.

and then turning to the Lords Westmoreland and Exeter announces that they will embark for France that evening.

Perceiving the change in the colour of the faces of the conspirators, Henry inquires the cause :

> Why, how now, gentlemen !
> What see you in those papers that you lose
> So much complexion ? Look ye, how they change !
> Their cheeks are paper. Why, what read you there,
> That hath so cowarded and chas'd your blood
> Out of appearance ?

and being self-convicted of treason the three traitors crave pardon of the king :

> *Cam.*   I do confess my fault,
> And do submit me to your highness' mercy.
> *Grey, Scroop.* To which we all appeal.

" You must not dare, for shame, to talk of mercy," sternly replies Henry, for you are like " dogs worrying their own masters " ; and then turning to Cambridge upbraids him for having for a " few light crowns " conspired to assassinate him.   Scroop he describes as a " cruel, Ingrateful, savage and inhuman creature " :

> Thou that didst bear the key of all my counsels,
> That knew'st the very bottom of my soul,
> That almost might'st have coin'd me into gold
> Would'st thou have practis'd on me for thy use,
> May it be possible that foreign hire
> Could out of thee extract one spark of evil
> That might annoy my finger ? 'tis so strange
> That, though the truth of it stands off as gross
> As black and white, my eye will scarcely see it.

Henry then orders them to be arrested for having conspired with their country's enemies to put him to death.   Being arrested by the Earl of Exeter on the charge of high treason, each of them again appeals for mercy, although admitting that they deserve death :

> *Scroop.* Our purposes God justly hath discover'd,
> And I repent my fault more than my death ;
> Which I beseech your highness to forgive,
> Although my body pay the price of it.
> *Cam.* For me, the gold of France did not seduce,
> Although I did admit it as a motive
> The sooner to effect what I intended :
> But God be thanked for prevention ;
> Which I in sufferance heartily will rejoice,
> Beseeching God and you to pardon me.
> *Grey.* Never did faithful subject more rejoice
> At the discovery of most dangerous treason
> Than I do at this hour joy o'er myself,
> Prevented from a damned enterprise.
> My fault, but not my body, pardon, sovereign.

but after reminding them again of their offences :

> You have conspir'd against our royal person,
> Join'd with an enemy proclaim'd, and from his coffers
> Receiv'd the golden earnest of our death ;

Henry sentences them to be beheaded :

>   Get you therefore hence,
> Poor miserable wretches, to your death ;
> The taste whereof, God of his mercy give you
> Patience to endure, and true repentance
> Of all your dear offences !   Bear them hence.

As they are led away, the king, turning to the lords bids them make preparations to embark, and the scene closes with Henry invoking the aid of God (" who has so graciously brought to light this dangerous treason ") on the expedition.   Cf. *Extract* 3 from Holinshed.

The next scene is enacted before Mistress Quickly's tavern.   She expresses a wish to accompany her husband—Pistol—as far as Staines, on his way to Southampton :

" Prithee, honey-sweet husband, let me bring thee to Staines." Pistol refuses to grant her wish, and then turning to his companions, bids Bardolph to be " blithe " ; Nym to " rouse his vaunting veins " ; and the boy to " bristle up his courage " although Falstaff has gone. Bardolph expresses a wish to be with Falstaff " either in heaven or in hell ! " to which Dame Quickly replies : " Nay, sure, he 's not in hell : he 's in Arthur's bosom, if ever man went to Arthur's bosom. A' made a finer end— and went away—after having called out ' God, three or four times '—an it had been any christom child ; a' parted even just between twelve and one, even at the turning o' the tide : for after I saw him fumble with the sheets and play with flowers and smile upon his fingers' ends, I knew there was but one way ; for his nose was as sharp as a pen, and a' babled of green fields." But " They say he cried out of sack," interposes Nym. " Ay, that a' did," replies Dame Quickly. " And of women," adds Bardolph. " Nay, that a' did not," is the hostess' reply. " Yes, that a' did " : enjoins the Boy, " and said they were devils incarnate." " A' could never abide carnation ; 'twas a colour he never liked," is the Dame's rejoinder. " A' said once," insists the boy, that the " devil would have him about women." " A' did in some sort, indeed, handle women," admits the hostess, " but then he was rheumatic, and talked of the whore of Babylon," and the boy gently reminds her that when Falstaff " saw a flea stick upon Bardolph's nose," he said it was a " black soul burning in hell-fire," whereupon Bardolph interposes with the remark that the " fuel that main- tained that fire " has passed away, and the conversation is brought to a close by Nym observing : " Shall we shog ? " [move off] ; or the king will have departed from Southampton.

Giving instructions to his wife to look after his house during his absence, and to give no credit : " My love, give me thy lips. Look to my chattels and my move- ables : Let senses rule, the word is ' Pitch and pay '," Pistol exhorts her to " Trust none ; For oaths are straws, men's faiths are wafer-cakes, And hold-fast is the only dog, my duck." Telling her to wipe her eyes : " Go, clear thy crystals," he bids Bardolph and Nym kiss his wife : " Touch her soft mouth, and march," and Bardolph bids the hostess farewell, but Nym declares he " cannot kiss, that is the humour of it ; but adieu." This done, Pistol again enjoins his wife to look after the house during his absence, to keep indoors, and attend to business : " Let housewifery appear : keep close, I thee command," after which taking an affectionate farewell of her, the three companions proceed forthwith to Southampton to join the army *en route* for France.

We are now transferred to France, the fourth scene opening in the French king's palace. Hearing of the projected invasion of France by the English forces, Charles gives orders to the French generals and the Dauphin " with all swift dispatch, To line and new repair our towns of war With men of courage and with means defendant." The Dauphin—although admitting that such preparations are necessary—considers that there is no more danger " than if we heard that England Were busied with a Whitsun morris-dance " : for being " so idly king'd " there is nothing to fear from such a " vain, giddy, shallow, humorous youth " as king Henry. But the Constable of France tells the Dauphin that he is " too much mistaken in the English king," and bids him to " question the late ambassadors " as to the dignity meted out to the French embassy at the English Court, " How well supplied with noble counsellors, How modest in exception, and withal How terrible in constant resolution," and the Dauphin excuses himself by saying that he favours the strengthening of the defences, as it is better to " weigh The enemy more mighty than he seems." On the other hand, the French king, calling to mind the defeat of France at Creçy and Poitiers, where a relative of Henry—Edward the Black Prince—won his spurs, is full of apprehension at the projected English invasion, and gives orders for strong forces to be mustered to meet the emergency, for Henry " is bred out of that bloody strain That haunted us in our familiar paths." At this point a messenger enters, and announces :

> Ambassadors from Harry King of England
> Do crave audience to your majesty.

Giving orders for them to be admitted, Charles remarks :

> You see this chase is hotly follow'd, friends,

to which the Dauphin exclaims that the time has come to " Turn head, and stop pursuit ; for coward dogs Most spend their mouths when what they seem to threaten Runs far before them. Good my sovereign, Take up the English short, and let them know Of what a monarchy you are the head." The ambassadors being ushered in, Lord Exeter demands the French king, on pain of war, to surrender to Henry the crown and kingdom of France, which claims he substantiates by handing to Charles the pedigree of Henry, who claims the crown as a descendant of Edward the Third. " Or else what follows ? " asks Charles, and Exeter replies : " Bloody constraint ; for if you hide the crown Even in your hearts, there will he rake for it " ; and proceeds to warn the French king solemnly of the consequences in case of his refusal to meet Henry's demands : " Deliver up the crown, and take mercy On the poor souls for whom this hungry war Opens his vasty jaws." This is " my message," concludes Exeter, unless the Dauphin is present to whom " expressly I bring greeting too." Charles promises to consider the demand, and give an answer on the morrow :

> For us, we will consider of this further :
> To-morrow shall you bear our full intent
> Back to our brother of England.

Asked by the Dauphin what Henry sends to him : " For the Dauphin, I stand here for him : what to him from England ? " and Exeter haughtily replies : " Scorn and defiance ; slight regard, contempt, And any thing that may not misbecome The mighty sender, doth he prize you at," adding, that if his father—Charles—does not grant all Henry's demands, and " Sweeten the bitter mock you sent his majesty," he will " call him to so hot an answer of it, That caves and womby vaultages of France Shall chide your trespass and return your mock In second accent of his ordinance," but the Dauphin replies that he is opposed to his father granting any of Henry's demands, desiring nothing but war with England. Again gravely warning him that he will bitterly regret his jest, for Henry will " make your Paris Louvre shake for it," the ambassadors depart, Exeter requesting the French king to give an answer

> with all speed, lest that our king
> Come here himself to question our delay ;
> For he is footed in this land already,

and Charles replies that they will soon be " dispatch'd with fair conditions " : for " A night is but small breath and little pause To answer matters of this consequence." The scene closes with a flourish of trumpets. Cf. *Extract* 4 from Holinshed.

The *Prologue* or *Chorus* which precedes the third Act describes the crossing over from Southampton of Henry's army ; his landing with thirty thousand men at Caux at the mouth of the River Seine, and his march upon Harfleur. In order, however, to raise the mind of the audience to the highest pitch of imagination, the *Chorus* alludes to the supposition of the return of the ambassadors from the French court, to tell the king of England " that the French king doth offer him Katharine his daughter ; and with her, to dowry, Some petty and unprofitable dukedoms " : but the proposal is not acceptable to Henry : " the offer likes not," for the " nimble gunner With linstock now the devilish cannon touches." There is an alarum and the discharge of chambers, and " down goes all before them," and another appeal is made to the audience to " Still be kind, And eche out our performance with your mind."

The first scene of the third Act is laid before the walls of Harfleur, which town the English are besieging. A breach having been made in the walls, Henry—in a resolute speech, which shows him a man of courage in the hour of danger—appeals to his soldiers to again assail the breach they have made, or close it up with their dead :

> Once more unto the breach, dear friends, once more,
> Or close the wall up with our English dead.
> . . . .
> And you, good yeomen,
> Whose limbs were made in England, show us here
> The mettle of your pasture ; let us swear
> That you are worth your breeding ; which I doubt not ;
> . . . . . .
> The game 's afoot :
> Follow your spirit ; and upon this charge
> Cry, " God for Harry, England, and Saint George ! "

Cf. *Extract* 5 from Holinshed.

We are still before Harfleur in the next scene. It opens with the entry of **Nym**, Bardolph, Pistol and Boy. Bardolph urges Nym on to the breach :

> On, on, on, on, on ! to the breach, to the
> breach !

but Nym tells him it is " too hot " :

> Pray thee, corporal, stay : the knocks are too
> hot ; and for mine own part, I have not a case of
> lives : the humour of it is too hot, that is the
> very plain-song of it.

This causes Pistol to break out in song :

> Knocks go and come, God's vassals drop and die ;
> And sword and shield,
> In bloody field,
> Doth win immortal fame.

while the boy wishes himself in " some alehouse in London ! " as he " would give all his fame for a pot of ale, and safety," to which Pistol adds : " And I."

Fluellen, a peppery Welsh captain enters in a rage, and attempts to drive the men to the attack :

> Up to the breach, you dogs ! avaunt, you cullions !

but Pistol asks for mercy :

> Be merciful, great duke, to men of mould !
> Abate thy rage, abate thy manly rage ;
> Abate thy rage, great duke !
> Good bawcock, bate thy rage ; use lenity, sweet chuck !

to which Nym adds :

> These be good humours ! your honour wins bad
> humours.

After they have gone, the boy makes comments on them, describing them as " three swashers." " As young as I am, I have observed these three swashers. I am boy to them all three, but all they three, though they would serve me, could not be man to me ; for indeed three such antics do not amount to a man." He describes Bardolph as " white-livered and red-faced ; by the means whereof a' faces it out, but fights not." Pistol " hath a killing tongue and a quiet sword ; by the means whereof a' breaks words, and keeps whole weapons." Nym " scorns to say his prayers, lest a' should be thought a coward : but his few bad words are matched with as few good deeds ; for a' never broke any man's head but his own, and that was against a post when he was drunk. Nym and Bardolph are sworn brothers in filching, and in Calais they stole a fire-shovel. All three are rogues, who " would have him as familiar with men's pockets as their gloves or their handkerchers," but their " villany goes against his weak stomach," and therefore he must leave them.

Fluellen, followed by Gower—an English officer—re-enters, and is ordered by the latter to proceed to the siege-mines, as the Duke of Gloucester wishes to speak with him. The Welshman replies that he will not go, as the " mines is not according to the disciplines of the war," but Gower reminds him that the siege is being conducted by the Duke under the direction of a very valiant Irish gentleman, named Macmorris. Fluellen describes Macmorris as " an ass " who has no " more directions in the true disciplines of the wars, . . . than a puppy-dog." At this point, Macmorris enters, accompanied by Captain Jamy, a hot-headed Scotchman, who, according to Fluellen is a " marvellous falorous gentleman, . . . and of great expedition and knowledge in th' aunchient wars, upon my particular knowledge of his directions : by Cheshu, he will maintain his argument as well as any military man in the world, in the disciplines of the pristine wars of the Romans." A colloquy on the " disciplines of the wars " follows, in which the nationality of the captains is evidenced by their oddities of speech. Asked by Gower if he has quitted the mines, the Irishman replies : " By Chrish, la ! tish all done : the work ish give over, the trumpet sound the retreat. By my hand, I swear, and my father's soul, the work ish ill done ; it ish give over : I would have blowed up the town, so Chrish save me, la ! in an hour : O ! tish ill done, tish ill done ; by my hand, tish ill done." " Captain Macmorris," enjoins the Welshman, " I beseech you now, will you voutsafe me, look you, a few disputations with you, as partly touching or concerning the disciplines of the war, the Roman wars, in the way of argument, look you, and friendly communication ; partly to satisfy my opinion, and partly for the satisfaction, look you, of my mind, as touching the direction of the military discipline : that is the point," in which argument, the Scotchman will, with their permission, answer them, or interpose with his ideas, as opportunity affords : " It sall be vary gud, gud feith, gud captains bath : and I sall quit you with gud leve, as I may pick occasion ; that sall I, marry, " but the Irishman replies that it is not the time to argue, for the " day is hot, and the weather, and the wars, and the dukes : it is no time to discourse." Fluellen is however so persistent in endeavouring to instruct Macmorris in the " true disciplines of the wars," and their argument becomes so heated that they are about to come to blows, when a trumpet in the town sounds a parley :

> *Gower.* The town sounds a parley.
> *Flu.* Captain Macmorris, when there is more better
> opportunity to be required, look you, I will be so
> bold as to tell you I know the disciplines of
> war ; and there is an end.

The third scene is enacted before the gates of Harfleur. A parley having been sounded, the Governor of Harfleur and some citizens appear on the walls. In a resolute speech [III. iii. 1–43] Henry demands the surrender of the city, offering the town mercy if it submits, but threatening in case of refusal, to lay it waste :

> How yet resolves the governor of the town ?
> This is the latest parle we will admit :
> Therefore to our best mercy give yourselves ;
> Or like to men proud of destruction
> Defy us to our worst : for, as I am a soldier,
> A name that in my thoughts becomes me best,
> If I begin the battery once again,
> I will not leave the half-achieved Harfleur
> Till in her ashes she lie buried.
>
> .   .   .   .   .
>
>   Therefore, you men of Harfleur,
> Take pity of your town and of your people,
> Whiles yet my soldiers are in my command ;
>
> .   .   .   .   .
>
> What say you ? will you yield, and this avoid ?
> Or, guilty in defence, be thus destroy'd ?

To this the Governor replies, that, owing to the failure of the Dauphin to come to their relief, they will throw themselves on Henry's mercy :

> Our expectation hath this day an end.
> The Dauphin, whom of succours we entreated,
> Returns us that his powers are yet not ready
> To raise so great a siege. Therefore, great king,
> We yield our town and lives to thy soft mercy.
> Enter our gates ; dispose of us and ours ;
> For we no longer are defensible.

Henry therefore bids that the gates of the city be opened, and orders the Duke of Exeter to enter, and " fortify it strongly 'gainst the French " : and to exercise clemency to the citizens :

> Open your gates ! Come, uncle Exeter,
> Go you and enter Harfleur ; there remain,
> And fortify it strongly 'gainst the French :
> Use mercy to them all.

Henry then announces that after one night's rest in Harfleur he will march for Calais

>   For us, dear uncle,
> The winter coming on and sickness growing
> Upon our soldiers, we will retire to Calais.
> To-night in Harfleur will we be your guest ;
> To-morrow for the march are we addrest.

The scene ends as the king and his train enter the town amid a fanfare of trumpets. Cf. *Extract* 6 from Holinshed.

The fourth scene is a Room in the French King's palace at Rouen. It shows us the Princess Katharine, daughter of the French king, taking lessons in English. As the question of a marriage between the king of England and herself has already been mooted in the *Prologue* or *Chorus* to this Act, this scene incidentally prepares us for the conversation between Henry and Katharine in Act V., Scene ii. It opens with Katharine questioning Alice—her maid—who has been in England, as to her knowledge of the English Language : " Alice, tu as esté en Angleterre, et tu parles bien le langage." [Alice, you have been in England, and are familiar with the language.]

On Alice admitting that she has an elementary knowledge of English : " Un peu, madame " [A little, madam,] the princess bids her give her a little instruction : " Je te prie, m'enseignez ; il faut que j'apprenne à parler." [I beg you, teach me ; I must learn to speak it,] asking the English for ' hand ' ' fingers ' ' nails ' ' arm ' ' elbow ' ' neck ' ' chin.' These she repeats after Alice several times more or less accurately, which makes Alice observe : " Sauf vostre honneur, en vérité, vous prononcez les mots aussi droict que les natifs d'Angleterre " [Pardon me, but truly, you pronounce the words as correctly as the English themselves] to which Katharine replies : " Je ne doute point d'apprendre par la grace de Dieu, et en peu de temps " [I have no doubt at all of being able to learn, by the Grace of God, and in a short time.] " N'avez vous déjà oublié ce que je vous ay enseigné ? [Have you not already forgotten what I have taught you ?] observes Alice. " Non, je reciteray à vous promptement," [No, I will recite to you promptly] replies Katharine. " De hand, de fingre, de mails,—" De nails, madame," rejoins Alice. " De nails, de arme, de ilbow," commences Katharine, and Alice observes : " Sauf vostre honneur, d'elbow," [Pardon me, the elbow.] " Ainsi dis je " ; [So I said] replies Katharine, " d'elbow, de nick, et de sin." Asking the English for " le pied et la robe [the foot and the gown] the princess again recites her lesson all together, which Alice considers " excellent " and the scene closes with Katharine remarking : C'est assez pour une fois : allons nous à diner. [That is enough for now : let's go to dinner.]

We are still in the French King's Palace at Rouen in the next scene. It shows us the French king and his nobles discussing the situation, Charles remarking that " 'Tis certain " that the English have already " pass'd the river Somme." The Constable opines that if they do not intend to arrest Henry's march it is better for them not to " live in France," but " quit all, And give their vineyards to a barbarous people." " O Dieu vivant ! " [O Living God] exclaims the Dauphin, shall a " few sprays of us . . . Spirt up so suddenly into the clouds " and look down upon them with scorn, while the Duke of Bourbon describes the English as " Normans, but bastard Normans, Norman bastards ! " and exclaiming " Mort de ma vie ! [Death of my life] declares that if Henry is allowed to march along unmolested he will " sell his dukedom, To buy a slobbery and a dirty farm In that nook-shotten isle of Albion." Exclaiming " Dieu de batailles ! " [God of battles] the Constable proceeds to pour ridicule upon Henry and his army, wondering where the English, who live in a " climate raw and dull " and drink " barley broth " get " their mettle from," while the French who are " spirited with wine Seem frosty," to which the Dauphin adds that " their women folk laugh at them," and tell them that their " mettle is bred out," and urges the king to raise an army to intercept the English forces :

Con.   O, for honour of our land,
Let us not hang, like roping icicles
Upon our houses' thatch, whiles a more frosty people
Sweat drops of gallant youth in our rich fields !
Poor we may call them in their native lords.
Dau.   By faith and honour,
Our madams mock at us, and plainly say
Our mettle is bred out ; and they will give
Their bodies to the lust of English youth
To new-store France with bastard warriors.

Encouraged by these remarks, Charles bids Montjoy, the French Herald carry to Henry a challenge :

Where is Montjoy the herald ? speed him hence :
Let him greet England with our sharp defiance,

afterwards ordering " High dukes, great princes, barons, lords, and knights " to intercept Henry in his passage to Calais, and bring him a prisoner to Rouen :

> Bar Harry England, that sweeps through our land
> With pennons painted in the blood of Harfleur :
>   .   .   .   .   .   .
> Go down upon him, you have power enough,
> And in a captive chariot into Roan
> Bring him our prisoner.

Elated at the French king's exhortation, the Constable remarks that he is sorry Henry's " numbers are so few, His soldiers sick and famish'd in their march," that on seeing such a large French force his courage will fail him, and he will offer to pay a large sum as a ransom :

> Sorry am I his numbers are so few,
> His soldiers sick and famish'd in their march,
> For I am sure when he shall see our army
> He 'll drop his heart into the sink of fear,
> And for achievement offer us his ransom.

Charles therefore bids the Constable hasten on the French Herald and ask the English king what ransom he is prepared to offer, and then turning to the Dauphin orders him to remain at Rouen :

> Therefore, lord constable, haste on Montjoy,
> And let him say to England that we send
> To know what willing ransom he will give.
> Prince Dauphin, you shall stay with us in Roan,

" Not so, I do beseech your majesty," rejoins the Dauphin, but the king insists upon his staying at home, and then turning to his nobles, charges the " lord constable and princes all," to " quickly bring him news of Henry's defeat. Cf. *Extract 7* from Holinshed.

The sixth scene shows us the English Camp in Picardy. Henry, as intimated at the end of Act III., Scene iii., pressed on towards Calais, which at this time was an English fortified town, and arriving at the river Somme found the fords in the possession of the enemy, who had broken down the bridges. Marching along the river, an unguarded spot was discovered at Nesle, and Henry, flinging his army rapidly across the stream, marched to Blangy, beyond which was the village of Agincourt, where a French army, estimated at 50,000 strong, was encamped to intercept the English forces. At Blangy the French offered a fierce resistance, but being driven back the English forces took charge of the bridge over the river Ternoise until the remainder of the army had crossed.

The scene opens with the entry of Gower and Fluellen who are loud in praise of the Duke of Exeter for his bravery in guarding the bridge over the river Ternoise at Blangy, Fluellen describing the Duke as " magnanimous as Agamemnon." With the Duke was Pistol, whom Fluellen refers to as " valiant a man as Mark Antony," and yet " a man of no estimation in the world." At this point Pistol enters, and appeals to Fluellen to use his influence with the Duke of Exeter to pardon Bardolph, who has been condemned to be hanged for stealing a pax from a church :

> Bardolph, a soldier firm and sound of heart,
> And of buxom valour, hath, by cruel fate
> And giddy Fortune's furious fickle wheel,
> That goddess blind,
> That stands upon the rolling restless stone—
>   :   :   :   .   .   ·   .

For he hath stol'n a pax, and hanged must a' be.
A damned death !
Let gallows gape for dog, let man go free
And let not hemp his wind-pipe suffocate.
But Exeter hath given the doom of death
For pax of little price.
Therefore, go speak ; the duke will hear thy voice ;
And let not Bardolph's vital thread be cut
With edge of penny cord and vile reproach :
Speak, captain, for his life, and I will thee requite.

but Fluellen will not listen to any meddling with military discipline, and remarks : " If he were my brother, I would desire the duke to use his good pleasure and put him to execution ; for discipline ought to be used," to which Pistol—in a violent temper—replies : " Die and be damn'd ; and figo for thy friendship ! " and forthwith departs. Having gone, Gower tells Fluellen that Pistol is " an arrant counterfeit rascal : . . . a bawd, a cut-purse, . . . a gull, a fool, a rogue, that now and then goes to the wars to grace himself at his return into London under the form of a soldier," for such fellows make themselves intimately acquainted with the names of the great generals, and learn off by heart where great deeds were performed, who were shot and disgraced, and are well conversant in all the " phrase of war, which they trick up with new-tuned oaths."

A drum sounds, heralding the approach of the king, who on entering enquires the news " from the bridge," only to learn that Exeter " very gallantly maintains the pridge," and " hath lost never a man but one that is like to be executed for robbing a church ; one Bardolph, if your majesty know the man : his face is all bubukles, and whelks, and knobs, and flames o' fire ; and his lips blows at his nose, and it is like a coal of fire, sometimes plue and sometimes red ; but his nose is executed, and his fire 's out." Henry who had given orders that the villages were not to be plundered, approves of the punishment meted out to Bardolph, and repeats his order to treat the inhabitants with consideration, and to take nothing but that for which they pay, " for when lenity and cruelty play for a kingdom, the gentler gamester is the soonest winner."

A tucket sounds, announcing the arrival of Montjoy, the French herald. " You know me by my habit," remarks Montjoy as he enters. " Well then I know thee : what shall I know of thee ? " rejoins Henry. " My master's mind," replies Montjoy. " Unfold it," whereupon Montjoy delivers the French king's message :

" Thus says my king : Say thou to Harry of England : Though we seemed dead, we did but sleep : advantage is a better soldier than rashness. Tell him we could have rebuked him at Harfleur, but that we thought not good to bruise an injury till it were full ripe : now we speak upon our cue, and our voice is imperial : England shall repent his folly, see his weakness, and admire our sufferance. Bid him therefore consider of his ransom : which must proportion the losses we have borne, the subjects we have lost, the disgrace we have digested ; which in weight to re-answer, his pettiness would bow under."

" What is thy name ? " asks Henry, " I know thy quality." " Montjoy," replies the herald. " Thou doest thy office fairly," remarks Henry, but " Turn thee back, And tell thy king I do not seek him now, But could be willing to march on to Calais Without impeachment " ; for I have no ransom to offer by my " frail and worthless trunk." Giving the herald a reward " for his labour " Henry—although his army is weakened on account of sickness—warns him that if he is hindered in his march to Calais he will dye the soil of France with French blood : " If we be hinder'd, We shall your tawny ground with your red blood Discolour." " I hope they will not come upon us now," remarks the Duke of Gloucester after Montjoy has departed, to which Henry replies they are in the hands of God and will march to the bridge and camp beyond the river :

> We are in God's hands, brother, not in theirs.
> March to the bridge ; it now draws toward night :
> Beyond the river we 'll encamp ourselves,
> And on to-morrow bid them march away.

Cf. *Extract* 8 from Holinshed.

The final scene of this Act is descriptive of the French Camp near Agincourt on the eve of the battle, where we see the Constable of France, the Dauphin and other nobles bragging in anticipation of victory over the English forces. The Constable prides himself that he has the " best armour in the world," and longs for the breaking of the day, while the Duke of Orleans, although agreeing that the Constable has an " excellent armour " considers that his " horse should have his due," adding " Will it never be morning ? " On the other hand, the Dauphin who bewails the length of the night, thinks that his steed outrivals those of the other nobles : " I will not change my horse " he remarks, " with any that treads but on four pasterns. . . . When I bestride him, I soar, I am a hawk : he trots the air ; the earth sings when he touches it ; the basest horn of his hoof is more musical than the pipe of Hermes. . . . It is a beast for Perseus : he is pure air and fire ; and the dull elements of earth and water never appear in him, . . . he is indeed a horse : and all other jades you may call beasts," boasting that he " once writ a sonnet in his praise and began thus : ' Wonder of nature,' "—So confident is the Dauphin of victory that he brags he will " trot to-morrow a mile, and his way will be paved with English faces," after which he departs, exclaiming : " 'Tis midnight : I 'll go arm myself." After he has gone, Orleans remarks : " The Dauphin longs for morning," to which Rambures adds : " He longs to eat the English," but the Constable, who has no faith in the Dauphin, observes that " he will eat all the English he kills," but Orleans tells him to " Give the devil his due," only to receive the answer that " A fool's bolt is soon shot." A messenger enters with the news that the " English lie within fifteen hundred paces of the French tents." " Alas ! poor Harry of England, he longs not for the dawning as we do," is the Constable's remark, " If the English had any apprehension, they would run away," while Orleans describes Henry as a " wretched and peevish fellow, to mope with his fat-brained followers so far out of his knowledge," but Rambures reminds them that the English are an indomitable breed who never run away, and like mastiffs, are of unmatchable courage. They are " Foolish curs ! " observes Orleans, " that run winking into the mouth of a Russian bear and have their heads crushed like rotten apples. You may as well say that's a valiant flea that dare eat his breakfast on the lip of a lion," to which the Constable rejoins : " Exactly ! give them great meals of beef and iron and steel, and they will eat like wolves and fight like devils," and the nobles depart with a self-confidence that the " English are shrewdly out of beef," and the scene closes with Orleans observing :

> It is now two o'clock : but, let me see, by ten
> We shall have each a hundred Englishmen.

Cf. *Extract* 9 from Holinshed.

The *Prologue* or *Chorus* to Act IV describes the night before the great battle. The two armies are lying fifteen hundred paces apart. Through the stilly night the hum of either army makes a low sound ; the fixed sentinels receive in a whisper their commands ; from the glow of the camp-fires each army can discern the other's faces ; the neighing of the horses pierce the night's dull air ; the busy hammers of the armourers denote the " dreadful note of preparation " ; while the " crowing cocks " and the " tolling of the clocks " announce the " third hour of the drowsy morning " :

> From camp to camp through the foul womb of night
> The hum of either army stilly sounds,
> That the fix'd sentinels almost receive
> The secret whispers of each other's watch :
> Fire answers fire, and through their paly flames
> Each battle sees the other's umber'd face ;
> Steed threatens steed, in high and boastful neighs
> Piercing the night's dull air ; and from the tents
> The armourers, accomplishing the knights,
> With busy hammers closing rivets up,
> Give dreadful note of preparation.

The French—so confident are they of victory—play at dice for the English prisoners :

> Proud of their numbers, and secure in soul,
> The confident and over-lusty French
> Do the low-rated English play at dice ;

The English sit patiently by their watch-fires, and sadly await the dawn of day, while Henry goes round the tents, his presence filling his men with courage :

> O ! now, who will be-
> hold
> The royal captain of this ruin'd band
> Walking from watch to watch, from tent to tent,
> Let him cry " Praise and glory on his head ! "
> For forth he goes and visits all his host,
> Bids them good-morrow with a modest smile,
> And calls them brothers, friends and country-
> men.

The ' Chorus ' closes with another apology for attempting to represent on the stage the great battle :

> Where, O for pity ! we shall much disgrace
> With four or five most vile and ragged foils,
> Right ill-dispos'd in brawl ridiculous,
> The name of Agincourt,

and another appeal to the imagination of the audience to

> sit and see ;
> Minding true things by what their mockeries be.

Cf. *Extract* 10 from Holinshed.

Scene one opens in the English camp at Agincourt, and is a striking contrast to the arrogance and bragging of the French as portrayed in Act III., Scene vii. Henry, apprehensive of his army's peril confesses that they are in great danger, but the greater the danger the greater must be their courage. Meeting Sir Thomas Erpingham—an old soldier—Henry addresses him : " Good morrow, old Sir Thomas Erpingham : A good soft pillow for that good white head Were better than a churlish turf of France," to which Erpingham replies : " Not so, my liege : this lodging likes me better, Since I may say ' Now lie I like a king.' " Borrowing of Erpingham an old cloak to disguise himself, Erpingham asks whether he shall attend on him, but Henry refuses his company, remarking : " I and my bosom must debate awhile." " The Lord in heaven bless thee, noble Harry ! " is Erpingham's remark as the king departs, who mutters to himself " God-a-mercy, old heart ! thou speak'st cheer-fully." In disguise Henry sallies forth in the camp, and immediately encounters Pistol, who, not recognising the king, challenges him : " Qui va là ? " [Who goes there ?] demands Pistol. " A friend," replies Henry. " Discuss unto me ; art thou officer ? Or art thou base, common and popular ? " " I am a gentleman of a company," replies the king, and " What art you ? " " As good a gentleman as the emperor," answers Pistol. " Then you are a better than the king," adds Henry, to which Pistol makes the insulting remark : " The king 's a bawcock, and a heart of gold, A lad of life, an imp of fame ; Of parents good, of fist most valiant : I kiss his dirty shoe, and from heart-string I love the lovely bully. What is thy name ? " " Harry le Roy," is the reply. " Le Roy ! a Cornish name : art thou of Cornish crew ? " enquires Pistol. " No, I am a Welshman," replies Henry. " Know'st thou Fluellen." " Yes." Then " Tell him I 'll knock his leek about his pate Upon Saint Davy's day." " Do not you wear your dagger in your cap that day, lest he knock that about yours," is Henry's rejoinder. A moment later Fluellen and Gower pass across the scene, the former remarking, in reply to Gower, who mentions how " very loud the enemy have been all night," that " If the enemy is an ass and a fool and a prating coxcomb," there is no need for the English to copy their example, and Gower, in whom Henry confesses there is much " care and valour " although it may be a " little out of fashion " promises to " speak lower." They are followed by three soldiers—Bates, Court and Williams. Court draws attention to the dawn which is just breaking, Bates opines that they have " no desire for the approach of day," while Williams expresses his opinion that " they will not live to see the end of it." On seeing the king, Williams challenges him, demanding to know under what captain he serves. " Under Sir Thomas Erpingham," is Henry's reply, to which Williams makes answer : " A good old commander and a most kind gentleman." The three soldiers then engage in conversation with the king. Bates deplores the critical position of the English army, and although Henry " may show what outward courage he will," he believes " cold a night as 'tis, he could wish himself in Thames up to the neck, and so I would he were, and I by him, at all adventures, so we were quit here," yet he is determined to fight lustily for him, while Williams speaks of the king's responsi-bilities for the suffering of his troops, whose orders compel them to fight in quarrels with which they are not concerned, at the same time they feel bound to obey their rightful sovereign. " I myself heard the king say he would not be ransomed," remarks Henry, to which Williams answers : " Ay, he said so, to make us fight cheer-fully," and when " our throats are cut he may be ransomed, and we ne'er the wiser." This leads to sharp words between Henry and Williams, and on the latter remarking : " Let it be a quarrel between us, if you live," Henry accepts a challenge from Williams to fight it out should they survive the battle, each agreeing to wear in his bonnet his adversary's glove so that when they met again they would recognise each other. " If ever thou come to me and say after to-morrow, ' This is my glove,' by this hand I will take thee a box on the ear," says Williams, to which Henry replies : " If ever I live to see it, I will challenge it."

The soldiers having gone, Henry soliloquises on the worthlessness of " idol cere-mony " with all its pomp and glory which surround a monarch, ceremony which when " laid in bed majestical, cannot sleep so soundly as the wretched slave." [*See* IV. i. 236–290.] This soliloquy—which is considered one of the most striking passages in the play—ending as it does with the words :

> but in gross brain little wots
> What watch the king keeps to maintain the peace,
> Whose hours the peasant best advantages,

is a paraphrase on the well-known and often-quoted passage : " Then happy low, lie down ! Uneasy lies the head that wears a crown," the concluding lines of the soliloquy uttered by Henry IV. in the *Second Part of King Henry the Fourth*, III. i. 4–31. This soliloquy is interrupted by the entry of Sir Thomas Erpingham, who tells the king that his nobles being " jealous of his absence " are seeking him throughout the camp. Henry therefore bids the " good old knight " collect them all together at his tent, and all being assembled, Henry in a fervent prayer prays that the " God of Battles will steel his soldiers' hearts," that they will not be possessed with fear on account of the overwhelming numbers against them :

> O God of battles ! steel my soldiers' hearts ;
> Possess them not with fear ; take from them now
> The sense of reckoning, if the opposed numbers
> Pluck their hearts from them,

and contemplating that divine retribution must be exacted for the wrongful deposition of Richard the Second by his father Henry the Fourth, beseeches heaven not to visit upon him the sin by which his father " compassed the crown " :

> Not to-day, O Lord !
> O ! not to-day, think not upon the fault
> My father made in compassing the crown,

for " Richard's body I have interred new," and wept over it many contrite tears " Than from it issued forced drops of blood. Five hundred poor I have in yearly pay, Who twice a day their wither'd hands hold up Toward heaven, to pardon blood " ; and " More will I do ; Though all that I can do is nothing worth, Since that my penitence comes after all, Imploring pardon."

Gloucester enters. " My liege ! " he exclaims, to which Henry rejoins : " My brother Gloucester's voice ! Ay " ; and remarking :

> I know thy errand, I will go with thee :
> The day, my friends, and all things stay for me,

the royal brothers quit the scene. Cf. *Extract* 10 from Holinshed.

We are back again in the French camp in scene two. It opens with the Duke of Orleans and the Dauphin again boasting of their armour and horses :

Orl. The sun doth gild our armour ; up, my lords !
Dau. Montez à cheval ! [Mount on horseback !] My horse ! valet ! lacquais ! [lackey], ha !
Orl. O brave spirit !
Dau. Via ! les eaux et la terre ! [Away ! water and earth !]
Orl. Rien puis ? l'air et le feu ! [Nothing more ? Air and fire !]
Dau. Ciel ! [Heaven !] cousin Orleans.

On the entry of the Constable who remarks : " Hark, how our steeds for present service neigh ! " the Dauphin—who is in a state of excitement—suggests that they make " incisions " in the hides of their horses so that they can sprinkle the English with their hot blood, but Rambures asks him whether he would have the English weep their horses' blood ? " in which case the French would not behold the " natural tears " of the English.

A messenger enters with the news that the English forces are " embattail'd " and the Constable, after exclaiming, " To horse, you gallant princes ! straight to horse ! " describes the English as a " poor and starved band," not having sufficient " blood in all their sickly veins," to wield a cutlass, and that " if blown upon, The vapour of their (French) valour would o'erturn them," adding that the approach of the French forces would so frighten them that they would surrender.   The Constable's speech is interrupted by the entry of Grandpré, who after enquiring " why they stay so long," contemptuously refers to the English army as " Yon island carrions," whose " steeds stand with drooped heads," and their " horsemen sit like fixed candlesticks, With torch-staves in their hand," while " knavish crows," hover impatiently over them only waiting to pick their bones.   To this the Constable adds that the English " have said their prayers," and only " wait for death," while the Dauphin—so sure is he of victory—suggests that they send them " dinners and fresh suits of armour, And give their fasting horses provender," and " after fight with them."   But the Constable, waving his hand in triumph, gives the order " On to the field ! " for :

> The sun is high, and we outwear the day.

Cf. *Extract* 11 from Holinshed.

We return to the English camp in the third scene.   The king, in order to infuse valour and courage into his army, rides forth into the camp, and inspires them with his own courage.   The English lords, apprehensive of the overwhelming force against them, realise that a determined stand will have to be made to secure victory, the French army being estimated to be five times greater than the English army.   "There's five to one ; besides, they all are fresh," is Exeter's comment.   " God's arm strike with us ! " exclaims the Earl of Salisbury, " 'tis a fearful odds."   Not expecting to survive the battle they take solemn farewell of one another :

> God be wi' you, princes all ; I 'll to my charge :
> If we no more meet till we meet in heaven,
> Then, joyfully, my noble Lord of Bedford,
> My dear Lord Gloucester, and my good Lord Exeter,
> And my kind kinsman, warriors all, adieu !

" Farewell, good Salisbury ; and good luck go with thee ! " is Bedford's reply, to which Exeter adds : " Farewell, kind lord.   Fight valiantly to-day " :

> And yet I do thee wrong to mind thee of it,
> For thou art fram'd of the firm truth of valour.

On the departure of Salisbury, Westmoreland exclaims : " O ! that we now had here But one ten thousand of those men in England That do no work to-day," just as the king appears.   " What 's he that wishes so ? " asks Henry.   " I would not have one man more," for if we are to die " we are enow To do our country's loss " ; but should we prove victorious, the " fewer men, the greater share of honour.   God's will !   I pray thee, wish not one man more."   Exclaiming again :

> No, faith, my coz, wish not a man from England :
> ' God's peace ! '   I would not lose so great an honour
> As one man more, methinks, would share with me,
> For the best hope I have.   O ! do not wish one more :

Henry orders it to be proclaimed through the camp that all who are afraid to fight can return home with their passport and their pay :

> Rather proclaim it, Westmoreland, through my host,
> That he which hath no stomach to this fight,
> Let him depart ; his passport shall be made,
> And crowns for convoy put into his purse :

proudly declaring that

> We would not die in that man's company
> That fears his fellowship to die with us.
> This day is call'd the feast of Crispian :
> He that outlives this day, and comes safe home,
> Will stand a tip-toe when this day is nam'd,
> And rouse him at the name of Crispian,

adding, that in generations to come, Englishmen would speak with pride of this encounter, and that their names would become " household words " :

> Then shall our names,
> Familiar in his mouth as household words,
> Harry the king, Bedford and Exeter,
> Warwick and Talbot, Salisbury and Gloucester,
> Be in their flowing cups freshly remember'd.
> This story shall the good man teach his son ;
> And Crispin Crispian shall ne'er go by,
> From this day to the ending of the world,
> But we in it shall be remembered ;
> We few, we happy few, we band of brothers ;
> For he to-day that sheds his blood with me
> Shall be my brother ; be he ne'er so vile
> This day shall gentle his condition :
> And gentlemen in England now a-bed
> Shall think themselves accurs'd they were not here,
> And hold their manhoods cheap whiles any speaks
> That fought with us upon Saint Crispin's day.

This speech of the king's, which so aroused the enthusiasm of his army, [*see* **IV. iii.** 18–67] is considered to be one of the most inspiring and intrepid exhortations in the English language, breathing as it does the spirit of comradeship, and gives the key-note as to why the English forces in France routed an army so many times their superior in point of numbers.

Salisbury re-enters, and announces that the French are " bravely in their battles set," and are ready to charge. " All things are ready, if our minds be so," rejoins Henry, whereupon Westmoreland expresses the hope that every man whose " mind is backward " will perish. " Thou dost not wish more help from England, coz ? " is Henry's query, and Westmoreland—upon whom the king's words have made a deep impression—wishes it were possible for " he and the king alone, Without more help, could fight this royal battle ! " · Henry is greatly pleased with the words of Westmoreland :

> Why, now thou hast unwish'd five thousand men ;
> Which likes me better than to wish us one.
> You know your places : God be with you all !

Almost immediately a Tucket sounds, and Montjoy the French herald re-appears, to give Henry another chance of ransom :

> Once more I come to know of thee, King Harry,
> If for thy ransom thou wilt now compound,
> Before thy most assured overthrow :
> For certainly thou art so near the gulf
> Thou needs must be englutted. Besides, in mercy,
> The constable desires thee thou wilt mind
> Thy followers of repentance ; that their souls
> May make a peaceful and a sweet retire
> From off these fields, where, wretches, their poor
> bodies
> Must lie and fester.

" Who hath sent thee now ? " demands Henry, and being told " The Constable of France," Henry, in a dignified speech [*see* IV. iii. 90–125], which again shows him to be a man of courage in the hour of danger, again rejects the terms, and reminds the herald of the man who was killed by the beast whose skin he sold while the beast was still alive :

> I pray thee, bear my former answer back :
> Bid them achieve me and then sell my bones.
> Good God ! why should they mock poor fellows thus ?
> The man that once did sell the lion's skin
> While the beast liv'd, was kill'd with hunting him.
>
> .   .   .   .   .
>
> Herald, save thou thy labour,
> Come thou no more for ransom, gentle herald :
> They shall have none, I swear, but these my joints ;
> Which if they have as I will leave 'em them,
> Shall yield them little, tell the constable.

" I shall, King Harry. And so fare thee well : Thou never shalt hear herald any more," is the herald's reply, only to receive from Henry the apt and prophetic retort : " I fear thou wilt once more come again for a ransom."

The Duke of York—called in *Richard the Second*, Aumerle—now enters, and " humbly begs " to lead the vanguard :

> My lord, most humbly on my knee I beg
> The leading of the vaward,

a request which is readily granted by Henry : " Take it, brave York," and again commending the battle to God, the king gives orders for the English army to advance :

> Now, soldiers, march away :
> And how thou pleasest, God, dispose the day !

Cf. *Extracts* 12 and 13 from Holinshed.

Scenes four, five and six are descriptive of the great battle of Agincourt, fought on the 25th of October, 1415, when the French army, estimated at 50,000 strong, was utterly defeated by the English forces, numbering approximately 9,000.

Scene four opens with Pistol taking captive a French soldier. " Yield, cur ! " demands Pistol, to which the French soldier remarks : " Je pense que vous estes gentilhomme de bonne qualité," [I think you are a gentleman of good quality] and Pistol being under the impression that the Frenchman himself is a man of rank, demands his name and quality : " Qualtitie calmie custure me ! [Quality call you me ?] Art thou a gentleman ? What is thy name ? discuss." The French soldier asks for mercy : " O, prenez misericorde ! ayez pitié de moy ! " [Oh, take pity ! Have pity on me !] and Pistol—who is not familiar with the French language—answers : " Moy shall not serve ; I will have forty moys ; Or I will fetch thy rim out of thy throat In drops of crimson blood. " Est il impossible d'eschapper la force de ton bras ? [Is it impossible to escape the power of your arm ?] asks the cowardly Frenchman, and Pistol retorts : " Brass, cur ! Thou damned and luxurious mountain goat, Offer'st me brass ? Upon the Frenchman again pleading for mercy, Pistol instructs the boy—who acts as interpreter—to ask this " slave in French " what his name is, and on the boy replying : " Master Fer," Pistol retorts : " Master Fer ! I 'll fer him, and firk him, and ferret him. Bid him prepare, for I will cut his throat. Que dit-il, monsieur ? [What does he say, sir ?] inquires the Frenchman, and the boy tells him that Pistol intends to cut his throat : " Il me commande à vous dire que vous faites vous prest ; car ce soldat icy est disposé tout à cette heure de couper vostre gorge," [He commands me to tell you to make ready, for this soldier is disposed to cut your throat immediately.] The French soldier again pleads for mercy, promising a ransom of two hundred crowns : " O ! ye vous supplie pour l'amour de Dieu, me pardonner. Je suis gentilhomme de bonne maison : gardez ma vie, et je vous donneray deux cents escus. [Oh, I beg of you, for the love of God, to pardon me. I am a gentle-man of good family, Spare my life, and I will give you two hundred crowns.] The matter being settled : " Tell him my fury shall abate, and I The crowns will take," the Frenchman in gratitude replies : " Sur mes genoux je vous donne mille remercie-mens ; et je m'estime heureux que je suis tombé entre les mains d'un chevalier, je pense, le plus brave, vaillant, et tres-distingué seigneur d'Angleterre." [On my knee I give you thousand thanks, and I feel myself happy in the thought that I have fallen in the hands of a knight whom I regard as the most bravest, the most valiant, and the most distinguished nobleman of England,] and the boy orders the Frenchman to " Suivez vous le grand capitaine," [Follow the great captain.] Pistol and the French soldier having taken their departure, the boy soliloquises that he never did " know so full a voice issue from so empty a heart : but the saying is true, ' The empty vessel makes the greatest sound.' Bardolph and Nym had ten times more valour than this roaring devil i' the old play, that every one may pare his nails with a wooden dagger ; and they are both hanged ; and so would this be if he durst steal any thing adventurously," and expresses his regret that as the baggage in the English camp is in an exposed condition he must remain to guard it : " I must stay with the lackeys, with the luggage of our camp : the French might have a good prey of us if he knew of it ; for there is none to guard it but boys."

We are in another part of the battlefield in scene five, where we find the Constable of France, the Dauphin and other French lords assembled. The French ranks have been thrown into hopeless disorder, and all is consternation. " O seigneur ! le jour est perdu ! tout est perdu ! " [Oh Lord ! the day is lost, all is lost] exclaims the Duke of Orleans, while the Dauphin suggests—when the Constable admits that all the French ranks are broken—that they " stab themselves " for are these the " wretches that we play'd at dice for ? " In spite of their heavy losses, however, the French still outnumber the English forces, and the Duke of Bourbon suggests that they all rush back into the fray, for there is nothing left but to die fighting :

> Shame, and eternal shame, nothing but shame !
> Let us die in honour : once more back again ;

" We are enow yet living in the field To smother up the English in our throngs, If any order might be thought upon," is Orleans' answer, but so great is the confusion in the French ranks, that no attempt at a rally is made, and in desperation, Bourbon exclaims :

> The devil take order now ! I 'll to the throng :
> Let life be short, else shame will be too long.

In scene six we are in another part of the battlefield. There are alarums, amid which Henry and Exeter with their respective forces enter. Henry pays a tribute to the bravery of his troops : " Well have we done, thrice-valiant countrymen " : but " all 's not done " ; for the French still hold the field. Enquiring for the Duke of York who three times within an hour had been struck down, and who from helmet to spur was covered with blood when last seen by the king, Exeter, with tears rolling down his cheeks announces the death of York, as well as the " noble Earl of Suffolk." He relates that " Suffolk first died," and York, all " haggled over " took his comrade by the " beard " and " kiss'd the gashes that bloodily did yawn upon his face," after which York cried aloud :

> Tarry, dear cousin Suffolk !
> My soul shall thine keep company to heaven ;
> Tarry, sweet soul, for mine, then fly abreast,
> As in this glorious and well-foughten field
> We kept together in our chivalry !

and then with a smile upon his face, he took Exeter by the hand, and with a feeble shake charged him to " commend his service to his sovereign," after which he threw his arms round Suffolk's neck, and kissing his lips the brave warrior passed away :

> So did he turn, and over Suffolk's neck,
> He threw his wounded arm, and kiss'd his lips ;
> And so espous'd to death, with blood he seal'd
> A testament of noble-ending love.
> The pretty and sweet manner of it forc'd
> Those waters from me which I would have stopp'd ;
> But I had not so much of man in me,
> And all my mother came into mine eyes
> And gave me up to tears.

The king is deeply affected by the news. There is an alarum, the French are rallying for a further attack, and Henry, in order that all his soldiers can be at liberty to fight, gives the stern order that all prisoners must be slain :

> The French have reinforc'd their scatter'd men :
> Then every soldier kill his prisoners !
> Give the word through.

Cf. *Extract* 14 from Holinshed.

Scenes seven and eight conclude the day of the great battle.

In scene seven we are again introduced to Fluellen and Gower. Fluellen is enraged with the French for having slain the boys in charge of the baggage : " Kill the poys and the luggage ! 'tis expressly against the law of arms : 'tis an arrant a piece of knavery, mark you now, as can be offer't in your conscience now, is it not ? " while Gower approves the king's action in ordering the killing of the prisoners : " 'Tis certain there 's not a boy left alive ; and the cowardly rascals that ran from the battle ha' done this slaughter : besides, they have burned and carried away all that was in the king's tent ; wherefore the king most worthily hath caused every soldier to cut his prisoner's throat. O ! 'tis a gallant king." This pleases Fluellen, who claims Henry—who was born at Monmouth castle—as his countryman : " Ay, he was porn at Monmouth, Captain Gower," and then attempts to prove a semblance between Henry and Alexander the Great : " What call you the town's name where Alexander the Pig was born ? " " I think Alexander the Great was born in Macedon : his father was called Philip of Macedon, as I take it," replies Gower. " I think it is in Macedon where Alexander is porn," retorts Fluellen, " I tell you, captain, if you look in the maps of the 'orld, I warrant you sall find, in the comparisons between Macedon and Monmouth, that the situations, look you, is both alike. There is a river in Macedon, and there is also moreover a river at Monmouth : it is called Wye at Monmouth ; but it is out of my prains what is the name of the other river ; but 'tis all one, 'tis alike as my fingers, is to my fingers, and there is salmons in both. If you mark Alexander's life well, Harry of Monmouth's life is come after it indifferent well ; for there is figures in all things. Alexander, God knows, and you know, in his rages, and his furies, and his wraths, and his cholers, and his moods, and his displeasures, and his indignations, and also being a little intoxicates in his prains, did, in his ales and his angers, look you, kill his best friend, Cleitus." To this Gower takes exception : " Our king is not like him in that : he never killed any of his friends," and Fluellen tells him he should not interrupt until he has finished his tale, and goes on to explain that whereas Alexander during a drunken passion, killed Cleitus, Henry " being in his right wits and his good judgments, turned away the fat knight with the great-belly doublet : he was full of jests, and gipes, and knaveries, and mocks ; I have forgot his name." " Sir John Falstaff," adds Gower. " That is he," replies Fluellen. " I 'll tell you there is good men porn at Monmouth."

At this point Henry enters. He is in angry mood with a body of Frenchmen on an adjoining hill who will neither fight nor fly : " I was not angry since I came to France Until this instant. Take a trumpet, herald ; Ride thou unto the horsemen on yon hill : If they will fight with us, bid them come down, Or void the field ; they do offend our sight. If they 'll do neither, we will come to them, And make them skirr away, as swift as stones Enforced from the old Assyrian slings. Besides, we 'll cut the throats of those we have, And not a man of them that we shall take Shall taste our mercy. Go and tell them so."

Montjoy, the French herald now appears, Gloucester remarking as he enters that his " eyes are humbler " than they were when he last appeared. Asked his errand, Montjoy asks permission to collect and bury the French dead ; to sort the " nobles from our common men " ; and to succour the wounded :

K. Hen. How now ? what means this, herald ? know'st thou
  not
That I have fin'd these bones of mine for ransom ?
Com'st thou again for ransom ?
Mont.   No great king :
I come to thee for charitable license,
That we may wander o'er this bloody field
To book our dead, and then to bury them ;

.   .   .   .
              O ! give us leave, great king,
To view the field in safety and dispose
Of their dead bodies.

Professing to be ignorant as to who has won the battle Henry remarks :

I tell thee, truly, herald,
I know not if the day be ours or no ;

and is assured by the French herald that the English have been victorious : " The day is yours." " Praised be God, and not our strength, for it ! " exclaims the king. " What is this castle call'd that stands hard by ? " asks Henry, and being told by Montjoy " They call it Agincourt " Henry declares that the battle shall be called by that name :

Then call we this the field of Agincourt,
Fought on the day of Crispin Crispianus.

Fluellen takes the opportunity of reminding Henry that his " grandfather of famous memory " and his " great-uncle Edward the Plack Prince of Wales, fought a most prave pattle here in France," to which Henry interposes : " They did, Fluellen," where the " Welshmen," continues Fluellen, " did good service in a garden where leeks did grow, wearing leeks in their Monmouth caps ; which, your majesty know, to this hour is an honourable badge of the service ; and I do believe your majesty takes no scorn to wear the leek upon Saint Tavy's day." " I wear it for a memorable honour ; For I am Welsh, you know, good countryman," at which the Welshman is highly pleased, adding : " I am your majesty's countryman, I care not who know it ; I will confess it to all the 'orld : I need not to be ashamed of your majesty, praised be God, so long as your majesty is an honest man." " God keep me so ! " is Henry's pious answer. After ordering his heralds to accompany Montjoy to ascertain the number of the slain, Henry's eyes fall upon Williams, and he asks him why he wears a glove in his cap ? Williams replies that it is the gage of a " rascal that swaggered with him last night," who, if alive, he had " sworn to give a box on his ear." Turning to Fluellen the king enquires if " it is fit for this soldier to keep his oath," and Fluellen having given his opinion that it is quite in order, Henry remarks that the glove may belong to a " gentleman of great sort, quite from the answer of his degree," and bids Williams to go and call his commander, Captain Gower. Williams having gone, Henry hands Williams' glove to Fluellen, bidding him to " wear thou this favour for me and stick it in thy cap," claiming to have plucked it from the helm of Alençon during the battle, and tells Fluellen that if any man challenge him he is a " friend to Alençon, and an enemy to our person," and he must apprehend him. Fluellen considers it a great honour : " Your grace doo's me as great honours as can be desired in the hearts of his subjects " : and placing the gage in his cap, departs. Fearing that the glove may obtain for Fluellen a box on the ear, and wishing no harm to result from what is merely a joke, the king commands the Lords Warwick and Gloucester to " Follow Fluellen closely at the heels," for knowing Fluellen to be " valiant, And touch'd with choler, hot as gunpowder," he fears some " sudden mischief may arise of it " ; for the glove which he had given the Welshman for a favour belongs to Williams, and he (Henry) by " bargain should Wear it himself."

> My Lord of Warwick, and my brother Gloucester,
> Follow Fluellen closely at the heels,
> The glove which I have given him for a favour
> May haply purchase him a box o' th' ear ;
> It is the soldier's ; I by bargain should
> Wear it myself. Follow, good cousin Warwick :
> If that the soldier strike him, as I judge
> By his blunt bearing he will keep his word,
> Some sudden mischief may arise of it ;
> For I do know Fluellen valiant,
> And touch'd with choler, hot as gunpowder,
> And quickly will return an injury :
> Follow and see there be no harm between them.

Scene eight opens before King Henry's Pavilion. Gower and Williams appear and Williams tells Gower of the king's summons, adding : " I warrant it is to knight you, captain. At this moment, Fluellen, wearing the glove in his cap, enters, and is forthwith challenged by Williams : " Sir, know you this glove ? " " Know the glove ! " replies Fluellen, " I know the glove is a glove," whereupon Williams strikes him. Fluellen—in accordance with the king's orders—attempts to arrest Williams, whom he describes as an '." arrant traitor as any 's in the universal world, or in France, or in England," being a " friend of the Duke Alençon's." The Dukes of Warwick and Gloucester now appear, and enquiring " what 's the matter ? " Fluellen is explaining to Warwick that a most " contagious treason has come to light," just as Henry enters, and demands to know the meaning of the trouble. " My liege," replies Fluellen, " here is a villain and a traitor, that, look your grace, has struck the glove which your majesty is take out of the helmet of Alençon." Williams on the other hand claims it as his glove, and says he had struck the man for " wearing it in his cap according to challenge." Fluellen denounces Williams as an " arrant, rascally, beggarly, lousy knave," whereupon Henry produces the " fellow glove " to the one which Williams carries : " Give me thy glove, soldier : look, here is the fellow of it," adding " 'Twas I, indeed, thou promised'st to strike ; And thou hast given me most bitter terms," to which Fluellen rejoins : " let his neck answer for it, if there is any martial law in the world." Henry then asks Williams what " satisfaction he is prepared to make " for having treated him as a " common soldier," to which Williams replies : " Your majesty came not like yourself : you appeared to me but as a common man ; witness the night, your garments, your lowliness ; and what your highness suffered under that shape, I beseech you, take it for your own fault and not mine : for had you been as I took you for, I made no offence ; therefore, I beseech your highness, pardon me," for " All offences, my lord, come from the heart : never came any from mine that might offend your majesty." Henry accepts Williams' simple and honest explanation, and bids Exeter return to him his glove full of crowns : " Here, uncle Exeter, fill this glove with crowns, And give it to this fellow. Keep it, fellow ; And wear it for an honour in thy cap Till I do challenge it. Give him the crowns," and turning to Fluellen, says : " And, captain, you must needs be friends with him." Fluellen offers to add " twelve pence " at the same time telling Williams to " serve God, and keep out of prawls, and prabbles, and quarrels, and dissensions," but Williams declares he will have none of Fluellen's money. Fluellen tells him not to be " pashful " for it will " serve to mend his shoes, which is not so good," adding " 'tis a good silling, I warrant you, or I will change it."

The English herald now enters, and hands to the king a roll giving the number of French killed in the battle as ten thousand, including " nobles bearing banners, One hundred and twenty-six ; knights, esquires, and gallant gentlemen, Eight thousand and four hundred " ; five hundred of whom were only " dubb'd knights yesterday " ; besides a number of " princes, barons, lords, knights, squires, And gentlemen of blood and quality." The herald then hands him another paper giving the death roll on the English side. The Dukes of York and Suffolk had fallen fighting side by side, Sir Richard Ketly and Davy Gam, esquires : and only twenty-five rank and file. As Henry's eyes fall on this short list, he exclaims :

> O God ! thy arm was here ;
> And not to us, but to thy arm alone,
> Ascribe we all. When, without stratagem,
> But in plain shock and even play of battle,
> Was ever known so great and little loss
> On one part and on the other ? Take it, God,
> For it is none but thine !

The king then orders them to go in procession to the neighbouring village church, and there to sing " Non nobis " [Not unto us, O Lord, not unto us, but unto Thy name give glory] and the " Te Deum " [We praise thee, O God] after which the army will depart to :

> Calais ; and to England then
> Where ne'er from France arriv'd more happy men.

Cf. *Extracts* 15 and 16 from Holinshed.

The *Prologue* or *Chorus* preceding Act V is an ' interim ' following Henry's return to England and his subsequent return to France.

Crossing over from Calais he lands at Dover where a crowd of " men, with wives, and boys," give him an enthusiastic welcome : " Behold, the English beach Pales in the flood with men, with wives, and boys, Whose shouts and claps out-voice the deep-mouth'd sea." On arriving at Blackheath he refuses the request that his " bruised helmet and his bended sword " should be borne before him in his progress through the streets of London. The capital receives him with exultation " The mayor and all his brethren in best sort, Like to the senators of the antique Rome, With the plebeians swarming at their heels, Go forth and fetch their conquering Cæsar in " : allusion being made at this point to the almost immediate expectation of the victorious return of Lord Essex from his Irish campaign.

Henry remains in England for a period of two years, during which time he receives a visit from the Emperor Sigismund who has come to England to try to arrange terms of peace between England and France.

The *Chorus* concludes with a reference to Henry's return to France in 1417 :

and omit

> All the occurrences, whatever chanc'd,
> Till Harry's back-return again to France :
> There must we bring him ; and myself have play'd
> The interim, by remembering you 'tis past.
> Then brook abridgement, and your eyes advance,
> After your thoughts, straight back again to France.

Cf. *Extract* 17 from Holinshed.

Scene one shows us the English camp in France. Fluellen and Gower enter, and the latter asks the former why he is wearing his leek in his cap, St. David's day being past. Fluellen, who mentions that " There is occasions and causes why and wherefore in all things " : tells Gower that the " rascally, scauld, beggarly, lousy, pragging knave, Pistol," who is no " petter than a fellow," bid him yesterday to " eat his leek," but being in a place where " contention " was forbidden he is wearing the national emblem in his cap until he again meets Pistol, and then he intends to " tell him a little piece of his desires." At this point, Pistol appears, and Gower remarks : " here he comes, swelling like a turkey-cock," to which Fluellen rejoins : " 'Tis no matter for his swellings nor his turkey-cocks," and a quarrel ensues between them. Fluellen calls Pistol a " scurvy, lousy knave," to which Pistol retaliates by asking Fluellen if he is mad, and tells him to be gone, for the " smell of leeks make him feel sick." Fluellen however requests Pistol to eat the leek : " I peseech you heartily, scurvy lousy knave, at my desires and my requests and my petitions, to eat, look you, this leek " ; but Pistol swears he will not eat it, not for " Cadwallader and all his goats." " There is one goat for you, [Strikes him]. Will you be so good, scauld knave, as eat it ? " " Base Trojan, thou shalt die," replies Pistol, " scauld knave, that 's true," rejoins Fluellen, " when God's will is, . . . eat your victuals," and striking him again, adds : " come, there is sauce for it. I pray you, fall to : if you can mock a leek you can eat a leek." " Enough, captain : you have astonished him," interposes Gower, but Fluellen is determined that Pistol shall " eat some part of his leek, or he will peat his pate four days," and bids Pistol to " Bite, I pray you ; it is good for your green wound and your ploody coxcomb." " Must I bite ? " asks Pistol. " Certainly, and out of doubt and out of question too and ambiguities," replies Fluellen, and Pistol begins to threaten : " By this leek, I will most horribly revenge. I eat and eat, I swear——" " Eat," demands Fluellen, " Will you have some more sauce to your leek ? there is not enough leek to swear by." " Quiet thy cudgel " ; pleads Pistol, " thou dost see I eat," and Fluellen tells him to " throw none away ; the skin is good for your broken coxcomb. When you take occasions to see leeks hereafter, I pray you, mock at 'em ; that is all," and forthwith departs, remarking : " God b' wi' you, and keep you, and heal your pate." Having gone, Pistol swears to be avenged on Fluellen : " All hell shall stir for this " ; but Gower reproves him for his insolence in " mocking at an ancient tradition, begun upon an honourable respect, and worn as a memorable trophy of predeceased valour, and dare not avouch in your deeds any of your words ? " calling Pistol a " counterfeit cowardly knave." Gower having taken his departure, Pistol observes that " Fortune plays the huswife with him," for he has received news of the death of his wife. He therefore resolves to " steal away " to England, vowing he will turn " bawd " and a " cut-purse " and " patch up his cudgell'd scars," and " swear that they are wounds received in fighting in the Gallia wars."

The final scene of the Play shows us an Apartment in the French King's Palace at Troyes in Champagne. The English and French monarchs—with their respective retinues—meet, and greet each other cordially :

> *K. Hen.* Peace to this meeting, wherefore we are met !
> Unto our brother France, and to our sister,
> Health and fair time of day ; joy and good wishes
> To our most fair and princely cousin Katharine ;
> And, as a branch and member of this royalty,
> By whom this great assembly is contriv'd,
> We do salute you, Duke of Burgundy ;
> And, princes French, and peers, health to you all !
> *Fr. King* Right joyous are we to behold your face,
> Most worthy brother England ; fairly met :
> So are you, princes English, every one.

after which Queen Isabella extends to Henry a special welcome, and expresses a hope that a happy issue may be the outcome of their meeting.

The Duke of Burgundy, who professes to be attached to both monarchs on " equal love " is proud of having been instrumental in bringing the two kings together, and pleads for reconciliation to heal the wounds of France, so as to restore her again to her former self. [*See* V. ii. 22–67.] Henry replies that he is prepared to come to terms conditionally upon his full and just demands—which have already been presented to the French king—being conceded :

> If, Duke of Burgundy, you would the peace,
> Whose want gives growth to the imperfections
> Which you have cited, you must buy that peace
> With full accord to all our just demands ;
> Whose tenours and particular effects
> You have, enschedul'd briefly, in your hands.

To this the French monarch replies that he has only with a " cursorary eye O'erglanc'd the articles " ; and suggests that a joint council be appointed—with power to act— to consider terms of peace, and the Dukes of Exeter, Clarence, and Gloucester, with the Earls of Warwick and Huntingdon are appointed to represent England. As they retire to an adjoining room, Isabella decides to accompany them in order to " avert attrition " :

> Our gracious brother, I will go with them.
> Haply a woman's voice may do some good
> When articles too nicely urg'd be stood on,

but—at the instigation of Henry—leaves behind her, her daughter, " our cousin " Katharine.

> Yet leave our cousin Katharine here with us :
> She is our capital demand, compris'd
> Within the fore-rank of our articles.

Being left alone with Katharine and her maid Alice, Henry declares himself in plain and blunt language : " Fair Katharine, and most fair, Will you vouchsafe to teach a soldier terms Such as will enter at a lady's ear And plead his love-suit to her gentle heart?" but Katharine excuses herself: "Your majesty shall mock at me; I cannot speak your England." "O fair Katharine! if you love me soundly with your French heart, I will be glad to hear you confess it brokenly with your English tongue. Do you like me, Kate?" asks Henry, to which Katharine replies: "Pardonnez-moy, I cannot tell vat is 'like me.'" "An angel is like you, Kate, and you are like an angel," rejoins Henry, and turning to her waiting-maid, Alice, Katharine asks: "Que dit-il? que je suis semblable à les anges?" [What did he say? that I am like the angels?] to which Alice replies: "Ouy, vrayment, sauf vostre grace, ainsi dit-il." [Yes, truly, saving your grace, so he said.] "O bon Dieu! les langues des hommes sont pleines de tromperies," [O good God! the language of men is full of deception] exclaims Katharine. "What says she, fair one?" interposes Henry, "that the tongues of men are full of deceits?" and Alice replies: "Ouy, dat de tongues of de mans is be full of deceits: dat is de princess." To this Henry affirms that the "princess is the better Englishwoman," expressing his pleasure that she cannot speak better English, for if she could she would find him such a very plain king, that she would be under the impression he had sold a farm to buy a crown. "Give me your answer; i' faith, do: and so clap hands and a bargain. How say you, lady?" enjoins Henry, and Katharine makes answer: "Sauf vostre honneur, me understand vell." Again urging his suit, Katharine asks: "Is it possible dat I sould love de enemy of France?" Henry replies: "No; it is not possible you should love the enemy of France, Kate; but, in loving me, you should love the friend of France, for I love France so well that I will not part with a village of it; I will have it all mine: and Kate, when France is mine and I am yours, then yours is France and you are mine." As Katharine pretends not to understand: "I cannot tell vat is dat," Henry essays to explain in French, but so stumbles in the attempt that he exclaims: "I shall never move thee in French, unless it be to laugh at me," but Katharine very graciously tells him he speaks French infinitely better than she speaks English: "Sauf vostre honneur, le François que vous parlez il est meilleur que l'Anglois lequel je parle." [Saving your honour, the French that you speak is better than the English that I speak.] His efforts proving fruitless, Henry falls back again into plain English, and after a little flirtation on the part of Katharine she finally accepts the "conqueror of Agincourt" on condition "Dat is as it sall please de roy mon père." Henry then kisses her hand to which Katharine objects, exclaiming: "Laissez, mon seigneur, laissez, laissez! Ma foy, je ne veux point que vous abaissiez vostre grandeur, en baisant la main d'une de vostre seigneurie indigne serviteur: excusez moy, je vous supplie, mon très puissant seigneur." [Don't, my lord, don't, don't. My faith, I do not wish you to lower your dignity by kissing the hand of one of your unworthy servants; excuse me, I beg of you, my most powerful lord.] "Then I will kiss your lips, Kate," is Henry's reply, only to be told by Katharine that it is not the fashion for the ladies of France to kiss before they are married, [Les dames et damoiselles, pour estre baisées devant leur nopces, il n'est pas le coutume de France] and Henry retorts by saying: "O Kate! nice customs curtsy to great kings." This wooing scene, which is a very pretty piece of comedy, although the quaintest of episodes, is ended by the return of the French King and Queen, with Burgundy and other lords, Burgundy good-humouredly enquiring if Henry is teaching the princess English, to which Henry makes answer: "I would have her learn, my fair cousin, how perfectly I love her; and that is good English." A little banter between Burgundy and Henry follows, Henry admitting that his "tongue is rough," and his "condition not smooth," but all ends happily, for the French monarch gives his consent to the match, after which it is announced that terms of peace have been concluded. The French king then presents his daughter to Henry, exclaiming : " Take her, fair son," and may France and England " cease their hatred, and live in Christian-like accord, so that never again shall war advance His bleeding sword 'twixt England and fair France," to which all present say " Amen " while the queen calls down the blessing of heaven upon them and upon both realms : " God, the best maker of all marriages, Combine your hearts in one, your realms in one ! " so " That English may be French, French Englishmen, Receive each other ! God speak this, Amen ! " to which all present again cry " Amen." Henry then announces that he will receive the oaths of all the French peers on his wedding-day, when he will :

> swear to Kate, and you to me ;
> And may our oaths well kept and prosperous be !

Cf. *Extract* 18 from Holinshed.

The Play concludes with an *Epilogue* or *Chorus*—consisting of fourteen lines only —which designates Henry as " This star of England " :

> Small time, but in that small most greatly liv'd
> This star of England : Fortune made his sword,
> By which the world's best garden he achiev'd,
> And of it left his son imperial lord,

and foreshadows the disasters that will befall England during the reign of King Henry the Sixth, who, on the death of his father, becomes King of France and England when only nine months old, and concludes with a reference to the three parts of *King Henry the Sixth*, which were written several years previously and which had been presented on the stage—Part I of which deals with the loss of the English possessions in France, and Parts II and III with the disastrous Civil War, known as the Wars of the Roses :

> Henry the Sixth, in infant bands crown'd king
> Of France and England, did this king succeed ;
> Whose state so many had the managing,
> That they lost France and made his England bleed :
> Which oft our stage hath shown ; and, for their sake,
> In your fair minds let this acceptance take.

Scene : England, afterwards France.

CHARACTERS, PLACE-NAMES, ETC.

Adam. I. i. 29.

> And whipp'd the offending Adam out of him, [1. i 29]

According to Biblical dictum *the old Adam* i.e. *the old man*, signified man in an unregenerated state.

Agamemnon. III. vi. 7.

King of Mycenæ, and Leader of the Greeks at the siege of Troy.

Agincourt. IV. Chorus 52 ; IV. vii. 91, 92 ; Prologue 14.

A village in Pas-de-Calais, where one of the more important battles in the Hundred years' war was fought on October 25th, 1415, the English, numbering about 9,000 under Henry V. defeating the French numbering about 50,000 under the Constable d'Albret.

Agincourt. Field of Battle.

The Scene of Act IV., Scene iv. Pistol takes captive a French soldier, who offers two hundred crowns for his freedom. This Pistol accepts and the Frenchman is so grateful that he describes Pistol as the " bravest, the most valiant and the most distinguished nobleman of England." The boy—who acts as interpreter—leaves to guard the baggage in the English camp which is in an exposed condition.

Agincourt. Another part of the field.

The Scene of Act IV., Scenes v., vi. and vii.

Act IV., Scene v. The French have been defeated and their ranks thrown into hopeless disorder. The Duke of Bourbon suggests that they rush back into the fight for there is nothing left but to die fighting.

Act IV., Scene vi. This scene shows us the deaths of the Dukes of York and Suffolk. The French make an attempt to rally, and Henry, in order that all his troops can be at liberty to fight, gives orders to kill the prisoners.

According to Holinshed the king gave as his reason for ordering the prisoners to be slain, that he expected another battle, and had not men enough to guard one army and fight another. Courtenay remarks : " This is Shakespear's version of the most lamentable incident of the battle of Agincourt, by which, in the opinion of many, the fame of the victorious Henry has been tarnished."

Act IV., Scene vii. Fluellen and Gower appear and approve the king's action in ordering the French prisoners to be slain. Henry is angry with a body of French horsemen on an adjoining hill who will neither fight nor retreat. Montjoy appears and asks permission to collect and inter the French who have been slain. He acknowledges to Henry that the English forces have been victorious, and Henry declares that the battle shall be called " Agincourt." The rest of the scene is occupied with the incident of the challenge as portrayed in Act IV., Scene i.

Albion. III. v. 14.

> To buy a slobbery and a dirty farm
> In that nook-shotten isle of Albion. [III. v. 13–14.]

= England. Albion was the Gaelic name for Scotland, and was later applied to the whole island of Britain. *nook-shotten* = probably a contemptuous term referring to the irregular coast-line of England.

Alençon. III. v. 42 ; IV. vii. 158, 161 ; IV. viii. 18, 28, 38, 98.

John, Duke of Alençon. Malone says : " Henry was felled to the ground at the battle of Agincourt by the Duke of Alençon, but recovered and slew two of the Duke's attendants. Afterwards Alençon was killed by the King's guard, contrary to Henry's intention, who wished to have saved him."

> When Alençon and
> myself were down together I plucked this glove
> from his helm :

This encounter with the Duke of Alençon is the only reference in the play we have as to the king's share in the fighting.

Alexander the Great. IV. vii. 15, 20, 23, 33, 35, 47.

Alexander the Pig. IV. vii. 14.

= Alexander the Great. Fluellen draws a parallel between Alexander born in Macedon, and Henry born at Monmouth.

Alexanders. III. i. 19.

Fathers that, like so many Alexanders,
Have in these parts from morn till even fought,
And sheath'd their swords for lack of argument.
[III. i. 19–21.]

An allusion to Alexander the Great, who, it is said, after making himself master of Asia, sat down and wept when told there were no more worlds to conquer. *sheath'd their swords for lack of argument* = because there were no longer any enemies left to fight.

Alice. III. iv. p.1, 1, 28 ; V. ii. p.1.

The Lady attending on Katharine. She appears in Act III., Scene iv., where she gives the princess a lesson in the English language.

Alps. III. v. 52.

The great mountain range of Europe, forming the boundary between France, Germany and Switzerland on the north and west, and Italy on the south.

Ambassadors to the King of England. I. ii. p.234.

Appear before King Henry and his Court, bringing a message of defiance from the Dauphin :

Your highness, lately sending into France,
Did claim some certain dukedoms, in the right
Of your great predecessor, King Edward the Third.
In answer of which claim, the prince our master
Says that you savour too much of your youth,
And bids you be advis'd : there 's nought in France
That can be with a nimble galliard won ;
You cannot revel into dukedoms there.
He therefore sends you, meeter for your spirit,
This tun of treasure ; and, in lieu of this,
Desires you let the dukedoms that you claim
Hear no more of you. This the Dauphin speaks.
[I. ii. 246–257.]

Several embassies were sent from France to Henry IV., but the personages on the present occasion were, Louis Earl of Vendôme ; Monsieur William Bouratin, the Archbishop of Bourges ; the Bishop of Lisieux ; the lords of Ivry and Braquemont, with Jean Andree and Master Gualtier Cole, the King's Secretaries. Grafton gives at much length the addresses of the ambassadors of whom the Archbishop was the chief speaker, telling Henry V., with great boldness, that his master, the King of France, did not consider him even to have any right to the crown of England, since it belonged to the true heir of the late King Richard. In the *Famous Victories* it is stated that ' the Archbishop of Bourges and Monsieur le Cole ' have been sent on the embassage, but the prelate only appears on the scene. *French.*

See also Grafton's *Chronicle*, vol. I., pp. 510–511.

Ancient Pistol. II. i. 3, 27.

Ancient = a corruption of ensign or standard-bearer.

Angleterre. IV. iv. 1, 39 ; IV. iv. 58.

= England.

Anthony, Duke of Brabant. IV. viii. 98.

See Duke of Brabant.

Archbishop of Canterbury. I. i. p.l. ; I. ii. p.l. p. 7.

Appears only in the first two scenes of the play.

While his eloquent speeches urging Henry to embark on the war in France at first seem to be the honest thoughts of a patriotic noble, we must remember that his first thoughts were to protect the property of the Church, and here was an opportunity to distract the king's attention from home affairs.

He exclaims to the Bishop of Ely, before they go into the king's presence,

My lord, I 'll tell you—that self bill is urg'd,
Which in the eleventh year of the last king's reign,
Was like, and had indeed against us pass'd,
But that the scambling and unquiet time
Did push it out of farther question. [I. i. 1–5.]

and on receiving the question " But how, my lord, shall we resist it now," replies " It must be thought on."

The opportunity soon comes, and the Archbishop in an impassioned speech determines to precipitate a war with France.

> Gracious lord,
> Stand for your own ; unwind your bloody flag ;
> Look back into your mighty ancestors :
> Go, my dread lord, to your great-grandsire's tomb,
> From whom you claim ; invoke his war-like spirit,
> And your great-uncle's, Edward the Black Prince.
> [I. ii. 100–105.]

" The King, for the honour of himselfe, and the aduancement of hys people, called this yere (1414) and the last day of Aprill, in the towne of Leycester his high Court of Parliament, in the which many good and profitable lawes were concluded, and many peticions moued, were for that tyme deferred. Among which petitions one was, that a bill exhibited in the xj yere of King Henry which by reason that the King was then troubled with Ciuill dissention, came to none effect, might nowe be considered and regarded : the effect of which petition was, that the temporall lands deuoutly geuen, & disordinately spent by the religious, and other of the clergie, might suffice to mainteyne to the honour of the king, and defence of the realme, xv. Erles, xv. C. Knightes, vj. thousande, two hundreth Esquiers, and one hundreth almose houses, for the reliefe of the impotent and nedy persons, and the King to haue cleerely into his Coffers, xx. thousand poundes, with many other prouisions and values of sundrie religious houses.

This before memembred bill (sayth Hall) much feared the religious, insomuch that fat Abbottes swet, the proude Priors frowned, the poore Friers cursed, the siely Nonnes wept, and all together were nothyng pleased nor yet content. But to finde a remedie for a mischiefe, and a tent to stop a wounde, the Clergie practised to put into the kinges heade, the title that he had to the Crowne and Kingdome of Fraunce, and howe honourable it should be for him to trauaile for the recouerie thereof, and howe willyng all the good people of the realme woulde be to ayde him in that honoyrable enterprice. And the next day after in most solempne and

learned maner, the Archebishop of Cantorbury, whose name then was Henry Chichley, made such an excellent Oration to moue, encourage, and perswade the king to take that voyage in hand, that nothing could be eyther more or better spoken. And when the Bishop had done, then the Nobilitie in like maner sayd to and fro their mindes, so that nowe there was vsed none other talke in euery mannes mouth in the Parliament house, but for the conqueryng of Fraunce, and the bill against the Clergie was lulled a sleepe, and nothing came thereof. And so soone as this voyage was agreed vpon, the parliament brake vp." Grafton's *Chronicle.*

Deighton remarks : " The Prelates—Canterbury and Ely—do not appear in a very favourable light. Reading between the lines we see them ready to plunge England into war in order to avert the threatened spoilation of the church possessions, and the Archbishop's harangue is as unprincipled as it is astute. Despite the King's appeal for a faithful settlement of his claim, Canterbury, backed up by Ely, strains every argument and appeals to every sentiment that will provoke the King to declare war."

[Henry Chichele, son of a yeoman of Higham Ferrers, called by Fuller " that skilful statefencer," and by Southey, in his *Joan of Arc :*

> " the proud prelate, the blood-guilty man,
> Who, trembling for the Church's ill-got wealth,
> Made our fifth Henry claim the crown of France.'

After filling many ecclesiastic positions was sent as envoy to Pope Innocent VII in 1405 and to Gregory XII in 1407 ; appointed Bishop of St. David's, 1408 ; translated to Canterbury, 1414. Accompanied Henry the Fifth on his second expedition to France ; upheld in council Humphrey, Duke of Gloucester, who refused to recognise Bishop Beaufort as papal legate. Founder of All Souls' College, Oxford. (1362–1443).]

Arthur's bosom.   II. iii. 9, 10.

> Nay, sure, he 's not in hell : he 's in Arthur's
> bosom, if ever man went to Arthur's bosom.
> [II. iii. 9–10.]

The Hostess's mistake for ' Abraham's bosom ' See *St. Luke* xvi. 19–31.

Assyrian slings. IV. vii. 64.

> as swift as stones
> Enforced from the old Assyrian slings,   [IV. vii. 64.]

The Assyrians were famous slingers. " The Assyrians trusted in their shields, bows and slings." *Judith*, IX. vii.

Attendants. I. ii. p.1 ; II. ii. p.12.

Aunchient Pistol. III. vi. 18, 30, 51 ; V. i. 18.

See Ancient Pistol.

Babylon. II. iii. 40.

> and talked of the whore
> of Babylon.   [II. iii. 39–40.]

According to the Apocalypse, the City of Anti-Christ.

Barbason. II. i. 53.

> I am not Barbason ; you cannot conjure me
>   [II. i. 53.]

The name of a devil. Cf. *Merry Wives of Windsor*, II. iii. 311–313 :

> Terms ! names !—
> Amaimon sounds well ; Lucifer, well ; Barbarson,
> well ; yet they are devils' additions, the names
> of fiends :

Bardolph. II. i. p.1, 2, 83 ; II. iii. p.1, 4, 42 ; II. ii. p.1, 32, 45, 46 ; III. vi. 25, 40, 48, 105 ; IV. iv. 71.

Lieutenant Bardolph was formerly in the service of Falstaff, and companion to Prince Henry in *King Henry the Fourth*. Although he is described by Pistol as being " a soldier, firm, and sound of heart," the Boy undoubtedly characterises him more authentically in the words :

> For Bardolph, he is
> white-livered and red-faced ; by the means
> whereof a' faces it out, but fights not.   [III. ii. 32–34.]

Bardolph's nose seems to be his chief feature, for Fluellen says :

> his lips blows at his nose, and
> it is like a coal of fire, sometimes plue and some-
> times red ; but his nose is executed, and his fire 's
> out.   [III. vi. 107–110.]

He ends his life in crime, being hanged for stealing a pax in spite of Henry's proclamation against sacrilege.

French says : " The theft for which Bardolph was condemned to die ' with edge of penny cord,' namely, for stealing a ' pix of little price,' is recorded by the contemporary historians, Elmham and Titus Livius, as having been committed by a soldier on the march, Oct. 17, 1415, who mistook a pix of copper-gilt for real gold, and stole it from the church at Corbie, for which sacrilege the king ordered him to be hanged on a tree, close to the church, in sight of the whole army."

Bardolph's nose. II. iii. 42.

> Do you not remember a' saw a flea stick upon
> Bardolph's nose, and a' said it was a black soul
> burning in hell-fire ?   [II. iii. 41–43.]

A reference to Bardolph's red nose.

Bartholomew-tide. V. ii. 328.

> for
> maids, well summered and warm kept, are like
> flies at Bartholomew-tide, blind, though they have
> their eyes ; and then they will endure handling,
> which before would not abide looking on.
>   [V. ii. 325–330.]

St. Bartholomew's day is August 24th, that is, the latter end of summer, or as an old rhyme has it : " St. Bartholomew brings the cold dew." Commenting on this passage, Emma Phipson in her Animal-Lore of Shakespeare's Time, says : " He (Mr. Patterson) imagines this allusion to have reference to some forgotten legend, some ancient superstition. By the end of August, especially if the season be wet, flies seek the shelter of houses in great numbers, and become drowsy and semi-torpid, or, as children call them, tame."

Basilisks. V. ii. 17.

> The fatal balls of murdering basilisks :
> The venom of such looks, we fairly hope,
> Have lost their quality,   [V. ii. 17–19.]

" The Queen means that the look from Henry's eye-balls has been a deadly influence to the French, taking, so to speak, the form of cannon-balls." *Verity*.

A Basilisk was (1) a fabulous serpent, the glance of whose eye was supposed to be fatal, and (2) a large cannon resembling a serpent and which would throw a shot of two hundred pounds in weight.

Bates. IV. i. p.85, 85.

A typical example of a common soldier of the period, brave and ever loyal to his sovereign.

" Bates, Court, and Williams are excellent specimens of the common soldier—' good yeomen, whose limbs were made in England ' (III. i. 25)—and right well do they prove at Harfleur and Agincourt ' the mettle of their pasture ' (III. i. 27). The cynical indifference which they show as to the rights or wrongs of their cause was typical of the stormy times in which they lived. It was enough for them to know that they were subjects of the king, and their whole duty was to ' fight lustily for him ' when required. Their sturdy independence and outspoken frankness are as conspicuous before the king in the midst of his court as when he appeared to them ' but as a common man.' From first to last they prove themselves well worthy of the fellowship of their great sovereign." *Academy edition.*

Beaumont. III. v. 44 ; IV. viii. 102.

A French lord killed at the battle of Agincourt.

Bedlam. V. i. 20.

A corruption of Bethlehem. The name given to the great London lunatic asylum.

Belzebub. IV. vii. 142.

Originally the name of the chief god of the Philistines. In the *New Testament* the name is applied to the prince of the devils. See *St. Matthew* xii. 24.

Bishop of Ely. I. i. p.1 ; I. ii. p.7.

Is one of the minor characters of the play, appearing only in the first two scenes, where he supports the Archbishop of Canterbury.

[John Fordham who, after being Dean of Wells, was appointed Bishop of Durham in 1381, and translated to Ely 1388. Was oné of the ambassadors to treat of Henry the Fifth's marriage. He died in 1425. *See also under* Archbishop of Canterbury.]

Blackheath. V. Chorus 16.

A common near London, where Henry the Fifth was met by the Mayor and many promi-nent citizens of London on his return from France, after defeating the French at the battle of Agincourt.

Blithild. I. ii. 67.

Shakespeare describes her as the daughter of Clothaire the Second, and ancestress of King Pepin.

Boy. II. i. p.81 ; II. iii. p.1 ; III. ii. p.1 ; IV. iv. p.1.

Is portrayed as being shrewd underneath his simple and innocent appearance. His observations on his masters are both entertaining and true. He says that he is a boy to all three, but they could not be a man to him, and announces his intention " to leave them and seek some better service," for their villany goes against his weak stomach.

Hudson says : " I have elsewhere observed somewhat upon the remarkable character of the Boy who figures as servant to ' these three swashers.' He is probably the same whom we met with as Page to Falstaff in the preceding Play. His arch and almost unconscious shrewdness of remark was even then a taking feature ; and it encouraged the thought of his having enough healthy keenness of preception to ward off the taints and corruptions that beset him. And he now translates the follies and vices of his employers into apt themes of sagacious and witty reflection, touching at every point the very pith of their distinctive features. The mixture of penetration and simplicity with which he moralizes their pretentious nothings is very charming. Thus Pistol's turbulent vapourings draw from him the sage remark, ' I did never know so full a voice issue from so empty a heart : but the saying is true, *The empty vessel makes the greatest sound*. Bardolph and Nym had ten times more valour than this roaring Devil i' the old play, and they are both hang'd ; and so would this be, if he durst steal any thing adventurously.' Shakespeare specially delights in thus endowing his children and youngsters with a kind of unsophisticated shrewdness, the free outcome of a native soundness that enables them to walk unhurt amid the contagions of bad example ; their own minds being kept pure, and even furthered in the course of manhood, by an instinctive oppugnance to the shams and meannesses which beset their path.''

Bridge. III. vi. 2.

The bridge over the river Ternoise at Blangy. Malone says : '' After Henry had passed the Some, the French endeavoured to intercept him in his passage to Calais ; and for that purpose attempted to break down the only bridge that there was over the small river of Ternois, at Blangi, over which it was necessary for Henry to pass. But Henry, having notice of their design, sent a part of his troops before him, who, attacking and putting the French to flight, preserved the bridge, till the whole English army arrived, and passed over it.''

Cadwallader. V. i. 29.

Not for Cadwallader and all his goats.   [V. i. 29.]

The last of the Welsh kings. He was the son of Cadwallon, king of Wales. According to the prophecy of Merlin he is one day to return to expel the Saxon from the land. He is supposed to have visited Rome where he was baptized and received the name of Bhendiged, or the Blessed.
Goats = a jibe at the poverty of the Welsh mountaineer.

Cæsar. V. Chorus 28.

Go forth and fetch their conquering Cæsar in :
[V. Chorus 28.]

Henry the Fifth's reception at Blackheath by the Mayor and citizens of London is here compared with that of ' conquering Cæsar ' at Rome.

Calais. III. ii. 47.

Nym and Bardolph are sworn brothers in filching, and in Calais they stole a fire-shovel ;   [III. ii. 46-48.]

Evidently a slip on Shakespeare's part. The army did not reach Calais, until after the battle of Agincourt.

Calais. III. iii. 56 ; III. vi. 147 ; IV. viii. 127 ; V. Chorus 7.

Captain James. III. ii. 88.

= Captain Jamy.

Caveto. II. iii. 54.

Beware ; take care.

Charlemain. I. ii. 75.

Charles the Bald ; who assumed his grandfather's title of '' Charles the Great.'' Lady Lingare is mentioned as his daughter.

Charles Delabreth. III. v. 40.

= Constable of France (q.v.).

Charles, Duke of Lorraine. I. ii. 70, 83.

Son of Louis the Fourth. Received from the Emperor Otto the Second, for services rendered, the dukedom of Lower Lorraine. On the death of Louis the Fifth made an effort to seize the throne of France, and, after several successes, captured Reims, but was betrayed by Adalberon, bishop of Laon, and imprisoned by Hugh Capet where he died 993, thus Hugh Capet is said to have '' usurped the crown of Charles the Duke of Lorraine.''

Charles the Great. I. ii. 46, 61, 71, 77, 84.

= Charlemagne, king of France 768–814, son of King Pepin.

Charles the Sixth, King of France. II. iv. p.1 ; III. v. p.1 ; V. ii. p.1 ; 2, 23, p.299, 355.

Takes no great part in the action of the play. He is depicted as a weak monarch, who seems to be mainly in the hands of his courtiers, especially the Dauphin, who generally takes the leading part in the scenes in which the king appears. His words show him to be weak-minded and easily swayed, for although he has sufficient insight to see that Henry is not the '' vain, giddy, shallow, humorous youth '' the Dauphin would have him believe, he lacks the strength of character needed in such a crisis, and consequently pays the penalty for the Dauphin's shallowness. In short the king appears as being a victim of the dread of the horrors of war, and is sincerely anxious to avoid bloodshed, for he readily agrees to the terms of Henry's treaty, gladly accepting peace on whatever terms are forthcoming.

"Like Richard II. of England, his contemporary, and almost at the same time, he suddenly declared himself of age in 1388, dismissed his uncles who had ruled during his minority, and governed well for four years. Then he went mad, and was never perfectly sane for the rest of his life. The rivalry between the Duke of Burgundy, his uncle, and Louis of Orleans, his younger brother, for the power which the king could no longer wield, was the chief cause of the misfortunes of France at this time. Charles was neither at Agincourt nor at Troyes ; it is said that his uncle, the Duc de Berri, who had served at Poictiers, kept him away, saying that ' it was better to lose a battle than a battle and a king too.' " *Blackfriars edition.*

[Charles the Sixth, succeeded his father Charles V. in 1380. He married Isabel, daughter of Stephen II., Duke of Bavaria, by whom he had three sons, successively Dauphins ; and five daughters, viz. : 1. Isabelle, the second queen of Richard II. ; 2. Marie, who became a nun ; 3. Michelle, who was the first wife of Philip, Count of Charolois, afterwards Duke of Burgundy ; 4. Jane, married to John de Montfort, Duke of Brittany ; 5. Katharine the Fair, who became the queen of Henry the Fifth. Charles VI. died Oct. 21, 1422, a few weeks after his English son-in-law, who had been declared his heir to the kingdom of France, as noticed in the play.]

Charolois.   III. v. 45.

A French lord killed at the battle of Agincourt.

Cheshu.   III. ii. 67, 74, 83.

Fluellen's blunder for ' Jesu.'

Childeric.   I. ii. 65.

Childeric the Third, son of Childeric the Second, last of the Merovingian kings, who reigned from 743 to 752. He was deposed by Pepin and died in the monastery of St. Omer in 755.

Chorus.   Prologue 32.

for the which supply,
Admit me Chorus to this history ;
Who prologue-like your humble patience pray,
Gently to hear, kindly to judge, our play.
[Prologue 31–34.]

" The duty of the Chorus is to explain the subject and action of the play, and to fill up with narrative the intervals between the Acts." *Wright.*

In this Play each Act is preceded by a Prologue or Chorus, and an Epilogue or Chorus concludes the play. *See* OUTLINE OF THE PLAY.

In the time of Shakespeare a Chorus was another name for a Prologue which was delivered by a single person, whereas in Greek drama the Chorus was composed of many persons.

Chrish.   III. ii. 91, 95, 108, 112, 116, 136.

Macmorris's pronunciation of Christ.

Citizens of Harfleur.   III. iii. p.1.

Appear with the Governor on the walls of Harfleur, and agree to open their gates to the English King.

Clarence.   V. ii. 84.

Thomas Plantagenet, Duke of Clarence, born 1388 and killed at the battle of Beaugé, 23rd March, 1421. He is one of the characters in the *Second Part of King Henry the Fourth* (q.v.).

Mentioned here as being appointed by Henry the Fifth to attend the Council at Troyes.

Cleitus.   IV. vii. 40, 47.

A favourite general of Alexander the Great. He saved the king's life on one occasion, but was killed by the latter in a fit of drunken passion :

as Alexander killed his friend Cleitus, being in his ales and his cups.

Clothair.   I. ii. 67.

Clothaire the Second, King of the Franks.

Constable of France.   II. iv. p.1 ;   III. v. p.1, 40 ;   III. vii. p.1 ;   IV. ii. p.7, 7 ;   IV. iii. 89 ;   IV. v. p.1 ;   IV. viii. 94.

This character is represented as a gallant soldier, and a man of shrewd judgment.

He feels that the Dauphin and the King of France are mistaken in their opinion of Henry and his forces ;

> O peace, Prince Dauphin !
> You are too much mistaken in this king. [II. iv. 29–30.]

At Agincourt he fought nobly, and was mortally wounded. In Act III., Scene vii., Lord Rambures addressing the Constable, says :

> My lord constable, the armour that I saw
> in your tent to-night, are those stars or suns
> upon it ?
> *Con.* Stars, my lord.
> *Dau.* Some of them will fall to-morrow, I hope.
> *Con.* And yet my sky shall not want.
> *Dau.* That may be, for you bear a many superfluously,
> and 'twere more honour some were away.
> *Con.* Even as your horse bears your praises; who
> would trot as well were some of your brags dismounted.

[Charles De-la-Bret, son of Charles the Bad, King of Navarre, and half-brother to Queen Joan, Henry the Fifth's step-mother. He was commander-in-chief of the French forces at Agincourt, where he was wounded, and died the day after the battle.]

Constantinople. V. ii. 218.

> that shall go to Constantinople and take the Turk by the beard ?
> [V. ii. 218–219.]

An anachronism. The Turks were not in possession of Constantinople until 1453, thirty-one years after the death of Henry the Fifth.

Court. IV. i. p.85.

Merely represents the common soldier in the rank and file of King Henry's army.
See also under Bates.

Cressid's kind. II. i. 76.

> No ; to the spital go,
> And from the powdering-tub of infamy
> Fetch forth the lazar kite of Cressid's kind,
> [II. i. 74–76.]

Probably an allusion to the punishment of Cressida, the heroine of *Troilus and Cressida* for her falsehood to Troilus. Henryson in his *Testament of Cresseid* tells us that having been turned out of doors by Diomede, she was struck with leprosy, and sent to the 'spittel hous' where she died.

Cressy. II. iv. 54.

> Witness our too much memorable shame
> When Cressy battle fatally was struck, [II. iv. 53–54.]

Battle of Crécy, August 26, 1346, where King Edward the Third with 30,000 troops defeated the French. Before the battle of Agincourt Charles the Sixth reminds his council of that fatal day.

Crispian. IV. iii. 40, 44.
Crispin Crispianus. IV. iii. 57 ; IV. viii. 93.
Crispin's day. IV. iii. 48.

Crispian and Crispin Crispianus were brothers, members of a noble Roman family, who fled to Soissons in France and suffered martyrdom under Diocletian. As during their missionary labours they exercised their trade of shoemaking, they were afterwards regarded as the patron saints of the shoemakers. The battle of Agincourt was fought on the festival of St. Crispin, the 25th October, 1415.

Dauphin. I. ii. 221, 235, 240, 245, 257, 259, 273, 280, 288, 291, 294, 308.

The title of the eldest son of heir-apparent to the French throne. Originally the title of the lords of Dauphiny, but Humbert II., the last of the Dauphin dynasty, ceded the province to King Philippe de Valois in 1349, on condition that the title of Dauphin should be perpetuated in the eldest son of the reigning monarch of France.

Davy Gam, esquire. IV. viii. 106.

A nickname (squinting David) applied to Davydd ab Llewelyn, a Welsh warrior. Rewarded by King Henry the Fourth during the revolt of Glendower, for fidelity. Accompanied Henry the Fifth to France, and was present at the battle of Agincourt, where he was killed. Sent by the king to reconnoitre the enemy on the eve of the battle, and on being questioned by Henry as to the strength of the French forces, replied : " May it please you, my liege, there are enough to be killed, enough to be taken prisoners, and enough to run away."

Doll Tearsheet. II. i. 77.

A disreputable character appearing in the *Second Part of King Henry the Fourth* in which play she is hailed to prison for brawling.

Duke of Bedford. I. ii. p.1 ; II. ii. p.1 ; III. i. p.1 ; IV. i. p.1, 3 ; IV. iii. p.1, 8, 53 ; V. ii. p.1.

Bedford's first appearance is in a State Room in the King's Palace, when Henry discusses his claims to certain dukedoms in France. In this scene, as during his future appearances he takes little or no part in the action of the play.

In the delineation of his part, however, there is one point to be noted, an evident error on Shakespeare's part, for although Bedford is elected to the position of Lieutenant of England for the period of Henry's absence in France, we find him with the king at Harfleur and at Agincourt.

He is a man of great courage, and after his distinguished career in *Henry IV.*, we would expect to hear more of him than is the case. But we are to meet him later in the *First Part of King Henry the Sixth*, adding to his fame until his death. Therefore we must accept his part in this play as one of the quieter episodes in his life, but one in which he is no less useful, and a part which there was no one better fitted to play.

[The Duke of Bedford is also a character in the *First Part of King Henry the Sixth* (q.v.).]

Duke of Berri. II. iv. p.1, 4 ; III. v. 41.

Uncle to Charles the Sixth, King of France. He had served at Poitiers, in 1356, and knowing how fatal that battle was to the nobility of France, persuades Charles not to be present at Agincourt, for " It is better," said he, " to lose the battle, than to lose the king and the battle."

Duke of Bourbon. III. v. p.1, 41 ; IV. v. p.1, 12 ; IV. viii. 79.

Takes no important part in the action of the play, following the same rôle as the other French princes. He is numbered among the French prisoners taken at Agincourt.

[" John, Duke of Bourbon, succeeded his father Louis the Good in 1410 ; served at Agincourt under the Constable Charles de-la-Bret, and

being taken prisoner was conveyed to England where he died in 1433, and was succeeded as Duke of Bourbon by his son, Charles Count of Clermont. He was buried at Christ-Church, Newgate Street, where so many illustrious persons of royal and noble rank were interred. Stow records the interment of the Duke : ' *John*, Duke of *Burbon* and *Angue*, Earl of *Claremond*, *Mont-pencier*, and Baron *Beaugen*, who was taken prisoner at *Agencourt*, kept prisoner eighteene yeeres and deceased in 1433.' " *French.*]

Duke of Brabant. II. iv. 5 ; III. v. 42.

Originally Brabant was a province of the Low Countries, but now divided between Belgium and Holland. In 1404 the whole of Brabant was handed over to the countess of Flanders, and in 1406 Anthony her son, who was subsequently killed at Agincourt—took the title of duke.

Duke of Bretagne. II. iv. p.1, 4.

John VI, Duke of Bretagne. Present at the council of war before the battle of Agincourt. He was not present at the battle, but was at that time at the head of several thousand men intended as reinforcements.

Duke of Burgundy. III. v. 42.

Jean Sans Peur, nephew of Charles V, enticed by the Armagnac party to a conference with the Dauphin Charles at the bridge of Montereau, September 10, 1419, and assassinated. No hint is given in the play that the Duke in Act V. is not the same as the Duke in Act III.

Duke of Burgundy. V. ii. p.1, 7, 68, p.299, 391.

The Duke of Burgundy, who appears at Troyes in the last Act was a most ardent striver for peace between the French and the English people. His speech extolling the blessings of peace is one of the fine passages in the play. [*See* Act V., Scene ii.]

[Philip, Count of Charolois, styled Philip the Good. He was the son of John the Fearless, Duke of Burgundy [Act III. v. 42], who was assassinated at Montereau in 1419, in consequence of which Philip went over to the English side. At Troyes, the Duke appeared in deep mourning for his murdered father ; King Henry on the same occasion was in a splendid suit of burnished armour, wearing in his helmet a fox's tail ornamented with jewels." *French.*]

[The Duke of Burgundy is also a character in the *First Part of King Henry the Sixth* (q.v.).]

Duke of Exeter. I. ii. p.1 ; II. ii. p.1, 39, 70 ; II. iv. p.75 ; III. i. p.1 ; III. iii. 51 ; III. vi. 5, 6, 22, 45, 92, 97 ; IV. iii. p.1, 9, 53 ; IV. vi. p.1 ; IV. vii. p.57, 188 ; IV. viii. p.23, 59 ; V. ii. p.1, 83.

Exeter first appears when the discussion takes place as to Henry's claim to the French crown. He supports the Archbishop of Canterbury in urging Henry to take up arms in support of his claim, saying ;

> Your brother kings and monarchs of the earth
> Do all expect that you shall rouse yourself,
> As did the former lions of your blood.   [I. ii. 122–124.]

We next meet him at Southampton, when Henry is about to embark for France. He is aware of the treacherous plot against Henry and remarks to the Duke of Bedford that,

> They shall be apprehended by and by.   [II. ii. 2.]

To Exeter falls the task of being spokesman in Henry's embassy to the French king, and he demands that his king's right shall be acknowledged in a determined speech, and when asked the sequel of receiving a refusal exclaims :

> if you hide the crown
> Even in your hearts, there will he rake for it :
> And therefore in fierce tempest is he coming,
> In thunder and in earthquake, like a Jove,
>   [II. iv. 97–100.]

That he was a brave soldier may be gathered from Fluellen's eulogy concerning his bravery at the bridge :

> The Duke of Exeter is as magnanimous as
> Agamemnon ; and a man that I love and honour
> with my soul, and my heart, and my duty, and
> my life, and my living, and my uttermost power :
> he is not,—God be praised and blessed !—any
> hurt in the world, but keeps the bridge most
> valiantly, with excellent discipline.   [III. vi. 6–12.]

Exeter is represented as being at Agincourt, and conveys to the king the news of the death of York and Suffolk, describing in graphic terms how these two died in loving embrace. This,

however, constitutes an error on the part of the dramatist for earlier (Act III., Scene iii.) Exeter is given charge of the town of Harfleur, Henry instructing him ;

> Come, uncle Exeter,
> Go you and enter Harfleur ; there remain,
> And fortify it strongly 'gainst the French :
> Use mercy to them all.   [III. iii. 51–54.]

He also appears with the king in the amusing scene between Henry and Williams, and gives the crowns to the latter.

After the battle of Agincourt he gives Henry particulars as to the number of prisoners taken by the English forces.

> Charles Duke of Orleans, nephew to the king ;
> John Duke of Bourbon, and Lord Bouciqualt :
> Of other lords and barons, knights and squires,
> Full fifteen hundred, besides common men.
>   [IV. viii. 78–81.]

[Sir Thomas Beaufort, a son of John of Gaunt and Catharine Swynford ; uncle to King Henry the Fifth. Under Henry IV. he held the offices of Admiral of the Fleet, Captain of Calais and Lord Chancellor of England, and was created Earl of Dorset and a K.G. by that king. On the surrender of Harfleur he was made captain of the town :

> Open your gates ! Come, uncle Exeter,
> Go you and enter Harfleur ; there remain,
> And fortify it strongly 'gainst the French :

Was not present at Agincourt ; lieutenant of Normandy 1416 ; created Duke of Exeter the same year ; was one of the ambassadors to treat of Henry the Fifth's marriage and was present at the Treaty of Troyes.]

[The Duke of Exeter is also a character in the *First Part of King Henry the Sixth* (q.v.).]

Duke of Gloucester. I. ii. p.1 ; III. i. p.1 ; III. ii. 59, 69 ; III. vi. p.90 ; IV. i. p.1, 1, p.312, 313 ; IV. iii. p.1, 9, 54 ; IV. vii. p.57, 175 ; IV. viii. p.18 ; V. ii. 84.

'The good Duke Humphrey' had a distinguished career throughout Henry's wars in France, and at the famous battle of Agincourt was in command of the second largest contingent on the English side. During the course of the encounter he led his men with great courage, and when he was wounded, Henry, seeing his gallant brother's plight, came to his aid and defends him until he can be borne from the field.

Gloucester is also present at the other important events in the course of the play, and is finally included by Henry in his Council at the signing of the Treaty of Troyes :

> K. Hen.   Go, uncle Exeter,
> And brother Clarence, and you, brother Gloucester,
> Warwick and Huntingdon, go with the king ;
>   [V. ii. 83–85.]

[The Duke of Gloucester is also a character in the *First Part of King Henry the Sixth* (q.v.).]

Duke of Orleans. II. iv. 5 ; III. v. 41 ; III. vii. p.1, 7 ; IV. ii. p.1, 6 ; IV. v. p.1 ; IV. viii. 78.

Takes but a small part in the action of the play. He is full of praises for the Dauphin, and is, like him, a shallow-minded boaster.

> By the white hand of my lady, he 's a gallant
>   prince.   [III. vii. 96–97.]

and

> He is simply the most active gentleman of France.
>   [III. vii. 99.]

His opinion of the English forces may be gathered from his remarks uttered before Agincourt,

> Foolish curs ! that run winking into the mouth of
> a Russian bear and have their heads crushed like
> rotten apples.   [III. vii. 143–145.]

but like the rest he is soon forced to change his opinion :

> Is this the king we sent to for his ransom ?   [IV. v. 9.]

and in Act IV., Scene viii., we find his name in the list of prisoners.

[Charles D'Angouleme, second Duke of Orleans, eldest son of the first duke. He married in 1406 his cousin Isabella, widow of Richard the Second of England, whose daughter Joan became the wife of John II. Duke of Alençon, a character in the *First Part of King Henry the Sixth*. The Duke married secondly Bona, daughter of Bernard, Count of Armagnac, and thirdly Mary, daughter of Adolph, Duke of Cleves. He commanded at Agincourt, was taken prisoner and carried to England, where he remained a prisoner for twenty-five years. In 1440

he was ransomed through the good offices of Philip the Good of Burgundy. He died at Amboise in 1465. His son by his third wife became Louis XII. of France, 1498.]

Duke of York. IV. iii. p.129, 131 ; IV. vi. 3, 11 ; IV. viii. 105.

Appears but once in the play, although we hear of his bravery at the battle of Agincourt from King Henry, and of his noble death from the Duke of Exeter.

Before Agincourt he exclaims to his king ;

> My lord, most humbly on my knee I beg
> The leading of the vaward.   [IV. iii. 129–130.]

and Henry complies with his request :[1]

> Take it, brave York.   [IV. iii. 131.]

Later, while the battle is in progress, the Duke of Exeter brings greeting to the king from York, and Henry asks,

> Lives he, good uncle ? thrice within this hour
> I saw him down ; thrice up again and fighting ;
> From helmet to the spur all blood he was. [IV. vi. 4–6.]

but Exeter has to reply that he is dead. This speech, describing the death of Suffolk and York is one of the most pathetic passages in the play (IV. vi. 7–32),

[Edward Plantagenet, second Duke of York, (the " Aumerle " in *King Richard II.*) eldest son of Edmund de Langley, first Duke of York, and cousin to King Henry the Fifth. Created Earl of Rutland and Duke of Albemarle (Aumerle) by Richard the Second ; deprived of the dignity of duke by Henry the Fourth, but was restored to favour in 1406. At Agincourt—where he was killed—he commanded the right wing of the English forces, and being struck down by the Duke of Alençon, was, owing to being so corpulent, unable to rise, and is said to have been ' pressed to death.' In stooping to assist York,

---

1. And in a poem of the fifteenth century, attributed to Lydgate, we have :—

> The Duke of York then full soon.
>   Before our king *he fell on knee.*
> My liege lord, *grant me a boon*
>   For His love that on cross did die !
> The foreward that you this day grant me,
>   To be before you in the field :
> By my banner, slain I will be,
>   Or I will turn my back, or me yield.

Henry was himself attacked by Alencon who knocked part of his crown from his head. The Duke of York married Philippa, eldest daughter of Sir John Mohun, Lord Mohun of Dunster, K.G., and there being no issue the title came to his nephew Richard Plantagenet who is the " Duke of York " in the *First, Second and Third Parts of King Henry the Sixth*. The Duchess Philippa married secondly Sir Walter Fitz-walter, Knight, and died in 1433.]

Earl of Cambridge. II. Chorus 23 ; II. ii. 13, 58, 66, 85, 93, 146.

Appears only in Act II., Scene ii., where with Scroop and Grey he is accused of high treason, having conspired to kill the King at Hampton (Southampton). He admits his guilt and begs for mercy :

> I do confess my fault,
> And do submit me to your highness' mercy.
> [II. ii. 77–78.]

Henry, however, offers none, and he is led away to execution.

" And then fell there a great disease and a foul mischief, for there were three lords which the King trusted much on and through false covet-ousness they had purposed and imagined the King's death and thought to have slain him and all his brethren or that he had taken the sea, which were named thus—Sir Richard, earl of Cambridge brother to the duke of York, the second was the lord Scrope Treasurer of England, the third was Sir Thomas Gray knight of the North Country, and these lords aforesaid, for lucre of money, had made promise to the Frenchmen for to have slain King Henry and all his worthy brethren by a false train suddenly or they had be-ware. But Almighty God of his great grace held his holy hand over them and saved them from this perilous mien. And for to have done this they received of the Frenchmen a million of gold and that there was proved openly. And for their false treason they were all judged unto the death. And this was the judgement, that they should be led through Hampton and without Northgate there to be beheaded, and thus they ended their life for their false covetousness and treason." Nicolas's *Battle of Agincourt*. [From Jones' *York and Lancaster*, 1399–1485.]

" The conspirators in the Play are represented as having been executed without trial. This was not the case. An inquest of twelve jurors of the county found that the Earl of Cambridge and Sir Thomas Grey had treasonably conspired to proclaim the Earl of March, and to call in a Scottish army ; and that Lord Scroop was guilty of misprison of treason. Grey was beheaded ; Cambridge and Scroop claimed the privilege of being tried by their peers ; this was granted, and all the lords in the army condemned them to the block." *Oxford and Cambridge edition*.

[Richard Plantagenet, second son of Edmund de Langley, first Duke of York (one of the charac-ters in *King Richard the Second*) and father of Richard, Duke of York, slain at the battle of Wakefield, 1460, and cousin to Henry the Fourth and brother to the Duke of York of this play. Created Earl of Cambridge 1414 ; married Anne, daughter of Roger de Mortimer and became the centre of a plot to place his wife's brother—Edmund Earl of March—on the throne, a scheme which was revealed to Henry. Attainted and executed 1415. His son Richard Plantagenet is the " Duke of York " in the *First, Second and Third Parts of King Henry the Sixth*.]

Earl of Salisbury. IV. iii. p.τ, 11, 54, p.68.

Appears but once in the play in Act IV., Scene iii., where, before the battle, he bids fare-well to the Lords Bedford, Gloucester and Exeter :

> God's arm strike with us ! 'tis a fearful odds.
> God be wi' you, princes all ; I 'll to my charge :
> If we no more meet till we meet in heaven,
> Then, joyfully, my noble Lord of Bedford,
> My dear Lord Gloucester, and my good Lord Exeter,
> And my kind kinsman, warriors all, adieu !
> [IV. iii. 5–10.]

and informs Henry that the " French are bravely in their battles set," and are ready to charge.

[This nobleman was Thomas de Montacute, eldest son of the loyal Earl of Salisbury in *King Richard II*. Took a prominent part in the French wars of Henry the Fifth by whom he was made a K.G. He was one of the ambassadors to treat of Henry's marriage with the Princess Katharine, and was his Lieutenant-General in Normandy.]

[The Earl of Salisbury is also a character in the *First Part of King Henry the Sixth* (q.v.).]

Earl of Suffolk. IV. vi. 10, 11, 15, 24 ; IV. viii. 105.

Michael de la Pole, third Earl of Suffolk ;

served with his father—who died during the siege of Harfleur—in France ; distinguished himself by his bravery at the battle of Agincourt where he was killed. His father died during the siege of Harfleur, September 4, 1415. *See Extract* 16 from Holinshed.

Earl of Warwick. IV. iii. 54 ; IV. vii. p.57, 175, 180 ; IV. viii. p.18, 20 ; V. ii. p.1, 85.

One of the minor characters of the play. He appears at the discussion of Henry's title to the French crown (I. ii.), at the battle of Agincourt (IV. vii.), and at the signing of the Treaty of Troyes.

Richard Beauchamp, Earl of Warwick, [the distinguished character in the preceding play] son of Thomas, Earl of Warwick, whom he succeeded in 1401 ; Lord high steward at the coronation of Henry the Fifth ; assisted in the suppression of the Lollard rising 1414 ; went with Henry the Fifth to France and was present at Harfleur, but not at Agincourt ; one of the ambassadors to treat of Henry's marriage, and was present at the treaty of Troyes. On his death-bed Henry the Fifth appointed him, tutor or governor to his infant son, for that " no fitter person could be provided to teach him all things becoming his rank."

[The Earl of Warwick is also a character in the *First Part of King Henry the Sixth* (q.v.).]

Earl of Westmoreland. I. ii. p.1 ; II. ii. p.1, 70 ; IV. iii. p.1, 19, 34 ; V. ii. p.1.

Appears on four occasions in the course of the play, firstly at the discussion on Henry's claim to the French crown, next at Southampton, at the battle of Agincourt, and finally at the signing of the Treaty of Troyes. He does not take any part in the development of the action.

[Ralph Neville, first Earl of Westmoreland, a character in the *First and Second Parts of King Henry the Fourth*. He was not present at Agincourt, because his duty as one of the Council of the Regent Bedford was to remain in England, therefore the wish attributed to him in Act IV., Scene iii., " O ! that we now had here But one ten thousand of those men in England That do no work to-day "*being really spoken by Sir Walter Hungerford. He died in 1425.]

Edward. I. i. 89.

Of his true titles to some certain dukedoms,
And generally to the crown and seat of France,
Deriv'd from Edward, his great-grandfather.
[I. i. 87–89.]

= King Edward the Third. The dukedoms referred to are Aquitaine, Anjou, Maine and Normandy.

Edward the Black Prince. I. ii. 105 ; II. iv. 56.

And your great-uncle's, Edward the Black Prince,
Who on the French ground play'd a tragedy,
Making defeat on the full power of France ;
[I. ii. 105–107.]

Son of King Edward the Third. An allusion to the battle of Crécy, fought on the 26th August, 1346, where the Black Prince lead the vanguard.

Edward the Black Prince of Wales. IV. vii. 96.

and your great-uncle Edward the
Plack Prince of Wales, as I have read in the
chronicles, fought a most prave pattle here in
France.   [IV. vii. 95–98.]

A reference to the battle of Crécy, where the Black Prince led the vanguard.

Edward, Duke of Bar. III. v. 42 ; IV. viii. 100.

Present at the battle of Agincourt, where he was killed.

Edward the Third. II. iv. 93.

Elbe. I. ii. 45, 52.

A river of northern Europe, the Roman Albis. It rises in the Riesengebirge, flows through Bohemia and Germany, and empties into the North Sea. Here mentioned as a boundary of the " Land Salique."

Elysium. IV. i. 280.

The land of the blest, where, according to ancient mythology the souls of the righteous passed without suffering death.

Emperor's coming. V. Chorus 38.

The emperor 's coming in behalf of France
To order peace between them ;   [V. Chorus 38.]

Refers to the visit of Sigismund—Emperor of Germany—to England in May 1416, to try to arrange terms of peace between England and France. Sigismund was married to Henry's second cousin. " This same yeer cam Sigismund, the emperour of Almayn, in to Englond forto speke with king Harri, to trete of certayn thyngiȝ touching the pees of Englond and of Fraunce : and also for the welfare and vnite of alle holi chirche. And the king and his lordis mette with him at saint Thomas wateryng, withoute Suthwerk, and him receyued withe greet reuerence and worshippe, and brouȝte him in to Londoun, and fro thenneȝ to Westmynstre, and there he was loggid in the paleis atte kyngis cost : and that tyme the king yaf him the liverey of the garter.[1] [*English Chronicle*, ed. Davies, Camden Society, No. 64.]

England. II. iv. 9 ; III. v. 37, 62 ; III. vi. 129 ; V. ii. 10, 12.

= King of England.

England. I. ii. 126, 128, 153, 169, 214, 269 ; II. Chorus 1, 16 ; II. ii. 193 ; II. iv. 24, 65, 75, 115, 116, 129 ; III. Chorus 19 ; III. i. 26, 34 ; III. vii. 134, 141 ; IV. i. 30 ; IV. ii. 37 ; IV. iii. 18, 30, 64, 73 ; IV. iv. 65 ; IV. viii. 10, 127 ; V. i. 91 ; IV. ii. 253, 350, 370, 375 ; Epilogue 6, 10, 12.

England. V. ii. 103.

Your majesty shall mock at me ; I cannot
Speak your England. [V. ii. 102-103.]

= English Language.

English Camp at Agincourt.

The Scene of Act IV., Scenes i and iii.

Act IV., Scene i. Henry confesses to Gloucester that they are in great danger on account of the odds against them. Disguising himself, he sallies forth in the camp, where he first meets Pistol with whom he bandies words, and after-

1. Walsingham says that Sigismund was installed Knight of the Garter on the Feast of St. George, having told us that he arrived in London on May 7th. This may seem strange, as St. George's day was on April 23rd. Fabyan perhaps explains this apparent contradiction, by saying that the *celebration* of the feast had been deferred on account of the Emperor.

wards meets Fluellen and Gower. Then follow three soldiers—Bates, Court and Williams—and a discussion arises on the critical position of the English army, and on the responsibility of monarchs. A dispute then ensues on the subject, and Henry accepts a challenge from Williams to fight it out should they survive the battle. The closing part of the scene shows us the king alone, musing on the heavy responsibility he has undertaken, and an appeal to heaven that his troops may prove victorious in the fight, and not to visit upon him the sin of his father,—an allusion to the usurpation of the crown by Henry the Fourth.

Act IV., Scene iii. Henry rides forth into the camp and encourages his troops. The English lords—Exeter, Salisbury and Bedford—take farewell of each other. Montjoy—the French herald—re-appears and gives Henry another chance of ransom, but Henry in a dignified manner refuses to surrender.

[The introduction of the Dukes of Bedford, and Exeter, and the Earl of Westmoreland as being among the commanders present is inaccurate. Bedford had been left as regent in England ; Exeter was in command at Harfleur and Westmoreland was at his post as Warden of the Scottish Marches.]

English Camp at Picardy.

The Scene of Act III., Scene vi. The French attempt to destroy the bridge over the river Ternoise at Blangy, but are driven away by the English troops. Henry crosses the bridge on the eve of the battle of Agincourt. Bardolph is condemned to be hanged for stealing a pax from a church. Montjoy—the French herald—arrives and delivers the French king's message, but Henry will not listen to any surrender.

English Mercuries. II. Chorus 7.

With winged heels, as English Mercuries. [II. Chorus 7.]

Mercury was the son of Jupiter and the messenger of the gods, represented with wings at his heels, hence a type of speed. The English people are represented here as hastily preparing to join the king forces for the invasion of France.

Europe. II. iv. 133 ; III. vii. 5.

Expectation. II. Chorus 8.

> For now sits Expectation in the air,
> And hides a sword from hilts unto the point
> With crowns imperial, crowns and coronets,
> Promised to Harry and his followers. [II. Chorus 8–11.]

" The imagery is wonderfully fine, and the thought exquisite," says Warburton. " *Expectation sitting in the air* designs the height of their ambition ; and the *sword hid from the hilt to the point* with crowns and coronets, that all sentiments of danger were lost in the thoughts of glory." Tollet remarks " In the Horse Armoury in the Tower of London, Edward III., is represented with two crowns on his sword, alluding to the two kingdoms, France and England, of both of which he was crowned heir. Perhaps the poet took the thought from a similar representation."

Falstaff. II. iii. 5.

Sir John Falstaff. The Falstaff of *Merry Wives of Windsor* and the two Parts of *King Henry the Fourth*. His death is mentioned here by Mrs. Quickly, hostess of an inn [the Boar's Head] in Eastcheap.

" For some cause or other the promise, already quoted [*see* Epilogue to the *Second Part of King Henry the Fourth*] touching the continuation of Sir John was not made good. Falstaff does not once appear in the play. I suspect that when the author went to planning the drama, he saw the impracticability of making any thing more out of him ; while there was at least some danger lest the part should degenerate into clap-trap. And indeed the very fact of such a promise being made might well infer a purpose rather too theatrical for the just rights of truth and art. At all events, Sir John's dramatic office and mission were clearly at an end when his connection with Prince Henry was broken off ; the design of the character being to explain the Prince's wild and riotous courses. Besides, Falstaff must have had so much of manhood in him as to love the Prince, else he were too bad a man for the Prince to be with ; and when he was so sternly cast off, the grief of this wound must in all reason have sadly palsied his sport-making powers. To have continued him with his wits shattered or crippled, had been flagrant injustice to him ; to have continued him with his wits sound and in good trim, had been something unjust to the Prince." *Hudson.*

Fauconberg. III. v. 44 ; IV. viii. 101.

A French lord killed at the battle of Agincourt.

Fig of Spain. III. vi. 60.

Probably an allusion to the use of poisoned figs in Spain for purposes of revenge. *See* Figo.

Figo. III. vi. 58 ; IV. i. 60.

> Die and be damn'd ; and figo for thy friendship !
> [III. vi. 58.]

An expression of contempt, used by Spaniards and accompanied by a contemptuous gesture. Douce in his *Illustrations of Shakespeare* has a long article on this passage. *See* Fig of Spain.

Flower-de-luce. V. ii. 220.

The Fleur-de-lys, the national emblem of France.

Fluellen. III. ii. p.21, p.58, 58, 87 ; III. vi. p.1, 91, 100 ; IV. i. 52, p.64, 64 ; IV. vii. p.1, 99, 135, 157, 176, 184 ; IV. viii. p.2 ; V. i. 9.1.

Represents the Welsh nation in Henry's forces, and is depicted as being brave, patriotic and honourable. Henry sums up his character admirably when he says of him :

> For I do know Fluellen valiant,
> And touch'd with choler, hot as gunpowder,
> And quickly will return an injury : [IV. vii. 184–186.]

but he has to admit that :

> Though it appear a little out of fashion,
> There is much care and valour in this Welshman.
> [IV. i. 83–84.]

We cannot fail to notice the many-sidedness of his character. He is courteous, and yet quick-tempered, exceptionally honest and thinks no evil of others, as exemplified by his being deceived by the boastful words of the cowardly Pistol. His open-mindedness is another of his characteristics, for he freely speaks his mind both to his superiors and followers. He praises the Duke of Exeter :

> The Duke of Exeter is as magnanimous as
> Agamemnon ; and a man that I love and honour
> with my soul, and my heart, and my duty, and
> my life, and my living, and my uttermost power :
> [III. vi. 6–9.]

and he does not conceal his devotion to King Henry, for he says :

> By Jeshu, I am your majesty's countryman, I care not who know it ; I will confess it to all the 'orld : I need not to be ashamed of your majesty, praised be God, so long as your majesty is an honest man.   [IV. vii. 115–119.]

Then there is the humorous side of his nature. His affair with Williams is particularly amusing, as is the scene where he vigorously chastises Pistol ; and he is quite as capable of using a cudgel as caustic phrases.

Hudson remarks : " But the comic life of the drama is mainly centred in a very different group of persons. Fluellen, Jamy, and Macmorris strike out an entirely fresh and original vein of entertainment ; and these, together with Bates and Williams, aptly represent the practical, working soldiership of the King's army. The conceited and loquacious Welshman, the tenacious and argumentative Scotchman, the hot and impulsive Irishman, with all whose nations the English have lately been at war, serve the further purpose of displaying how smoothly the recent national enmities have been reconciled, and all the parties drawn into harmonious co-operation, by the King's inspiring nobleness of character, and the catching enthusiasm of his enterprise. All three are as brave as lions, thoroughly devoted to the cause, and mutually emulous of doing good service ; each entering into the work with as much heartiness as if his own nation were at the head of the undertaking. All of them too are completely possessed with the spirit of the occasion, where ' honour's thought reigns solely in the breast of every man ' ; and as there is no swerving from the line of earnest warlike purpose in quest of any sport or pastime, so the amusement we have of them results purely from the spontaneous working-out of their innate peculiarities ; and while making us laugh they at the same time win our respect, their very oddities serving to set off their substantial manliness.

Fluellen is pedantic, pragmatical, and somewhat querulous, but withal a thoroughly honest and valiant soul. He loves to hear himself discourse touching ' the true discipline of the wars,' and about ' Alexander the Pig,' and how ' Fortune is painted plind, with a muffler afore her eyes, to signify to you that Fortune is plind ;

and she is painted also with a wheel, to signify to you, which is the moral of it, that she is turning and inconstant, and mutability, and variation ' : but then he is also prompt to own that ' Captain Jamy is a marvellous falorous gentleman, and of great expedition and knowledge in th' aunchient wars ' : and that ' he will maintain his argument as well as any military man in the 'orld, in the disciplines of the pristine wars of the Romans.' He is indeed rather easily gulled into thinking Pistol a hero, on hearing him ' utter as prave 'ords at the pridge as you shall see in a Summer's day ' : this lapse, however, is amply squared when he cudgels the swagger out of the ' counterfeit rascal,' and persuades him to eat the leek, and then makes him accept a groat to ' heal his proken pate ' ; which is one of Shakespeare's raciest and most spirited comic scenes. Herewith should be noted also his cool discretion in putting up with the mouthing braggart's insolence, because the time and place did not properly allow his resenting it on the spot : and when he calls on him to ' eat his victuals,' and gives him the cudgel for sauce to it ; and tells him, ' You called me yesterday mountain-squire, but I will make you to-day a squire of low degree ' ; there is no mistaking the timber he is made of.

On another occasion, Fluellen sharply reproves one of his superior officers for loud-talking in the camp at night : ' If you would take the pains but to examine the wars of Pompey the Great, you shall find, I warrant you, that there is no tiddle-taddle nor pibble-pabble in Pompey's camp ' : and the King, overhearing this reproof, hits the white of his character when he says to himself,—

> Though it appear a little out of fashion,
> There is much care and valour in the Welshman.

But perhaps the man's most characteristic passage is in his plain and downright style of speech to the King himself : the latter referring to the place of his own birth, which was in Wales, addresses him as ' my good countryman,' and he replies, ' I am your Majesty's countryman, I care not who know it : I will confess it to all the 'orld : I need not be ashamed of your Majesty, praised be God, so long as your Majesty is an honest man.' On the whole, Fluellen is a capital instance of the Poet's consideration for the rights of manhood irrespective of rank and title or any adventitious regards. Though a very subordinate person in the drama, there is more wealth of genius shown in the delineation of him than of any other except the King."

See also Gower.

Foix. III. v. 45 ; IV. viii. 101.

A French lord killed at the battle of Agincourt.

Fortune's furious fickle wheel. III. vi. 27, 32, 38, 40.

Fortune's wheel was a favourite subject of Allegory. Steevens says : " *Fortune the goddess is represented blind, to show that fortune, or the chance of life, is without discernment,*" and Farmer : " The picture of *Fortune* is taken from the old history of *Fortunatus ;* where she is described to be a fair woman, *muffled over the eyes.*"

France. Prologue 12.

can this cockpit hold
The vasty fields of France ? [Prologue i. 11–12.]

Cockpit is used contemptuously here, as the small area of the Globe Theatre was better suited for a cock-fight than for the representation of the battle of Agincourt. Malone remarks that the Phœnix Theatre in Drury Lane had formerly been a cockpit.

France. I. i. 79.

For I have made an offer to his majesty,
Upon our spiritual convocation,
And in regard to causes now in hand,
Which I have open'd to his grace at large,
As touching France. [I. i. 75–79.]

For the Archbishop's speech, see *Extract* 2 from Holinshed.

France. I. i. 88.

The severals and unhidden passages
Of his true titles to some certain dukedoms,
And generally to the crown and seat of France,
  [I. i. 87–89.]

The details and clear evidences by which Henry's claims to certain French dukedoms could be established. The dukedoms were Aquitaine, Anjou, Maine, and Normandy.

France. I. ii. 6, 11, 41, 55, 68, 80, 85, 90, 107, 112, 129, 147, 157, 161, 213, 215, 224, 227, 246, 251, 262, 275, 279, 302 ; II. Chorus 26, 27, 30, 37 ; II. i. 12, 91 ; II. ii. 16, 90, 155, 182, 193 ; II. iii. 56 ; II. iv. 22, 84, 124, 139 ; III. Chorus 24 ; III. iv. 56 ; III. v. 3, 31 ; III. vi. 157, 163 ; IV. vii. 99 ; IV. i. 15 ; IV. ii. 38 ; IV. iii. 98, 103 ; IV. vii. 57, 98 ; IV. viii. 10, 128 ; V. Chorus 38, 41, 45 ; V. i. 86 ; V. ii. 37, 38, 176, 178, 179, 180, 182, 183, 189, 191, 231, 254, 279, 282, 370, 375 ; Epilogue 10, 12.

France. I. ii. 167.

If that you will France win,
Then with Scotland first begin. [I. ii. 167–168.]

" Westmoreland was one of the lords of the northern border, which is another proof that this speech belongs to him, and not, as others represent it, to the Duke of Exeter or the Bishop of Ely. Perhaps the Poet intended, by making Westmoreland speak according to the wisdom of Proverbs, and reason from the habits of wild animals, to exhibit a specimen of the native and natural eloquence of one born and brought up far from the court and city. He makes the Archbishop afterwards adopt the same style of oratory to give utterance to refined and just sentiments, to shew how a highly cultivated mind can, on occasion given, beat the less cultivated, even at their own peculiar eloquence." *Hunter.*

France. I. ii. 265.

Tell him he hath made a match with such a wrangler
That all the courts of France will be disturb'd
with chases. [I. ii. 264–266.]

A *chace* at tennis is that spot where a ball falls, beyond which the adversary must strike his ball to gain a point or *chace*. The King probably quibbles on the word, its secondary meaning being that he will play such a game in France that the whole country will be disturbed by the flight and chasing of armies. *Halliwell.*

France. II. Chorus 20.

= King of France.

France. Before Harfleur.

The Scene of Act III., Scenes i and ii.

Act III., Scene i., comprises a single speech by Henry in which he exhorts his soldiers to break down the walls of Harfleur.

Act III., Scene ii. In this scene we return to the underplot, and get a glimpse of the rank and file of the attacking army. They include the three swash-bucklers—Bardolph, Nym and Pistol —the shrewd boy, and four captains, Gower, Macmorris, Fluellen and Jamy representatives of England, Ireland, Wales and Scotland respectively, characteristic types of their respective nationalties showing the popularity of the war.

France. Before King Henry's Pavilion.

The Scene of Act IV., Scene viii. Opens with a quarrel between Williams and Fluellen, but on the appearance of Henry the quarrel is brought to a happy ending. An English herald hands to Henry a list of the slain on both sides. The English loss is so small and the French loss so enormous that Henry ascribes the victory to God and orders his troops to go to a neighbouring village church to give thanks, after which they will depart for Calais on their way to England.

France. Before the Gates [of Harfleur].

The Scene of Act III., Scene iii. Owing to the failure of the Dauphin to come to the relief of the town, the governor surrenders to the English forces. The Duke of Exeter is placed in charge, Henry announcing that after one night's rest in the town he will march to Calais. Harfleur surrendered on the 22nd of September, 1415, after a siege of thirty-seven days.

France. The English Camp.

The Scene of Act V., Scene i. The last of the comic scenes. Pistol insults Fluellen by deriding the custom of wearing the leek, the Welsh national emblem. Fluellen makes Pistol eat the leek. Pistol receives the news of the death of his wife which makes him hasten back to England, and the comic characters are dismissed from the stage. Johnson observes : " The comick scenes of *The History of Henry the Fourth and Fifth* are now at an end, and all the comick

personages are now dismissed. Falstaff and Mrs. Quickly are dead ; Nym and Bardolph are hanged ; Gadshill was lost immediately after the robbery ; Poins and Peto have vanished since, one knows not how ; and Pistol is now beaten into obscurity. I believe every reader regrets their departure."

France. The French King's Palace.

The Scene of Act II., Scene iv. In this scene King Charles of France (he was not present at the audience, being insane, the Dauphin acting as Regent) is represented as being much concerned at the invasion of France by the English forces. The English Embassy is introduced and the Duke of Exeter as spokesman demands that Charles surrenders to Henry the crown and kingdom of France. The French king decides to reserve his answer until the following day.

[Shakespeare here takes great liberty with history. Exeter's mission, as related by Holinshed, took place a considerable time before Henry went to France, or even to Southampton. Exeter does not appear to have been in any one of Henry's missions to the French king ; nor was there any mission, after the landing of the English in France.]

French Camp, near Agincourt.

The Scene of Act III., Scene vii. Act IV., Scene ii.

Act III., Scene vii. Describes the French camp near Agincourt on the eve of the battle. It shows the French princes outrivaling one another in their boastfulness, so sure are they of defeating the English. A messenger brings word that the English are within fifteen hundred paces of the French tents.

Act IV., Scene ii. The French camp where we find the French princes again boasting of their horses and armour, and of their self-confidence of an easy victory.

Gallia. I. ii. 216.

= France.

Gallia Wars. V. i. 93.

= French wars.

Germany. I. ii. 44, 53.

Gordian knot. I. i. 46.

> Turn him to any cause of policy,
> The Gordian knot of it he will unloose,
> Familiar as his garter ;					[I. i. 45–47.]

The Archbishop here infers that Henry by his ingenuity is able to solve any question of public policy.

An allusion to the story of the famous knot in Gordium, Phyria. According to Legend, Gordius, king of Phyria dedicated his chariot to Jupiter in the Acropolis of Gordium. An intricate knot fastened the pole of the yoke, and an oracle declared that whoever should untie it would rule over all Asia. Alexander the Great solved the difficulty by cutting the knot with one stroke of his sword, and applied the oracle's prophecy to himself.

Governor of Harfleur. III. iii. p.1.

From the walls of the city of Harfleur the Governor and citizens announce to King Henry that it is their intention " to yield their town to his soft mercy."

" Jean lord D'Estouteville held the chief command at Harfleur when it was first invested by the English, but a reinforcement of 300 lances having been thrown in under Raoul, Sieur de Gaucourt, that leader seems thereupon to have assumed the direction of the defence ; thus Lydgate speaks of him as Governor,—

> ' The Lord Gaucourt certyenly,
> For he was capteyn in that place.'

Gaucourt was the principal spokesman for his side in the parleys with the English lords, appointed to treat for the surrender of the town, after a siege of thirty-six days, September 22, 1415. D'Estouteville and Gaucourt were both sent as prisoners to England ; the latter wrote a narrative of the siege. A Robert D'Estouteville was appointed by Louis XI., to the command of a force in Artois to oppose the landing of Edward IV., when he meditated the conquest of France. *French.*

Gower. III. ii. p.58 ; III. vi. p.1, 84 ; IV. i. p.64 ; IV. vii. p.1, 12, 152, 153, 170 ; IV. viii. p.1, 13 ; V. i. p.1, 5.

Is the representative of the English nation in Henry's army, and a typical English soldier of the period. He appears at the siege of Harfleur, where we find him well in the thick of the fight. For the most part he is in the company of Fluellen, of whom he stands in awe, for he accepts Fluellen's rebuke for speaking loudly most submissively :

> *Flu.* So ! in the name of Jesu Christ, speak lower.
>
> *Gow.* I will speak lower.					[IV. i. 65–81.]

He is also present at Agincourt, where he bravely upheld the traditions of the English troops.

The conjunction of the four captains—Gower (England), Jamy (Scotland), Macmorris (Ireland), Fluellen (Wales)—fighting side by side in a common cause is regarded by many critics as typifying the union of the crowns, which, at the date of the composition of this play, all felt to be imminent. The fiery Macmorris, the ' marvellous falorous ' Jamy, the impulsive Fluellen, and the self-restrained Gower are singularly characteristic types of their respective nationalities. *Academy Shakespeare.*

Gower, Fluellen, Macmorris, and Jamy represent the four nations, English, Welsh, Irish, and Scottish, of which Henry's army was composed, though there were very few Irish or Scots in it, particularly the latter, who were much readier to fight for the French. There was, however, a Scotchman of the name of James in Henry's last expedition to France—no less a personage than the King of Scotland, James I., who had been a prisoner in England since 1405. Jamy does not take much part in the play, and speaks more like a Yorkshireman than a Scotchman : Macmorris, the Irishman is a fair example of the excitable Celt, though his speech bears no resemblance to a modern Irish brogue : Gower is a good specimen of a solid, rather stupid Englishman—who does not see why he should not speak loud if the enemy does, but accepts Fluellen's rebuke meekly, and evidently has a great admiration for him. *Blackfriars edition.*

Grandpré. III. v. 44 ; III. vii. 129 ; IV. ii. p.38 ; IV. viii. 101.

Appears only in one scene of the play. He led the main body of the French army with the Dukes of Alençon and Bar. He fell on the field of Agincourt,

[One of the twelve great Peers of France. At the battle of Agincourt he was a leader in the main body of the French forces with the Dukes of Bar and Alençon.]

Hampton. II. ii. 91.

And sworn unto the practices of France,
To kill us here in Hampton :   [II. ii. 90–91.]

= Southampton. The Earl of Cambridge, Lord Scroop and Sir Thomas Grey had entered into a conspiracy to kill Henry at Hampton. *An English Chronicle*, ed. Davies, [Camden Society, No. 64,] says : " Thanne made the kyng redy his ordenaunce necessary forto the warre, commaundyng alle menne that sholde go with him to be redy att Suthamptoun, at Lammesse thanne next folowyng, the iij yeer of his regne. At whiche day, whan the king was redy to take his passage, it was there publisshid and openli knowe that iij lordis, that is to say, ser Richard erlle of Cambrigge brothir to the duke of York, the lord Scroope tresorer of Englond, and ser Thomas Grey, knyghte, hadde receyued an huge summe of money, that is to say, a milion of gold, forto betraie the king and his bretheryn to the Frenshemen ; wherfore thair heddis were smyte of, withoute the northgate at Suthamptoun."

Hampton pier. III. Chorus 4.

Suppose that you have seen
The well-appointed king at Hampton pier
Embark his royalty ;   [Chorus iii. 3–5.]

= Southampton. Warton says : " Among the records of the town of Southampton, they have a minute and authentick account (drawn up at that time) of the encampment of Henry the Fifth near the town, before his embarkment for France. It is remarkable, that the place where the army was encamped, then a low level or a down, is now entirely covered with sea, and called Westport."

Harfleur. III. Chorus 17 ; III. iii. 8, 27, 52, 57 ; III. v. 49 ; III. vi. 126.

A seaport on the northern coast of France on the estuary of the Seine. It was taken after a six months' siege by the English under Henry (1415).

" Whanne this was don, the king sailled forth in to Normandie with xvc shippis, and landid at Kitcaux, in the vigily of Assumpcion of our Lady, and fro thenne3 he wente to Harfleiu, and it besegid be lond and be watir, and commaundyng him forto delyuer the toun, and he saide he wolde not. Wherfore the king commaundid his gonners to bete doun the wallis on euery side, and anon thay of the toune sente out to the king prayyng him of viij daie3 respit in hope of rescu, and yf non wolde come, thay wolde delyver the toun : and so thay dede. And thanne the kyng made his vncle, the erl of Dorset, capteyn therof, and commaundid him to put out alle the Frensshe peple, man womman and child, and stuffe the toun with English peple." *An English Chronicle*, ed. Davies, [Camden Society, No. 64]. *See also* Grafton's *Chronicle*, vol. I., pp. 512–514.

Harfleur. III. Chorus 27.

With fatal mouths gaping on girded Harfleur.
                        [III. Chorus 27.

Harfleur was besieged on every side.

Harry. Prologue 5.

Then should the warlike Harry, like himself,
Assume the port of Mars ; and at his heels,
Leash'd in like hounds, should famine, sword, and fire
Crouch for employment.   [Prologue i. 5–8.]

= King Henry the Fifth. Tollet says : " This image of the war-like Henry very much resembles Montfaucon's description of the Mars discovered at Bresse, who leads a lion and a lioness in couples, and crouching as for employment." Holinshed says that when the citizens of Rouen petitioned Henry V., " he declared that the goddesse of battell, called Bellona, had three handmaidens, euer of necessitie attending vpon hir, as blood, fire, and famine."

Harry. II. Chorus 11.

= King Henry the Fifth. *See* Expectation.

Harry. III. Chorus 29 ; III. i. 34 ; IV. i. 33 ; V. Chorus 35.

= King Henry the Fifth.

Harry. IV. Chorus 47.

A little touch of Harry in the night.   [Chorus iv. 47.]

= King Henry the Fifth. Theobald says : " The poet, addressing himself to every degree of his audience, tells them he'll show (as well as his unworthy pen and powers can describe it) a little touch or sketch of this hero in the night ; a faint resemblance of that cheerfulness and resolution which this brave prince expressed in himself, and inspired in his followers."

Harry England. III. v. 48.

= King Henry the Fifth.

Harry le Roy. IV. i. 49.

= Harry the King.

Harry Monmouth. IV. vii. 48.

= Henry the Fifth, from the place of his birth.

Harry of England. III. vi. 123 ; III. vii. 131 ; V. ii. 250, 296.

= King Henry the Fifth.

Harry of Monmouth. IV. vii. 33.

Henry the Fifth, so-called because he was born at Monmouth.

Harry's back-return. V. Chorus 41.

An allusion to Henry the Fifth's return to France in 1417.

Harry the King. IV. iii. 53.

= King Henry the Fifth.

Henry Plantagenet. V. ii. 254.

= King Henry the Fifth.

Henry the Sixth. Epilogue 9.

> Henry the Sixth, in infant bands crown'd King
> Of France and England, did this king succeed.
> [Epilogue 9–10].

Henry the Sixth was only nine months old when his father—Henry the Fifth—died.

Herald, A. IV. viii. p.75.

English Herald. Informs the king of the number of the French slain and taken prisoners in the battle, as well as the number of the English dead.

Three heralds attended Henry V. at Agincourt, namely, Lancaster, Guienne, and Ireland, Kings at Arms. In 1419, March 4, Henry created a new herald, called " Agincourt, king at arms," in honour of his great achievement. In this reign " Lancaster, king at arms," was John Ashwell ; " Guienne," was John Wrexworth ; and " Ireland," was John Kitteby. Weever, *Ancient Funeral Monuments.* The king also employed " Dorset " herald, on embassies ; he is named in a writ, May 13, 1413, " William Bois, Armiger, Dorset le Heraud." Rymer's *Fœdera.*

Hermes. III. vii. 18.

> the basest horn of his hoof
> is more musical than the pipe of Hermes.
> [III. vii. 17–18.]

The shepherd's pipe invented by the god Hermes or Mercury, the music of which was so sweet that it charmed to sleep the hundred-eyed Argus.

Herod's bloody - hunting slaughtermen. III. iii. 41.

An allusion to the slaughter of the innocents. See *St. Matthew,* ii. 16–18.

Hostess of a tavern, formerly Mistress Quickly, and now married to Pistol. II. i. 19, p.27, 78, p.117 ; II. iii. p.1.

Appears with Nym, Bardolph and her future husband Pistol, in a street before the Boar's Head Tavern in Eastcheap. A quarrel takes place between Nym and Pistol, who are rivals for the hand of the hostess, but it is interrupted by the entry of Falstaff's boy who announces that his master has been taken very ill. Mistress Quickly forthwith departs, and later returns, bidding them come quickly as the old knight is dying :

> As ever you came of women, come in quickly
> to Sir John. Ah, poor heart ! he is so shaked
> of a burning quotidian tertian, that it is most
> lamentable to behold. Sweet men, come to him.
> [II. i. 117–120.]

Hound of Crete. II. i. 73.

An allusion to the blood-hounds of Crete which were much prized in antiquity. The expression here is one of Pistol's high-sounding phrases, insinuating that Nym is thirsting for his blood,

Hugh Capet. I. ii. 69, 78, 87.

The founder of the Capetian dynasty of France, son of Hugh the Great whom he succeeded in the duchy of France. Proclaimed king in 987 and reigned till his death in 996. His reign was a troubled one by the revolt of the party that had raised him to the throne and who refused to acknowledge his supremacy. Adelbert, a count of Perigueux usurped the titles of Count of Poitiers and of Tours, and Capet sent a messenger to ask " who made you count ? " and got for answer the counter-challenge " who made you king ? " According to the Archbishop of Canterbury Capet " usurped the crown of Charles the Duke of Lorraine " and " to find his title with some shows of truth, Though, in pure truth, it was corrupt and naught," claimed descent from " Charles the Great " [Charlemagne] through " Lady Lingare."

Huntingdon. V. ii. 85.

John Holland, Earl of Huntingdon ; distinguished himself at the battle of Agincourt, 1415 ; K.G. 1416 ; took part in the siege of Caen and Rouen 1419, and after won the battle of Fresney. Constable of the Tower of London 1429 ; English representative at Arras, 1438, and Governor of Aquitaine 1440. He died in 1447.

Mentioned here as being appointed by Henry the Fifth to attend the Council at Troyes.

Hydra-headed. I. i. 35.

> Nor never Hydra-headed wilfulness
> So soon did lose his seat and all at once
> As in this king.   [I. i. 35-37.]

The Hydra was a celebrated monster with nine heads—one of which was immortal—which infested the neighbourhood of Lake Lerna in Peloponnesus. As Hercules cut off one of its heads, two new ones sprang up in its place, but with the help of Iolaus he succeeded in conquering the monster by burning away the heads and thus preventing the growth of more. He then struck off the immortal head and buried it under a rock. Cf. *First Part of King Henry the Fourth,* V. iv. 25 : " Another king ! they grow like Hydra's heads " :

Hyperion. IV. i. 281.

> next day after dawn,
> Doth rise and help Hyperion to his horse,
>   [IV. i. 280-281.]

One of the Titans, represented as the son of Heaven and earth, and father of the sun and moon. Often used by poets to signify the sun. Cf. *Titus Andronicus,* V. ii. 56-57 :

> Even from Hyperion's rising in the east
> Until his very downfall in the sea :

Iceland dog. II. i. 41.

> Pish for thee, Iceland dog ! thou prick-ear'd cur of
> Iceland.   [II. i. 41.]

A curly, rough-haired dog, used as a lap-dog. In the time of Shakespeare they were fashionable pets.

Ireland. V. Chorus 31.

> Were now the general of our gracious empress,
> As in good time he may, from Ireland coming,
> Bringing rebellion broached on his sword,
>   [V. Chorus 29-31.]

The allusion is to Robert Devereux, Earl of Essex. Macgillivray remarks : " In the spring of 1599 the Earl of Essex was sent to Ireland with a large force to suppress Tyrone's rebellion. His departure was the occasion for such a great outburst of popular enthusiasm that it is said to have aroused the jealousy of the queen. For various reasons, the campaign was a failure, and Essex was recalled in disgrace. This allusion to Essex practically settles the limits of the date of the play—after the spring of 1599 and before the autumn of the same year ; *i.e.* between the departure in triumph and the return in disgrace of Essex."

Ireland. V. ii. 253.

Isabel, Queen of France. V. ii. p.1, p.299.

As Isabel appears but once in the play it is difficult to gather any definite opinion of her character.

She appears to be deeply interested in the affairs of her country, however, as it is by her own wish that she is present at the council convened to arrive at terms of peace, exclaiming ;

> Our gracious brother, I will go with them ;
> Haply a woman's voice may do some good
> When articles too nicely urg'd be stood on.
>   [V. ii. 92-94.]

Her approval of Henry's marriage to Katharine is voiced in a speech which expresses a hope that thus a friendship may be formed between England and France, showing that she believed the power of amity to be stronger than that of arms.

> God, the best maker of all marriages,
> Combine your hearts in one, your realms in one !
> As man and wife, being two, are one in love,
> So be there 'twixt your kingdoms such a spousal
> That never may ill office, or fell jealousy,
> Which troubles oft the bed of blessed marriage,
> Thrust in between the paction of these kingdoms,
> To make divorce of their incorporate league ;
> That English may as French, French Englishmen,
> Receive each other !   God speak this Amen !
>   [V. ii. 379–388.]

Daughter of Stephen the Second, Duke of Bavaria. Married King Charles of France in 1385. She was a woman of very dissolute habits. Miss Strickland describes her as the " wicked queen Isabeau " and calls her a " vile woman," while Hallam styles her the " most infamous of women."

Jack-an-napes.   V. ii. 144.

An imprudent fellow.

Jack-sauce.   IV. vii. 145.

= A saucy fellow.

Jacques of Chatillon.   III. v. 43 ;   IV. viii. 95.

Admiral of France, killed at the battle of Agincourt.

Jamy.   III. ii. p.78, 79, 80.

Takes but a little part in the play, but it is evident that Shakespeare intended him to represent the Scottish nation in King Henry's troops. Fluellen describes him as " a marvellous falorous gentleman, of great expedition and knowledge in the disciplines of war," who will " maintain his argument as well as any military man in the world."

For Hudson's comment on the character of Jamy *see under* Fluellen.

Jeshu.   IV. vii. 115.

Jewry.   III. iii. 40.

Judea. *See* Herod's bloody-hunting slaughtermen.

Jove.   II. iv. 100.

> In thunder and in earthquake like a Jove,   [II. iv. 100.]

Jupiter, represented as having his throne in heaven, and as wielding a thunderbolt in his right hand.   King Henry in his invasion of France is here described as descending upon the land like Jove.

Jove.   IV. iii. 24.

> By Jove, I am not covetous for gold,   [IV. iii. 24.]

Probably used as a substitute for a profane term, as an act was passed in the reign of James the First against profanity on the stage.   Johnson remarks : " The king prays like a christian, and swears like a heathen ! "

Kate.   V. ii. 107, 109, 122, 135, 145, 150, 157, 167, 178, 181, 185, 192, 199, 202, 205, 209, 210, 213, 224, 233, 241, 263, 264, 273, 285, 286, 288, 293, 343, 377, 393.

= Katharine, daughter of Charles and Isabel, King and Queen of France ; afterwards Queen to King Henry the Fifth.   *See* Katharine.

Katharine.   III. Chorus 30 ; III. iv. p.1 ; V. ii. p.1, 4, 95, 98, 104, 113, 228, 247, 259.

Appearing only in two scenes of the play, Katharine appears to us as a simple French maid, an impression undoubtedly intended to be formed by the introduction of the English lesson scene.

Although she has some affection for Henry, it seems that she enters the marriage compact rather from a sense of duty than love.

Heine remarks : " We wonder whether Shakespeare really wrote that scene in which Princess Katharine takes an English lesson ; and I question whether the French forms of speech so pleasing to the ear of John Bull, are actually Shakespeare's. . . .   It was probably an Englishman's ill-will which caused the artist of the portrait before us to give this French princess rather a comical than a beautiful expression. She has the face of a bird, and her eyes look as if they belonged to someone else. Does she wear parrots' feathers on her head, and do they signify her powers of chattering? Her small white hands have an inquisitive look. She is made up of a vain love of display and a desire to please, and she knows how to play with her fan. I think her feet flirt with the very ground on which she treads."

[Katharine was the youngest daughter of Charles the Sixth and Isabel, and was born at Paris 1401. Married Henry the Fifth at Troyes on the 2nd June, 1420, and was crowned at Westminster 1421; accompanied Henry to France in 1422 and returned with his corpse to England the same year. She subsequently married Owen Tudor, a poor Welch gentleman who is said to have been one of Davy Gam's retinue at Agincourt, and to have saved the life of Henry V. who made him one of his " esquires of the body," an office which he afterwards held to the infant king, Henry VI.]

Kern of Ireland. III. vii. 54.

　　　　　　　　　　and you
　rode, like a kern of Ireland, your French hose
　off, and in your strait strossers.　[III. vii. 53-55.]

The kern was a light-armed Irish soldier, who rode without breeches, and therefore *strait trossers.*

King Edward's fame. I. ii. 162.

　To fill King Edward's fame with prisoner kings,
　　　　　　　　　　[I. ii. 162.]

= King Edward the Third. *prisoner kings =* David the Second, and King John of France who was captured at the battle of Poitiers, 1356.

King Edward the Third. I. ii. 248.

= King of England (1327–1377), son of Edward the Second.

King Harry. II. iv. 48, 65; IV. iii. 79, 126.

= King Henry the Fifth.

King Henry the Fifth. Prologue 5; I. ii. p.1; II. Chorus 11; II. ii. p.12; II. iv. 48, 65; III. Chorus 29; III. i. p.1, 34; III. iii. p.1; III. v. 48; III. vi. p.90, 123; III. vii. 131; IV. Chorus 47; IV. i. p.1, 33; IV. iii. p.17, 53, 70, 126; IV. vi. p.1; IV. vii. p. 57; IV. viii. p.23; V. Chorus 35, 37, 41; V. ii. p.1, 23, 250, 296, 359, 361.

It is considered by many that in King Henry V., Shakespeare has created the finest character in all his historical plays. He is represented as possessing all the great qualities of a king, a statesman and a gentleman. His individuality is perfect, for he stands out clearly against the background of his court, a court which is itself composed of some very fine figures.

At the commencement of the play he is discussing his claims to the lands in France, and it is significant of his nature, that instead of immediately rushing to arms against the French king he first of all seeks the advice of the Archbishop of Canterbury as to the exact interpretation of the Salique Law, and his own position in the light of that Statute, in order firmly to establish in his own mind as well as in the minds of his nobles, that the course he is constrained to take is right.

Before going further into the character of Henry as a king, it is well to consider him as we found him in *King Henry IV.* Here he was wild, headstrong and careless of his position, or at least so it then appeared, but was not the experience of life that he so gained the basis of his perfect character as a king? He had learnt to understand the minds of the common people, to share in their very thoughts and so learn to judge between the counsels of the wise and the foolish so that when we see him as a king he is firm, resolute, and inspiring in his words, a man perfectly fitted to govern in a perfectly fearless and impartial way. He had learnt that to favour unduly did not always mean true allegiance, for many unscrupulous men would take advantage of any favour shown them against the giver.

He is depicted as a man of the greatest courage, and we find him throughout the course of the wars in France ever urging his men on, and inspiring them to gallant deeds.

Also Henry's piety is to be noted ; he trusts in the power of God always. On leaving for France he exclaims :

> let us deliver
> Our puissance into the hands of God
> [II. ii. 189–190.]

and again when the English army is seriously depleted through sickness and the remainder of the men worn out with continued marching, he replies to Gloucester, who has expressed a hope that the enemy will not attack at such a time,

> We are in God's hand, brother, not in theirs.
> [III. vi. 175.]

Once more his trust is shown when, just before the battle he offers up that inspiring prayer,

> O God of battles ! steel my soldiers' hearts ;
> Possess them not with fear ; take from them now
> The sense of reckoning, if the opposed numbers
> Pluck their hearts from them.   [IV. i. 295–298.]

and the victory having been won he turns once more to Heaven with words of true thankfulness on his lips ;

> O God ! thy arm was here ;
> And not to us, but to thy arm alone,
> Ascribe we all.   [IV. viii. 108–110.]

Instances exemplifying Henry's qualities as a statesman, scholar, soldier and even as a lover could be quoted, and the sum of the opinions formed on study of his character can best be expressed by saying that Henry was a great man and a great king.

Commenting on the character of King Henry, Hudson says : " The King is the most complex and many-sided of all Shakespeare's heroes, with the one exception of Hamlet ; if indeed even Hamlet ought to be excepted. He is great alike in thought, in purpose, and in performance ; all the parts of his character drawing together perfectly, as if there were no foothold for distraction among them. Truth, sweetness, and terror build in him equally. And he loves the plain presence of natural and homely characters, where all is genuine, forthright, and sincere. Even in his sternest actions as king, he shows, he cannot help showing, the motions of a brotherly heart : there is a certain grace and suavity in his very commands, causing them to be felt as bene-dictions. To be frank, open, and affable with all sorts of persons, so as to call their very hearts into their mouths, and move them to be free, plain-spoken, and simple in his company, as losing the sense of inferior rank in an equality of manhood,—all this is both an impulse of nature and a rule of judgment with him. Nothing contents him short of getting heart to heart with those about or beneath him : all conventional starch, all official forms, all the facings of pride, that stand in the way of this, he breaks through ; yet he does this with so much natural dignity and ease, that those who see it are scarcely sensible of it : they feel a peculiar graciousness in him, but know not why. And in his practical sense of things, as well as in his theory, inward merit is the only basis of kingly right and rule : yet he is so much at home in this thought, that he never emphasizes it at all ; because he understands full well that such merit, where it really lives, will best make its way when left to itself, and that any boasting or putting on airs about it can only betray a lack of it.

Thus the character of this crowned gentlemen stands together in that native harmony and beauty which is most adorned in being un-adorned. And his whole behaviour appears to be governed by an instinctive sense of this. There is no simulation, no disguise, no study for appearances, about him : all got-up dignities, any thing put on for effect, whatever savours in the least of sham or shoddy, is his aversion ; and the higher the place where it is used, the more he feels it to be out of place ; his supreme delight being to seem just what he is, and to be just what he seems. In other words, he has a sted-fast, living operative faith in the plenipotence of truth : he wants nothing better ; scorns to rely on any thing else : this is the soul of all his thoughts and designs. The sense of any dis-crepancy between his inward and his outward parts would be a torment to him. Hence his unaffected heartiness in word and deed. What-soever he cannot enter into with perfect whole-ness and integrity of mind, that he shrinks from having any thing to do with. Accordingly in all that flows from him we feel the working of a heart so full that it cannot choose but overflow. Perhaps indeed he has never heard it said that ' an honest man 's the noblest work of God ' ; perhaps he has never even thought it conscious-ly ; but it is the core of his practical thinking ;

he lives it, and therefore knows it by heart, if not by head. . . .

The character of Shakespeare's Henry the Fifth may almost be said to consist of piety, honesty, and modesty. And he embodies these qualities in their simplest and purest form ; all sitting so easy and natural in him that he thinks not of them. Then too, which is well worth the noting, they so draw and work together, that each may be affirmed of the others ; that is, he is honest and modest in his piety, pious and modest in his honesty ; so that there is nothing obtrusive or showy in his acting of these virtues : being solid and true, they are therefore much within and little without, and are perfectly free from any air of pretence or design. And all the other manly virtues gather upon him in the train of these ; while, as before remarked, at the centre of the whole stands a serene faith in the sufficiency of truth. . . .

In respect of piety, the King exemplifies whatever was best in the teaching and practice of his time. Nor, upon the whole, is it altogether certain that any thing better has arisen since his time. What appears as modesty in his dealings with men here takes the form of humility, deep and unaffected ; he thinks, speaks, and acts in fear of God : this trait is indeed the central point, the very core of the whole delineation."

[King Henry the Fifth, surnamed Monmouth from the place of his birth, was the eldest son of Henry the Fourth ; born 1387, acceded 1413, died 1422. His youthful escapes and his associations with that marvellous creation, Sir John Falstaff form the leading incidents in the *First Part of King Henry the Fourth.* He accompanied his father to Wales in 1400 and succeeded in checking Glendower, assisted his father at Shrewsbury in 1403 where he was wounded ; afterwards being appointed the king's lieutenant in Wales. On his accession he claimed the French crown and invaded France, captured Harfleur, and on the 25th of October, 1415, won the battle of Agincourt. Three years later he married the Princess Katharine, daughter of the French king, and in 1420 concluded the peace of Troyes under which he was recognised as regent and heir to the French throne. Returned to France for a third campaign in 1421 when he was seized with illness and died at Vincennes, August 31st, 1422.]

King Lewis, his satisfaction. I. ii. 88.

= the satisfaction of King Lewis' conscience. As mentioned in lines 77–83 Lewis could not wear the crown with a clear conscience " till satisfied That fair Queen Isabel, his grandmother, Was lineal to the Lady Ermengare, Daughter to Charles the foresaid Duke of Lorraine : By the which marriage the line of Charles the Great was reunited to the crown of France."

King of England. V. Chorus 37.

= King Henry the Fifth.

King of Scots. I. ii. 161.

> But taken and impounded as a stray
> The King of Scots ; whom she did send to France,
> [I. ii. 160–161.]

David the Second, captured at the battle of Neville's Cross, October 17, 1346, by the English army under Queen Philippa, during the absence of Edward the Third in France. In the anonymous Play of *Edward III.*, John Copland, to whom David surrendered, is represented as taking his prisoner to Calais and handing him over to the king. David was not sent to France, but was held in captivity for eleven years.

King Pepin. I. ii. 65, 87.

" The Short," son of Charles Martel, and founder of the Carlovingian dynasty. He deposed Childeric in A.D. 751. According to the Archbishop, Pepin claimed the crown of France through female descent.

Ladies. V. ii. p.1.

Lady Ermengare. I. ii. 82.

According to Shakespeare, the daughter of Charles, Duke of Lorraine, and an ancestress of King Lewis the Tenth. The name is not mentioned in history.

Lady Lingare. I. ii. 74.

> Convey'd himself as heir to the Lady Lingare,
> Daughter to Charlemain, [I. ii. 74–76.]

Supposed ancestress of Hugh Capet. The name is not mentioned in history. Ritson says : " But then Charlechauve (Charlemain) had only one daughter, named Judith, married, or, as some say, only betrothed, to our King Ethelwuld, and carried off, after his death, by Baldwin the forester, afterward Earl of Flanders, whom, it is very certain, Hugh Capet was neither heir to, nor any way descended from. This Judith, indeed, had a great-grand-daughter called Luitgarde, married to a Count Wichman, of whom nothing further is known. It was likewise the name of Charlemagne's fifth wife ; but no such female as Lingare is to be met with in any French historian. In fact, these fictitious personages and pedigrees seem to have been devised by the English heralds, to ' find a title with some show of truth,' which, ' in pure truth was corrupt and naught.' It was manifestly impossible that Henry, who had no hereditary title to his own dominions, could derive one, by the same colour, to another person's. He merely proposes the invasion and conquest of France, in prosecution of the dying advice of his father :

> to busy giddy minds
> In foreign quarrels ; that action, thence borne out,
> Might waste the memory of former days :

that his subjects might have sufficient employment to mislead their attention from the nakedness of his title to the crown. The zeal and eloquence of the Archbishop are owing to similar motives."

Le Fer, Monsieur. IV. iv. 26, 27, 28.

A French soldier taken prisoner by Pistol who exhorts a ransom of two hundred crowns from him.

Lestrale. III. v. 45 ; IV. iii. 102.

A French nobleman killed at the battle of Agincourt.

Lewis the Dauphin. II. iv. p.1, 6, 29, 111, 115 ; III. iii. 45 ; III. v. p.1, 64 ; III. vii. p.1, 93 ; IV. ii. p.1 ; IV. v. p.1.

An unworthy youth whose shallowness was mainly responsible for the French defeat. He is dissolute, boastful and arrogant, and his obstinate refusal to be turned from the idea that England

> is so idly king'd
> Her sceptre so fantastically borne
> By a vain, giddy, shallow, humorous youth,
> That fear attends her not.   [II. iv. 26–29.]

shows plainly the shallowness of his nature.

We find that even his nobles doubt his courage, and the Constable freely states his mind when he says that the Dauphin " will eat all he kills in the battle."

He appears for the last time at Agincourt, and in the hour of defeat wildly exclaims ;

> Mort de ma vie ! all is confounded, all !
> Reproach and everlasting shame
> Sits mocking in our plumes. O meschante fortune !
> Do not run away.   (IV. v. 3–6.]

and

> O perdurable shame ! let 's stab ourselves.
> Be these the wretches that we play'd at dice for ?
>   [IV. v. 7–8.]

Gervinus says : " Among the French leaders there is hardly one who does not vie with another in empty boasting and bragging ; not one who does not share the childish delight in dress and military decoration, not one whom the seriousness of things can draw away from insipid witicisms and vain debates, not one who showed even a tinge of the seriousness and of the calm courage and devotion of the English. But the Dauphin surpasses them all in shallow self-complacency, in frivolous arrogance, and in this merry bragging from natural narrowness of capacity."

[The Dauphin was the eldest son of Charles the Sixth of France. He died in 1415 soon after the battle of Agincourt where he was not allowed to be present on account of his impetuousness. Succeeded as Dauphin by his brother John who died in 1417 and then by his brother Charles, afterwards Charles the Seventh, who figures in the *First Part of King Henry the Sixth* under both characters.]

Lewis the emperor. I. ii. 76.

> who was the son
> To Lewis the emperor, and Lewis the son
> Of Charles the Great.   [I. ii. 75–77.]

Lewis the Tenth. I. ii. 77.

This should be Lewis the Ninth. Holinshed misled Shakespeare.

London. II. Chorus 34 ; III. ii. 12 ; III. vi. 70 ; V. Chorus 14, 24, 35.

London. An Antechamber in the King's Palace.

The Scene of Act I., Scene i. Opens with a discussion between the Archbishop of Canterbury and the Bishop of Ely relative to a Bill, which, if passed into law, would deprive the Church of a great portion of its wealth. With a view to gaining the support of the king, the Archbishop announces that he has offered on behalf of the Church a large subsidy for the prosecution of the war with France. Comment is also made on the marked change in the king's character since his accession. [According to Holinshed this scene took place at Leicester, where a Parliament was held on the 30th of April, 1414. See *Extract* 1 from Holinshed.]

London. Before a Tavern.

The Scene of Act II., Scene iii. We are back in London. The principal themes in this scene are the death of Sir John Falstaff, and the departure of Nym, Bardolph and Pistol for Southampton to join the army for France.

London. The Presence Chamber.

The Scene of Act I., Scene ii. The Archbishop of Canterbury is summoned by the king who asks him whether the Salique Law bars him from claiming the throne of France. The Archbishop satisfies the king that his claim is just, as the Salique Law originated in Germany, and therefore does not apply to France, and urges the king to stand for his own. Canterbury is supported in this by the Bishop of Ely and the Duke of Exeter, who incite Henry to war, the archbishop again offering a large sum of money, on behalf of the clergy. The king mentions the possibility of a Scottish invasion during the army's absence in France, but this objection is overcome. The French ambassadors are admitted and tell Henry that his claim to certain French dukedoms is rejected, and that the Dauphin has sent him a present of tennis-balls. Henry resents this insult, and war is declared between England and France.

Courtenay remarks : " Modern historians are apt to treat them [Henry's claims] as altogether unrighteous, and dictated by an inordinate ambition ; and of this opinion, I fear, is Sir Harris Nicolas, who has so ably described the king's warlike achievements. Now it appears to me that though the claim to the crown could not be sustained, Henry had a just cause of war with France, from her breach of the treaty of Bretigny ; and a just right to demand, at the least, all that had been lost since the renewal of hostilities on the part of France, for the provinces taken from his predecessors had not been ceded by any treaty of peace. England had been wrongfully dispossessed of them, and had never renounced her right to recover them."

London. A Street.

The Scene of Act II., Scene i. This comic interlude serves a two-fold purpose. First it acts as a relief to Act I., and secondly it reintroduces those comic characters who appeared in the Play of *King Henry the Fourth.*

Lord Bouciqualt. III. v. 45 ; IV. viii. 79.

Jean de Meingre, a celebrated Marshal of France. Taken prisoner at the battle of Agincourt ; died in England being unable to pay the sum fixed for his ransom.

Lords. II. iv. p.1, p.75 ; V. ii. p.1, p.299.

Lord Scroop. II. Chorus 24 ; II. ii. p.12, 13, 58, 67, 94, 148.

One of the three conspirators against Henry's person, and who, with Cambridge and Grey, is accused of high treason. He admits being a party to the conspiracy, and begs Henry's mercy. The king, however, answers him :

> But O !
> What shall I say to thee, Lord Scroop ? thou cruel,
> Ingrateful, savage and inhuman creature !
> Thou that didst bear the key of all my counsels,
> That knew'st the very bottom of my soul,
> That almost might'st have coin'd me into gold.
> [II. ii. 93–98.]

and orders his arrest and, subsequently, his execution.

[Henry, third Baron Scrope of Masham, eldest son of Sir Stephen Scrope (one of the characters in *Richard the Second*), second Lord Scrope of Masham, whom he succeeded in 1406 ; went on a mission with Henry Beaufort to France 1409 ;

arrested for conspiring to dethrone Henry the Fifth, and, being found guilty was executed in 1415 and his head fixed on one of the gates of York. *See also under* Earl of Cambridge.]

Lucifer. IV. vii. 142.

The morning star. Macgillivray quotes Gr. Phosphoros. " The name is applied by Isaiah to the King of Babylon, and from the time of St. Jerome (331–420) it has been bestowed upon the prince of darkness, whose kingdom in the Apocalypse is denoted by Babylon."

Macedon. IV. vii. 21, 23, 26, 28.

Macedonia, in ancient geography a country of south-eastern Europe. Alexander was born at Pella the capital of Macedonia.

Macmorris. III. ii. 72, p.78, 89, 99, 123, 129, 140.

Is regarded by Fluellen as " an ass, as in the world," having " no more directions in the true disciplines of the wars, than is a puppy-dog." He appears only in Act III., Scene ii., where we find him engaged in a heated argument,—which almost ends in a fight,—concerning " the disciplines of war."

For Hudson's comment on the character of Macmorris *see under* Fluellen.

Mark Antony. III. vi. 15.

                                          I think
in my very conscience he is as valiant a man as
Mark Antony ;   [III. vi. 13–15.]

Grandson and a warm partisan of Julius Cæsar. After the assassination of the latter, defeated Brutus and Cassius at Philippi, and with Octavius and Lepidus formed a triumvirate. Pistol is considered by Fluellen to be as valiant a man as Mark Antony.

Marle. IV. viii. 102.

A French lord killed at the battle of Agincourt.

Mars. Prologue 6.

The Roman god of war. *See* Harry, Prologue 5.

Mars. IV. ii. 43.

Big Mars seems bankrupt in their beggar'd host,
                                          [IV. ii. 43.]

= The god of war. A contemptuous term applied to Henry by Grandpré.

Masham. II. Chorus 24 ; II. ii. 13, 67, 148.

A small town in the North Riding of Yorkshire.

May-morn. I. ii. 120.

                    and my thrice-puissant liege
Is in the very May-morn of his youth,   [I. ii. 119–120.]

" His May of youth." *Deighton.* Henry was born in 1387, and was at this time in his twenty-seventh year.

Meisen. I. ii. 53.

Which Salique, as I said, 'twixt Elbe and Sala,
Is at this day in Germany call'd Meisen   [I. ii. 52–53.]

Meissen on the Elbe, near Dresden, famous for the manufacture of China.

Messengers. II. iv. p.65 ; III. vii. p.126 ; IV. ii. p.14.

Monmouth. IV. vii. 12, 26, 29, 55.

The county town of Monmouthshire and the birthplace of Prince Henry, afterwards King Henry the Fifth.

Monmouth caps. IV. vii. 103.

Monmouth was famous for the manufacture of caps which were formerly much worn by soldiers. The following stanza is from an old ballad *The Caps*, printed in *The Antidote against Melancholy*, 1661 :

The soldiers that the *Monmouth* wear,
On castle's tops their ensigns rear.
The seaman with the thumb doth stand
On higher parts than all the land.

Montjoy, a French Herald. III. v. 36, 61 ; III. vi. p.119, 144, 164, 168 ; IV. iii. p.79, 121, 122 ; IV. vii. p.68.

The name Montjoy is really a title, meaning King-at-arms, or chief herald.

On his first appearance he bears a message of defiance to Henry from the French king ; secondly he appears as a messenger from the Constable of France before Henry asking a ransom " before his most assured overthrow." To this Henry replies in a stirring speech, concluding with the words ;

I fear thou wilt once more come again for a ransom.
[IV. iii. 128.]

and these words are soon to be fulfilled, for on Montjoy's next appearance he says ;

I come to thee for charitable license,
That we may wander o'er this bloody field,
To book our dead, and then to bury them ;
[IV. vii. 73–75.]

According to French Montjoy was taken prisoner at Agincourt, and it was from him that Henry V. learned that he had gained the field, and the name of the place, as stated in the play. " Mont-joie " was the battle-cry of the French, as " St. George " was of the English ; and in the *Famous Victories* the former are represented as crying : " St. Dennis Mont-joye, St. Dennis ! "

Muse of fire.   Prologue 1.

O ! for a Muse of fire, that would ascend
The brightest heaven of invention ;   [I. Prologue 1–2.]

Shakespeare asks for inspiring influence after the manner of great epic poets. " This goes upon the notion of the Peripatetic system, which imagines several heavens one above another ; the last and highest of which was one of fire." *Warburton.* " It alludes likewise," remarks Johnson, " to the aspiring nature of fire, which, by its levity, at the separation of the chaos, took the highest seat of all the elements."

Nell.   II. i. 31.

= Dame Quickly, Hostess of a tavern in Eastcheap.

Nell.   V. i. 85.

News have I that my Nell is dead i' the spital
Of malady of France ;   [V. i. 85–86.]

= Mrs. Quickly, wife of Pistol, who at this point receives news of her death.

Non nobis.   IV. viii. 125.

' Not unto us.' The words are from *Psalm* cxv.

Northumberland.   II. Chorus 25 ; II. ii. 68.

Numbers.   I. ii. 98.

For in the book of Numbers is it writ :
" When a man dies, let the inheritance
Descend unto the daughter."   [I. ii. 98–100.]

The reference is to Zelophehad, a Manassite, who died during the journey of the Israelites in the wilderness, leaving no male issue. His five daughters successfully asserted their claim to their father's inheritance. See *Numbers* xxvii. 1–11.

Nym.   II. i. p.1, 1, 13, 42, 102, 110, 123 ;   II. iii. p.1, 4 ; III. ii. p.1, 37, 46 ;   IV. iv. 71.

Like Pistol, the chief characteristics of Nym are his cowardice and his boastfulness, but he attempts to conceal his cowardice in an " impressive silence " rather than in a display of highsounding phrases. The boy admirably characterises him when he says :

For Nym, he hath
heard that men of few words are the best men ;
[III. ii. 37–38.]

He invariably appears accompanied by Bardolph, and the Boy describes them as " sworn brothers in filching."

French observes : " The name of Nym is a verb which signifies ' to filch,' or as Pistol softens the expression, ' convey the wise it call.' Nym's peculiar ' humour ' may have been taken by Shakespeare from actual observation."

Officers.

Parca's fatal web.   V. i. 21.

Ha ! art thou bedlam ? dost thou thirst, base Trojan
To have me fold up Parca's fatal web ?   [V. i. 19–20.]

Pistol's bombastic phrase for ' to die ' or ' to kill.' The Three Fates, daughters of Nox and Erebus, all-powerful goddesses who presided over the destiny of man. They dwelt in the deep abyss of Demogorgon. Their names were Clotho, who held the distaff ; Lachesis, who spun the thread of human life ; and Atropos, who cut it.

Sad Clotho held the rocke, the whiles the thrid
By griesly Lachesis was spun with paine,
That cruell Atropos eftsoones undid,
With cursed knife cutting the twist in twaine.
Most wretched men, whose dayes depend on
    thrids so vaine !
                    Spenser : *Faerie Queene*, IV. ii.

Paris balls. II. iv. 131.

I did present him with the Paris balls.   [II. iv. 131.]

= Tennis balls, as mentioned in Act I., Scene ii. " And at this time, as some writers reporte, the Dolphyn, who heering this message sent to the French king his father, and disdeyning the youth of King Henry, and thinking it was an enterprise farre vnmete for him to take in hande, did therefore in mockage send to him a Tonne of Tennys balles to play with all, meaning that he had better skill in a Tennys courte, and handling of a Ball, then in the martiall affayres of warre. But the King after he had receyued from the Dolphin his former present, aunswered : that before he had ended with him and his father, he purposed by Gods ayde to tosse as many Balles of Yron with him, which ye best racket he had should not be hable to resist nor returne." Grafton's *Chronicle*.

" And his lords gave him [Henry V.] counsel, to send ambassadors unto the King of France and his council, and that he should give up to him his right heritage, that is to say Normandy, Gascony, and Guienne, the which his predecessors had held before him, or else he would it win with dint of sword, in short time, with the help of Almighty God. And then the Dauphin of France answered our ambassadors, and said in this manner, that the king was over young and too tender of age to make war against him, and was not like yet to be no good warrior to do and to make such a conquest there upon him ; and somewhat in scorn and despite he sent to him a toune full of tennis balls because he would have somewhat for to play withal for him and for his lords, and that became him better than to maintain any war ; and then anon our lords that was ambassadors took their leave and came to England again, and told the King and his

Council of the ungoodly answer that they had of the Dauphin, and of the present which he had sent unto the King ; and when the King had heard their words and the answer of the Dauphin, he was wondrous sore aggrieved . . . and thought to avenge him upon them as soon as God would send him grace and might, and anon made tennis balls for the Dauphin, in all haste ; and they were great gun-stores for the Dauphin to play withal." *Chronicle of King Henry V.*, printed in Nicolas's *Battle of Agincourt*. [From Jones' *York and Lancaster*, 1399–1485.]

Paris Louvre. II. iv. 132.

He 'll make your Paris Louvre shake for it, [II. iv. 132.]

The Louvre was the ancient palace of the French kings on the bank of the Seine, built in the seventh century.

Pegasus. III. vii. 14.

The fable steed of Bellerophon, which sprung from the blood of Medusa. Immediately he was born he flew up into heaven, or, according to Ovid he fixed his residence on Mount Helicon, where; by striking the ground with his hoof he caused water to spring forth, which formed the fountain called Hippocrene.

Perseus. III. vii. 21.

In Greek mythology the son of Jupiter and Danae. He slew the gorgon Medusa from whose blood Pegasus sprung, and rescued Andromeda, daughter of Cepheus from a dragon and won her as his bride.

Pharamond. I. ii. 37, 41, 58.

A king of the Franks, and the supposed founder of the Salique law. It is said that he visited incognito, the court of King Arthur, and was made a knight of the Round Table.

Philip of Macedon. IV. vii. 21.

King of Macedon, son of Amyntas II. and father of Alexander the Great. Assassinated at Ægae, Macedonia, 336 B.C.

Phœbus. III. Chorus 6.

> and his brave fleet
> With silken streamers the young Phœbus fanning :
> [III. Chorus 5–6.]

= Fanning the face of the sun-god Phœbus, or Apollo.

Phœbus. IV. i. 279.

> from the rise to set
> Sweats in the eye of Phœbus,   [IV. i. 278–279.]

= Under the sun's rays. Phœbus was the sun-god.

Pistol. II. i. 3, p.27, 27, 28, 51, 55, 81 ; II. iii. p.1 ; III. ii. p.1, 35 ; III. vi. 18, p.20, 30, 51 ; IV. i. p.35, 62 ; IV. iv. p.1 ; V. i. 6, p.15, 18.

A bully, and as we might expect him to be, a coward as well. He is very much given to boasting, attempting to hide his cowardice under imposing language. He is described by Gower as " an arrant counterfeit rascal, a bawd, a cut-purse." Pistol is also fond of indulging in a display of classical allusions, which although ridiculous, are laughable, and were undoubtedly appreciated by the audiences of Shakespeare's time. Pistol, however, meets his superior in Fluellen, who humbles him by making him eat his Welsh leek, and soundly chastising him.

Dr. Johnson remarks : " " His character has been the model of all the bullies that have yet appeared on the English stage. . . . His language is reminiscent of the playhouse scraps and tags of the period, and, provided the words fill the mouth well, he lets the sense take care of itself. He has a passion for ' alliteration's artful aid,' but with him it is seldom ' apt.' "

Pistol's cock. II. i. 51.

> For I can take, and Pistol's cock is up,
> And flashing fire will follow.   [II. i. 51–52.]

Mason remarks : " I can take fire. Though Pistol's cock was up, yet if he did not take fire, no flashing would ensue." The sentence is a play on Pistol's name.

Pompey the Great. IV. i. 70, 72.

Cneius Pompey, surnamed the Great, Roman General. He served in the social war in 89 B.C.,

and in the Mithridatic war. Formed against the Senate of Rome—in conjunction with Julius Cæsar and Crassus—the first triumvirate in 60 A.D. and six years later began the civil war against Cæsar, and after a struggle was totally defeated by Cæsar at Pharsalia. He escaped to Egypt and was assassinated by order of Ptolemy XII.

Queen Isabel. I. ii. 81.

Wife of Philippe Auguste, grandmother of Lewis the Ninth.

Quondam Quickly. II. i. 78.

Formerly Mrs. Quickly, Hostess of the Boar's Head Tavern in Eastcheap, now married to Pistol.

Rambures. III. v. 43 ; III. vii. p.1 ; IV. ii. p.1 ; IV. v. p.1 ; IV. v. p.1 ; IV. viii. 96.

Appears in three scenes, but does not take a prominent part in the action of the play. His name appears among those slain in the battle of Agincourt.

[A French lord who at the battle of Agincourt was " Master of the Crossbows." Probably the same person alluded to by Rymer in his *Fœdera* as " David, Seigneur de Ramouxes nostre Cambellain and Maister de Arbalestriers de France," in a treaty between Charles VI and Henry V., dated at Paris, August 22, 1413.]

Richard's body. IV. i. 301.

> I Richard's body have interred new,   [IV. i. 301.]

The body of Richard the Second—who had been deposed and murdered at Pontefract Castle —had been buried at Langley in Hertfordshire, but Henry V. transferred it to Westminster Abbey. " When all thinges were thus setled and framed to his purpose, he caused the bodie of king Richard the seconde to be remoued, with all funerall pompes conuenient for his estate, from Langley to Westminster, where he was honourably enterred with Queene Anne his first wife, in a solempne Tombe, erected and set vp at the costes and charges of this Noble Prince King Henrie." *Grafton.*

Richard's soul. IV. i. 309.

and I have built
Two chantries, where the sad and solemn priests
Sing still for Richard's soul.   [IV. i. 307-309.]

A chantry was a foundation for the chanting
of masses. *Two chantries.* One of these monasteries was for Carthusian monks, and was called
Bethlehem ; the other was for religious men and
women of the order of Saint Bridget, and was
named Sion. They were on opposite sides of the
Thames, and adjoined the royal manor of Sheen,
now called Richmond. Aldis Wright points out
that " according to the charters of foundation of
the two religious houses of Bethlehem at Shene
and of Sion on the opposite side of the river that
Henry did not establish them that masses might
be sung for the repose of Richard's soul, yet it is
possible that Shakespeare may have derived his
information from the following narrative in
Fabyan's *Chronicle* (ed. Ellis), ' For asmoche as
he knewe well that his fader had laboured the
meanes to depose the noble prynce Richarde the
Seconde, and after was consentyng to his deth,
for which offence his said fader had sent to Rome,
of yᵗ great cryme to be assayled [absolved], and
was by yᵉ pope enioyned, yᵗ lyke as he had
beraft hym of his naturall and bodely lyfe for
euer in this world, that so, by contynuel prayer
& suffragies of the churche, he shuld cause his
soule to lyue perpetuelly in the celestyall worlde :
Which penaunce, for that his fader by his lyfe
dyd nat perfourme, this goostly knyght in most
habundaunt maner perfourmyd it : for first he
buyldyd .iii. houses of relygyon, as the Charter-
hous of monkes called Shene, the house of close
nunnes called Syon, and the thirde was an house
of Obseruauntes buyldyd vpon that other syde
of Thamys, & after let fall by hym for the skyll
that foloweth, as testyfieth the boke or regyster
of mayres. . . . And ouer this great acte of
foundyng of thise .ii. religious houses, he ordeyned
at Westminster to brenne perpetuelly wᵗout
extinccon .iiii. tapers of waxe vpon yᵉ sepulture
of kyng Richarde ; & ouer yᵗ he ordeyned ther,
to be contynued for euer, one day in yᵉ weke, a
solempn dirige to be songe, & vpon yᵉ morowe a
masse ; after which masse endid, certayn money
to be gyuen, as before is expressyd, wᵗ other
thynges in ye begynnyng of this kynges reign̄.'

Roan. III. v. 53, 64.

= Rouen, the former capital of Normandy.

Roman Brutus. II. iv. 37.

And you shall find his vanities forespent
Were but the outside of the Roman Brutus,
Covering discretion with a coat of folly ; [II. iv. 36-38.

The reference is to Lucius Junius Brutus who
to escape the fate of his brother at the hands of
his uncle Tarquinius Superbus feigned madness.

Rome. V. Chorus 26.

Rouen.   A Room in the Palace.

The Scene of Act III., Scenes iv. and v.

Act III., Scene iv. Shows us the French
princess, Katharine, taking lessons in English
from her maid Alice. Critics consider that this
scene was not written by Shakespeare. " I have
left this ridiculous scene as I found it ; and am
sorry to have no colour left from any of the
editions, to imagine it interpolates." *Warburton.*
Johnson says : " Sir T. Hanmer has rejected it.
The scene is indeed mean enough, when it is
read ; but the grimaces of two French women,
and the odd accent with which they uttered the
English, made it divert upon the stage. It may
be observed, that there is in it not only the
French language, but the French spirit. Alice
compliments the princess upon her knowledge of
four words, and tells her that she pronounces like
the English themselves. The princess suspects
no deficiency in her instructress, nor the instructress in herself. Throughout the whole scene
there may be found French servility, and French
vanity."

Act III., Scene v. The French king and his
nobles discuss the position after which Charles
sends Montjoy, his herald, to Henry with a
message of defiance, afterwards ordering his
nobles to intercept Henry in his march towards
Calais.

Roussi. III. v. 44 ; IV. viii. 101.

A French noble killed at the battle of Agincourt.

Saint Crispian. IV. iii. 46.

See Crispian.

Saint Crispian's day. IV. iii. 67.

See Crispian.

Saint Davy's day. IV. i. 55 ; V. i. 2.

Tell him, I 'll knock his leek about his pate
Upon Saint Davy's day.   [IV. i. 54–55.]

Saint David's day is March 1st. The leek is the national emblem of the Welsh and is still worn by Welshmen in their hats on St. David's day. Tradition states that the wearing of the leek dates from a famous victory gained by King Arthur over the Saxons on March 1st, 540. The battle was fought ' in a garden ' where leeks were growing and St. David, whose birthday it was, commanded the Welsh soldiers to wear a leek in their caps in commemoration of the victory.

Saint Denis. V. ii. 190, 216.

Saint Denis be my speed   [V. ii. 190.]

= May the patron saint of France help me. Dionysius, Bishop of Paris and patron Saint of France. One of the missionaries sent from Rome in the third century to convert the Gauls. By order of the Roman governor he was tortured and put to death about 270 A.D.

Saint George. III. i. 34 ; V. ii. 217.

The patron saint of England. ' England and Saint George ' was the English battle cry.

Saint Tavy's day. IV. vii. 107.

= Saint David's day (q.v.).

Sala. I. ii. 45, 52, 63.

= the Saale, a tributary of the Elbe. The great part of the kingdom of Saxony lies " between the floods of Sala and of Elbe."

Salique land. I. ii. 39, 40, 44, 51, 52, 56.

" No woman shall succeed in Salique land : "
Which Salique land the French unjustly gloze
To be the realm of France, and Pharamond
The founder of this law and female bar.
Yet their own authors faithfully affirm
That the land Salique is in Germany,   [I. ii. 39–44.]

The Salique land was originally a part of Germany, and did not become a part of France until centuries after the death of Pharamond :

Nor did the French possess the Salique land
Until four hundred one and twenty years
After defunction of King Pharamond.   [I. ii. 56–58.]

As Pharamond died A.D. 426 and Charles the Great occupied the land beyond the Sala in 805 the interval was 379 years and not 421.

Salique Law. I. ii. 11, 54, 91.

An ancient law in force among the Salic tribes of the Franks—who finally settled in France under their leader Pharamond—which forbad the succession to pass through the female line. On the death of Charles IV. of France, Edward the Third claimed the crown of France through his mother Isabella, but the Salic Law debarred her and her heirs, and Philip the Long acceded to the throne. Queen Victoria was excluded from the throne of Hanover in 1837 by the operation of this law. Cf. *Extract* 2 from Holinshed.

Scotland. I. ii. 168.

See France. I. ii. 167.

Sir Guichard Dauphin. IV. viii. 97.

Great Master of France, killed at the battle of Agincourt.

Sir John. II. i. 118.

= Sir John Falstaff. The hostess at this point enters with the news that Falstaff has suddenly been taken ill.

Sir John. II. iii. 18 ; IV. vii. 53.

= Sir John Falstaff. *See also under* Falstaff.

Sir Richard Ketly. IV. viii. 106.

Killed at the battle of Agincourt, fighting on the side of the English.

Sir Thomas Erpingham. IV. i. p.13, 13, 24, 94, p.291 ; IV. iii. p.1.

Is described by Williams as a " good old commander and a most kind gentleman." He is present at the battle of Agincourt, where he is placed in command of the archers. Henry greets him before the battle :

> Good morrow, old Sir Thomas Erpingham :
> A good soft pillow for that good white head
> Were better than a churlish turf of France.
> [IV. i. 13–15.]

but the brave old knight answers :

> Not so, my liege : this lodging likes me better,
> Since I may say ' Now lie I like a king,'   [IV. i. 16–17.]

and adds his blessing on his king :

> The Lord in heaven bless thee, noble Harry ! [IV. i. 33.]

[Sir Thomas Erpingham of Erpingham, Norfolk ; was in the service of John of Gaunt whom he accompanied to Spain in 1386 ; landed with Bolingbroke at Ravenspur and was made by him a K.G., Chamberlain of the Household, and Lord Warden of the Cinque Ports ; distinguished himself at Agincourt, 1415. He was the builder of the Erpingham gate-way at Norwich, which forms one entrance to the Cathedral Close. He married first, Joan Walton, and secondly Joan, daughter of Sir William Clopton, knight, and died without issue in 1428. He was a supporter of Wycliffe, for which he incurred some persecution as a " Lollard."]

Sir Thomas Grey. II. Chorus 25 ; II. ii. p.12, 58, 68, 150.

One of the conspirators against Henry, who, with Scroop and Cambridge, is arrested at Southampton for high treason, and subsequently executed.
[Sir Thomas Grey was the son-in-law to the Earl of Westmoreland. This associate of the Earl of Cambridge and Lord Scroop in the conspiracy to dethrone Henry the Fifth was the second son of Sir Thomas Grey of Berwick, Constable of Norham Castle. He was executed at Southampton 1415. See also under Earl of Cambridge.]

Soldiers, English. III. i. p.1 ; III. iii. p.1 ; III. vi. p.90 ; IV. i. p.85 ; IV. iii. p.1 ; IV. vi. p.1 ; IV. vii. p.57.

Soldiers, French. IV. iv. p.1.

Somme. III. v. 1.

The ancient Samara. A river in northern France which flows into the English Channel, north-west of Dieppe. See *Extract* 7 from Holinshed, and Grafton's *Chronicle*, vol. I, page 514.

Song.

> The plain-song is most just, for humours do abound :
> Knocks go and come, God's vassals drop and die ;
>   And sword and shield,
>   In bloody field,
> Doth win immortal fame   [III ii. 7–11.]

A snatch of some old ballad.
Plain-song = the simple melody of the song without variations.

Song.

> If wishes would prevail with me,
> My purpose should not fail with me,
>   But thither would I hie.
>   As duly,
>   But not as truly,
> As bird doth sing on bough. [III. ii. 15–20.]

A snatch of some old ballad.

Southampton. II. Chorus 30, 35, 42 ; II. iii. 47.

A seaport in Hampshire from whence Henry the Fifth embarked for France. *See also Hampton.*

Southampton. A Council-chamber.

The Scene of Act II., Scene ii. The English army at Southampton prepares for the crossing to France when a conspiracy to put the king to death is discovered. Henry gives orders for a man imprisoned for insulting him to be liberated. The three conspirators—the Earl of Cambridge, Lord Scroop, and Sir Thomas Grey—unaware that their conspiracy is known, urge the king not to pardon the man, and by so doing pronounce their own doom for Henry hands to each of them a paper which reveals their plot. They are apprehended and sentenced to be beheaded.

Staines. II. iii. 1.

A town near Windsor on the road from London to Southampton,

Talbot. IV. iii. 54.

Fifth Baron Talbot, elder brother of John Talbot, first Earl of Shrewsbury. He is mentioned as one of those who would become "familiar as household words." Wright mentions that "Henry in his will (24th July, 1415) left Gilbert Lord Talbot, 'consanguineo nostro,' a bason and ewer of gold worth a hundred marks."

Tartar. II. ii. 123.

= Tartarus, the classical name for the infernal regions. Cf. *Twelfth Night*, II. v. 212–213 :

> To the gates of Tartar, thou most excellent
> devil of wit ?

Te Deum. IV. viii. 125.

A hymn of praise so-called from its first words Te Deum laudamus (We praise Thee, O God).

Thames. IV. i. 116.

= River Thames.

Train. II. iv. p.75.

A body of attendants ; a retinue.

Trojan. V. i. 20, 32.

= used here as a term of reproach or abuse.

Troyes in Champagne. An Apartment in the French King's Palace.

The Scene of Act V., Scene ii. The conference was held in St. Peter's Church, Troyes—but for dramatic purposes it is staged in the French King's Palace—in 1420, five years after Henry returned to England after his victory at Agincourt, so that Shakespeare has omitted the campaign of 1417–18 in which campaign Rouen was besieged and taken and Normandy conquered.

[This final scene of the Play shows the meeting of the English and French monarchs at Troyes, the meeting having been brought about by Philip, Duke of Bergundy. A joint Council is appointed to consider terms of peace and retire to an adjoining room. Henry suggests that Katharine—daughter of the French king— remain behind. Henry woos Katharine and is successful. On the return of the Council the Duke of Burgundy announces that the King of France had acceded to all Henry's demands. This settled, Henry asks for Katharine's hand which is granted, and the play ends with Henry announcing that he will receive the oath of all the French nobles on his wedding-day when he will pledge his own word to Katharine.

" And aftir meny and dyvers treteeȝ, the xij kalendis of Juyne, the xl yere of king Charlis regne, in the cathedralle chirche of Nogent, kyng Harri withe the duke of Clarence his brothir and othir princeȝ and noblis, and Ysabelle quene of Fraunce with the duke of Burgoyne, beyng there for kyng Charlis, thanne labouryng in his seeknesse forsaid, and in thair owen nameȝ also, and the iij statis of Fraunce, peeȝ betuene the ij remes of Englond and of Fraunce was maad, and with certayn condicions approued. And kyng Charlis charged alle his liegemenne on peyne of forfaiture of thair ligeaunceȝ to kepe the said peeȝ ; and therto thay made thair othe, and plight thair troutheȝ in the handeȝ of kyng Harri. And anon quene Ysabelle of Fraunce, and Philippe duke of Burgoyne, in the name of kyng Charlis, swoor vpon the holy gospellis to kepe the said peeȝ so concludid for thaym and for their heiris and successours withoute fraude and male engyne for euermore ; and this same oth made quene Ysabel, and the duke of Burgoyne, and the iij statis of Fraunce to kyng Harri, to his heiris and successours. And atte ix kalendis of Juyne, befor quene Ysabel and kyng Charlis counsel, befor the parlement and the iij statis of Fraunce, and othir English princeȝ and lordis, contract of matrimony be present wordis betuene kynge Harri and dame Katerine, kyng Charlis doughtir of Fraunce, was there maad and solemnyȝid. *An English Chronicle*, ed. Davies, [Camden Society, No. 64.] For the full Text of the Treaty of Troyes, see *inter alia* Grafton's *Chronicle ; or, History of England ;* and Rapin's *History of England.*

Tucket. III. vi. p.119 ; IV. iii. p.79.

A flourish on a trumpet.

Turk. V. ii. 219.

' and take the Turk by the beard ' is merely a colloquial expression, as the Turks did not gain possession of Constantinople until 1453, when it was taken after fifty-three days' siege by Mahmud II.

Turkish mute. I. ii. 232.

Like Turkish mute, shall have a tongueless mouth,
[I. ii. 232.]

An allusion to the practice in Turkey of employing attendants at courts whose tongues had been cut out to prevent them betraying secrets.

Vaudemont. III. v. 43 ; IV. viii. 102.

A French noble, killed at the battle of Agincourt.

Whitsun morris-dance. II. iv. 25.

Originally a Moorish dance. These dances were used on festive, or on festival occasions such as May-day and Whitsuntide. Considered to have been introduced to England from Spain in the time of King Edward the Fourth. For full description see A Dissertation on the Ancient English Morris Dance, by Francis Douce.

Williams. IV. i. p.85 ; IV. viii. p.1.

A soldier in the ranks of Henry's army.

He is on sentry duty when Henry appears, and he challenges the king as he does not recognise him. Henry seizes the opportunity to make him talk in order to find out what the common soldiers think of the campaign. Williams is very outspoken, and challenges the king, after which they exchange gages, each vowing to challenge the other to combat should they meet at a more convenient time.

Later Henry gives the gage to Fluellen, and Williams, seeing his gage in Fluellen's cap, strikes him. Henry appears and explanations follow, the king bidding Exeter fill Williams' glove with crowns.

See also under Bates.

Wooden O. Prologue 13.

The Globe Theatre on the Bankside. It was built of wood, was circular within and octagonal without. It is supposed that the Play of King Henry the Fifth was first performed at the opening of this Theatre.

Wye. IV. vii. 29, 110.

The river Wye which runs through Monmouth, the birthplace of Prince Henry, who was afterwards Henry the Fifth.

APPENDIX I.

EXTRACTS FROM HOLINSHED[1] THAT ILLUSTRATE *The Life of King Henry the Fifth.*

1. In the second years of his reigne, king Henrie called his high court of parlement, the last daie of Aprill, in the towne of Leicester ; in which parlement manie profitable lawes were concluded, and manie petitions mooued were for that time deferred. Amongst which, one was, that a bill exhibited in the parlement holden at Westminster, in the eleuenth yeare of king Henrie the fourth (which by reason the king was then troubled with ciuill discord, came to none effect), might now with good deliberation be pondered, and brought to some good conclusion. The effect of which supplication was, that *the temporall lands* (deuoutlie *giuen*, and discordinatlie spent by religious, and other spirituall persons) should be seized into the kings hands ; *sith the same might suffice to maineteine, to the honor* of the king, and defense of the realme, *fifteene earles, fifteene hundred knights, six thousand and two hundred esquiers,* and a *hundred almesse-houses,* for *reliefe* onelie *of* the poore, impotent, and needie persons ; *and the king* to haue cleerelie *to* his *coffers* twentie *thousand pounds :* with manie other prouisions and values of religious houses, which I passe ouer.

2. This bill was much noted, and more feared, among the religious sort, whom suerlie it touched verie neere ; and therefore to find remedie against it, they determined to assaie all waies to put by and ouerthrow this bill : wherein they thought best to trie if they might mooue the kings mood with some sharpe inuention, that he should not regard the importunate petitions of the commons. Wherevpon, on a daie in the parlement, Henrie Chichelie archbishop of Canterburie made a pithie oration, wherein he declared, how not onelie the duchies of Normandie and Aquitaine, with the counties of Aniou and Maine, and the countrie of Gascoigne, were by vndoubted title apperteining to the king, as to the lawfull and onelie heire of the same ; but also the whole realme of France, as heire to his great grandfather king Edward the third.

[Chichele inveighed] against the surmised and false fained law Salike, which the Frenchmen alledge euer *against* the kings of England in *barre* of their iust title *to* the crowne of *France.* The verie words of that supposed law are these : ' *In terram Salicam mulieres ne succedant* ' *;* that is to saie, ' *Into* the *Salike land* let not women *succeed.*' *Which* the *French* glossers expound *to be* the *realme of France, and* that *this law* was made by king *Pharamond ;* whereas *yet their owne authors affirme, that the land Salike is in Germanie, betweene* the riuers *of Elbe and Sala ;* and that when *Charles the great* had ouercome *the Saxons,* he placed there certeine *French*men, which hauing *in disdeine the dishonest maners of the Germane women,* made a *law, that the females should* not succeed to any inheritance with*in* that *land, which at this daie is called Meisen :* so that, if this be true, this *law was not* made *for the realme of France, nor the Frenchmen possessed the land Salike, till foure hundred* and *one and twentie yeares after* the death *of Pharamond,* the *supposed* maker *of this* Salike *law ;* for this Pharamond deceassed *in the yeare* 426, *and Charles the great subdued the Saxons, and* placed *the French*men in those parts *beyond the riuer* of *Sala, in the yeare* 805.

Moreouer, it appeareth by *their* owne *writers,* that *king Pepin, which deposed Childerike,* claimed *the crowne of France,* as *heire generall,* for that he was *descended of Blithild, daughter to king Clothair* the first. *Hugh Capet also,* (who *vsurped the crowne* vpon *Charles duke of Loraine,* the *sole heire male of the line and stocke of Charles the great,*) to *make his title* seeme true, and appeare good, (though in deed *it was* starke *naught,*) *conueied himselfe as heire to the ladie Lingard, daughter to* king *Charlemaine, sonne to Lewes the emperour, that was son to Charles the great. King Lewes also, the tenth,[2]* (otherwise called saint Lewes,) being verie *heire to the* said *vsurper* Hugh *Capet, could* neuer be *satisfied in his conscience* how he might iustlie keepe and possesse *the crowne of France, till* he was persuaded and fullie instructed, that *queene Isabell his grandmother was lineallie* descended *of the ladie Ermengard, daughter* and heire *to the* aboue named *Charles duke of Loraine ; by the which marriage, the* bloud and *line of Charles the great was* againe *vnited* and restored *to the crowne* & scepter *of France :* so that more *cleere* then *the sunne* it openlie *appeareth, that the title* of *king Pepin, the claime of Hugh Capet,* the possession *of Lewes ;* yea, and *the* French *kings to this daie,* are deriued and conueied from *the* heire *female ;* though *they would,* vnder the colour of such a fained *law, barre* the kings and princes of this realme of England of their right and lawfull inheritance.

The archbishop further alledged out of *the booke of Numbers* this saieng : ' When a man *dieth* without a sonne, *let the inheritance descend to* his *daughter.*'

1. Shakespeare's Holinshed, by W. B. Boswell-Stone.   2. ninth.

[*Chichele*] hauing said sufficientlie for the proofe of the kings iust and lawfull title to the crowne of France, he exhorted him to aduance foorth his banner to fight for his *right*, to conquer his inheritance, to spare neither *bloud, sword*, nor *fire ;* sith his warre was iust, his cause good, and his claime true.   And to the intent his louing chapleins and obedient subiects *of the spiritualtie* might shew themselues willing and desirous to aid his maiestie, for the recouerie of his ancient right and true inheritance, the archbishop declared that, in their spirituall conuocation they had granted to his *highnesse such a summe* of monie, *as neuer* by no spirituall persons was to any prince before those daies giuen or aduanced.

When the archbishop had ended his prepared tale, Rafe Neuill, earle of Westmerland, and as then lord Warden of the marches against Scotland, vnderstanding that the king, vpon a couragious desire to recouer his right in France, would suerlie take the wars in hand, thought good to mooue the king to begin first with Scotland ; and therevpon declared how easie a matter it should be to make a conquest there, and how greatlie the same should further his wished purpose for the subduing of the Frenchmen ; concluding the summe of his tale with this old saieng : that, ' Who so *will France win, must with Scotland first begin.*'

Whilest in the Lent season the king laie at Killingworth, there came to him from Charles Dolphin of France certeine ambassadors, that brought with them a barrell of Paris balles ; which from their maister they presented to him for a token that was taken in verie ill part, as sent in scorne, to signifie, that it was more meet for the king to passe the time with such childish exercise, than to attempt any worthie exploit.

Wherfore the K. wrote to him, that yer ought long, he would tosse him some London balles that perchance should shake the walles of *the* best *court* in France.

3.   When king Henrie had fullie furnished his nauie with men, munition, & other prouisions perceiuing that his capteines misliked nothing so much as delaie, determined his souldiors to go a ship-boord and awaie.   But see the hap !   the night before the daie appointed for their departure, he was crediblie informed, that Richard earle of Cambridge, brother to Edward duke of Yorke, and Henrie lord Scroope of Masham, lord treasuror, with Thomas Graie, a knight of Northumberland, being confederat togither, had conspired his death : wherefore he caused them to be apprehended.

The said lord Scroope was in such fauour with the king, that he admitted him sometime to be his bedfellow ; in whose fidelitie the king reposed such trust, that, when anie priuat or publike councell was in hand, this lord had much in the determination of it.   For he represented so great grauitie in his countenance, such modestie in behauiour, and so vertuous zeale to all godlinesse in his talke, that whatsoeuer he said was thought for the most part necessarie to be doone and followed.   Also the said Thomas Graie (as some write) was of the kings priuie councell.

These prisoners, vpon their examination, confessed, that for a great summe of monie which they had receiued of the French king, they intended verelie either to haue deliuered the king aliue into the hands of his enimies, or else to haue murthered him before he should arriue in the duchie of Normandie.   When king Henrie had heard all things opened, which he desired to know, he caused all his nobilitie to come before his presence ; from whome he caused to be brought the offenders also, and to them said : " Hauing thus *conspired* the death and destruction of me, which " am the head of the realme and gouernour of the people, it maie be (no doubt) but that you like- " wise haue sworne the confusion of all that are here with me, and also the *desolation* of your owne " countrie.   To what horror (O lord !) for any true English hart to consider, that such an exe- " crable iniquitie should euer so bewrap you, as for pleasing of a forren enimie to imbrue your " hands in your bloud, and to ruine your owne natiue soile.   *Reuenge* herein *touching* my *person,* ." though I *seeke* not ; yet for the safegard of you my deere freends, & for due preseruation of all " sorts, I am by office to cause example to be shewed.   *Get ye hence therefore,* ye *poore miserable* " *wretches,* to the receiuing of *your* iust reward ; wherein *Gods* maiestie *giue you* grace *of his mercie,* " *and repentance of your* heinous *offenses.*"   And so immediatlie they were had to execution.

4.   [Henry] first princelie appointing to aduertise the French king of his comming, therefore dispatched Antelope his purseuant at armes with letters to him for restitution of that which he wrongfully withheld ; contrarie to the lawes of God and man : the king further declaring how sorie he was that he should be thus compelled for repeating of his right and iust title of inheritance, to make warre to the destruction of christian people ; but sithens he had offered peace which could not be receiued, now, for fault of iustice, he was forced to take armes.   Neuerthelesse exhorted the French king, *in the bowels* of Iesu Christ, to render him that which was his owne ; whereby effusion of Christian bloud might be auoided.   These letters, cheeflie to this effect and purpose, were written and dated from Hampton the fift of August.   When the same were presented to the French king, and by his councell well perused, answer was made, that he would take aduise, and prouide therein as time and place should be conuenient : so the messenger [was] licenced to depart at his pleasure.

The Dolphin, who had the gouerance of the realme, bicause his father was fallen into his old disease of frensie, sent for the dukes of Berrie and Alanson, and all the other lords of the councell of France : by whose aduise it was determined, that they should not onelie prepare a sufficient armie to resist the king of England, when so euer he arriued to inuade France, but also to stuffe and furnish the townes on the frontiers and sea coasts with conuenient garrisons of men : . . .

The French king, being aduertised that king Henrie was arriued on that coast, sent in all hast the lord de la Breth constable of France, the seneshall of France, the lord Bouciqualt marshall of France, the seneshall of Henault, the lord Lignie, with other ; which fortified townes with men, victuals, and artillerie, on all those frontiers towards the sea.

[At Winchester,] before the kings presence, sitting in his throne imperiall, the archbishop of Burges made an eloquent and a long oration, dissuading warre, and praising peace ; offering to the king of England a great summe of monie, with diuerse countries, being in verie deed but base and poore, as a dowrie with the ladie Catharine in mariage ; so that he would dissolue his armie, and dismisse his soldiers, which he had gathered and put in a readinesse.

5. The Duke of Glocester, to whome the order of the siege was committed, made three mines vnder the ground ; and, approching to the wals with his engins and ordinance, would not suffer them within to take anie rest.

For although they with their countermining somwhat disappointed the Englishmen, & came to fight with them hand to hand within the mines, so that they went no further forward with that worke ; yet they were so inclosed on ech side, as well by water as land, that succour they saw could none come to them.

6. The king, aduertised hereof, sent them word, that, except they would surrender the towne to him the morow next insuing, without anie condition, they should spend no more time in talke about the matter. But yet at length through the earnest sute of the French lords, the king was contented to grant them truce untill nine of the clocke the next sundaie, being the two and twentith of September ; with condition, that, if in the meane time no rescue came, they should yeeld the towne at that houre, with their bodies and goods to stand at the kings pleasure. . . .

[During the truce,] the lord Bacqueuill was sent vnto the French king, to declare in what point the towne stood. To whome the Dolphin answered, *that* the kings *power* was *not yet* assembled, in such number as was conuenient *to raise so great a siege.* This answer being brought vnto the capteins within the towne, they rendered it vp to the king of England, after that the third daie was expired ; which was on the daie of saint Maurice, being the seuen and thirtith daie after the siege was first laid. The souldiors were ransomed, and the towne sacked, to the great gaine of the Englishmen. . . .

The king ordeined capteine of the towne his vncle the duke of Excester, who established his lieutenant there, one sir Iohn Fastolfe ; with fifteene hundred men, or (as some haue) two thousand, and thirtie six knights.

King Henrie, after the winning of Harflue, determined to haue proceeded further in the winning of other townes and fortresses ; but, because the dead time of the winter approched, it was determined by aduise of his councell, that he should in all conuenient speed set forward, and march through the countrie towards Calis by land, least his returne as then homewards should of slanderous toongs be named a running awaie ; and yet that iournie was adiudged perillous, by reason that the number of his people was much minished by the flix and other feuers, which sore vexed and brought to death aboue fifteene hundred persons of the armie : and this was the cause that his returne was the sooner appointed and concluded.

7. The French king, being at Rone, and hearing that king Henrie was passed the riuer of Some, was much displeased therewith, and, assembling his councell to the number of fiue and thirtie, asked their aduise what was to be doone. There was amongst these fiue and thirtie, his sonne the Dolphin, calling himselfe king of Sicill ; the dukes of Berrie and Britaine, the earle of Pontieu the kings yoongest sonne, and other high estates. At length thirtie of them agreed, that the Englishmen should not depart vnfought withall, and fiue were of a contrarie opinion, but the greater number ruled the matter : and so Montioy king at armes was sent to the king of England to defie him as the enimie of France, and to tell him that he should shortlie haue battell.

The noble men had deuised a chariot, wherein they might triumphantlie conueie the king captiue to the citie of Paris ; crieng to their soldiers : " Haste you to the spoile, glorie and honor ! " little weening (God wot) how soone their brags should be blowne awaie.

The Dolphin sore desired to haue beene at the battell, but he was prohibited by his father.

8. The king of England, (hearing that the Frenchmen approched, and that there was an other riuer for him to passe with his armie by a bridge, and doubting least, if the same bridge should be broken, it would be greatlie to his hinderance,) appointed certeine capteins with their bands, to

go thither with all speed before him, and to take possession thereof, and so to keepe it, till his comming thither.

Those that were sent, finding the Frenchmen busie to breake downe their bridge, assailed them so vigorouslie, that they discomfited them, and tooke and slue them; and so the bridge was preserued till the king came, and passed the riuer by the same with his whole armie. This was on the two and twentith day of October.

[During Henry's march there was no] outrage or offense doone by the Englishmen, except one, which was, that a souldiour took a pix out of a church, for which he was apprehended, & the king not once remooued till the box was restored, and the offendor strangled.

[Henry] caused proclamation to be made, that no person should be so hardie, on paine of death, either to take anie thing out of anie church that belonged to the same; or to hurt or doo anie violence either to priests, women, or anie such as should be found without weapon or armor, and not readie to make resistance : . . .

Yet in this great necessitie, the poore people of the countrie were not spoiled, nor anie thing taken of them without paiment, . . .

King Henrie aduisedlie answered : " Mine intent is to doo as it pleaseth God : I will *not seeke* " your maister at this time ; but, if he or his seeke me, I will meet with them, God willing. If " anie of your nation attempt once to stop me in my iournie now towards Calis, at their ieopardie " be it ; and yet wish I not anie of you so vnaduised, as to be the occasion that I die *your tawnie* " *ground with your red bloud."*

When he had thus answered the herald, he gaue him a princelie reward, and licence to depart.

9. The cheefe leaders of the French host were these : the constable of France, the marshall, the admerall, the lord Rambures, maister of the crosbowes, and other of the French nobilitie ; which came and pitched downe their standards and banners in the countie of saint Paule, within the territorie of Agincourt, . . .

They were lodged euen in the waie by the which the Englishmen must needs passe towards Calis ; and all that night, after their comming thither, made great cheare, and were verie merie, pleasant, and full of game.

10. [The French were] incamped not past two hundred and fiftie pases distant from the English.

Fiers were made to giue light on euerie side, as there likewise were in the French host, . . .

[The French,] as though they had beene sure of victorie, made great triumph ; for the capteins had determined before how to diuide the spoile, and the soldiers the night before had plaid the Englishmen at dice.

The Englishmen also for their parts were of good comfort, and nothing abashed of the matter ; and yet they were both hungrie, wearie, sore trauelled, and vexed with manie cold diseases. Howbeit, reconciling themselues with God by hoossell and shrift, requiring assistance at his hands that is the onelie giuer of victorie, they determined rather to die, than to yeeled, or flee.

Order was taken by commandement from the king, after the armie was first set in battell arraie, that no noise or clamor should be made in the host ; so that, in marching foorth to this village, euerie man kept himselfe quiet : . . .

11. When the messenger was come backe to the French host, the men of warre put on their helmets, and caused their trumpets to blow to the battell. They thought themselues so sure of victorie, that diuerse of the noble men made such hast towards the battell, that they left manie of their seruants and men of warre behind them, and some of them would not once staie for their standards : as, amongst other, the duke of Brabant, when his standard was not come, caused a baner to be taken from a trumpet and fastened to a speare ; the which he commanded to be borne before him in steed of his standard.

Their armie (as some write) [extended] to the number of threescore thousand horsemen, besides footmen, wagoners, and other.

12. [Henry] determined to make haste towards Calis, and not to seeke for battell, except he were thereto constreined ; bicause that his armie by sicknesse was sore diminished : in so much that he had but onelie two thousand horssemen, and thirteene thousand archers, bilmen, and of all sorts of other footmen.

It is said, that as he heard one of the host vtter his wish to another thus : " I would to God " there were with vs now so manie good soldiers as are at this houre within England ! " the king answered : " I would not wish a man more here than I haue ; we are indeed in comparison to the " enimies but a few, but if God of his clemencie doo fauour vs, and our iust cause, (as I trust he " will,) we shall speed well inough. But let no man ascribe victorie to our owne strength and " might, but onelie to Gods assistance ; to whome I haue no doubt we shall worthilie haue cause " to giue thanks therefore. And if so be that for our offenses sakes we shall be deliuered into the

" hands of our enimies, the lesse number we be, the lesse damage shall the realme of England
" susteine ; but if we should fight in trust of multitude of men, and so get the victorie, (our minds
" being prone to pride,) we should thervpon peraduenture ascribe the victorie not so much to the
" gift of God, as to our owne puissance, and thereby prouoke his high indignation and displeasure
" against vs : and if the enimie get the vpper hand, then should our realme and countrie suffer
" more damage and stand in further danger. But be you of good comfort, and shew your selues
" valiant ! God and our iust quarrell shall defend vs, and deliuer these our proud aduersaries
" with all the multitude of them which you see (or at the least the most of them) into our hands."

13. Here we may not forget how the French, thus in their iolitie, sent an herald to king
Henrie, to inquire what ransome he would offer. Wherevnto he answered, that within two or
three houres he hoped it would so happen, that the Frenchmen should be glad to common rather
with the Englishmen for their ransoms, than the English to take thought for their deliuerance ;
promising for his owne part, that his dead carcasse should rather be a prize to the Frenchmen,
than that his liuing bodie should paie anie ransome.

[The king] appointed a vaward, of the which he made capteine, Edward duke of Yorke, who
of an haulite courage had desired that office, . . .

14. When the Frenchmen perceiued his intent, they were suddenlie amazed and ran awaie
like sheepe ; without order or arraie. Which when the king perceiued, he incouraged his men,
and followed so quickelie vpon the enimies, that they ran hither and thither, casting awaie their
armour : manie on their knees desired to haue their liues saued.

The Englishmen had taken a great number of prisoners, certeine Frenchmen on horssebacke,
whereof were capteins Robinet of Borneuill, Rifflart of Clamas, Isambert of Agincourt, and other
men of armes, to the number of six hundred horssemen, (which were the first that fled,) hearing
that the English tents & pauilions were a good waie distant from the armie, without anie sufficient
gard to defend the same, either vpon a couetous meaning to gaine by the spoile, or vpon a desire
to be reuenged, entred vpon the kings campe ; and there spoiled the hails, robbed the tents, brake
vp chests, and caried awaie caskets, and slue such seruants as they found to make anie resistance.

But when the outcrie of the lackies and boies, which ran awaie for feare of the Frenchmen thus
spoiling the campe, came to the kings eares, he, (doubting least his enimies should gather togither
againe, and begin a new field ; and mistrusting further that the prisoners would be an aid to his
enimies, or the verie enimies to their takers in deed if they were suffered to liue,) contrarie to his
accustomed gentlenes, commanded by sound of trumpet, that euerie man (vpon paine of death)
should incontinentlie slaie his prisoner.

15. When this lamentable slaughter was ended, the Englishmen disposed themselues in order
of battell, readie to abide a new field, and also to inuade, and newlie set on, their enimies : with
great force they assailed the earles of Marle and Fauconbridge, and the lords of Louraie, and of
Thine, with six hundred men of armes ; who had all that daie kept togither, but [were] now slaine
and beaten downe out of hand.

Some write, that the king, perceiuing his enimies in one part to assemble togither, as though
they meant to giue a new battell for preseruation of the prisoners, sent to them an herald, commanding them either to depart out of his sight, or else to come forward at once, and giue battell :
promising herewith, that if they did offer to fight againe, not onelie those prisoners which his
people alreadie had taken, but also so manie of them as, in this new conflict, which they thus
attempted, should fall into his hands, should die the death without redemption.

The Frenchmen, fearing the sentence of so terrible a decree, without further delaie parted out
of the field.

In the morning, Montioie king at armes and foure other French heralds came to the K., to
know the number of prisoners, and to desire buriall for the dead. Before he made them answer
(to vnderstand what they would saie) he demanded of them whie they made to him that request ;
considering that he knew not whether the victorie was his or theirs ? When Montioie by true
and iust confession had cleered that doubt to the high praise of the king, he desired of Montioie to
vnderstand the name of the castell neere adioining : when they had told him that it was called
Agincourt, he said, " Then shall this conflict be called the battell of Agincourt."

The daie following was the fiue and twentith of October in the yeare 1415 ; being then fridaie,
and the feast of Crispine and Crispinian : a day faire and fortunate to the English, but most
sorrowful and vnluckie to the French.

[The King] feasted the French officers of armes that daie, and granted them their request ;
which busilie sought through the field for such as were slaine. But the Englishmen suffered them
not to go alone, for they searched with them, & found manie hurt, but not in ieopardie of their
liues ; whom they tooke prisoners, and brought them to their tents.

The king that daie shewed himselfe a valiant knight, albeit almost felled by the duke of Alanson ; yet with plaine strength he slue two of the dukes companie, and felled the duke him-selfe ; whome, when he would haue yelded, the kings gard (contrarie to his mind) slue out of hand.

16.   There are taken prisoners : *Charles duke of Orleance, nephue to the* French king ; *Iohn duke of Burbon ;* the *lord Bouciqualt*, one of the marshals of France (he after died in England) ; with a number of *other lords, knights, and esquiers*, at the least *fifteene hundred, besides* the *common* people.   There were *slaine* in all of the French part to the *number of ten thousand* men ; whereof were *princes* and noble men *bearing baners one hundred twentie and six ; to these, of knights, esquiers, and gentlemen*, so manie as made vp the number of *eight thousand and foure hundred* (*of the which fiue hundred were dubbed knights* the night before the battell) : so as, of the meaner sort, not past *sixteene hundred*.   Amongst those of the nobilitie that were slaine, these were the cheefest : *Charles* lord *de la Breth*, high constable of France ; *Iaques of Chatilon*, lord of Dampier, *admerall of France ; the lord Rambures, master of the crossebowes ; sir Guischard Dolphin, great master of France ; Iohn duke of Alanson ; Anthonie duke of Brabant, brother to the duke of Burgognie ; Edward duke of Bar ;* the earle of Neuers, an other brother to the duke of Burgognie ; with the *erles of Marle, Vaudemont, Beaumont, Grandpree, Roussie, Fauconberge, Fois*, and *Lestrake ;* besides a great number of lords and barons of name.

Of Englishmen, there died at this battell, *Edward duke of Yorke ; the earle of Suffolk ; sir Richard Kikelie ;* and *Dauie Gamme, esquier ; and, of all other*, not aboue *fiue and twentie persons*,
.   .   .
And so, about foure of the clocke in the after noone, the king, when he saw no apperance of enimies, caused the retreit to be blowen ; and, gathering his armie togither, gaue thanks to al-mightie God for so happie a victorie ; causing his prelats and chapeins to sing this psalme : " In exitu Israel de Aegypto " ; and commanded euerie man to kneele downe on the ground at this verse : " *Non nobis*, Domine, non nobis, sed nomini tuo da gloriam." Which doone, he caused *Te Deum*, with certeine anthems to be soong ; giuing laud and praise to God, without boasting of his owne force or anie humane power.

17.   When the king of England had well refreshed himselfe, and his souldiers, (that had taken the spoile of such as were slaine,) he, with his prisoners, in good order, returned to his towne of Calis.
After that the king of England had refreshed himselfe, and his people at Calis, . . . the sixt [16th] daie of Nouember, he with all his prisoners tooke shipping, and the same daie landed at Douer, . . . In this passage, the seas were so rough and troublous, that two ships belonging to sir Iohn Cornewall, lord Fanhope, were driuen into Zeland ; howbeit, nothing was lost, nor any person perisht.
The maior of London, and the aldermen, apparelled in orient grained scarlet, and foure hundred commoners clad in beautifull murrie, (well mounted, and trimlie horssed, with rich collars, & great chaines,) met the king on Blackheath ; reioising at his returne : and the clergie of London, with rich crosses, sumptuous copes, and massie censers, receiued him at saint Thomas of Waterings with solemne procession.
The king, like a graue and sober personage, and as one remembring from whom all victories are sent, seemed little to regard such vaine pompe and shewes as were in triumphant sort deuised for his welcomming home from so prosperous a iournie : in so much that he would not suffer his helmet to be caried with him, whereby might haue appeared to the people the blowes and dints that were to be seene in the same ; neither would he suffer anie ditties to be made and soong by minstrels of his glorious victorie, for that he would wholie haue the praise and thanks altogither giuen to God.
[On or about May 1, 1416,] the emperour Sigismund . . . came into England, to the intent that he might make an attonement betweene king Henrie and the French king : . . .
There came to him eftsoones ambassadours from the French king and the duke of Burgognie to mooue him to peace.   The king, minding not to be reputed for a destroier of the countrie, which he coueted to preserue, or for a causer of christian bloud still to be spilt in his quarell, began so to incline and giue eare vnto their sute and humble request, that at length, (after often sending to and fro,) and that the bishop of Arras, and other men of honor had beene with him, and likewise the earle of Warwike, and the bishop of Rochester had beene with the duke of Burgognie, they both finallie agreed vpon certeine articles ; so that the French king and his commons would thereto assent.

18.   Now was the French king and the queene with their daughter Katharine at Trois in Champaigne ; gouerned and ordered by them, which so much fauoured the duke of Burgognie, that they would not, for anie earthlie good, once hinder or pull backe one iot of such articles as the same duke should seeke to preferre.   And therefore what needeth manie words ? a truce

tripartite was accorded betweene the two kings and the duke, and their countries ; and order taken that the king of England should send, in the companie of the duke of Burgognie, his ambassadours vnto Trois in Champaigne ; sufficientlie authorised to treat and conclude of so great matter. The king of England, being in good hope that all his affaires should take good successe as he could wish or desire, sent to the duke of Burgognie, his vncle the duke of Excester, the earle of Salisburie, the bishop of Elie, the lord Fanhope, the lord Fitz Hugh, sir Iohn Robsert, and sir Philip Hall, with diuerse doctors, to the number of fiue hundred horsse ; which in the companie of the duke of Burgognie came to the citie of Trois the eleuenth of March. The king, the queene, and the ladie Katharine them receiued, and hartilie welcomed ; shewing great signes and tokens of loue and amitie.

After a few daies they fell to councell, in which at length it was concluded, that king Henrie of England should come to Trois, and marie the ladie Katharine ; and the king hir father after his death should make him heire of his realme, crowne, and dignitie. It was also agreed, that king Henrie, during his father in lawes life, should in his steed haue the whole gouernement of the realme of France, as regent thereof : with manie other couenants and articles, as after shall appeere.

[Henry,] mistrusting that the duke of Burgognie was the verie *let* and stop of his desires, said vnto him before his departure : " Coosine, we will haue your kings daughter, and *all* things that " we demand with hir, or we will driue your king and you out of his realme."

[Henry went to Troyes,] accompanied with his brethren the dukes of Clarence and Glocester, the earles of Warwike, Salisburie, Huntington, . . .

The two kings and their councell assembled togither diuerse daies ; wherein the first concluded agreement was in diuerse points altered and brought to a certeinetie, according to the effect aboue mentioned.

1. First, it is accorded betweene our father and vs, that forsomuch as by the bond of matrimonie made for the good of the peace betweene vs and our most deere beloued Katharine, daughter of our said father, & of our most deere moother Isabell his wife, the same Charles and Isabell beene made our father and moother : therefore them as our father and moother we shall haue and worship, as it fitteth and seemeth so worthie a prince and princesse to be worshipped, principallie before all other temporall persons of the world.

25. Also *that* our said father, during his life, *shall name*, call, and *write* vs *in French in this* maner : *Nostre treschier filz Henry roy d'Engleterre heretere de France. And in Latine* in this maner : *Præclarissimus filius noster Henricus rex Angliæ & hæres Franciæ.*

[Henry] went to visit the French king, the queene, and the ladie Katharine, whome he found in saint Peters church, where was a verie ioious meeting betwixt them ; (and this was on the twentith daie of Maie ;) and there the king of England and the ladie Katharine were affianced.

The kings sware for their parts to obserue all the couenants of this league and agreement. Likewise the duke of Burgognie, and a great number of other princes and nobles which were present, receiued an oth, . . .

APPENDIX II.

Extracts from *The Famous Victories of Henry the Fifth, conteining the Honorable Battell of Agincourt*, utilised by Shakespeare in the *Life of King Henry the Fifth*.[1]

Hen. V.	Now my good Lord Archbishop of Canterbury,
	What say you to our Embassage into France ?
Archb.	Your right to the French Crowne of France,
	Came by your great grandmother Izabel,
	Wife to King Edward the third,
	And sister to Charles the French King :
	Now if the French king deny it, as likely inough he wil,
	Then must you take your sword in hand,
	And conquer the right.
	Let the vsurped Frenchman know,
	Although your predecessors haue let it passe, you wil not :
	For your Countrymen are willing with purse and men,
	To aide you.
	Then my good Lord, as it hath bene alwaies knowne,
	That Scotland hath bene in league with France,
	By a sort of pensions which yearly come from thence,
	I thinke it therefore best to conquere Scotland,
	And thē I think that you may go more easily into France :
	And this is all that I can say, My good Lord.
Hen. V.	I thanke you, my good lord Archbishop of Canterbury.
	What say you my good Lord of Oxford ?
Oxf.	And, And please your Maiestie,
	I agree to my Lord Archbishop, sauing in this,
	He that wil Scotland win, must first with France begin :
	According to the old saying.
	Therefore my good Lord, I think it best to inuade France,
	For in conquering Scotland, you conquer but one,
	And conquere France, and conquere both.

Enter Lord of Exeter.

Exe.	And please your Maiestie,
	My Lord Embassador is come out of France.
Hen. V.	Now trust me my Lord,
	He was the last man that we talked of,
	I am glad that he is come to resolue vs of our answere,
	Commit him to our presence.

Enter Duke of Yorke.

York.	God saue the life of my soueraign Lord the king.
Hen. V.	Now my good Lord the Duke of York,
	What newes from our brother the French King ?
York.	And please your Maiestie,
	I deliuered him my Embassage,
	Whereof I tooke some deliberation,
	But for the answere he hath sent,
	My Lord Embassador of Burges, the Duke of Burgony,
	Monsieur le Cole, with two hundred and fiftie horsemen,
	To bring the Embassage.
Hen₁ V.	Commit my Lord Archbishop of Burges Into our presence.

---

1. Shakespeare's Library, edited by Hazlitt.

Enter Archbishop of Burges

Now my Lord Archbishop of Burges,
We do learne by our Lord Embassador,
That you haue our message to do
From our brother the French King :
Here my good Lord, according to our accustomed order,
We giue you frée libertie and license to speake,
With good audience.

Archb.   God saue the mightie King of England,
My Lord and maister, the most Christian king,
Charles the seuenth, the great & mightie king of France.
As a most noble and Christian king,
Not minding to shed innocent blood, is rather content
To yéeld somewhat to your vnreasonable demaunds,
That if fiftie thousand crownes a yeare with his daughter
The said Ladie Katheren, in marriage,
And some crownes which he may wel spare,
Not hurting of his kingdome,
He is content to yéeld so far to your vnreasonable desire.

Hen. V.   Why then belike your Lord and maister,
Thinks to puffe me vp with fifty thousand crowns a yere,
No tell thy Lord and maister,
That all the crownes in France shall not serue me,
Except the Crowne and kingdome it selfe :
And perchance hereafter I wil haue his daughter.

Archb.   And may it please your maiestie,
My Lord Prince Dolphin greets you well,
With this present.

         He deliuereth a Tunne of Tennis Balles.

Hen. V.   What a guilded Tunne ?
I pray you my Lord of Yorke, looke what is in it ?

Yorke.   And it please your Grace,
Here is a Carpet and a Tunne of Tennis balles.

Hen. V.   A Tunne of Tennis balles ?
I pray you good my Lord Archbishop,
What might the meaning thereof be ?

Archb.   And it please you my Lord,
A messenger you know, ought to kéepe close his message,
And specially an Embassador.

Hen. V.   But I know that you may declare your message
To a king, the law of Armes allowes no lesse.

Archb.   My Lord, hearing of your wildnesse before your
Fathers death, sent you this my good Lord,
Meaning that you are more fitter for a Tennis Court
Then a field, and more fitter for a Carpet then the Camp.

Hen. V.   My lord Prince Dolphin is very pleasant with me :
But tel him, that in stéed of balles of leather,
We wil tosse him balles of brasse and yron,
Yea such balles as neuer were tost in France,
The proudest Tennis Court shall rue it.
I and thou Prince of Burges shall rue it.
Therefore get thée hence, and tel him thy massage quickly,
Least I be there before thee : Away priest, be gone.

    .   .   .   .

Now my Lords, to Armes, to Armes,
For I vow my heauen and earth, that the proudest
French man in all France, shall rue the time that euer
These Tennis balles were sent into England.
My Lord, I wil y^t there be prouided a great Nauy of ships,
With all spéed, at South-Hampton.

Enter a Captaine, Iohn Cobler and his wife.

Cap.	Come, come, there 's no remedie,
	Thou must néeds serue the King.
Iohn.	Good maister Captaine let me go,
	I am not able to go so farre.
Wife.	I pray you good maister Captaine,
	Be good to my husband.
Cap.	Why I am sure he is not too good to serue ye king ?
Iohn.	Alasse no : but a great deale too bad,
	Therefore I pray you let me go.
Cap.	No, no, thou shalt go.
Iohn.	Oh sir, I haue a great many shooes at home to Cobble.
Wife.	I pray you let him go home againe.
Cap.	Tush I care not, thou shalt go.
Iohn.	Oh wife, and you had been a louing wife to me,
	This had not bene, for I haue said many times,
	That I would go away, and now I must go
	Against my will. *He weepeth.*

. . . . , ... ,

Enters the Theefe.

. . . . . . , . . .

Cap.	How now good fellow, doest thou want a maister.
Theefe.	I truly sir.
Cap.	Hold thée then, I presse thée for a souldier,
	To serue the King in France.
Der.	How now Gads, what doest knowes thinkest ?
Theefe.	I, I knew thée long ago.
Der.	Heare you maister Captaine ?
Cap.	What saist thou ?
Der.	I pray you let me go home againe.
Cap.	Why what wouldst thou do at home ?
Der.	Marry I haue brought two shirts with me,
	And I would carry one of them home againe,
	For I am sure héele steale it from me,
	He is such a filching fellow.
Cap.	I warrant thée he wil not steale it from thée,
	Come lets away.
Der.	Come maister Captaine lets away,
	Come follow me.
Iohn.	Come wife, lets part lovingly.
Wife.	Farewell, good husband.
Der.	Fie what a kissing and crying is here ?
	Sownes, do ye thinke he wil neuer come againe ?
	Why Iohn come away, doest thinke that we are so base
	Minded to die among French men ?
	Sownes, we know not whether they will laie
	Vs in their Church or no : Come M. Captain, lets away.
Cap.	I cannot staie no longer, therefore come away. *[Exeunt omnes.*

Enter the King, Prince Dolphin, and Lord
high Constable of France.

King.	Now my Lord high Constable,
	What say you to our Embassage into England ?
Con.	And it please your Maiestie, I can say nothing,
	Vntil my Lords Embassadors be come home,
	But yet me thinkes your grace hath done well,
	To get your men in so good a readinesse,
	For feare of the worst.
King.	I my Lord we haue some in a readinesse,
	But if the King of England make against vs,
	We must haue thrice so many moe.

Dol.	Tut my Lord, although the King of England Be yoong and wild headed, yet neuer think he will be so Vnwise to make battell against the mightie King of France.
King.	Oh my sonne, although the King of England be Yoong and wilde headed, yet neuer thinke but he is rulde By his wise Councellors.

Enter Archbishop of Burges.

Archb.	God saue the life of my soueraign lord the king.
King.	Now my good Lord Archbishop of Burges, What news from our brother the English King ?
Archb.	And please your Maiestie, He is so far from your expectation, That nothing wil serue him but the Crowne And kingdome it selfe, besides, he bad me haste quickly, Least he be there before me, and so far as I heare, He hath kept promise, for they say, he is alreadie landed At Kidcocks in Normandie, vpon the Riuer of Sene, And laid his siege to the Garrison Towne of Harflew.
King.	You have made great haste in the meane time, Haue you not ?
Dol.	I pray you my Lord, how did the King of England take my presents ?
Archb.	Truly my Lord, in very ill part, For these your balles of leather, He will tosse you balles of brass and yron. Trust me my Lord, I was verie affraide of him, He is such a hautie and high minded Prince, He is as fierce as a Lyon.
Con.	Tush, we wil make him as tame as a Lambe, I warrant you.

Enter a Messenger.

Mess.	God saue the mightie King of France.
King.	How Messenger, what newes ?
Mess.	And it please your Maiestie, I come from your poore distressed Towne of Harflew, Which is so beset on euery side, If your Maiestie do not send present aide, The Towne will be yeelded to the English King.
King.	Come my Lords, come, shall we stand still Till our Country be spoyled vnder our noses ? My Lords, let the Normanes, Brabants, Pickardies, And Danes, be sent for with all spéede : And you my Lord high Constable, I make Generall Ouer all my whole Armie. Monsieur le Colle, Maister of the Boas, Signior Deuens, and all the rest, at your appointment.
Dol.	I trust your Maiestie will bestow, Some part of the Battell on me, I hope not to present any otherwise then well.
King.	I tell thée my sonne, Although I should get the victory, and thou lose thy life, I should thinke my selfe quite conquered, And the English men to haue the victorie.
Dol.	Why my Lord and father, I would haue the pettie king of England to know, That I dare encounter him in any ground of the world.
King.	I know well my sonne, But at this time I will haue it thus : Therefore come away. ⌊*Exeunt omnes.*

Enters Henry the fifth, with his Lords.

Hen. V.	Come my Lords of England,
	No doubt this good lucke of winning this Towne,
	Is a signe of an honourable victorie to come.
	But good my Lord, go and speake to the Captaines
	With all spéed, to number the hoast of the French men,
	And by that meanes we may the better know
	How to appoint the battell.
Yorke.	And it please your Maiestie,
	There are many of your men sicke and diseased,
	And many of them die for want of victuals.
Hen. V.	And why did you not tell me of [it before ?
	If we cannot haue it for money,
	We will haue it by dint of sword,
	The lawe of Armes allow no lesse.
Oxf.	I beséech your grace, to graunt me a boone.
Hen. V.	What is that my good Lord ?
Oxf.	That your grace would give me the
	Euantgard in the battell.
Hen. V.	Trust me my Lord of Oxford, I cannot :
	For I haue alreadie giuen it to my vnc[l]e ye Duke of York,
	Yet I thanke you for your good will.

A Trumpet soundes.

	How now, what is that ?
Yorke.	I thinke it be some Herald of Armes.

Enters a Herald.

Her.	King of England, my Lord high Constable,
	And others of the Noble men of France,
	Sends me to defie thée, as open enemy to God,
	Our Countrey, and vs, and hereupon,
	They presently bid thée battell.
Hen. V.	Herald tell them, that I defie them,
	As open enemies to God, my Countrey, and me,
	And as wron[g]full vsurpers of my right :
	And whereas thou saist they presently bid me battell.
	Tell them that I thinke they knowe how to please me :
	But I pray thée what place hath my lord Prince Dolphin
	Here in battell.
Her.	And it please your grace,
	My Lord and King his father,
	Will not let him come into the field.
Hen V.	Why then he doth me great iniurie,
	I thought that he & I shuld haue plaid at tennis togither
	Therefore I haue brought tennis balles for him,
	But other maner of ones then he sent me.
	And Herald, tell my Lord Prince Dolphin,
	That I haue inured my hads with other kind of weapons
	Then tennis balles, ere this time of day,
	And that he shall finde it, ere it be long,
	And so adue my friend :
	And tell my Lord that I am readie when he will. [*Exit Herald.*
	Come my Lords, I care not and I go to our Captaines,
	And ile sée the number of the French army my selfe.
	Strike up the Drumme. [*Exeunt omnes.*

Enter French souldiers.

1 Soul.	Come away Jack Drummer, come away all,
	And me will tel you, what me wil doo,
	Me wil tro one chance on the dice,
	Who shall haue the king of England and his lords.
2 Soul.	Come away Iacke Drummer,
	And tro your chance, and lay downe your Drumme.

Enter Drummer.

Drum.	Oh the braue apparrel that the English mans
	Hay broth ouer, I wil tel you what
	Me ha donne, me ha prouided a hundreth trunkes,
	And all to put the fine parel of the English mans in.
1 *Soul.*	What do thou meane by trunkea (*sic*) ?
2 *Soul.*	A shest man, a hundred shests.
1 *Soul.*	Awee, awee, awee, Me wil tel you what,
	Me ha put fiue children out of my house,
	And all too litle to put the fine apparel of the
	English mans in.
Drum.	Oh the braue, the braue apparel that we
	Haue anon, but come, and you shall sée what we wil tro
	At the kings Drummer and Fife,
	Ha, me ha no good lucke, tro you.
3 *Soul.*	Faith me wil tro at yᵉ Earle of Northumberland
	And my Lord a Willowby, with his great horse,
	Snorting, farting, oh braue horse.
1 *Soul.*	Ha, bur Ladie you ha reasonable good lucke,
	Now I wil tro at the king himselfe,
	Ha, me haue no good lucke.

Enters a Captaine.

Cap.	How now what make you here,
	So farre from the Campe ?
2 *Soul.*	Shal me tel our captain, what we haue done here ?
Drum.	Awée, awée. [*Exeunt Drum and one souldier.*
2 *Soul.*	I wil tel you what whe haue doune,
	We haue bene troing on shance on the Dice,
	But none can win the king.
Cap.	I thinke so, why he is left behind for me,
	And I haue set thrée or foure chaire-makers a worke,
	To make a new disguised chaire to set that womanly
	King of England in, that all the people may laugh
	And scoffe at him.
2 *Soul.*	Oh braue Captaine.
Cap.	I am glad, and yet with a kindle of pitie,
	To sée the poore king.
	Why, who euer saw a more flourishing armie in France
	In one day, then here is ? Are not here all the Péeres
	of France ?
	Are not here the Normans with their firie hand-
	Gunnes, and slaunching Curtleaxes ?
	Are not here the Barbarians with their bard horses,
	And lanching speares ?
	Are not here Pickardes with their crosbowes & piercing Dartes.
	The Henues with their cutting Glaues, and sharpe Carbuckles
	Are not here the Lance knights of Burgondie ?
	And on the other side, a site of poore English scabs ?
	Why take an English man out of his warme bed
	And his stale drinke, but one moneth,
	And alas what wil become of him ?
	But giue the Frenchman a Reddish roote,
	And he wil liue with it all the dayes of his life. [*Exit.*
2 *Soul.*	Oh the braue apparel that we shall haue of the English mans.
	[*Exit.*

Enters the king of England, and his Lords.

Hen. V.	Come my Lords and fellows of armes,
	What company is there of the French men ❧
Oxf.	And it please your Maiestie,
	Our Captaines haue numbred them,
	And so neare as they can iudge,
	They are about thréescore thousand horsemen,
	And fortie thousand footemen.

Hen. V. They thréescore thousand,
   And we but two thousand.
   They thréescore thousand footemen,
   And we twelue thousand.
   They are a hundred thousand,
   And we fortie thousand, ten to one.
   My Lords and louing Countrey men,
   Though we be fewer, and they many,
   Feare not, your quarrel is good, and God wil defend you :
   Plucke vp your hearts, for this day we shall either haue
   A valiant victorie, or a honourable death.
   Now my Lords, I wil that my vncle the Duke of Yorke,
   Haue the auantgard in the battell.
   The Earle of Darby, the Earle of Oxford,
   The Earle of Kent, the Earle of Nottingham,
   The Earle of Huntingdon, I wil haue beside the army,
   That they may come fresh vpon them.
   And I my self with the Duke of Bedford.
   The Duke of Clarence and the Duke of Gloster,
   Wil be in the midst of the battell.
   Furthermore, I wil that my Lord of Willowby,
   And the Earle of Northumberland,
   With their troupes of horsemen, be cõtinually running
    like Wings on both sides of the army :
   My Lord of Northumberland, on the left wing.
   Then I wil that euery archer prouide him a stake of
   A trée, and sharpe it at both endes,
   And at the first encounter of the horsemen,
   To pitch their stakes downe into the ground before them,
   That they may gore themselues vpon them,
   And then to recoyle backe, and shoote wholly altogither,
   And so discomfit them.
Oxf. And it please your Maiestie,
   I wil take that in charge, if your grace be therwith cõtent.
Hen. V. With all my heart, my good Lord of Oxford :
   And go and prouide quickly.
Oxf. I thanke your highnesse.   *[Exit.*
Hen. V. Well my Lords, our battels are ordeined,
   And the French making of bonfires, and at their bankets,
   But let them looke, for I meane to set vpon them.
             The Trumpet soundes.
   Soft, here comes some other French message.

Enters Herald.

Her. King of England, my Lord high Constable,
   And other of my Lords, considering the poore estate of thée
   And thy poore Countrey men,
   Sends me to know what thou wilt giue for thy ransome ?
   Perhaps thou maist agrée better cheape now,
   Then when thou art conquered.
Hen. V. Why then belike your high Constable,
   Sends to know what I wil giue for my ransome ?
   Now trust me Herald, not so much as a tun of tennis-bals
   No not so much as one poore tennis-ball,
   Rather shall my bodie lie dead in the field to féed crowes,
   Then euer England shall pay one penny ransome For my bodie.
Her. A kingly resolution.
Hen. V. No Herald, tis a kingly resolution,
   And the resolution of a king :
   Here take this for thy paines.   *[Exit Herald.*
   But stay my Lords, what time is it ?
All. Prime my Lord.

Hen. V.	Then it is good time no doubt,
	For all England praieth for vs :
	What my Lords, me thinks you looke chéerfully vpon me ?
	Why then with one voice and like true English hearts,
	With me throw vp your caps, and for England,
	Cry S. George, and God and S. George helpe vs.

             Strike Drummer. [*Exeunt omnes.*
   The Frenchmen crie within, S. Dennis, S. Dennis,
       Mount Ioy, S. Dennis.

The Battell.

Enters King of England, and his Lords.

Hen. V.	Come my Lords come, by this time our
	Swords are almost drunke with French blood,
	But my Lords, which of you can tell me how many of our
	Army be slaine in the battell ?
Oxf.	And it please your Maiestie,
	There are of the French armie slaine
	Aboue ten thousand, twentie six hundred
	Whereof are Princes and Nobles bearing banners :
	Besides, all the Nobilitie of France are taken prisoners.
	Of your Maiesties Armie, are slaine none but the good
	Duke of Yorke, and not aboue fiue or six and twentie
	Common souldiers.
Hen. V.	For the good Duke of Yorke my vnckle,
	I am heartily sorie, and greatly lament his misfortune,
	Yet the honourable victorie which the Lord hath giuen vs,
	Doth make me much reioyce. But staie,
	Here comes another French message.

                Sound Trumpet
    Enters a Herald and kneeleth.

Her.	God saue the life of the most mightie Conqueror,
	The honourable king of England.
Hen. V.	Now Herald, me thinks the world is changed
	With you now, what I am sure it is a great disgrace for a
	Herald to kneele to the king of England,
	What is thy message ?
Her.	My Lord & maister, the conquered king of France,
	Sends thée long health, with heartie gréeting.
Hen. V.	Herald, his greetings are welcome,
	But I thanke God for my health :
	Well Herald, say on.
Her.	He hath sent me to desire your Maiestie,
	To giue him leaue to go into the field to view his poore
	Countrymen, that they may all be honourably buried.
Hen. V.	Why Herald, doth thy Lord and maister
	Send to me to burie the dead ?
	Let him bury them a Gods name.
	But I pray thée, Herald, where is my Lord hie Constable,
	And those that would haue had my ransome ?
Her.	And it please your maiestie,
	He was slaine in the battell.
Hen. V.	Why you may sée, you will make your selues
	Sure before the victorie be wonne, but Herald,
	What Castle is this so néere adioyning to our Campe ?
Her.	And it please your Maiestie,
	'Tis cald the Castle of Agincourt.
Hen. V.	Well then my lords of England,
	For the more honour of our English men,
	I will that this be for euer cald the battell of Agincourt.
Her.	And it please your Maiestie,
	I haue a further message to deliuer to your Maiestie.
Hen. V.	What is that Herald ? say on.

Her. And it please your Maiestie, my Lord and maister,
    Craues to parley with your Maiestie.
Hen. V. With a good will, so some of my Nobles
    View the place for feare of trecherie and treason.
Her. Your grace néeds not to doubt that.
Hen. V. Well, tell him then, I will come.
                 [*Exit Herald.*
    Now my lords, I will go into the field my selfe,
    To view my country men, and to haue them honourably
    Buried, for the French King shall neuer surpasse me in
    Curtesie, while I am Harry King of England.
    Come on my lords.   [*Exeunt omnes.*

     Enters Iohn Cobler and Robbin Pewterer.

Robin. Now Iohn Cobler,
    Didst thou sée how the King did behaue himselfe ?
Iohn. But Robin, didst thou see what a pollicie
    The King had, to sée how the French men were kild
    With the stakes of the trées.
Robin. I Iohn, there was a braue pollicie.

     Enters an English Souldier roming.

Soul. What are you my maisters ?
Both. Why we be English men.
Soul. Are you English men, then change your language
    For all the Kings Tents are set a fire,
    And all they that speake English will be kild.
Iohn. What shall we do Robin ? faith ile shift,
    For I can speake broken French.
Robin. Faith so can I, lets heare how thou canst speak.
Iohn. Commodeuales Monsieur.
Iohn. Thats well, come lets be gone. *Drum and Trumpet sounds.*

   Enters Dericke roming. After him a Frenchman, and
       takes him prisoner

Der. O good Mounser.
French. Come, come, you villeaco.
Der. O I will sir, I will.
French. Come quickly you pesant.
Der. I will sir, what shall I giue you ?
French. Marry, thou shalt giue me,
    One, to, tre, foure hundred Crownes.
Der. Nay sir, I will giue you more,
    I will giue you as many crowns as will lie on your sword.
French. Wilt thou giue me as many crowns
    As will lie on my sword ?
Der. I marrie will I, but you must lay downe your
    Sword, or else they will not lie on your sworde.
      Here the Frenchman layes downe his sword, and
        the clowne takes it vp, and hurles him downe.
Der. Thou villaine, darest thou looke vp ?
French. O good Mounsier comparteue
    Monsieur pardon me.
Der. O you villaine, now you lie at my mercie,
    Doest thou remember since thou lambst me in thy short el ?
    O villaine, now I will strike off thy head.
        Here whiles he turns his back, the French-
          man runnes his wayes.
Der. What is he gone, masse I am glad of it,
    For if he had staid, I was afraid he wold haue sturd again,
    And then I should haue béene spilt,
    But I will away, to kill more Frenchmen.

Enters King of France, King of England, and
attendants.

Hen. V.	Now my good brother of France,
	My comming into this land was not to shead blood,
	But for the right of my Countrey, which if you can deny.
	I am content peaceably to leaue my siege,
	And to depart out of your land.
Char.	What is it you demand,
	My louing brother of England.
Hen. V.	My Secretary hath it written, read it.
Sec.	Item, that immediately Henry of England
	Be crowned King of France.
Char.	A very hard sentence.
	My good brother of England.
Hen. V.	No more but right, my good brother of France.
Fr. King.	Well, read on.
Sec.	Item, that after the death of the said Henry,
	The Crowne remaine to him and his heires for euer.
Fr. King.	Why then you do not onely meane to
	Dispossesse me, but also my sonne.
Hen. V.	Why my good brother of France,
	You haue had it long inough :
	And as for Prince Dolphin,
	It skils not though he sit beside the saddle :
	Thus I haue set it downe, and thus it shall be.
Fr. King.	You are very peremptorie,
	My good brother of England.
Hen. V.	And you as peruerse, my good brother of France.
Char.	Why then belike, all that I haue here is yours.
Hen. V.	I euen as far as the kingdom of France reaches.
Char.	I for by this hote beginning,
	We shall scarce bring it to a calme ending.
Hen. V.	It is as you please, here is my resolution.
Char.	Well my brother of England,
	If you will, giue me a copie,
	We will meet you againe to-morrow.
	[*Exit King of France, and all their attendants.*
Hen. V.	With a good will my good brother of France.
	Secretary deliuer him a coppie.
	My lords of England goe before,
	And I will follow you. [*Exeunt Lords. Speaks to himselfe.*
Hen. V.	Ah Harry, thrice vnhappie Harry.
	Hast thou now conquered the French King,
	And begins a fresh supply with his daughter,
	But with what face canst thou seeke to gaine her loue,
	Which has sought to win her fathers Crowne ?
	Her fathers Crowne said I, no it is mine owne :
	I but I loue her, and must craue her,
	Nay I loue her and will haue her.

Enters Lady Katheren and her Ladies.

	But here she comes :
	How now faire Ladie Katheren of France,
	What newes ?
Kathren.	And it please your Maiestie,
	My father sent me to know if you will debate any of these
	Vnreasonable demands which you require.
Hen. V.	Now trust me, Kate,
	I commend thy fathers wit greatly in this,
	For none in the world could sooner haue made me debate it
	It it were possible :
	But tell me swéete Kate, canst thou tell how to loue ?
Kate.	I cannot hate my good Lord,
	Therefore far vnfit were it for me to loue.

Hen. V.	Tush Kate, but tell me in plaine termes,
	Canst thou loue the King of England ?
	I cannot do as these Countries do,
	That spend halfe their time in woing :
	Tush wench, I am none such,
	But wilt thou go ouer to England ?
Kate.	I would to God, that I had your Maiestie,
	As fast in loue, as you haue my father in warres,
	I would not vouchsafe so much as one looke,
	Vntill you had related all these vnreasonable demands.
Hen. V.	Tush Kate, I know thou wouldst not vse me so hardly :
	But tell me, canst thou loue the King of England ?
Kate.	How should I loue him, that hath dealt so hardly
	With my father ?
Hen. V.	But ile deale as easily with thee,
	As thy heart can imagine, or tongue can require,
	How saist thou, what will it be ?
Kate.	If I were of my owne direction,
	I could giue you answere :
	But séeing I stand at my fathers direction,
	I must first know his will.
Hen. V.	But shal I haue thy good wil in the mean season ?
Kate.	Whereas I can put your grace in no assurance,
	I would be loth to put you in any dispaire.
Hen. V.	Now before God, it is a sweete wench.

She goes aside, and speaks as followeth.

Kate.	I may thinke my selfe the happiest in the world,
	That is beloued of the mighty King of England.
Hen. V.	Well Kate, are you at hoast with me ?
	Swéete Kate, tel thy father from me,
	That none in the world could sooner haue perswaded me to
	It then thou, and so tel thy father from me.
Kate.	God kéepe your Maiestie in good health. [*Exit Kate.*
Hen. V.	Farwel swéet Kate, in faith it is a swéet wench,
	But if I knew I could not haue her fathers good wil,
	I would so rowse the Towers ouer his eares,
	That I would make him be glad to bring her me,
	Vpon his hands and knées. [*Exit King.*

Enter Dericke with his girdle full of shooes.

Der.	How now ? Sownes it did me good to see how
	I did triumph ouer the French men.

Enters Iohn Cobler rouing, with a packe full of apparell.

Iohn.	Whoope Dericke, how doest thou ?
Der.	What Iohn, Comedeuales, aliue yet.
Iohn.	I promise thée Dericke, I scapte hardly,
	For I was within halfe a mile when one was kild.
Der.	Were you so ?
Iohn.	I trust me, I had like bene slaine.
Der.	But once kild, why it is nothing,
	I was foure or fiue times slaine.
Iohn.	Foure or fiue times slaine.
	Why how couldst thou haue béene aliue now ?
Der.	O Iohn, neuer say so,
	For I was cald the bloodie souldier amongst them all.
Iohn.	Why what didst thou ?
Der.	Why, I will tell thée Iohn,
	Euery day when I went into the field,
	I would take a straw, and thrust it into my nose,
	And make my nose bléed, and then I wold go into the field,
	And when the Captaine saw me, he would say,
	Peace a bloodie souldier, and bid me stand aside,

Der.	Whereof I was glad :
(contd.)	But marke the chance Iohn.
	I went and stood behinde a tree, but marke then Iohn,
	I thought I had béne safe, but on a sodaine,
	There steps to me a lustie tall Frenchman,
	Now he drew, and I drew,
	Now I lay here, and he lay there,
	Now I set this leg before, and turned this backward,
	And skipped quite ouer a hedge,
	And he saw me no more there that day,
	And was not this well done Iohn ?
Iohn.	Masse Dericke, thou hast a wittie head.
Der.	I Iohn, thou maist sée, if thou hadst taken my coūsel,
	But what hast thou there ?
	I thinke thou hast bene robbing the Frenchman.
Iohn.	I faith Dericke, I haue gotten some reparrell,
	To carry home to my wife.
Der.	And I haue got some shooes,
	For ile tel thee what I did, when they were dead,
	I would go take off all theyr shooes.
Iohn.	I, but Dericke, how shall we get home ?
Der.	Nay sownds and they take thée, They wil hang thée,
	O Iohn, neuer do so, if it be thy fortune to be hangd,
	Be hangd in thy owne language whatsoeuer thou doest.
Iohn.	Why Dericke the warres is done,
	We may go home now.
Der.	I but you may not go before you aske the king leaue,
	But I know a way to go home, and aske the king no leaue.
Iohn.	How is that Dericke ?
Der.	Why Iohn, thou knowest the Duke of Yorkes
	Funerall must be carried into England, doest thou not ?
Iohn.	I that I do.
Der.	Why then thou knowest wéele go with it.
Iohn.	I but Dericke, how shall we do for to méet them ?
Der.	Sownds if I make not shift to méet them, hang me.
	Sirra, thou knowst that in euery Towne there wil
	Be ringing, and there wil be cakes and drinke,
	Now I wil go to the Clarke and Sexton
	And kéepe a talking, and say, O this fellow rings well,
	And thou shalt go and take a péece of cake, then ile ring,
	And thou shalt say, oh this fellow kéepe a good stint,
	And then I will go drinke to thée all the way :
	But I maruel what my dame wil say when we come home,
	Because we haue not a French word to cast at a Dog
	By the way ?
Iohn.	Why what shall we do Dericke ?
Der.	Why Iohn, ile go before and call my dame whore,
	And thou shalt come after and set fire on the house,
	We may do it, Iohn, for ile proue it,
	Because we be souldiers. *The Trumpets sound.*
Iohn.	Dericke helpe me to carry my shooes and bootes.

Enters King of England, Lord of Oxford and Exeter,
then the King of France, Prince Dolphin, and the
Duke of Burgondie, and attendants.

Hen. V.	Now my good brother of France,
	I hope by this time you haue deliberated of your answere ?
Fr. King.	I my welbeloued brother of England,
	We haue viewed it ouer with our learned Councell,
	But cannot finde that you should be crowned King of France
Hen. V.	What not King of France, then nothing,
	I must be King : but my louing brother of France,
	I can hardly forget the late iniuries offered me,
	When I came last to parley,

Hen. V.	The French men had better a raked
(*contd.*)	The bowels out of their fathers carkasses,
	Then to haue fiered my Tentes,
	And if I knew thy sonne Prince Dolphin for one,
	I would so rowse him, as he was neuer so rowsed,
Fr. King.	I dare sweare for my sonnes innocencie
	In this matter.
	But if this please you, that immediately you be
	Proclaimed and crowned heire and Regent of France,
	Not King, because I my selfe was once crowned King.
Hen. V.	Heire and Regent of France, that is well,
	But that is not all that I must haue.
Fr. King.	The rest my Secretary hath in writing.
Sec.	Item, that Henry King of England,
	Be Crowned heire and Regent of France,
	During the life of King Charles, and after his death,
	The Crowne with all rights to remaine to King Henry
	Of England, and to his heires for euer.
Hen. V.	Well my good brother of France,
	There is one thing I must néeds desire.
Fr. King.	What is that my good brother of England ?
Hen. V.	That all your Nobles must be sworne to be true to me.
Fr. King.	Whereas they haue not stucke with greater
	Matters, I know they wil not sticke with such a trifle,
	Begin you my Lord Duke of Burgondie.
Hen. V.	Come my Lord of Burgondie,
	Take your oath vpon my sword.
Burgon.	I Philip Duke of Burgondie,
	Sweare to Henry King of England,
	To be true to him, and to become his league-man,
	And that if I Philip, heare of any forraigne power
	Comming to inuade the said Henry or his heires,
	Then I the said Philip to send him word,
	And aide him with all the power I can make,
	And thereunto I take my oath. *He kisseth the sword.*
Hen. V.	Come Prince Dolphin, you must sweare too. *He kisseth the sword.*
Hen. V.	Well my brother of France,
	There is one thing more I must néeds require of you,
Fr. King.	Wherein is it that we may satisfie your Maiestie ?
Hen. V.	A trifle my good brother of France.
	I meane to make your daughter Quéene of England,
	If she be willing, and you therewith content :
	How saist thou Kate, canst thou loue the King of England ?
Kate.	How should I loue-thee, which is my fathers enemy ?
Hen. V.	Tut stand not vpon these points,
	Tis you must make vs friends :
	I know Kate, thou art not a litle proud, that I loue thée :
	What wench, the King of England ?
Fr. King.	Daughter let nothing stand betwixt the
	King of England and thée, agree to it.
Kate.	I had best while he is willing.
	Least when I would, he will not :
	I rest at your Maiesties commaund.
Hen. V.	Welcome swéet Kate, but my brother of France.
	What say you to it ?
Fr. King.	With all my heart I like it,
	But when shall be our wedding day ?
Hen V.	The first Sunday of the next moneth,
	God willing. [*Sound Trumpets. Exeunt omnes.*

The First Part of King Henry the Sixth.

Written. 1589–1591. In the *Diary* of Philip Henslowe, edited by Collier, the following entry appears : " Rd at henery the vj, the 3 of marche 1591 . . . iij^li xvj^s v^d." It was acted by ' my lord Stranges mene,' and proved extremely popular and profitable, the receipts at the first performance amounting to £3 16s. 5d.

The only external piece of evidence is the reference in Thomas Nash's *Pierce Penniless's Supplication to the Devil :* " How would it haue joy'd braue Talbot (the terror of the French) to thinke that after he had lyne two hundred yeare in his tomb, he should triumph againe on the stage, and haue his bones new embalmed with the teares of ten thousand spectators at least, (at seuerall times), who, in the tragedian that represents his person, imagine they behold him fresh bleeding.

Published. 1623. Considered to be an old Play by one or more authors, which has been re-modelled by Shakespeare. Greene seems to have had the chief hand in the play, and others mentioned are Peele, Marlowe and Nash. It is not mentioned by Meres in his *Palladis Tamia, or, Wit's Treasury.*

Source of the Plot. The *Chronicles* of Raphael Holinshed[1] and Edward Hall. The latter has been extensively used, as his Chronicle *The Union of the two Noble and Illustre Families of Lancaster and York* was specially devoted to the wars between the houses of York and Lancaster.

Henry the Fifth died at Vincennes in France and was buried in Westminster Abbey with great pomp. Before he died he gave instructions for the future ruling of the two kingdoms, his infant son being only nine months old. To his elder brother, the Duke of Bedford, Henry committed the Regency of Kingdom of France ; nominated his uncle, Thomas Beaufort Duke of Exeter, as regent of the Kingdom of England and guardian to his son ; and appointed the Earl of Warwick as his governor.[2]

Outline of the Play. The *First Part of King Henry the Sixth* continues the story of *King Henry the Fifth.* It covers a period of twenty-two years from the funeral of Henry the Fifth, November 1422, to the overture of marriage made by Suffolk to Margaret of Anjou on behalf of Henry the Sixth towards the end of 1444.

The first Act opens in Westminster Abbey during the funeral of Henry the Fifth. Realising the calamity that has fallen upon the kingdom by the premature death of the king, Bedford very sorrowfully enjoins the " heavens hang themselves with black, yield day to night ! " for England has lost the greatest king that ever ruled over her, while Gloucester remarks that " England ne'er had a king until his time," a king whose " deeds exceeded all speech " for he " ne'er lifted up his hand but conquered." Exeter on the other hand advances the opinion that the " subtle-witted French " whom he describes as " conjurers and sorcerers," had by " magic verses contriv'd his

1. *See* Appendix I.   2. *See* Appendix II.

end." The Bishop of Winchester claims that Henry's victories were due to the prayers of the church, averring that the " dreadful judgment-day " will not be so awful to the French, as was the sight of Henry :

> He was a king bless'd of the King of kings.
> Unto the French the dreadful judgment-day
> So dreadful will not be as was his sight.
> The battles of the Lord of hosts he fought :
> The church's prayers made him so prosperous.

but Gloucester—Winchester's rival—tells him that the " church's prayers " were the cause of the king's decline in health, and denounces Winchester as a hypocrite who desires a weak monarch, so that he may have him in subjection :

> The church ! where is it ? had not churchmen pray'd
> His thread of life had not so soon decay'd :
> None do you like but an effeminate prince,
> Whom, like a school-boy, you may over-awe.

Winchester retorts by telling Gloucester that as protector he wants to " rule the prince and realm," and that his wife, who is proud, " holds him in awe, More than God or religious churchmen," and the face of the haughty prelate flushes with rage as Gloucester, in scornful accents, hurls at him :

> Name not religion, for thou lov'st the flesh,
> And ne'er throughout the year to church thou go'st
> Except it be to pray against thy foes.

" Cease, cease these jars and rest your minds in peace ! " entreats Bedford, who earnestly beseeches the " ghost of the dead king " will " Prosper this realm, and keep it from civil broils ! " for Henry's soul will make a " far more glorious star Than Julius Cæsar or bright ——." This speech is interrupted by the entry of a messenger with tidings that the English provinces in France : " Guienne, Champaigne, Rheims, Orleans, Paris, Guysors, and Poictiers," have been captured by the French with heavy loss of life. " What say'st thou, man, before dead Henry's corse ? " interposes Bedford, " Speak softly " for the " loss of those great towns " would " before dead Henry's corse make him burst his lead and rise from death." Is Paris Lost ? is Roan yielded up ? " enquires Gloucester, " If Henry was recall'd to life again These news would cause him once more yield the ghost." " How were they lost ? " demands Exeter, " what treachery was us'd ? " and the messenger replies there was no treachery, but the calamity was due to " want of men and money," owing, as the " soldiers mutter " to the " several factions " in England who are at loggerheads as to who should be appointed generals, instead of showing a united front to the enemy. " Were our tears wanting to this funeral These tidings would call forth her flowing tides," observes Exeter, while Bedford, as Regent of France, immediately calls for his " steeled coat " intending to depart for France forthwith, when a second messenger enters with the news that the Dauphin Charles has been crowned king of France at Rheims ; " The Bastard of Orleans with him is join'd ; Reignier, Duke of Anjou, doth take his part ; The Duke of Alençon flieth to his side." " The Dauphin crowned king ! exclaims Exeter with surprise, then all the French will now flock to their king's standard, and " whither shall we fly from this reproach ? " " We will not fly, but to our enemies' throats," retorts Gloucester, for if " Bedford be slack, he himself will fight it out," and Bedford asks Gloucester if he doubts his eagerness to meet the emergency, assuring him that he has already mustered in his thoughts an army which will overrun France. This messenger is followed by a third who bears the evil tidings that at the siege of Orleans, the valiant Talbot with scarce " six thousand men " had been attacked by twenty-three thousand Frenchmen, and after fighting for over three hours, had, owing to the treachery of Sir John Fastolfe, been wounded and taken prisoner, together with the Lords Scales and Hungerford ; and further, that the Earl of Salisbury owing to want of reinforcements could " hardly keep his men from mutiny," being so greatly outnumbered by the French. Bedford, who declares that if Talbot had been slain, he would have slain himself, decides to start for France without delay, and " hale the Dauphin headlong from his throne." On Bedford's departure, Gloucester purposes paying a " hasty visit " to the Tower, to " view th' artillery and munition " ; after which he will " proclaim young Henry king," while Exeter, as " special governor to the young king " proceeds to Eltham. Having gone, Winchester muses to himself that each has his rank and his duty to perform, yet for himself " nothing remains " being " left out," and declaring that he will not be " Jack out of office for long " for he will remove the young king from Eltham, and be the dictator of the realm :

> Each hath his place and function to attend :
> I am left out ; for me nothing remains,
> But long I will not be Jack out of office.
> The king from Eltham I intend to send,
> And sit at chiefest stern of public weal.

In the next scene we are before Orleans, which town the English forces are besieging. At the sound of a trumpet, King Charles with his forces appears, and declares that Mars, whose " true moving " both in the " heavens And in the earth " is unknown, and who had hitherto " smiled " upon the English, has transferred his affections to the French, by whose pleasure they occupy Orleans, and describes the English as " pale ghosts," who " Faintly besiege them one hour in a month." Alençon considers that the unsuccessful efforts of the English to capture Orleans is due to their " want of porridge and their fat bull-beeves " : while Reignier is in favour of " raising the siege " and not " live idly here," for as Talbot is a prisoner there is nothing to fear from the " mad-brain'd Salisbury," who has neither " men nor money to make war." Charles, however, gives the order for attack : " Sound, sound alarum ! we will rush on them," avowing that he will pardon the man who kills him when he sees him retreat " one foot or fly." The Frenchmen are however beaten back by the English with great loss, and Charles, in a rage exclaims :

> Who ever saw the like ? what men have I !
> Dogs ! cowards ! dastards ! I would ne'er have fled
> But that they left me 'midst my enemies.

Reignier describes Salisbury as a " desperate homicide " ; who " fighteth as one weary of his life " ; while the " other lords " he likens to " lions wanting food " who being so famished do " rush upon them as their hungry prey." Alençon quotes Froissart the French chronicler, that during the reign of Edward the Third, England bred none but " Olivers and Rowlands " yet none but " Samsons and Goliases " are sent forth to battle. Charles is however so angry at his men running away that he is in favour of abandoning Orleans, declaring that " hunger will enforce the citizens " —whom he describes as " hare-brain'd slaves "—to be more eager in its defence. At this point the Duke of Orleans enters and addressing Charles, whose " looks are sad," tells him not to be " dismay'd, for succour is at hand," as a " holy maid who claims to have had a vision from heaven, and whose spirit of deep prophecy exceeds the nine sibyls of old Rome," for " What 's past and what 's to come " she can reveal, begs an audience of his majesty. Ordering her to be admitted, Charles, in order to test her prophetic vision, directs Reignier to take his place as monarch, and with stern countenance question the maid, for " By this means shall we sound what skill she hath." Being ushered in by Orleans, she is asked by Reignier : " Fair maid, is 't thou wilt do these wondrous feats ? " and addressing him by his name, asks if he thinks he can " beguile her " : " Where is the Dauphin ? " demands the maid, and turning round, addresses Charles :

Come, come from behind ;
I know thee well, though never seen before.
Be not amazed, there 's nothing hid from me :
In private will I talk with thee apart.
Stand back, you lords, and give us leave awhile.

" She takes upon her bravely at first dash," observes Reignier, and going aside the maid informs Charles that she is by birth a shepherd's daughter, to whom the Virgin Mary has appeared and told her to leave her " base vocation and free her country from calamity." She assures Charles that she will answer unpremeditated any question he puts to her, and if he will try her courage by combat he will find that she " exceeds her sex." " Thou hast astonish'd me with thy high terms," remarks Charles, and forthwith challenges the prophetess to " single combat," and if she vanquishes him, he will believe her " words are true ; Otherwise he will renounce all confidence." " I am prepared : here is my keen-edg'd sword, Deck'd with five flower-de-luces on each side : The which at Touraine, in Saint Katharine's church-yard, Out of a great deal of old iron I chose forth," is the maid's reply. They fight and Charles being promptly overcome, calls out : " Stay, stay thy hands ! thou art an Amazon, And fightest with the sword of Deborah," but the maid unobtrusively replies that it was " Christ's mother who had helped her." Charles then beseeches her aid, offering to be her " servant and not her sovereign," but the maid declares she will not " yield to any rites of love, For my profession 's sacred from above " : nor will she " think upon a recompense " until she has " chased all his foes from hence." As Charles and the maid are " very long in talk, " Reignier suggests that they " disturb them " for, according to Alençon, " women are shrewd tempters with their tongues." " My lord, where are you ? " enquires Reignier, " shall we abandon Orleans, or no ? " " Why, no, I say : distrustful recreants ! Fight till the last gasp ; I will be your guard," interposes the maid, for as she has been specially appointed by heaven to be the " English scourge " she will that very night assuredly relieve Orleans, for " Glory is like a circle in the water, Which never ceaseth to enlarge itself Till by broad spreading it disperse to nought," adding, that " With Henry's death the English circle ends," and with it are " Dispersed the glories it included." Sinking on one knee and addressing the maid, Charles says : " Was Mahomet inspired with a dove ? Thou with an eagle art inspired then. Helen, the mother of great Constantine, Nor yet Saint Philip's daughters were like thee. Bright star of Venus, fall'n down on the earth, How may I reverently worship thee enough ? " " Leave off delays and let us raise the siege," exclaims Alençon, while Reignier appeals to the maid to do her utmost to save their honour, adding " Drive the English from Orleans and be immortalized," to which Charles retorts " Presently we 'll try," declaring that " No prophet will he trust if she prove false."

We are before the Tower of London in the next scene. The Duke of Gloucester, with his Servingmen in blue coats arrives, in order to " view th' artillery and munition," as, since Henry's death, he fears there has been some artifice, at the same time demanding to know why the warders are not present to open the gates. Arriving on the scene, the first Warder enquires who " knocks so imperiously ? " and being told it is the " noble Duke of Gloucester," the second Warder answers that " Whoe'er he be, you may not be let in." " Villains, answer you so the lord protector ? " asks the first Servingman. " The Lord protect him ! so we answer him : We do no otherwise than we are will'd," is the first Warder's reply. " Who willed you ? " demands Gloucester, " There 's none protector of the realm but I," and orders his men to " break up the gates," for which he will hold himself responsible, adding : " Shall I be flouted thus by dunghill grooms ? " As Gloucester's men rush at the gates, the Lieutenant appears on the scene. " What noise is this ? what traitors have we here ? " is the Lieutenant's query, and on Gloucester peremptorily demanding admittance, the Lieutenant informs him that he has " express commandment " from Winchester that " neither thou nor none of thine " must be allowed to enter. Gloucester denounces Winchester as an " arrogant haughty prelate " whom Henry the Fifth could never tolerate, and charges the lieutenant with being " faint-hearted " and no " friend to God or to the king," and again demands the gates to be opened or he will " shut him out shortly." At this point Winchester appears with his men in tawny coats, and addresses Gloucester in a very curt fashion : " How now, ambitious Humphrey ! what means this ? and receives an equally insolent reply : " Peel'd priest, dost thou command me to be shut out ? " Winchester accuses Gloucester of being a most " usurping proditor, And not protector, of the king or realm," while Gloucester retorts by telling Winchester he is a " manifest conspirator " and threatens to " canvass him in his broad cardinal's hat " if he persists in his insolence. " Stand thou back " ; demands Winchester, " I will not budge a foot : This be Damascus, be thou cursed Cain, To slay thy brother Abel, if thou wilt." " I will not slay thee," retorts Gloucester, but will drive thee back, and describes the Cardinal's " scarlet robes " as nothing but a " child's christening-cloth I 'll use to carry thee out of this place." " Do what thou dar'st ; I beard thee to thy face," answers Winchester, and Gloucester tells him to " beware of his beard, . . . I mean to tug it, and to cuff him soundly," for in spite of pope and church dignitaries he will stamp his cardinal's hat beneath his feet, and " drag him up and down by his cheeks." " Thou wilt answer this before the pope," is Winchester's remark, to which Gloucester retaliates by " Winchester goose, thou wolf in sheep's array," and commands his men to attack his opponent : " Out, tawny coats ! out, scarlet hypocrite ! " During the skirmish, in which the Cardinal's men are beaten back, the Lord Mayor appears, and severely reproves them for contumeliously breaking the peace, being " supreme magistrates." Gloucester tells the Lord Mayor that Winchester " regards neither God nor king," having seized the Tower for his own purpose, while Winchester describes Gloucester as a " foe to citizens," who always supports war and never peace, inflicts heavy fines, seeks to overthrow religion, and would " crown himself king." This causes them to renew their skirmish : " I will not answer thee with words, but blows," is Gloucester's retort, and the Lord Mayor has no alternative but to order the riot act to be read :

> *May.* Nought rests for me in this tumultuous strife
> But to make open proclamation.
> Come, officer ; as loud as e'er thou canst,
> Cry.
>
> *Off.* " All manner of men, assembled here in arms
> this day against God's peace and the king's, we
> charge and command you, in his highness' name,
> to repair to your several dwelling-places ; and not
> to wear, handle, or use any sword, weapon, or
> dagger, henceforward, upon pain of death."

Addressing Winchester, Gloucester tells him " he will be no breaker of the law," but when opportunity affords he will " meet him and break their minds at large." Eager for revenge, Winchester declares he will have " Gloucester's heart-blood " and the Lord Mayor threatens to " call for clubs " if they do not depart, describing Winchester as being " more haughty than the devil." " Abominable Gloucester !

guard thy head : for I intend to have it ere long," is Winchester's parting shot as he and his men leave the scene. The Lord Mayor then gives orders to his officer to " See the coast clear'd, and then they will depart," expressing surprise that nobles " should such stomachs bear " ; when he himself " fights not once in forty year."

In the next scene we are back again before Orleans, which is invested by the English forces. A Master-gunner and his boy appear on the ramparts of the city, which is in danger of being captured by the English who have already the " suburbs won." The lad is aware of this having shot at the English with his gun, but has been unfortunate in his aim. " Now be ruled by me," enjoins his father, and then you will not fail next time, for I am " Chief master-gunner of this town," and must achieve some success to win favour. He then tells his son that as the spies report having seen English officers overpeering the city " through a secret grate of iron bars," he has trained a " piece of ordnance " on that gate, and although he has watched three days " if he could see them " he can now stay no longer, and therefore charges his son to keep a strict watch, and " If thou spy'st any, run and bring me word, And thou shalt find me at the governor's," but the boy, on his father's departure, mutters to himself : " Father, I warrant you ; take you no care ; I 'll never trouble you if I may spy them."

At this point the Lords Salisbury and Talbot, with Sir William Glansdale and Sir Thomas Gargrave appear on the English turrets. Talbot has been released by his captors in exchange for a French nobleman. Salisbury rejoices at Talbot's release, and enquires how he was treated by the French, and how he came to be released :

> Talbot, my life, my joy ! again return'd !
> How wert thou handled being prisoner,
> Or by what means got'st thou to be releas'd,
> Discourse, I prithee, on this turret's top.

and Talbot explains that he was " exchang'd and ransomed " for the " brave Lord Ponton de Santrailles " captured by Bedford, and mentions how wounded at heart he is when he thinks of the treachery of Sir John Fastolfe, whom he threatens to " execute " with his " bare fists " if he only had him in his power. " Yet tell'st thou not how thou wert entertain'd," observes Salisbury, and Talbot replies " With scoffs and scorns and contumelious taunts," being exposed as a public spectacle in the open market-place guarded by a " guard of chosen shot " who had orders to " shoot him to the heart " if he attempted to escape. Salisbury is grieved at the treatment meted out to " brave Talbot " and vows revenge.

Being " supper-time in Orleans " Salisbury invites Talbot to " view through the grate " the French busily fortifying the city, a sight which will " much delight him," and invites Gargrave and Glansdale to give their " express opinions " as to the best place to attack the city. " I think at the north gate ; for there stand lords," is Gargrave's opinion, but Glansdale considers the " bulwark of the bridge " is the better place, while Talbot opines that the city must be famished, or can be easily reduced. As they gaze through the " grate," they are observed by the boy on the ramparts. Applying a torch to his cannon there is a flash of light, and a cannon ball bursting on the English fortifications, Salisbury and Gargrave fall mortally wounded : " O Lord ! have mercy on us, wretched sinners," mutters Salisbury, and Gargrave : " O Lord ! have mercy on me, woeful man." " What chance is this that suddenly hath cross'd us ? " observes Talbot, and turning to Salisbury—whom he describes as the " mirror of all martial men " is horrified to see that one of his eyes and cheeks have been blown away. Woefully exclaiming : " Accursed tower ! accursed fatal hand That hath contriv'd this woeful tragedy ! In thirteen battles Salisbury o'ercame " ; Talbot endeavours to cheer his stricken comrade : " Salisbury, cheer thy spirit with this comfort : Thou shalt not die whiles——" but Salisbury, who is past all human aid, can only faintly smile and beckon with his hand, a token which Talbot interprets as a token for revenge :

> He beckons with his hand and smiles on me,
> As who should say " When I am dead and gone,
> Remember to avenge me on the French."

" Plantagenet, I will be avenged," exclaims Talbot, when there is an alarum, and a terrible storm of thunder and lightning breaks over the scene :

> What stir is this ? what tumult 's in the heavens ?
> Whence cometh this alarum and the noise ?

and a messenger hastily enters with the news that the Dauphin, accompanied " with one Joan la Pucelle A holy prophetess new risen up " is advancing at the head of a large French force to raise the siege. This makes Salisbury rouse himself and groan aloud : " Hear, hear how dying Salisbury doth groan ! It irks his heart he cannot be reveng'd," remarks Talbot, and then turning towards the beleaguered city threatens dire reprisals on the enemy :

> Frenchmen, I 'll be a Salisbury to you ;
> Pucelle or puzzel, dolphin or dogfish,
> Your hearts I 'll stamp out with my horse's heels
> And make a quagmire of your mingled brains,

and giving orders for Salisbury to be conveyed to his tent, Talbot takes Salisbury's place as leader of the English forces.

We are still before Orleans in the next scene. There is an alarum, and French soldiers rush across the bridge and attack the English. There is great commotion, and Talbot enters and pursues the Dauphin, but is discouraged to see his men beaten back by the " holy maid " :

> Where is my strength, my valour, and my force ?
> Our English troops retire, I cannot stay them ;
> A woman clad in armour chaseth them.

Meeting Joan he offers to fight her :

> Here, here she comes. I 'll have a bout with thee ;
> Devil, or devil's dam, I 'll conjure thee :
> Blood will I draw on thee, thou art a witch,
> And straightway give thy soul to him thou serv'st.

With the remark : " Come, come ; 'tis only I that must disgrace thee," she accepts the challenge. They fight, and Talbot, who gets the worst of it, cries out :

> Heaven, can you suffer hell so to prevail ?
> My breast I 'll burst with straining of my courage,
> And from my shoulders crack my arms asunder,
> But I will chastise this high-minded strumpet.

They fight again, and although she is Talbot's equal in the fray, leaves him with the remark :

> Talbot, farewell ; thy hour is not yet come :
> I must go victual Orleans forthwith.

and " scorning his strength " tells him to go and cheer up his half-starved men, and help Salisbury to make his testament, for " This day is ours, as many more shall be." " My thoughts are whirled like a potter's wheel ; I know not where I am, nor what I do " : exclaims Talbot, and declaring that his troops have been beaten back by a

" witch " and not by " force," orders them either to " renew the fight Or tear the lions out of England's coat ; Renounce your soil, give sheep in lions' stead." The fight is therefore renewed, but notwithstanding the bravery of Talbot's men the English are driven back, the siege is raised, and Talbot gives the order for his forces to retire :

. . . .

retire into your trenches :

. . . .

Pucelle is enter'd into Orleans
In spite of us or aught that we could do,

declaring that if he

were to die with Salisbury,
The shame hereof would make him hide his head.

In the final scene of this Act we are still before Orleans. Joan, with Charles, Reignier, Alençon and soldiers, appear on the ramparts of the city, and Joan gives orders for the French colours to be raised on the walls, as the city is now rescued from the English :

Advance our waving colours on the walls
Rescued is Orleans from the English.

Charles loudly praises the maid for this great triumph : " Divinest creature, Astræa's daughter, How shall I honour thee for this success ? Thy promises are like Adonis' garden, That one day bloom'd and fruitful were the next." Reignier wishes the bells in the city to be rung in honour of the " victory that God hath given them," while Alençon remarks that " All France will be replete with mirth and joy, When they shall hear how we have play'd the men." But Charles attributes the success to Joan : " 'Tis Joan, not we, by whom the day is won " ; and offers to " divide his crown with her," while " priests and friars in his realm Shall in possession sing her endless praise," promising her at her death to erect a statelier pyramis than " Rhodope's or Memphis' ever was," and her " ashes enclosed in an urn more precious Than the rich-jewell'd coffer of Darius." Declaring that in future she shall be France's patron saint instead of Saint Denis, he invites all present to a banquet to celebrate this " golden day of victory."

We are still before Orleans at the opening of the second Act. Although the English have been defeated and Orleans relieved, Talbot was too an intrepid a general to be disheartened by this reverse. A French Sergeant and two sentinels appear, and the former orders the latter to mount vigilant guard, and report should they hear any noise or see any soldiers near the walls. The Sergeant gone, the first sentinel complains of their hard lot in being " constrain'd to watch in darkness, rain, and cold," when others " sleep upon their quiet beds."

Talbot, Bedford and Burgundy advance quickly with forces and scaling-ladders, their drums beating a dead march. Talbot opines that their opportunity has arrived, as the " Frenchmen are secure, Having all day caroused and banqueted " ; in honour of their victory, while Bedford describes Charles as the " Coward of France," for, instead of being resolute, he had " joined with witches " and invoked the " help of hell ! " to gain success, to which Burgundy adds that " Traitors have never other company." The scaling-ladders having been placed in position, Bedford requests Talbot to ascend and they will follow him, but Talbot considers it would be far better to attack the city from several points, so that if by " chance the one of us do fail " another may succeed. " Agreed : I 'll to yond corner," remarks Bedford, " And I to this," adds Burgundy, while Talbot " will mount here, or make his grave." All being ready, Talbot remarks : " Now, Salisbury, for thee, and for the right of

English Henry, shall this night appear How much in duty I am bound to both," and the signal being given, the English scale the ladders and reach the ramparts of the city. The sentinel gives the alarm : " Arm, arm ! the enemy doth make assault ! " The English, shouting their battle-cry, " St. George," " A Talbot " leap over the walls, and the French, being taken by surprise snatch up their clothes and weapons and scramble over the walls in their shirts. Later Orleans, Alençon and Reignier appear, half ready and half unready, and Alençon remarks : " How now, my lords ! what ! all unready so ? " " Unready ! " ejaculates Orleans. " Yes ! " and lucky they are to have " 'scaped so well," while Reignier observes that it was time to leave their beds when they heard " alarums at their chamber-doors." Alençon confesses that since he " follow'd arms " he has never heard of a " war-like enterprise More venturous or desperate than this." Orleans considers Talbot must be a " fiend of hell," while Reignier is of opinion that if he is not a " fiend " the " heavens, sure, favour him."

Later, Charles and Joan enter, and the former denounces the latter as a " cunning and deceitful dame " :

> Is this thy cunning, thou deceitful dame ?
> Didst thou at first, to flatter us withal,
> Make us partakers of a little gain,
> That now our loss might be ten times so much ?

and Joan implores Charles not to be so " impatient with his friend ? " for if the " watch had been good This sudden mischief never could have fallen." Alençon, Orleans and Reignier all declare that their respective watches were secure, while Charles himself acknowledges having " most part of all this night " passed to and fro to see if the sentinels were on guard. " The English must have found some place, But weakly guarded," is Joan's remark, and suggests that they gather their " scatter'd and dispers'd soldiers together and formulate new plans " to regain the city, when there is an alarum, and an English soldier suddenly enters, crying " A Talbot ! A Talbot ! " The French flee, leaving their clothes behind, which the soldier hastily gathers up, gloating over the fact that his artful trick has been so successful :

> I 'll be so bold to take what they have left.
> The cry of Talbot serves me for a sword ;
> For I have loaden me with many spoils,
> Using no other weapon but his name.

Scene two is enacted within the town of Orleans. It opens with Bedford giving orders to " sound retreat, and cease their hot pursuit." Talbot then orders the body of Salisbury to be brought in the " market-place, The middle centre of this cursed town," and having paid his " vow unto his soul " proclaims that he will, in order that future generations may know the cause the city was despoiled, erect within their chiefest temple, a " tomb wherein his corpse shall be interr'd " : on which shall be " engraved the sack of Orleans, The treacherous manner of his mournful death, And what a terror he had been to France," for every drop of blood drawn from Salisbury's body, at least five Frenchmen have met their death. He then enquires the where-abouts of Charles and Joan. Bedford replies that it was thought that when the fight began they escaped from the city by leaping over the walls for refuge in the field, to which Burgundy facetiously enjoins that he saw them " arm in arm, . . . swiftly running, Like to a pair of loving turtle-doves That could not live asunder day or night," adding, that after they have put matters in order in Orleans, they will " follow them with all the power they have." At this point a messenger enters, and after enquiring " Which of this princely train Call ye the war-like Talbot," informs Talbot

that the " virtuous lady " Countess of Auvergne " modestly " invites him to visit
her :

> The virtuous lady, Countess of Auvergne,
> With modesty admiring by renown,
> By me entreats, great lord, thou would'st vouchsafe
> To visit her poor castle where she lies,
> That she may boast she hath beheld the man
> Whose glory fills the world with loud report.

Burgundy—who observes that when " ladies crave to be encounter'd with " wars will
turn into a " peaceful comic sport "—tells Talbot he must not " despise her gentle
suit," and Talbot bids the messenger to convey to the Countess his " great thanks "
and to say he will have pleasure in waiting upon her presently.   He then invites his
companions to accompany him, but Bedford tells him that " unbidden guests Are
often welcomest when they are gone."   " Then I must go alone," is Talbot's reply,
for I mean to " prove this lady's courtesy," and calling a captain whispers to him
" You perceive my mind," to which the captain answers " I do, my lord, and mean
accordingly."

The Court of the Castle of Auvergne supplies the next scene.   It opens with the
Countess ordering the porter to lock the castle gate, and bring the keys to her immediately Talbot has entered.   On his departure, she soliloquises on how she will exceed
that barbarous woman Tomyris when she gets Talbot into her power :

> The plot is laid : if all things fall out right,
> I shall as famous be by this exploit
> As Scythian Tomyris by Cyrus' death.

Accompanied by the messenger, Talbot enters : " Madam, according as your ladyship
desir'd, By message crav'd, so is Lord Talbot come."   On being admitted she taunts
him on the meanness of his stature : " What ! is this the man ? "   " Madam, it is,"
replies the messenger.

> Is this the scourge of France ?
> Is this the Talbot, so much fear'd abroad
> That with his name the mothers still their babes ?
> I see report is fabulous and false :
> I thought I should have seen some Hercules,
> A second Hector, for his grim aspect,
> And large proportion of his strong-knit limbs.
> Alas ! this is a child, a silly dwarf :
> It cannot be this weak and writhled shrimp
> Should strike such terror to his enemies.

Annoyed at her unflattering remarks, Talbot reminds the Countess that he has been
" bold to trouble her " but since her " ladyship is not at leisure " he will choose a
more fitting occasion to visit her, and forthwith takes his departure.   Ordering the
messenger to follow Talbot, and enquire " whither he goes," the messenger entreats Talbot to stay, for " my lady craves To know the cause of your abrupt
departure," and Talbot tells him that as the Countess is labouring under a miscon-
ception, he goes to prove to her that " Talbot is really here."   Just then the Porter
re-enters bringing with him the keys, and turning to Talbot she tells him he is her
prisoner now.   " Prisoner ! " repeats Talbot in surprise, " to whom ? "   " To me,
blood-thirsty lord " ; retorts the Countess, adding that she intends to wreak vengeance upon him for having " wasted our country, slain our citizens, And sent our
sons and husbands captivate."   " Ha, ha, ha ! " laughs Talbot, to which she retorts :
" Laughest thou, wretch ? thy mirth shall turn to moan."   But Talbot tells her
" that she has aught but Talbot's shadow," adding that " were the whole frame here,"

her castle would not be large enough to contain it, language which she describes as only coined for the occasion :

> This is a riddling merchant for the nonce ;
> He will be here, and yet he is not here :
> How can these contrarieties agree ?

Winding his horn, drums strike up, there is a peal of ordnance, and soldiers burst into the castle :

> How say you, madam ? are you now persuaded
> That Talbot is but shadow of himself ?
> These are his substance, sinews, arms, and strength,
> With which he yoketh your rebellious necks,
> Razeth your cities, and subverts your towns,
> And in a moment makes them desolate.

Seeing her treacherous designs defeated she craves pardon :

> Victorious Talbot, pardon my abuse :
>
> .   .   .   .
>
> For I am sorry that with reverence
> I did not entertain thee as thou art.

Talbot assures her that she has not offended him, and requests her not to be dismayed, nor misconstrue his mind as she did mistake the outward composition of his body, for the only satisfaction he craves is that they may " Taste of her wine and see what cates she has ; For soldiers' stomachs always serve them well." " With all my heart," is the Countess' reply, and " think me honoured To feast so great a warrior in my house."

We are now transferred to London, the next scene being the Temple Garden.   A Council meeting has been held in the Temple Hall at which a dispute has arisen between Richard Plantagenet—heir to Mortimer—and the Earl of Somerset, and the nobles adjourn to the garden as a more fitting place to continue the dispute :

> *Plan.*   Great lords and gentlemen, what means this silence ?
>   Dare no man answer in a case of truth ?
> *Suf.*   Within the Temple hall we were too loud ;
>   The garden here is more convenient,

whereupon Plantagenet enjoins Suffolk to declare at once that he is right, and the " wrangling " Somerset wrong, but Suffolk answers evasively :

> *Plan.*   Then say at once if I maintain'd the truth,
>   Or else was wrangling Somerset in the error ?
> *Suf.*   Faith, I have been a truant in the law,
>   And never yet could frame my will to it ;
>   And therefore frame the law unto my will.

Somerset then invites Warwick to judge who is right, but Warwick, not to be beguiled, replies :

> Between two hawks, which flies the highest pitch ;
> Between two dogs, which hath the deeper mouth ;
> Between two blades, which bears the better temper ;
> Between two horses, which doth bear him best ;
> Between two girls, which hath the merriest eye ;

he has " some shallow spirit of judgment " ; but " in these nice sharp quillets of the law," he is " no wiser than a daw."   " Tut, tut ! " retorts Plantagenet, " here is a mannerly forbearance " : the " truth is so naked on my side," that a short-sighted man can see it, and it is " So well apparell'd, so clear, so shining, and so evident on my side " exclaims Somerset, that even a blind man can catch a glimmer of it.

Plantagenet persists that he is in the right, and as the nobles are " tongue-tied and
so loath to speak " he invites them " In dumb significants " to " proclaim their
thoughts," and plucks a white rose from a neighbouring bush :

> Let him that is a true-born gentleman
> And stands upon the honour of his birth,
> If he suppose that I have pleaded truth,
> From off this brier pluck a white rose with me,

whereup₍ n Somerset invites those who maintain he is in the right to pluck a red rose
from another bush :

> Let him that is no coward nor no flatterer,
> But dare maintain the party of the truth,
> Pluck a red rose from off this thorn with me.

Warwick who " loves no colours " plucks a white rose :

> I love no colours, and without all colour
> Of base insinuating flattery
> I pluck this white rose with Plantagenet,

while Suffolk plucks a red one :

> I pluck this red rose with young Somerset,
> And say withal I think he held the right.

Vernon then suggests that " upon whose side The fewest roses are cropp'd . . .
Shall yield the other in the right opinion."   To this both parties agree, whereupon
Vernon declares himself on the side of Plantagenet :

> Then for the truth and plainness of the case,
> I pluck this pale and maiden blossom here,
> Giving my verdict on the white rose side,

and Somerset retorts :

> Prick not your finger as you pluck it off,
> Lest bleeding you do paint the white rose red,
> And fall on my side so, against your will,

to which Vernon replies :

> If I, my lord, for my opinion bleed,
> Opinion shall be surgeon to my hurt,
> And keep me on the side where still I am.

" Well, well, come on : who else ? " impatiently asks Somerset.   The next is a Lawyer
who considers that Somerset is in the wrong :

> Unless my study and my books be false,
> The argument you held was wrong in you ;
> In sign whereof I pluck a white rose too.

This makes Plantagenet remark : " Now, Somerset, where is your argument ? "
" Here in my scabbard ; meditating that Shall dye your white rose in a bloody red,"
excitedly exclaims Somerset, and Plantaganet tells Somerset that already his cheeks
are so pale with fear that they imitate the white rose, thus showing that the truth is
on the side of Plantagenet, and Somerset retorts that it is " not for fear but anger
that Plantagenet's cheeks for pure shame do counterfeit the red rose," and yet his
tongue will not confess his error.   " Hath not thy rose a canker, Somerset ? " taunts
Plantagenet, to which Somerset curtly replies : " Hath not thy rose a thorn,
Plantagenet ? " and Plantagenet, holding the white rose in his hand, scorns Somerset,
calling him a " peevish boy."   These and other reproaches cause unpleasantness
between the parties, which is accentuated by Somerset accusing Plantagenet of being

the son of a " yeoman," which Warwick repudiates by proving his descent from Lionel, Duke of Clarence. Somerset, who declares he will sustain his words on any " plot of ground in Christendom," then charges Plantagenet with being the son of a traitor, his father, Richard, Earl of Cambridge, having been executed for treason, and Plantagenet resents this accusation, maintaining that his father was " attached and not attainted, condemn'd to die for treason, but no traitor " : declaring that he has " noted both Suffolk and Somerset in his book of memory " and will, when the time is ripe, " scourge them for their apprehension : look to it well and say you are well warn'd," to which Somerset retorts that Plantagenet will find both himself and Suffolk ready. Plantagenet swears by his " soul " that he will as " cognizance of his blood-drinking hate " always wear this " pale and angry rose," until it either " wither with him to his grave Or flourish to the height of his degree," whereupon Suffolk takes his departure, remarking to Plantagenet as he leaves : " Go forward, and be chok'd with thy ambition : And so farewell until I meet thee next." Suffolk is followed by Somerset with the parting shot : " Farewell, ambitious Richard." When they are gone, Plantagenet remarks to Warwick how he is insulted, and " must perforce endure it ! " and Warwick tells him that the blot against his house shall be wiped out in the next parliament or he will not "live to be accounted Warwick ; " adding, that this " brawl " which originated in the Temple Hall and " grown to this faction in the Temple Garden," will

> send between the red rose and the white
> A thousand souls to death and deadly night.

Warwick, Vernon and the Lawyer pledge themselves always to wear the white rose as a token of love and fidelity to Plantagenet. Plantagenet thanks them for their loyalty, afterwards inviting them to dine with him : " Come, let us four to dinner " : for he has no doubt that :

> This quarrel will drink blood another day.

The final scene of this Act shows us the Tower of London. Mortimer—a prisoner in the Tower—is brought in a chair by two gaolers :

> Kind keepers of my weak decaying age,
> Let dying Mortimer here rest himself.
> Even like a man new haled from the rack,
> So fare my limbs with long imprisonment ;
> And these grey locks, the pursuivants of death,
> Nestor-like aged in an age of care,
> Argue the end of Edmund Mortimer.

Owing to his long imprisonment he is in a weak condition, and is therefore anxious to see his nephew—Richard Plantagenet—before he dies. Being assured by the first gaoler that Plantagenet, whom they have sent for to the Temple will presently arrive, Mortimer remarks that his " soul will then be satisfied," and proceeds to point out to his gaolers how he has been deprived of his just honour and inheritance, and wishes that the troubles of young Plantagenet were over, so that he could regain that which he [Mortimer] had lost. Plantagenet now appears :

> Ay, noble uncle, thus ignobly used,
> Your nephew, late-despised Richard, comes,

and is affectionately embraced by Mortimer :

> Direct mine arms I may embrace his neck,
> And in his bosom spend my latter gasp :
> O ! tell me when my lips do touch his cheeks,
> That I may kindly give one fainting kiss.

" Sweet stem from York's great stock, Why didst thou say of late thou wert despised ? " asks Mortimer, and Plantagenet replies : " First, lean thine aged back against mine arm, And in that ease I 'll tell thee my disease," and then relates to his uncle the quarrel between himself and Somerset, who has upbraided him with being the son of a traitor. He then asks his uncle the reason his father was executed :

> Therefore, good uncle, for my father's sake,
> In honour of a true Plantagenet,
> And for alliance sake, declare the cause
> My father, Earl of Cambridge, lost his head.

" That cause, fair nephew," replies Mortimer, " that imprison'd me, And hath detain'd me all my flow'ring youth Within a loathsome dungeon, there to pine, Was cursed instrument of his decease," and Plantagenet asks his uncle to be more explicit " what cause that was," for he is " ignorant and cannot guess," and Mortimer goes on to explain that Richard the Second, grandson of Edward the Third, and lawful heir to the crown, was deposed by his uncle, Henry the Fourth, grandfather of the present king Henry the Sixth. " Finding his usurpation most unjust " the war-like lords endeavoured to place him—Mortimer—as the next heir by birth and parentage—on the throne. As a result these war-like lords lost their lives, and he [Mortimer] was sent a prisoner to the Tower, while the Earl of Cambridge—brother-in-law to Mortimer and father to Plantagenet—was beheaded as a traitor by Henry the Fifth. " Thus the Mortimers, In whom the title rested, were suppress'd." Whispering to Plantagenet that the " fainting words " he has just uttered " warrant death " he tells him " Thou art my heir ; the rest I wish thee gather : But yet be wary in thy studious care," and Plantagenet—who promises to regard with care his uncle's " grave admonishments "—infers that his " father's execution Was nothing less than bloody tyranny." Mortimer counsels caution as the House of Lancaster is firmly fixed upon the throne :

> With silence, nephew, be thou politic :
> Strong-fixed is the house of Lancaster,
> And like a mountain, not to be removed.

Mortimer then tells his nephew that owing to his long incarceration he is at the point of death :

> But now thy uncle is removing hence,
> As princes do their courts, when they are cloy'd
> With long continuance in a settled place,

and Plantagenet wishes he could give " some part of his young years " to prolong his uncle's days, but Mortimer tells him he " wrongs him, as that slaughterer doth Which giveth many wounds when one will kill," and a few moments later—after telling his nephew to " Mourn not, except thou sorrow for my good ; Only give order for my funeral "—bids Plantagenet farewell :

> And so farewell ; and fair be all thy hopes ,
> And prosperous be thy life in peace and war !

Death having extinguished the " dusky torch " of Mortimer, Plantagenet—after musing that he will " lock in his breast " the counsel he has just received—gives the gaolers orders to bear away the body :

> Keepers, convey him hence ; and I myself
> Will see his burial better than his life,

and vowing to avenge himself on Somerset for his insults :

> And for those wrongs, those bitter injuries,
> Which Somerset hath offer'd to my house,
> I doubt not but with honour to redress ;

he forthwith hurries away to the Parliament House :

> Either to be restored to my blood,
> Or make my ill the advantage of my good.

The third Act opens in the Parliament House in London. Gloucester " offers to put up a bill "—a statement of accusations against Winchester. Snatching it out of his hand and tearing it to pieces, Winchester tells Gloucester that if he has anything to lay to his charge, to do it " without invention, suddenly " and not " with deep premeditated lines " and " with written pamphlets studiously devis'd " so that he can answer with " sudden and extemporal speech." Gloucester, who addresses Winchester as " Presumptuous priest ! " tells him that the Parliament House " commands my patience Or thou should'st find thou hast dishonour'd me," and although he preferred to put in writing the " manner of his vile outrageous crimes," Winchester must not consider that he is unable to rehearse them verbatim. Telling Winchester that his " audacious wickedness " is such, that his " lewd, pestiferous, and dissentious pranks, As very infants prattle of his pride," he charges him with being a " most pernicious usurer, Froward by nature, enemy to peace ; Lascivious, wanton, more than well beseems A man of his profession and degree," and accuses him of having at " London Bridge and at the Tower laid a trap to take his life." " Gloucester, I do defy thee," shouts Winchester, and craving permission to speak, tells the nobles that Gloucester is incensed against him because he wants to " sway the realm." " But," adds Winchester, " he shall know I am as good——" " As good ! " ejaculates Gloucester, " Thou bastard of my grandfather ! " " Ay, lordly sir " ; retorts Winchester, " for what are you, I pray, But one imperious in another's throne ? " " Am I not protector, saucy priest ? " demands Gloucester. " And am not I a prelate of the church ? " shouts Winchester. " Yes ! " and like an outlaw keeps in his castle, and uses it to " patronage his theft," is Gloucester's sarcastic retort, to which Winchester ejaculates : " Unreverent Gloucester ! " " Thou are reverent, Touching thy spiritual function, not thy life," angrily retorts Gloucester, and Winchester tells him that " Rome shall remedy this." Somerset considers that Winchester " should be religious," and know the " office that belongs to such," while Warwick expresses the opinion that Winchester should be " humbler " as it is not fitting for a " prelate so to plead." As the quarrel proceeds, Plantagenet [aside] discreetly mutters :

> Plantagenet, I see, must hold his tongue,
> Lest it be said ' Speak, sirrah, when you should ;
> Must your bold verdict entertalk with lords ? '
> Else would I have a fling at Winchester.

Henry then appeals to Gloucester and Winchester as " special watchmen of the weal " to " join their hearts in love and amity " as " Civil dissension is a viperous worm, That gnaws the bowels of the commonwealth." At this point there is a noise and shouts " Down with the tawny coats ! " and on Henry asking what is the meaning of the tumult, Warwick answers " An uproar, I dare warrant, Begun through malice of the bishop's men." This is followed by the throwing of stones, and the Mayor enters and complains that Winchester's and Gloucester's men, who have been " forbidden to carry any weapon Have fill'd their pockets full of pebble stones," and " Do pelt so fast at one another's pate, That many have their giddy brains knock'd out " ; that windows are broken in every street, in consequence of which they have been compelled to close their shops. Servingmen, with bloody pates, now enter, and Henry charges them to keep the peace, and then turning to Gloucester appeals to him to put an end to this strife, but Gloucester's men assert that they are so resolute, that if " forbidden stones, they 'll fall to it with their teeth," and the skirmish breaks out again. Gloucester appeals to his men to cease fighting, but the first servingman replies that although they know Gloucester to be a " just and upright man " and inferior to none but the king, they and their wives and children are determined to fight to the death, and the tumult being renewed, Gloucester again appeals to his men that if they " love him, as they say they do," to cease fighting. Henry, who enjoins that this " discord doth afflict his soul " then appeals to Winchester to interfere in the interest of peace, for " who should study to prefer a peace If holy churchmen take delight in broils ? " in which he is supported by Warwick, but Winchester refuses to yield unless Gloucester submits. Gloucester therefore, out of compassion for the young king, offers Winchester his hand in token of reconciliation :

> Compassion on the king commands me stoop ;
> Or I would see his heart out ere the priest
> Should ever get that privilege of me,

but as Winchester is very reluctant to meet Gloucester, the king reproaches him for not practising what he preaches :

> Fie, uncle Beaufort ! I have heard you preach
> That malice was a great and grievous sin ;
> And will not you maintain the thing you teach,
> But prove a chief offender in the same ?

Winchester still hesitating, Warwick appeals to him :

> For shame, my lord of Winchester, relent !
> What ! shall a child instruct you what to do ?

whereupon Winchester offers his hand to Gloucester :

> Well, Duke of Gloucester, I will yield to thee ;
> Love for thy love and hand for hand I give,

Gloucester, however, fears that Winchester does not give his hand in good faith, for [aside] he mutters : " Ay ; but, I fear me, with a hollow heart," and then turning to the other lords, he, while clasping Winchester's hand, declares that " This token serveth for a flag of truce Betwixt ourselves and all our followers. So help me God, as I dissemble not ! " and Gloucester's fears are justified, for Winchester [aside] mutters : " So help me God, as I intend it not ! " Henry is " joyful " over this " contract of peace," and urges them to " join in friendship and trouble him no more." Two of the servingmen then repare to the surgeon's to have their wounds dressed, while a third proceeds to the nearest tavern to see what " physic " it can supply.

A petition is then presented to the king by Warwick urging his majesty to restore to Plantagenet his father's titles and estates, which petition Gloucester supports. Plantagenet having sworn " obedience And humble service till the point of death " the king commands him to kneel :

> Stoop then and set your knee against my foot ;
> And, in reguerdon of that duty done,
> I girt thee with the valiant sword of York :
> Rise, Richard, like a true Plantagenet,
> And rise created princely Duke of York.

Rising from his knee, Plantagenet again swears fidelity to the king : " And so thrive Richard as thy foes may fall ! And as my duty springs, so perish they That grudge one thought against your majesty ! " " Welcome, high prince, the mighty Duke of York ! " is the shout of acclamation from all the peers present, save Somerset, who murmurs aside, " Perish, base prince, ignoble Duke of York ! "

Preparations having been made for the crossing over to Paris where the coronation of Henry as King of France is to be solemised, all depart with the exception of Exeter, who soliloquises that the dissension between the peers which " Burns under feigned ashes of forg'd love," will at last break out into a flame, for he fears the realisation of that

> fatal prophecy
> Which in the time of Henry nam'd the Fifth
> Was in the mouth of every sucking babe ;
> That Henry born at Monmouth should win all ;
> And Henry born at Windsor should lose all ;
> Which is so plain that Exeter doth wish
> His days may finish ere that hapless time.

We are before Rouen in the next scene. Joan disguised, and four soldiers with sacks upon their backs, enter. Joan warns the soldiers :

> These are the city gates, the gates of Roan,
> Through which our policy must make a breach :
> Take heed, be wary how you place your words ;
> Talk like the vulgar sort of market men
> That come to gather money for their corn,

otherwise they will be detected, intimating that if they gain entrance owing to the weakness of the watch, she is to give a preconcerted signal to Charles when to attack the city. After one of the soldiers has made the punning remark : " Our sacks shall be a mean to sack the city, And we be lords and rulers over Roan " ; he knocks at the gate, and the watch within demands : " Qui est là ? " [Who is there ?] " Paysans, pauvres gens de France : [Peasants, poor folk of France]. Poor market folks that come to sell their corn," is the reply. Being satisfied the watch opens the gate : " Enter, go in ; the market bell is rung," and as they pass in, Joan with delight, mutters : " Now, Roan, I 'll shake thy bulwarks to the ground."

Charles and his followers enter, and the king invokes St. Denis to bless this happy stratagem, and " once again we 'll sleep secure in Roan," while Alençon, in reply to Orleans adds, that Joan will give the signal for attack by thrusting out a torch from the tower. Almost immediately Joan appears on the tower, and with the remark : " Behold ! this is the happy wedding torch That joineth Roan unto her countrymen, But burning fatal to the Talbotites," thrusts the brand through the casement. " See, noble Charles, the beacon of our friend, The burning torch in yonder turret stands," cries Orleans, and the signal being given the gates are burst open, and the forces under Charles enter. There is an alarum and Talbot, who swears vengeance, enters :

> France, thou shalt rue this treason with thy tears,
> If Talbot but survive thy treachery.
> Pucelle, that witch, that damned sorceress,
> Hath wrought this hellish mischief unawares,
> That hardly we escap'd the pride of France.

There is another alarum and excursions, and Bedford is brought in sick in a chair. Joan, with Charles and others, now appear on the ramparts, and the maid, delighted that her ruse has been so successful, scoffs at the English :

> Good morrow, gallants ! Want ye corn for bread ?
> I think the Duke of Burgundy will fast
> Before he 'll buy again at such a rate.
> 'Twas full of darnel ; do you like the taste ?

and Burgundy bids her " Scoff on, vile fiend and shameless courtesan ! " for before long he will " choke her," and " make her curse the harvest of that corn," to which

Charles enjoins : " Your grace may starve perhaps before that time." Bedford suggests " deeds " and not " words " to avenge this treason, and Joan mockingly retorts :

> What will you do, good grey-beard ? break a lance,
> And run a tilt at death within a chair ?

and is reproved by Talbot for her insult to a man who is lying sick unto death :

> Foul fiend of France, and hag of all despite,
> Encompass'd with thy lustful paramours !
> Becomes it thee to taunt his valiant age
> And twit with cowardice a man half dead ?

after which he challenges her to fight :

> Damsel, I'll have a bout with you again,
> Or else let Talbot perish with this shame,

and Joan asks him whether he is so " hot," yet she must hold her peace, for " If Talbot do but thunder, rain will follow." The English leaders then " whisper together in council," after which Talbot challenges the French to meet them in open battle, and Joan tells him that he must " take them for fools, To try if that our own be ours or no." Talbot reminds her that he is not addressing her : " I speak not to that railing Hecate," but to " Alençon, and the rest," whom he describes as " base muleters of France ! " who " Like peasant foot-boys do they keep the walls, And dare not take up arms like gentlemen." " God be wi' you, my lord : we came but to tell you That we are here," is Joan's retort, as she with Charles and others leave the walls, declaring that " Talbot means no goodness by his looks."

Talbot then appeals to Burgundy to assist him in regaining the town consecrated as the place where the " Great Cordelion's heart was buried," but before doing so wishes to remove the dying Bedford to a place of safety, but Bedford, having in mind the " stout Pendragon," who " in his litter sick Came to the field and vanquished his foes," refuses to be moved, preferring to remain beside the walls of the town in order to " revive the soldiers' hearts," a spirit which draws forth the admiration of Talbot :

> Undaunted spirit in a dying breast !
> Then be it so : heavens keep old Bedford safe !

There is an alarum, followed by excursions, and Sir John Fastolfe and a captain appear. " Whither away, Sir John Fastolfe, in such haste ? " demands the captain. " Whither away ! " repeats Fastolfe, why " to save myself by flight, We are like to have the overthrow again." " What ! " exclaims the captain in surprise, " will you fly, and leave Lord Talbot ? " and the dishonourable knight replies : " Ay, All the Talbots in the world, to save my life," and is denounced by the captain as a " Cowardly knight ! ill fortune follow thee ! " More excursions follow, and the French being driven back, Joan, Alençon, and Charles flee from the city, and Bedford, seeing the enemy in flight passes away :

> Now, quiet soul, depart when heaven please,
> For I have seen our enemies' overthrow.
> What is the trust or strength of foolish man ?
> They that of late were daring with their scoffs
> Are glad and fain by flight to save themselves.

As the corpse is borne away into the town, Talbot remarks to Burgundy that it is a double honour for Rouen to be lost and recovered in a day, to which Burgundy enjoins that " Talbot's noble deeds are enshrined in his heart." Thanking Burgundy for his compliment, Talbot inquires for Joan and the French, remarking that Roan hangs her head in grief now such a " valiant company are fled." Talbot then purposes placing some " expert officers " in charge of the town, after which they will depart for Paris to be present at the coronation of the king, in which Burgundy acquiesces, but before doing so they must not forget to celebrate the " exequies " of the " noble Duke of Bedford late-deceas'd," declaring that

> A braver soldier never couched lance,
> A gentler heart did never sway in court ;
> But kings and mightiest potentates must die,
> For that 's the end of human misery.

The third scene shows us the Plains near Rouen where the scattered French forces have gathered together. Joan exhorts Charles and his princes not to be dismayed over " this accident " the loss of Rouen, as " Care is no cure, but rather corrosive, For things that are not to be remedied," adding that Talbot is quite entitled like a " peacock to sweep along his tail " at his temporary triumph, but they will " pull his plumes and take away his train " if Charles will only be ruled by her. To this the Dauphin replies that as they have been guided by her hitherto, and assuring her that " One sudden foil shall never breed distrust," he asks what she purposes doing to retrieve this defeat, and her agile mind devises a plan to weaken Talbot by making use of " fair persuasions mix'd with sugar'd words " to entice Burgundy from the English side. The sound of a drum is heard afar off, and Talbot with his forces marches out of Rouen on their way to Paris to attend the coronation of Henry :

> Hark ! by the sound of drum you may perceive
> Their powers are marching unto Paris-ward.
> There goes the Talbot, with his colours spread,
> And all the troops of English after him.

Presently Burgundy appears at the head of his forces : " Now in the rearward comes the duke and his : Fortune in favour makes him lag behind. Summon a parley ; we will talk with him." A parley is sounded, and Burgundy halts and asks : " Who craves a parley with the Burgundy ? " " The princely Charles of France, thy countryman," replies Joan. Being asked what is his message, Charles turns to Joan and tells her to " Speak, Pucelle, and enchant him with thy words," and, stepping forward, Joan addresses Burgundy :

> Brave Burgundy, undoubted hope of France !
> Stay, let thy humble handmaid speak to thee.

" Speak on ; but be not over-tedious," replies Burgundy, and in a very skilful and captivating speech, the maid addresses him :

> Look on thy country, look on fertile France,
> And see the cities and the towns defaced
> By wasting ruin of the cruel foe.
> As looks the mother on her lowly babe
> When death doth close his tender dying eyes,
> See, see the pining malady of France ;
> Behold the wounds, the most unnatural wounds,
> Which thou thyself hast given her woeful breast.
> O ! turn thy edged sword another way ;
> Strike those that hurt, and hurt not those that help.
> One drop of blood drawn from thy country's bosom
> Should grieve thee more than streams of foreign gore.
> Return thee therefore with a flood of tears
> And wash away thy country's stained spots.

" Either she hath bewitch'd me with her words, Or nature makes me suddenly relent," remarks Burgundy, and seeing his indecision, she, in very subtle language tells him, that in consequence of his assisting the English all " French and France " throws doubt on his " birth and lawful progeny " ; that Talbot is only using him for " profit's sake," and when he has achieved the end he has in view and " English Henry is lord of France," he will be cast on one side :

> Who join'st thou with but with a lordly nation
> That will not trust thee but for profit's sake ?
> When Talbot hath set footing once in France,
> And fashion'd thee that instrument of ill,
> Who then but English Henry will be lord,
> And thou be thrust out like a fugitive ?
> Call we to mind, and mark but this for proof,
> Was not the Duke of Orleans thy foe,
> And was he not in England prisoner ?
> But when they heard he was thine enemy,
> They set him free without his ransom paid,
> In spite of Burgundy and all his friends.
> See then, thou fight'st against thy countrymen,
> And join'st with them will be thy slaughter-men.
> Come, come, return ; return, thou wand'ring lord ;
> Charles and the rest will take thee in their arms.

Unable to withstand the bewitching words of the maid, Burgundy is won over, and Talbot loses his ally :

> I am vanquished ; these haughty words of hers
> Have batter'd me like roaring cannon-shot,
> And made me almost yield upon my knees.
> Forgive me, country, and sweet countrymen !
> And, lords, accept this hearty kind embrace :
> My forces and my power of men are yours.
> So, farewell, Talbot ; I 'll no longer trust thee.

This makes Joan turn aside and murmur : " Done like a Frenchman : turn, and turn again ! " Charles welcomes the Duke : " Welcome, brave duke ! thy friendship makes us fresh, to which Alençon adds that Joan has played her part very well, and deserves a coronet of gold. The scene closes with Charles inviting the lords to :

> join our powers,
> And seek how we may prejudice the foe.

The final scene of this Act is the Palace at Paris. It opens with Talbot addressing the king and the nobles present, that having heard of their arrival in France he has proclaimed a truce in order to pay homage to his sovereign, and laying his sword at the feet of Henry, and afterwards kneeling in token of obedience, boasts of the many fortresses, cities and walled towns of strength he has subdued :

> In sign whereof, this arm, that hath reclaim'd
> To your obedience fifty fortresses,
> Twelve cities, and seven walled towns of strength,
> Beside five hundred prisoners of esteem,
> Lets fall his sword before your highness' feet ;

He is welcomed by the young king, after being assured by Gloucester that it is " Lord Talbot, That hath so long been resident in France " :

> Welcome, brave captain and victorious lord !
> When I was young, as yet I am not old,
> I do remember how my father said
> A stouter champion never handled sword,

As a reward for his martial services in France, Henry creates him Earl of Shrewsbury :

> Therefore, stand up ; and for these good deserts,
> We here create you Earl of Shrewsbury ;
> And in our coronation take your place.

This done, all leave except Vernon and Basset who quarrel, Vernon taking exception to Basset " Disgracing the colours he wears in honour of the noble Duke of York," while Basset objects to Vernon's " envious barking of his saucy tongue Against my lord the Duke of Somerset." Basset considers Somerset " as good a man as York." " Not so " retorts Vernon " in witness, take ye that " whereupon he strikes Basset, and Basset calling Vernon a " villain," tells him that he knows that " the law of arms is such That whoso draws a sword, 'tis present death, Or else this blow should broach thy dearest blood," but he will crave the king's permission to resort to combat :

> But I 'll unto his majesty, and crave
> I may have liberty to venge this wrong ;
> When thou shalt see I 'll meet thee to thy cost,

to which Vernon replies :

> Well, recreant, I 'll be there as soon as you ;
> And, after, meet you sooner than you would.

The fourth Act opens in a Hall of State in Paris. It opens with the coronation of Henry by Winchester, after which Gloucester requests the Governor of Paris to take the oath of allegiance. Fastolfe now enters with a letter from the Duke of Burgundy : " My gracious sovereign, as I rode from Calais, To haste unto your coronation, A letter was deliver'd to my hands, Writ to your grace from the Duke of Burgundy." Calling Fastolfe a " base knight," Talbot steps forward, and tears from his knee the Insignia of the Garter, declaring how, at the battle of Patay, he shamefully deserted, before even a " stroke was given " :

> Shame to the Duke of Burgundy and thee !
> I vow'd, base knight, when I did meet thee next,
> To tear the garter from thy craven leg ;   *[Plucks it off.*
> Which I have done, because unworthily
> Thou wast installed in that high degree.
> Pardon me, princely Henry, and the rest :
> This dastard, at the battle of Patay,
> When but in all I was six thousand strong,
> And that the French were almost ten to one,
> Before we met or that a stroke was given,
> Like to a trusty squire did run away :
> In which assault we lost twelve hundred men ;
> Myself and divers gentlemen beside
> Were there surpris'd and taken prisoners.
> Then judge, great lords, if I have done amiss ;
> Or whether that such cowards ought to wear
> This ornament of knighthood, yea or no.

Gloucester also denounces Fastolfe, describing his act as " infamous " and unworthy even of a common soldier " Much more a knight, a captain and a leader," while Talbot reminds all present that when this noble order was instituted " Knights of the garter were of noble birth, Valiant and virtuous, and full of haughty courage," and Henry tells Fastolfe to be " packing " and banishes him from court :

> Stain to thy countrymen ! thou hear'st thy doom.
> Be packing therefore, thou that wast a knight :
> Henceforth we banish thee on pain of death.

Fastolfe gone, Henry orders Gloucester to read the letter from the Duke of Burgundy. Gazing at the superscription, Gloucester expresses surprise at the blunt manner in which Burgundy addresses Henry :

> What means his grace, that he hath chang'd his style ?
> No more but, plain and bluntly, *To the King !*

" Hath he forgot he is his sovereign ?   Or doth this churlish superscription Pretend some alteration in good will ? "   " What 's here ? " he exclaims, and proceeds to read :

> " I have, upon especial cause,
> Moved with compassion of my country's wrack,
> Together with the pitiful complaints
> Of such as your oppression feeds upon,
> Forsaken your pernicious faction
> And join'd with Charles, the rightful King of France."

" O monstrous treachery !   Can this be so, That in alliance, amity, and oaths, There should be found such false dissembling guile ? " exclaims Gloucester, and Henry suggests that Lord Talbot shall " talk with Burgundy, And give him chastisement for this abuse," and Talbot having replied that if he had not been ordered, he would have " begg'd to be so employ'd," Henry orders him to

> gather strength and march unto him straight :
> Let him perceive how ill we brook his treason,
> And what offence it is to flout his friends.

and Talbot departs, remarking as he does so :

> I go, my lord ; in heart desiring still
> You may behold confusion of your foes.

Talbot having gone, Vernon and Basset enter, and crave the king's permission to resort to combat to settle their differences, in which they are supported by York and Somerset.   Henry requests to be informed of the nature of their quarrel : " Say, gentlemen, what makes you thus exclaim ?   And wherefore crave you combat ? or with whom ?   First let me know, and then I 'll answer you."   Basset—who belongs to the red-rose or Lancaster faction—complains that when crossing the sea from England into France " this fellow here, with envious carping tongue, Upbraided him in vile and ignominious terms about the rose he wears, Saying, the sanguine colour of the leaves Did represent the colour of his master's blushing cheeks."   Vernon— a white-rose or York adherent—tells the king that Basset took " exceptions to his badge, Pronouncing that the paleness of the flower Bewray'd the faintness of his master's heart."   Henry considers it nothing but madness for men to quarrel over so slight and frivolous a cause, and implores them to be at peace :

> Good Lord ! what madness rules in brainsick men,
> When for so slight and frivolous a cause
> Such factious emulations shall arise !
> Good cousins both, of York and Somerset,
> Quiet yourselves, I pray, and be at peace.

But York and Somerset will not let the matter drop, and request the king to let the dissension be determined by a duel, for the quarrel is " betwixt themselves."   As they continue to wrangle, Gloucester exclaims :

> Confirm it so !   Confounded be your strife !
> And perish ye, with your audacious prate !
> Presumptuous vassals ! are you not asham'd
> With this immodest clamorous outrage
> To trouble and disturb the king and us ?

to which Exeter adds : " It grieves his highness : good my lords, be friends." The king then charges them that if they " love him to forget this quarrel and the cause " and " think upon the conquest of his father, His tender years, and let us not forgo That for a trifle that was bought with blood." With the remark : " Let me be umpire in this doubtful strife " he puts on a red rose, and lest any suspicion should arise that he is more inclined to Somerset than York, he claims both as kinsmen, and appoints York " To be our regent in these parts of France," and tells Somerset to " unite His troops of horsemen with his bands of foot " ; and " like true subjects, . . . go cheerfully together and digest their angry choler on their enemies." The king then announces that he will return forthwith to Calais and thence to England where he hopes ere long to hear that they have been victorious over " Charles, Alençon, and that traitorous rout."

The king having gone, Warwick addressing York says : " My Lord of York, I promise you, the king Prettily, methought, did play the orator," to which York replies : " And so he did ; but yet I like it not In that he wears the badge of Somerset," and Warwick tells him it " was but his fancy, blame him not " for he was sure the king meant no harm, and all, with the exception of Exeter, take their departure.

Left alone, Exeter murmurs that York did well to suppress his voice, for if the passions of his heart had burst out, every " simple man would have seen that This jarring discord of nobility, This shouldering of each other in the court, This factious bandying of their favourites, . . . doth presage some ill event," for when

> sceptres are in children's hands ;
> But more when envy breeds unkind division :
> There comes the ruin, there begins confusion.

We are now transferred to Talbot's camp before Bourdeaux. Talbot gives orders to a trumpeter to summon the General in charge of the city to the walls, after which he demands surrender of the city :

> Open your city gates,
> Be humble to us, call my sovereign yours,
> And do him homage as obedient subjects,
> And I 'll withdraw me and my bloody power ;

The General, however, refuses to surrender, and warns Talbot—whom he describes as an " ominous and fearful owl of death "—that he is in great danger, as a large French army under Charles is approaching :

> Thou ominous and fearful owl of death,
> Our nation's terror and their bloody scourge !
> The period of thy tyranny approacheth.
>
> . . . . . .
>
> Ten thousand French have ta'en the sacrament
> To rive their dangerous artillery
> Upon no Christian soul but English Talbot.

A drum is heard afar off, and the General exclaims : " Hark ! hark ! the Dauphin's drum, a warning bell, Sings heavy music to thy timorous soul, And mine shall ring thy dire departure out." Realising the danger, which is due to " negligent and heedless discipline," Talbot despatches some light horsemen to " peruse the enemy's wings," and then making an appeal to his soldiers to " sell their lives as dear as his own," prays that " God and Saint George, Talbot and England's right," will

> Prosper our colours in this dangerous fight !

We are on the Plains of Gascony in the next scene, where York, with forces, are assembled. Inquiring whether the " speedy scouts " have returned, a messenger replies that they have returned, and report that the " mighty army of the Dauphin has march'd to Bourdeaux " to give battle to Talbot, and further that " Two mightier troops than that the Dauphin led " have joined with him. York denounces Somerset for not sending him the promised supply of horsemen :

> A plague upon that villain Somerset,
> That thus delays my promised supply
> Of horsemen that were levied for this siege !

and tells the messenger he is unable to march to the assistance of the " noble cheva-lier " Talbot, being " louted by a traitor villain," and prays that God will " comfort Talbot in this necessity ! " for " If he miscarry, farewell wars in France."

At this point Sir William Lucy spurs into the camp, and telling York that his assistance was never more urgently needed than at this moment, urges him to

> Spur to the rescue of the noble Talbot,
> Who now is girdled with a waist of iron
> And hemm'd about with grim destruction.
> To Bourdeaux, war-like duke ! to Bourdeaux, York !
> Else, farewell Talbot, France, and England's honour.

But York repeats he is helpless without Somerset's promised levies, and wishes Somerset were in Talbot's place, for " we should save a valiant gentleman By for-feiting a traitor and a coward." " O ! send some succour to the distress'd lord," pleads Lucy, and York exclaims : that if " Talbot dies, we lose ; . . . We mourn, France smiles ; we lose, they daily get ; All long of this vile traitor Somerset." " Then God take mercy on brave Talbot's soul ; And on his son young John, whom two hours since I met in travel toward his war-like father. This seven years did not Talbot see his son ; And now they meet where both their lives are done," is Lucy's comment, and York, although professing that " vexation almost stops his breath " that the " noble Talbot should bid his young son welcome to his grave," bids Lucy farewell, and with his soldiers marches away with the words " no more my fortune can But curse the cause I cannot aid the man," while Lucy dashes away to meet Somerset, observing that " Lives, honours, lands, and all hurry to loss," while the " vulture of sedition Feeds in the bosom of such great commanders " as York and Somerset.

We are in another part of the Plains in Gascony in the fourth scene. Somerset, with one of Talbot's captains, enters, and the former tells the latter that it is now too late to send reinforcements to assist Talbot, who has, by his rashness, tarnished all his former honour, by this " unheedful, desperate, wild adventure." He declares that the expedition was too " rashly plotted " by York and Talbot, the former setting the latter on to fight and die in shame so that York—on Talbot's death—might bear the name. At this moment Sir William Lucy enters. " How now, Sir William ! whither were you sent," asks Somerset, and Lucy, in angry tones replies :

> Whither, my lord ? from bought and sold Lord Talbot ;
> Who, ring'd about with bold adversity,
> Cries out for noble York and Somerset,
> To beat assailing death from his weak legions :
> And whiles the honourable captain there
> Drops bloody sweat from his war-wearied limbs,
> And, in advantage lingering, looks for rescue,
> You, his false hopes, the trust of England's honour,
> Keep off aloof with worthless emulation.

> Let not your private discord keep away
> The levied succours that should lend him aid,
> While he, renowned noble gentleman,
> Yields up his life unto a world of odds :
> Orleans the Bastard, Charles, Burgundy,
> Alençon, Reignier, compass him about,
> And Talbot perisheth by your default.

Somerset blames York : " York set him on ; York should have sent him aid," to which Lucy retorts that York blames him : " And York as fast upon your grace exclaims ; Swearing that you withhold his levied host Collected for this expedition." " York lies," shouts Somerset, adding that if York had sent he could have had the promised reinforcements, although he " owes him little duty, and less love," and Lucy in despair exclaims that it is the " fraud of England, not the force of France," that " Hath now entrapp'd the noble-minded Talbot. Never to England shall he bear his life, But dies, betray'd to fortune by your strife." Being conscience-stricken, Somerset promises to despatch reinforcements forthwith, but Lucy declares it is too late, by now he is a prisoner or slain, for fly he never would, declaring that :

> His fame lives in the world, his shame in you.

We are back again in the English Camp near Bourdeaux in the fifth scene, which consists of a conversation between Talbot and his son John. It opens with the father telling his son that he has sent for him " To tutor him in stratagems of war, That Talbot's name might be in him reviv'd When sapless age and weak unable limbs Should bring his father to his drooping chair," but having now come unto a " feast of death," he urges the boy to " mount the swiftest horse " and seek safety in flight. " Is my name Talbot ? and am I your son ? And shall I fly ? " asks the boy, and requests his father not to make a " slave of him " for " The world will say, he is not Talbot's blood That basely fled when noble Talbot stood." " Fly, to revenge my death if I be slain," urges his father, but the boy replies that " He that flies so will ne'er return again," and when his father tells him that if they both stay they are both sure to die, the boy implores his father to let him stay, and urges his father to escape himself, for " Flight cannot stain the honour he has won." Talbot, however, refuses to leave his followers to fight and die without him, as his age was never tainted with such shame. " Why should my youth be guilty of such blame ? " asks the boy, and tells his father to

> Stay, go, do what you will, the like do I ;
> For live I will not if my father die.

Both having decided to remain the father takes an affectionate farewell of his son :

> Then here I take my leave of thee, fair son,
> Born to eclipse thy life this afternoon,
> Come, side by side together live and die,
> And soul with soul from France to heaven fly.

Scenes six and seven show us the Field of Battle. Scene six opens with Talbot crying : " Saint George and victory ! fight, soldiers, fight ! " for York not having sent the promised reinforcements they are left to the rage of France. Talbot's son is hemmed in by the foe, and is rescued by his father from the sword of Orleans. " Art thou not weary, John ? how dost thou fare ? " enquires the old man, and is again urged by his father to escape in order to avenge his [Talbot's] death, and to preserve the house of Talbot :

> Wilt thou yet leave the battle, boy, and fly,
> Now thou art seal'd the son of chivalry ?
> Fly, to revenge my death when I am dead ;
> .   .   .   .

> If I to-day die not with Frenchmen's rage,
> To-morrow I shall die with mickle age :
> By me they nothing gain an if I stay ;
> 'Tis but the short'ning of my life one day.
> In thee thy mother dies, our household's name,
> My death's revenge, thy youth, and England's fame.
> All these and more we hazard by thy stay ;
> All these are sav'd if thou wilt fly away.

but young Talbot refuses to quit the battle-field, declaring that if he flies he is not Talbot's son, and therefore tells his father " to talk no more of flight," for if he is " son to Talbot, he will die at Talbot's foot." The old man is proud at the bravery shown by his young son, and rushing back into the fight, exclaims :

> Thy life to me is sweet :
> If thou wilt fight, fight by thy father's side,
> And, commendable proved, let 's die in pride.

Scene seven shows us another part of the Field of Battle. Led in by a servant, Talbot enquires for his son :

> Where is my other life ? mine own is gone ;
> O ! where 's young Talbot ? where is valiant John ?
> Triumphant death, smear'd with captivity,
> Young Talbot's valour makes me smile at thee.

The servant replies : " O ! my dear lord, lo ! where your son is borne," and soldiers enter bearing the body of young Talbot. Talbot gives them orders to lay the body in his arms, and embracing his son bids him an affectionate farewell :

> Come, come, and lay him in his father's arms :
> My spirit can no longer bear these harms,

and then crying :

> Soldiers, adieu ! I have what I would have,
> Now my old arms are young John Talbot's grave,

the brave old man passes away.

Charles, Alençon, Burgundy, Orleans and La Pucelle, with forces, enter. Charles admits that the day would have been a bloody one had York and Somerset come to the aid of Talbot. Orleans relates how valiantly young Talbot fought, and the maid tells how he disdained to encounter her, considering it unworthy to fight with a " giddy wench " :

> Once I encounter'd him, and thus I said :
> ' Thou maiden youth, be vanquish'd by a maid ' ;
> But with a proud majestical high scorn,
> He answer'd thus : ' Young Talbot was not born
> To be the pillage of a giglot wench.'
> So, rushing in the bowels of the French,
> He left me proudly, as unworthy fight.

" Doubtless he would have made a noble knight," exclaims Burgundy, and noticing young Talbot lying dead in the arms of his father, adds : " See, where he lies in-hearsed in the arms Of the most bloody nurser of his harms." Orleans proposes the bodies be quartered : " Hew them to pieces, hack their bones asunder, Whose life was England's glory, Gallia's wonder," but Charles enjoins him to refrain : " O, no ! forbear ; for that which we have fled During the life, let us not wrong it dead."

Preceded by a French herald, Lucy now enters and requests to be conducted to Charles' tent. " On what submissive message art thou sent ? " asks Charles. " Submission, Dauphin ! " remarks Lucy with surprise, " 'tis a mere French word " ; and we English warriors do not know what it means, adding that he had come to ascertain what prisoners have been taken, and to inspect the bodies of the slain. " For prisoners ask'st thou ? hell our prison is," remarks Charles, but whom dost thou seek ? Lucy replies that he seeks Lord Talbot, and forthwith proceeds to call out the numerous titles borne by that warrior :

> But where 's the great Alcides of the field,
> Valiant Lord Talbot, Earl of Shrewsbury ?
> Created, for his rare success in arms,
> Great Earl of Washford, Waterford, and Valence ;
> Lord Talbot of Goodrig and Urchinfield,
> Lord Strange of Blackmere, Lord Verdun of Alton,
> Lord Cromwell of Wingfield, Lord Furnival of Sheffield,
> The thrice-victorious Lord of Falconbridge,
> Knight of the noble order of Saint George,
> Worthy Saint Michael and the Golden Fleece,
> Great marshal to Henry the Sixth
> Of all his wars within the realm of France ?

Joan describes these as " a silly stately style indeed ! " for even the " Turk, that two-and-fifty kingdoms hath, Writes not so tedious a style as this," adding that the man he " magnifiest with all these titles Stinking and fly-blown lies here at our feet." Learning that Talbot the " Frenchmen's only scourge " lies dead, Lucy wishes his " eyeballs might into bullets be turned " so that he could " in a rage shoot them at their faces," after which he begs the bodies in order to give them fitting burial. Joan describes Lucy as an " upstart " who " speaks with such a proud commanding spirit," that he must be " old Talbot's ghost," and advises that for " God's sake " he be given permission to remove the bodies, as their presence " would but stink and putrefy the air." As they are being carried away, Lucy remarks that " from their ashes shall be rear'd A phœnix that shall make all France afeard." Charles retorts " So we be rid of them, do with him what thou wilt," and then announces that they will proceed to Paris in this conquering vein ; for :

> All will be ours now bloody Talbot's slain.

We are transferred to London at the opening of the fifth Act, the first scene being enacted in the Palace. It opens with the king enquiring if Gloucester has perused the letters from the pope, the emperor and the Earl of Armagnac. Gloucester replies in the affirmative, adding that the letters are entreaties for a peace between England and France. Realising the hopelessness of the struggle, Gloucester is in favour of accepting the terms as the " only means To stop effusion of our Christian blood," in which he is supported by the king who considers it " impious and unnatural " for " professors of one faith " to shed each other's blood. To further " bind this knot of amity " Gloucester announces that the Earl of Armagnac, a near relative of Charles, has offered his daughter in marriage with Henry, together with a large and sumptuous dowry, and the king although " his years are young and fitter is his study and his books than wanton dalliance with a paramour " is prepared to be " well content with any choice " which " Tends to God's glory and his country's weal," and forthwith gives orders for the ambassadors to be admitted. Winchester in Cardinal's habit, a Legate and two ambassadors being ushered in, Exeter expresses surprise to see that Winchester has been made a Cardinal :

> What ! is my lord of Winchester install'd,
> And call'd unto a cardinal's degree ?
> Then I perceive that will be verified
> Henry the Fifth did sometime prophesy :
> ' If once he come to be a cardinal,
> He'll make his cap co-equal with the crown.'

Henry then informs the ambassadors that their " several suits Have been consider'd and debated on," and they are prepared to conclude a peace with France, to which Gloucester adds that the king, having been informed of the " virtuous gifts, the beauty, and the value of her dower," is willing to accept the daughter of Armagnac in marriage. Henry confirms this by handing to Gloucester for the lady " a jewel, the pledge of his affection," afterwards giving him orders to see them safe to Dover and there to " Commit them to the fortune of the sea," and all, except Winchester and the Legate, leave the chamber.

Winchester and the Legate being left alone, the former pays the sum of money promised to the pope for exalting him to the rank of cardinal :

> Stay, my lord legate : you shall first receive
> The sum of money which I promised
> Should be deliver'd to his holiness
> For clothing me in these grave ornaments,

after which he [aside] mutters that in his new sphere he will not be " inferior to the proudest peer " neither will he be overborne " in birth or for authority " by Humphrey of Gloucester, but on the other hand will

> either make him stoop and bend his knee,
> Or sack this country with a mutiny.

The Plains in Anjou supply the next scene. Charles announces that news—which will " cheer their drooping spirits "—has been received that the " stout Parisians " have revolted against the English. Alençon and Joan are therefore urging Charles to march to Paris, when a Scout enters, and reports that the " English army, that divided was Into two parties, is now conjoin'd in one, And means to give battle presently." Charles considers the " warning very sudden " but they will " presently provide for them," while Burgundy trusts the ghost of Talbot will not be there, and then they will have nothing to fear. Joan describes " fear " as the " most accurs'd " of all " base passions," and prophesies victory for the French :

> Command the conquest, Charles, it shall be thine ;
> Let Henry fret and all the world repine.

We are before Angiers in the next scene, where a battle is in progress. There are alarums and excursions, and desperate fighting follows, during which the French are beaten back. Seeing the French forces retreating, Joan calls up " ye charming spells and periapts " and " ye choice spirits " that inform her of future events to aid her in her " enterprise." To the accompaniment of thunder and lightning the Fiends appear, their " speedy and quick appearance " being proof how diligent they are in her service. Addressing them as " ye familiar spirits " that are gathered from the infernal regions she asks them for their help in order that the French may conquer, but they " walk and speak not." Appealing to them not to hold her in suspense she offers in place of her blood with which she was accustomed to feed them, to cut off one of her limbs and give it to them, if they will " condescend to help her " but the fiends hang down their heads. Then " My body shall Pay recompense if you will grant my suit," but the spirits shake their heads. " Then take my soul " ; she exclaims, my body, soul, and all before that England give the French the foil, but the fiends depart, and Joan remarks :

> See ! they forsake me. Now the time is come
> That France must vail her lofty plumed crest,
> And let her head fall into England's lap.
> My ancient incantations are too weak.
> And hell too strong for me to buckle with :
> Now, France, thy glory droopeth in the dust.

There are more excursions, followed by hand-to-hand fighting, and York takes Joan captive :

> Damsel of France, I think I have you fast :
> Unchain your spirits now with spelling charms,
> And try if they can gain your liberty.
> A goodly prize, fit for the devil's grace !
> See how the ugly witch doth bend her brows,
> As if with Circe she would change my shape.

" Chang'd to a worser shape thou canst not be," retorts the maid, and York retaliates by telling her that only the shape of Charles the Dauphin can please her " dainty eye." As she is led away she curses both York and Charles, hoping that both of them will be murdered while sleeping on their beds :

> A plaguing mischief light on Charles and thee !
> And may ye both be suddenly surpris'd
> By bloody hands, in sleeping on your beds !

" Fell banning hag, enchantress, hold thy tongue ! " demands York, and Joan craves permission to " curse awhile," but York retorts by telling her she can curse when she is brought to the stake.

More alarums follow, and Suffolk enters with Lady Margaret of Anjou as his prisoner. " Be what thou wilt, thou art my prisoner. O fairest beauty ! do not fear nor fly, For I will touch thee but with reverent hands. I kiss these fingers for eternal peace, And lay them gently on thy tender side." " Who art thou ? say, that I may honour thee," asks Suffolk, and she replies " Margaret my name, and daughter to a king, The King of Naples, whosoe'er thou art," and Suffolk makes answer : " An earl I am, and Suffolk am I call'd. Be not offended, nature's miracle, Thou art allotted to be ta'en by me : So doth the swan her downy cygnets save, Keeping them prisoner underneath her wings. Yet, if this servile usage once offend, Go and be free again, as Suffolk's friend." As she attempts to leave, Suffolk exclaims : " O, stay ! I have no power to let her pass ; My hand would free her, but my heart says no." Muttering to himself that he would be glad to woo her, but as he dare not speak, he will call for " pen and ink and write his mind," and exclaiming " Fie, de la Pole ! I have a tongue " he asks himself why he should destroy the power of action, or be " daunted at a woman's sight ? " Perplexed at his unusual manner, she asks what ransom she must pay in order to go free. As he does not answer her, she enquires " Why speak'st thou not ? what ransom must I pay ? " " She 's beautiful and therefore to be woo'd ; She is a woman, therefore to be won," he mutters. " Wilt thou accept of ransom, yea or no ? " demands Margaret, and Suffolk mutters to himself that he must remember that " he has a wife " otherwise he would marry Margaret. " He talks at random ; sure, the man is mad," observes Margaret, and as he will not hear she will leave him. " I 'll win this Lady Margaret. For whom ? Why, for my king : tush ! that 's a wooden thing," he again mutters to himself, to which Margaret ejaculates : " He talks of wood : it is some carpenter," and turning to her Suffolk tells her he has a " secret to reveal " and asks her to condescend to listen to what he has to say. " Perhaps I shall be rescu'd by the French ; And then I need not crave his courtesy," mutters Margaret to herself. Again appealing to her to hear him, she retorts : " Tush ! women have been captivate ere now," and when asked why she speaks so disdainfully she apologises, still it is only *quid* for *quo*. " Would you not suppose Your bondage happy to be made a queen ? " asks Suffolk, and Margaret tells him that a " queen in bondage " is more worthless than a " slave in base servility ; For princes should be free." " And so shall you," exclaims Suffolk, " If happy England's royal king be free," and when she enquires of what concern is the king of England's freedom to her, Suffolk undertakes to make her queen of England, and put a golden sceptre in her hand, and set a precious crown upon her head. But when she replies that she is " unworthy to be Henry's queen," Suffolk tells her he is unworthy to " woo so fair a dame to be Henry's wife," and earnestly begs of her to consent to be queen of England. Replying that she is willing if it please her father, a parley is sounded and Reignier appears on the walls. Seeing his daughter captive, he asks what remedy there is, as he is a " soldier, and unapt to weep Or to exclaim on fortune's fickleness," and Suffolk tells him that the remedy is that he gives consent for his " daughter to be wedded to his king." Trumpets sound, and Reignier descends from the walls to discuss the matter with Suffolk, and eventually gives his consent conditionally upon being allowed to

> Enjoy mine own, the country Maine and Anjou,
> Free from oppression or the stroke of war.

Setting Margaret free : " That is her ransom ; I deliver her " ; and guaranteeing Reignier that his stipulation in respect to the two counties of Maine and Anjou shall be carried out, Suffolk promises to return to England forthwith and make arrangements for the marriage to be solemnised. He then bids Reignier farewell, enjoining upon him to

> set this diamond safe
> In golden palaces, as it becomes.

and Reignier embraces Suffolk as he would

> embrace
> The Christian prince, King Henry, were he here.

Margaret too bids Suffolk farewell :

> Farewell, my lord. Good wishes, praise and prayers
> Shall Suffolk ever have of Margaret,

and Suffolk takes leave of her, but before doing so asks her if she has

> No princely commendations to his king ?

" Such commendations," replies Margaret, as " becomes a maid, A virgin and his servant." Suffolk considers her words are " sweetly placed and modestly directed," and apologising for troubling her again enquires if she has

> No loving token to his majesty ?

to which she replies :

> Yes, my good lord ; a pure unspotted heart,
> Never yet taint with love, I send the king.

" And this withal," rejoins Suffolk, at the same time kissing her, and Margaret tells him that is for himself, for she would not be so presumptuous as

> To send such peevish tokens to a king.

Reignier and Margaret having gone, Suffolk soliloquises that although he cannot win her for himself :

> O ! wert thou for myself. But, Suffolk, stay ;
> Thou may'st not wander in that labyrinth ;
> There Minotaurs and ugly treasons lurk,

he will " Solicit Henry with her wondrous praise," her " virtues " and her " natural graces," so that when

> thou com'st to kneel at Henry's feet,
> Thou may'st bereave him of his wits with wonder,

The Camp of the Duke of York in Anjou supplies the next scene. It opens with York ordering that "sorceress, condemn'd to burn," to be brought forth. As she enters guarded, a shepherd—her father—appears, who exclaims :

Ah, Joan, this kills thy father's heart outright !
Have I sought every country far and near,
And, now it is my chance to find thee out,
Must I behold thy timeless cruel death ?
Ah, Joan, sweet daughter Joan, I 'll die with thee !

but to his surprise she repudiates him, calling him a " Decrepit miser ! base ignoble wretch ! Thou art no father nor no friend of mine," claiming to have " descended of a gentler blood." But the old shepherd tells York and the other lords that her mother is still alive who can testify to Joan being their daughter. " Graceless ! " exclaims Warwick, " wilt thou deny thy parentage ? " to which York adds that it " argues what her kind of life hath been : Wicked and vile ; and so her death concludes." Another appeal is made to her by her father to admit her parentage, but Joan tells him to be gone, and turning to York declares that the old man has been " suborn'd Of purpose to obscure her noble birth." Her father then asks her to kneel down and take his blessing, but as she refuses the old man calls down imprecations on her head, wishing that " some ravenous wolf had eaten her," and finally casts her off as a " cursed drab," and bids them " burn her, burn her : hanging is too good." York then gives orders for her to be taken away having lived too long already " To fill the world with vicious qualities," but before being led away she claims that she is descended from the " progeny of kings, virtuous and holy " and " chosen from above, By inspiration of celestial grace " to work miracles upon earth. She declares she has been a " virgin from her tender infancy, Chaste and immaculate in very thought," and that her " maiden blood, thus rigorously effused, Will cry for vengeance at the gates of heaven." But York with a wave of the hand orders her away to execution, while Warwick gives orders to " Spare for no faggots, let there be enow : Place barrels of pitch upon the fatal stake, that so her torture may be shortened."· She then claims the " privilege of the law " declaring herself to be with child, and when Warwick suggests that any progeny of Charles should not be allowed to live, Joan tells them she has deceived them, and names Alençon and Reignier. But York replies that all her entreaty is in vain, for " Strumpet, thy words condemn thy brat and thee," As she is led away she curses York, hoping that the sun will never shine upon that country where he " makes abode " and that the shadow of death may so haunt him and the other lords that they will either " break their necks," or be driven to self-destruction :

Then lead me hence ; with whom I leave my curse :
May never glorious sun reflex his beams
Upon the country where you make abode ;
But darkness and the gloomy shade of death
Environ you, till mischief and despair
Drive you to break your necks or hang yourselves !

and York wanly retorts :

Break thou in pieces and consume to ashes
Thou foul accursed minister of hell !

Winchester now enters, and after greeting York " With letters of commission from the king " informs him that the king earnestly implores that peace shall be concluded with France. This does not meet with York's approval, after the

slaughter of so many peers,
So many captains, gentlemen, and soldiers,
That in this quarrel have been overthrown,
And sold their bodies for their country's benefit,

and turning to Warwick, exclaims :

> O ! Warwick, Warwick, I forsee with grief
> The utter loss of all the realm of France.

Warwick counsels patience : " Be patient, York " : for

> if we conclude a peace,
> It shall be with such strict and severe covenants
> As little shall the Frenchmen gain thereby.

    Charles, accompanied by Alençon, Orleans, Reignier and others now enters, and asks to be informed of the conditions of peace.   York requests Winchester to speak, for

> boiling choler chokes
> The hollow passage of my poison'd voice,
> By sight of these our baleful enemies.

Winchester then informs Charles that Henry " gives consent Of mere compassion and of lenity " to conclude a peace with France, conditionally upon France " become true liegemen to his crown," and that Charles, provided he will " swear to pay tribute and submit himself," shall be appointed " viceroy under him, And still enjoy his regal dignity."   Alençon considers these conditions as " absurd and reasonless " as Charles would be nothing more than a " shadow of himself," but Charles reminds him that he is already " possess'd with more than half the Gallian territories. " Insulting Charles ! " retorts York, " hast thou by secret means Us'd intercession " to obtain a peace, and now wish to compromise ; adding, that he must, without challenge, accept the conditions as laid down, or be " plagued with incessant wars." Reignier opines that they should not be " obstinate " and " cavil " at the terms offered, for another opportunity may not present itself if they allow this one to pass, and Alençon—who admits it is " policy for Charles to save his subjects from massacre "—advises him to agree to the terms, adding " Although you break it when your pleasure serves."   Charles accepts the conditions offered with one reservation, that England

> claim no interest
> In any of our towns of garrison,

after which Charles swears allegiance, and peace is concluded.

    The final scene of the Play is enacted at the Royal Palace in London.   It opens with Henry expressing to Suffolk—who has given the king a brilliant account of Margaret of Anjou's charm and beauty—his astonishment at the " wondrous rare description " the noble earl has related of her " virtues graced with external gifts," virtues and gifts which do " breed love's settled passions in his heart " ; but Suffolk replies : " Tush ! my good lord," this superficial tale is but a " preface of her worthy praise," for if he had " sufficient skill to utter the chief perfections of that lovely dame " it would make a " volume of enticing lines."   Henry then asks Gloucester as Lord Protector to give his consent that " Margaret may be England's royal queen," and Gloucester reminds him that he is already " betrothed to another lady of esteem," and therefore cannot " dispense with that contract," without " defacing his honour with reproach."   Suffolk describes her as a " poor earl's daughter," unfit to be England's queen, and therefore the " contract may be broken without offence." Gloucester considers Margaret is scarcely more, her " father being no better than an earl, Although in glorious titles he excel," but Suffolk retorts : " Yes, my lord, her father is a king, The king of Naples and Jerusalem ; And of such great authority in France As his alliance will confirm our peace, And keep the Frenchmen in allegiance."

Gloucester claims the same authority for the Earl of Armagnac on account of being a near kinsman to Charles, to which Exeter adds that the Earl being wealthy had offered a large and sumptuous dowry with his daughter. " A dower, my lords ! " exclaims Suffolk, " disgrace not so your king," for Henry is able to " enrich his queen, And not to seek a queen to make him rich," adding :

> Whom should we match with Henry, being a king,
> But Margaret, that is daughter to a king ?
> Her peerless feature, joined with her birth,
> Approves her fit for none but for a king :
> Her valiant courage and undaunted spirit,
> More than in women commonly is seen,
> Will answer our hope in issue of a king ;
> . . . .
> Then yield, my lords ; and here conclude with me
> That Margaret shall be queen, and none but she.

To this speech Henry remarks that he cannot tell whether it is the " force of Suffolk's report " or his " tender youth which was never yet attaint with any passion of inflaming love," but he is so " sick of such fierce alarums of hope and fear working in his thoughts," that he forthwith decides the matter himself, and straightway gives Suffolk orders to " take shipping " and cross over to France, and safely conduct Margaret to England to be " crown'd King Henry's faithful and anointed queen," and authorising him to " gather up a tenth " of the kingdom's revenue for his " expenses and sufficient charge," tells him to " Be gone " ; for " till you do return I rest perplexed with a thousand cares," and begging Gloucester to " excuse This sudden execution of his will," forthwith leaves the room with the words :

> And so conduct me, where from company
> I may resolve and ruminate my grief,

to which Gloucester sadly exclaims :

> Ay, grief, I fear me, both at first and last.

All having left, Suffolk, exalted at the victory he has gained, triumphantly declares : " Thus Suffolk hath prevail'd " ; and like Paris who carried off to Troy Helen the wife of Menelaus, the most beautiful woman in the world, so he will cross over to France with hope to " prosper better than the youthful Trojan did " ; and as there flashes through his mind visions of still greater triumphs to come, in an ecstasy of joy, exclaims :

> Margaret shall now be queen, and rule the king ;
> But I will rule both her, the king, and realm.

Scene : Partly in England and partly in France.

CHARACTERS, PLACE-NAMES, ETC.

Abel. I. iii. 40.

> This be Damascus, be thou accursed Cain,
> To slay thy brother Abel, if thou wilt. [I. iii. 39–40.]

See Damascus.

Adonis. I. vi. 6.

> Thy promises are like Adonis' garden,
> That one day bloom'd and fruitful were the next.
> [I. vi. 6–7.]

In Greek mythology a youth, a model of beauty, beloved by Aphrodite. The allusion is to the pots of earth, planted with fennel and lettuce by the ancient Greeks, called 'Adonis' garden,' on account of these plants being reared for the annual festival of Adonis which was a special favourite with women. Spenser in his *Faerie Queene* gives an account of the Garden of Adonis, and Pliny in his *Natural History* makes reference to them.

Alarum. I. ii. p.22 ; I. v. p.1, p.15 ; II. i. p.78 ; III. ii. p.36, p.41, p.104, p.115 ; IV. vi. p.1 ; IV. vii. p.1 ; V. iii. p.1, p.45.

A summons to arms ; to give notice of approaching danger.

Alcides. IV. vii. 60.

Hercules, the son of Alcæus, noted for his great strength. Sir William Lucy here compares Talbot with Alcides : " But where 's the great Alcides of the field."

Alton. IV. vii. 65.

See Earl of Washford.

Amazon. I. ii. 104.

> Stay, stay thy hands ! thou art an Amazon, [I. ii. 104.]

The Amazons were a fabled race of female warriors. According to Herodotus they were inhabitants of Scythia. The term is now applied to a woman of masculine habits.

Ambassadors. V. i. p.28.

Messengers from France who bring to Henry letters praying for peace between England and France, and the Earl of Armagnac's offer of his daughter's hand in marriage.

On Gloucester's advice the proposals are accepted, and Henry orders the ambassadors to be escorted to Dover bearing a jewel, " In argument and proof of his contract " with the daughter of Armagnac.

Angiers, Before.

The Scene of Act V., Scene iii. A battle is in progress between the English and French forces. Joan calls up familiar spirits to aid her, offering her " body, soul and all " if only France can gain the victory, but the spirits shake their heads and leave, which Joan takes as a symbol of defeat. York and Joan fight hand to hand, and York takes her captive. Later Suffolk enters with Margaret of Anjou as a prisoner, and proposes her union with Henry, which ultimately receives the approval of her father—Reignier, duke of Anjou—and Suffolk returns home and suggests the proposed alliance to the king. [Needless to say Suffolk did not take Margaret prisoner, and it was not until 1444—or some fourteen years after Joan of Arc was captured—that Suffolk was employed as the king's proxy to negotiate the marriage between Margaret and Henry.]

Anjou. V. iii. 147.

An old province of France. In V. iii. 154 it is called " County." By the marriage of Geoffrey Plantagenet Count of Anjou with Matilda, daughter of Henry I., their son Henry II. became Count of Anjou. The province was lost in 1203 during the reign of John, and again came into the possession of the English during the reigns of Henry V. and VI., but reverted to France in 1444, and in 1584 it passed under the direct rule of the kings of France.

Anjou. V. iii. 154.

See Maine.

Artois. II. i. 9.

An ancient province of France. It came into the possession of the Dukes of Burgundy in 1384. Mentioned here as being friendly to the English.

Astræa, I. vi. 4.

> Divinest creature, Astræa's daughter,
> How shall I honour thee for this success?   [I. vi. 4–5.]

In classical mythology the goddess of Justice, daughter of Astræus and Eos, or according to another account, of Zeus and Themis. She lived among men on earth during the golden age, and in the brazen age was the last to withdraw into the sky, where she shines as the constellation of Virgo. Should the golden age ever return it is believed she will re-establish her home on earth again. Many poets make reference to this theory, but the best known is Dryden's *Astræa Redux.*

Attendants. IV. vii. p.1.

Auvergne. Court of the Castle.

The Scene of Act II., Scene iii. There is no historical authority for the story of Talbot's visit to the Countess of Auvergne.

Basset, of the Red-Rose or Lancaster Faction. III. iv. p.1 ; IV. i. p.78.

Only appears in two scenes, with Vernon, with whom he quarrels over their allegiance.

[French says : " The family of Basset was one of great eminence in the 13th, 14th, and 15th, centuries, and several of its members were barons, highly distinguished in the wars of Henry III., and of the three Edwards. The person in this play may have been one of the heroes of Agincourt, either Robert Basset, who was one of the lances in the train of the earl marshal, or Philip Basset, a lance in the retinue of Lord Botreaux.

A Red Rose was the badge of John of *Gaunt*, as the White Rose was of his brother, Edmund of *Langley* ; hence the origin of their adoption afterwards by the partizans of their families, as symbols of strife. These badges are found as illustrations in the Missal of Nicholas Litlington, Abbot of Westminster, written between A.D. 1373

and 1377. Shakespeare has given a poetical charm to the selection of the Red and White Roses, by the Lancaster and York factions, in the Temple Garden.]

Bastard of Orleans. I. i. 93 ; I. ii. p.46, 47, p.64 ; II. i. p.39 ; III. ii. p.18, p.41, 123 ; III. iii. p.1, 69 ; IV. iv. 26 ; IV. vi. 14, 16, 25, 42 ; IV. vii. p.33 ; V. ii. p.1 ; V. iv. p.116.

First appears before Charles the Dauphin with the news that he has discovered Joan La Pucelle, saying :

> A holy maid hither with me I bring,   [I. ii. 51.]

He does not take any important part in the development of the action of the play, but appears with the French forces on several occasions.

[This renowned warrior, " the brave Dunois," was John, an illegitimate son of Louis, Duke of Orleans, by Marie D'Engheim, wife of his chamberlain, Albert, Lord of Cawny. In 1439 he was legitimated as of the blood-royal, and created Count of Dunois and Longueville. It is under the first title that he is known as the best knight in France, and one of the greatest captains of the age ; Monstrelet calls him, " one of the most eloquent men in all France." He compelled the Earl of Warwick to raise the siege of Montargis in 1429, and chiefly directed the sallies of Joan of Arc from Orleans. Dunois gained many important victories in Normandy and Guienne, and his martial exploits have made him hero of song and romance. The count by his second wife, Mary, daughter of James, Count of Tancarville, had a son, Francis, Count of Dunois, nearly as famous a soldier as his warlike father ; he is introduced by Sir Walter Scott in *Quentin Durward.* He married Agnes of Savoy, a younger sister of the " Lady Bona," in the *Third Part of King Henry VI.,* and their son, Francis II., was created Duke of Longueville. *French.*]

Blois. IV. iii. 45.

Capital of the department of Loire on the river Loire. Mentioned here as being lost to England.

Bolingbroke. II. v. 83.

Henry Bolingbroke, Duke of Hereford, afterwards King Henry the Fourth.

Bourdeaux. IV. ii. 1 ; IV. iii. 4, 8, 22.

Bourdeaux was the birthplace of Richard the First, his father Edward the Black Prince having had his residence here when Governor of Aquitaine. The attack on Bourdeaux by Talbot as here related is unhistorical.

Bourdeaux, Before.

The Scene of Act IV., Scene ii. [Between Act IV., Scene i., and Act IV., Scene ii., there is a lapse of over twenty years, from Henry's coronation in 1431 to Talbot's last campaign in 1453, during which period the English lost nearly the whole of their English possessions.] In Act IV., Scene ii., Talbot appears before Bourdeaux and demands surrender of the town. The General in charge of the garrison refuses to surrender, and warns Talbot that he is in great danger due to the approach of a large French force. [According to history, Talbot was admitted into Bourdeaux without resistance.]

Bourdeaux.   A Field of Battle.

The Scene of Act IV., Scenes vi. and vii.

In Act IV., Scene vi., young Talbot is hemmed in by the enemy, and is rescued by his father from the sword of Orleans.

In Act IV., Scene vii., both father and son are among the slain. Sir William Lucy enters and begs the bodies in order to give them fitting burial, to which Charles consents.

Cæsar.   I. ii. 139.

Now am I like that proud insulting ship
Which Cæsar and his fortune bare at once.
[I. ii. 138–139.]

Probably an allusion to the story in the *Life of Julius Cæsar*, by Plutarch (North's translation). During the war with Pompey, when the latter's navy had command of the seas, Cæsar " In the end, followed a dangerous determination, to imbark unknown in a little pinnace of 12 oars only, to pass over the sea again unto Brundusium, the which he could not do without great danger, considering that all that sea was full of Pompey's ships and armies. So he took ship in the night, apparelled like a slave, and went aboard upon this little pinnace, and said never a word, as if he had been some poor man of mean condition. The pinnace lay in the mouth of the river of

Anius, the which commonly was wont to be very calm and quiet, by reason of a little wind that came from the shore, which every morning drave back the waves far into the main sea. But that night (by ill fortune) there came a great wind from the sea, that overcame the landwind, insomuch as, the force and strength of the river fighting against the violence of the rage and waves of the sea, the encounter was marvellous dangerous, the water of the river being driven back, and rebounding upward, with great noise and danger, in turning of the water. Thereupon the master of the pinnace, seeing that he could not possibly get out of the mouth of this river, bade the mariners to cast about again, and to return against the stream. Cæsar hearing that, straight discovered himself unto the master of the pinnace, who at the first was amazed when he saw him ; but Cæsar then taking him by the hand, said unto him : " Good fellow, be of good cheer, and forwards hardily ; fear not, for thou hast Cæsar and his fortune with thee."

Cain.   I. iii. 39.

This be Damascus, be thou cursed Cain,
To slay thy brother Abel, if thou wilt.   [I. iii. 39–40.]

See Damascus.

Calais.   IV. i. 9, 170.

A seaport on the Strait of Dover. Edward III., invested it in September, 1346, and after enduring a siege for nearly a year surrendered in August, 1347. The French made an unsuccessful attempt to regain possession in 1349. At the close of Henry VI's reign it remained as the sole vestige of the English conquests in France. The privilege of representation in the English Parliament was granted to Calais by Henry VIII., which was continued until 1558 when it was captured by the Duke of Guise. On April 24th, 1596, the town was taken by the Spaniards and two years later was restored to France.

Camp of the Duke of York in Anjou.

The Scene of Act V., Scene iv. Shows us the condemnation of Joan of Arc to be burned as a witch, which took place on the 31st of May, 1431. Beaufort announces that Henry is ready to conclude peace with France, but this does not meet with York's approval. Terms of peace are, however, concluded, Charles consenting to pay tribute and act as Henry's Viceroy. [There are several inaccuracies in this scene. Beaufort is substituted for Suffolk, who was the real negotiator of the treaty, and York did not oppose it, neither was Charles compelled to agree to ignominious terms. The terms of the truce are extant, and contain no condition of allegiance or submission on either side.]

Cardinal's Men. I. iii. p.57.

See Men in tawny coats.

Champaigne. I. i. 60.

An ancient province of France. Mentioned here as being lost to England, but this is unhistorical.

Charles, Dauphin, and afterwards King of France. I. i. 92, 96, 137, 149, 163 ; I. ii. p.1, p.22, 47, 66, 72, 112 ; I. iv. 101 ; I. v. p.1 ; I. vi. p.1 ; II. i. 48, p.50, 55 ; II. ii. 19, 28 ; III. ii. 9, p.18, 29, 34, p.41, p.110, 123 ; III. iii. p.1, 8, 38, 39, 77 ; IV. i. 60, 173 ; IV. ii. 21, 39 ; IV. iii. 2, 7 ; IV. iv. 26 ; IV. vi. 10 ; IV. vii. p.33, 51, 54 ; V. i. 17 ; V. ii. p.1, 4, 19 ; V. iii. 37, 39 ; V. iv. 68, 71, 77, 100, p.116, 123, 129, 147, 165 ; V. v. 45.

Seeking to overthrow the English rule in France, Charles attacks Orleans, and when we first meet him before that city he remarks that England's power is waning.

> Mars his true moving, even as in the heavens
> So in the earth, to this day is not known.
> Late did he shine upon the English side ;
> Now we are victors ; upon us he smiles.   [I. ii. 1-4.]

The Bastard of .Orleans enters saying :

> Methinks your looks are sad, your cheer appaled.
> Hath the late overthrow wrought this offence ?
> Be not dismay'd, for succour is at hand :
> A holy maid hither with me I bring,
> Which by a vision sent to her from heaven
> Ordained is to raise this tedious siege,
> And drive the English forth the bounds of France.
>   [I. ii. 48-54.]

Charles receives La Pucelle, and on her inviting him to " try her courage by combat, if he dar'st," accepts the challenge, only to be overcome at which he acknowledges her power, and at first wishes to make her his love rather than his leader, saying :

> Whoe'er helps thee, 'tis thou that must help me.
> Impatiently I burn with thy desire ;
> My heart and hands thou hast at once subdued.
>   [I. ii. 107-109.]

She refuses his advances and vigorously repudiates the suggestion of abandoning Orleans, to which Charles readily agrees.

The town is taken, and Charles attributes their success to Joan, exclaiming :

> 'Tis Joan, not we, by whom the day is won ; [I. vi. 17.]

Later, when Orleans is recaptured by the English forces, Charles declares that the first victory was but a trick of Joan's :

> Is this thy cunning, thou deceitful dame ?
> Didst thou at first, to flatter us withal,
> Make us partakers of a little gain,
> That now our loss might be ten times so much.
>   [II. i. 50-54.]

and then accuses the Duke of Alençon of negligence in setting the guard.

We next meet Charles before Rouen which is also taken by the French, but is speedily recaptured by the English, and the Dauphin, although a little mistrustful of La Pucelle, remarks :

> We have been guided by thee hitherto,
> And of thy cunning had no diffidence ;
> One sudden foil shall never breed distrust.
>   [III. iii. 9-11.]

Burgundy is now won over to the French side and is welcomed by Charles.

> Welcome, brave duke ! thy friendship makes us fresh.
>   [III. iii. 86.]

Later, before Bordeaux, Charles secures a further victory, and cries :

> And now to Paris, in this conquering vein ;
> All will be ours now bloody Talbot's slain.
>   [IV. vii. 95-96.]

News is brought that ' the stout Parisians do revolt And turn again unto the war-like French,' but immediately another messenger enters with the tidings that the English army is united, and ready for battle.

In the fight which ensues the French are routed, and we next find that terms of peace between France and England are being sought.

Charles appears before the Duke of York, and says :

> Since, lords of England, it is thus agreed
> That peaceful truce shall be proclaim'd in France,
> We come to be informed by yourselves
> What the conditions of that league must be.
>   [V. iv. 116-119.]

to be informed by Winchester :

> Charles, and the rest, it is enacted thus :
> That, in regard King Henry gives consent,
> Of mere compassion and of lenity,
> To ease your country of distressful war,
> And suffer you to breathe in fruitful peace,
> You shall become true liegemen to his crown.
> And, Charles, upon condition thou wilt swear
> To pay him tribute, and submit thyself,
> Thou shalt be placed as viceroy under him,
> And still enjoy thy regal dignity.   [V. iv. 123–132.]

Charles demurs at the terms, but ultimately agrees, being advised to do so by Alençon, who remarks in an undertone :

> And therefore take this compact of a truce,
> Although you break it when your pleasure serves.
>   [V. iv. 163–164.]

The scene closes with Charles and his followers swearing allegiance to Henry.

[This prince, third son of Charles VI., became Dauphin in 1417, in succession to his brothers, Louis and John. Although at the date when the second scene of this play occurred he was really king by the death of his father, and had been crowned at Poitiers in 1423, he continued to be styled the Dauphin, until he was conducted by Joan of Arc, according to her promise, to be solemnly inaugurated at Rheims, where the kings of France had been usually crowned. This ceremony occurred July 17, 1429, although it is prematurely alluded to in the first scene.

Charles VII., married Mary of Anjou, sister of King René, and by her was father of Louis XI., who is a character in the *Third Part of King Henry the Sixth.*]

Circe.   V. iii. 35.

> See how the ugly witch doth bend her brows,
> As if with Circe she would change my shape.
>   [V. iii. 34–35.]

An allusion to Circe the enchantress, who lived on the island of Æææ, described by Homer as " fair-haired, a clever goddess, possessing human speech." When Ulysses on his return from the Trojan war visited her coasts, Circe turned his companions into swine, but Ulysses resisted this metamorphosis by a herb called Moly which he had received from Mercury.

Constantine.   I. ii. 142.

Roman Emperor 306–337 A.D.

Cordelion's heart.   III. ii. 83.

> As sure as in this late-betrayed town
> Great Cordelion's heart was buried,
> So sure I swear to get the town or die.   [III. ii. 82–84.]

King Richard the First, surnamed Cœur-de-Lion. Holinshed says that Richard " willed his heart to be conueied vnto Rouen, and there buried ; in testimonie of the loue which he had euer borne vnto that citie for the stedfast faith and tried loialtie at all times found in the citizens there," and Grafton : " And within three dayes after the king was hurt, he dyed that is to say, the ix. day of Aprill, and was buryed as he himselfe willed at Fount Ebrard or Euerard at the Feete of his father. Howbeit his hart was buryed at Roan, and his bowelles in Poytiers, when he had reigned ix. yeres, ix. monethes and odde dayes, leauing after him none issue."

Countess of Auvergne.   II. ii. 38 ; II. iii. p.1.

Anxious to secure notoriety the Countess causes a messenger to be sent to Lord Talbot, desiring his presence at her castle so that she may congratulate him on his valiant deeds, and claim the honour of having had an interview with so famous a man. The messenger states :

> The virtuous lady, Countess of Auvergne,
> With modesty admiring thy renown,
> By me entreats, great lord, thou would'st vouchsafe
> To visit her poor castle where she lies,
> That she may boast she hath beheld the man
> Whose glory fills the world with loud report.
>   [II. ii. 38–43.]

and Talbot says to the messenger :

> I return great thanks,
> And in submission will attend on her.   [II. ii. 51–52.]

This message is all part of a plot by which the Countess hopes to secure the capture of Talbot, and she gives orders to her porter to :

> remember what I gave in charge ;
> And when you have done so, bring the keys to me.
>   [II. iii. 1–2.]

On the porter's departure she soliloquises :

> The plot is laid ; if all things fall out right,
> I shall as famous be by this exploit
> As Scythian Tomyris by Cyrus' death.   [II. iii. 4–6.]

Talbot now enters, accompanied by a messenger, and the Countess exclaims :

> Is this the scourge of France ?
> Is this the Talbot, so much fear'd abroad
> That with his name the mothers still their babes ?
>   [II. iii. 14–16.]

continuing in a sarcastic vein :

> I see report is fabulous and false :
> I thought I should have seen some Hercules,
> A second Hector, for his grim aspect,
> And large proportion of his strong-knit limbs.
> Alas ! this is a child, a silly dwarf :
> It cannot be this weak and writhled shrimp
> Should strike such terror to his enemies. [II. iii. 17–23.]

At this Talbot turns to go, and the Countess exclaims :

> If thou be he, then art thou prisoner.   [II. iii. 32.]

and goes on to say how she will :

> chain these legs and arms of thine,
> That hast by tyranny these many years
> Wasted our country, slain our citizens,
> And sent our sons and husbands captivate.
> [II. iii. 38–41.]

Lord Talbot then says he is " but shadow of himself " and " were the whole frame here, It is of such a spacious lofty pitch, Your roof were not sufficient to contain it."

The Countess is mystified at these riddling words and demands an explanation which Talbot gives by blowing a horn, and without there is a sound of gun-fire and his soldiers march into the castle.

Seeing her plot defeated the Countess weakly craves indulgence, saying :

> Victorious Talbot, pardon my abuse :
>
> .   .   .   .
>
> For I am sorry, that with reverence
> I did not entertain thee as thou art. [II. iii. 66–71.]

and Talbot says he will be quite satisfied if he and his men, " may Taste of your wine and see what cates you have " :

Thus the Countess was humiliated as she well deserved to be, for presuming that she could so easily trap the brave Lord Talbot.

[Courtenay remarks : " I do not know where Shakespeare found the story of Talbot and the Countess of Auvergne." This lady, introduced in Act II., Scene iii., may be intended for Mary, daughter of Godefroi D'Auvergne, wife of Bertrand III., Lord de la Tour, Count of Auvergne ; from a branch of this house have descended the Princes De la Tour-Auvergne.]

Crete. IV. vi. 54.

> Then follow thou thy desperate sire of Crete,
> Thou Icarus.   [IV. vi. 54–55.]

See Icarus.

Cyrus. II. iii. 6.

> I shall as famous be by this exploit
> As Scythian Tomyris by Cyrus' death..   [II. iii. 5–6.]

The founder of the Persian Empire, son of Cambyses a Persian noble, and of a daughter of Astyages, king of Media ; defeated Astyages and took him prisoner and united Media with Persia, B.C. 559 ; conquered the kingdom of Lydia and took Crœsus prisoner, B.C. 546 ; conquered Babylon, B.C. 538. He then marched with a great army against the Massagetæ in Scythia. Tomyris, queen of the Massagetæ, met and defeated him, and cutting off his head threw it into a vessel filled with human blood, remarking as she did so, ' There, drink thy fill.'   Dante refers to this incident in his *Purgatorio*, xii. 55–57 :

> Displayed the ruin and the cruel carnage
> That Tomyris wrought, when she to Cyrus said,
> ' Blood didst thou thirst for, and with blood I glut thee !'

And in Sackville's *A Mirrour for Magistraytes* (The Complaynt, 1587) we read :

> Consyder Cyrus . . .
> He whose huge power no man might overthrowe.
> Tomyris queen with great despite hath slowe,
> His head dismembered from his mangled corps,
> Herself she cast into a vessel fraught
> With clotted blood of them that felt her force,
> And with these words a just reward she taught—
> ' Drynke now thy fyll of thy desired draught.'

Damascus. I. iii. 39.

> This be Damascus, be thou cursed Cain,
> To slay thy brother Abel, if thou wilt. [I. iii. 39–40.]

An allusion to the legend that Damascus was built on the site of Abel's grave.

" About four miles from Damascus is a high hill, reported to be the same on which Cain slew his brother Abel."   Maundrel's *Travels*.

" And in that place where *Damascus* was founded, *Kaym* sloughe *Abel* his brother." Maundeville's *Travels*, 1725.

" *Damascus* is as moche to saye as shedynge of blood.   For there *Chaym* slowe *Abell*, and hidde hym in the sonde."   *Polychronicon*.

Darius. I. vi. 25.

> Her ashes, in an urn more precious
> Than the rich-jewell'd coffer of Darius. [I. vi. 24.25.]

" When Alexander the Great took the city of Gaza, the metropolis of Syria, amidst the other spoils and wealth of Darius treasured up there, he found an exceeding rich and beautiful little chest or casket, and asked those about him what they thought fittest to be laid up in it. When they had severally delivered their opinions, he told them, he esteemed nothing so worthy to be preserved in it as Homer's Iliad." *Plutarchum in Vitâ Alexandri Magnie. Theobald.*

The very words of the text are found in Puttenham's *Arte of English Poesie,* 1589: "In what price the noble poems of Homer were holden with Alexander the Great, insomuch as everie night they were layd under his pillow, and by day were carried in *the rich jewel coffer of Darius,* lately before vanquished by him in battaile." *Malone.*

See Plutarch's *Life of Alexander the Great.*

Deborah. I. ii. 105.

> Stay, stay thy hands! thou art an Amazon,
> And fightest with the sword of Deborah. [I. ii. 104–105.]

An allusion to the story of Deborah and Barak. *See* Judges, chapters iv. and v.

Dover. V. i. 49.

> And so, my lord protector, see them guarded
> And safely brought to Dover;   [V. i. 48–49.]

Henry gives orders for the ambassadors to be " guarded And safely brought to Dover ; ".

Duke of Alençon. I. i. 95 ; I. ii. p.22 ; I. vi. p.1 ; II. i. p.39, 60 ; III. ii. p.18, p.41, 65, p.110 ; III. iii. p.1, p.33, 36, 37 ; IV. i. 173 ; IV. iv. 26 ; IV. vi. 14 ; IV. viii. p.33 ; V. ii, p.1 ; V. iv. 73, 74, p.116.

A noble who assists the Dauphin in his actions against the English.

He appears with the French forces at Orleans and Rouen, and at the latter city, exclaims to La Pucelle, urging her to assist them :

> We'll set thy statue in some holy place,
> And have thee reverenced like a blessed saint :
> Employ thee then, sweet virgin, for our good.
>   [III. iii. 14–16.]

On the plains in Anjou, hearing that the Parisians are revolting in favour of the French, Alençon urges the Dauphin :

> Then march to Paris, royal Charles of France,
> And keep not back your powers in dalliance.
>   [V. ii. 4–5.]

He finally appears with the Dauphin and others before York and Warwick when the peace terms are presented, and advises Charles, in the words :

> To say the truth, it is your policy
> To save your subjects from such massacre
> And ruthless slaughters as are daily seen
> By our proceeding in hostility ;
> And therefore take this compact of a truce,
> Although you break it when your pleasure serves.
>   [V. iv. 159–164.]

[The Duke of Alençon, was John II., son of the brave prince, John I., who was slain at Agincourt, after his personal encounter with Henry V., who endeavoured to save the life of his noble enemy. He was released on *parole* after he was taken prisoner by Fastolfe, in 1424, at Verneuil ; and he commanded the French forces in 1429 at Jergeau, where the Earl of Suffolk was taken prisoner. He was present at the coronation of Charles VII., at Rheims, but joined the faction of Louis the Dauphin against the royal authority in 1440, but was allowed to retire to his *apanage.* In 1456 Alençon was arrested on a charge of intriguing with the English cabinet, tried and pronounced guilty of treason, October 10, 1448, and condemned to die ; but though his life was spared, he was kept in close confinement, and did not regain his liberty until the accession of his friend the Dauphin as Louis XI., in 1461, against whom in turn he rebelled, and being once more arrested, this time by the celebrated Tristan l'Hermite, this turbulent prince ended his days in prison, in 1476. By his wife Joan, daughter of Charles, Duke of Orleans, and Isabel of France, he left a son, René, who succeeded as Duke of Alençon. *French.*]

Duke of Anjou. I. i. 94 ; V. iii. 95.

= Reignier, Duke of Anjou (q.v.), and father of Margaret.

Duke of Bedford. Uncle to the King, and Regent of France. I. i. p.1, 99 ; I. iv. 27 ; II. i. p.8, 8 ; II. ii. p.1 ; III. ii. p.41, 87, 93, 100, 132.

Bedford opens the play with a speech bemoaning the death of King Henry V., saying :

> England ne'er lost a king of so much worth. [I. 1-7.]

Messengers enter with news that the French have revolted, and Bedford, exclaiming ' I'll hale the dauphin headlong from his throne ' immediately departs for France.

We next meet him before Orleans and with Talbot he attacks the town. The assault being successful, Bedford orders the retreat to be sounded.

His next appearance is before Rouen. La Pucelle and a number of soldiers having gained admission to the town by a ruse, it is taken by the forces under Charles. Bedford is brought in sick in a chair, and urges the nobles around him to ' let no words, but deeds, revenge this treason.'

Talbot endeavours to persuade him to let them ' bestow him in some better place, Fitter for sickness and for crazy age,' but Bedford stubbornly refuses, saying :

> Lord Talbot, do not so dishonour me,
> Here will I sit before the walls of Roan,
> And will be partner of your weal and woe.
> [III. ii. 90–92.]

Further encounters take place between the opposing forces and finally the French are routed, Bedford at this point exclaiming :

> Now, quiet soul, depart when heaven please ;
> For I have seen our enemies' overthrow.
> [III. ii. 110–111.]

and passes away.

After his body has been borne out Talbot pays tribute to his sterling qualities in the words :

> A braver soldier never couched lance,
> A gentler heart did never sway in court.
> [III. ii. 134–135.]

[In this part the ' Prince John of Lancaster,' of former plays, closes his career of military glory and wise administration, sullied, however, by one blot,—his treatment of the heroine, Joan of Arc. Hume calls him ' the most accomplished prince of the age." This great general gained the famous battle of Verneuil, August 27, 1424, against the combined French and Scots, and after achieving many other victories died at Rouen, the seat of his government, September 14, 1435, *after* the execution of Joan of Arc, although in the play his own death is made to occur before that of the Maid of Orleans. Bedford's first wife, 1423, was Anne, sister of Philip the *Good*, Duke of Burgundy, the character of this play ; she died November 14, 1432, and very shortly after he married secondly Jacqueline, daughter of Peter, Count of Luxemburg, a vassal of the Duke of Burgundy, who was highly offended at the hasty alliance. The Duke had no children by either of his wives, and his widow Jacqueline soon after his death, being then only seventeen, married Richard Woodville, and one of their children, Elizabeth, became the Queen of Edward the Fourth.

The duke was buried in the church of St. Marie at Rouen, and the following inscription was placed on his tomb : " Cy gist fu de noble memoire tres-haut & puissant prince Johan en son vivant Regent le Roialme de France, Duc de Bedford ; pour lequel est fondre une Messe estre chez un jour perpetuellement celebre a cest autel par le college des Clementines incontinent apres prime. Et tres-passa le xiv jour de Septembre 1, an Mill. ccccxxxv, au quel xiv jour semblablement est fonde pour luy une solempnele en ceste Eglise. Dieu face pardon a son ame." *Buswell.* Greatly to his praise, Louis XI. refused to deface the monument to Bedford's memory when urged to do so, declaring,—" Let his body rest in quiet, which when he was living would have disquieted the proudest of us all ; and as for his tomb, which I assure you is not so worthy as his acts deserve, I account it an honour to have his remains in my dominions." *Banks.*]

Duke of Burgundy. II. i. p.8, 8 ; II. ii. p.1 ; III. ii. p.41, 42, 77, 101, p.115, 116, 118, 130 ; III. iii. 19, p.41, 73 ; IV. i. 12, 13, 49, 64 ; IV. iv. 26 ; IV. vi. 14 ; IV. vii. p.33 ; V. ii. p.1.

A noble, who appears first on the side of the English, but later forsakes his allegiance and supports the Dauphin.

After Rouen has been finally captured by the English forces and Talbot and Burgundy and their forces are marching away, La Pucelle orders a parley to be sounded that she may speak with Burgundy.

She flatters him at first to gain his confidence :

> Brave Burgundy, undoubted hope of France !
> Stay, let thy humble handmaid speak to thee.
> [III. iii. 41–42.]

and then goes on to describe how France, his country, has been despoiled by the wars, and seeing he is inclining to her view continues :

> thou fight'st against thy countrymen,
> And join'st with them will be thy slaughter-men.
> [III. iii. 74–75.]

Her earnest appeal succeeds, and Burgundy exclaims :

> I am vanquished ; these haughty words of hers
> Have batter'd me like roaring cannon-shot,
> And made me almost yield upon my knees.
> Forgive me, country, and sweet countrymen !
> And, lords, accept this hearty kind embrace :
> My forces and my power of men are yours.
>
> [III. iii. 78–83.]

He sends a letter to Henry announcing his decision, and Talbot is sent to fight him.

After this he appears but twice, and does not take any further part in the action of the play.

[In this play the duke is the Count de Charolois, the same Duke of Burgundy that appears in the last act of *Henry V.*, Philip, called the " Good," born in 1396, who succeeded his father, John the *Fearless*, in 1418. Duke Philip for a long time was in alliance with England, and the Duke of Bedford resigned to him the Regency of France in 1429 ; but though the defection of Burgundy from the English is in the play made to occur through the persuasion of Joan of Arc, he did not really fall off, and become reconciled to France, until 1435.

In reality the only interview between Burgundy and Joan of Arc was at her capture ; the " fair persuasions, mix'd with sugar'd words," employed by the heroine in Act III., Scene iii., were addressed to the duke in a letter, wherein she implored him, as first vassal to the crown of France, to return to his allegiance. *Barante.*

The Duke of Burgundy's first wife was Michelle, daughter of Charles VI., she died in 1422 ; he married secondly, Bona, daughter of Philip, Count of Eu, who died in 1425 ; and thirdly, in 1430, Isabella of Portugal, daughter of John I., and Philippa, the daughter of John of *Gaunt* by his first duchess, Blanche of Lancaster. By his third wife, a woman of great talent and spirit, Duke Philip had two sons, who died during infancy, and a third son, who succeeded at his father's death in 1467 as Duke of Burgundy, and is known in history as " Charles the Bold " ; he is alluded to in the *Third Part of King Henry VI.*, Act IV., Scene vi.—" I like not of this flight of Edward's ; For doubtless Burgundy will yield him help." Charles *the Bold's* third wife was Margaret Plantagenet, 1467, sister of Edward IV., she was the Duchess of Burgundy, who supported, if she did not suggest, the impostures of Lambert Simnel, and Perkin War-

beck. In honour of his third marriage Philip *the Good* established the Order of the Golden Fleece of Burgundy, at Bruges, January 18, 1430. He was elected a Knight of the Garter in the reign of Henry V., as his son, Charles the Bold, was in that of Edward IV.]

Duke of Gloucester. Uncle to the King, and Protector. I. i. p.1, 37, 100 ; I. iii. p.1, 4, 6, 8, 16, 18, p.29, 29, 52, 62, 82, 87 ; II. iv. 118 ; III. i. p.1, 3, 27, 49, 65, 78, 89, 134, 142, 184 ; III. iv. p.1, 13 ; IV. i. p.1 ; V. i. p.1, 58 ; V. v. p.1.

In this play we see a good deal of the rivalry between Gloucester and Henry Beaufort, Bishop of Winchester.

Both are anxious to secure supreme and unquestioned power and the determined efforts of Winchester to override Gloucester being continually to the fore.

Gloucester is the one who would rather work amicably and this is shown in Act III. when he offers to present a bill against Winchester, but finally after the two have been appealed to by Henry he offers his hand in reconciliation which is reluctantly, and then formally, accepted.

He is in favour of Henry's marriage with the daughter of the Earl of Armagnac rather than with Margaret of Anjou, and reminds the king of his previous betrothal when Suffolk is persuading him to accept Margaret as his queen, perceiving that Suffolk intends to further his own ends in arranging the match.

[The brave Humphrey Plantagenet, who fought so well at Agincourt, figures in this play as the chief guardian to the young king, his nephew ; and in the very first scene he is brought into collision with the proud priest, the Bishop of Winchester, better known as Cardinal Beaufort, in foretaste of the bitter hatred and struggle for power between them, which ceased not until the ' good Duke Humphrey ' came to an untimely end by his envious rival's means.]

[The Duke of Gloucester is also a character in the *Second Part of King Henry the Sixth* (q.v.).]

Duke of Maine. V. iii. 95.

= Reignier (q v.).

Earl of Armagnac. V. i. 2, 17 ; V. v. 44.

> The Earl of Armagnac, near knit to Charles,
> A man of great authority in France,
> Proffers his only daughter to your grace
> In marriage, with a large and sumptuous dowry.
>
> [V. i. 17–20.]

= John IV., Count of Armagnac, who offered his daughter in marriage to Henry VI.

Holinshed says : " He (Armagnac) sent solemne ambassadours to the king of England, offering him his daughter in mariage, with promise to be bound (beside great summes of monie, which he would giue with hir) to deliuer into the king of Englands hands, all such castels and townes, as he or his ancestors deteined from him within anie part of the duchie of Aquitaine, either by conquest of his progenitors, or by gift and deliuerie of anie French king : and further to aid the same king with monie for the recouerie of other cities within the same duchie, from the French king ; or from anie other person that against king Henrie vniustlie kept, and wrongfullie withholden them." See *Extract* 38 from Holinshed, *and under* Emperor and Pope.

Armagnac was part of Gascony, now mostly included in the department of Gers.

After the murder of the Duke of Orleans, in 1407, France became a prey to two rival factions, the Burgundians and the Armagnacs. The latter received this name from their leader, Bernard, Count of Armagnac, father-in-law to the Duke of Orleans. The Armagnacs, in May, 1412, entered into negotiations with Henry IV., of England. Their leader was massacred by the Burgundians and the citizens of Paris, with four thousand of his adherents, June 12, 1418. Louis XI., before he came to the French throne, put himself at the head of a body of ruffians, called Armagnacs, the disbanded mercenaries of the English war, and invaded Switzerland, where he was defeated in 1444. The Armagnacs were almost exterminated by Louis XI., in 1473. *Townsend.*

Earl of Cambridge. II. v. 54, 84.

Second son of Edmund of Langley, Duke of York. Created Earl of Cambridge in 1414. Executed at Southampton for conspiracy against Henry V. in 1415. Hall says : " For diuerse write that Richard earle of Cambridge did not conspire with the lorde Scrope and sir Thomas Graye to murther kyng Henry to please the Frenche kyng withal, but onely to theintent to exalte to the croune his brotherinlawe Edmond earle of Marche as heyre to duke Lyonel. After whose death consideryng that the earle of Marche for diuerse secrete impediments was not hable to haue generacion, he was sure that the croune should come to him by his wife, or to his children. And therefore it is to be thought that he rather cofessed him selfe for nede of money to be corrupted by the Freche kyng, then he would declare his inwarde mynd and open his very entent. For surely he sawe that if his purpose were espied, the earle of March should haue dronken of the same cup that he did, and what should haue come to his owne children he muche doubted. And therfore beyng destitute of comfort and in dispayre of life, to saue his children he fayned that tale, desiryng rather to saue his succession then him selfe, which he did in dede. For Richard duke of Yorke his sonne not priuely but openly claimed the croune, and Edward his sonne both claimed and gained it as hereafter you shall heare, which thyng at this time if kyng Henry had foresene I doubt whether either euer that line should haue either claimed the garlande or gained the game." In II. v. 88–89, Mortimer says that Cambridge " Levied an army, weening to redeem and have install'd me [Mortimer] in the diadem." In respect to this passage Malone says : " Here is again another falsification of history. Cambridge levied no army, but was apprehended at Southampton, the night before Henry sailed from that town for France, on the information of this very Edmund Mortimer, Earl of March." Grafton remarks : " Shortly after the king beyng in a readinesse to aduaunce forwarde, sodeinly, he was credibly informed, that Richard, Erle of Cambridge, brother to Edward Duke of Yorke, and Henry Lordè Scrope, and Sir Thomas Gray had conspired his death and vtter destruction, wherfore he caused them forthwith to be apprehended. And after these prisoners were examined, they not onely confessed the conspiracie but also declared that for a great somme of money which they had receyued of the French king, they entended eyther to delyuer the king alive into the handes of his enemyes, or else to murther him before that he shoued arriue in Normandie."

Earl of Salisbury. I. i. 159 ; I. ii. 15, 25 ;
I. iv. p.23, 73, 78, 82, 86, 90, 104,
106, 110 ; I. v. 17, 34, 38 ; II. i. 35 ;
II. ii. 4.

The Earl of Salisbury is in charge of the English
forces at Orleans at the commencement of the
play, and a messenger reports that he is in dire
need :

> The Earl of Salisbury craveth supply,
> And hardly keeps his men from mutiny,
> Since they, so few, watch such a multitude.
> [I. i. 159–161.]

He is not taken to be of much account by the
French leaders who are assaulting the city.
Reigner remarks :

> Remaineth none but mad-brain'd Salisbury,
> And he may well in fretting spend his gall ;
> Nor men not money hath he to make war.
> [I. ii. 15–17.]

and further :

> Salisbury is a desperate homicide ;
> He fighteth as one weary of his life :   [I. ii. 25–26.]

Later when in a chamber of a tower over-
looking the walls of the town, he greets Talbot
who has been released by the French, and while
they are talking with Sir Thomas Gargrave, and
Sir William Glansdale as to which is the best
point to attack the town, a shot rings out, and
Salisbury and Sir Thomas fall to the ground
mortally wounded.

[In this play the valiant Thomas Montacute
closes his long and glorious career at Orleans in
1428. He has been styled " a person more of
an old Roman courage, than one of his age."
Camden states that he was the first English
gentleman that was slain by a cannon-ball. The
earl was a patron of Lydgate the poet and historian, who dedicated his works to Salisbury,
and the copy in the British Museum has in the
frontispiece portraits of the earl and the poet.
Thomas Montacute married first, Eleanor Holland, daughter of Thomas, second Earl of Kent,
and their only daughter, Alice Montacute,
married Richard Nevill, who is the " Earl of
Salisbury " in the *Second Part of King Henry the
Sixth*. The Earl in this play married secondly,
Alice, daughter of Thomas Chaucer (the poet's
son) but had no issue by her. His daughter,
Alice Nevill, inherited her father's baronies of
Montacute and Monthermer. *French.*]

Earl of Suffolk. II. iv. p.1, 78, 80, 100,
114, 122 ; III. i. p.1 ; III. iv. p.1 ;
IV. i. p.1 ; V. iii. p.45, 53, 59, 67,
72, 132, 141, 142, 174, 187 ; V. v.
p.1, 80, 103.

First appears in the Temple garden, and plucks
a red rose in token of his allegiance to the house
of Lancaster.

He does not take any important part until he
appears before Angiers and leads in Reigner's
daughter Margaret, whom he has taken prisoner.

He is at first disposed to make love to her, but
decides that he will make her Henry's queen, and
makes this offer to her father, saying :

> Consent, and for thy honour give consent,
> Thy daughter shall be wedded to my king,
> [V. iii. 136–137.]

This is readily agreed to, and Suffolk determines to :

> Solicit Henry with her wondrous praise : [V. iii. 190.]

He returns to the king and extols Margaret's
virtues, and Henry remarks :

> Your wondrous rare description, noble earl,
> Of beauteous Margaret hath astonish'd me :
> [V. v. 1–2.]

Suffolk exercises his influence over the king by
his flattering words, and he is sent to France to
fetch Margaret for the marriage.

At the close of the play we are told in his
own words why Suffolk was so anxious to arrange
the match :

> Thus Suffolk hath prevail'd ; and thus he goes,
> As did the youthful Paris once to Greece ;
> With hope to find the like event in love,
> But prosper better than the Trojan did.
> Margaret shall now be queen, and rule the king ;
> But I w.ll rule both her, the king, and realm.

[This noble was William de la Pole, fourth
earl, brother and successor of Michael de la Pole,
third earl, who fell gloriously at Agincourt, and
to whose large possessions the fourth earl eventually became heir. At the death of Henry V.
he was left in France, and held a high command
at the famous battle of Verneuil, second only in
importance to Agincourt, under the regent, Bedford, and with Salisbury for a colleague, at whose
death Suffolk succeeded to the chief command
at Orleans. At the siege of Jergeau, May 18,
1429, he was taken prisoner by a French esquire,
to whom Suffolk yielded his sword, having first
knighted him with it ; his captor was named

Guillaume Renaud. The earl was present in Paris at the coronation of Henry VI., and was sent into Sicily to negociate that king's marriage with Margaret of Anjou ; this *First Part* concludes with Suffolk's departure on his embassy. He is continued in the *Second Part* with increase of rank, the consequence of his successful mission. He was made a K.G. in the reign of Henry V *French.*]

[The Earl—as Duke—of Suffolk is also a character in the *Second Part of King Henry the Sixth.*]

Earl of Valence. IV. vii. 63.

One of Lord Talbot's titles. Valence is the name of a city in France. *See* Earl of Washford.

Earl of Warwick. I. i. p.1 ; II. iv. p.1, 10 ; II. iv. 120 ; III. i. p.1, 152 ; III. iv. p.1 ; IV. i. p.1 ; V. iv. p.1, 111.

Warwick is the Duke of York's champion throughout the play, and is the first to show his allegiance to him in the Temple garden, promising to see that his rights are asserted :

> This blot that they object against your house
> Shall be wip'd out in the next parliament,
>   [II. iv. 116–117.]

and presents the petition to Henry :

> Accept this scroll, most gracious sovereign,
> Which in the right of Richard Plantagenet
> We do exhibit to your majesty.   [III. i. 149–151.]

and when York is about to burst out at Henry's donning Somerset's colour, quietly rebukes him for his own good, saying :

> Tush ! that was but his fancy, blame him not ;
> I dare presume, sweet prince, he thought no harm.
>   [IV. i. 178–179.]

knowing that a brawl at this point would be most impropitious to his cause.

He finally appears with York when Joan La Pucelle is brought before him for trial, and later in the same scene when Cardinal Beaufort appears asking for peace on behalf of the dauphin, appeals to his leader to :

> Be patient, York : if we conclude a peace,
> It shall be with such strict and severe covenants
> As little shall the Frenchmen gain thereby.
>   [V. iv. 113–115.]

[The Richard Beauchamp of the two preceding plays is appropriately continued in this *First Part of King Henry VI.*, whom he carried in his arms

at fourteen months old, on being presented to his Peers in Parliament. In the " Rous Roll," the Earl of Warwick is depicted holding his young charge on his arm. He succeeded the Duke of Bedford as lieutenant-general in France and Normandy, and died at Rouen, April 30, 1439 ; he was buried at Warwick, where his tomb, in the Church of St. Mary, is considered to be the most magnificent and beautiful of its kind in England He married first, Elizabeth, only daughter and heir of Thomas, fifth Lord Berkeley, Viscount Lisle, and by her had three daughters : (1) Margaret Beauchamp, who was the second wife of the illustrious Talbot of this play ; (2) Alianor Beauchamp, who married first, Thomas, ninth Lord de Ros, and secondly, Edmund Beaufort, second Duke of Somerset ; (3) Elizabeth Beauchamp, who married George Nevill, Lord Latimer. The Earl of Warwick's second wife was Isabel le Despencer, daughter of Thomas, Earl of Gloucester, by whom he had one son, his successor, Henry Beauchamp, created Duke of Warwick, and a K.G. ; and one daughter, Anne Beauchamp, who became the wife of Richard Nevill, who is the great " Earl of Warwick " in the two next Parts. Fuller says of Richard Beauchamp, " His deeds of charity, according to the devotion of those days, were little inferior to the achievements of his valour." *French.*]

[According to the *Henry Irving Edition of Shakespeare* " There are supposed to be two Earls of Warwick introduced in this play. The first, who, according to this supposition, appears only in Act I., Scene i., and is a *persona muta*, was, undoubtedly, Richard Beauchamp, who succeeded to the title, in 1401, on the death of his father, Thomas Beauchamp, condemned as a traitor in the reign of Richard II., but not executed. He was made lieutenant and deputy-regent in France by the Duke of Bedford when he was sent for into England by Cardinal Beaufort in 1425. In 1427 he was recalled from France and appointed ' governor ' of the young king, Henry VI., and held this office nine years. In 1437 he was appointed Regent of France, and died at Rouen in 1439. He is the same Warwick who appears in Henry V., and also frequently in Henry IV., where Shakespeare makes the mistake of causing the king to address him as ' Nevil,' and not as ' Beauchamp.'

The second Earl of Warwick of this play is

supposed to be Richard Neville, called ' the king-maker,' who is undoubtedly one of the principal characters in the *Second and Third Parts of Henry VI.*"]

Earl of Washford.   IV. vii. 63.

> But where 's the great Alcides of the field,
> Valiant Lord Talbot, Earl of Shrewsbury ?
> Created, for his rare success in arms,
> Great Earl of Washford, Waterford, and Valence ;
> Lord Talbot of Goodrig and Urchinfield,
> Lord Strange of Blackmere, Lord Verdun of Alton,
> Lord Cromwell of Wingfield, Lord Furnival of Sheffield,
> The thrice-victorious Lord of Falconbridge,
> Knight of the noble order of Saint George,
> Worthy Saint Michael and the Golden Fleece,
> Great marshal to Henry the Sixth
> Of all his wars within the realm of France ?
>   [IV. vii. 60–71.]

This long list of Talbot's titles is taken from the *Epitaph* on his tomb at Roüen in Normandy. It appears in Richard Crompton's *Mansion of Magnanimitie,* 1599, and is given by Boswell-Stone in his *Shakespeare's Holinshed :* " Here lieth the right noble knight, *Iohn Talbott Earle of Shrewsbury, Washford, Waterford, and Valence, Lord Talbot of Goodrige, and Vrchengfield, Lord Strange of the blacke Meere, Lord Verdon of Alton, Lord Crumwell of Wingfield,* Lord Louetoft of Worsop, *Lord Furniuall of Sheffield, Lord Faul-conbri[d]ge, knight of the* most *noble order of S. George, S. Michaell, and the Golden fleece, Great Marshall to* king *Henry the sixt of his realme of France ;* who died in the battell of Burdeaux in the yeare of our Lord 1453." Burke says that " The Earl's Monument at Whitchurch repeats nearly the whole of this list of honours."

Camden in his *Britannia,* says : " and next, White-church, or the White Monaſtery, famous for ſome monuments of the Talbots, but more particularly for that of our Engliſh Achilles *John Talbot,* the firſt Earl of Shrewſbury of this family, whoſe Epitaph I here infert, not that it comes up to the character of ſuch an Hero, but only for a Specimen, how the ſtile of every age varies in framing their monumental Inſcrip-tions." Camden gives the inscription in Latin and English, " ORATE PRO ANIMA PRÆNOBILIS DOMINI," etc., that is : " Pray for the foul of the right honourable Lord, Lord John Talbott, ſometime Earl of Shrewsbury, Lord Talbott, Lord Furnivall, Lord Verdon, Lord Strange of Blackmere, and Marſhal of France, who died in battel, at Burdews, VII. of July, MCCCCLIII.

Earl of Waterford.   IV. vii. 63.

One of Lord Talbot's titles. Burke says that " He was subsequently re-constituted lord-lieutenant of Ireland, and elevated to the peerage of that kingdom, 17 July, 1446, as *Earl of Water-ford,* having been appointed at the same time lord-high-steward of Ireland." *See* Earl of Washford.

Edmund Langley, Duke of York.   II. v. 85.

Fifth son of King Edward the Third ; accom-panied his father to the French wars ; created Earl of Cambridge, 1362 ; and Duke of York, 1385. He is one of the characters in *King Richard the Second.*

Edmund Mortimer, Earl of March.   II. v. p.1, 2, 7, 122.

Mortimer is a prisoner in the Tower of London, and we see him brought in by gaolers. He is in a very weak condition owing to his long imprison-ment, and feeling that he is about to die, ex-presses his wish to see his nephew Richard Plantagenet.

The gaoler tells him that Plantagenet has promised to come, and presently he arrives with the words :

> Your nephew, late-despised Richard comes. [II. v. 36.]

Mortimer enquires the meaning of these words, and is told of the dissention between Somerset and himself, and of the disparaging terms used concerning his father's (Richard, Earl of Cam-bridge) death.

Mortimer then tells of how his house is in the direct line for the sovereignty of England, and Plantagenet having sworn he will see that all these wrongs are expiated, the aged earl dies, and his body is borne out by the keepers.

[Shakespeare has varied from the truth of history, to introduce this scene (II. v.) between Mortimer and Richard Plantagenet. Edmund Mortimer served under Henry V., in 1422, and died unconfined in Ireland in 1424. Holinshed says, that Mortimer was one of the mourners at the funeral of Henry V. His uncle, Sir John Mortimer, was indeed a prisoner in the Tower, and was executed not long before the Earl of March's death, being charged with an attempt to make his escape in order to stir up an insurrection in Wales. *Steevens.*

The error concerning Edmund Mortimer, brother-in-law to Richard, Earl of Cambridge, having been ' kept in captivity until he died,' seems to have arisen from the legend of Richard Plantagenet, Duke of Yorke, in *The Mirrour for Magistrates,* 1575. *Malone.*]

Edward King. II. v. 66.

= King Edward the Third.

Edward, King of England. II. iv. 84.

= King Edward the Third.

Edward the Third. I. ii. 31.

Eltham. I. i. 170.

> To Eltham will I, where the young king is,
> Being ordain'd his special governor ;   [I. i. 170–171.]

Grafton says : " The Citie of Mouns thus being reduced into the English mens hands, the lorde Talbot departed to the towne of Alanson. After which marciall feate manfully acheeued, the Erle of Warwike departed into Englande, to be gouernour of the yong king, in stead of Thomas duke of Excester, late departed to God. In whose steede was sent into Fraunce, the lord Thomas Mountacute Erle of Salisburie, with fiue thousand men, which landed at Calice, and so came to the Duke of Bedford in Paris."

Eltham. I. i. 176.

Eltham, a town in Kent, now part of the Borough of Woolwich. It contains the ruins of a palace which was a royal residence from Henry III to Henry VIII. It was much frequented by Elizabeth and other monarchs for hunting purposes. In *The Paston Letters* under date A.D. 1460, 12 Oct., we have : " As for tythyngs here, the Kyng is way at Eltham and at Grenewych to hunt and to sport hym there, bydyng the Parlement and the Quene and the Prynce byth in Walys alway.   And is with hir the Duc of Excestre and other, with a fewe mayne, as men seythe here."

Henry Beaufort, Bishop of Winchester, afterwards Cardinal, planned to remove Henry VI. from Eltham to Windsor some four years after the young king's accession. Item 2 of the Articles of Accusation says : " My sayde Lorde of Winchester, without the aduise and assent of my sayde Lorde of Gloucester, or of the kings counsayle, purposed and disposed him to set hand on the kings person, and to haue remoued him from Eltham, the place that he was in, to Windsore, to the entent to put him in gouernaunce as him liste."

Eltham-place. III. i. 156.

See Eltham.

Emperor. V. i. 2.

> Have you perused the letters from the pope,
> The Emperor, and the Earl of Armagnac ?   [V. i. 1–2.]

Sigismund, king of the Romans, son of Charles IV. In 1435 he arrived in England to mediate between England and France. He was a distant relative of Henry by marriage and had visited England in 1416 to mediate between Henry V. and Charles VI. of France. Cf. *Henry V.,* Act V., Chorus 37–39.

See also under Earl of Armagnac and Pope.

England. I. i. 7, 8 ; I. ii. 30 ; III. i. 187 ; IV. i. 89, 171 ; IV. iv. 38 ; V. i. 6 ; V. iii. 23, 167 ; V. iv. 116, 171, 172 ; V. v. 90.

England. III. iii. 70.

> Was not the Duke of Orleans thy foe,
> And was he not in England prisoner ?
> But when they heard he was thine enemy,
> They set him free without his ransom paid,
> In spite of Burgundy and all his friends.
> [III. iii. 69–73.]

Inaccurate. The Duke of Orleans captured at Agincourt 1415 was kept a prisoner in England for twenty-five years, being released at the end of 1440, or about five years after the Duke of Burgundy had deserted the English forces.

England. IV. iv. 36.

> The fraud of England, not the force of France,
> Hath now entrapp'd the noble-minded Talbot.
> [IV. iv. 36–37.]

The quarrel between the Red and White Rose factions, and not the might of France has " entrapp'd the noble-minded Talbot."

England's coat. I. i. 81.

> Cropp'd are the flower-de-luces in your arms
> Of England's coat, one half is cut away. [I. i. 80–81.]

Hart (*Arden edition*) says : " Your arms of England's *coat* " is equivalent to " your English *coat* of arms," spoken by a foreign messenger who already uses English nobility in a foreign manner.

England's coat. I. v. 28.

> Hark, countrymen ! either renew the fight
> Or tear the lions out of England's coat : [I. v. 27–28.]

An allusion to the armorial dress of the kings of England.

England's fame. IV. vi. 39.

England's glory. IV. vii. 48.

England's honour. IV. iii. 23 ; IV. iv. 20.

England's lap. V. iii. 26.

England's queen. V. i. 45.

> He doth intend she shall be England's queen. [V. i. 45.]

Daughter of the Earl of Armagnac. See *Extract* 38 from Holinshed.

England's right. IV. ii. 55.

> *See* Talbot, A ! a Talbot !

England's royal king. V. iii. 115.

= King Henry the Sixth.

England's royal queen. V. v. 24.

= Margaret, daughter of Reignier, Duke of Anjou. See *Extracts* 46, 47, 48 *and* 49 from Holinshed.

England's timorous deer. IV. ii. 46.

English Camp near Bourdeaux.

The Scene of Act IV., Scene v. The whole scene is a conversation between Talbot and his son John.

English Henry. II. i. 36.

= King Henry the Sixth.

Europe. I. i. 156.

Fiends appearing to Joan la Pucelle. V. iii. p.8.

Seeing the French forces fleeing, Joan calls upon the ' choice spirits that admonish her, and give her signs of future accidents ' to aid her. They appear but do not speak, and when Joan offers them even her body and soul if they will come to her aid, they shake their heads and depart. This Joan takes as a sign of France's defeat and says :

> Now the time is come
> The France must vail her lofty plumed crest,
> And let her head fall into England's lap
> My ancient incantations are too weak,
> And hell too strong for me to buckle with :
> Now, France, thy glory droopeth to the dust.
> [V. iii. 24–29.]

France. I. i. 58, 84, 90, 102, 139, 153 ; I. ii. 54 ; I. iv. 97 ; I. vi. 8, 15, 27 ; II. i. 16 ; II. ii. 17, 36 ; III. i. 180, 187 ; III. ii. 14, 36, 40, 52, 68, 78 ; III. iii. 22, 25, 41, 44, 49, 60, 64 ; III. iv. 13 ; IV. i. 89, 147, 163 ; IV. iii. 16, 18, 23, 32 ; IV. v. 55 ; IV. vi. 48 ; IV. vii. 71, 82, 93 ; V. i. 6, 40 ; V. ii. 21 ; V. iii. 12, 25, 29, 30 ; V. iv. 112, 117 ; V. v. 41, 87.

France. II. iii. 14.

> Is this the scourge of France ?
> Is this the Talbot, so much fear'd abroad
> That with his name the mothers still their babes ?
> [II. iii. 14–16.]

See *Extract* 21 from Holinshed.

France. IV. i. 138.

> And you, my lords, remember where we are ;
> In France, amongst a fickle wavering nation.
> [IV. i. 137–138.]

Hart (*Arden edition*) quotes Dr. Johnson : " The inconstancy of the French was always the subject of satire : I have read a dissertation written to prove that the index of the wind upon our steeples was made in form of a cock, to ridicule the French for their frequent changes."

France. IV. iv. 36.

See England, IV. iv. 36.

France. Before Orleans.

The Scene of Act I., Scenes ii., iv., v., and vi. Act II., Scene i.

Act I., Scene ii. The French army under Charles marching to the relief of Orleans, which is being besieged by the English forces under Salisbury, is repulsed. Charles is in favour of retiring, when Joan of Arc is introduced, who promises that by nightfall she will assuredly raise the siege.

Act I., Scene iv. A master-gunner and his son appear on the ramparts of the city. Talbot is released in exchange for a French nobleman and returns to the English camp. The Earl of Salisbury and Sir Thomas Gargrave are killed by a shot from the walls. Talbot takes Salisbury's place as leader of the English forces.

Act I., Scene v. An encounter takes place between the English and French forces, and the French being victorious, succeed in gaining an entrance into Orleans. During the skirmish, a hand to hand fight takes place between Talbot and Joan of Arc.

Act I., Scene vi. Joan and Charles appear on the walls of the city, and the French colours are raised over the ramparts. Charles loudly praises Joan for this great triumph.

[In the preceding four scenes we have the same contempt for dates, the French before Orleans; the Dauphin, Alençon, Reignier, rejoice at the capture of Talbot; they are then beaten by Salisbury, and Joan is introduced. Salisbury who came over in 1428, obtained some successes before Orleans, and was killed, with Sir Thomas Gargrave by a shot from the town as described in Scene iv. Apparently Talbot was under the command of Salisbury, who was succeeded by the Earl of Suffolk. Talbot's release from a French prison is imaginary as he was not taken prisoner until after the death of Salisbury, and not released until 1431.]

Act II., Scene i. In this scene Orleans is recovered by Talbot, the English scaling the walls by means of scaling-ladders. Taken by surprise, the French escape in their night attire, and when next heard of are before Rouen in Act III., Scene ii.

[The recovery of Orleans by Talbot is a stretch of the imagination, for it was not long after the abandonment of Orleans that he was defeated and taken. The story of the French leaping from the walls in their shirts is transferred to Orleans from Mans.]

France. Before Rouen.

The Scene of Act III., Scene ii. Joan by strategy succeeds in gaining an entrance into Rouen. [There does not appear to be any historical foundation for this story, unless it be a story which Holinshed relates of the capture of Evreux, by six strong fellows, apparelled like men of the country, with sack and baskets, as carriers of corn and victuals.] The Duke of Bedford is brought in a chair sick. Joan and Charles appear on the walls and taunt the English. More fighting follows, and the English succeed in recovering the city. Bedford passes away, and Talbot gives orders for his burial after which preparations are made to depart for Paris to attend the coronation of Henry as King of France.

[Courtenay remarks: "Of all this I find no trace in the Chronicle, except that this brave duke died in September, 1435, and was buried at Rouen. The Duke of Burgundy is made to cheer him in his dying moments: but the defection of that prince had, in truth, occurred upon inducements connected with the English part of our history to which I have referred, *before* the Duke of Bedford's death. There is, therefore, a compound anachronism in the following scene, in which *Joan* is made to persuade Burgundy to separate himself from the English cause."]

France his sword. IV. vi. 3.

The regent hath with Talbot broke his word,
And left us to the rage of France his sword.

[IV. vi. 2-3.]

= The King of France's sword.

France. Plains in Anjou.

The Scene of Act V., Scene ii. News is received that the Parisians have revolted against the English. A scout enters, and reports the conjunction of the two parts of the English army, an event which happened some years previously than represented in this scene,

Courtenay says : " Here the chronology makes an attempt to right itself, by carrying us back to the year 1436, when soon after the death of the Duke of Bedford, the Parisians returned under the allegiance of their native king. 'But then comes an event (the conjunction of the two parts of the English army) which happened in the year 1430."

France.   The Plains near Rouen.

The Scene of Act III., Scene iii. Talbot marches out of Rouen at the head of the English forces on his way to Paris to attend the coronation of Henry. He is followed by the Duke of Burgundy who, being intercepted by Joan, is won over to the side of Charles. *See* Extract from Courtenay, *under* France. Before Rouen.

France's saint.   I. vi. 29.

But Joan la Pucelle shall be France's saint.
[I. vi. 29.]

Joan of Arc shall be France's patron saint in place of Saint Denis.

French Sergeant.   II. i. p.1.

Froissart.   I. ii. 29.

Jean Froissart, French historian. His history deals with the period between 1326 and 1400. He was secretary for many years to Philippa of Hainault, wife of Edward III.

Funeral of King Henry the Fifth.   I. i. p.1.

The play opens with the Playing of the Dead March, during which the corpse of Henry the Fifth is brought in, in state.

Gallia.   IV. vi. 15.

Beat down Alençon, Orleans Burgundy,
And from the pride of Gallia rescu'd thee.
[IV. vi. 14–15.]
= Full power of France.

Gallia's wonder.   IV. vii. 48.

= Talbot, the wonder of France.

Gascony, Plains in.

The Scene of Act IV., Scene iii. A messenger meets the Duke of York and reports that a large French army is marching towards Bourdeaux to intercept Talbot.   Sir William Lucy appears and urges York to send aid to Talbot but York replies that he is unable to succour him owing to the failure of Somerset in sending himself the promised levies. [The presence of York in this scene is not in accordance with history ; he was at this time in England fomenting civil strife.]

Gascony, Other Plains in.

The Scene of Act IV., Scene iv. In this scene we meet Somerset in another part of the plains of Gascony. Sir William Lucy appears and urges Somerset to send reinforcements to Talbot, but Somerset declares his inability to spare any part of his force, declaring that the expedition was too hastily planned by York and Talbot. [The presence of Somerset in this scene is not historical ; he was at this time in England fomenting civil strife.]

General of the French Forces in Bourdeaux.   IV. ii. p.3.

Is called to the walls by Talbot, who demands immediate surrender, which terms are stubbornly refused by the General :

On us thou canst not enter but by death ;
For, I protest, we are well fortified,
And strong enough to issue out and fight :
[IV. ii. 18–20.]
[French says : " The great Talbot surprised the garrison of Bordeaux, and captured the city, October 23rd, 1452. At the battle of Castillon, where he and his son John Talbot were slain, fighting against overwhelming numbers, the French forces were commanded by two Marshals, Andreas de Valle, Lord of Loheauc, and the Sieur de Jalognes, July 7th, 1453."]

Golden Fleece.   IV. vii. 69.

A distinguished Order of Knighthood, held by Lord Talbot. It was founded by Philip the Good, Duke of Burgundy, on the occasion of his marriage with the Infanta Isabella of Portugal.

Goliases.   I. ii. 33.

For none but Samsons and Goliases
It sendeth forth to skirmish.   [I. ii. 33–34.]

Goliath was a Philistine giant whose spear " was like a weaver's beam."

Goodrig. IV. vii. 64.

Probably Goodrich in Herefordshire. *See* Earl of Washford.

Governor of Paris. IV. i. p.1, 3.

At the coronation in Paris of King Henry the Sixth as King of France, the Governor is required by Gloucester to take the oath of allegiance to the new king.

> Now, governor of Paris, take your oath,
> That you elect no other king but him,
> Esteem none friends but such as are his friends,
> And none your foes but such as shall pretend
> Malicious practices against his state :
> This shall ye do, so help you righteous God !
> [IV. i. 3–8.]

[John, Duke of Bedford, when Paris was captured by the English, appointed as its governor, John of Luxemburg, who may therefore be the person introduced, as present at the coronation of Henry VI., December 7, 1431, to take the oath of fealty to him, as King of France, in Act IV., Scene i.]

Greece. V. v. 104.

See Paris.

Guienne. I. i. 60.

With Gascony the ancient Aquitania, an old province in the south-west of France. By the marriage of Henry II. of England with Eleanor of Aquitaine in 1152 Guienne became an English province. It remained an English possession until 1451, although the messenger who enters declares it to be lost in 1422.

Guysors. I. i. 61.

> Paris, Guysors, Poictiers, all are quite lost. [I. i. 61.]

The ancient capital of the Norman Vexin. It was surrendered in 1449, or twenty-seven years later than represented in the play.

Hannibal. I. v. 21.

> A witch, by fear, not force, like Hannibal,
> Drives back our troops and conquers as she lists :
> [I. v. 21–22.]

An allusion to Hannibal's stratagem of affixing blazing torches to the horns of two thousand oxen and driving them against the Romans in order to divert their attention, while he made his escape.

Hecate. III. ii. 64.

In Mythology Hecate was the goddess of witchcraft.

Hector. II. iii. 19.

An allusion to Hector " the bravest of the Trojans."

Helen. I. ii. 142.

> Helen, the mother of great Constantine,
> Nor yet Saint Philip's daughters were like thee.
> [I. ii. 142–143.]

" This was St. Helena, the first wife of Constantius Chlorus, and mother of Constantine the Great. Little is known of her origin except that she was not of high birth. In A.D. 292 according to some, according to others 296, Constantius divorced her at the bidding of Diocletian, in order to marry Theodora. Some of the historians say she was not married to him ; but if so, she could not be divorced from him. One legend makes her the daughter of King Coel of Colchester and a native of Britain. When she was 64 years old she is said to have discovered, buried on Mount Calvary, the true cross on which our Lord was crucified. [In the time of Shakespeare two frescoes representing this legend adorned the Guild Chapel at Stratford-on-Avon.] She died about the age of 80." *Irving edition.*

Joan of Arc is here declared by Charles as being greater than Helen,

Henry. III. i. 196, 198.

> And now I fear that fatal prophesy
> Which in the time of Henry nam'd the Fifth.
> [III. i. 195–196.]

= King Henry the Fifth. For the fatal prophecy see *Extract* 27 from Holinshed.

Henry. I. i. 47.

= King Henry the Fifth.

Henry. I. i. 162.

> Remember, lords, your oaths to Henry sworn,
> Either to quell the Dauphin utterly,
> Or bring him in obedience to your yoke. [I. i. 162–164.]

See *Extract* 5 from Holinshed.

Henry. I. i. 169.

= King Henry the Sixth.

Henry. I. iii. 24.

> Arrogant Winchester, that haughty prelate,
> Whom Henry, our late sovereign, ne'er could brook ?
> [I. iii. 23–24.]

= Henry the Fifth. Hart (*Arden edition*) says : " The Duke of Bedford . . . landed at Calice, with whome also passed the seas, Henry Bishop of Winchester, which in the sayde towne was invested with the Habite, Hat, and dignitie of a Cardinall, with all Ceremonies to it apperteynyng. Which degree King Henrie the fift, knowying the haute courage, and the ambicious minde of the man, prohibited him on his allegeance once [altogether], either to sue for or to take : meaning y^t [that] Cardinals Hats should not presume to be egal with princes. But now the king beyng yong, and the Regent his friend, he obteyned that dignitie . . . so was he surnamed the rich Cardinall of Winchester, and neyther called learned Bishop, nor virtuous Priest." See *Extracts* 39 *and* 40 from Holinshed.

Henry Beaufort, Great-uncle to the King, Bishop of Winchester, and afterwards Cardinal. I. i. p.1 ; I. iii. 19, 23, p.29, 53, 60, 80 ; II. iv. 118 ; III. i. p.1, 64, 65, 78, 107, 112, 122, 126, 127, 132, 162 ; III. iv. p.1 ; IV. i. p.1 ; V. i. p.28, 28, 39, 56 ; V. iv. p.93, 120.

Depicted as being extremely ambitious and unscrupulous, Winchester is one of the principal characters in the play.

He is anxious to secure absolute power over the young king, and to override Gloucester who is protector of the realm.

At the end of the first scene we learn his intentions, for he says :

> Each has his place and function to attend ;
> I am left out ; for me nothing remains.
> But long I will not be Jack out of office.
> The king from Eltham I intend to send,
> And sit at chiefest stern of public weal.   [I. i 173–177.]

He persuades Woodville the lieutenant of the Tower to refuse Gloucester admission to view the armaments, and appears on the scene with his men, who engage in a fight with Gloucester's followers.

This is followed by the appearance of the Lord Mayor of London who causes the riot act to be read, and the tumult dies down while Winchester remarks :

> Abominable Gloucester ! guard thy head ;
> For I intend to have it ere long.   [I. iii. 87–88.]

A further battle of words takes place in the Parliament House and Henry appeals to Winchester and Gloucester to ' join their hearts in love and amity ' when a tumult is heard outside, which proves to be a skirmish between the followers of the dissenting nobles.

On Henry further appealing to them they agree to cease their enmity, but Winchester remarks, aside :

> So help me God, as I intend it not !   [III. i. 140.]

Winchester succeeds in obtaining a Cardinal's degree from the Pope in order to secure more power, and pays the Pope's legate remarking :

> you shall first receive
> The sum of money which I promised
> Should be deliver'd to his holiness
> For clothing me in these grave ornaments,   [V. i. 51–54.]

and then, soliloquising, remarks :

> [*Aside.*] Now Winchester will not submit, I trow,
> Or be inferior to the proudest peer.
> Humphrey of Gloucester, thou shalt well perceive
> That neither in birth or for authority
> The bishop will be overborne by thee :
> I 'll either make thee stoop and bend thy knee,
> Or sack this country with a mutiny.   [V. i. 56–62.]

At the end of the play Winchester appears and announces that the king desires peace to be concluded with France, and Charles, having agreed to ' pay tribute and submit himself ' is allowed to ' still enjoy his regal dignity.'

[This eminent ecclesiastic was the second son of *Gaunt* and Catharine Swynford, and Humphrey of Gloster takes care to remind his rival of the bar-sinister attaching to his birth,— ' Thou bastard of my grand-father,' for no Act of Parliament can change a *natural taint of blood* in a person, though it may restore him to forfeited honours.

Henry Beaufort was born about the year 1370, and in 1402 succeeded the illustrious William of Wickham in the see of Winchester, and in the same year was appointed Lord High Chancellor. He became extremely rich, and he lent to his nephew, Henry V., the large sum (for those days) of £28,000 for his French wars. His abilities, as well as his birth, qualified him for the leading part he took in state affairs during the long minority of his great-nephew. In 1426, June 23rd, Pope Martin V. made him ' Cardinal of St. Eusebius.' In opposition to the Duke of Gloster, who wished the young king to marry a daughter of the Count of Armagnac, Cardinal Beaufort recommended Margaret of Anjou, and his interest prevailed. The character of this prelate, as drawn in the play, agrees with the account given of him by the old chroniclers,— ' Haughty in stomach, and high in countenance,' says Holinshed, ' and strong in malice and mischief.' *French.*]

[Henry Beaufort—as Cardinal—is also a character in the *Second Part of King Henry the Sixth* (q.v.).]

Henry Monmouth. II. v. 23.

= King Henry the Fifth so-called from the place of his birth.

Henry's corse. I. i. 62.

= King Henry the Fifth.

Henry's death. I. i. 5 ; I. ii. 136.

= King Henry the Fifth.

Henry's death. I. iii. 2.

Since Henry's death, I fear there is conveyance. [I. iii. 2.]

Since the death of Henry the Fifth there has been theft, jugglery and conspiracy.

Henry the Fifth. I. i. 52 ; I. iv. 79 ; II. v. 82 ; IV. iii. 52.

Henry the Fifth. V. i. 31.

Henry the Fifth did sometime prophesy :
' If once he come to be a cardinal,
He 'll make his cap co-equal with the crown.'

See *Extract* 39 from Holinshed.

Henry the Fourth. II. v. 63.

Heralds. I. i. p.1 ; IV. vii. p.51.

Hercules. II. iii. 18.

I thought I should have seen some Hercules, [II. iii. 18.]

Son of Jupiter, celebrated for his great strength.

Icarus. IV. vi. 55 ; IV. vii. 16.

Then follow thou thy desperate sire of Crete,
Thou Icarus. [IV. vi. 54–55.]

In Greek mythology the son of Dædalus who was confined—with his father—in the famous labyrinth of Crete. With his father, escaped by taking a winged flight, but Icarus soared so high that the sun melted the wax which cemented his wings and he fell into the sea, which was afterwards named after him—the Icarian Sea.

Jack. I. i. 175.

But long I will not be Jack out of office. [I. i. 175.]

A term of contempt. Cf. Riche *his Farewell to Militarie profession : conteining verie pleasaunt discourses fit for a peaceable tyme :* " To become a courtier, there is as little gaines to be gotten ; for liberalitie, who was wont to be a principall officer, as well in the court as in the country, by whose meanes wel doyng could never go unrewarded, is tourned Jacke out of office, and others appointed to have the custodie of hym, to hold him short, that he range no more abroad, so that no man can speake with him ; and thei saie the poore gentleman is so fleest from tyme to tyme, by those that bee his keepers, that he hath nothing to give that is good but it falls to their shares," and in Heywood's *Proverbs*, we have :

And Jacke out of office she may bid me walke,
And thinke me as wise as Waltham's calfe, to talke.

Joan la Pucelle. I. ii. p.64, 110 ; I. iv. 101, 107 ; I. v. p.1, p.3, 36 ; I. vi. p.1, 3, 17, 29 ; II. i. 20, 49, p.50 ; II. ii. 20 ; III. ii. p.1, 20, p.26, 38, p.41, 58, p.110, 121 ; III. iii. p.1, 17, 40, 88 ; IV. vii, p.33 ; V. ii. p.1 ; V. iii. p.1, p.30 ; V. iv. p.2, 2, 6, 17, 20, 49, 60.

Joan comes to the Dauphin at Orleans fired with a fierce ambition to save her country from the English, and claims to have been divinely appointed to this mission.

She tells of a vision which has come to her :

> Lo ! whilst I waited on my tender lambs,
> And to sun's parching heat display'd my cheeks,
> God's mother deign'd to appear to me,
> And, in a vision full of majesty
> Will'd me to leave my base vocation
> And free my country from calamity :
> Her aid she promis'd, and assur'd success ;
>
> [I. ii. 76–82.]

Charles is ultimately convinced of her sincerity, and invokes her aid.

In this scene Shakespeare shows us Joan of Arc as we are accustomed to think of her in the light of history, but later the characterisation dwindles into the view taken by contemporary writers, depicting Joan as an evilly guided woman, indeed we see her in converse with fiends, who are represented as being her helpers.

When she is captured she begs leave ' to curse awhile,' hardly the thing we should expect of the " saintly maid " we meet at first.

While on her first appearance she indicates that she is of but humble birth, at the time of her trial she vehemently denounces her father as an impostor, and declares she is of noble birth.

Such inconsistences as these lead one to believe that, although Shakespeare at first endeavours to give this character that which she deserves, gradually allows himself to show her as other authors of his time have depicted her, and thus she goes to her death leaving none but evil impressions, her former saintliness being obscured in her later actions and words.

" An old chronicle covering the period 1405–1449, under the title *The diary of a bourgeois of Paris under Charles VI., and VII.*, which throws an interesting light on Joan of Arc has been published in Paris," says the *Daily Chronicle* of the 18th of September, 1929. " The name of the author is now known, but he appears to have been a member of the clergy, and closely connected with Paris University. There are references to the British domination and the chronicler, describing the State entry of the little Henry VI., ' King of England and France,' into Paris, records how he was greeted from a balcony by his grandmother, Isabeau of Bavaria, who then ' turned away weeping.' "

[Joan of Arc was born in 1409 at Domrémy. She was the daughter of Jacques D'Arc, and was herself employed as a shepherdess up to the age of eighteen years. At that age she left her home to seek Charles VII., inspired with a divine mission to rescue France, her country, from the hands of the English. Her great success was at the battle of Patay, on February 17th, 1429, after which she wished to retire : but at the entreaty of the king she remained with the army. The next year she was taken prisoner at Compiègne by the Burgundians, on the 24th May, in a sortie. To the eternal disgrace of the English, to whose custody she was surrended, she was condemned to death and burned alive at Rouen, May 14th, 1431. Her story furnished Schiller with the subject of one of his finest tragedies, and our English poet Southey wrote a long poem on her life. *Irving edition.*]

Joan's denial of her father at the trial seems to be an invention of the dramatist.

John Beaufort, Earl, afterwards Duke, of Somerset. II. iv. p.1, 6, 37, 59, 68, 82, 98, 122 ; IV. v. 46, 125 ; III. i. p.1 ; III. iv. p.1, 34 ; IV. i. p.1, 108, 114, 120, 154, 164, 177 ; IV. iii. 9, 24, 33, 46 ; IV. iv. p.1, 15 ; IV. vii. 33.

Somerset first appears in the Temple Garden, accompanied by Richard Plantagenet and other nobles.

It is in this scene that the followers of the houses of Lancaster and York pluck red and white roses respectively to show their allegiance.

Somerset is the leader in this, for his side, saying :

> Let him that is no coward nor no flatterer,
> But dare maintain the party of the truth,
> Pluck a red rose from off this thorn with me.
>
> [II. iv. 31–33.]

King Henry shows himself to incline to Somerset, when, on his coronation in Paris, he, while urging the two leaders to abandon their strife says :

> I see no reason, if I wear this rose,
>
> [*Putting on a red rose.*
>
> That any one should therefore be suspicious
> I more incline to Somerset than York :
>
> [IV. i. 152–154.]

and turning to Somerset says :

> And, good my Lord of Somerset, unite
> Your troops of horsemen with his bands of foot ;
>
> [IV. i. 164–165.]

Later, on the Plains of Gascony we find Somerset being urged by Sir Henry Lucy to go to the aid of Lord Talbot. He refuses, saying :

> York set him on ; York should have sent him aid.
>
> [IV. iv. 29.]

and being reminded that York declares that he is to blame, retorts with : " York lies : "

At length he promises to send the much-needed reinforcements, exclaiming :

> I will despatch the horsemen straight :
> Within six hours they will be at his aid. [IV. iv. 40-41.]

but Lucy expresses the opinion that it will be too late.

From the scenes later in the play in which Somerset appears we see how bitter the feeling between him and York has become and are thus prepared for the strife which breaks out in the second part of the play.

He entirely ignores the welfare of his country in his desire to see his personal enemies vanquished, and this is the chief characteristic of Somerset as exemplified in the play.

[This character was third Earl, succeeding his brother Henry in that title, and was second son of John Beaufort, first Earl of Somerset, the eldest of the children of John of *Gaunt* and Catharine Swynford. The first Earl was a distinguished soldier under his father, and in the reign of Richard II., was Constable of Dover Castle, and Warden of the Cinque Ports ; he died in 1410, leaving by his wife Margaret Holland, daughter of Thomas Earl of Kent, the two sons already mentioned, and a third son, Edmund Beaufort, afterwards Duke of Somerset, a character in the *Second Part of King Henry VI.*, and also two daughters. (1) Joanna Beaufort, who became the Queen of James the First, King of Scots, so long a prisoner in England ; and (2) Margaret Beaufort, who married Thomas Courtenay, fifth Earl of Devon. The character of this play served with great honour in the French wars, was a K.G., and created by Henry VI., in 1443, Duke of Somerset ; he died in the next year, leaving by his wife Margaret, daughter of Sir John Beauchamp of Bletsho, an only child, the great heiress, Margaret Beaufort, who married first Edmund Tudor, Earl of Richmond, and their only son sat on the throne as Henry the Seventh ; the Countess of Richmond married secondly Sir Henry Stafford, knight, and thirdly Thomas, Lord Stanley, a character in *King Richard III.*, but had no issue by either of these two husbands.

John Beaufort, Duke of Somerset, and his wife, Margaret Beauchamp, are buried under a rich monument at Wimborne Minster, co. Dorset, where their daughter, the Countess of Richmond, founded a grammar-school in 1497. *French.*]

John of Gaunt. II. v. 77.

Fourth son of King Edward the Third.

John Talbot, his son. IV. iii. 35 ; IV. v. p.1, 1, 12 ; IV. vi, p.1, 4, 27, 46 ; IV. vii. 2, 4, p.18, 21, 32, 40.

We first make the acquaintance of this character in the English camp near Bordeaux.

He has come to his father that he might, ' tutor him in stratagems of war,' but Lord Talbot is at the moment in grave danger, and urges his son to escape :

> Therefore, dear boy, mount on my swiftest horse,
> And I 'll direct thee how thou shalt escape
> By sudden flight :   [IV. v. 9-11.]

This he stubbornly refuses to do, saying :

> Is my name Talbot ? and am I your son ?
> And shall I fly ?   [IV. v. 12-13.]

and the remainder of the scene consists of a conversation which shows clearly that the younger Talbot has all the fiery determination so strikingly exemplified in his father, and the two finally go off together, Talbot remarking :

> Come, side by side together live and die ;
> And soul with soul from France to heaven fly.
>   [IV. v. 54-55.]

In the next scene young Talbot is in great danger but is rescued by his father, and in the following scene we see the body of the courageous young soldier brought in, and his father, who is mortally wounded, holding him in his arms dies, remarking :

> Soldiers, adieu ! I have what I would have,
> Now my old arms are young John Talbot's grave.
>   [IV. vii. 31-32.]

[This young soldier, whom his father proudly calls " valiant John," was created in 1443 Baron, and in 1452 Viscount L'Isle, his mother, Margaret, being eldest daughter and co-heir of Richard Beauchamp, the " Earl of Warwick " in this play, by Elizabeth, only child of Thomas, fifth Lord Berkeley, Viscount L'Isle. The admirable scene wherein the elder Talbot in vain implores his son to quit the field is from Hall. As the death of young Talbot—who was killed by his father's side at Castillon,—not at Bordeaux, as represented by the dramatist in 1453

—occurred twenty-two years after the execution of Joan of Arc, it was impossible that they could meet in single combat, as hinted at by her in the play, Act IV., Scene vii.,—" Once I encounter'd him, and thus I said," etc.

The Viscount L'Isle married Joan, daughter of Sir Thomas Cheddar, Knight, and had by her one son, who died without issue in 1469, and two daughters, of whom the youngest, Margaret Talbot, married Sir George Vere, and the eldest, Elizabeth Talbot, married Sir Edward Grey, who was created Viscount L'Isle, and their daughter, Elizabeth Grey, by her marriage with Edmund Dudley, carried the ancient barony of L'Isle to that family, from whom it descended by marriage to the Sydneys ; and the lineal representative of those two families, and of young John Talbot, is the present Lord De L'Isle and Dudley, Philip Sidney (1865) who has also taken the name of his lady, daughter and heir of the late Sir William Foulis, Bart., of Ingilby." *French.*]

Julius Cæsar.   I. i. 56.

> A far more glorious star thy soul will make
> Than Julius Cæsar or bright—   [I. i. 55–56.]

The blank has been filled in by various commentators, with the name of Drake, Berenice, etc.

" I can't guess the occasion of the hemistich and imperfect sense in this place ; 'tis not impossible it might have been filled up with— *Francis Drake,* though that were a terrible anachronism (as bad as Hector's quoting Aristotle in Troilus and Cressida) ; yet perhaps at the time that brave Englishmen was in his glory, to an English-hearted audience, and pronounced by some favourite actor, the thing might be popular, though not judicious ; and, therefore, by some critick in favour of the author, afterwards struck out. But this is a mere slight conjecture." *Pope.*

" To confute the slight conjecture of Pope, a whole page of vehement opposition is annexed to this passage by Theobald. Sir Thomas Hanmer has stopped at *Cæsar*—perhaps more judiciously. It might, however, have been written—*or bright Berenice.*" *Johnson.*

" Pope's conjecture is confirmed by this peculiar circumstance, that two blazing stars (the *Julium sidus*) are part of the arms of the *Drake* family." *Mason.*

Cf. Ovid's *Metamorphoses* (Golding's translation) The Epistle 292–293 : " The turning to a blazing starre of Julius Cesar showes, That fame and immortalitie of vertuous doing growes," and Book XV. 944–956.

King Edward the Third.   II. v. 76.

King Henry's hearse.   I. i. 104.

> Wherewith you now bedew King Henry's hearse.
>   [I. i. 104.]

Cf. 2 *Henry IV.,* IV. v. 114 : " Let all the tears that should bedew my hearse Be drops of balm to sanctify thy head " :

King Henry the Fifth.   I. i. 6.

King Henry the Sixth.   I. i. 169 ; III. i. p.1, 76, 184, 199 ; III. ii. 80, 129 ; III. iii. 22, 66 ; III. iv. p.1 ; IV. i. p.1, 2, 18, 81, 146 ; IV. ii. 4 ; IV. vii. 70 ; V. i. p.1 ; V. ii. 20 ; V. iii. 117, 122, 156, 160, 172, 190, 194 ; V. iv. 124 ; V. v. p.1, 21, 22, 66, 73, 91.

At the time the play opens King Henry VI was but nine months old, and his uncle the Duke of Gloucester was Protector of the realm.

Thus in the earlier part of the drama the king plays but an unimportant part, and indeed, even when he is grown up he takes but little interest in the affairs of state leaving everything to the nobles, who naturally do not hesitate to further their own ends whenever possible.

Henry's first appearance is in Act III., Scene i., when we find him in the Parliament House. A quarrel takes place between Gloucester and Winchester, and the Lord Mayor enters with the news that the followers of these two nobles are pelting one another with stones.

To this Henry replies with words of mild reproof and although the dissenting nobles are at last reconciled it is but for a short time only, neither really meaning what he says.

This is but one instance of Henry's weakness, he had not the strength of character to rule efficiently and firmly in those difficult times when civil war was about to break out at any moment.

All through the play we see that he is entirely in the hands of the nobles. He allows Gloucester to decide his coronation in Paris, and Suffolk makes him an easy victim to his extravagant talk by persuading him to take Margaret in marriage in preference to his former choice.

Not in one single instance do we find Henry asserting himself, he always accedes to any request the nobles make and one is almost led to believe that he is oblivious of the turmoil which is ever threatening to break out and involve the country in the throes of civil war.

[Of this most unfortunate monarch Fuller says in his quaint fashion,—" This Henry was twice crowned, twice deposed, and twice buried, first at Chertsey, and then at Windsor, and once half-sainted." Henry V. had expressly directed that his son's birth should not take place at Windsor, but the event occurred there December 6, 1421, and when the young king came to the throne he was only eight months old. The scenes in this play are much confused as to order of time, and the youthful sovereign is brought upon the stage long before he could take any active share in the realities of government. This *First Part* is made to commence with the funeral of Henry V. in Westminster Abbey, November 11, 1422 ; and it closes with the departure of the Earl of Suffolk to treat for the hand of Margaret of Anjou ; this commission was given in 1443. Henry VI., was crowned by Archbishop Chicheley, November 6, 1429. *French.*]

[King Henry the Sixth is also a character in the *Second Part of King Henry the Sixth* (q.v.).]

King of Jerusalem. V. v. 40.

See King of Naples.

King of Naples. V. iii. 52, 94 ; V. iv. 78 ; V. v. 40.

= Reignier, Duke of Anjou, and father of Margaret of Anjou. According to Holinshed " This Reiner duke of Aniou named himselfe king of Sicill, Naples, and Ierusalem ; hauing onlie the name and stile of those realmes, without anie penie, profit, or foot of possession."

King Richard. II. v. 71.

young King Richard thus remov'd,
Leaving no heir begotten of his body—   [II. v. 71 72.]

An allusion to the deposition of King Richard the Second.

Lancaster. II. v. 102.

With silence, nephew, be thou politic :
Strong-fixed is the house of Lancaster,
And like a mountain, not to be removed.
           [II. v. 101–103.]

The descendants of John of Gaunt, Duke of Lancaster, and the rival of the York House in the Wars of the Roses.

Lawyer, A. II. iv. p.1.

Appears in the Temple Garden in company with Somerset, Plantagenet, and other lords. They all show to which leader they incline by plucking red or white roses from the bushes, the lawyer remarking to Somerset that :

Unless my study and my books be false,
The argument you held was wrong in you ;
           [II. iv. 56–57.]

and plucks a white rose showing his allegiance to Plantagenet.

Legate. V. i. p.28.

A Pope's ambassador to a foreign prince or state. The legate here only speaks one line : " I will attend upon your lordship's leisure."

Lionel, Duke of Clarence. II. iv. 83.

His grandfather was Lionel, Duke of Clarence,
           [II. iv. 83.]

" The author mistakes. Plantagenet's paternal grandfather was Edmund of Langley, Duke of York. His maternal grandfather was Roger Mortimer, Earl of March, who was the son of Philippa the daughter of Lionel, Duke of Clarence. The duke therefore was his maternal great-great-grandfather." *Malone.*

Lionel, Duke of Clarence. II. v. 75.

For by my mother I derived am
From Lionel, Duke of Clarence,   [II. v. 74–75.]

Duke of Antwerp, and Duke of Clarence, third son of King Edward the Third. *Mother* : should be grandmother.

London. III. i. 77.

London. Before the Tower.

The Scene of Act I., Scene iii. The Duke of Gloucester arrives at the Tower and demands admission. Being refused admittance, he orders his men to ' rush the gates.' During the tumult the Bishop of Winchester appears and a quarrel takes place between Gloucester's and Winchester's men. Gloucester's men beat back Winchester's men. The Mayor of London appears on the scene and reproves them for committing a breach of the peace. The quarrel being renewed the Mayor orders the riot act to be read, after which the conflicting parties disperse.

London Bridge.   III. i. 23.

> In that thou laid'st a trap to take my life,
> As well at London Bridge as at the Tower.
> [III. i. 22–23.]

The famous old bridge across the Thames. Brooke says : " Gloucester's third charge against Winchester, as reported by the chroniclers, was that he had put men at arms and archers in ambush at the Southwark end of London Bridge, with intent to slay the Protector if he attempted to pass that way to the young king at Eltham."

Item 3 of the Articles of Accusation says : " My sayde Lord of Winchester, vntruely and agaynst the kinges peace, to the entent to trouble my sayde Lorde of Gloucester goyng to the king, purposing his death in case that he had gone that way, set men of armes and Archers at the ende of London bridge next Southwarke : and in forbarring of the kings high way, let drawe the cheyne of the Stulpes there, and set vp Pypes and Hardels, in maner and forme of Bulwarkes ; and set men in Chambers, Sellers, and Windowes, with Bowes and arrowes and other weapons, to the entent to bring to finall destruction my sayde Lorde of Gloucesters person, as well as of those that then should come with him."

London.   The Palace.

The Scene of Act V., Scene i   There are two events here, separated by a considerable interval. The first is the intervention of the pope and the emperor Sigismund to secure a reconciliation between England and France ; and the second is, that the Earl of Armagnac—who had recently quarrelled with his kinsman, Charles of France— had offered his daughter in marriage with Henry, together with a large dowry. Henry accepts the proposed alliance. Beaufort, in cardinal's robes is made to appear in this scene, but this is not in accordance with history, as he was not in any way connected with the marriage arrangements

of Henry. Cf. Grafton's *Chronicle*, The XIIJ. Yere, 1434, vol. I., pp. 602–603.

London.   The Parliament House.

The Scene of Act III., Scene i. [The historical place of this scene was Leicester where Parliament assembled in 1426.] It opens with a dispute between Winchester and Gloucester, which, on the king's entreaty, supported by the Earl of Warwick, is brought to a close. A petition is then presented to the king by Warwick, which Gloucester supports, and Somerset opposes, urging his majesty to restore to Plantagenet his father's titles and estates, and the king creates him Duke of York. Preparations are then made for Henry's departure to Paris to be crowned king of France.

London.   The Royal Palace.

The Scene of Act V., Scene v. Suffolk having given Henry a brilliant account of Margaret of Anjou's virtues, Henry asks Gloucester, as Lord Protector, to give his consent to the marriage, and York reminds him that he is already betrothed to the daughter of the Earl of Armagnac. [According to Rapin the English Government grew cold with respect to the match, when Armagnac had been stripped of his territories by the French king. *See* Earl of Armagnac.] An argument ensues between Gloucester and Suffolk. Suffolk considers an earl's daughter is unworthy to be Henry's queen, and when Gloucester remarks that Margaret of Anjou is scarcely more, Suffolk tells Henry that Margaret's father is a king,—the king of Naples and of Jerusalem. This so works on the imagination of the king that he gives Suffolk orders to cross over to France and conduct Margaret to England, to be " crown'd King Henry's faithful and anointed queen," and the play closes with Suffolk triumphantly announcing that he has prevailed :

> Margaret shall not be queen, and rule the king ;
> But I will rule both her, the king, and realm.

Cf. Grafton's *Chronicle*, The XXIIJ. Yere, 1443, vol. I., pp. 623–625.

London.   The Temple Garden.

The Scene of Act II., Scene iv. Here were plucked the red and white roses which formed the badges of Lancaster and York respectively.

[There does not, however, appear to be any historical foundation for this story.] *See* Temple Garden.

Lord Cromwell of Wingfield. IV. vii. 66.

One of Lord Talbot's titles. *See* Earl of Washford.

Lord Furnival of Sheffield. IV. vii. 66.

One of Lord Talbot's titles. Talbot held the barony of Furnival through his wife Maud Neville, whose mother was Joan Furnival. Burke says that " having married Maud, eldest daughter and co-heir of Thomas Nevil, Lord Furnival, had been summoned to parliament in 1409, as ' Johannes Talbot de Furnyvall.' "

Long Hungerford. I. i. 146.

Sir Walter Hungerford. Was present at the battle of Agincourt, but no mention of him is made by Holinshed in the account of the battle· Taken prisoner at the battle of Patay on the 18th of June, 1429. He was appointed Lieutenant of Cherbourg in 1418 in place of Lord Grey, and was Steward of the Household in the beginning of the reign of Henry VI., and afterwards Lord Treasurer.

Lord of Falconbridge. IV. vii. 67.

See Earl of Washford.

Lord Ponton de Santrailles. I. iv. 28.

> The Duke of Bedford had a prisoner
> Called the brave Lord Ponton de Santrailles ;
> For him I was exchang'd and ransomed. [I. iv. 27–29.]

A French captain who was taken prisoner in 1431 at Beauvais. Talbot was captured at Patay in June, 1429, and was not released until 1433.

Lord Scales. I. i. 146.

Thomas, seventh Lord Scales. Taken prisoner at the battle of Patay, 18th June, 1429. As Governor of the Tower of London he appears in the *Dramatis Personæ* in the *Second Part of King Henry the Sixth*, and notes on his character will be found in that play.

Lord Strange of Blackmere. IV. vii. 65.

One of Lord Talbot's titles. French says that

Talbot was born at Blackmere, near Whitchurch. *See* Earl of Washford.

Lords.

Lord Talbot, afterwards Earl of Shrewsbury. I. i. 106, 107, 108, 121, 128, 138, 141 ; I. ii. 14 ; I. iv. p.23, 23, 89 ; I. v. p.1, 13 ; II. i. p.8, 28, 34, 46, 79 ; II. ii. p.1, 22, 35, 37 ; II. iii. p.11, 12, 15, 28, 31, 45, 61, 66, 73 ; III. ii. p.36, 37, p.41, 57, 59, 72, 76, 90, 107, 108, p.115, 118, 130 ; III. iii. 5, 20, p.31, 31, 64, 84 ; III. iv. p.1, 13, 26 ; IV. i. p.1, 68 ; IV. ii. p.1, 3, 30, 55 ; IV. iii. 5, 12, 19, 23, 25, 34, 37, 39 ; IV. iv. 2, 5, 9, 13, 28, 37, 44, 45 ; IV. v. p.1, 3, 16 ; IV. vi. p.1, 2, 24, 46, 51, 53 ; IV. vii. p.1, 21, 35, 61, 64, 77, 87, 96 ; V. ii. 16.

Shakespeare presents in Talbot the finest character in this play, and as we follow his actions we find him to be an example of a brave, patriotic soldier, willing to fight to the last for his country, daring anything, and never daunted.

The arrival of his son displays a new light on his character, he is now shown as an ideal father, devoted to his son, and anxious only for his safety, regardless of the extreme danger he himself is in.

The death of Talbot is an episode exquisitely portrayed and may be described as the most appealing moment in the play, which is otherwise taken up with ' wars and rumours of wars ' and party strife within the kingdom.

On studying Talbot's part in the play we can say that here is a man to whom party strife means nothing, his country and its welfare are all that matter to him, and to his death he does his utmost to uphold its honour and traditions.

He is a fearless fighter, holding his enemies in terror even of his name, and as a soldier once exclaims :

> The cry of Talbot serves me for a sword ;
> For I have loaden me with many spoils,
> Using no other weapon but his name. [II. i. 79–81.]

The Countess of Auvergne matches her cunning against him, endeavouring to trap him by inviting him to her castle, but his shrewdness enables him to construe her intentions and he turns the tables on her by calling in his men just when she appears to have succeeded in her plot, after having jested :

> I am but shadow of myself :
> You are deceiv'd, my substance is not here ;
> For what you see is but the smallest part
> And least proportion of humanity.
> I tell you, madam, were the whole frame here,
> It is of such a spacious lofty pitch,
> Your roof were not sufficient to contain it.
> [II. iii. 49–55.]

and exclaims triumphantly :

> How say you, madam ? are you now persuaded
> That Talbot is but shadow of himself ?
> These are his substance, sinews, arms, and strength,
> [II. iii. 60–62 .]

Now another trait in his character is revealed, he does not make her his prisoner, or become enraged at the trick which she has endeavoured to play on him, but merely says :

> Be not dismayed, fair lady ; nor misconster
> The mind of Talbot as you did mistake
> The outward composition of his body.
> What you have done hath not offended me :
> No other satisfaction do I crave,
> But only, with your patience, that we may
> Taste of your wine, and see what cates you have :
> For soldiers' stomachs always serve them well.
> [II. iii. 72–79.]

Talbot appears in many exciting scenes of battle, and his victories far outweigh his losses. His many honours are learned when Sir Henry Lucy seeks him on the battlefield :

> But where 's the great Alcides of the field,
> Valiant Lord Talbot, Earl of Shrewsbury ?
> Created, for his rare success in arms,
> Great Earl of Washford, Waterford, and Valence ;
> Lord Talbot of Goodrig and Urchinfield,
> Lord Strange of Blackmere, Lord Verdun of Alton,
> Lord Cromwell of Wingfield, Lord Furnival of Sheffield,
> The thrice-victorious Lord of Falconbridge ;
> Knight of the noble order of Saint George,
> Worthy Saint Michael and the Golden Fleece ;
> Great marshal to Henry the Sixth
> Of all his wars within the realm of France ?
> [IV. vii. 60–71.]

The English are all proud of Talbot, whatever their personal feelings may be, and the French as unanimously hate him, and the dauphin expresses the latters' feeling of relief at his death in the words :

> All will be ours now bloody Talbot's slain. [IV. vii. 96.]

[This is the renowned captain, Sir John Talbot, whose ancestor, Richard de Talbot, came in with the Conqueror, and from whom lineally descended Gilbert Talbot, summoned to Parliament, 4 Edward III., 1330, as Baron Talbot, and his grandson, of the same name, third Lord Talbot, married Petronilla Butler, daughter of James, first Earl of Ormonde by his wife, Eleanor de Bohun, a granddaughter of Edward the First, and was father of Richard, fourth Lord Talbot, who by his wife Ankaret, daughter of John, fourth Lord Strange of Blackmere, had four sons, the eldest of whom, Sir Gilbert Talbot, K.G., one of the heroes of Agincourt, was fifth lord, and the second son, Sir John Talbot, is the character in this play, who became sixth Lord Talbot, at the death of his brother Gilbert in 1419.　His career was a series of successes against the French until he was defeated by their great heroine, Joan of Arc, at Pataye, in 1429, when he was taken prisoner.　This affair is mentioned in the first scene, although that opens with the funeral of Henry V., which was in 1422.　Talbot was detained captive four years, and was exchanged for a famous French leader, who is named in the play,—" The brave Lord Ponton de Santrailles," the very same knight who had taken Lord Talbot prisoner at Pataye.　His creation as Earl of Shrewsbury was in 1442, although placed much earlier in the play, where in Act III., Scene iv., the king says to him,— " We here create thee Earl of Shrewsbury, And in our coronation take your place " ; but that ceremony occurred in Paris in 1431.

This great soldier's name was used by the French women to quiet their unruly children, as Southey says, in *Joan of Arc,*—" Talbot, at whose dread name the froward child Clings mute and trembling to his nurse's breast."　This effect upon children is alluded to in the play by the Countess of Auvergne, when she fancies that Talbot is in her power, and she taunts him with the meanness of his stature, Act II., Scene iii. " Is this the Talbot so much fear'd abroad, That with his name the mothers still'd their babes ? "

After taking Bordeaux he was killed, when more than eighty years of age, with his son, " valiant John," at Castillon, July 7, 1453, long *after* Joan of Arc had suffered her cruel fate, although in the play her death is placed after that of the Talbots.　Most writers place the death of the great captain as July 20th, but the 7th is the date which was recorded on his monument at Whitechurch, co. Salop.　" Orate pro anima prænobolis domini, domini Johannis

Talbot quondam Comitis Salopiæ, domini Furnivall, domini Verdon, domini Strange de Blackmere, & Mareschelli Franciæ, qui obiit in bello apud Burdews vij Julii, MCCCCLIII." *Buswell.* The great Talbot was born at Blackmere, which derives its name from one of the three fine lakes in the neighbourhood of Whitechurch.

The Earl of Shrewsbury married first, Maud Nevill, eldest daughter of Thomas, fifth Lord Furnival, by whom he had three sons : (1) Thomas, *ob. vitâ patris ;* (2) John ; (3) Sir Christopher Talbot ; the two latter were slain at Northampton, July 10, 1460, fighting for the house of Lancaster. The second son, John Talbot, succeeded his father as second earl, and from his second son, Sir Gilbert Talbot of Grafton, descended the later Earls of Shrewsbury, and also the Earls Talbot, both which titles are now united in Sir Gilbert's lineal descendants. The character of this play married secondly, Margaret Beauchamp, by whom he had one daughter, Joan, married to James, sixth Lord Berkeley, and three sons, John, Sir Humphrey, and Sir Lewis ; his eldest son by this marriage is the " valiant " John Talbot, a character in this play.]

[The famous sword of Talbot, alluded to by Fuller in his *Worthies,* as having " good steel within, and bad Latin without," is no longer in existence. Camden states that " it was found not long since in the river of Dordon, and sould by a peasant to an amorer of Bordeaux." A portrait of Talbot was long preserved in a castle built by him in France, in which he is represented with his drawn sword, on the blade of which is engraved :

> Sum Talboti miiii⁴ xliii
> Pro Vincere Inimico Meo.

This date is ten years before the great captain's death. The picture was engraved as early as the year 1584, in *The True Portraits and Lives of Illustrious Men,* written by André Thevet. French.]

Lord Verdun of Alton. IV. vii. 65.

One of Lord Talbot's titles. *See* Earl of Washford.

Machiavel. V. iv. 74.

An allusion to Machiavel a crafty Italian statesman and historian, born at Florence ; was secretary of the Florentine Republic, 1498–1512. He was opposed to the restoration of the Medici family, and on return of the banished Medici in 1512 was deprived of office, imprisoned and put to the torture on suspicion of conspiring against Giovanni de Medici. The allusion is an anachronism as Machiavel's *Il Principe* was not published until 1513. There are in Elizabethan literature many references to Machiavel as a type of wickedness.

Mahomet. I. ii. 140.

Was Mahomet inspired with a dove ? [I. ii. 140.]

An allusion to the dove which fled from Mahomet's ear. The training of this dove to feed from his ear was an artifice to delude his followers into the belief that he was inspired by the Holy Ghost. Cf. Raleigh's *History of the World.* " *Mahomet* had a dove, which he used to feed with wheat out of his ear ; which dove, when it was hungry, lighted on Mahomet's shoulder, and thrust its bill in to find its breakfast ; Mahomet persuading the rude and simple Arabians, that it was the Holy Ghost that gave him advice," and Scot's *Discovery of Witchcraft,* XII. xv., " or *Mahomet's* Pigeon, which would refort unto him, being in the midſt of his Camp, and pick a Peaſe out of his ear ; in ſuch ſort that many of the people thought that the Holy-Ghoſt came and told him a tale in his ear : the ſame Pigeon alſo brought him a ſcroll, wherein was written *Rex eſto,* and laid the ſame in his neck." Cf. France. *King Henry the Fourth*—Part ii, p. 587.

Maine. IV. iii. 45.

An old province of France. Mentioned here as being lost to England.

Maine. V. iii. 154.

Reignier is willing for his daughter Margaret to marry Henry conditionally upon his being allowed to " Enjoy his own, the country Maine and Anjou, Free from oppression or the stroke of war."

Margaret, Daughter to Reignier, afterwards married to King Henry. V. iii. p.45, 51, 82, 89, 141, 174, 175 ; V. v. 2, 24, 36, 67, 76, 78, 89.

The Duke of Suffolk captures Margaret in the

battle before Angiers, and inquiring her name, is told :

> Margaret my name ; and daughter to a king,
> The King of Naples, whosoe'er thou art. [V. iii. 51–52.]

She asks ' What ransom must I pay before I pass ? ' and Suffolk, after first considering if he shall make love to her himself, offers her her freedom if she will consent to be Henry's queen. " An if my father please, I am content," she replies, and Suffolk sounds a parley in answer to which Reignier, Margaret's father, appears on the walls, and agrees to Suffolk's terms in the words :

> Since thou dost deign to woo her little worth
> To be the princely bride of such a lord,
> Upon condition I may quietly
> Enjoy mine own, the country Maine and Anjou,
> Free from oppression or the stroke of war,
> My daughter shall be Henry's, if he please.
> [V. iii. 151–156.]

Suffolk prepares to depart for England to arrange the match with Henry and Margaret says :

> a true unspotted heart,
> Never yet taint with love, I send the king.
> [V. iii. 182–183.]

Margaret does not appear again, but we hear Suffolk's flattering description of her to Henry, and the king consents to marry her, much to Suffolk's satisfaction, for he remarks :

> Margaret shall now be queen and rule the king ;
> But I will rule both her, the king, and realm.
> [V. v. 107–108.]

[Miss Strickland observes : " The history of Margaret of Anjou from her cradle to the tomb, is a tissue of the most striking vicissitudes, and replete with events of more powerful interest than are to be found in the imaginary career of any heroine or romance."

She was the daughter of Reignier, Duke of Anjou, and was born March 23, 1429 ; married by proxy in 1445 to Henry VI., and crowned queen at Westminster the same year.

" She may be said virtually to have governed England and to have been the leader of the Lancastrian party ; for all that was done both in the government of the country, and in the management of the campaign against the Yorkists, was done under her directions." *Irving edition.* Her history, however, belongs to the next part of the play.]

[Queen Margaret is also a character in the *Second Part of King Henry the Sixth* (q.v.).]

Mars. I. ii. 1.

> Mars his true moving, even as in the heavens
> So in the earth, to this day is not known. [I. ii. 1–2.]

Previous to Kepler's work on Mars, published in 1609, the movements of the planet Mars were —owing to its irregular course—very puzzling to astronomers. Cf. Nash's *Preface to Gabriel Harvey's Hunt is up,* 1596 : " You are as ignorant in the true movings of my muse, as the astronomers are in the true movings of Mars. which to this day they could never attain to."

Master-Gunner of Orleans, and his son. I. iv. p.1, p.57.

The gunner puts his son in charge of a gun on the walls of Orleans, telling him that it has been trained on a gate occupied by the English spies. He leaves him with instructions to watch carefully and fetch him if he should see any movement on the part of the enemy, but the boy makes up his mind that he will use the gun himself if the opportunity arises.

> Father, I warrant you ; take you no care ;
> I 'll never trouble you if I may spy them.
> [I. iv. 21–22.]

[According to tradition, Maître Jean was the Master-Gunner of Orleans at this time. See *Life of Joan of Arc,* by T. J. Serle.]

Mayor of London. I. iii. p.57, 59, 86 ; III. i. p.76.

A skirmish is in progress between the followers of the Duke of Gloucester and the Bishop of Winchester, when the Lord Mayor and his officers appear. The Mayor reproves the nobles :

> Fie, lords ! that you, being supreme magistrates,
> Thus contumeliously should break the peace !
> [I. iii. 57–58.]

whereupon they both declare the reasons for their quarrel and the fight is renewed.

At this the Lord Mayor causes the Riot Act to be read, and the dissenting nobles depart with threats of future revenge, while the Mayor, giving orders to his men to see that the coast is cleared, remarks on leaving :

> Good God ! these nobles should such stomachs bear ;
> I myself fight not once in forty year. [I. iii. 90–91.]

He again appears before the King in the Parliament House declaring :

O ! my good lords, and virtuous Henry,
Pity the city of London, pity us.
The bishop and the Duke of Gloucester's men,
Forbidden late to carry any weapon,
Have fill'd their pockets full of pebble stones ;
And banding themselves in contrary parts,
Do pelt so fast at one another's pate,
That many have their giddy brains knock'd out :
Our windows are broke down in every street,
And we for fear compell'd to shut our shops.
[III. i. 76–85.]

and ultimately the disturbance is quelled.

[This is the first time that this important functionary is introduced in Shakespeare's plays. The events in Act I., Scene iii., and Act III., Scene i., both really occurred in 1425, during the time that the Lord Mayor was John Coventry, citizen and mercer ; and it is recorded in history that he behaved manfully on the occasions, and put the Bishop of Winchester's faction to flight. The title of " Lord Mayor " was first allowed 28 Edward III., 1354. In Act I , Scene iii , the stage direction in the Folio of 1623 reads,— " *Enter in the hurly burly the Maior of London, and his officers* " ; among whom no doubt the sheriffs would appear ; these in 1425 were William Milred and John Brockle, who became Mayor in 1433. *Stow.*]

Mayor of London's Officers. I. iii. p.57.

See *under* Mayor of London.

Memphis. I. vi. 22.

See Rhodopes.

Men in tawny coats. I. iii. p. 29, p.57.

The tawny coat was the livery of an apparitor, or officer who serves the process of an ecclesiastical court. Stow describes the Bishop of London as " attended on by a goodly company of gentlemen in tawny coats." Hart (*Arden edition*) quotes from Harington's *Brief View of the Church*, 1608 : " Doctor Whitegyte was made Bishop of Worcester . . . though the revenew of that be not very great, yet this custom was to come to the Parliament very well attended, which was a fashion the Queen liked exceeding well. It happened one day Bishop Elmer of London, meeting this Bishop with such an orderly troop of Tawny Coats, and demanding

of him how he could keep so many men, he answered it was by reason he kept so few women."

Messengers. I. i. p.57, p.89, p.103 ; I. iv. p. 100 ; II. ii. p.34 ; II. iii. p.11 ; IV. iii. p.1.

Minotaurs. V. iii. 189.

The Minotaur was a fabled monster, half-man, half-bull, confined in the famous labyrinth in Crete.

Monmouth. III. i. 198.

That Henry born at Monmouth should win all,
[III. i. 198.]

See *Extract* 27 from Holinshed.

Mortimer's Keepers. II. v. p.1.

The warders deputed to attend on Mortimer, Earl of March, during his imprisonment in the Tower.

One of them tells Mortimer that his nephew has been summoned at his request :

Richard Plantagenet, my lord, will come :
We sent unto the Temple, unto his chamber ;
The answer was return'd that he will come.
[II. v. 18–20.]

Mortimers. II. v. 91.

Thus the Mortimers,
In whom the title rested, were suppress'd.
[II. v. 91–92.]

= The Family of Mortimer.

Nemesis. IV. vii. 78.

The Greek goddess of retribution.

Nero. I. iv. 95.

and like thee, Nero,
Play on the lute, beholding the towns burn :
[I. iv. 95–96.]

Roman emperor, A.D. 54–68, a tyrant and a man of infamous character. He claimed to be an actor, poet and musician, which led him to appear publicly in the theatre. One of the chief events of his reign was the burning of Rome in A.D. 64 which is said to have been the result of his orders, and during the conflagration the story relates that he watched the scene from his palace where he amused himself by singing to his lyre. The senate having declared him an enemy to his country the tyrant committed suicide A.D. 68.

Nestor-like. II. v. 6.

Nestor-like aged in an age of care,　　　[II. v. 6.]

Nestor King of Pylos in Greece the oldest and most experienced of all the Greek Generals who went to the siege of Troy ; hence the name is symbolical of an old and wise man.

Officers. II. ii. p.11 ; III. ii. p.103 ; IV. iv. p.1.

Old Shepherd, Father to Joan la Pucelle. V. iv. p.2.

On his entry with Joan before York and Warwick he exclaims :

Ah, Joan, this kills thy father's heart outright !
Have I sought every country far and near,
And, now it is my chance to find thee out,
Must I behold thy timeless cruel death ?
Ah, Joan, sweet daughter Joan, I 'll die with thee !
　　　　　　　　　　　　[V. iv. 2–6.]

She denies him despite his earnest entreaties to her :

Peasant, avaunt ! You have suborn'd this man,
Of purpose to obscure my noble birth. [V. iv. 21–22.]

Finally he exclaims :

Dost thou deny thy father, cursed drab ?
O ! burn her, burn her ; hanging is too good.
　　　　　　　　　　　　[V. iv. 32–33.]
and thus leaves her to her fate.

[The parents of the French heroine were Jacques D'Arc, a small farmer, and his wife, Isabel Romee, who lived at Domrémy, a village near Vaucouleurs, on the Marches of Bar, Champagne. *De Serres, etc.* Charles VI., in grateful testimony of Joan's vast services, granted a patent of nobility to her father, brothers, and their descendants, even in the female line ; they were to take the sur-name of De Lys, and the village of Domrémy was to be for ever free from taxation. Montaigne, writing in 1580, saw the house in which Joan's father lived : " Ses descendans furent ennoblés par faveur du Roi, et nous monstrerent les Armes que le Roi leur donna, qui sont, D'Azur a une espée droite couronnée et poignée d'or, et deux fleurs de lis d'or au coté de ladite espée." *Voyages.* The last male descendant of the family is said to have died in 1761, namely Coulombe De Lys, Prior of Coutras. *French.*]

Olivers and Rowlands. I. ii. 30.

Froissart, a countryman of ours, records,
England all Olivers and Rowlands bred
During the time Edward the Third did reign.
　　　　　　　　　　　　[I. ii. 29–31.]

These were two of the most famous in the list of Charlemagne's twelve Peers ; and their exploits are rendered so ridiculously and equally extravagant by the old romancers, that from thence arose that saying amongst our plain and sensible ancestors, of giving one a Rowland for his Oliver, to signify the matching one incredible lie with another. Walsh says : " The etymologies connecting the proverb with Charles II., General Monk, and Oliver Cromwell are wholly unworthy of credit, for even Shakespeare alludes to it : ' England all Olivers and Rolands bred,' and Edward Hall, the historian, a century before Shakespeare, writes,—But to have a Roland to resist an Oliver he sent solempne ambassadors to the kyng of Englande [Henry VI.], offeryng hym hys doughter in mariage."

Orleans. I. i. 60.

Guienne, Champaigne, Rheims, Orleans,
Paris, Guysors, Poictiers, all are quite lost.
　　　　　　　　　　　　[I. i. 60–61.]

Unhistorical. Orleans was not an English possession.

Orleans. I. i. 111.

The tenth of August last this dreadful lord,
Retiring from the siege of Orleans,　[I. i. 110–111.]

These lines are descriptive of the battle of Patay fought on the 18th of June, 1429. Orleans was not an English possession at this time.

Orleans. I. i. 157.

So you had need ; for Orleans is besieg'd ;
The English army is grown weak and faint ;
　　　　　　　　　　　　[I. i. 157–158.]

Orleans. I. ii. 6.

At pleasure here we lie near Orleans ;　[I. ii. 6.]

Grafton says : " After this in the Moneth of September, he [Salisbury] layde his siege on the one side of the water of Loyre and besieged the towne of Orleaunce, before whose comming, the Bastard of Orleaunce, and the Byshop of the Citie and a great number of Scottes hering of the Erles intent, made divers fortifications about the towne, and destroyed the suburbs, in the which were xij. Parishe Churches, and foure orders of Friers. They cut also downe all the Vines, trees and bushes within fiue leagues of the towne, so that the Englishe men should haue neyther comfort, refuge, nor succour."

Orleans. I. ii. 125, 148.

Shall we give over Orleans, or no ? [I. ii. 125.]

Unhistorical. Orleans was not in possession of the English.

Orleans. I. iv. 1, 59 ; I. v. 14, 36 ; II. ii. 15.

Orleans. I. vi. 2, 9.

Rescued is Orleans from the English. [I. vi. 2.]
Recover'd is the town of Orleans : [I. vi. 9.]

The account of the raising of the siege of Orleans, which took place in the year before the battle of Patay, is thus given by Hall : " Then the erle of Suffolke, the Lorde Talbot, the Lorde Scales, and other capitaines, assembled together, where causes wer shewed, that it was bothe necessary and conueniente either to leue the siege for euer, or to deferre it till another tyme, more luckey and conuenient. And to the intent that thei should not seme either to flie or to be driuen from the siege by their enemies, they determined to leaue their fortresses and Bastyles, and to assemble in the plain feld and there to abyde all the daie, abidying the out-comming and battaile of their enemies. This conclusion taken, was accordyngly executed. The Frenchmen, weried with the last bickerying, held in their heddes and durste not once appere : and so thei set fire in their lodgynges, and departed in good ordre of battail from Orleaunce." *Irving edition.* See also *A Collection of the Chronicles and Ancient Histories of Great Britain, now called England,* by John De Waurin, Lord of Forestel.

Orleans. Within the Town.

The Scene of Act II., Scene ii We are within the city of Orleans. Talbot orders the body of Salisbury to be buried in the " middle centre of this cursed town." [This is unhistorical, Salisbury's body was brought to England, and buried at Bissam.] A messenger enters and tells Talbot that the Countess of Auvergne wishes him to visit her.

Paris. I. i. 61, 65.

Mentioned here as being lost to England.

Paris. III. ii. 128.

And then depart to Paris to the king ; [III. ii. 128.]

Henry VI was at this time in Paris, having arrived there some time previously to be crowned King of France.

Paris. IV. vii. 95.

And now to Paris, in this conquering vein :
[IV. vii. 95.]

Having defeated and slain Talbot, Charles suggests that they now proceed " to Paris, in this conquering vein : All will be ours now bloody Talbot's slain."

Paris. V. ii. 4.

Then march to Paris, royal Charles of France,
And keep not back your powers in dalliance.
[V. ii. 4-5.]

News having been received that the Parisians have revolted against the English, Alençon suggests that the army shall march to Paris. " The Parisians, and in especiall the Master of the Hales, and some of the Vniuersitie, and Michael Laillier, and many notable Burgesses of the towne (which euer with an Englishe countenaunce couered a French heart) perceiuyng the weakenesse of the Englishemen, and the force and strength of the Frenchmen, signifiyng to the Frenche Captaynes theyr mindes and intentes, willed them to come with all diligence, to receiue so rich a pray, to them without any difficultie offered and geuen. The Constable delaiyng no tyme, came with his power, and lodged by the Charterhouse : and the Lorde Lisleadam, approchyng the walles, shewed to the Citizens, a Charter, sealed with the great seale of king Charles, by the which he had pardoned them their offences, and graunted them all the olde liberties and auncient priuileges, so they would hereafter be to him obedient, true and seruiceable : which thing to them declared, they ranne about the towne criyng : Saint Denise, liue king Charles. The Englishe men perceiuying this, determined to kepe the gate of Saint Denise, but they were deceyued, for the Cheynes were drawen in euery strete, & women and children cast downe stones, and scaldyng water on the Englishe mens heades, and the Citizens persecuted them, from strete to strete, and frome lane to lane, and slue & hurt, diuers and many of them. The Bishop of Tyrwine, Chauncelor there for king Henry, and the Lord Willoughby, and Sir Simon Moruier, tooke great paine to appease the people, and represse their fury : but when they saw that all auayled not, they withdrew themselues, to the Bastile of Saint Anthony, which Fortresse they had well vittayled and furnished, wyth men and municions.

Whiles this rumor was in the towne, the Erle of Dumoys and other scaled the walles, and some passed the riuer by Boates, and opened the gate of Saint Iames, at the which the constable with his Banner displayed entered, at whose entrie the Parisians were verye glad, and made great ioy. The Bishop and the Lorde Willoughby, with their small companie, defended their fortresse, tenne dayes, loking for ayde, but when they sawe that no comfort appered, they yelded their fortresse, so that they and theirs with certain baggage, might peaceably returne to Roan, which desire was to them gaūted. Then as they departed, the Parisians rayled, mocked, and taunted the English men, with the most spitefull wordes, and shamefull termes, that could be inuented or deuised : so that all men may apparauntly perceyue, that their heartes neuer thought, as their tongues vttered." *Grafton.*

Paris. V. v. 104.

> As did the youthful Paris once to Greece ;
> With hope to find the like event in love,
> [V. v. 104–105.]

A legendary prince of Troy, son of Priam and Hecuba. His abduction of Helen, wife of Menelaus, king of Sparta led to the Trojan war. Suffolk here compares himself with Paris going into Greece, but hopes he will be more successful.

Paris. A Hall of State.

The Scene of Act IV., Scene i. The coronation of Henry as King of France. Fastolfe enters with a letter from the Duke of Burgundy announcing his defection from the English side. Talbot reproaches Fastolfe for his cowardice at the battle of Patay, and tears the ensignia of the Garter from his knee. Fastolfe is banished by Henry. A quarrel arises between Vernon—a

white rose adherent—and Basset—a red rose adherent—and Henry, supported by Gloucester and Warwick appeals for reconciliation. Henry dons a red rose, and to allay any suspicion appoints York as " Regent in these parts of France " and tells Somerset " to unite his troops of horsemen with his bands of foot." [There are several inaccuracies in this scene. Henry was crowned King of France in 1431, long before the death of the Duke of Bedford, or the defection of the Duke of Burgundy who was present at the coronation. Gloucester was not present at the ceremony being in England at the time, and the Duke of Exeter—represented as being present— had been dead some five years.]

Paris. The Palace.

The Scene of Act III., Scene iv. Talbot presents himself before Henry, who creates him Earl of Shrewsbury. [This scene is purelȳ imaginary. The coronation of Henry took place in 1431, Talbot at this time being a prisoner in the hands of the French. Talbot was created Earl of Shrewsbury in 1442.]

Paris-ward. III. iii. 30.

Towards Paris to attend the coronation of King Henry the Sixth.

Patay. IV. i. 19.

A village in the Department of Loiret, France, near Orleans, where the French under Dunois and Joan of Arc defeated the English under Talbot on the 18th June, 1429. The Folios have ' Poictiers.' Steevens says : " The battle of Poictiers was fought in the year 1357, the 31st of King Edward III., and the scene now lies in the 7th year of the reign of King Henry VI., *viz.* 1428. This blunder may be justly imputed to the players or transcribers ; nor can we very well justify ourselves for permitting it to continue so long, as it was too glaring to have escaped an attentive reader. The action of which Shakespeare is now speaking, happened (according to Holinshed) ' neere unto a village in Beausse called Pataie ' which we should read, instead of Poictiers."

Pendragon. III. ii. 95.

> for once I read
> That stout Pendragon in his litter sick
> Came to the field and vanquished his foes. [III. ii. 94–96.]

The father of King Arthur, and brother of Aurelius Ambrosianus. Geoffrey of Monmouth attributes this heroic deed to Pendragon, but according to Holinshed it was " Aurelius Ambrosius, euen *sicke* as he was, caused himselfe to be caried forth *in a litter ;* with whose presence his people were so incouraged, that, incountring with the Saxons, they wan the victorie, . . . " Harding gives the following account of Uther Pendragon :

For which the king ordain'd a horse-litter
To bear him so then unto Verolame,
Where Ocea lay, and Oysa also in fear,
That saint Albones now hight of noble fame,
Bet down the walles ; but to him forth they came,
Where in battayle Ocea and Oysa were slayn.
The fielde he had, and thereof was full fayne.

Percies. II. v. 67.

= The House of Northumberland.

Phœnix. IV. vii. 93.

I 'll bear them hence ; and from their ashes shall be rear'd
A phœnix that shall make all France afeard.
[IV. vii. 92-93.]

See *As You Like It*, page 51.

Picardy. II. i. 10.

Walloon, and Picardy, are friends to us, [II. i. 10.]

An old province of France. Picardy was friendly to the English on account of the Duke of Burgundy being an ally of Henry VI.

Plantagenet. I. iv. 95.

Plantagenet, I will ; [I. iv. 95.]

Salisbury's real name was Montacute.

Plantagenet. II. v. 52.

Poictiers. I. i. 61 ; IV. iii. 45.

Mentioned as being lost to England, but this is unhistorical as Poictiers was not an English possession at this period of history.

Pope. V. i. 1.

Have you perused the letters from the pope,
The Emperor, and the Earl of Armagnac ? [V. i. 1-2.]

" This probably refers to two attempts on the part of the pope to put an end to the disastrous war between England and France. One was made a year after the king's coronation. Hall, after describing the terrible sufferings which the war inflicted upon both nations, says ' for whiche cause Euginye the fourth, beyng bishopp of Rome, intendying to bryng this cruel warre, to a friendly peace, sent his Legate, called Nicolas, Cardinall of the holy crosse, into Fraunce to thentent to make an amitie, and a concord betwene the two princes and their realmes. This wise cardinall, came first to the Frenche kyng, and after to the duke of Bedford beyng at Paris ; exhortyng concord, and persuadyng vnitie, shewyng, declaryng and arguyng, peace to be moste honorable and more profitafle to christian princes, then mortall warre, or vncharitable discencion ' ; and further on he says : " The Cardinal beyng in vtter dispaire, of cōcludyng a peace betwene the two realmes, (least he should seme to departe empty of all thynges, for the whiche he had taken so muche trauaill) desired a truce for sixe yeres to come, which request, as it was to him, by bothe parties hardly graunted, so was it of the Frenchmen, sone and lightly broken, after his returne.' " *Irving edition.* See also under Earl of Armagnac and Emperor

Porter, A. II. iii. p.1, p.32.

Servitor to the Countess of Auvergne, who assists his mistress in making Talbot a prisoner.

Pucelle or puzzel, dolphin or dogfish. I. iv. 107.

Pucelle = Joan of Arc. *Puzzel* = a dirty wench or a drab. *Dolphin* = Dauphin. *Dogfish* = a term of reproach. In *Robert Laneham's Letter : describing a part of the entertainment unto Queen Elizabeth at the castle of Kenilworth in* 1575 we read : " Then, three pretty puzels az bright az a breast of bacon, of a thirtie yéere old a pées, that carried thrée speciall spisecakes of a bushell of wheat, (they had it by meazure oout of my Lord's backhouse,) before the Bryde " :

Reignier, Duke of Anjou, and titular King of Naples. I. i. 94 ; I. ii. p.1, p.22, 61, 65 ; I. iv. p.1, 12 ; II. i. p.39 ; III. ii. p. 41 ; IV. iv. 26 ; V. ii. p.1 ; V. iii, 52, 94, p.131, 131, p.146, 148, 163, 169 ; V. iv. 78, p.116 ; V. v. 47.

Is on the side of the Dauphin, and is with him

on most of his appearances. He takes the place of Charles when Joan La Pucelle first appears and attempts to deceive her, but is unsuccessful, for she says :

> Reignier, is 't thou that thinkest to beguile me ?
> Where is the Dauphin ? Come, come from behind ;
> [I. ii. 65–66.]

His daughter is taken prisoner by Suffolk and Reignier appears on the walls of Angiers in reply to a parley sounded by the former.

Suffolk asks his consent for Margaret to be married to Henry, and Reignier replies that :

> Upon condition I may quietly
> Enjoy mine own, the country Maine and Anjou,
> Free from oppression or the stroke of war,
> My daughter shall be Henry's, if he please.
> [V. iii. 153–156.]

To this Suffolk agrees and hastens away to obtain Henry's consent to the marriage.

[This prince, usually called " le bon Roi René," was second son of Louis II., King of both the Sicilies, Naples, Arragon, and Jerusalem, Duke of Calabria and Anjou, and Count of Provence. René married Isabella, daughter and heir of Charles, Duke of Lorraine, at whose death his brother Anthony de Vaudemont claimed that province, and a war ensued between them and his nephew René, who was taken prisoner in 1429 at the battle of Balgenville, after fighting valiantly, and he was not released until 1438 ; he is therefore out of place in some of the scenes of the play. His eldest daughter Yolande married her cousin Ferrand, son of Anthony de Vaudemont ; his youngest Margaret of Anjou became the Queen of Henry VI. Of this alliance Holinshed remarks : " the Earl of Suffolk condescended that the duchy of Anjou, and the county of Maine, should be delivered to the king, the bride's father, demanding for the marriage neither penny nor farthing." The " good King René," who was an excellent poet and musician, died in 1480 ; his character is well sketched by Sir Walter Scott in *Anne of Geierstein*.]

Rheims. I. i. 69.

> Guienne, Champaigne, Rheims, Orleans,
> Paris, Guysors, Poictiers, all are quite lost.
> [I. i. 60–61.]

An ancient city of France. Rheims was held by the English for a period of nine years, being lost in 1429 or seven years later than represented in the play.

Rheims. I. i. 92.

> The Dauphin Charles is crowned king in Rheims ;
> [I. i. 92.]

An anachronism. Charles VII was crowned on the 12th July, 1429, or seven years after the death of King Henry the Fifth. Charles had, however, been crowned at Poitiers in 1422.

Rhodopes. I. vi. 22.

A celebrated Greek courtezan, a Thracian by birth, said to have been a fellow-slave of Æsop. She was taken to Egypt where Psammetichus, king of Egypt fell in love with her and ransomed her. She is supposed to have erected the costly pyramid near Memphis.

Richard, Earl of Cambridge. II. iv. 90.

> Was not thy father, Richard, Earl of Cambridge,
> For treason executed in our late king's days ?
> [II. iv. 90–91.]

See Earl of Cambridge.

Richard Plantagenet, Son of Richard, late Earl of Cambridge, afterwards Duke of York. II. iv. p.1, 36, 64, 69, 74, 77, 114, 119 ; II. v. 18, 26, p.33, 34, 36, 41 ; III. i. p.1, 61, 150, 154, 159, 160, 163, 165, 171, 172, 173, 174, 177, 178 ; III... iv. p.1, 30, 36 ; IV. i. p.1, 96, 109, 114, 154, 162, 174, 182 ; IV. iii. p.1, 22 ; IV. iv. 2, 9, 15, 29, 30 ; IV. vii. 33 ; V. iii. p.30 ; V. iv. p.1 ; V. iv. 113.

Makes his first appearance with Somerset and other nobles in the Temple Garden, and invites his followers to pluck a white rose, saying :

> Since you are tongue-tied and so loath to speak,
> In dumb significants proclaim your thoughts ;
> Let him that is a true-born gentleman
> And stands upon the honour of his birth,
> If he suppose that I have pleaded truth,
> From off this brier pluck a white rose with me.
> [II. iv. 25–30.]

An altercation ensues between Plantagenet and Somerset, in which the latter refers to him as a ' yeoman.' Warwick interposes with :

> Now, by God's will, thou wrong'st him, Somerset ;
> His grandfather was Lionel, Duke of Clarence,
> Third son to the third Edward, King of England.
> Spring crestless yeomen from so deep a root ?
> [II. iv. 81–85.]

and later Warwick exclaims :

> And here I prophesy : this brawl to-day,
> Grown to this faction in the Temple garden,
> Shall send between the red rose and the white
> A thousand souls to death and deadly night.
>
> [II. iv. 124–127.]

which later only proved to be too true.

Plantagenet visits his aged uncle in prison in the Tower, and hears from him his claim to the English crown, and Richard thereupon declares his intention of claiming his titles and forwarding his rights without delay, saying :

> And for those wrongs, those bitter injuries,
> Which Somerset hath offer'd to my house,
> I doubt not but with honour to redress ;
> And therefore haste I to the parliament,
> Either to be restored to my blood,
> Or make my ill the advantage of my good.
>
> [II. v. 124–129.]

We next find him before Parliament, and Warwick presents a scroll bearing Plantagenet's claims, to which Henry replies :

> our pleasure is
> That Richard be restored to his blood. [III. i. 158–159.]

Plantagenet, having sworn allegiance, the King bids him,

> Stoop then and set your knee against my foot ;
> And, in reguerdon of that duty done,
> I girt thee with the valiant sword of York :
> Rise, Richard, like a true Plantagenet,
> And rise created princely Duke of York.
>
> [III. i. 169–173.]

Later, when Henry is crowned in Paris, he endeavours to pacify the opposing leaders, but York is annoyed that the king should show his inclinations by putting on a red rose, remarking :

> but yet I like it not
> In that he wears the badge of Somerset. [IV. i. 175–177.]

In Gascony, York is awaiting reinforcements which he says were promised him by Somerset, and he cannot go to the aid of Lord Talbot at Bordeaux on account of their non-arrival.

Sir Thomas Lucy, who has come to seek his aid on behalf of Talbot, exclaims :

> Thus, while the vulture of sedition
> Feeds in the bosom of such great commanders,
> Sleeping neglection doth betray to loss
> The conquest of our scarce cold conqueror,
> That everliving man of memory,
> Henry the Fifth : whiles they each other cross,
> Lives, honours, lands, and all hurry to loss.
>
> [IV. iii. 47–53.]

It is York who captures Joan La Pucelle in the fight before Angiers, and as he takes her, he exclaims :

> Damsel of France, I think I have you fast :   [V. ii. 30.]

and on her saying :

> I prithee, give me leave to curse awhile.   [V. iii. 43.]

retorts with :

> Curse, miscreant, when thou comest to the stake.
> [V. iii. 44.]

Joan is brought before York for trial, and is condemned to be burned at the stake, York remarking as she is led away :

> Break thou in pieces and consume to ashes,
> Thou foul accursed minister of hell !   [V. iv. 92–93.]

Throughout the play the civil strife is brewing, and we are led to anticipate by the occasional outbursts during York's appearances, the bitter struggle which is about to ensue.

[This Prince was the only son of Richard of *Coningsburg* and Anne Mortimer. As his father had been attainted it was necessary that he should be restored in blood, thus Somerset taunts him,—" Till thou art restor'd, thou art a yeoman." This taint was removed in the Parliament held April, 30, 1425, Act III., Scene i., where King Henry, though only in his fourth year, is made to express his pleasure,—" That Richard be restored to his blood."

He was at the same time created Duke of York, the title which had been held by his uncle, who fell at Agincourt, and by his grandfather, Edmund of *Langley*. In 8 Henry VI., he was made Constable of England during the absence of the Duke of Bedford in France ; and at the death in 1435 of that warlike prince succeeded him as Regent of France, conjointly with the Duke of Somerset. The introduction, however, of the Duke of York in Act IV., Scene i, is premature, as he did not arrive in France until 1436. He had been elected a K.G. in 1433. As his sons, although really too young for such scenes, are introduced in the *Second Part of King Henry the Sixth*, it will be most in place here to notice the marriage of Richard Plantagenet with Cicely Nevill, the " Rose of Raby," an alliance which brought to the House of York the powerful support of her father's numerous family connections. By this lady, youngest child of Ralph, Earl of Westmoreland, the Duke of York had, besides four sons who died young, four other sons, and four daughters ; of the latter, (1) Anne, married first Henry Holland, second and last Duke of Exeter, a character in the *Third Part of King Henry the Sixth*, and secondly Sir Thomas St. Leger, and their daughter Anne married Sir George Manners, ancestor of the Dukes of Rutland ; (2) Elizabeth, married to John de la Pole, son of the Duke of Suffolk in this play ; (3) Margaret, who became the third wife, in 1467, of Charles the *Bold*, Duke of Burgundy ; (4) Ursula, who died young.

The surviving sons were (1) Edward, born in 1442, afterwards king ; (2) Edmund, Earl of Rutland, born 1443 ; (3) George, the ill-fated Clarence, born 1449 ; and (4) Richard, *youngest* of all the eight sons, born 1452, afterwards king. The eldest of all, Henry, born 1441, died quite young ; William, the fourth son, born 1447 ; John, fifth son, born 1448 ; and Thomas, born before Richard, all died in their infancy. *French.*]

[Richard Plantagenet, Duke of York, is also a character in the *Second Part of King Henry the Sixth.*]

Richard, Edward's son. II. v. 64.

= King Richard the Second.

Roan. I. i. 65.

= Rouen. The ancient capital of Normandy. It was an English possession from 1419 to 1449, when it was captured by the French under Charles VII. It was, during the occupation by the English, that Joan of Arc was, in 1431, burned alive as a witch in the square of the city, called in memory of her " Place de la Pucelle "

Roan. III. ii. 1, 11, 17, 19, 27, 91, 124, 133.

= Rouen, a former capital of Normandy. The story of its capture in Act III., Scene ii., is entirely fictitious. It was an English possession from 1419 to 1449.

Roan. III. iii. 2.

= Rouen.

Rome. I. ii. 56.

Rowlands. I. ii. 30.

See Olivers.

Saint Denis. I. vi. 28 ; III. ii. 18.

The Patron Saint of France.

Saint George. IV. ii. 55 ; IV. vi. 1.

The Patron Saint of England. The name of the leader coupled with St. George, was the usual battle-cry. See *Extract* 18 from Holinshed.

Saint George. IV. vii. 68.

A distinguished Order of Knighthood.

Saint George's feast. I. i. 154.

Bonfires in France forthwith I am to make,
To keep our great Saint George's feast withal :
[I. i. 153–155.]

The 23rd of April, and traditionally the day of Shakespeare's birth and death.

Saint Katharine's churchyard. I. ii. 100.

See Touraine.

Saint Martin's summer. I. ii. 131.

Expect Saint Martin's summer, halcyon's days. [I. ii. 131]

Summer in late autumn. St. Martin's day (November 11th) was associated with the halcyon days, *i.e.* calm weather after storms. Joan here infers that " after the winter of misfortune will come the summer of success."

Saint Michael. IV. vii. 69.

A distinguished Order of Knighthood. The attribution by the dramatist of the Order of St. Michael to Talbot is an anachronism, as the French Order was not instituted until some sixteen years after his death.

Saint Philip's daughters. I. ii. 143.

Nor yet Saint Philip's daughters were like thee.
[I. ii. 143]

The four daughters of Philip ' that did prophesy.' See *Acts* xxi 9.

Samsons. I. ii. 33.

In Biblical history, Samson was a Judge of Israel, endowed with supernatural strength.

Scout. V. ii. p.8.

= A soldier who is sent out to gain information and bring in tidings of the movements of the enemy. The scout here enters and reports that the English army will presently give battle.

Scythian Tomyris. II. iii. 6.

See Cyrus.

Sennet. III. i. p.187 ; V. i. p.1.

A call on a trumpet for entrance or exit on the stage. It occurs chiefly in the stage directions of old plays. The word is now obsolete.

Servingmen in blue coats. I. iii. p.1 ; III. i. p.86.

Servants or attendants. Boswell-Stone in his *Shakespeare's Holinshed* quotes from Fabian : " Fabian says that the Parliament which witnessed the reconciliation of Gloucester and Winchester was clepyd of the Comon people the Parlyament of Battes : the cause was, for Proclamacyons were made, that men shulde leue theyr Swerdes & other wepeyns in theyr Innys, the people toke great battes & stauys in theyr neckes, and so folowed theyr lordes and maisters vnto the Parlyament. And whan that wepyn was Inhybyted theym, then they toke stonys & plummettes of lede, & trussyd them secretly in theyr sleuys & bosomys."

Sibyls. I. ii. 56.

Exceeding the nine sibyls of old Rome ;   [I. ii. 56]

Supposed to be an allusion to the nine sibylline books, offered by the Cumæan Sibyl to King Tarquin. The number of all the sibyls is variously stated at from two to twelve, and contained predictions of our Saviour, and taught the doctrine of the resurrection, the last judgment and hell torments. They are supposed to be work of some Christian, and clouded with the heathen and Jewish superstitions, on purpose to disguise the true intent of the author.

Sir John Fastolfe. I. i. 131 ; I. iv. 35 ; III. ii. p.103, 104 ; IV. i. p.9.

Is represented as being cowardly, for we first meet him fleeing from the battle before Rouen, saying in answer to a Captain's query :

Whither away ! To save myself by flight ;
We are like to have the overthrow again.
                                [III. ii. 105–106.]

and on being asked, What ! will you fly, and leave Lord Talbot ? replies :

                                        Ay,
All the Talbots in the world, to save my life.
                                [III. ii. 108.]

to which the captain ejaculates :

Cowardly knight ! ill fortune follow thee ! [III. ii. 109.]

On his next appearance at Henry's coronation in Paris, Talbot exclaims :

I vow'd, base knight, when I did meet thee next,
To tear the garter from thy craven's leg ; [*Plucks it off.*
                                [IV. i. 14–15.]

and tells of how he forsook him when hard pressed at the battle of Patay.

Henry is amazed at these revelations, and banishes him forthwith, taking away his title of knight,

Stain to thy countrymen ! thou hear'st thy doom ;
Be packing therefore, thou that wast a knight :
Henceforth we banish thee on pain of death.
                                [IV. i. 45–47.]

[This knight, son of John Fastolfe and his wife, Mary, daughter of Nicholas Parke, was born on St. Leonard's day, November 6, 1380, at Great Yarmouth, co. Norfolk ; he was educated as a page in the household of Thomas Mowbray, the " Duke of Norfolk" in *King Richard II.* and afterwards attended Prince Thomas of Lancaster to Ireland in 1405. He accompanied Henry V. in his expedition to France in 1415, with a retinue of " 10 lances and 30 archers," and served at Harfleur, where he was left to form part of the garrison, so that he could not be at Agincourt, as often asserted. After the death of Henry V., the regent, Bedford, made Fastolfe Grand Master of his household, and Seneschal of Normandy ; and in 1423 appointed him Governor of Anjou and Maine. He took several strong places from the French, and in 1426 was rewarded with the honour of a K.G. In 1428 he achieved his great exploit, called " the Battle of the Herrings," before Orleans ; but in the next year he was defeated at Pataye by Joan of Arc, who caused such a panic among the English that they fled in dismay, and Monstrelet mentions the behaviour of Sir John Fastolfe and his companions, who " had not dismounted, and to save their lives, they with many other knights set off full gallop." This blot on his escutcheon is alluded to in Act III., Scene ii. According to the same French author, the knight was reproached by

Bedford for having thus fled " before a stroke
was given," and was by him deprived of his
" Garter," which was restored in after time.
This degradation is, in the play, performed by
Talbot, who pronounces a glowing eulogy on
" this most honourable order," Act IV., Scene i.
The Duke of Bedford continued his favour to
Fastolfe, appointed him Governor of Caen, and
named him as one of the executors to his ·vill.
He remained in France under the Duke of York,
who rewarded his services with a pension, and
he at length retired from active service in 1440,
to his estate at Caistor, near Great Yarmouth,
where the remains exist of the stately castellated
brick mansion, which he built from the proceeds,
as alleged, of the ransom of John II., Duke of
Alençon (son of the prince killed at Agincourt),
who was taken prisoner by Fastolfe, at the battle
of Verneuil, in 1424. Sir John died at Caistor,
Nov. 6, 1459. *French.*]

The *Paston Letters* contain many interesting
accounts of his private life.

Sir Thomas Gargrave.   I. iv. p.23, 63, 88.

Appears on the turrets before Orleans during
the siege, accompanied by Lords Salisbury and
Talbot, Sir William Glansdale and others.

They are debating as to which is the best
place for the next assault on the town when a
shot is heard, and Gargrave and Salisbury fall
to the ground mortally wounded. Cf. Grafton's
Chronicle, vol. I, V.J. Yere, p. 577.

[The fatal shot which struck down the Earl of
Salisbury, before Orleans, also wounded one of
his chief officers, Sir Thomas Gargrave, who died
from the blow within two days. The family
was seated at Gargrave and Nosthall, in the
West Riding of Yorkshire, of which county
another Thomas Gargrave was sheriff 7 and 11
Queen Elizabeth ; and afterwards the office was
filled by members of the family. *Monasticon.*]

Sir William Glansdale.   I. iv. p.23, 63.

Appears before the walls of Orleans during
the siege with the Lords Salisbury and Talbot,
and Sir Thomas Gargrave.

He expresses the opinion that the best place
for the next assault on the town is ' here, at the
bulwark of the bridge.'

[This knight is called by French historians

" Glacidas," by Stow " Gladesdale " ; and
Southey, in his *Joan of Arc*, speaks of him, under
the name of " Gladdisdale," as—

> " the last of all his race,
> Slain in a foreign land, and doom'd to share
> A common grave."

This alludes to his fate at Orleans, where he
perished by the breaking of a draw-bridge, struck
by a cannon-shot, when he was drowned, with
many knights and soldiers, who sank in the
Loire, oppressed by the weight of their armour.
Shakespeare makes Glansdale, in the only·words
spoken by him, take up his position at the place
whence he was to assault the town, and where he
lost his life, Act I., Scene iv.

Serle calls this character " a stern rude soldier
of fortune," which may account for the com-
piler of these memoirs not finding the name of
Glansdale, or Glasdale, as he is sometimes styled,
in any Ordinary of Arms : and in answer to an
enquiry, Mr. J. W. Papworth says—" I believe
you will not find anywhere, except by the
merest accident, a coat for Gladdesdale or Glansdale. *French.*]

Sir William Lucy.   IV. iii. p.17 ; IV. iv.
10, p.12, 12 ; IV. vii. p.51.

First appears on the plains in Gascony before
the Duke of York as a messenger to ask for help
for Lord Talbot at Bordeaux.

York says he cannot send any reinforcements
as he himself cannot obtain much-needed aid
from Somerset. At this Lucy remarks :

> Thus, while the vulture of sedition
> Feeds in the bosom of such great commanders,
> Sleeping neglection doth betray to loss
> The conquest of our scarce cold conqueror,
> That ever living man of memory,
> Henry the Fifth : whiles they each other cross,
> Lives, honours, lands, and all hurry to loss.
> [IV. iii. 47–53.]

He then rushes to Somerset to appeal for help
and meeting him and being asked ' Whither were
you sent ? ' cries :

> Whither, my lord ? from bought and sold Lord Talbot ;
> [IV. iv. 13.]

and begs him to put aside personal disputes in
the national cause :

> Let not your private discord keep away
> The levied succours that should lend him aid,
> [IV. iv. 22–23.]

Somerset then blames York for the plight Talbot is in, and Lucy, in a rage, exclaims :

> The fraud of England, not the force of France,
> Hath now entrapp'd the noble-minded Talbot.
> Never to England shall he bear his life,
> But dies, betray'd to fortune by your strife.
> [IV. iv. 36–39.]

and declaring that help must now be too late, departs.

Lucy next appears on the battlefield near Bordeaux, and demands from the Dauphin which force has won the day, and begs permission to " know what prisoners thou hast ta'en, And to survey the bodies of the dead.'

Enquiring :

> But where 's the great Alcides of the field,
> Valiant Lord Talbot, Earl of Shrewsbury ?
> [IV. vii. 60–61.]

to be told by La Pucelle that :

> Him that thou magnifiest with all these titles
> Stinking and fly-blown lies here at our feet.
> [IV. vii. 75–76.]

Lucy exclaims, ' Is Talbot slain ? ' and asks to take the bodies away, saying as this is done :

> I 'll bear them hence ; but from their ashes shall be rear'd
> A phœnix that shall make all France afeard.
> [IV. vii. 92–93.]

[This character, says French, may be intended for Sir William Lucy, knight, of Charlecote, co. Warwick, whereof he was sheriff, in the 14, 28, and 31 of Henry VI., and who died 6 Edward IV., 1466. His family had been seated at Charlecote from the time of King John, when Walter de Cherlcote's son, William, assumed the name of Lucy, 1 Henry III., 1216. From him descended in the seventh generation Thomas Lucy, who died 3 Henry V., and by his wife Alesia, sister and heir of William Hugford of Hugford, co. Salop, was father of Sir William Lucy, supposed to be the character in this play, who married Alianor, daughter of Reginald Lord Grey de Ruthyn ; and their lineal descendant, Sir Thomas Lucy, is the person celebrated by Shakespeare to all time as " Justice Shallow," placing him however in the reign of Henry IV., though he flourished in that of Queen Elizabeth.]

Soldiers, English. I. v. p.15 ; II. i. p.8, p.78 ; II. iii. p.60 ; III. iii. p.31 ; III. iv. p.1 ; IV. iii. p.1 ; IV. iv. p.1 ; IV. vii. p.18.

Soldiers, French. I. ii. p.1 ; I. vi. p.1 ; III. ii. p.1, p.18 ; III. iii. p.1, p.33 ; IV. vii. p.33 ; V. ii. p.1.

Talbot, a Talbot ! I. i. 128 ; II. iii. 15.

Hart (*Arden edition*) says : " The name of the leader, coupled with St. George, was the usual battle-cry. So in Grafton : ' And in lyke manner the Duke of Bedford, encouraged his people, and foorthwith they gave the onset upon their enimies, crying, Saint George, Bedford.' And again : ' the Englishe men came out . . . by the gate of the towne, cryeng Saint George, Salisburie : and set on their enimies both before and behinde.' And again : ' About sixe of the clock in the morning they issued out of the Castell, cryeng Saint George, Talbot,' " See *Extract* 18 from Holinshed.

Temple garden. II. iv. 125.

The garden of the Temple Hall, London. Here were plucked the red and white roses which formed the badges of the Houses of Lancaster and York respectively, during the Wars of the Roses. There is, however, no historical foundation for this scene.

" The *Red Rose* of Lancaster was, says Camden, the accepted badge of Edmund Plantagenet, second son of Henry III., and of the first Duke of Lancaster, surnamed Crouchback. It was also the cognizance of John of Gaunt, second Duke of Lancaster, in virtue of his wife, who was godchild of Edmund Crouchback, and his sole heir ; and, in later times, of the Richmonds. . . . The *White Rose* was not first adopted by the Yorkists during the contest for the crown, as Shakespeare says. It was an hereditary cognizance of the House of York, and had been borne by them ever since the title was first created. It was adopted by the Jacobites as an emblem of the Pretender, because his adherents were obliged to abet him *sub rosa* (in secret). Cecily Nevill, wife of Richard, Duke of York, and mother of Edward IV. and Richard III., was known as *The White Rose of Raby.*" *Brewer.*

Temple hall. II. iv. 3 ; II. v. 18.

> Within the Temple hall we were too loud ;
> The garden here is more convenient. [II. iv. 3–4.]

The Hall of the Middle Temple, London, one of the Inns of Court. The dispute carried on in the Temple garden was begun here.

Thomas Beaufort, Duke of Exeter, Great-uncle to the King. I. i. p.1 ; III. i. p.1, 200 ; III. iv. p.1 ; IV. i. p.1 ; V. i. p.1 ; V. v. p.1.

Exeter is fully aware of the growing dissension between the Lancastrians and Yorkists, and foresees that as a result of the inevitable climax Henry will be overthrown.

This is shown by his soliloquy after Richard Plantagenet has been created Duke of York :

> This late dissension grown betwixt the peers
> Burns under feigned ashes of forg'd love,
> And will at last break out into a flame :
> As fester'd members rot but by degree,
> Till bones and flesh and sinews fall away,
> So will this base and envious discord breed.
> And now I fear that fatal prophecy
> Which in the time of Henry, nam'd the Fifth,
> Was in the mouth of every sucking babe,—
> That Henry, born at Monmouth should win all ;
> And Henry, born at Windsor should lose all :
>   [III. i. 189–199.]

and finally he expresses his own desire to escape the catastrophe :

> Which is so plain that Exeter doth wish
> His days may finish ere that hapless time.
>   [III. i. 200–201.]

He does not take much part in the action of the play, but remains in the background, only coming forward to remind those about him of what has been prophesied as in the above instance, and as when he sees Winchester has realised his ambition and been made cardinal, he remarks :

> What ! is my lord of Winchester install'd,
> And call'd unto a cardinal's degree ?
> Then I perceive that will be verified
> Henry the Fifth did sometime prophesy :
> " If once he come to be a cardinal,
> He 'll make his cap co-equal with the crown."
>   [V. i. 28–33.]

[The Duke of Exeter is a character in the last play, but as he died December 27th, 1426, his introduction is out of place in many of the scenes, as in Act IV., Scene i., his nephew's coronation in Paris, which did not occur till 1431. Thomas Beaufort had no issue by his wife Margaret, daughter of Sir Thomas Nevill, and his large estates passed to his nephew, John Beaufort, first Duke of Somerset. *French.*]

Tomyris. II. iii. 6.

See Cyrus

Touraine. I. ii. 100.

Although alluded to here as a ' town ' Touraine was an ancient province of France   On her way to the court of Charles, Joan of Arc found in Saint Katharine's churchyard among " a great deal of old iron " a sword engraved " with five flower-de-luces on each side " with which she afterwards fought.

Tours. IV. iii. 45.

Capital of the government of Touraine. Mentioned here as being lost to England.

Tower. I. i. 167.

= The Tower of London.

Tower. I. iii. 1, 61, 67.

> I am come to survey the Tower this day ;   [I. iii. 1.]

The Tower of London. See *Extracts* 11 *and* 12 from Holinshed.

Tower. III. i. 23.

> In that thou laid'st a trap to take my life,
> As well at London Bridge as at the Tower.
>   [III. i. 23–23.]

The reference is to the incidents in Act I., Scene iii., where Gloucester demands entrance to the Tower.

Tower of London.

The Scene of Act II , Scene v. Shows Mortimer a prisoner in the Tower. Richard Plantagenet who now appears is Mortimer's nephew, his father—the Earl of Cambridge—having married Mortimer's sister. Mortimer explains to Plantagenet the reason his father was executed, and tells him he is heir to the throne, but counsels caution. After bidding his nephew farewell, Mortimer passes away. [There is some confusion in this scene. Edmund Mortimer, Earl of March, having served in the French wars of Henry V., died at his home in Ireland in 1425 at an early age. His uncle, Sir John Mortimer was imprisoned in the Tower and executed. The dramatist was doubtless misled by the historians of his time.]

Trojan. V. v. 106.

See Paris, V. v. 104.

Two Sentinels. II. i. p.1.

A sentinel is a soldier whose duty it is to watch or guard an army or camp from surprises

Urchinfield. IV. vii. 64.

See Earl of Washford.

Venus. I. ii. 144.

> Bright star of Venus, fall'n down on the earth,
> [I. ii. 144.]

The goddess of love. She is called Urania, *i.e.* Celestial, because she was believed to have dropped from heaven at Paphos in the isle of Cyprus.

Vernon, of the White-Rose or York Faction. II. iv. p.1, 44, 128 ; III. iv. p.1 ; IV. i. p.78.

Appears in the Temple garden, and there shows his allegiance to Plantagenet by plucking a white rose, remarking :

> Then for the truth and plainness of the case,
> I pluck this pale and maiden blossom here,
> Giving my verdict on the white rose side. [II. iv. 46–48.]

after having first suggested that the party strongest in number by counting the roses plucked shall be declared to be in the right :

> Stay, lords and gentlemen, and pluck no more
> Till you conclude that he, upon whose side
> The fewest roses are cropp'd from the tree,
> Shall yield the other in the right opinion. [II. iv. 39–42.]

He has a heated argument with Basset in the palace in Paris, which nearly ends in bloodshed, Vernon striking his rival, and later the two appear before Henry, both claiming the right to a duel, and championed by their respective leaders.

Henry endeavours to quieten them but does not succeed in making more than a temporary truce between Plantagenet and Somerset.

[Courtenay says : " I presume that the person intended is Sir Richard Vernon, Speaker of the House of Commons in the Leicester Parliament, ancestor of Lord Vernon ; he died 1452." This character, therefore, was Sir Richard Vernon, of Haddon, Knight of the Shire of Derby in 1433. He married his cousin, Benedicta, daughter of William Ludlow, by whom he had a son, Sir William Vernon, Treasurer of Calais, and Constable of England for life, who died in 1467, and was succeeded by his son, Sir Henry Vernon, K.G., who was Governor and Treasurer to Prince Arthur, eldest son of Henry VII., and who by his wife Anne, daughter of John Talbot, second Earl of Shrewsbury, was father of Humphrey Vernon, whose second son, Thomas, was ancestor of the present Lord Vernon. In the east window of the chapel at Haddon, which was built by Sir Richard Vernon, there is an inscription,—" Orate pro animabus Ricardi Vernon militis et Benedictæ uxoris ejus, qui fecerunt istam capellam, A.D. 1427 " : Duke's *Shropshire*, under Tong, in which church there is a splendid effigy of Sir Richard Vernon, in armour, one of the finest examples of the kind ; it is given in Shaw's *Decor. of Mid. Ages. French.*]

Walloon. I. i. 137.

> A base Walloon, to win the Dauphin's grace,
> Thrust Talbot with a spear into the back ;
> [I. i 137–138.]

A people of mixed Teutonic and Celtic stock descended from the Belgæ of ancient Gaul. Talbot is here represented as having been stabbed in the back by ' a base Walloon.'

Walloon. II. i. 10.

> Walloon, and Picardy, are friends to us,   [II. i. 10.]

The ancient inhabitants of Artois, Hainault, Namur, Luxemburg and parts of Flanders and Brabant. Mentioned here as being friendly to the English.

Wardens of the Tower. I. iii.

Warders under Lieutenant Woodvile, who refuse Gloucester's men admission to the Tower.

Westminster Abbey.

The Scene of Act I., Scene i. The Play opens with the funeral of King Henry the Fifth. A succession of messengers enter, and announce the loss of Guienne, Champaigne, Rheims, Orleans, Paris, Guysors and Poictiers, the coronation of the Dauphin as Charles VII. and the defeat and capture of Lord Talbot at the siege of Orleans. [The anachronisms of this scene are manifold, as most of the events which are announced by the messengers took place many years afterwards. Courtenay says : " King Charles the Sixth did not die, nor did his son assume the title until October. Nor were the places enumerated lost at this time, or all at once ; indeed, the events of the war were for some time favourable to England. . . . Above all Talbot was not taken prisoner till the year 1429, when he was defeated at Patay."]

Winchester goose. I. iii. 53–54.

Winchester goose ! I cry, a rope ! a rope ! [I. iii. 53.]

Winchester was noted for its geese. *I cry, a rope ! a rope !* alludes to a cry which a parrot was taught to utter. Cf *Troilus and Cressida*, V. x. 55–56 : " It should be now, but that my fear is this, Some galled goose of Winchester would hiss."

Windsor. III. i. 199.

That Henry born at Windsor should lose all ;
[III. i. 199.]

See *Extract* 27 from Holinshed.

Wingfield. IV. vii. 66.

In Derbyshire. *See* Earl of Washford.

Woodvile, Lieutenant of the Tower. I. iii. p.15, 16, 22.

The Duke of Gloucester with his serving-men approaches the Tower of London and demands to be admitted when Woodvile appears within and informs Gloucester that :

I may not open ;
The Cardinal of Winchester forbids :   [I iii. 18–19]

This enrages the Duke who exclaims :

Faint-hearted Woodvile, prizest him 'fore me ?
[I. iii. 22.]

and one of his servants demands :

Open the gates unto the lord protector,
Or we 'll burst them open, if that you come not quickly.
[I. iii. 27–28.]

Winchester now appears with his men, and a skirmish takes place which is only brought to an end by the reading of the Riot Act.

[Richard de Widvill, or Woodvile, of a good Northamptonshire family, of whom several had served as sheriff, was 7 Henry IV., Governor of Northampton Castle ; he was afterwards one of the esquires of the body of Henry V., and subsequently became chamberlain and councillor to the Duke of Bedford, under whom he served in the French wars. In 3 Henry VI., he was appointed Constable of the Tower, he was therefore of higher rank than " Lieutenant," as he is styled in the play (and in the year 1424 Robert Scot was the Lieutenant) ; Woodvile was created a K.G., by Henry VI., and in 1448 Baron Rivers. Monstrelet calls him the handsomest man in all England. In 1436 he married the youthful widow of his patron the Duke of Bedford, Jacqueline of Luxembourg, by whom he had five sons and six daughters. The former were : (1) Sir Anthony Woodvile, who is the " Earl Rivers " in *King Richard III.* ; (2) Sir John Woodvile, who was slain with his father in 1469 ; (3) Lionel Woodvile, Bishop of Salisbury ; (4) Sir Edward Woodvile, K.G. ; (5) Sir Richard, afterwards third Earl Rivers, at whose death in 1491, without issue, the title became extinct.

Of the other children of Earl Rivers by the Duchess Jacqueline, Fuller says,—" Almost all our ancient nobility may be traced to his six daughters." These were : (1) Elizabeth, the wife first of Sir John Grey, afterwards Queen to Edward IV. ; (2) Margaret, who married Thomas Fitz-alan, sixteenth Earl of Arundel ; (3) Anne, thrice married, *viz.* to William Lord Bourchier, George Grey, Earl of Kent, and Sir Anthony Wingfield ; (4) Jacquetta, who married John Lord Strange ; (5) Mary, the wife of William Herbert, Earl of Huntingdon ; (6) Katharine, who married first Henry Stafford, Duke of Buckingham, secondly Jaspar Tudor, and thirdly Sir Richard Wingfield, K.G. Richard Woodvile was created Earl Rivers by his son-in-law, Edward IV., in 1466, and was beheaded by Robin of Riddesdale at Northampton, 1469. The Duchess Jacqueline died in 1472. *French.*]

APPENDIX I.

1. And suerlie the death of this king Charles caused alterations in France. For a great manie of the nobilitie, which before, either for feare of the English puissance, or for the loue of this king Charles, (whose authoritie they followed,) held on the English part, did now reuolt to the Dolphin ; with all indeuour to driue the English nation out of the French territories. Whereto they were the more earnestlie bent, and thought it a thing of greater facilitie, because of king Henries yoong yeares ; whome (because he was a child) they esteemed not, but with one consent reuolted from their sworne fealtie : . . .

2. But heere is one cheefe point to be noted, that either the disdeine amongest the cheefe peeres of the realme of England, (as yee haue heard,) or the negligence of the kings councell, (which did not foresee dangers to come,) was the losse of the whole dominion of France, betweene the riuers of Somme and Marne ; and, in especiall, of the noble citie of Paris. For where before, there were sent ouer thousands for defense of the holds and fortresses, now were sent hundreds, yea, and scores ; some rascals, and some not able to draw a bowe, or carrie a bill : . . .

3. The Dolphin, which lay the same time in the citie of Poitiers, after his fathers deceasse, caused himselfe to be proclaimed king of France, by the name of Charles the seuenth ; and, in good hope to recouer his patrimonie, with an haultie courage preparing war, assembled a great armie : and first the warre began by light skirmishes, but after it grew into maine battels.

4. Betweene twentie and three and twentie thousand men, . . . fought with the lord Talbot (who had with him not past six thousand men) neere vnto a village in Beausse called Pataie : at which battell the charge was giuen by the French so vpon a sudden, that the Englishmen had not leisure to put themselues in araie, after they had put vp their stakes before their archers ; so that there was no remedie but to fight at aduenture. This battell continued by the space of three long houres ; for the Englishmen, though they were ouerpressed with multitude of their enimies, yet they neuer fled backe one foot, till their capteine the lord Talbot was sore wounded at the backe, and so taken.

Then their hearts began to faint, and they fled ; in which flight were slaine about twelue hundred, and fortie taken, of whome the lord Talbot, the lord Scales, the lord Hungerford, & sir Thomas Rampston were cheefe. . . . From this battell departed without anie stroke striken sir Iohn Fastolfe ; the same yeare for his valiantnesse elected into the order of the garter.

5. [When Henry V. lay a-dying at Bois de Vincennes, he was visited by] the dukes of Bedford and Glocester, & the earles of Salisburie and Warwike, whome the king louinglie welcomed, and seemed glad of their presence.

Now, when he saw them pensife for his sicknesse and great danger of life wherein he presentlie laie, he, with manie graue, courteous, and pithie words, recomforted them the best he could ; and therewith exhorted them to be trustie and faithfull vnto his sonne, and to see that he might be well and vertuouslie brought vp. And, as concerning the rule and gouernance of his realms, during the minoritie and yoong yeares of his said sonne, he willed them to ioine togither in freendlie loue and concord, keeping continuall peace and amitie with the duke of Burgognie ; and neuer to make treatie with Charles that called himselfe Dolphin of Vienne, by the which anie part, either of the crowne of France, or of the duches of Normandie and Guien, may be lessened or diminished ; and further, that the duke of Orleance and the other princes should still remaine prisoners, till his sonne came to lawfull age ; least, returning home againe, they might kindle more fire in one daie than might be quenched in three.

He further aduised them, that if they thought it necessarie, that it should be good to haue his brother Humfreie duke of Glocester to be protector of England, during the nonage of his sonne, and his brother the duke of Bedford, with the helpe of the duke of Burgognie, to rule and to be regent of France ; commanding him with fire and sword to persecute the Dolphin, till he had either brought him to reason and obeisance, or else to driue and expell him out of the realme of France. . . .

---

1. *Shakespeare's Holinshed*, by W. G. Boswell-Stone.

The noble men present promised to obserue his precepts, and to performe his desires ; but their hearts were so pensife, and replenished with sorrow, that one could not for weeping behold an other.

6. The custodie of this yoong prince was appointed to Thomas duke of Excester, & to Henrie Beauford bishop of Winchester.

7. 2 Item, my said lord of Winchester, without the aduise and assent of my said lord of Glocester, or of the kings councell, purposed and disposed him to set hand on the kings person, and to haue remooued him from Eltham, the place that he was in, to Windsor, to the intent to put him in gouernance as him list.

THE SIEGE OF ORLEANS.

8. After the siege had continued full three weekes, the bastard of Orleance issued out of the gate of the bridge, and fought with the Englishmen ; but they receiued him with so fierce and terrible strokes, that he was with all his companie compelled to retire and flee backe into the citie. But the Englishmen followed so fast, in killing and taking of their enimies, that they entered with them. The bulworke of the bridge, with a great tower standing at the end of the same, was taken incontinentlie by the Englishmen, who behaued themselues right valiantlie vnder the conduct of their courageous capteine, as at this assault, so in diuerse skirmishes against the French ; partlie to keepe possession of that which Henrie the fift had by his magnanimitie & puissance atchiued, as also to inlarge the same. . . .

In this conflict, manie Frenchmen were taken, but more were slaine ; and the keeping of the tower and bulworke was committed to William Glasdale esquier. By the taking of this bridge the passage was stopped, that neither men nor vittels could go or come by that waie.

9. In time of this siege at Orleance (French stories saie) the first weeke of March 1428, vnto Charles the Dolphin, at Chinon, as he was in verie great care and studie how to wrestle against the English nation, by one Robert Badricourt, capteine of Vacouleur, (made after marshall of France by the Dolphins creation,) was caried a yoong wench of an eighteene yeeres old, called Ione Arc, by name of hir father (a sorie sheepheard) Iames of Arc, and Isabell hir mother ; brought vp poorelie in their trade of keeping cattell ; borne at Domprin (therefore reported by *Bale*, Ione Domprin) vpon Meuse in Lorraine, within the diocesse of Thoule. Of fauour was she counted likesome, of person stronglie made and manlie, of courage great, hardie, and stout withall ; an vnderstander of counsels though she was not at them ; great semblance of chastitie both of bodie and behauiour ; the name of Iesus in hir mouth about all hir businesses ; humble, obedient ; and fasting diuerse daies in the weeke. A person (as their bookes make hir) raised vp by power diuine, onelie for succour to the French estate then deepelie in distresse ; in whome, for planting a credit the rather, first the companie that toward the Dolphin did conduct hir, through places all dangerous, as holden by the English, (where she neuer was afore,) all the waie and by nightertale safelie did she lead : then at the Dolphins sending by hir assignement, from saint Katharins church of Fierbois in Touraine, (where she neuer had beene and knew not,) in a secret place there among old iron, appointed she hir sword to be sought out and brought hir, (that with fiue floure delices was grauen on both sides,) wherewith she fought and did manie slaughters by hir owne hands On warfar rode she in armour cap a pie & mustered as a man ; before hir an ensigne all white, wherin was Iesus Christ painted with a floure delice in his hand.

Unto the Dolphin into his gallerie when first she was brought ; and he, shadowing himselfe *behind*, setting other gaie lords before him to trie hir cunning, from all the companie, with a salutation, (that indeed marz all the matter,) she pickt him out alone ; who therevpon had hir to the end of the gallerie, where she held him an houre *in* secret and priuate *talke*, that of his priuie chamber was thought *verie long*, and therefore would haue broken it off ; but he made them a signe to let hir saie on. In which (among other), as likelie it was, she set out vnto him the singular feats (for sooth) giuen hir to vnderstand by reuelation diuine, that in vertue of that sword shee should atchiue ; which were, how with honor and victorie shee would raise the siege of Orleance, set him in state of the crowne of France, and driue the English out of the countrie, thereby he to inioie the kingdome alone. Heerevpon he hartened at full, appointed hir a sufficient armie with absolute power to lead them, and they obedientlie to doo as she bad them. Then fell she to worke, and first defeated, indeed, the siege at Orleance ; by and by incouraged him to crowne himselfe king of France at Reims, that a little before from the English she had woone. Thus after pursued she manie bold enterprises to our great displeasure a two yeare togither ; for the time she kept in state vntill she were taken and for heresie and witcherie burned ; as in particularities hereafter followeth.

10. [In 1425] fell a great diuision in the realme of England ; which of a sparkle was like to haue grown to a great flame. For whether the bishop of Winchester, called Henrie Beaufort, (sonne to Iohn duke of Lancaster by his third wife,) enuied the authoritie of Humfreie duke of

Glocester, protectour of the realme ; or whether the duke disdained at the riches and pompous estate of the bishop ; sure it is that the whole realme was troubled with them and their par-takers : . . .

CHARGES AGAINST WINCHESTER.

11.   1 First, whereas he, being protectour, and defendour of this land, desired the Tower to be opened to him, and to lodge him therein, Richard Wooduile esquier (hauing at that time the charge of the keeping of the Tower) refused his desire ; and kept the same Tower against him vndulie and against reason, by the commandement of my said lord of Winchester ;   . . .

12.   4 Item, my said lord of Glocester saith and affirmeth, that our souereigne lord, his brother, that was king Henrie the fift, told him on a time, (when our soueriegne lord, being prince, was lodged in the palace of Westminster, in the great chamber,) by the noise of a spaniell, there was on a night a man spied and taken behind a tapet of the said chamber ; the which man was deliuered to the earle of Arundell to be examined vpon the cause of his being there at that time ; the which so examined, at that time confessed that he was there by the stirring and procuring of my said lord of Winchester ; ordeined to haue slaine the said prince there in his bed : wherefore the said earle of Arundell let sacke him foorthwith, and drowned him in the Thames :

13.   And lykely it was to haue ensued great Effucyon of blode shortly therupon, ne had ben the discressyon of the Mayre, and his Brether, that exorted the people, by all Polytike meane, to kepe the kynges peas.

THE FRENCH WAR.

14.   Amongst other of the cheefest prisoners, that valiant capteine, Poton de Santrails, was one ; who without dalaie was exchanged for the lord Talbot, before taken prisoner at the battell of Pataie.

15.   [Bedford] appointed the earle of Suffolke to be his lieutenant and capteine of the siege ; and ioined with him the lord Scales, the lord Talbot, sir Iohn Fastolfe, and diuerse other right valiant capteins.

16.   In the tower that was taken at the bridge end (as before you haue heard) there was an high chamber, hauing a grate full of barres of iron, by the which a man might looke all the length of the bridge into the citie ; at which grate manie of the cheefe capteins stood manie times, viewing the citie, and deuising in what place it was best to giue the assault. They within the citie well perceiued this tooting hole, and laid a peece of ordinance directlie against the window.

It so chanced, that the nine and fiftith daie after the siege was laid, the earle of Salisburie, sir Thomas Gargraue, and William Glasdale, with diuerse other went into the said tower, and so into the high chamber, and looked out at the grate ; and, within a short space, the sonne of the maister-gunner, perceiuing men looking out at the window, tooke his match, (as his father had taught him ; who was gone downe to dinner,) and fired the gun ; the shot whereof brake and shiuered the iron barres of the grate, so that one of the same bars strake the earle so violentlie on the head, that it stroke awaie one of his eies, and the side of his cheeke. Sir Thomas Gargraue was likewise stricken, and died within two daies.

17.   [Joan] roade from Poictiers to Blois, and there found men of warre, vittels, and munition, readie to be conueied to Orleance.

Heere was it knowne that the Englishmen kept not so diligent watch as they had been accus-tomed to doo, and therefore this maid (with other French capteins) comming forward in the dead time of the night, and in a great raine and thunder, entred into the citie with all their vittels, artillerie, and other necessarie prouisions. The next daie the Englishmen boldlie assaulted the towne, but the Frenchmen defended the walles, so as no great feat worthie of memorie chanced that daie betwixt them, though the Frenchmen were amazed at the valiant attempt of the Englishmen : wheruppon the bastard of Orleance gaue knowledge to the duke of Alanson, in what danger the towne stood without his present helpe ; who, comming within two leagues of the citie, gaue knowledge to them within, that they should be readie the next daie to receiue him.

18.   [The English] withdrew without any tarriance into the castell, which standeth at the gate of saint Vincent, whereof was constable Thomas Gower esquier ; whither also fled manie Englishmen ; so as for vrging of the enimie, prease of the number, and lacke of vittels, they could not haue indured long : wherfore they priuilie sent a messenger to the lord Talbot, which then laie at Alanson, certifieng him in how hard a case they were. The lord Talbot, hearing these newes, like a carefull capteine, in all hast assembled togither about seuen hundred men ; & in the euening departed from Alanson, so as in the morning he came to a castell called Guierch, two miles from Mans, and there staied a while, till he had sent out Matthew Gough, as an espiall, to vnder-stand how the Frenchmen demeaned themselues.

Matthew Gough so well sped his businesse, that priuilie in the night he came into the castell, where he learned that the Frenchmen verie negligentlie vsed themselues, without taking heed to their watch, as though they had beene out of all danger : which well vnderstood, he returned againe, and within a mile of the citie met the lord Talbot, and the lord Scales, and opened vnto them all things, according to his credence.   The lords then, to make hast in the matter, (bicause the daie approched,) with all speed possible came to the posterne gate ; and, alighting from their horsses, about six of the clocke in the morning, they issued out of the castell, crieng, " *saint George ! Talbot !* "

    The Frenchmen, being thus suddenlie taken, were sore amazed ; in so much that some of them, being not out of their beds, got vp *in their shirts*, and lept *ouer the walles*   Other ran naked out of the gates to saue their liues, leauing all their apparell, horsses, armour, and riches behind them : none was hurt but such as resisted.

    19.   Lord Talbot, being both of noble birth, and of haultie courage, after his comming into France, obteined so manie glorious victories of his enimies, that his onelie name was & yet is dreadfull to the French nation ; ánd much renowned amongst all other people.
    20.   This earle was the man at that time, by whose wit, strength, and policie, the English name was much fearefull and terrible to the French nation ; which of himselfe might both appoint, command, and doo all things in manner at his pleasure ; in whose power (as it appeared after his death) a great part of the conquest consisted : for, surelie, he was a man both painefull, diligent, and readie to withstand all dangerous chances that were at hand, prompt in counsell, and of courage inuincible ; so that in no one man, men put more trust ; nor any singular person wan the harts so much of all men.
    21.   This man was to the French people a very *scorge* and a daily *terror ;* in so muche that as his person was fearfull and terrible to his aduersaries present, so his name and fame was spitefull and dreadfull to the common people absent ; in so much that women in Fraunce, to feare their yong children, would crye, " the Talbot commeth, the Talbot commeth ! "

    22.   The duke of Yorke, perceiuing his euill will, openlie dissembled what which he inwardlie minded, either of them working things to the others displeasure ; till, through malice and diuision betweene them, at length by mortall warre they were both consumed, with almost all their whole lines and o(spring.

    23.   During the same season. Edmund Mortimer, the last earle of March of that name, (which long time had beene restreined from his libertie, and finallie waxed lame,) deceassed without issue ; whose inheritance descended to the lord Richard Plantagenet, sonne and heire to Richard earle of Cambridge, beheaded (as before yee haue heard) at the towne of Southampton.

    24.   [In 1425, when Gloucester and Winchester were at open strife,] the citizens of London were faine to keepe dailie and nightlie watches, *and to shut* vp their *shops, for feare* of what which was doubted to haue insued of their [Gloucester's and Winchester's] assembling of people about them.
    25.   That the said lord of Winchester should haue these words that follow vnto my said lord of·Glocester : " My lord of Glocester, I haue conceiued to my great heauinesse, that yee should " haue receiued by diuerse reports that I should haue purposed and imagined against your person, " honor, and estate, in diuers maners ; for the which yee haue taken against me great displeasure : " Sir, I take God to my witnesse, that what reports so euer haue beene to you of me, peraduenture " of such as haue had no great affection to me, God forgiue it them !) I neuer imagined, ne pur- " posed anie thing that might be hindering or preiudice to your person, honor, or estate ; and " therefore I praie you, that yee be vnto me good lord from this time foorth : for, by my will, I " gaue neuer other occasion, nor purpose not to doo hereafter, by the grace of God."   The which words so by him said, it was decreed by the same arbitrators, that my lord of Glocester should answer and saie : " Faire vncle, sith yee declare you such a man as yee saie, I am right glad that " it is so, and for such a man I take you."   And when this was doone, it was decreed by the same arbitrators, that euerie each of my lord of Glocester, and Winchester, should take either other by the hand, in the presence of the king and all the parlement, in signe and token of good loue & accord ; the which was doone, and the parlement adiorned till after Easter.
    26.   But, when the great fier of this dissention, betweene these two noble personages, was thus by the arbitrators (to their knowledge and iudgement) vtterlie quenched out, and laid vnder boord, all other controuersies betweene other lords, (taking part with the one partie or the other,) were appeased, and brought to concord ; so that for ioy the king caused a solemne fest to be kept on Whitsundaie ; on which daie he created Richard Plantagenet, sonne and heire to the erle of Cambridge, (whome his father at Southampton had put to death, as before yee haue heard,) duke of Yorke ; not foreseeing that this preferment should be his destruction, nor that his seed should of his generation be the extreame end and finall conclusion.

    27.   This yeare [1421] at Windsore, on the daie of saint Nicholas [Dec. 6], in December, the queene was deliuered of a sonne named Henrie ; whose godfathers were Iohn duke of Bedford,

and Henrie bishop of Winchester, and Iaquet, or (as the Frenchmen called hir) Iaqueline, of Bauier, countesse of Holland, was his godmother. The king, being certified hereof, as he laie at siege before Meaux, gaue God thanks ; in that it had pleased his diuiue prouidence to send him a sonne, which might succeed in his crowne and scepter. But, when he heard reported the place of his natiuitie, were it that he [had been] warned by some prophesie, or had some foreknowledge, or else iudged himselfe of his sonnes fortune, he said vnto the lord Fitz Hugh, his trustie chamberlaine, these words : " My lord, I *Henrie, borne at Monmouth*, shall small time reigne, & much get ; " and *Henrie, borne at Windsore*, shall long reigne, and *all loose :* but, as God will, so be it."

28. Sir Francis the Arragonois, hearing of that chance [the loss of Evreux], apparelled six strong fellowes, like men of the countrie, with sacks and baskets, as cariers of corne and vittels ; and sent them to the castell of Cornill, in the which diuerse Englishmen were kept as prisoners ; and he, with an ambush of Englishmen, laie in a vallie nigh to the fortesse.

The six counterfet husbandmen entered the castell vnsuspected, and streight came to the chamber of the capteine, & laieng hands on him, gaue knowledge to them that laie in ambush to come to their aid. The which suddenlie made foorth, and entered the castell, slue and tooke all the Frenchmen, and set the Englishmen at libertie : . . .

29. Philip, duke of Burgognie, partlie mooued in conscience to make amends to Charles duke of Orleance (as yet prisoner in England) for the death of duke Lewes his father, whome duke Iohn, father to this duke Philip, cruellie murthered in the citie of Paris ; and partlie intending the aduancement of his neece, the ladie Marie, daughter to Adolfe duke of Cleue, (by the which aliance, he trusted, that all old rancor should ceasse,) contriued waies to haue the said duke of Orleance set at libertie, vpon promise by him made to take the said ladie Marie vnto wife. This duke had beene prisoner in England euer since the battell was fought at Agincourt, vpon the daie of Crispine and Crispinian, in the yeare 1415, and was set now at libertie in the moneth of Nouember, in the yeare 1440 ; paieng for his ransome foure hundred thousand crownes, though other saie but three hundred thousand.

The cause whie he was deteined so long in captiuitie, was to pleasure thereby the duke of Burgognie : for, so long as the duke of Burgognie continued faithfull to the king of England, it was not thought necessarie to suffer the duke of Orleance to be ransomed, least vpon his deliuerance he would not ceasse to seeke meanes to be reuenged vpon the duke of Burgognie, for the old grudge and displeasure betwixt their two families ; and therefore such ransome was demanded for him as he was neuer able to pay. But, after the duke of Burgognie had broken his promise, and was turned to the French part, the councell of the said king of England deuised how to deliuer the duke of Orleance, that thereby they might displeasure the duke of Burgognie. Which thing the duke of Burgognie perceiuing, doubted what might follow if he were deliuered without his knowledge, and therefore to his great cost practised his deliuerance, paid his ransome, and ioined with him amitie and aliance by mariage of his neece.

30. About this season, Iohn, the valiant lord Talbot, for his approued prowesse and wisdome, as well in England as in France, both in peace & warre so well tried, was created earle of Shrewesburie ; and with a companie of three thousand men sent againe into Normandie, for the better defense of the same.

31. There were in his companie of his owne nation, his vncle the cardinall of Winchester, the cardinall and archbishop of Yorke, the dukes of Bedford, Yorke, and Norffolke, the earles of Warwike, Salisburie, Oxenford, Huntington, Ormond, Mortaigne, and Suffolke.

He was crowned king of France, in our ladie church of Paris, by the cardinall of Winchester : the bishop of Paris not being contented that the cardinall should doo such an high ceremonie in his church and iurisdiction.

32. The duke of Burgognie, to set a veile before the king of Englands eies, sent Thoison Dore his cheefe herald to king Henrie with letters ; excusing the matter by way of information, that he was constreined to enter in this league with K. Charles, by the dailie outcries, *complaints*, and lamentations of his people, alledging against him that he was the onelie cause of the long continuance of the wars, to the vtter impouerishing of his owne people, and the whole nation of France. . . .

. . . The superscription of this letter was thus : " *To the* high and mightie prince, Henrie, " by the grace of God, *king* of England, his welbeloued cousine." Neither naming him king of France, nor his souereigne lord, according as (euer before that time) he was accustomed to doo. This letter was much maruelled at of the councell, after they had throughlie considered all the contents thereof, & they could not but be much disquieted ; so far foorth that diuerse of them stomaked so muche the vntruth of the duke, that they could not temper their passions, but openlie called him traitor.

33. In the beginning of this twentith yeare, Richard duke of Yorke, regent of France, and gouernour of Normandie, determined to inuade the territories of his enimies both by sundrie armies, and in seuerall places, and therevpon without delaie of time he sent the lord of Willoughbie with a great crue of soldiers to destroie the countrie of Amiens ; and Iohn lord Talbot was appointed to besiege the towne of Diepe ; and the regent himselfe, accompanied with Edmund duke of Summerset, set forward into the duchie of Aniou. . . .

The dukes of Yorke and Summerset . . . entered into Aniou and Maine, and there destroied townes, and spoiled the people, and with great preies and prisoners repaired againe into Normandie, . . .

34. [The French] left the siege, and retired in good order into the place which they had trenched, diched, and fortified with ordinance. The earle, aduertised how the siege was remoued, hasted forward towards his enimies, doubting most least they would haue beene quite fled and gone before his comming. But they, fearing the displeasure of the French king (who was not far off) if they should haue fled, abode the earles comming, and so receiued him : who though he first with manfull courage, and sore fighting wan the entrie of their camps, yet at length they compassed him about, and shooting him through the thigh with an handgun, slue his horsse, and finallie killed him lieng on the ground ; whome they durst neuer looke in the face, while he stood on his feet.

35. It was said, that after he perceiued there was no remedie, but present losse of the battell, he counselled his sonne, the lord Lisle, to saue himselfe by flight, sith the same could not redound to anie great reproch in him, this being the first iournie in which he had beene present. Manie words he vsed to persuade him to haue saued his life ; but nature so wrought in the son, that neither desire of life, nor feare of death, could either cause him to shrinke, or conueie himselfe out of the danger, and so there manfullie ended his life with his said father.

36. Motion was made among Sigismund the emperour and other christen kings . . . that, sith such horror of bloudshed betweene the two nations continuallie so lamentablie raged in France, some mediation might be made for accord : . . .

37. [The cardinal of S. Crosse . . .] declared to the three parties the innumerable mischeefes, that had followed to the whole state of the chiristian common-wealth by their continuall dissention and dailie discord ; exhorting them, for the honour of God, & for the loue which they ought to beare towards the aduancement of his faith and true religion, to conforme themselues to reason, and to laie aside all rancor, malice, and displeasure ; so that, in concluding *a godlie peace*, they might receiue profit and quietnesse heere in this world, and of God an euerlasting reward in heauen.

38. In this yeare died in Guien the countesse of Comings, to whome the French king and also the earle of Arminacke pretended to be heire, in so much that the earle entred into all the lands of the said ladie. And bicause he knew the French king would not take the matter well, to haue a Rouland for an Oliuer he sent solemne ambassadours to the king of England, offering him his daughter in mariage, with promise to be bound (beside great summes of monie, which he would giue with hir) to deliuer into the king of Englands hands all such castels and townes, as he or his ancestors deteined from him within anie part of the duchie of Aquitaine, either by conquest of his progenitors, or by gift and deliuerie of anie French king ; and further to aid the same king with monie for the recouerie of other cities, within the same duchie, from the French king ; or from anie other person that against king Henrie vniustlie kept, and wrongfullie withheld them.

This offer seemed so profitable and also honorable to king Henrie and the realme, that the ambassadours were well heard, honourablie receiued, and with rewards sent home into their countrie. After whome were sent, for the conclusion of the marriage, into Guien, sir Edward Hull, sir Robert Ros, and Iohn Grafton, deane of S. Seuerines ; the which (as all the chronographers agree) both concluded the mariage, and by proxie affied the yoong ladie.

39. Kynge Henry the fifth, knowynge the haute corage, and the ambicious mynde of the man [Winchester], proh bited hym on hys allegeaunce once either to sue for or to take ; meanynge that Cardinalles Hattes shoulde not presume to bee *egall with* Princes.

40. Habit, hat, and dignitie of a cardinall, with all ceremonies to it apperteining : which promotion, the late K. (right deeplie persing into the vnrestrainable ambitious mind of the man, that euen from his youth was euer [wont] to checke at the highest ; and [having] also right well asserteined with what intollerable pride his head should soone be swoollen vnder such a hat) did therefore all his life long keepe this prelat backe from that presumptuous estate. But now, the king being yoong and the regent his freend, he obteined his purpose, to his great profit, and the impouerishing of the spiritualtie of this realme. For by a bull legatine, which he purchased from Rome, he gathered so much treasure, that no man in maner had monie but he : so that he was called the rich cardinall of Winchester,

41   Thus was the citie of Paris brought into possession of Charles the French king, through the vntrue demeanour of the citizens, who, contrarie to their oths, and promised allegiance, like false and inconstant people, so reuolted from the English.

42.   England was vnquieted, . . . and France by spoile, slaughter, and burning sore defaced ; (a mischeefe in all places much lamented ;) therefore, to agree the two puissant kings, all the princes of christendome trauelled so effectuouslie by their oratours and ambassadors, that a diet was appointed to be kept at the citie of Tours in Touraine ; where for the king of England appeared William de la Poole earle of Suffolke, . . .

43.   In treating of this truce, the earle of Suffolke, aduenturing somewhat vpon his commission, without the assent of his associats, imagined that the next waie to come to a perfect peace was to contriue a mariage betweene the French kings kinsewoman, the ladie Margaret, daughter to Reiner duke of Aniou, and his souereigne lord king Henrie.

THE CONFESSION OF JOAN.

44.   For hir pranks so vncouth and suspicious, the lord regent, by Peter Chauchon bishop of Beauuois, (in whose diocesse she was taken,) caused hir life and beleefe, after order of law, to be inquired vpon and examined.   Wherein found though a virgin, yet first, shamefullie reiecting hir sex abominablie in acts and apparell, to haue counterfeit mankind, and then, all damnablie faithlesse, to be a pernicious instrument to hostilitie and bloudshed in diuelish witchcraft and sorcerie, sentence accordinglie was pronounced against hir.   Howbeit, vpon humble confession of hir iniquities with a counterfeit contrition pretending a carefull sorow for the same, execution spared and all mollified into this, that from henceefoorth she should cast off hir vnnaturall wearing of mans abilliments, and keepe hir to garments of hir owne kind, abiure hir pernicious practises of sorcerie and witcherie, and haue life and leasure in perpetuall prison to bewaile hir misdeeds. Which to performe (according to the maner of abiuration) a solemne oth verie gladlie she tooke.

But herein (God helps vs !) she fullie afore possest of the feend, not able to hold her in anie towardnesse of grace, falling streight waie into hir former abominations, (and yet seeking to eetch out life as long as she might,) stake not (though the shift were shamefull) to confesse hir selfe a strumpet, and (vnmaried as she was) to be with child.   For triall, the lord regents lenitie gaue hir nine moneths staie, at the end wherof she (found herein as false as wicked in the rest, an eight daies after, vpon a further definitiue sentence declared against hir to be relapse and a renouncer of hir oth and repentance) was thereupon deliuered ouer to secular power, and so executed by consumption of fire in the old market place at Rone, in the selfe same steed where now saint Michaels church stands : hir ashes afterward without the towne wals shaken into the wind.   Now recounting altogither, hir pastorall bringing vp, rude, without any vertuous instruction, hir campestrall conuersation with wicked spirits, whome, in hir first salutation to Charles the Dolphin, she vttered to be our Ladie, saint Katharine, and saint Anne, that in this behalfe came and gaue hir commandements from God hir maker, as kept hir fathers lambs in the fields . . .

These matters may verie rightfullie denounce vnto all the world hir execrable abhominations, and well iustifie the iudgement she had, and the execution she was put to for the same.   A thing yet (God wot) verie smallie shadowed and lesse holpen by the verie trauell of the Dolphin, whose dignitie abroad [was] foulie spotted in this point, that, contrarie to the holie degree of a right christen prince (as he called himselfe), for maintenance of his quarels in warre would not reuerence to prophane his sacred estate, as dealing in diuelish practises with misbeleeuers and witches.

45.   The Englishmen would that king Charles should haue nothing but what it pleased the king of England, and that not as dutie, but as a benefit by him of his meere liberalitie giuen and distributed.   The Frenchmen, on the other part, would that K. Charles should haue the kingdome franklie and freelie, and that the king of England should leaue the name, armes, and title of the king of France, and to be content with the dukedomes of Aquitaine and Normandie, and to forsake Paris, and all the townes which they possessed in France, betweene the riuers of Some and Loire ; being no parcell of the duchie of Normandie.   To be breefe, the demands of all parts were betweene them so farre out of square, as hope of concord there was none at all.

46.   The earle of Suffolke with his companie returned into England, where he forgat not to declare what an honourable truce he had taken, out of the which there was a great hope that a finall peace might grow the sooner for that honorable mariage, which he had concluded ; omitting nothing that might extoll and set foorth the personage of the ladie, or the nobilitie of hir kinred.

But although this mariage pleased the king and diuerse of his councell, yet Humfrie duke of Glocester protector of the realme was much against it ; alledging that it should be both contrarie to the lawes of God, and dishonorable to the prince, if he should breake that promise and contract of mariage, made by ambassadours sufficientlie thereto instructed, with the daughter of the earle of Arminacke, vpon conditions both to him and his realme, as much profitable as honorable. But the dukes words could not be heard, for the earles doings were onelie liked and allowed.

47.   This Reiner duke of Aniou named himselfe king of Sicill, Naples, and Ierusalem ; hauing onlie the name and stile of those realmes, without anie penie, profit, or foot of possession.

48.   But on the other parte, the Quene his [Henry's] wyfe was a woman of a great witte, and yet of no greater wytte then of haute stomacke desirous of glory and couetous of honor ; and of reason, pollicye, counsaill, and other giftes and talentes of nature belongyng to a man, full and flowyng : of witte and wilinesse she was not vnexperte ; but yet she had one poynt of a very woman, for, often tyme, when she was vehement & fully bente in a matter, she was sodainly, lyke a wethercocke, mutable and turnyng.

49.   This ladie excelled all other, as well in beautie and fauour, as in wit and policie ; and was of stomach and courage more like to a man than a woman.

APPENDIX II.

THE DEATH OF HENRY V (1422).

(Monstrelet's *Chronicles*, translated by Johnes.)[1]

KING HENRY, finding himself mortally ill, called to him his brother the Duke of Bedford, his uncle of Exeter, the earl of Warwick, sir Louis de Robesart and others, to the number of six or eight of those in whom he had the greatest confidence, and said that he saw with grief it was the pleasure of his Creator that he should quit this world.   He then addressed the Duke of Bedford : ' John, my good brother, I beseech you, on the loyalty and love you have ever expressed for me, that you show the same loyalty and affection to my son Henry, your nephew, and that, so long as you shall live, you do not suffer him to conclude any treaty with our adversary Charles, and that on no account whatever the duchy of Normandy be wholly restored to him.   Should our good brother of Burgundy be desirous of the regency of the Kingdom of France, I would advise that you let him have it ; but should he refuse, then take it yourself.   My good uncle of Exeter, I nominate you sole regent of the Kingdom of England, for that you well know how to govern it ; and I entreat that you do not, on any pretence whatever, return to France ; and I likewise nominate you as guardian to my son,—and I insist, on your love to me, that you do very often personally visit and see him.   My dear cousin of Warwick, I will that you be his governor, and that you teach him all things becoming his rank, for I cannot provide a fitter person for the purpose.   I entreat you all as earnestly as I can, that you avoid all quarrels and dissensions with our fair brother of Burgundy ; and this I particularly recommend to the consideration of my fair brother Humphrey,—for should any coolness subsist between you, which God forbid, the affairs of this realm, which are now in a very promising state, would soon be ruined . . .'' The King then sent for his physicians, and earnestly demanded of them how long they thought he had to live.   They delayed answering the question directly ; but, not to discourage hope, they said that it depended solely on the will of God whether he would be restored to health.   He was dissatisfied with this answer, and repeated his request, begging of them to tell the truth.   Upon this they consulted together, and one of them, as spokesman, falling on his knees, said, ' Sire, you must think on your soul ; for, unless it be the will of God to decree otherwise, it is impossible that you should live more than two hours.'   The King, hearing this, sent for his confessor, some of his household and his chaplains, whom he ordered to chant the seven penitential psalms.   When they came to *Benigne fac Domine* where mention is made *Muri Hierusalem*,[2] he stopped them, and said aloud, that he had fully intended, after he had wholly subdued the realm of France to his obedience, and restored it to peace, to have gone to conquer the Kingdom of Jerusalem, if it had pleased his Creator to have granted him a longer life.   Having said this, he allowed the priests to proceed, and shortly after, according to the prediction of his physicians, gave up the ghost.

1. Jones' *York and Lancaster*, 1399–1485.

2. " Do good in thy good pleasure unto Zion : build thou the walls of Jerusalem " (*Psalm* li. 18).   The king's words were : " Good Lord, thou knewest that my mind was to re-edify the walls of Hierusalem."   Leland's *Collectanea*.

The Second Part of King Henry the Sixth

Written. 1591–1592.

Published. 1594. Considered to be a recast of an old Play, known as "The | First Part of the Con- | tention betwixt the two famous houses of Yorke | and Lancaster, with the death of the good | Duke Humphrey : | And the banishment and death of the Duke of | *Suffolke*, and the Tragicall end of the proud Cardinall | of *Winchester*, with the notable Rebellion | of *Iacke Cade :* | *And the Duke of Yorkes first claime vnto the* | *Crowne.* LONDON Printed by Thomas Creed, for Thomas Millington, | and are to be sold at his shop vnder Saint Peters | Church in Cornwall. 1594." This was entered in the Registers of the Stationers' Company under date 12 March, 1593-4. In 1600 a reprint appeared under the same title, printed by Valentine Simmes for Thomas Millington. In 1619 a third edition—and including also *The True Tragedy of Richard, Duke of York*—appeared with the following title : "The | Whole Contention | betweene the two Famous—Houses, LANCASTER and YORKE.—*With the Tragicall ends of the good Duke*—Humfrey, Richard Duke of Yorke, | *and King Henrie the* | *Sixt.* Diuided into two Parts ; And newly corrected and | enlarged. Written by *William Shake* | speare, Gent.—Printed at LONDON, for T.P. | " The revised version known as the *Second Part of King Henry the Sixth* was first published in the first Folio of 1623.

In the *Transactions of the New Shakspere Society*, 1875–76, Part II, will be found a Paper on the authorship of the Play by Miss Jane Lee.

Source of the Plot. The *Chronicles* of Raphael Holinshed and Edward Hall.[1]

The connection between the *Second and Third Parts of King Henry the Sixth* is such, that they should—as in the case of *King Henry the Fourth*—be read as one Play. The principal theme in the First Part is the events in France. The subject of the Second and Third Parts is the contention of the Houses of York and Lancaster ; the decline of England's power under Henry VI., and the rise of the Duke of York.

This, and the Second Part, which is a direct continuation of Part I., cover a period of about ten years, from the arrival of Queen Margaret in England in 1445 to the first battle of St. Albans, 1455.

Outline of the Play. The First Act opens in the Palace in London. It opens with Suffolk's introduction of Queen Margaret to the King and his court. Suffolk who has been sent to France to marry her as the king's proxy, humbly delivers up on bended knee to Henry " The fairest queen that ever king received." Bidding Suffolk rise, Henry welcomes Margaret : " Welcome, Queen Margaret : I can express no kinder sign of love Than this kind kiss," and expresses the hope that as her " beauteous face " has brought to his " soul " a " world of earthly blessings " so " love unite our thoughts." Margaret reciprocates his greetings, depicting Henry as her " alderliefest sovereign." Henry is enraptured at Margaret's beauty and her gracious speech :

1. *See* Appendix I.

> Her sight did ravish, but her grace in speech,
> Her words y-clad with wisdom's majesty,
> Makes me from wondering fall to weeping joys ;

after which he bids the nobles do her homage :

> Lords, with one cheerful voice welcome my love.

"Long live Queen Margaret, England's happiness !" is the shout of acclamation from all the peers present, to which the queen replies "We thank you all."

Suffolk then delivers to Gloucester the Articles of Contracted Peace between Henry and the French king Charles. In a fluent voice Gloucester reads the marriage contract, but when he comes to the clause surrendering the "duchy of Anjou and the county of Maine" to Reignier—father of Margaret—he, under the pretext that "Some sudden qualm hath struck me at the heart And dimmed mine eyes," lets the paper fall, and Beaufort, at the king's request, takes the scroll and reads on.

Pleased with the bargain, Henry creates Suffolk a duke :

> Lord marquess, kneel down :
> We here create thee the first Duke of Suffolk,
> And girt thee with the sword,

discharges the Duke of York from his regency "I' the parts of France, till term of eighteen months Be full expired," and after thanking the nobles for their attendance to welcome Margaret, leaves the room with the queen and Suffolk, after having given orders for preparations to be made for the queen's coronation.

After they have gone, Gloucester vehemently protests against any of the English possessions in France being surrendered, and asks the other peers present whether the victories of Henry the Fifth, the vigilance of Bedford, and their own deeds of valour and honour shall die, declaring that the marriage is a fatal one to England :

> O peers of England ! shameful is this league,
> Fatal this marriage, cancelling your fame,
> Blotting your names from books of memory,
> Razing the characters of your renown,
> Defacing monuments of conquered France,
> Undoing all, as all had never been.

Beaufort—Suffolk's chief supporter—rebukes Gloucester for his bold speech, for :

> France, 'tis ours ; and we will keep it still,

but Gloucester maintains that it is impossible to hold France, now that

> Suffolk, the new-made duke that rules the roast,
> Hath given the duchy of Anjou and Maine
> Unto the poor King Reignier, whose large style
> Agrees not with the leanness of his purse.

Salisbury declares that Anjou and Maine are the keys to Normandy, and turning to Warwick asks him why he weeps. Warwick replies that he weeps for grief that these two provinces which he himself did win should be delivered up so peacefully.

Gloucester considers it a joke for Suffolk to demand such a large sum for costs and transporting Margaret, who he declares should have stayed in France :

> A proper jest, and never heard before,
> That Suffolk should demand a whole fifteenth
> For costs and charges in transporting her !
> She should have stayed in France, and starved in France,
> Before—

" It was the pleasure of my lord the king," interjects Beaufort, and chides Gloucester for being too outspoken, but Gloucester retorts by telling the Cardinal that it is his—Gloucester's—presence that he dislikes, and fearing if he stays they would doubtless renew their " ancient bickerings " leaves the room with the remark :

> Lordings, farewell ; and say, when I am gone,
> I prophesied France will be lost ere long.

On Gloucester's departure, Beaufort remarks that Gloucester is no great friend to the king ; and on account of his being next heir to the crown he is courting the favour of the common people who call him " Humphrey, the good Duke of Gloucester," and " God preserve the good Duke Humphrey ! ", adding that for all this " flattering gloss, He will be found a dangerous protector." Buckingham however reminds them that as the king is old enough to assume the reins of government, he needs no protector, and invites Somerset to join with him, and with the aid of Suffolk, remove Gloucester from his protectorship. This is upheld by Beaufort who immediately leaves with the purpose of winning over Suffolk, for

> This weighty business will not brook delay.

Beaufort having gone, Somerset remarks that they must " watch the haughty cardinal " for his " insolence is more intolerable Than all the princes' in the land beside," for if Gloucester be displaced, Beaufort will be protector, but Buckingham replies that

> thou or I, Somerset, will be protector,
> Despite Duke Humphrey or the cardinal.

They too having taken their leave, Salisbury observes : " Pride went before, ambition follows him," and as Beaufort, Somerset and Buckingham are only labouring for their own preferment, it behoves the others to labour for the good of the realm, and declaring that he had always seen Gloucester " bear himself like a noble gentleman " and often, had seen the " haughty cardinal More like a soldier than a man o' the church, . . . Swear like a ruffian and demean himself Unlike the ruler of a commonweal," invites his son—the Earl of Warwick—and his brother—the Duke of York—to unite with him to " bridle and suppress The pride of Suffolk and the cardinal, With Somerset's and Buckingham's ambition." Warwick gladly accepts this proposition, and York mutters aside " And so says York, for he hath greatest cause." " Then let's make haste away, and look unto the main," is Salisbury's remark, and Warwick cries out :

> Unto the Main ! O father, Maine, is lost !
> That Maine which by main force Warwick did win,
> And would have kept so long as breath did last :
> Main chance, father, you meant ; but I meant Maine,
> Which I will win from France, or else be slain.

Left alone, York soliloquises over the lost provinces : " Anjou and Maine are given to the French : Paris is lost ; while the " state of Normandy Stands on a tickle point now they are gone." They have given away that which was not their own, but in the meanwhile he must abide his time, for the day will come when " York shall claim his own," for when Henry is absorbed in his " new bride and England's dear-bought queen," and Gloucester and the peers be " fallen at jars " he will

> raise aloft the milk-white rose,
> With whose sweet smell the air shall be perfumed,
> And in my standard bear the arms of York,
> To grapple with the house of Lancaster ;
> And, force perforce, I'll make him yield the crown,
> Whose bookish rule hath pulled fair England down.

The second scene is enacted at the Duke of Gloucester's house, and shows the loyalty of the duke, and the duchess' ambition.   It opens with the duchess enquiring why her husband " droops, like over-ripened corn " when he might assume " King Henry's diadem," and suggests that he " Put forth thy hand," and " reach at the glorious gold," in which she will assist him.   Gloucester, who attributes his sadness to a dream, bids her banish from her mind those ambitious thoughts.   She then asks him to tell her the nature of his dream and she will " requite it With sweet rehearsal of my morning's dream."   He then relates how he dreamed that his " staff " his " office-badge in court Was broke in twain, methought by a cardinal," and on the pieces of the broken wand Were placed the heads of the Dukes of Somerset and Suffolk.   The duchess who exclaims " Tut ! " considers that his dream is " nothing but an argument," for he that is so presumptuous as to attempt to break a " stick of Gloucester's grove," would certainly " lose his head," and goes on to relate that she dreamed she sat in " seat of majesty " in the Cathedral Church of Westminster, where Henry and Margaret kneeled to her, and set the diadem upon her head.   Gloucester is angry with her, and calls her " Presumptuous dame ! ill-nurtured Eleanor !" telling her she ought to be satisfied, as she is the " second woman in the realm," adding that if she is not more cautious she will " tumble down thy husband and thyself From top of honour to disgrace's feet," and implores her to go away and let him hear no more. But the duchess asks him not to be so choleric with her, for she was " telling but her dream," and in future she will keep her dreams to herself, but Gloucester requests her not to be angry, for he is pleased again.   At this point a messenger enters and invites Gloucester to Saint Albans where the king and queen intend to hawk.   Gloucester invites his wife to accompany him, but the duchess promises to " follow presently," and Gloucester and the messenger depart forthwith.   After they have gone, she mutters :

> Follow I must ; I cannot go before,
> While Gloucester bears this base and humble mind,

adding, that if she were a " man, a duke, and next of blood," she would

>   remove these tedious stumbling-blocks
> And smooth my way upon their headless necks ;
> And, being a woman, I will not be slack
> To play my part in Fortune's pageant.
> Where are you there ?   Sir John ! nay, fear not, man,
> We are alone ; here 's none but thee and I.

Her chaplain, John Hume, enters and addresses her as " your royal majesty ! " She expresses surprise, telling him " I am but grace," but Hume, who has been suborned by Suffolk and the cardinal to undermine the duchess, replies that it has been promised her by an enchantress, and offers to call up the spirit from the nether-world.   This offers the duchess accepts, and telling him to " make merry, take this reward," departs forthwith for Saint Albans.   After she has gone Hume mutters to himself that he will " make merry with her gold," for knowing the duchess' aspirations he has been hired by Suffolk and Beaufort to " buz these conjurations in her brain," and although " A crafty knave does need no broker," yet he himself is " Suffolk's and the cardinal's broker," whom he describes as a " pair of crafty knaves," adding that his " knavery " will be the duchess' ruin, and her " attainture will be Humphrey's fall."

We return to the Palace in the next scene, where we find petitioners, of whom Peter the Armourer's man is one, awaiting the arrival of the Lord Protector.   Suffolk, accompanied by the Queen, enters, and Peter observes : " Here a' comes, methinks, and the queen with him. I 'll be the first, sure," to which the second petitioner replies : " Come back, fool ! this is the Duke of Suffolk, and not my lord protector." Suffolk's attention being arrested he questions the petitioner : " How now, fellow ! would'st any thing with me ? " to which the petitioner replies : " I pray, my lord, pardon me : I took ye for my lord protector." " To my Lord Protector ! " "Are your supplications to his lordship ? Let me see them " demands the queen. The petitions contain a series of accusations. One accuses the Lord Cardinal's man, and another the Duke of Suffolk with dishonesty, while a third is an accusation against Thomas Horner for saying that York is the rightful heir to the crown. Servants enter, and Suffolk orders the last petitioner to be detained, and a pursuivant to be sent to arrest Horner, to be brought before the king, after which the queen, in order to suppress the petition against her favourite, Suffolk, tears it to pieces.

Turning to Suffolk, this proud and headstrong woman asks whether it is the " fashion in the court of England ? " the " government of Britain's isle " the " royalty of Albion's king " for her husband " still to be a pupil under the surly Gloucester's governance," declaring that she would never have married him had she not thought he resembled Suffolk " In courage, courtship, and proportion," poignantly adding that Henry's time is spent in numbering Ave-Maries on his beads, and praying to brazen images of canonised saints, and wishes the " college of the cardinals Would choose him pope, and carry him to Rome, And set the triple crown upon his head." She further complains that Beaufort, Somerset, Buckingham and York are more powerful in the realm than the king. Suffolk counsels patience, but Margaret, whose pride raised enemies against her, angrily confesses that all the peers together do not madden her as does that " proud dame, the lord protector's wife " sweeping through the court with a troop of ladies, flaunting her wealth. Strangers in court take her for the queen, bearing on her back the revenues of a duke, whilst in her heart she scorns at the poverty of the queen, boasting to her minions that the train of her worst wearing gown is worth more than all her (the queen's) father's estates, and calling her a "Contemptuous base-born callat," vows to be avenged on the duchess. Suffolk advises Margaret to leave the matter to him, for he has already laid a trap for the duchess :

> Madam, myself have limed a bush for her,
> And placed a quire of such enticing birds
> That she will light to listen to the lays,
> And never mount to trouble you again,

adding, that Gloucester would soon be disgraced, and her enemies weeded out one by one, and she herself " shall steer the happy helm."

A sennet is sounded, and the king, with nobles, enters. Henry remarks that he cares not whether Somerset or York holds the reins of office, for " all 's one to me." York announces that if he did misdemean himself in France he should be " denayed the regentship," while Somerset is willing to yield to York if the latter is more worthy. Warwick considers York the worthier of the two and is told by Beaufort to " let thy betters speak." High words ensue, and when Salisbury asks why " Somerset should be preferred to York " the Queen, remarks " Because the king, forsooth, will have it so." " Madam," replies Gloucester, the " king is old enough himself To give his censure : these are no women's matters " whereupon the queen retorts " If he be old enough, what needs your grace To be protector of his excellence ? " Gloucester reminds the queen that he is the protector of the realm, which office he will resign at Henry's pleasure, and Suffolk tells him to " Resign, and leave thine insolence," for since " thou wert King, as who is king but thou ? The commonwealth hath daily run to wrack." Beaufort accuses Gloucester of " racking " the Commons, while the " clergy's bags Are lank and lean with thy extortions " ; Somerset of squandering public money on sumptuous buildings and his wife's attire ; and Buckingham of cruelty to offenders against the law, but when the queen charges him with surrendering the English possessions in France :

> Thy sale of offices and towns in France,
> If they were known, as the suspect is great,
> Would make thee quickly hop without thy head

Gloucester leaves the room.

After he has gone the queen drops her fan :

> Give me my fan : what, minion ! can ye not ?

and as the Duchess of Gloucester does not proceed forthwith to pick it up, the queen gives the duchess a box on the ear, with the remark : " I cry you mercy, madam ; was it you ? ", and the Duchess indignantly answers :

> Was 't I ! yea, I it was, proud Frenchwoman :
> Could I come near your beauty with my nails
> I 'd set my ten commandments in your face.

" Sweet aunt, be quiet ; 'twas against her will," interposes Henry, but the Duchess replies

> Against her will !   Good king, look to 't in time ;
> She 'll hamper thee and dandle thee like a baby :
> Though in this place most master wear no breeches,
> She shall not strike Dame Eleanor unrevenged,

and forthwith takes her departure.   She is hurriedly followed by Buckingham, who, whispering to Beaufort, says :

> She 's tickled now ; her fume needs no spurs,
> She 'll gallop far enough to her destruction.

Immediately after, Gloucester, who has cooled his choler by walking in the quadrangle of the castle, re-enters, and informs the king that " York is meetest man To be your regent in the realm of France." Suffolk considers " York is most unmeet of any man " for the office, and York rejoins that the reason is that he refuses to " flatter Suffolk in his pride " adding, that if he were appointed, Somerset would do his utmost to detain him at home " Till France be won into the Dauphin's hands, for

> Last time I danced attendance on his will
> Till Paris was besieged, famished, and lost.

This is borne out by Warwick for a " fouler fact Did never traitor in the land commit," to which Suffolk retorts : " Peace, headstrong Warwick ! ", and Warwick curtly rejoins : " Image of pride, why should I hold my peace ? "

At this point Horner and his man Peter are brought in, and Suffolk suggests that as they accuse York of treason, York should leave the room, but when York asks who doth accuse him of treason, the king, turning to Suffolk, requests to know the reason why the two prisoners are brought before him. Suffolk replies that Peter accuses his master of high treason :

> His words were these : that Richard Duke of York
> Was rightful heir unto the English crown,
> And that your majesty was an usurper.

Being questioned by Henry, Peter swears by his " ten bones " that his master did " speak them," while Horner denies it, saying that his accuser is his prentice, who had vowed upon his knees to be even with him for correcting him for a fault.

Being perplexed the king asks Gloucester's advice, and Gloucester recommends Henry to appoint Somerset regent of France, and to fix a day for the two men to fight a duel in order to establish which has spoken the truth. Somerset humbly thanks his majesty, Horner willingly accepts the combat, and Peter declares he cannot fight, and asks for mercy, but Henry orders the two men away to prison, and appoints " the last of the next month," as the day for the duel to be fought.

The Duke of Gloucester's Garden supplies the next scene. Margery Jourdain, a witch ; Hume and Southwell, two priests, and a cunning necromancer named Boling-broke enter, in order to carry out their incantations, and raise a spirit to utter certain prophecies. Hume, who is an hireling of Suffolk's, tells Bolingbroke to fear not the duchess' courage. Bolingbroke assures him that all is ready, adding that he has heard that she is a woman of invincible spirit, and suggests that Hume keep the duchess company " aloft while we be busy below." Hume having gone, Bolingbroke commands Jourdain to throw herself upon the ground and grovel. Immediately the duchess, accompanied by Hume, appears " aloft," and after welcoming them, bids them to get along with their business, to which Bolingbroke replies :

> Patience, good lady ; wizards know their times :
> Deep night, dark night, the silent of the night,
> The time of night when Troy was set on fire ;
> The time when screech-owls cry, and ban-dogs howl,
> And spirits walk, and ghosts break up their graves,
> That time best fits the work we have in hand.
> Madam, sit you, and fear not : whom we raise
> We will make fast within a hallowed verge,

after which he makes a circle, and amid thunder and lightning a spirit slowly rises. Addressing the spirit, the witch says :

> By the eternal God, whose name and power
> Thou tremblest at, answer that I shall ask ;
> For till thou speak thou shalt not pass from hence,

to which the spirit replies : " Ask what thou wilt. That I had said and done ! "

The spirit is then asked three questions, which, as it reads aloud, are written down by Southwell. The first is :

> " First, of the king : what shall of him become ? "

to which the answer is given :

> The duke yet lives that Henry shall depose ;
> But him outlive, and die a violent death.

The second question is :

> " What fates await the Duke of Suffolk ? "

and the answer comes :

> By water shall he die and take his end.

and to the third question :

> " What shall befall the Duke of Somerset ? "

the spirit rejoins :

> Let him shun castles :
> Safer shall he be upon the sandy plains
> Than where castles mounted stand.

As it refuses to speak more : " Have done, for more I hardly can endure " Boling-broke commands the spirit to " Descend to darkness and the burning lake : False fiend, avoid ! " and amid thunder and lightning the apparition disappears.

At this point York and Buckingham, with a guard, rush into the garden and York gives orders to " Lay hands upon these traitors and their trash," for the practising of sorcery was treasonable. Glancing towards the balcony, and seeing the duchess, York says :

> What ! madam, are you there ? the king and commonweal
> Are deeply indebted for this piece of pains :
> My lord protector will, I doubt it not,
> See you well guerdoned for these good deserts,

and the duchess who treats the threat with contempt because her husband is Protector, replies :

> Not half so bad as thine to England's king,
> Injurious duke, that threatest where 's no cause,

and Buckingham asks : " What call you this ? " after which he orders all of them to be arrested :

> Away with them ! let them be clapped up close,
> And kept asunder. You, madam, shall with us :
> Stafford, take her to thee.
> 　　　　*[Exeunt above Duchess and Hume, guarded.*
> We 'll see your trinkets here all forthcoming.
> All, away !
> 　　　　*[Exeunt guard, with Southwell, Bolingbroke, etc.*

Turning to Buckingham, York says : " Lord Buckingham, methinks you watched her well : A pretty plot, well chosen to build upon ! " They then seize the papers containing the spirit's answers, which are despatched to the king who is hunting at Saint Albans with the Duke of Gloucester, to whom the news will be a "sorry breakfast," after which York sends a servant to

> Invite my Lords of Salisbury and Warwick
> To sup with me to-morrow night. Away !

The Second Act opens at Saint Alban's, and shows the king, the queen and the court, with Falconers halloing : They comment upon the sport, the queen observing that she had not seen " better sport these seven years' day ", while the king comments on Gloucester's falcon which flew above the rest. To this Suffolk remarks that Gloucester's hawks, like their master, love to soar high, and Gloucester tells him that it is only a base mind that can mount no higher than a bird can soar. " I thought as much ; he 'd be above the clouds " ejaculates Beaufort, and Gloucester asks him whether it is not good he could fly to heaven ? to which Beaufort retorts that Gloucester's eyes and thoughts are on the crown, and calls him a " Pernicious protector " and a " dangerous peer." The queen joins in the quarrel, and the king implores them to be at peace, telling Margaret to " whet not on these furious peers ; For blessed are the peacemakers on earth." Gloucester and Beaufort agree to fight a duel to settle the quarrel, and the king once again implores them to be at peace :

> The winds grow high ; so do your stomachs, lords,
> How irksome is this music to my heart !
> When such strings jar, what hope of harmony ?
> I pray, my lords, let me compound this strife.

At this point, a man enters, crying " A miracle ! " and being asked by Gloucester " what miracle dost thou proclaim ? " replies that a blind man, " within this half hour hath received his sight at Saint Alban's shrine," and the king exclaims " God be praised." The Mayor of Saint Alban's now enters, followed by a number of townsmen, who carry on a chair the man on whom the miracle is supposed to have been conferred. Commanded by the king to relate the " circumstance," so that " we for thee may glorify the Lord," the man answers that he was " born blind " and this is confirmed by his wife, although Gloucester remarks that if she had been his mother instead of his wife " thou could'st have better told." Asked by the queen how he came to visit the holy shrine, he replies that he was called " A hundred times and oftener " in his sleep by Saint Alban : " Simpcox, come ; Come, offer at my shrine, and I will help thee," to which his wife adds that she herself had " heard a voice to call him so." Being asked by Beaufort whether he is lame, the man answers in the affirmative, due to a " fall off of a tree " while gathering plums, to which Gloucester remarks that he must " love plums well " to venture to climb a tree when blind, and the man replies that his wife " desired some damsons, And made me climb with danger of my life." Gloucester describes him as a " subtle knave " and the " lyingest knave in Christendom," and asks " My masters of Saint Alban's, have you not beadles in your town, and things called whips ? " The mayor having replied in the affirmative, an attendant is despatched to fetch a beadle. Having had a stool brought, Gloucester tells the man that if he wishes to save himself from being whipped he must leap over the stool and run away. Just as the man is asserting he cannot stand alone, the beadle enters, and Gloucester commands him to whip the man. At the first stroke of the whip, the man " leaps over the stool and runs away," followed by his confederates, who cry " A miracle ! " and Gloucester, perceiving the imposition, orders both the man and his wife to be whipped through every market-town till they come to Berwick.

Buckingham now enters, and the king enquires what tidings he brings. Buckingham replies " Such as my heart doth tremble to unfold " for he has arrested a number of " naughty persons, lewdly bent,"—of whom Gloucester's wife is the head—for practising dangerously against the state and against the life of the king :

> *King.*   What tidings with our cousin Buckingham ?
> *Buck.*   Such as my heart doth tremble to unfold.
>   A sort of naughty persons, lewdly bent,
>   Under the countenance and confederacy
>   Of Lady Eleanor, the protector's wife,
>   The ringleader and head of all this rout,
>   Have practised dangerously against your state,
>   Dealing with witches and with conjurers :
>   Whom we have apprehended in the fact ;
>   Raising up wicked spirits from underground,
>   Demanding of King Henry's life and death,
>   And others of your highness' privy council,
>   So more at large your grace shall understand.

Beaufort is highly pleased at the news, and severely reproaches Gloucester, affirming that the news " hath turned your weapon's edge " ; and Gloucester addressing Beaufort as " Ambitious churchman," requests him not to " afflict my heart " : declaring that he has always loved his king above any one else, adding that if his wife had forgotten " Honour and virtue " he would " give her as a prey to law and shame, That hath dishonoured Gloucester's honest name."

The king then announces that he will " repose " at Saint Albans for the night, and " To-morrow toward London back again :

> To look into this business thoroughly,
> And call these foul offenders to their answers ;
> And poise the cause in justice' equal scales,
> Whose beam stands sure, whose rightful cause prevails.

We are in the Duke of York's Garden in the next scene, where we find the duke in conversation with the Lords Salisbury and Warwick with regard to his " infallible " title to England's crown :

> Now, my good Lords of Salisbury and Warwick,
> Our simple supper ended, give me leave
> In this close walk to satisfy myself,
> In craving your opinion to my title,
> Which is infallible, to England's crown.

Being asked to explain, York proves his descent from the Duke of Clarence, third son of King Edward the Third, while the present king (Henry the Sixth) has descended from John of Gaunt, the fourth son of that monarch. This they cannot deny, Warwick remarking:

> What plain proceeding is more plain than this ?
> Henry doth claim the crown from John of Gaunt,
> The fourth son ; York claims it from the third.
> Till Lionel's issue fails, his should not reign ;

and invites Salisbury to kneel and salute York as their rightful monarch:

> Then, father Salisbury, kneel we together,
> And in this private plot be we the first
> That shall salute our rightful sovereign
> With honour of his birthright to the crown.

York thanks them for their loyalty, but reminds them that he is not their king " Till I be crowned " and

> my sword be stained
> With heart-blood of the house of Lancaster ;

In the meantime he counsels caution, and advises his adherents to do as he does in these " dangerous days " and " Wink at the Duke of Suffolk's insolence, At Beaufort's pride, at Somerset's ambition, At Buckingham and all the crew of them," until they have " snared " the Duke of Gloucester, the " shepherd of the flock," whose death they seek, and whose death, if " York can prophesy," will be to their own undoing.

Before taking leave of each other, Warwick predicts that he will some day make York a king:

> My heart assures me that the Earl of Warwick
> Shall one day make the Duke of York a king,

to which York promises to make Warwick the greatest subject in the realm:

> And, Nevil, this I do assure myself:
> Richard shall live to make the Earl of Warwick
> The greatest man in England but the king.

We next behold a Hall of Justice, where the Duchess of Gloucester, with Margery Jourdain the witch ; Southwell and Hume the two priests ; and Bolingbroke the cunning necromancer, who have been tried and found guilty of practising witchcraft are under guard. Commanding the Duchess to " stand forth " to " Receive the sentence of the law for sins Such as by God's book are adjudged to death," informs her that as she is " more nobly born " than the other prisoners, she has been sentenced to undergo " three days' of open penance " and subsequent banishment to the Isle of Man ; Southwell, Hume and Bolingbroke to be " strangled on the gallows," and Margery Jourdain the witch to be " burned to ashes " in Smithfield.

The duchess welcomes banishment, while the duke declares he " cannot justify whom the law condemns," and the duchess and other prisoners guarded are led away. Turning to the king, Gloucester asks leave to depart, since " Sorrow would solace and mine age would ease." Before he goes, Henry requests him to deliver up his staff of office, as he (Henry) intends in the future to be his own Protector:

> Stay, Humphrey, Duke of Gloucester : ere thou go,
> Give up thy staff : Henry will to himself
> Protector be ; and God shall be my hope,
> My stay, my guide, and lantern to my feet.
> And go in peace, Humphrey, no less beloved
> Than when thou wert protector to thy king.

to which the queen observes that she sees no reason why a " king of years Should be to be protected like a child."

Handing the king his staff of office, Gloucester remarks :

> My staff ? here, noble Henry, is my staff :
> .   .   .   .
> Farewell, good king ! when I am dead and gone,
> May honourable peace attend thy throne,

and forthwith departs.   When he has gone both the queen and Suffolk express their delight at Eleanor's shame and Gloucester's abasement, after which York reminds the king that this is the day appointed for the duel between Horner the armourer and his man Peter, and the king give orders for the lists to be set in order.

Horner, accompanied by his neighbours, and Peter attended by Prentices, enter, and after they have drunk liberally of sack, charneco and double beer, the signal is given for the duel to commence.   They fight, and Peter fatally wounds Horner, who, before expiring confesses treason :

> Hold, Peter, hold !   I confess, I confess treason.

Peter joyfully exclaims that " right has prevailed " :

> O God ! have I overcome mine enemies in this
> presence ?   O Peter ! thou hast prevailed in right,

and the king orders that Horner's corpse be removed forthwith, and commands Peter to follow him to receive his reward :

> Go, take hence that traitor from our sight ;
> For by his death we do perceive his guilt :
> And God in justice hath revealed to us
> The truth and innocence of this poor fellow,
> Which he had thought to have murdered wrongfully.
> Come, fellow, follow us for thy reward.

A London Street supplies the concluding scene of this Act.   It opens with Gloucester enquiring the time of the day, and being told it is ten o'clock, remarks :

> Ten is the hour that was appointed me
> To watch the coming of my punished duchess :

The duchess, barefoot, clad in a white sheet and carrying a burning taper, accompanied by Sir John Stanley, the Sheriff and officers, and followed by a jeering crowd, enters.   The servant suggests rescuing their mistress from the sheriff, but Gloucester bids them to " stir not, for your lives."   Seeing her husband, the duchess asks him whether he has come to see her " open shame," and drawing his attention to the " giddy multitude " who " point, And nod their heads, and throw their eyes on thee," reminds him that it is penance for him too.   " Be patient, gentle Nell ; forget this grief," is Gloucester's reply, but his wife tells him that as he is a " prince and protector of this land," he should not have allowed her to suffer such humiliation, and counsels him to beware

> For Suffolk, he that can do all in all
> With her that hateth thee, and hates us all,
> And York, and impious Beaufort, that false priest,
> Have all limed bushes to betray thy wings;
> And, fly thou how thou canst, they 'll tangle thee :
> But fear not thou, until thy foot be snared,
> Nor never seek prevention of thy foes.

but Gloucester tells her that she is mistaken, for

> I must offend before I be attainted ;
> And had I twenty times so many foes,
> And each of them had twenty times their power,
> All these could not procure me any scath,
> So long as I am loyal, true, and crimeless.

At this point, a Herald enters and summons Gloucester to attend Parliament at Bury St. Edmunds on the first of the next month, which he promises to do, although it has been called without his consent, adding : " This is close dealing." Turning to Sir John Stanley, Gloucester entreats him to treat his wife well, and expresses a hope that he (Gloucester) may live to reward him for his kindness :

> Entreat her not the worse in that I pray
> You use her well. The world may laugh again ;
> And I may live to do you kindness if
> You do it her : and so, Sir John, farewell.

The Duchess then asks her husband why he does not bid her farewell, and Gloucester exclaims " Witness my tears, I cannot stay to speak," and with his Servingmen departs forthwith to Bury St. Edmunds where his enemies were then disposing his downfall, Eleanor remarking : " All comfort go with thee ! "

The Duchess bids the Sheriff farewell, " Although thou hast been the conduct of my shame," and the Sheriff asks her to " pardon him," for " it is my office." Then turning to Stanley she requests him to " lead the way," for she " longs to see her prison."

The Third Act opens in the Abbey at Bury St. Edmunds, where a Parliament is being held. Henry muses at Gloucester's delay in arriving as it is not his custom to be the " hindmost man," while the Queen, Suffolk, Beaufort and Buckingham accuse Gloucester of evil charges against the realm. The queen accuses him of being insolent, proud, and peremptory, and being next heir to the throne, is plotting against Henry. Suffolk charges him with being " full of deep deceit " ; Beaufort with visiting small offences with severe punishments contrary to law ; and York that he had levied large sums of money to pay the army in France and had never sent it, in consequence of which mutiny had broken out ; while Buckingham describes these as " petty faults " compared with those that would reveal themselves later. The king considers it " worthy praise " for the lords " To mow down thorns that would annoy our foot," but deems Gloucester as innocent as the " sucking lamb " and " harmless dove." To this the queen rejoins that that makes him all the more dangerous, for " Seems he a dove ? his feathers are but borrowed, . . . Is he a lamb ? his skin is surely lent him," and charges Henry to " Take heed, my lord ; the welfare of us all Hangs on the cutting short that fraudful man."

Somerset now enters, and announces the loss of the English possessions in France, which the king describes as " Cold news, but God's will be done ! " while York, aside, mutters it is " Cold news for me," but he will " remedy this gear ere long, Or sell my title for a glorious grave."

Gloucester now enters, and apologising for his lateness in arriving, is immediately arrested by Suffolk on the charge of high treason, to which Gloucester rejoins that he will not blush nor change his countenance for this arrest for " A heart unspotted is not easily daunted," and demands to know of what he is guilty. The charges being repeated, Gloucester strenuously denies his guilt, but is cut short by Suffolk who for " mightier crimes " arrests him, and hands him over to Beaufort to keep until the day of trial, and Henry, whose " special hope " is, that Gloucester will clear himself from all the accusations of which he is accused, confesses that " My conscience tells me you are innocent." " Ah ! gracious lord, these days are dangerous," exclaims Gloucester, for " Beaufort's red sparkling eyes blab his heart's malice ; And Suffolk's cloudy brow his stormy hate ; Sharp Buckingham unburthens with his tongue The envious load that lies upon his heart ; And dogged York, that reaches at the moon, Whose overweening arm I have plucked back, By false accuse doth level at my life " ; and knowing they seek his downfall, declares that false witnesses will not be wanting to condemn, for

> The ancient proverb will be well effected :
> A staff is quickly found to beat a dog !

As he is led away by the guards, Gloucester exclaims :

> Ah ! thus King Henry throws away his crutch
> Before his legs be firm to bear his body :
> Thus is the shepherd beaten from thy side,
> And wolves are gnarling who shall gnaw thee first.
> Ah ! that my fear was false : ah ! that it were ;
> For, good King Henry, thy decay I fear.

When Gloucester has gone, the weak-kneed monarch tells the nobles to " do or undo, as if ourself were here, what to your wisdoms seemeth best," and telling his wife that his " heart is drowned with grief," for Gloucester is no " traitor," leaves the room followed by some of his courtiers. Turning to Beaufort, Suffolk and York, the queen remarks that her husband is " Too full of foolish pity " and hints that in order to rid themselves of the one they fear " Gloucester should be quickly rid the world." Beaufort considers his death is " worthy policy " but some semblance should be found to make it appear legitimate. To this Suffolk remarks that there is no " policy " in Beaufort's suggestion, for both Henry and the Commons would do their utmost to save his life, adding " we have but trivial argument." York interprets in this remark that Suffolk "would not have him die" but is assured that no one is more " fain " than he is, in the carrying out of which he would " not stand on quillets how to slay him : Be it by gins, by snares, by subtility, Sleeping or waking, 'tis no matter how, So he be dead." The queen, who is bitterly opposed to Gloucester, approves of all that Suffolk says, and Beaufort offers to supply his " executioner " if only Suffolk will " consent and censure well the deed." " Here is my hand, the deed is worthy doing," is Suffolk's rejoinder in which he is supported by Margaret and York.

A messenger enters with the news that rebellion has broken out in Ireland, and to York is given the task of proceeding thither to suppress it, a task he cheerfully undertakes as it will remove him from the fury that will follow the murder of Duke Humphrey, for in the words of Beaufort " I will deal with him That henceforth he shall trouble us no more, And so break off ; the day is almost spent."

All leave with the exception of York, who mutters to himself that a golden opportunity has presented itself, for while he is in Ireland he will raise a " mighty band " and " stir up in England some black storm Shall blow ten thousand souls to heaven or hell " ; which shall not cease till he has obtained the crown, and reveals that he has seduced a " headstrong Kentishman " John Cade of Ashford to personify John Mortimer, to make " commotion " in England, during which commotion he will return from Ireland with all his strength

> And reap the harvest which that rascal sowed ;
> For Humphrey being dead, as he shall be,
> And Henry put apart, the next for me.

Scene two shows us a Room of State at Bury St. Edmunds. Two murderers, hired by Suffolk hastily enter. Whispering to his comrade, the first murderer tells him to " Run to my Lord of Suffolk," and let him know we have dispatched the duke, to which the second assassin replies : " What have we done ? Didst ever hear a man so penitent ? " At this moment Suffolk enters and on learning that Gloucester is dead promises to reward them for this " venturous deed," after satisfying himself that all things have been done according to his directions.

Trumpets sound, and the king, accompanied by the queen, and courtiers enters, and Henry summons Gloucester to appear for his trial. Suffolk having gone to fetch the duke, the king bids the nobles take their places, and entreats them to :

> Proceed no straiter 'gainst our uncle Gloucester
> Than from true evidence, of good esteem,
> He be approved in practice culpable.

A moment later, Suffolk, in an agitated condition, re-enters, and the king addressing him, says :

> How now ! why look'st thou pale ? why tremblest thou ?
> Where is our uncle ? what 's the matter, Suffolk ?

and Suffolk replies : " Dead in his bed, my lord ; Gloucester is dead." Winchester considers this as " God's secret judgment " for he himself did " dream to-night The duke was dumb and could not speak a word." The king swoons, and the queen cries : " Help, lords ! the king is dead," but eventually recovering consciousness, Henry—who is suspicious of Suffolk—tells him to

> Lay not thy hands on me ; forbear, I say :
> Their touch affrights me as a serpent's sting.
> Thou baleful messenger, out of my sight !
> Upon thy eye-balls murderous tyranny
> Sits in grim majesty to fright the world.

The queen is defending her favourite against her husband's imputations, when there is a noise, and Warwick, Salisbury and many of the Commons enter. Addressing the King, Warwick demands to know if it is true that Gloucester has been murdered :

> It is reported, mighty sovereign,
> That good Duke Humphrey traitorously is murdered
> By Suffolk and the Cardinal Beaufort's means.
> The commons, like an angry hive of bees
> That want their leader, scatter up and down,
> And care not who they sting in his revenge.
> Myself have calmed their spleenful mutiny,
> Until they hear the order of his death.

Henry having given orders for Warwick to enter the death chamber in order to ascertain the cause of death, Warwick charges Salisbury to keep the Commons in check until he returns. With tears rolling down his cheeks the king is praying for God's judgment on the murderers, when Warwick and others re-enter, bearing the dead body on a bed. Laying it at the king's feet, Warwick boldly announces that " violent hands have been laid Upon the life of this thrice-famed duke." Describing this as a " dreadful oath " Suffolk demands what proof he has to make that assertion, and Warwick points out that his " face is black and full of blood," his " eye-balls further out than when he lived," and the hands displayed as one that grasped and tugged for life, all of which point to foul play. Suffolk hotly denies that either he or Beaufort is a murderer, and Warwick retorts that both of them were vowed enemies of Gloucester. " Then you, belike, suspect these noblemen As guilty of Duke Humphrey's timeless death " ejaculates the queen, and Warwick hotly retorts :

> Who finds the heifer dead, and bleeding fresh,
> And sees fast by a butcher with an axe,
> But will suspect 'twas he that made the slaughter ?

The queen then asks Suffolk whether he is a "butcher," and Suffolk replies that he "wears no knife to slaughter sleeping men," but if " proud Lord of Warwickshire " dare slander him with " murder's crimson badge " he is prepared to prove his innocence with his " vengeful sword, rusted with ease." Beaufort and others are on the point of leaving, when Warwick announces he is prepared to accept Suffolk's challenge, and calling him a " pernicious blood-sucker of sleeping men ! " they both leave the room, the king remarking that a heart untainted is a man's strongest breastplate.

There is a noise within and Suffolk and Warwick re-enter with drawn swords, and the king rebukes them for their boldness in his presence, and Suffolk excuses himself by saying, that the " traitorous Warwick, with the men of Bury, Set all upon me, mighty sovereign."

Immediately afterwards the Commons enter and are told by Salisbury to " stand apart ; the king shall know your mind." Turning to Henry he then states that the Commons demand that " Unless false Suffolk straight be done to death " or banished the kingdom, they will take him by force and " torture him with grievous lingering death," as " They say, by him the good Duke Humphrey died ; They say, in him they fear your highness' death." Suffolk describes them as " rude unpolished hinds " as to send such a message to their sovereign, a " sort of tinkers," while the king bids Salisbury to thank the Commons for their " tender loving care " and will banish Suffolk within the next three days. Salisbury gone, the queen pleads for her favourite, calling him " Gentle Suffolk," but Henry tells her his word is irrevocable, and calls her " Ungentle queen, to call him gentle Suffolk ! " and then turning to Suffolk bids him take his departure, warning him that

> If after three days' space thou here be'st found
> On any ground that I am ruler of,
> The world shall not be ransom for thy life.

and bidding Warwick to " go with me " as " I have great matters to impart to thee," leaves the room.

His Majesty gone, Margaret, in strong language, denounces her husband, but when Suffolk bids her to cease her execrations and let him take his heavy leave, she gives away to tears :

> O ! let me entreat thee, cease. Give me thy hand,
> That I may dew it with my mournful tears ;
> Nor let the rain of heaven wet this place,
> To wash away my woeful monuments.
> O ! could this kiss be printed in thy hand,
> That thou might'st think upon these by the seal,
> Through whom a thousand sighs are breathed for thee.
> So, get thee gone, that I may know my grief ;
> 'Tis but surmised whiles thou art standing by,
> As one that surfeits thinking on a want.
> I will repeal thee, or, be well assured,
> Adventure to be banished myself ;
> And banished I am, if but from thee.
> Go ; speak not to me ; even now be gone.
> O ! go not yet. Even thus two friends condemned
> Embrace and kiss and take ten thousand leaves.
> Loather a hundred times to part than die.
> Yet now farewell ; and farewell life with thee.

to which Suffolk replies :

> Thus is poor Suffolk ten times banished,
> Once by the king, and three times thrice by thee.
>
> .   .   .   .
> I can no more : live thou to joy thy life ;
> Myself no joy in nought but that thou livest.

At this point a messenger hastily enters with the news that Beaufort, at the point of death, is " Blaspheming God, and cursing men on earth," and calling for the king. Being told to " tell this heavy message to the king," he hastily departs, and turning to Suffolk, the queen tells him :

> Now get thee hence : the king, thou know'st, is coming ;
> If thou be found by me thou art but dead,

and Suffolk begs her to let him stay and face death rather than die in a foreign land :

> From thee to die were torture more than death.
> O ! let me stay, befall what may befall.

But Margaret insists on his leaving, for in whatever part of the globe he might be her messenger would find him :

> Away ! though parting be a fretful corrosive,
> It is applied to a deathful wound.
> To France, sweet Suffolk : let me hear from thee ;
> For wheresoe'er thou art in this world's globe,
> I 'll have an Iris that shall find thee out.

" I go," is Suffolk's reply, and " take my heart with thee," rejoins the queen, and Suffolk passes to an exile shorter than either of them anticipates.

The concluding Scene of this Act shows us a Bedchamber where Beaufort is lying on his death-bed in agony of conscience. Entering with Salisbury and Warwick, the king, leaning over the dying man asks : " How fares my lord ? speak, Beaufort, to thy sovereign." But Beaufort does not recognise the king :

> If thou be'st death, I 'll give thee England's treasure,
> Enough to purchase such another island,
> So thou wilt let me live, and feel no pain.

To this the king remarks :

> Ah, what a sign it is of evil life
> Where death's approach is seen so terrible !

" Beaufort, it is thy sovereign speaks to thee," exclaims Warwick, but the dying man can only stammer that he will confess all if brought to trial :

> Bring me unto my trial when you will.
> Died he not in his bed ? where should he die ?
> Can I make men live whe'r they will or no ?
> O torture me no more ! I will confess.
> Alive again ? then show me where he is :
> I 'll give a thousand pound to look upon him.
> He hath no eyes, the dust hath blinded them.
> Comb down his hair ; look ! look ! it stands upright,
> Like lime-twigs set to catch my winged soul.
> Give me some drink ; and bid the apothecary
> Bring the strong poison that I bought of him.

To those present these words are evidence that Beaufort is guilty of the murder of Gloucester, and the king calls upon Heaven to purge his soul of this foul deed :

> O thou eternal Mover of the heavens !
> Look with a gentle eye upon this wretch ;
> O ! beat away the busy meddling fiend
> That lays strong siege unto this wretch's soul,
> And from his bosom purge this black despair.

" See how the pangs of death do make him grin ! " remarks Warwick, and Salisbury replies " Disturb him not ; let him pass peacefully," and as the king watches him sink into silence bids Beaufort to lift a hand in token of the hope of salvation :

> Peace to his soul ! if God's good pleasure be.
> Lord cardinal, if thou think'st on heaven's bliss,
> Hold up thy hand, make signal of thy hope.

But the hand is not lifted and Henry cries :

> He dies, and makes no sign.   O God, forgive him !

to which Warwick adds :

> So bad a death argues a monstrous life,

but Henry solemnly charges them to

> Forbear to judge, for we are sinners all.
> Close up his eyes, and draw the curtain close ;
> And let us all to meditation.

The Fourth Act opens on the Coast of Kent.   Suffolk, bidden to leave the realm forthwith, reached Dover in disguise, and took a ship for France, but being intercepted was, along with others, taken prisoner.   Being brought ashore, the First Gentleman asks : " What is my ransom, master ? let me know," and the answer is : " A thousand crowns, or else lay down your head," to which the Mate adds : " And so much shall you give, or off goes yours."   But the captain considers that such a paltry sum does not " counterpoise the lives of those which we have lost in fight," and commands that their throats be cut.   The two gentlemen offer to pay their ransoms, but Whitmore tells them they shall die in revenge of his having lost an eye in " laying the prize aboard."   " Be not so rash : take ransom ; let them live," interposes the captain.   Suffolk then offers to pay any amount of ransom, for he is a gentlemen.   " And so am I ; my name is Walter Whitmore," a name which Suffolk considers " affrights me, in whose sound is death."   Hoping to escape, Suffolk discloses his identity :

> Stay, Whitmore ; for thy prisoner is a prince,
> The Duke of Suffolk, William de la Pole.

" The Duke of Suffolk muffled up in rags ! " is Whitmore's remark, and Suffolk tells him his blood must not be shed by a jaded groom, but turning to the captain, Whitmore asks : " Speak, captain, shall I stab the forlorn swain ? " to which the captain replies : " Convey him hence, and on our long-boat's side Strike off his head." Suffolk considers his " words are blunt," but the captain calls him a :

> puddle, sink ; whose filth and dirt
> Troubles the silver spring where England drinks.
> .   .   .   .
> Thy lips, that kissed the queen, shall sweep the ground ;
> And thou that smiled'st at good Duke Humphrey's death,
> .   .   .   .

By thee Anjou and Maine were sold to France,

.   .   .   .

And to conclude, reproach and beggary
Is crept into the palace of our king,
And all by thee. Away ! convey him hence.

Wishing he was a god to shoot forth thunder, Suffolk charges the captain to convey him in safety across the channel, but the captain gives orders for him to be taken away and let him hear no more. As he is led away, Suffolk mutters to himself that a

Roman sworder and banditto slave
Murdered sweet Tully ; Brutus' bastard hand
Stabbed Julius Cæsar ; savage islanders
Pompey the Great ; and Suffolk dies by pirates.

The captain then gives orders for the other prisoners to be released, and all except the first gentleman, depart. Whitmore re-enters, and throwing Suffolk's body on the sand, remarks :

There let his head and lifeless body lie,
Until the queen his mistress bury it,

and the first gentleman exclaims :

O barbarous and bloody spectacle !
His body will I bear unto the king :
If he revenge it not, yet will his friends ;
So will the queen, that living held him dear.

The second scene is Blackheath. Two men—George Bevis and John Holland—enter, and discuss the changes Jack Cade will make in the land : " I tell thee, Jack Cade the clothier means to dress the commonwealth, and turn it, and set a new nap upon it," is Bevis' remark. " So he had need, for 'tis threadbare. Well, I say it was never merry world in England since gentlemen came up," adds Holland, for " nobility think scorn to go in leather aprons, . . . but " let the magistrates be labouring men ; and therefore should we be magistrates." Cade, accompanied by Dick the Butcher, Smith the Weaver and other followers, enters, and declares his father was a Mortimer and his mother a Plantagenet—although aside Dick mutters that Cade is of common birth, having been born " under a hedge ; for his father had never a house but a cage." Cade promises a reformation in the realm, for when he is king " There shall be in England seven half-penny loaves sold for a penny ; the three-hooped pot shall have ten hoops, and I will make it felony to drink small beer." Dick the Butcher then proposes to kill all the lawyers. To this Cade agrees for it is a " lamentable thing, that of the skin of an innocent lamb should be made parchment ? that parchment, being scribbled o'er, should undo a man ? "

At this point a prisoner is brought in. It is the Clerk of Chatham, who has been arrested because he " can write and read and cast accompt." " Monstrous ! " is Cade's retort. Declaring that he has been so well brought up that he can write his name, he is denounced as a " villain and a traitor," and is sentenced to death : " Away with him ! I say : hang him with his pen and ink-horn about his neck."

Another of Cade's followers now appears, and counsels him to seek refuge in flight, as Sir Humphrey Stafford and his brother with forces are at hand, but Cade replies that only knights can fight with men equal to themselves and kneeling down, knights himself as Sir John Mortimer.

Sir Humphrey and his brother with forces now enter, and he promises pardon to all who lay down their arms :

> Rebellious hinds, the filth and scum of Kent,
> Marked for the gallows, lay your weapons down ;
> Home to your cottages, forsake this groom :
> The king is merciful, if you revolt,

but Cade argues that he is the rightful heir to the crown, although aside he acknowledges his claim is fictitious. Stafford declares Cade's father was a plasterer, but as Cade is so insistent there is a suspicion that the Duke of York—although at this time in Ireland—has fostered the insurrection, for Stafford's brother remarks : " Jack Cade, the Duke of York hath taught you this." Stafford then bids the Herald to proclaim " throughout every town " that Cade and his followers—even their wives and children—are traitors, and forthwith departs :

> Herald, away ; and throughout every town
> Proclaim them traitors that are up with Cade ;
> That those which fly before the battle ends
> May, even in their wives' and children's sight,
> Be hanged up for example at their doors.
> And you that be the king's friends, follow me.

Stafford having gone, Cade urges his followers to follow him, and " fight for liberty, . . . Spare none but such as go in clouted shoon, For they are thrifty honest men, and such As would, but that they dare not, take our parts. . . . Come : march ! forward ! "

Scene three shows us another part of Blackheath, where a skirmish takes place between the royal troops and the followers of Cade, in which both the Staffords are slain. Enquiring for Dick the Butcher, Cade tells him that " thou behaved'st thyself as if thou hadst been in thine own slaughter-house " : for Stafford's men " fell before thee like sheep and oxen." Cade then proposes that the bodies of the victims be dragged at his horses' heels until he come to London, " where we will have the mayor's sword borne before us," and Dick suggests that they break open the gaols and let out the prisoners.

The Palace in London supplies the next scene. The king, with a supplication, the queen with Suffolk's head, and others enter. It opens with the queen, in grief, wondering how anyone can look upon the head of Suffolk and cease to weep. Buckingham then enquires what answer the king intends to make to the rebel's petition, and Henry replies that in order to save bloodshed he purposes sending some " holy bishop to entreat " ; and he himself will " parley with Jack Cade their general." Then turning to the queen, the king observes : " Still lamenting and mourning for Suffolk's death ? I fear me, love, if that I had been dead, Thou wouldst not have mourned so much for me," to which the queen answers " No, my love ; I should not mourn, but die for thee."

A messenger enters with the news that Cade has arrived at Southwark, had proclaimed himself Lord Mortimer, and vows he will crown himself at Westminster :

> The rebels are in Southwark ; fly, my lord !
> Jack Cade proclaims himself Lord Mortimer,
> Descended from the Duke of Clarence's house,
> And calls your grace usurper openly,
> And vows to crown himself in Westminster.

Buckingham suggests that the king retire to Kenilworth until the insurrection has been crushed :

> My gracious lord, retire to Killingworth,
> Until a power be raised to put them down,

while the queen remarks that if Suffolk were alive the rebellion would soon be crushed :

> Ah, were the Duke of Suffolk now alive,
> These Kentish rebels would be soon appeased !

Another messenger enters and reports that Cade has taken possession of London Bridge, and that many of the citizens have joined him :

> Jack Cade hath gotten London bridge ;
> The citizens fly and forsake their houses ;
> The rascal people, thirsting after prey,
> Join with the traitor ; and they jointly swear
> To spoil the city and your royal court.

Buckingham urges the king to linger not, and the king in bidding him farewell, counsels him to " trust not the Kentish rebels," and Buckingham replies " Trust nobody, for fear you be betrayed."

We are at the Tower of London in the next scene, where the governor—Lord Scales—enquires if Cade has been slain. One of the citizens replies that Cade has captured London bridge and is slaying all who offer resistance, in consequence of which the Lord Mayor craves the governor's assistance to defend the city from the rebels. Scales therefore sends Matthew Goffe with as many as can be spared, and tells them to

> Fight for your king, your country, and your lives ;
> And so farewell, for I must hence again.

We are in Cannon Street, London in the next scene, where Cade, along with his forces, has arrived. Striking London-stone with his sword, he announces : " Now is Mortimer Lord of this city" ; orders claret wine to flow from all the conduits to commemorate the " first year of our reign" , and proclaims it to be treasonable to address him other than as " Lord Mortimer : "

> Now is Mortimer lord of this city. And here, sitting
> upon London-stone, I charge and command that, of
> the city's cost, the pissing-conduit run nothing but
> claret wine this first year of our reign. And now
> henceforward it shall be treason for any that calls me
> other than Lord Mortimer.

A soldier enters, crying " Jack Cade ! Jack Cade ! " and Cade ordering him to be " Knocked down," he is immediately slain. Dick the Butcher then informs Cade that an army has gathered together at Smithfield, and Cade orders London Bridge to be set on fire, and if possible the Tower too, after which they will march to Smithfield and give battle to the king's forces.

In Scene seven we are at Smithfield. Having defeated the royal forces—in which encounter Matthew Goffe is slain—Cade orders his followers to pull down the Savoy, the Inns of Court, and to burn all the records of the realm, declaring that " my mouth shall be the parliament of England.

A messenger enters crying : " My lord, a prize, a prize ! here's the Lord Say, which sold the towns in France ; he that made us pay one-and-twenty fifteens, and one shilling to the pound, the last subsidy." " Well, he shall be beheaded for it ten times," is Cade's remark, as Lord Say, in charge of Bevis, enters. Addressing Say, Cade accuses him of having sold Normandy, for having traitorously corrupted the youth by erecting a grammar-school, and that his pupils talk of a " noun " and a " verb " and other abominable things as no Christian ear can endure to hear. Say denies that he sold Maine and lost Normandy, and " seeing ignorance is the curse of God " had given large gifts to spread knowledge. Being a tottering old man shaken with palsy, Dick the Butcher asks why he quivers, and Say replies that it is the palsy, and not fear, that provokes him. Declaring that his head would stand steadier on a pole, Cade orders him to be taken away and beheaded, after which he gives orders for the house of Say's son-in-law—Sir James Cromer—to be entered and to strike off his head, and the two heads to be brought upon two poles.

The executioners re-enter bearing the two heads, and Cade orders them to " kiss one another " for " they loved well when they were alive " and bids his followers that as they ride through the streets of the city the heads shall precede them and at every corner shall embrace :

> Soldiers, defer
> the spoil of the city until night ; for with these
> borne before us, instead of maces, will we ride through
> the streets ; and at every corner have them kiss.
> Away !

We are transferred to Southwark in the next Scene. Cade enters and calls upon his followers to " kill and knock down ! throw them into Thames ! " all who resist. A parley sounds, and Cade asks : " What noise is this I hear ? Dare any be so bold to sound retreat or parley, when I command to kill ? " Immediately Buckingham and Clifford appear and offer, on behalf of the king, pardon to all who disperse and go home in peace. When Clifford asks those who " loves the king, and will embrace his pardon," to throw up their caps and say " God save his majesty ! " they all cry out : " God save the king ! God save the king ! " Turning to his followers Cade upbraids them : " do ye believe him ? will you needs be hanged with your pardons about your necks ? Hath my sword therefore broke through London gates, that you should leave me at the White Hart in Southwark ? " and threatens to " make shift for one, and so, God's curse light upon you all ! ", they all cry out : "We 'll follow Cade, we 'll follow Cade ! " Asked by Clifford if Cade would conduct them through the heart of France as did Henry the Fifth—father of the present king—he appeals to them to end this civil broil and " To France, to France ! and recover what you have lost " ; they once more veer round and shout " A Clifford ! a Clifford ! we 'll follow the king and Clifford."

Seeing his followers wavering, Cade exclaims : " Was ever feather so lightly blown to and fro as this multitude ? " and considering himself unsafe, breaks through their ranks and makes his escape. Finding he has fled Buckingham offers a reward of a thousand crowns for his capture :

> What, is he fled ? go some, and follow him ;
> And he that brings his head unto the king
> Shall have a thousand crowns for his reward.

Kenilworth Castle supplies the next Scene. Trumpets sound, and the King, Queen and Somerset appear on the terrace. Henry laments his unhappy position, observing that " No sooner was I crept out of my cradle But I was made a king at nine months old " : and expresses the wish to be a " subject." Buckingham and Clifford enter, with the " glad tidings " that the insurrection has been crushed, that Cade has fled, and his followers, with halters on their necks, await "your highness' doom, of life or death." The king grants pardon to them and dismisses them to their " several countries " and as they disperse they all shout with delight : " God save the king ! God save the king ! "

No sooner have they dispersed, than a messenger enters and announces that the Duke of York has returned from Ireland with a " mighty power of gallowglasses and stout kerns." with the sole purpose of removing Somerset—his inveterate enemy, whom he terms a traitor—from the king's counsel.   Henry compares the state to a ship that having escaped a tempest, is now boarded by a pirate, and bids Buckingham go and meet York and tell him that Duke Edmund shall be committed to the Tower;   and then turning to Somerset, adds: " And, Somerset, we will commit thee thither, Until his army be dismissed from him."   Somerset cheerfully accepts this humiliation: " My lord, I 'll yield myself to prison willingly, Or unto death, to do my country good," after which Henry departs, remarking to the queen, as he does :

> Come, wife, let 's in, and learn to govern better ;
> For yet may England curse my wretched reign.

The concluding Scene of this Act shows us Iden's garden in Kent.   Desperate with famine, Cade, who has " These five days have I hid in these woods and durst not peep out, for all the country is laid for me," enters the garden of the Kentish squire in quest of food.   He is encountered by Iden.   " Here 's the lord of the soil come to seize me for a stray, for entering his fee-simple without leave.   Ah, villain, thou wilt betray me, and get a thousand crowns of the king by carrying my head to him ; but I 'll make thee eat iron like an ostrich, and swallow my sword like a great pin, ere thou and I part."   Iden, who does not recognise Cade, answers: " I know thee not ;   why then should I betray thee ? " and describes him as a " rude companion," for he is not content with breaking into his garden to rob, but " brave me with these saucy terms," and forthwith accepts his challenge.   They fight, and Cade falling mortally wounded reveals himself: " O, I am slain !   Famine and no other hath slain me :   let ten thousand devils come against me, and give me but the ten meals I have lost, and I 'd defy them all.   Wither, garden ;   and be henceforth a burying-place to all that do dwell in this house, because the unconquered soul of Cade is fled," and Iden resolves to " hallow " his sword for having slain " that monstrous traitor."   " Iden, farewell ;   and be proud of thy victory.   Tell Kent from me, she hath lost her best man," are Cade's dying words, and dragging the body " headlong by the heels " to a dunghill Iden cuts off his " ungracious head."

> Which I will bear in triumph to the king,
> Leaving thy trunk for crows to feed upon.

The Fifth Act opens in the Fields between Dartford and Blackheath.   York, with his army of Irish, with drum and colours, enters, and proclaims that he has come to " pluck the crown from feeble Henry's head " :

> From Ireland thus comes York to claim his right,
> And pluck the crown from feeble Henry's head :
> Ring, bells, aloud ; burn, bonfires, clear and bright,
> To entertain great England's lawful king.
> Ah ! sancta majestas, who would not buy thee dear ?
> Let him obey that know not how to rule ;
> This hand was made to handle nought but gold :
> I cannot give due action to my words,
> Except a sword or sceptre balance it.
> A sceptre shall it have, have I a soul,
> On which I 'll toss the flower-de-luce of France.

Buckingham appears, and greeting York informs him that the king has sent to know why he comes in arms :

> A messenger from Henry, our dread liege,
> To know the reason of these arms in peace ;
> Or why thou, being a subject as I am,
> Against thy oath and true allegiance sworn,
> Should'st raise so great a power without his leave,
> Or dare to bring thy force so near the court.

Although angry at the words of Buckingham, York aside mutters that his " choler is so great, he scarce can speak,"

> The cause why I have brought this army hither
> Is to remove proud Somerset from the king,
> Seditious to his grace and to the state.

Buckingham declares that York is very presumptuous, but if thy " arms be to no other end " than to " remove proud Somerset " informs him that the king has yielded to his demand and has sent Somerset to the Tower. Hearing this York dismisses his army and sends his two sons—Edward and Richard—to the king as " pledges of my fealty and love."

Buckingham then induces York to accompany him to the tent of the king, just as Henry and attendants appear, and noticing Buckingham "arm-in-arm" Henry concludes that York " intends no harm to us." Henry then asks York why he comes with an armed force, to which York replies : " To heave the traitor Somerset from hence, And fight against that monstrous rebel, Cade, Who since I heard to be discomfited."

Iden now enters, bearing the head of Cade, and addressing the king, says :

> If one so rude and of so mean condition
> May pass into the presence of a king,
> Lo ! I present your grace a traitor's head,
> The head of Cade, whom I in combat slew.

Henry is so pleased at Iden's brave deed, that he creates him a knight, and rewards him with a thousand marks, the price set on the head of Cade :

> The head of Cade ! Great God, how just art Thou !
> O, let me view his visage, being dead,
> That living wrought me such exceeding trouble.
> Tell me, my friend, art thou the man that slew him ?
> *Iden.* I was, an 't like your majesty.
> *King.* How art thou called, and what is thy degree ?
> *Iden.* Alexander Iden, that 's my name ;
> A poor esquire of Kent, that loves his king.
> *Buck.* So please it you, my lord, 'twere not amiss
> He were created knight for his good service.
> *King.* Iden, kneel down. [*He kneels.*] Rise up a knight.
> We give thee for reward a thousand marks ;
> And will that thou henceforth attend on us.
> *Iden.* May Iden live to merit such a bounty,
> And never live but true unto his liege.

Henry then observing Somerset—accompanied by the queen—approaching, bids Buckingham go and bid him hide from the Duke of York. As they enter, the queen remarks :

> For thousand Yorks he shall not hide his head,
> But boldly stand and front him in his face.

and York seeing Somerset at liberty, observes :

> How now ! is Somerset at liberty ?
> Then, York, unloose thy long-imprisoned thoughts
> And let thy tongue be equal with thy heart,

and charges Henry with a breach of faith, telling him he is not fit to govern the realm, and swears " thou shalt rule no more O'er him whom heaven created for thy ruler." Somerset therefore arrests York for high treason, and orders him to kneel to Henry for pardon :

> O monstrous traitor ! I arrest thee, York,
> Of capital treason 'gainst the king and crown.
> Obey, audacious traitor ; kneel for grace.

but York refuses to kneel and calls for his two sons to be his bail. Interposing, the queen requests that Clifford be called :

> To say if that the bastard boys of York
> Shall be the surety for their traitor father,

and York denounces her, calling her a " blood-bespotted Neapolitan," and declares that his two sons—her betters in their birth—shall be surety for their father. York's two sons now enter, followed by Clifford and his son. Kneeling before the king, Clifford is rebuked by York, who tells him that he (York) is their rightful sovereign. Clifford asks whether the " man has gone mad," and declaring him a traitor, counsels them to hale him to the Tower " And chop away that factious pate of his." " He is arrested, but will not obey," remarks the queen, and being asked by their father, the two sons of York declare their willingness to be surety for their father " if our words will serve, And if words will not, then our weapons shall." Clifford denounces them as a " brood of traitors " and York retaliates by calling Clifford a " false-heart traitor," and forthwith summons the Lords Salisbury and Warwick to his assistance.

As Warwick and Salisbury enter, Clifford remarks : " Are these thy bears ? we 'll bait thy bears to death, And manacle the bear-ward in their chains, If thou dar'st bring them to the baiting-place," and as Warwick and Salisbury refuse to do homage to the king, Henry reproves them :

> Why, Warwick, hath thy knee forgot to bow ?
> Old Salisbury, shame to thy silver hair,
> Thou mad misleader of thy brain-sick son !
> What ! wilt thou on thy death-bed play the ruffian,
> And seek for sorrow with thy spectacles ?
> O ! where is faith ?   O ! where is loyalty ?
> .   .   .   .
> For shame ! in duty bend thy knee to me,
> That bows unto the grave with mickle age.

To this Salisbury replies that he considers that York is the rightful heir to the crown .

> My lord, I have considered with myself
> The title of this most renowned duke ;
> And in my conscience do repute his grace
> The rightful heir to England's royal seat,

and the king thereupon bids Buckingham arm in defence of himself and the realm, while York declares he is resolved for " death or dignity." Young Clifford urges his " victorious father " to take up arms and " quell the rebels and their complices," after which they depart, York falling back upon Saint Albans, and Clifford and Somerset to the north to get together an army to oppose him.

Saint Albans supplies the next Scene, where a battle takes place between the forces of Lancaster and York. It opens with Warwick calling for Clifford to come forward and fight him :

> Clifford of Cumberland, 'tis Warwick calls :
> And if thou dost not hide thee from the bear,
> Now, when the angry trumpet sounds alarum,
> And dead men's cries do fill the empty air,
> Clifford, I say, come forth and fight with me !
> Proud northern lord, Clifford of Cumberland,
> Warwick is hoarse with calling thee to arms.

York suddenly appears, and reports having had a duel with Clifford in which each of their steeds were slain. Clifford now enters and Warwick challenges him, declaring that " Of one or both of us the time is come," but York requests Warwick to yield him first claim: " Hold, Warwick! seek thee out some other chase, For I myself must hunt this deer to death," and Warwick departs, exclaiming: " It grieves my soul to leave thee unassailed." York and Clifford combat each other and Clifford being slain, York exclaims:

> Thus war hath given thee peace, for thou art still.
> Peace with his soul, heaven, if it be thy will!

Young Clifford now enters, and seeing his father dead, in fierce anger vows vengeance on the House of York:

> O! let the vile world end,
>
> Even at this sight
> My heart is turned to stone: and while 'tis mine
> It shall be stony.   York not our old men spares;
> No more will I their babes: tears virginal
> Shall be to me even as the dew to fire;
> And beauty, that the tyrant oft reclaims,
> Shall to my flaming wrath be oil and flax.
> Henceforth I will not have to do with pity:
> Meet I an infant of the house of York,
> Into as many gobbets will I cut it
> As wild Medea young Absyrtus did:
> In cruelty will I seek out my fame.
> Come, thou new ruin of old Clifford's house:
> As did Æneas old Anchises bear,
> So bear I thee upon my manly shoulders;
> But when Æneas bare a living load,
> Nothing so heavy as these woes of mine,

and forthwith departs bearing away the body of his father.

Immediately afterwards Richard and Somerset enter fighting, in which Somerset is killed, and Richard, exulting over his body says:

> So, lie thou there;
> For underneath an alehouse' paltry sign.
> The Castle in Saint Alban's, Somerset
> Hath made the wizard famous in his death.
> Sword, hold thy temper; heart, be wrathful still:
> Priests pray for enemies, but princes kill.

More excursions follow, during which the king, queen, and others enter. The queen charges her husband with " being slow " and asks: " What are you made of? you 'll nor fight nor fly,"

> If you be ta'en, we then should see the bottom
> Of all our fortunes; but if we haply 'scape,
> As well we may, if not through your neglect,
> We shall to London get, where you are loved,
> And where this breach now in our fortunes made
> May readily be stopped.

Young Clifford re-enters and urges the king to flee:

> Away, for your relief! and we will live
> To see their day and them our fortune give.
> Away, my lord, away!

The final scene of the Play is enacted in the Fields near Saint Alban's. There is an alarum, and York, with forces enter. Inquiring the whereabouts of Salisbury, Richard tells his father how he rescued him from the enemy:

> Three times to-day I holp him to his horse,
> Three times bestrid him ; thrice I led him off,
> Persuaded him from any further act :
> But still, where danger was, still there I met him ;
> And like rich hangings in a homely house,
> So was his will in his old feeble body.

At this point Salisbury enters, thanks Richard for having rescued him and announces the retreat of the Lancastrian forces.   Hearing that the king has fled to London in order to call Parliament together, York decides to follow him :

> I know our safety is to follow them ;
> For, as I hear, the king is fled to London,
> To call a present court of parliament :
> Let us pursue him ere the writs go forth.
> What says Lord Warwick ? shall we after them ?

To this Warwick agrees :

> After them ! nay, before them, if we can.

but before departing, Warwick declares that this " glorious day " shall be immortalised throughout all ages.

> Saint Alban's battle, won by famous York,
> Shall be eternized in all age to come.
> Sound drums and trumpets ! and to London all :
> And more such days as these to us befall !

Scene : In various Parts of England.

CHARACTERS, PLACE-NAMES, ETC.

Abbey at Bury St. Edmunds.

The Scene of Act III., Scene i. The Parliament scene at Bury St. Edmunds. Gloucester is attacked by false accusations of his enemies, in which they are supported by the queen. He is arrested for high treason, and given in custody of Cardinal Beaufort, who conspires his murder. News arrives that the Irish are in rebellion, and York is appointed Regent to proceed to Ireland with troops to suppress the uprising, an opportunity which he gladly accepts as it will enable him to foment sedition in England.

Absyrtus. V. ii. 59.

> Meet I an infant of the house of York,
> Into as many gobbets will I cut it
> As wild Medea young Absyrtus did : [V. ii. 57–59.]

The Duke of York having slain Lord Clifford, his son,—the young Clifford—swears vengeance on the house of York.

Absyrtus was the son of King Æetes and brother of Medea. When Jason the Argonaut flew from Colchis, accompanied by Absyrtus and Medea, Medea cut her brother into pieces, and scattered them along the way so that her father in stopping to pick them up, might be delayed in pursuing her.

Achilles' spear. V. i. 100.

> Whose smile and frown, like to Achilles' spear,
> Is able with the change to kill and cure. [V. 1. 100–101.]

When Telephus, King of Mysia, who had married the daughter of the King of Troy, opposed the landing of the Greeks in his country, he was wounded by Achilles. An oracle having declared that the wound could never be cured save by the same weapon which had inflicted it, Telephus visited the camp of the Greeks. Ulysses, who had been informed by an oracle that Troy could not be captured without the assistance of Telephus, scraped rust from the spear, made it up into a plaster and applying it to the sore, cured the sufferer.

Cf. *King Edward III.*, ii., i.

> The poets write, that great Achilles' spear
> Could heal the wound it made : the moral is,
> What mighty men misdo, they can amend.

Greene, in his *Orlando Furioso*, 1599, has the same allusion :

> Where I took hurt, there have I heal'd myself ;
> As those that with Achilles' launce were wounded,
> Fetch'd help at self-same pointed speare.

Achilles was the chief hero of the Greeks in the Trojan war.

Adam. IV. ii. 133.

> And Adam was a gardener. [IV. ii. 133.]

Hart remarks : " Why should we be kept in servitude and bondage ? We be all come from one father and one mother, *Adam* and Eve."

Adsum. I. iv. 24.

" I am here."

Æneas. V. ii. 62, 64.

> Come, thou new ruin of old Clifford's house :
> As did Æneas old Anchises bear,
> So bear I thee upon my manly shoulders ;
> But then Æneas bare a living load,
> Nothing so heavy as these woes of mine.
> [V. ii. 61–65.]

See Anchises.

Æolus. III. ii. 92.

> Was I for this nigh wrecked upon the sea,
> And twice by awkward wind from England's bank
> Drove back again unto my native clime ?
> What boded this, but well forewarning wind
> Did seem to say " Seek not a scorpion's nest,
> Nor set no footing on this unkind shore ? "
> [III. ii. 82–87.]
> Yet Æolus would not be a murderer,
> But left that hateful office unto thee :
> [III. ii. 92–93.]

In Greek mythology the god of the winds which he kept confined in a cave. He resided in the islands of the Tyrrhenian Sea which were called the Æolian islands.

" Aio te, Æacida, Romanos vincere posse."
I. iv. 62.

" I say that you, descendant of Æneas, the Romans can conquer." The ambiguous reply the Oracle at Delhi gave Pyrrhus King of Epirus when he inquired whether he would vanquish Rome.

Hart quotes Puttenham *Arte of English Poesie*, under the heading of *Amphibologia*, or the Ambiguous : " these doubtfull speaches were vsed much in the old times by their false Prophets as appeareth by the Oracles of Delphos and of the Sybilles prophecies deuised by the religious persons of those days to abuse the superstitious . . . Lucianus, the merry Greeke, reciteth a great number of them devised by a coosening companion, one Alexander, to get himselfe the name and reputation of the God Æsculapius, and in effect all our old Brittish and Saxon prophecies be of the same sort, that, turne them on which side ye will, the matter of them may be verified . . . by the comfort of those blinde prophecies many insurrections and rebellions have bene stirred up in this Realme, as that of Iacke Strawe and Iacke Cade in Richard the seconds time."

Ajax Telamonius. V. i. 26.

And now, like Ajax Telamonius,
On sheep or oxen could I spend my fury. [V. i. 26–27.]

Son of Telamon a Greek hero of the Trojan War. In a state of madness at not receiving the armour of Achilles he slew a flock of sheep, mistaking them for his foes. He afterwards committed suicide. He is a character in *Troilus and Cressida*.

Hart quotes from Harington's *Metamorphoses*, 1596 : " First he killed all the horned beasts he met, which made Agamemnon and Menelaus now more afraid then Ulysses ; whereupon he was banished the towns presently, and then he went to the woods and pastures, and imagining all the fat sheep he met to be of kin to the coward Ulysses, because they ran away from him, he massacred a whole flock of sheep not ewes. Last of all, having nobody else to kill, poor man killed himself."

Alarums. IV. iii. p.1 ; IV. vii. p.1 ; IV. viii. p.1 ; V. ii. p.1 ; V. iii. p.1.

A summons to arms, as on the approach of an enemy.

Albion's king. I. iii. 44 ; III. ii. 113.

King of England. Albion was the ancient name of Britain.

Alderliefest. I. i. 28.

= Most beloved ; dearest of all.

Aldermen. II. i. p.68.

Alexander Iden, a Kentish Gentleman. IV. x. p.16, 43, 72 ; V. i. p.64, 74, 78, 81.

It is in Iden's garden that we next meet Cade after the defeat of his men at Southwark. Cade climbs over the wall, and is seen by Iden who challenges him for trespass. They fight and Iden mortally wounds Cade. " For, after a Proclamacion made that whosoeuer could apprehende the saied Iac Cade should haue for his pain a M. markes, many sought for hym, but few espied hym, til one Alexander Iden, esquire of Kent, found hym in a garden, and there in hys defence manfully slewe the caitife Cade, & brought his ded body to London, whose hed was set on London bridge." *Holinshed.*

Althæa. I. i. 232.

As did the fatal brand Althæa burned
Unto the prince's heart of Calydon. [I. i. 232–233.]

An allusion to the story of Meleager, Prince of Calydon. When he was born Althæa was warned by the Fates that he would live no longer than a brand burning upon the hearth. She contrived to keep the log unconsumed for many years, but being incensed at the slaying of her two brothers, threw the brand into the fire, and it was consumed in a few moments, and Meleager died at the same time. Cf. Ovid *Metamorphoses* (Golding's translation), viii., 594–614 :

There was a certaine firebrand which when *Oenies* wife did lie
In childebed of *Meleagar*, she chauned to espie
The Destnies putting in the fire : and in the putting in,
She heard them speake these words, as they his fatall threede did spin :
O lately borne, like time we give to thee and to this brand.
And when they so had spoken, they departed out of hand.
Immediatly the mother caught the blazing bough away.
And quenched it. This bough was kept full charely many a day :
And in the keeping of the same she kept hir sonne alive.
And now intending of his life him clearely to deprive,
She brought it forth, and causing all the coales and shivers to
Be layëd by, she like a foe did kindle fire thereto.
Fowre times she was about to cast the firebrand in the flame :
Fowre times she pulled backe hir hand from doing of the same.
As moother and as sister both she strove what way to go;
The divers names drew diversly hir stomacke to and fro.

Hir face waxt often pale for feare of mischiefe to ensue :
And often red about the eies through heate of ire she
grew.
One while hir looke resembled one that threatened
cruelnesse :
Another while ye would have thought she minded
pitiousnesse.
And though the cruell burning of hir heart did drie hir
teares,
Yet burst out some,

and *Second Part of King Henry the Fourth*, II.,
ii., 84–86 :

Marry, my lord, Althæa dreamed she was delivered of a fire-brand ; and therefore I call him her
dream.

Anchises. V. ii. 62.

In Greek legend a prince of the royal house of
Troy. He was of such a beautiful complexion
that Aphrodite fell in love with him and he had
by her a son named Æneas. But having, in
spite of her warnings boasted of her favour he
was struck blind. When Troy was sacked and
burnt, Anchises was an old man and Æneas
carried him through the flames upon his
shoulders and thus saved his life. He accompanied his son to Italy and died in Sicily in the
eightieth year of his age, and was buried on
Mount Eryx. Virgil in his Æneid, Book vi.,
introduces him in the Elysian fields :

" Meanwhile Æneas sees in the retired winding vale, a
grove situate by itself, shrubs rustling in the woods, and
the river Lethe which glides by those peaceful dwellings.
Around this *river* unnumbered tribes and nations of
ghosts were fluttering ; as in meadows on a serene
summer's day, when the bees sit on the various blossoms,
and swarm around the snow-white lilies, all the plain
buzzes with their humming noise. Æneas, confounded,
shudders at the unexpected sight, and asks the cause *of
that appearance*, what those rivers yonder are, or what
ghosts have in such crowds filled the banks. Then
father Anchises *said*, Those souls, from whom other
bodies are destined by fate, at the streams of Lethe's
flood quaff care-expelling draughts and lasting oblivion.
Long indeed have I wished to give you a detail of these,
pointing them out before you, and enumerate this my
future race, that you may rejoice the more with me in
the possession of Italy. O father, is it to be imagined
that any souls of an exalted nature will go hence to the
world above, and enter again into *clumsy* inactive
bodies ? What cursed love of life possesses the miserable
beings ? I, indeed, replied Anchises, will inform you,
my son, nor hold you longer in suspense ; and thus be
unfolds each particular in order." Davidson's *Translation*.

Anjou. I. i. 49, 57, 108, 234.

Item, that the duchy of Anjou and
the county of Maine shall be released and delivered
to the king her father "—   [I. i. 49–51.]

Grafton says : " This mariage seemed to
many, both infortunate and vnprofitable to the
realme of England, and that for many causes.
First the king had with her not one pennie,
and for the fetchyng of her, the Marques of
Suffolke demaunded a whole fiftene in open
Parliament : also for her mariage, the Duchie
of Aniow, the Citie of Mauns, and the whole
Countie of Mayne, were deliuered and released
to king Reyner her father, which Countries
were the very stayes, and backestandes to the
Duchie of Normandie.

See also Reigner.

Anjou. I. i. 117.

Sal. But wherefore weeps Warwick, my valiant son ?
War. For grief that they are past recovery :
For, were there hope to conquer them again,
My sword should shed hot blood, mine eyes no tears.
Anjou and Maine ! myself did win them both ;
                                [I. i. 112–117.]

Warwick's indignation is natural.

Anjou. I. i. 212 ; IV. i. 86.

Anjou and Maine are given to the French ;
Paris is lost ; the state of Normandy
Stands on a tickle point now they are gone.
                                [I. i. 212 *et seq.*]

Lines 212-235 of this Soliloquy are original,
the remainder is taken almost verbatim from
The Contention.

Grafton says : "Wherefore they (not mindyng
to be more charged, then their backes would
beare, and perceiuying that by negligent prouision and improuident pollicie, the affayres and
businesse in the partes beyonde the sea, dayly
decayed, and more were like to do) began first
to make exclamacion agaynst the Duke of
Suffolke, affirmyng him, to be the onely cause
of the deliuery of Aniow, and Main, the chiefe
procurer of the death of the good Duke of
Glouester, the very occasion of ye losse of
Normandie, the most swallower vp & consumer of
the kings treasure (by reason whereof, the
warres of Frauce were not mainteyned) the
expeller from the king of all good & vertuous
counsailors, and the bringer in & aduaunver of
vicious persons, common enemies, and apparaunt
aduersaries to the publike wealth : So that the
Duke was called in euery mans mouth a traytor,
a murtherer, a robber of the kings treasure,
and worthy to be put to most cruell punishe-
ment : By reason of this exclamacion, the
Queene somewhat fearyng the destruction of
the Duke, but more the confusion of herselfe,
caused the Parliament, before begon at the

black Friers in London, to be adiourned to Leycester, thinkyng there by force and rigor of the lawe, to subdue and represse all the malice and euill will, conceyued agaynst the Duke and her: at which place fewe of the Nobility would appere, wherefore it was againe adiourned to Westminster, where was a whole companie and a full apperaunce."

Anne. II. ii. 38, 44.

Daughter of Roger Mortimer, fourth Earl of March; married Richard, Earl of Cambridge and became the mother of Richard Plantagenet, Duke of York, who claimed the throne of England.

See also under Roger, Earl of March.

Argo. IV. ii. 30.
Corrupt for *Ergo.*

Ascanius. III. ii. 116.

> To sit and witch me, as Ascanius did
> When he to madding Dido would unfold
> His father's acts, commenced in burning Troy!
> [III. ii. 116-118.]

It was Cupid, in the shape of Ascanius who sat in Dido's lap, and played the witchcraft upon her; and it was Æneas who narrated to Dido the destruction of Troy.

Ashford. III. i. 356; IV. iii. 1.

A town in Kent. According to III., i., 356, it was the reputed birthplace of Jack Cade; and in IV., iii., 1, Dick the Butcher was a butcher in this town.

Asmath. I. iv. 24.

The name of a Spirit, invoked by Margery Jourdain. Cf. *Tobit,* iii., 6–8.

Attendants. III. ii. p.15; IV. viii. p.6; V. i. p.56.

Ave-Maries. I. iii. 55.

> But all his mind is bent to holiness,
> To number Ave-Maries on his beads;
> His champions are the prophets and apostles,
> His weapons holy saws of sacred writ,
> His study is his tilt-yard, and his loves
> Are brazen images of canonised saints. [I. iii. 54–59.]

An invocation to the Virgin Mary. Grafton says: "During the time of this truce or abstinence of warre, while there was nothing to vexe or trouble the mindes of men within the Realme, a sodayne mischiefe, and a long discorde, sprange out, by the meanes of a woman:

for king Henry, which raigned at this tyme, was a man of a meeke spirite, and of a simple witte, preferring peace before warre, rest before businesse, honestie before profite, and quietnesse before laboure. And to the intent, that all men might perceiue, that there coulde be none, more chaste, more meeke, more holye, nor a better creature: In him raigned shamefastnesse, modesty, integritie, and pacience to be maruayled at, taking and suffering all losses, chaunces, displeasures, and such worldly tormentes in good parte, and wyth a pacient maner, as though they had chaunced by his owne faulte, or negligent ouersight: and he was gouerned of them whome he shoulde haue ruled: and brideled of such, whom he sharpely shoulde haue spurred: He gaped not for honor, nor thristed for riches, but studied onelye for the health of hys soule: the sauing whereof, he esteemed to be the greatest wisedome, and the loss thereof, the extremest folie that coulde be. But on the other parte, the Queene his wife was a woman of a great witte, and yet of no greater wit, then of haute stomacke, desirous of glory, and couetous of honor, and of reason, pollicye, counsaill, and other giftes, and talentes of nature, she lacked nothing, nor of diligence, studie, and businesse, she was not vnexpert: but yet she had one pointe of a very woman: for often times, when she was vehement & fully bent in a matter, she was sodainly like to a wethercock, mutable and turning. This woman perceyuing that her husbande did not frankely rule as he would, but did all thing by the aduise and counsayle of Humfrey Duke of Gloucester, and that he passed not much on the aucthoritie and gouernaunce of the realme, determined wyth her selfe, to take vppon her the rule and regiment, both of the king and his kingdome, and to depriue and remoue out of all rule and aucthoritie the sayde Duke, then called the Lord Protectour of the realme: least men should say and report, that she had neyther wyt nor stomack, which would permit and suffer her husband, being of perfite age and mans estate, like a yong Scholer or innocent Pupile, to be gouerned by the disposition of an other man."

Bargulus. IV. i. 108.

> this villain here,
> Being captain of a pinnace, threatens more
> Than Bargulus the strong Illyrian pirate.
> [IV. i. 106-108.]

An Illyrian robber or pirate, who rose to be King of Illyria. In *The Contention* the corresponding passage is :

> This villain being but Captain of a Pinnais,
> Threatens more plagues then mightie Abradas,
> The great Masadonian Pyrate,
> Thy words addes fury and not remorse in me.

Bargulus is mentioned by Cicero in his *De Officiis.*

Beadle, A. II. i. p.142.

Summoned by the Mayor of St. Albans, and ordered by Gloucester to whip the impostor Simpcox.

Bedchamber, A.

The Scene of Act III., Scene iii. The scene shows the death of Cardinal Beaufort, six weeks after the death of the Duke of Gloucester. [Courtenay remarks : " This scene has stamped the name of Beaufort with the character of profligate and murderer ; and as if the poet's art were not sufficient, the sister art has been called in aid " ; while Stubbs observes : " On the 11th of April, six weeks after the death of Gloucester, the cardinal of England passed away ; not, as the great poet has described him, in the pangs of melodramatic despair, but with the same businesslike dignity in which for so long as he lived and ruled. As he lay dying in the Wolvesey palace at Winchester he had the funeral service and the mass of requiem solemnised in his presence ; in the evening of the same day he had his will read in the presence of his household, and the following morning confirmed it in an audible voice ; after which he bade farewell to all, and so died ; leaving, after large legacies, the residue of his great wealth to charity."]

Bedford. I. i. 81, 94.

The Duke of Bedford, Uncle to the King, and Regent of France. See *First Part of King Henry the Sixth.*

Bedlam. V. i. 131.

> To Bedlam with him ! is the man grown mad ?
> [V. i. 131.]

Bethlehem Hospital was used as a lunatic asylum at this time. Stow in his *Survey of London,* says : " Next unto the parish church of St. Buttolph is a fair inn for receipt of travellers ; then an hospital of St. Mary of Bethlehem, founded by Simon Fitz Mary, one of the sheriffs of London, in the year 1246 : he founded it to have been a priory of canons, with brethren and sisters ; and King Edward III., granted a protection, which I have seen, for the brethren, *Miliciæ beatæ Mariæ de Bethlem,* within the city of London, the 14th year of his reign. It was an hospital for distracted people : "

Beldam. I. iv. 42.

A hag ; a witch ; an enchantress.

Berwick. II. i. 83, 156.

A town in Northumberland. Saunder Simpcox, the impostor, was born here, and he and his wife were sentenced to be whipped from Saint Albans to this town :

> Let them be whipped through every market-town
> till they come to Berwick, from whence they came.

See Saint Alban's Shrine.

Best's son the tanner of Wingham. IV. ii. 23.

Blackheath.

The Scene of Act IV., Scene ii. The insurrection of Jack Cade, who personates Mortimer, stirred up by the Duke of York. [The connection between the rising of Cade and the design of the Duke of York are very obscure.] It is considered that Shakespeare borrowed his account of Cade's insurrection from that which is given of the rebellion of Wat Tyler and Jack Straw in the reign of Richard the Second. Cade and his followers are declared traitors by Sir Humphrey Stafford who has been sent by the king to offer pardon to all who lay down their arms.

Blackheath, Another part of.

The Scene of Act IV., Scene iii. A skirmish takes place between the king's forces and the followers of Cade, and both Sir Humphrey and his brother are slain. [Irving edition quotes Holinshed : " It appears that the defeat of the Staffords and their forces, which must have been very inconsiderable in number, took place owing to the royal party being deceived as to the movements of Cade. The king, according to Holinshed, had gone against the rebels with 15,000 men well equipped ; but the rebels fled into the wooded country near Sevenoaks ; and the king returned to London, upon which, as

Hall relates ; The Queene, which bare the rule, beyng of his retrayte well aduertised, sent Syr Humfrey Stafford knyght, and William his brother with many other gentelmen, to folow the chace of the Kentishmen, thinkynge that they had fledde, but verely, they were de- sceyued ; for at the fyrst skyrmish, both the Staffordes were slayne, and all their companye shamfully discomfited. . . . When the Kentish capitayn, or ye couetous Cade, had thus obteyned victory, and slayne the two valeaunt Staffordes, he appareled hym selfe in their rich armure, and so with pompe and glory returned agayn toward London ; in which retrayte diuers idle and vacabonde persons, resorted to him from Sussex and Surrey, and from other partes to a great number."]

Bolingbroke. II. ii. 39.

Henry Bolingbroke, eldest son of John of Gaunt, afterwards King Henry the Fourth.

Bolingbroke, a Conjuror. I. ii. 76 ; I. iv. p.1 ; II. iii. p.1.

First appears in the Duke of Gloucester's garden in response to a summons by the Duchess, accompanied by Margery Jourdain, a witch, and others.

He summons the spirit, and when it appears puts several questions to it, asking what shall become of the king, the Duke of Suffolk, and the Duke of Somerset.

Having answered these questions, the spirit exclaims :

> Have done for more I hardly can endure.   [I. iv. 38.]

and Bolingbroke commands it to depart :

> Descend to darkness and the burning lake :
> False fiend, avoid !   [I. iv. 39–40.]

He next appears, with the others who had taken part in this seance, before the king and is condemned to death by hanging, along with Hume and Southwell.

See also John Hume.

Brethren. II. i. p.68.

Citizens of Saint Albans, who enter with the Mayor of that town.

Bristol. III. i. 328.

> My Lord of Suffolk, within fourteen days
> At Bristol I expect my soldiers ;
> For these I 'll ship them all for Ireland.
> [III. i. 327–329.]

The Duke of York prepares to sail thence for Ireland.

Britain's isle. I. iii. 43.

= England.

Brutus' bastard hand Stabbed Julius Cæsar. IV. i. 136.

Servilia, mother of Brutus, was Cæsar's mistress, but not until after the birth of Brutus.

Brutus could not be called a *bastard*, for his mother Servilia was married to Marcus Junius Brutus, and by him became the mother of Cæsar's murderer. Her husband was put to death by order of Pompey, after which she became the favourite mistress of Julius Cæsar, and Brutus was said, absurdly enough, by some to have been the result of this connection. But Cæsar was only fifteen years older than Brutus, and it seems clear that Servilla did not become his mistress till some time after the birth of her son. She was married, a second time, to Junius Silanus, consul, B.C. 62. *Irving edition.*

Bury. II. iv. 71 ; III. ii. 240.

> I summon your grace to his majesty's parliament,
> holden at Bury the first of this next month.
> [II. iv. 70–71.]

Bury St. Edmunds. Grafton says : " So for the furtheraunce of their purpose, a parliament was sommoned to be kept at Bury, whether resorted all the peeres of the realme, and amongst them the Duke of Gloucester, which on the second day of the session, was by the Lorde Beamonde then high Constable of Englande, accompanied with the Duke of Buckyngham and other, arrested, apprehended, and put in warde, and all his seruaunts sequestred from him and xxxij., of the chiefe of his retinue, were sent to diuers prisons, to ye great admiration of the common people."

Bury St. Edmunds.   A Room of State.

The Scene of Act III., Scene ii. Under the direction of Suffolk, Gloucester is murdered. Salisbury and Warwick accuse Suffolk in the presence of the king with being guilty of the deed, and the Commons enter and demand his punishment, and Suffolk is banished by the king. The scene closes with the leave taking of the queen and Suffolk.

Cade of Herrings. IV. ii. 35.

Nash speaks of having weighed one of Gabriel Harvey's books against a *cade of herrings*, and ludicrously says, " That the rebel Jacke Cade was the first that devised to put redde herrings in *cades*, and from him they have their name." *Praise of the Red Herring.* 1599.

A *cade* is less than a *barrel*. The quantity it should contain is ascertained by the accounts of the Celeress of the Abbey of Berking. " Memorandum that a *barrel* of herryng shold contene a thousand herryngs, and a *cade* of herryng six hundreth, six score to the hundreth." *Malone.*

Cade's head. V. i. p.64.

Hall says : " After a proclamation made that whosoever could apprehende the saied Jack Cade should have for his pain a m. markes, many sought for hym, but few espied hym, til one Alexander Iden, esquire of Kent, found hym in a garden, and there in his defence manfully slewe the caitife Cade, and brought his ded body to London, whose hed was set on London bridge."

Cæsar. IV. vii. 60.

Kent, in the Commentaries Cæsar writ,
Is termed the civil'st place of all this isle :
[IV. vii. 60–61.]

The *Commentaries* of Cæsar, the only one of his literary works extant, contain the history of the first seven years of the Gallic War, and a history of the Civil War with Pompey.

Callat. I. iii. 82.

Contemptuous base-born callat as she is. [I. iii. 82.]

= a scold, a shrew.

Calydon. I. i. 233.

Calydon was a city of Ætolia famed in Grecian story of the hunting of the enormous bear which Artemis, to punish Œneus for neglecting to offer up sacrifices to the goddess, sent to ravage his vineyards. Meleager, Prince of Calydon killed the animal and presented the hide to Atalanta. *See* Althæa.

Cardinal Beaufort, Bishop of Winchester, Great-uncle to the King. I. i. p.1, 55, 66, 86, 137, 177, 183, 199 ; I. ii. 27, 94 ; I. iii. 67, p.100 ; II. i. p.1, 48 ; II. ii. 71 ; IV. iv. 53 ; III. i. p.1, 187 ; III. ii. p.15, 124, 180, 196, 369 ; III. iii. p.1, 1, 7, 26.

In the first scene of the Play we are given an insight into Beaufort's character when he openly admits his feelings towards Gloucester, and cunningly hints at the desirability of removing him :

So, there goes our protector in a rage.
'Tis known to you he is mine enemy,
Nay, more, an enemy unto you all,
And no great friend, I fear me, to the king.
[I. i. 145–148.]

On his next appearance he accuses Gloucester of extorting money from the clergy :

the clergy's bags
Are lank and lean with thy extortions. [I. iii. 127–128.]

and before the king accuses him of coveting the crown.

Beaufort is one of the leaders in the plot against Gloucester, and he allows no opportunity to escape when he might assist in his overthrow.

Gloucester's death, however, fills Beaufort with remorse, and we find him on his deathbed in a state of terror. He is delirious and his utterances convince those around him of his connivance at Gloucester's murder.

He cries :

Bring me unto my trial when you will.
Died he not in his bed ? where should he die ?
Can I make men live, whe'r they will or no ?
O, torture me no more, I will confess.
[III. iii. 8–11.]

and dies in an agony of remorse.

Castle in Saint Alban's. V. ii. 68.

So, lie thou there ;
For underneath an alehouse' paltry sign,
The Castle in Saint Alban's, Somerset
Hath made the wizard famous in his death.
[V. ii. 66–69.]

The name of a Tavern in Saint Albans. The death of Somerset here accomplishes that equivocal prediction given by Jourdain, the witch, concerning this duke ; which we meet with at the close of the First Act of this play :

Let him shun castles :
Safer shall he be upon the sandy plains
Than where castles mounted stand. [I. iv. 35–37.]

The corresponding passage in *The Contention* reads thus :

So Lie thou there, and breathe thy last.
Whats here, the signe of the Castle ?
Then the prophesie is come to passe,
For Somerset was forewarned of Castles,
The which he alwaies did obserue.

And now, behold, vnder a paltry Ale-house signe,
The Castle in Saint Albones,
Somerset hath made the Wissard famous by his death.

Grafton says : " Then came the Duke of Sommerset, and all the other Lordes with the kinges power, which fought a sore and cruell battaile, in the which many a tall man lost his life : but the Duke of Yorke sent euer fresh men, to succor the werie, and put new men in places of the hurt persons, by which onely pollecie, the kinges armie was ouerthrowne and dispersed, and all the Chieftaynes of the fielde almost slaine and brought to confusion. For there dyed vnder the signe of the Castel, Edmond Duke of Sommerset, who long before was warned to eschew all Castelles, and besyde him, lay Henry the seconde Erle of Northumberlande, Humfrey Erle of Stafford, sonne to the Duke of Buckingham, Iohn Lord Clifford, and viij thousand men and more. Humfrey Duke of Buckingham beyng wounded, and Iames Butler Erle of Wilshire and Ormond, seyng Fortunes lowryng chaunce, left the King post alone, and with a great number fled away. This was the ende of the first battaile at Saint Albones, which was fought on the Thursday before the feast of Pentecost, beyng the xxiij day of May."

Ceres'. I. ii. 2.

Why droops my lord, like over-ripened corn,
Hanging the head at Ceres' plenteous load ?
[I. ii. 1–2.]

The goddess of agriculture and of the fruits of the earth. Ceres was represented with a beautiful countenance ; tall and majestic ; her complexion fair ; her eyes languishing ; and her hair flaxen. Her head was crowned, with a garland of poppies intermixed with ears of corn, holding in her right hand a bunch of the same materials and in the left a flaming torch.

Channel. IV. i. 114.

The English Channel.

Charneco. II. iii. 63.

A Sweet wine. From a pamphlet entitled *The Discovery of a London Monster, called the Black Dog of Newgate,* 1612, we have : " Some drinking the neat wine of Orleance, some the Gascony, some the Bourdeaux. There wanted neither sherry, sack, nor *charneco,* maligo, nor amber-colour'd Candy, nor liquorish ipocras, brown beloved bastard, fat Aligant, or any quick-spirited liquor." *Warburton.*

In *Wit's Miserie, or the World's Madness,* 1596 : " the only medicine for the fleghm, is three cups of *charneco,* fasting."

Again, in Beaumont and Fletcher's *Wit without money :* " Where no old *charneco* is, nor no anchovies."

Again, in *The Fair Maid of the West,* 1615 : " Aragoosa, or Peter-see-me, canary, or *charneco.*" *Steevens.*

Charneco is the name of a village near Lisbon, where this wine was made.

Cheapside. IV. ii. 69 ; IV. vii. 124.

A thoroughfare in the City of London, originally a large open common, where markets and public assemblies were held. Harben in his *Dictionary of London* says : " In the old days before the Fire it was a handsome street, and was ornamented by the Cross, the Standard, and the Conduit. It must have been of considerable width, as the market was held in the middle of the street, while justings also took place in it from time to time. In process of time the street has been raised several feet, so that it is 28 ft. higher than where St. Paul's was first built, as appears by marks discovered when the new foundations were laid. Some houses at the south-west corner, near St. Paul's Churchyard, were taken down *c.* 1760 to widen the street. This was the site of the great market of London, and the several trades were represented by their selds in it. The street was named from the market, A.S. " ceap "=" barter," " purchase."

Citizens. II. i. p.68 ; IV. v. p.1.

Clerk of Chatham. IV. iii. p.84, 84.

Is brought in a prisoner before Jack Cade by Smith the weaver, who exclaims :

The clerk of Chatham : he can write and read
and cast accompt.   [IV. ii. 84–85.]

For his " crime " of being learned, he is condemned to death, and Cade orders :

Away with him ! I say : hang him with his pen and
ink-horn about his neck.   [IV. ii. 108–109.]

Coast of Kent.

The Scene of Act IV., Scene i. The murder of the Duke of Suffolk. It is a mysterious affair. [Shakespeare represents the execution as having been done by pirates, but according to Holinshed he was intercepted in transporting himself to France by a ship of war called the *Nicholas of the Tower* belonging to the Duke of Exeter, Constable of the Tower of London.]

Commons. III. ii. p.123, 125.

The commons, like an angry hive of bees
That want their leader, scatter up and down,
And care not who they stink in his revenge.
[III. ii. 125–127.]

Cf. George Peele's *Jack Strawe :*

It was a world to see what troops of men
Like bees that swarm about the honey hive,
'Gan strew the gravel ground and sandy plain.

Cumberland. V. ii. 1, 6.

Clifford of Cumberland, 'tis Warwick calls :

. . . .

Proud northern lord, Clifford of Cumberland,
[V. ii. 1–6.]

It was Henry, the eleventh Baron [great grandson of the Lord Clifford of this play] who was created Earl of Cumberland, in 1525.

Dauphin. I. iii. 124.

The Dauphin hath prevailed beyond the seas ;
And all the peers and nobles of the realm
Have been as bondmen to thy sovereignty.
Car. The Commons hast thou racked ; the clergy's bags
Are lank and lean with thy extortions.
[I. iii. 124–128.]

These charges are the same as contained in the Articles of treason " put vp to the king and the lordes by the Commons of the nether house agaynst the Duke of Suffolke." *See* Kent, IV., i., 100, and Grafton's *Chronicle*, Vol. i., pages 638–639.

Dauphin's hands. I. iii. 169.

Dick, the Butcher. IV. ii. 26, p.32 ; IV. iii. p.1 ; IV. vi. p.1 ; IV. vii. p.1 ; IV. viii. p.1.

One of Cade's followers, appearing with him in all the scenes describing the rebellion.

Dido. II. ii. 117.

To sit and witch me, as Ascanius did
When he to madding Dido would unfold
His father's acts, commenced in burning Troy !
[III. ii. 116–118.]

See Ascanius.

Downs. IV. i. 9.

For whilst our pinnace anchors in the Downs
Here shall they make their ransom on the sand,
[IV. i. 9–10.]

Downs is a term applied to the roadstead for shipping off the coast of Kent, between the North and South Forelands.

"On the 11th of June, 1771, we run up the channel . . . at noon we were abreast of Dover, and about three came to an anchor in the *Downs*, and went ashore at Deal." Cook's *Voyages.*

Duke Edmund. IV. ix. 38:

= The Duke of Somerset.

Duke of Alencon. I. i. 7.

Mentioned here as being present at the espousal of Margaret to Henry VI. Cf. *Extract* 1 from Holinshed.

Duke of Bretagne. I. i. 7.

Francis the First. Mentioned here as being present at the espousal of Queen Margaret. Cf. *Extract* 1 from Holinshed.

Duke of Buckingham. I. i. p.1, 67, 83, 170, 200 ; I. iii. 68, p.100, 112 ; I. iv. p.41, 55 ; II. i. p.162, 162 ; II. ii. 72 ; III. i. p.1, 39, 156 ; IV. iv. p.1 ; IV. viii. p.6, 20 ; IV. ix. p.7, 8, 36 ; V. i. p.12, 12, 15, 32, 44, 56, 83, 192, 193.

The Duke of Buckingham is one of the nobles who assists in the removal of Gloucester. It is he who first suggests the project, and invites Somerset to join him. On being warned by Somerset that Cardinal Beaufort would assume Gloucester's role, he replies, indicating his own ambitions :

Or thou or I, Somerset, will be protector,
Despite Duke Humphrey, or the cardinal.
[I. i. 176–177.]

He takes part in the arrest of the Duchess of Gloucester, and reports to the king of the witchcraft practised in her garden.

Later, when news of Cade's insurrection is brought to the king, Buckingham counsels him to retire to Kenilworth.

Buckingham, with Clifford, acts as envoy from the king to the rebels, and offers them pardon if they will disperse. Cade sees his followers are about to accept the offers made to them, and makes good his escape, upon which Buckingham offers a thousand crowns for his capture.

Then Buckingham and Clifford proceed to

Kenilworth, where they advise the king that the rebellion has been crushed, when news arrives that York has landed with an army for the alleged purpose of removing Somerset, and Buckingham is ordered to go to meet him and discover the true object of his arrival.

Having met York, Buckingham delivers the king's message, and requests York to accompany him to the king's tent. On seeing Somerset at liberty, York denounces the king and is arrested for treason. Thus a conflict is precipitated, and Buckingham is bidden by the king to arm and defend himself and the kingdom against the forces of York.

Humphrey Stafford, first Duke of Buckingham was the only son of Edmund Stafford, fifth Earl of Stafford, killed at the battle of Shrewsbury fighting on the side of the King Henry IV. Created Duke of Buckingham in 1444. The Duke married Anne Neville, daughter of Ralph first Earl of Westmoreland. He was killed at the battle of Northampton on the 27th of July, 1460.

Duke of Calabar. I. i. 7.

John of Anjou, Duke of Calabria, and brother of Margaret. Mentioned here as being present at the espousal of his sister—Margaret—at Tours. Cf. *Extract* 1 from Holinshed.

Duke of Clarence' daughter. IV. ii. 136.

Marry, this : Edmund Mortimer, Earl of March,
Married the Duke of Clarence' daughter, did he not ?
[IV. ii. 135–136.]

See Roger, Earl of March.

Duke of Clarence' house. IV. iv. 29.

Jack Cade proclaims himself Lord Mortimer,
Descended from the Duke of Clarence' house,
[IV. iv. 28–29.]

See John Mortimer.

Duke of Gloucester's House.

The Scene of Act I., Scene ii. Shows the loyalty of the Duke of Gloucester and the ambition of the Duchess. Gloucester is in a state of melancholy, due to a dream that his " office badge in Council was broke in twain " which the duchess interprets to mean that he will crush his enemies ; and goes on to relate that she herself has dreamed that she was being crowned queen in the Cathedral Church of Westminster. Gloucester rebukes his wife for her ambition.

A messenger enters inviting Gloucester to St. Alban's to hawk with the king and queen, and the scene closes with the entry of Hume—who has been suborned by Suffolk and Beaufort—to draw the duchess into practices of witchcraft and treason.

Duke of Orleans. I. i. 7.

Son of Lewis, Duke of Orleans (brother to Charles the Sixth). Taken prisoner at the battle of Agincourt, 1415, and brought to England, where he remained captive until 1440. Mentioned here as being present at the espousal of Margaret at Tours. Cf. *Extract* 1 from Holinshed.

Duke of Somerset. I. i. p.1, 67, 83, 165, 176, 200 ; I. ii. 29 ; I. iii. 68, p.100, 101, 104, 113, 167, 205, 220 ; I. iv. 34, 66 ; II. ii. 71 ; III. i. p.82, 83, 86, 290, 304 ; III. ii. p.15 ; IV. ix. p.1, 30, 39 ; V. i. 36, 41, 53, 61, 83, p.84, 87, 90 ; V. ii. p.66, 68.

In the first scene of the Play we find Buckingham inviting Somerset and Suffolk to join him in removing the Duke of Gloucester from his position as Protector. To this Somerset remarks that Cardinal Beaufort should be regarded as a danger in the way of such a project, but he throws in his lot with Buckingham.

Later, Somerset is appointed by the king to act as his regent in France, a post which he accepts, and departs for France forthwith.

He next appears before the king in Parliament at Bury St. Edmunds, and announces that the English territories in France have all been lost, which information Henry receives in a matter-of-fact way, but not so York, who is Somerset's bitterest enemy.

At Kenilworth Somerset accompanies the king when a messenger enters with the news that York has returned from Ireland with an army :

to remove from thee
The Duke of Somerset, whom he terms a traitor.
[IV. ix. 29–30.]

The king is at a loss as to what he should do, and then decides to commit Somerset to the Tower, while Buckingham is sent to inform York of what has been done. Somerset readily accepts this degradation, saying :

My lord,
I 'll yield myself to prison willingly,
Or unto death, to do my country good.
[IV. ix. 41–43.]

York is brought before Henry and is confronted by Somerset, who appears in company with the Queen. At this York exclaims that Henry is no king and not fit to reign, and Somerset thereupon arrests York on a charge of treason.

We next find Somerset engaged in combat with Richard Plantagenet at the Battle of St. Albans, and is killed by the son of him whom he had accused of being a traitor.

[Edmund Beaufort, second Duke of Somerset, and younger brother of John Beaufort, Earl of, and afterwards first Duke of Somerset, a character in the *First Part of King Henry the Sixth.* He was killed at the first battle of St. Albans, 22nd May, 1455.]

Duke of Suffolk. I. i. p.1, 17, 44, 62, 107, 122, 131, 169, 199, 215 ; I. ii. 30, 95, 101 ; I. iii. p.6, 8, 19, 39, 41, 49, 86, 164, 179 ; I. iv. 32, 64 ; II. i. p.1, 31 ; II. ii. 70 ; II. iii. p.1 ; II. iv. 51 ; III. i. p.1, 39, 98, 155, 246, 266, 273, 326, 327 ; III. ii. 1, p.6, p.27, 28, 39, 56, 114, 124, 195, 203, 206, p.237, 244, 266, 284, 289, 290, 306, 329, 357, 361, 382, 383, 405 ; IV. i. p.1, 45, 46, 69, 116, 139 ; IV. iv. p.1, 22, 41, 56.

The Play commences with Suffolk's announcement that he has carried out the king's instructions to marry in his behalf Margaret of Anjou, and he is created the first Duke of Suffolk :

> Lord marquess, kneel down :
> We here create thee the first Duke of Suffolk,
> And girt thee with the sword. [I. i. 61–63.]

At the end of the scene we are made aware of the plot between Buckingham, Somerset and Suffolk to depose Gloucester, and on Suffolk's next appearance he assures the Queen of his determination to put aside all the obstacles in the way until :

> You yourself shall steer the happy helm. [I. iii. 99.]

Later he openly demands Gloucester's resignation, and at the Parliament at Bury St. Edmunds arrests him on a charge of high treason.

It has been obvious from the beginning of the play that Suffolk intended to remove Gloucester, and as this scene closes is revealed the plot to murder him.

In the next scene the two murderers enter and inform Suffolk that they have duly carried out his orders, and Gloucester is dead. The king soon demands that Gloucester be brought before him, and Suffolk goes, only to return to say that he has found Gloucester dead in his bed. The king suspects foul play, and Warwick boldly accuses Suffolk of the deed.

Suffolk challenges him to combat and they leave the presence of the king to return a moment later with drawn swords. Salisbury enters and exclaims that the Commons demand Suffolk's banishment :

> Dread lord, the commons send you word by me,
> Unless false Suffolk straight be done to death,
> Or banished fair England's territories,
> They will by violence tear him from your palace
> And torture him with grievous lingering death.
> [III. ii. 243–247.]

and the king thereupon orders him to leave the country within three days :

> He shall not breathe infection in this air
> But three days longer, on the pain of death.
> [III. ii. 287–288.]

Suffolk embarks at Dover for France, but his boat is held up and he, in spite of his disguise, is taken prisoner with others and brought back to the shore. The leader of the captors hands Suffolk over to one Walter Whitmore. Suffolk, in abject fear, pleads for his life, but the Captain roundly condemns him and his affairs, and orders him to be executed. Suffolk is led away and in a few moments, Whitmore re-enters bearing the dead body of his captive.

So dies Suffolk, ambitious statesman, close companion of the queen and the instigator of the murder of Gloucester. His zeal to serve the queen's wishes and his own desires led him to remove the Protector to his own undoing. His is a sorry picture ; he had a certain amount of courage and power over his fellows, but he became a tool to the queen, and so brought about his own downfall. See *Paston's Letters* [Letter XXVII., dated 5th of May, 1450.]

For the Articles proposed by the Commons against the Duke of Suffolk, *see* Grafton's *Chronicle*, Vol. I., p. 638.

[This character the fourth Earl of Suffolk is William de la Pole, son of Michael de la Pole, second Earl of Suffolk, and brother and successor of Michael de la Pole, third Earl of Suffolk. Created Duke of Suffolk in 1448.]

Earl of Salisbury. I. i. p.1, 68, 84 ; I. iii. 75, p.100 ; I. iv. 79 ; II. ii. p.1, 1, 59 ; II. iii. p.1 ; III. i. p.1 ; III. ii. p.123, 134, 270, 275, 279 ; III. ii. p.1 ; V. i. 147 ; p.148, 162 ; V. iii. 1, 7, p.14.

Like his son, the Earl of Warwick, Salisbury is at first a supporter of Henry, but he recognises York's claim to the throne, and throws in his lot with him.

He appears as the leader of the Commons who are determined to learn the truth about Gloucester's death, and is ordered to announce to them that Suffolk has been banished for conspiring to murder the Protector.

When Salisbury and Warwick appear with the forces of York, the king upbraids them, and Salisbury replies :

> My lord, I have considered with myself
> The title of this most renowned duke ;
> And in my conscience do repute his grace
> The rightful heir to England's royal seat.
> [V. i. 175–178.]

He takes part in the first battle of St. Albans, and expresses his thanks to York for so nobly helping him, at the same time indicating that it is not enough to have won the battle, but they must pursue the king's forces towards London.

See also Earl of Warwick.

[Richard Neville, son of Ralph Neville, first Earl of Westmoreland. Married Alice, only child of Thomas de Montacute, Earl of Salisbury in the *First Part*, and had that title revived in his favour, May 4th, 1442. At first he was a supporter of Henry VI., but he deserted the royal cause for that of his brother-in-law, the Duke of York. Wounded and taken prisoner at the battle of Wakefield, 1460, and executed at Pontefract Castle.]

Earl of Warwick. I. i. p.1, 68, 84, 113, 188, 203, 208 ; I. iii. 73, p.100, 108, 110, 111, 174 ; I. iv. 79 ; II. ii. p.1, 1, 78, 81 ; III. i. p.1 ; III. ii. p.123, 130, p.148, 159, 179, 201, 203, p.237, 240, 298 ; III. iii. p.1 ; IV. i. 90 ; V. i. 147, p.148, 156, 161 ; V. ii. p.1, 1, 7, 14 ; V. iii. p.1, 27.

Warwick, one of the most powerful nobles in the land, takes his stand with the king and the Duke of Gloucester against the ambitions of the Duke of Suffolk, Buckingham and Somerset.

He deeply regrets the handing over of Anjou and Maine according to Henry's marriage deed, but covers his grief by emphasising his patriotism.

However, with his father Salisbury, he is invited by York to meet him at supper, when York expounds his claim to the throne, and Warwick, recognising the validity of the argument, exclaims :

> What plain proceeding is more plain than this ?
> .   .   .   .
> Then, father Salisbury, kneel we together,
> And in this private plot be we the first
> That shall salute our rightful sovereign
> With honour of his birthright to the crown.
> [II. ii. 53–62.]

and throws in his lot with the house of York.

Following the discovery of Gloucester's death, Warwick voices the suspicion of the Commons that he has been murdered, and is commanded by Henry to examine the body. This done, Warwick declares that he died a violent death, and accuses Suffolk of the deed, accepting his challenge to a resort to arms. The king averts a duel and banishes Suffolk, ordering Warwick to accompany him.

Warwick's next important appearance is on the fields between Dartford and Blackheath, when he is summoned by York to come forward as his supporter. The king is amazed to find Salisbury and Warwick opposed to him, and exclaims :

> Why, Warwick, hath thy knee forgot to bow ?
> Old Salisbury, shame to thy silver hair,
> Thou mad misleader of thy brain sick son !
> [V. i. 161–163.]

In the first battle of St. Albans, Warwick appears calling Clifford to combat, but York asks him to leave the honour of vanquishing Clifford to him, and Warwick departs.

The battle over and won, Warwick exclaims :

> Saint Alban's battle, won by famous York,
> Shall be eternized in all age to come.   [V. iii. 30–31.]

and thus the play ends.

See also Earl of Salisbury.

[Richard Nevill, Earl of Warwick and Salisbury, son of Richard Nevill, first Earl of Salisbury, a character in this play ; married Anne, only daughter of Richard de Beauchamp, Earl of Warwick. He is a character in the *Third Part of King Henry the Sixth*, in which Play he figures prominently (q.v.).]

Edmund. II. ii. 38, 39.

> This Edmund, in the reign of Bolingbroke,
> As I have read, laid claim unto the crown ;
> And, but for Owen Glendower, had been king,
> Who kept him in captivity till he died.
> [II. ii. 39–42.]

Edmund Mortimer, fifth Earl of March, son of Roger Mortimer, fourth Earl. Recognised as heir presumptive by King Richard the Second. Fought at Agincourt. Appointed Lieutenant of Ireland, 1423. He died in 1425.

In the *First Part of King Henry the Sixth*, Act II., Scene v., York is present at the death of Edmund Mortimer in prison, and the reader will recollect him to have been married to Owen Glendower's daughter in the *First Part of King Henry the Fourth*.

Malone says : " The historians as well as the dramatick poets have been strangely mistaken concerning this Edmond Mortimer, Earl of March, who was so far from being ' kept in captivity till he died.' that he appears to have been at liberty during the whole reign of King Henry the Fifth, and to have been trusted and employed by him ; and there is no proof that he ever was confined, as a *state-prisoner*, by King Henry IV. Being only six years of age at the death of his father in 1398, he was delivered by Henry in ward to his son Henry Prince of Wales ; and during the whole of that reign, being a minor and related to the family on the throne, both he and his brother Roger were under the particular care of the King. At the age of ten years, in 1402, he headed a body of Herefordshire men against Owen Glendower ; and they being routed, he was taken prisoner by Owen, and is said by Walsingham to have entered into a contract of marriage with Glendower's daughter, and to have been with him at the battle of Shrewsbury ; but I believe the story of his being affianced to Glendower's daughter is a mistake, and that the historian has confounded Mortimer with Lord Grey of Ruthvin, who was likewise taken prisoner by Glendower, and actually did marry his daughter. In the *First Part of King Henry the Sixth*, the aged and grey-hair'd Mortimer is introduced in the Tower, and made to say—

> Since Harry Monmouth first began to reign,
> Before whose glory I was great in arms,
> This loathsome sequestration I have had :

Yet here we are told, he was kept in captivity by Owen Glendower till he died. The fact is, that Hall having said that Glendower kept his son-in-law, Lord Grey of Ruthvin, *in captivity till he died*, and this Lord March having been said by some historians to have married Owen's daughter, the author of this play has confounded them with each other. Edmund Mortimer, Earl of March, married Anne Stafford, the daughter of Edmond Earl of Stafford. If he was at the battle of Shrewsbury he was probably brought there against his will, to grace the cause of the rebels.''

Edmund Langley. II. ii. 15, 46, 49.

First Duke of York, son of King Edward the Third (q.v.). See *King Richard the Second*, pp. 446–448.

Edmund Mortimer, [Third] Earl of March. II. ii. 36, 37, 49 ; IV. ii. 135.

Son of Roger Mortimer, second Earl of March, and Philippa, daughter of William Montacute, first Earl of Salisbury. He married Philippe, daughter of Lionel, Duke of Clarence, third son of King Edward the Third. See *Extract* 13 from Holinshed.

Edward, son to Richard Plantagenet, Duke of York. V. i. p.122.

Edward Plantagenet, later to become Edward IV., appears in the play with his brother Richard before the king at Blackheath, to be bail for his father when York is arrested for high treason by Somerset.

Being asked by their father if they will give their word for him, Edward replies :

> Ay, noble father, if our words will serve.
> [V. i. 139.]

to which Richard adds :

> And if words will not, then our weapons shall.
> [V. i. 140.]

[Edward and Richard Plantagenet are also characters in the *Third Part of King Henry the Sixth*, in which Play they figure prominently (q.v.).]

Edward the Black Prince, Prince of Wales. II. ii. 11, 18.

See *Extract* 13 from Holinshed.

Edward the Third. II. ii. 10, 20, 46.

York here (lines 10 *et seq.*) gives his genealogy proving that he is the rightful heir to the crown. See *Extract* 13 from Holinshed.

Eleanor, Duchess of Gloucester. I. ii. p.1, 17, 41, 42, 52, 59, 91, 97, 105 ; I. iii. p.100, 146, 147 ; I. iv. p.13 ; II. i. 166 ; II. iii. p.1, 1, 15, 46 ; II. iv. 10, 17, 26, 58, 67, 74 ; III. ii. p.15, 26, 79, 100, 120.

It would be difficult to discover a more ambitious character than Eleanor. She is bitterly jealous of the queen, and would leave no stone unturned to place herself in her position. At every opportunity she urges her husband to seize the crown, as her whole thoughts are centred on self-advancement.

An instance of her insistent demand to be the first woman in the land is given on her first appearance in the play, and these few lines give us the keynote to her character in an unmistakable manner.

She enquires,

> Why droops my lord, like over-ripened corn
> .   .   .   .
> Why are thine eyes fixed to the sullen earth,
> .   .   .   .
> What seest thou there ?   King Henry's diadem
> Enchased with all the honours of the world ?
> If so, gaze on, and grovel on thy face,
> Until thy head be circled with the same.
> Put forth thy hand, reach at the glorious gold.
>   [I. ii. 1–11.]

and continues, to assure him of her most willing assistance,

> What ! is 't too short ?   I 'll lengthen it with mine ;
> And, having both together heaved it up,
> We 'll both together lift our heads to heaven,
> And never more abase our sight so low
> As to vouchsafe one glance unto the ground.
>   [I. ii. 12–16.]

Her husband rebukes her for her ambition :

> Banish the canker of ambitious thoughts ;   [I. ii. 18.]

for he knows only too well her obsession, and no doubt fears that tragedy will be the outcome of it.

He proceeds to tell her of a dream he has had, which he fears is an omen of impending disaster, but she retorts by relating a dream of hers in which of course her one eternal ambition is realised.

> Methought I sat in seat of majesty
> In the cathedral church of Westminster,

> And in that chair where kings and queens are crowned ;
> Where Henry and Dame Margaret kneeled to me,
> And on my head did set the diadem.   [I. ii. 36–40.]

The Duchess on state occasions always endeavours to appear most dignified and likes to imagine that the courtiers take her for the queen, and on one occasion her airs are effectually belittled by Queen Margaret who purposely drops her fan when close to the Duchess. Of course Eleanor does not pick it up, and she receives the terse reproof from the queen who pretends not to recognise her,

> Give me my fan : what, minion ! can ye not ?
>   [I. iii. 137.]

This enrages Eleanor, who heatedly retorts :

> yea, I it was, proud Frenchwoman :
> Could I come near your beauty with my nails
> I 'd set my ten commandments in your face.
>   [I. iii. 139–141.]

This episode causes Buckingham to utter words containing a very true prophecy :

> She 's tickled now ;   her fume needs no spurs,
> She 'll gallop far enough to her destruction.
>   [I. iii. 149–150.]

Eleanor's next appearance is in her garden, when Jourdain calls up the spirit as has been arranged between the Duchess and Hume. She is anxious for the " seance " to commence remarking :

>   To this
> gear, the sooner the better.   [I. iv. 13–14.]

When the spirit has departed, York, Buckingham and guards rush upon the scene, and those who have been taking part are arrested.

The Duchess, with the others, is brought before King Henry to be sentenced for this trangression of the law, and Henry decrees that she shall

> after three days' open penance done,
> Live in your country here in banishment,
> With Sir John Stanley, in the Isle of Man. [II. iii. 11–13.]

and Eleanor, seeing that this is the end of all her lofty ambitions, exclaims :

> Welcome is banishment ; welcome were my death.
>   [II. iii. 14.]

In a street in London, the broken-hearted duke awaits the coming of his wife, who is to pass that way doing her penance, and he wishes to see her once more before she departs into banishment. On her appearance it is evident that a change has befallen her, as she is utterly broken in spirit, and when the duke has gone she exclaims to Sir John Stanley,

Go, lead the way ; I long to see my prison.
[II. iv. 110.]

Thus Eleanor passes, and having seen a glimpse of her nature as portrayed on her last appearance one cannot but think what a noble and useful life hers could have been if her extravagant ambition had not so completely obliterated her other characteristics.

Eleanor. II. ii. 38.

Daughter of Roger Mortimer, fourth Earl of March.

Eleanor. III. ii. 79, 100, 120.

Margaret. It is evident that the author was thinking of Eleanor, Duchess of Gloucester, instead of Margaret the queen.

Elysium. III. ii. 399.

In classical mythology the supposed abode of the blessed after death. Æneas was given a description of it by one of its inhabitants, and Virgil tells us that it abounds with all the delights that the most pleasant plains, the most verdant fields, the shadiest groves, and the finest and most temperate air, can produce.

Emmanuel. IV. ii. 98.

Cade.	What is thy name ?
Clerk.	Emmanuel.
Dick.	They use to write it on the top of letters. 'Twill go hard with you. [IV. ii. 97–100.]

= " God with us," formerly prefixed to letters and deeds to convey the impression of piety. Here given as the name of the Clerk of Chatham. Cf. *The Famous Victories of Henry the Fifth*, where the Archbishop after delivering the impertinent message from the Dauphin to Henry V., says :

I beseech your grace, to deliuer me your safe
Conduct vnder your broad seale Emanuel.

and a little further on, the king says :

My Lorde of Yorke, deliuer him our safe conduct,
Vnder our broad seale Emanuel.

Staunton remarks : " An exemplification of Dick's remark is found in the following letter from John Speed, the historian, to Sir Robert Cotton, written about 1609 or 1610, and published by the Camden Society in *Original Letters of Eminent Literary Men*, 1843 :

Emanuell.
Worshipfull Sir, my thoughts runnyng upon the well performance of this worke, and fearfull to comitt any thing disagreeing from the truth, I have sent you a coppy of some part of that which you have alredy sene, because you left in writing at the Printers that with a fast eye you had overune it, and your leasure better affording that busines in the contrey then here you had ; this therefore hath caused me to send you as much as my Printer can espare, beseiching your Worshipe to read it more attentyvly, to place the Coynes, and what adicssions you will before you returne it ; and I pray you to past a paper where you doe adde, and not to intirline the coppy, for somewhere we cannot read your Notes because the place geves your pene not rome to exprese your mynd. I have sent such Coynes as are cutt, and will weekly supply the same ; so much therefore as you shall perfect I praye you send againe with as much speed as you can ; but where you do want the Coynes, kepe that coppy still with you, untill I send them : for I shall not be sattisfied with your other directions or Mr. Coles helpe. Good Sir, afford me herein your assistance as you have begune, and remember my suit to my L. privy-seall, wherein you shall binde me in all dutifull service and affection to your Worship's command. So beseiking the Almighty to prosper our indevours I humbly take my leave, and leave your Worship to the Lordes protection. Your Worships to command in all dutifull service, JOH. SPEED."

England. I. i. 11, 73, 96, 230, 257 ; I. iii. 42, 65, 66, 70, 72 ; II. i. 31 ; II. ii, 82 ; III. i. 20, 88, 111, 123, 349 ; IV. i. 72 ; IV. ii. 161 ; IV. x. 42 ; V. i. 118.

England. IV. ii. 8.

Well, I say it
was never merry world in England since gentlemen
came up. [IV. ii. 7–9.]

The same phrase was used by the Duke of Suffolk in the time of King Henry the Eighth : " Then stept forth the Duke of Suffolke from the King, and spake with a hault countenance these words : *It was never merry in England* while we had any Cardinals among us." *Stow*.

England. IV. ii. 65.

> There shall be in England seven half-
> penny loaves sold for a penny ; the three-hooped pot
> shall have ten hoops ; and I will make it felony to drink
> small beer.   [IV. ii. 65–68.]

The old drinking-pots, being of wood, were
bound together, as barrels are, with hoops.

England. IV. vii. 6, 15.

> Only that the laws of England may come out of
> your mouth.   [IV. vii. 6–7.]

From the Wat Tyler rebellion of 1381. On
June 14th, 1381, Wat Tyler, it is alleged,
boasted, " putting his hands to his lips, that
within foure daies all the lawes of England
should come foorth of his mouth." *Boswell
Stone.*

England. IV. viii. 50.

> Spare England, for it is your native coast.
> Henry hath money, you are strong and manly ;
> God on our side, doubt not of victory. [IV. viii. 50–52.]

Dr. Warburton reads : " Henry hath mercy."
Commenting on this, Johnson remarks : " Dr.
Warburton does not seem to have attended to
the speaker's drift, which is to lure them from
their present design by the hope of French
plunder. He bids them spare England, and go
to France, and encourages them by telling them
that all is ready for their expedition ; that they
have *strength*, and the king has *money*."

England. IV. ix. 49.

> Come, wife, let 's in, and learn to govern better ;
> For yet may England curse my wretched reign.
>   [IV. ix. 48–49.]

In *The Contention*, the corresponding passage
reads :

> Come let vs haste to London now with speed,
> That solemne prosessions may be sung,
> In laud and honour of the God of heauen,
> And triumphs of this happie victorie.

England's royal seat. V. i. 178.

> My lord, I have considered with myself
> The title of this most renowned duke ;
> And in my conscience do repute his grace
> The rightful heir to England's royal seat.
>   [V. i. 175–178.]

Salisbury tells the king that Richard Plantagenet, Duke of York is the rightful heir to the
crown.

England's soil. I. i. 236.

> Cold news for me, for I had hope of France,
> Even as I have of fertile England's soil.
>   [I. i. 235–236.]

See France, I., i., 235.

England's treasure. III. iii. 2.

> If thou be'st death, I 'll give thee England's treasure,
> Enough to purchase such another island,
> So thou wilt let me live, and feel no pain.
>   [III. iii. 2–4.]

The corresponding passage in *The Contention*
is :

> Oh death, if thou wilt let me liue but one whole yeare,
> Ile giue thee as much gold as will purchase such another
> Iland.

Malone remarks : The following passage in
Hall's *Chronicle* probably suggested these lines :
" During these doynges, Henry Beaufford,
byshop of Winchester, and called the riche
Cardynall, departed out of this worlde.—This
man was—haut in stomach and hygh in countenance, ryche above measure of all men, and to
fewe liberal ; disdaynful to his kynne, and
dreadful to his lovers. His covetous insaciable
and hope of long lyfe made hym bothe to forget
God, his prynce, and hymselfe, in his latter
dayes ; for Doctor John Baker, his pryvie
counsailer and his chapellayn, wrote, that lying
on his death-bed, he said these words : ' Why
should I dye, having so muche riches ? If the
whole realme would save my lyfe, I am able
either by pollicie to get it, or by ryches to bye
it. Fye will not death be hyred, nor will money
do nothynge ? When my nephew of Bedford
died, I thought my selfe halfe up the whele, but
when I sawe myne other nephew of Gloucester
disceased, than I thought my selfe able to be
equal with kinges, and so thought to increase
my treasure in hope to have worne a trypple
croune. But I se nowe the worlde fayleth me,
and so I am deceyved ; praying you all to pray
for me.' " *See also* Grafton's *Chronicle*, Vol. I.,
pp. 631–632.

Envy. III. ii. 315.

> As lean-faced Envy in her loathsome cave.
>   [III. ii. 315.]

A personification of the Evil one.

Excursions. V. ii. 72.

Sallies ; Sorties : an issuing of troops from a
besieged place to attack the besiegers.

Falconers. II. i. p.1.

Fields between Dartford and Blackheath.

The Scene of Act V., Scene i. This scene opens with the arrival of York from Ireland at the head of a large army. Being met by Buckingham on behalf of the king to know why he comes in arms, York replies "to remove the traitor Somerset from the king's counsel." Buckingham tells York that the king has yielded to his demand and sent Somerset to the Tower, and York dismisses his army and sends his two sons—Edward and Richard—to the king as hostages. [For the arrival of Edward and Richard Plantagenet at this critical moment, there is no foundation, but the opinion of a Chronicler that it was the rumour of the Earl of March's coming that prevented York's arrest. But Edward was at this time only fourteen years old at the most, and Richard not four. *Courtenay.*] Iden appears with the head of Cade, and is knighted by Henry for his valiant deed in slaying the caitiff. Somerset now appears, and York charges Henry with a breach of faith. High words ensue between the parties, and the scene closes with preparations being made for the battle which immediately follows.

Fields near Saint Alban's.

The Scene of Act V., Scene iii. Stubbs remarks : " A battle followed, in which the Duke of Somerset, the earl of Northumberland, the earl of Stafford, son of Buckingham, and the lord Clifford, on the king's side, were slain, and he himself was wounded. Although in itself little more than a skirmish which lasted half an an hour, and cost comparatively little bloodshed, the first battle of S. Alban's sealed the fate of the kingdom ; the duke of York was completely victorious ; the king remained a prisoner in his hands, and he recovered at once all the power that he had lost. The battle of S. Alban's had one permanent result : it forced the queen forward as the head of the royal party."

La fin couronne les œuvres. V. ii. 28.

> *Clif.* La fin couronne les œuvres.
> [*They fight, and Clifford falls and dies.*]
> *York.* Thus war hath given thee peace, for thou art still.
> Peace with his soul, heaven, if it be thy will !
> [V. ii. 28–30.]

" The end crowns the work." The story departs from historical accuracy here. Lord Clifford was not killed by York. For the true historical account of Clifford's death see the *Third Part of King Henry the Sixth*, I., i., 7–9 :

> Lord Clifford, and Lord Stafford, all abreast,
> Charged our main battle's front, and breaking in
> Were by the swords of common soldiers slain.

Fish Street. IV. viii. 1.

> Up Fish Street ! down Saint Magnus' Corner !
> [IV. viii. 1.]

" Both these places (Fish Street and Saint Magnus' Corner) are on the opposite side of the river to Southwark, where the scene is supposed to take place. The name of *Fish Street* is preserved in *Fish Street Hill*, on which the Monument stands. There is a church of *Saint Magnus* in Lower Thames Street. Perhaps these directions were intended to be given to bands of the rebels who were to cross the bridge." *Irving edition.*

Fortune's Pageant. I. ii. 67.

> And, being a woman, I will not be slack
> To play my part in Fortune's pageant [I. ii. 66–67.]

Hart remarks : " This *pageant plaied*, the Regent sent Peter of Luxenborough . . . to besiege the toune of Sainct Valerie." And again : " The Erle of Warwickes doynges, which must needes *play a pageaunt* in this enterlude, or else the plai wer at a poynt."

France. I. i. 80, 85, 90, 100, 104, 133, 144, 194, 211, 230 ; I. iii. 160, 169 ; III. ii. 405 ; IV. i. 113 ; IV. vii. 131 ; IV. viii. 17 ; IV. viii. 36, 49 ; V. i. 11.

France. I. i. 2.

> As by your high imperial majesty
> I had in charge at my depart for France,
> As procurator to your excellence,
> To marry Princess Margaret for your grace,
> [I. i. 1–4.]

Grafton says : " This noble company came to the Citie of Toures in Tourayne, where they were honorably receyued, both of the French king, and of the king of Sicile. Where the Marques of Suffolke, as procurator to king Henry, espoused the sayde Lady, in the Church of saint Martins. At which mariage were present, the father and mother of the bride, the French king himselfe, which was Vncle to the husbande, and the French Quene also, which was Awnte to the wyfe. There were also the

Dukes of Orleaunce, of Calabar, of Alaunson, and of Britayne, seauen Erles, xij Barons, xx Bishops, beside knightes and gentlemen. There were triumphant Iustes, costly feastes, and delicate banquets : but all pleasure hath an ende, and euery ioye is not continuall. So that after these high solempnities finished, and these honorable ceremonies ended, the Marques had the Lady Margaret to him delyuered, which in great estate, he conueyed through Normandy to Deepe, and so transported her into Englande, where she landed at Portesmouth, in the Moneth of Aprill. This woman excelled all other, as well in beautie and fauour, as in wyt and pollicie, and was of stomacke and courage, more lyke to a man, then a woman. Sone after her arriuall, she was conueyed to the towne of Southwike in Hamshire, where she with all nupciall ceremonies, was coupled in matrimonie to king Henry the sixt of that name. After which mariage, she was with great triumph, conueyed to London, and so to Westminster, where vpon the xxx day of May, she with all solemnitie therevnto apperteyning, was crowned Queene of this Noble realme of Englande." Cf. *Extract* 1 from Holinshed.

France. I. i. 65.

> Cousin of York,
> We here discharge your grace from being regent
> I' the parts of France, till term of eighteen months
> Be full expired.　　　　　[I. i. 63–66.]

Cf. *Extract* 9 from Holinshed.

France. I. i. 235 ; III. i. 87.

> Cold news for me, for I had hope of France,
> Even as I have of fertile England's soil.
> 　　　　　[I. i. 235–236.]

York hoped to be king of France as well as of England, as Henry the Fifth had been, and his son—Henry the Sixth—before the possessions and conquests of the English had been lost.

France. I. iii. 51.

> I tell thee, Pole, when in the city Tours
> Thou rann'st a tilt in honour of my love,
> And stol'st away the ladies' hearts of France,
> I thought King Henry had resembled thee
> In courage, courtship, and proportion :
> 　　　　　[I. iii. 49–53.]

See Grafton's *Chronicle*, Vol. I., page 625 ; and *Extract* 1 from Holinshed.

France. I. iii. 102, 134.

> If York have ill demeaned himself in France,
> Then let him be denayed the regentship.
> 　　　　　[I. iii. 102–103.]

> Thy sale of offices and towns in France,
> If they were known, as the suspect is great,
> Would make thee quickly hop without thy head.
> 　　　　　[I. iii. 134–136.]

Hart quotes from Polydore Vergil : " There was forthwith a companye readie to sedition . . . who . . . did urge forwarde, exhorte, and perswade her, to looke into the revenewes of the Crowne, to call for an accompt thereof, and so should she well understande that the duek had used the same, not for the common wealth but for his owne private commoditie." This is Somerset's charge.

France. II. ii. 25.

> Sent his poor Queen to France, from whence she came,
> And him to Pomfret.　　　[II. ii. 25–26.]

See under Queen.

France. III. i. 62, 104, 106, 109.

> And did he not, in his protectorship,
> Levy great sums of money through the realm
> For soldiers' pay in France, and never sent it ?
> 　　　　　[III. i. 60–62.]

> *York.* Tis' thought, my lord, that you took bribes in France,
> And, being protector, stayed the soldiers' pay ;
> By means whereof his highness hath lost France.
> *Glou.* Is it but thought so ? What are they that think it ?
> I never robbed the soldiers of their pay,
> Nor ever had one penny bribe from France.
> 　　　　　[III. i. 104–109.]

One of the charges brought against the Duke of Gloucester by the Duke of York. Somerset was also charged with the same offence.

France. III. i. 83.

> *King.* Welcome, Lord Somerset. What news from France ?
> *Som.* That all your interest in those territories
> Is utterly bereft you : all is lost. [III. i. 83–85.]

The Duke of Somerset was Regent in France. Cf. *Extract* 9 from Holinshed.

Hart quotes Hall : At the yielding of Caen, the Duke of Somerset . . . made an agrement with the Frenche kyng, that he would rendre the toun so that he and all of his might depart in sauegard with all their goodes and substaunce ; whiche offre the Frenche kyng gladly accepted . . . Sir Davie Hall . . . departed to Chierburgh and from thence sailed into Irelande to the Duke of Yorke, making relacion to hym . . . whiche thyng kyndeled so greate a rancoure in his harte & stomache that he never left persecutynge of the Duke of Somersette . . . Now rested English onely the toune of Chierburgh. . . . Thus was the duchie of Normandy lost ye whiche had continued in the english-mennes possession xxx. yeres, by the conquest of Kyng Henry the fifth . . . Others say, that the Duke of Somerset, for his owne peculiar profit, kept not halfe his nombre of souldiors, and put their wages in his purse."

France. III. i. 292, 295.

York. That Somerset be sent as regent thither.
'Tis meet that lucky ruler be employed ;
Witness the fortune he hath had in France.

Som. If York, with all his far-fet policy,
Had been the regent there instead of me,
He never would have stayed in France so long.
[III. i. 290–295.]

In *The Contention* the passage is :

York. To keepe in awe the stubborne Irishmen,
He did so much good when he was in France.

Som. Had Yorke bene there with all his far fecht
Pollices, he might haue lost as much as I.

York. I, for Yorke would haue lost his liue before
That France should haue reuolted from Englands rule.

France. IV. i. 86.

By thee Anjou and Maine were sold to France.
[IV. i. 86.]
See Anjou, I., i., 212 ; IV., i., 86.

France. IV. vii. 21.

here 's the Lord Say,
which sold the towns in France ; [IV. vii. 20–21.]

Holinshed says : " The Commons in the Parliament of 1450 charged with being principal parties to the cession of Anjou and Maine the duke of Suffolke, with William bishop of Salisburie, and sir Iames Fines, lord Saie, and diuerse others.

Gallowglasses. IV. ix. 26.

And with a puissant and a mighty power
Of gallowglasses and stout kerns
Is marching hitherward in proud array ;
[IV. ix. 26–28.]

Stanihurst in his *Description of Ireland*, says : " The *galloglasse* useth a kind of pollax for his weapon. These men are grim of countenance, tall of stature, big of limme, and lusty of body,

wel and strongly timbered. The *kerne* is an ordinary souldier, using for weapon his sword and target, and sometimes his peece, being commonly good marksmen. Kerne signifieth a shower of hell, because they are taken for no better than for rake-hells, or the devils blacke garde." *See also* Kerns.

Gelidus timor occupat artus. IV. i. 117.

" Cold fear seizes my limbs " ; probably a reminiscence from the Eleventh Book of Virgil.

George. IV. i. 29.

Look on my George ; I am a gentleman.
Rate me at what thou wilt, thou shalt be paid.
[IV. i. 29–30.]

A jewelled figure of St. George forming part of the insignia of the Order of the Garter. Cf. *The Tragedy of King Richard the Third*, IV., iv., 369–376 :

K. Rich. Now, by my George, my garter, and my crown,—

Q. Eliz. Profan'd, dishonour'd, and the third usurp'd.

K. Rich. I swear—

Q. Eliz. By nothing ; for this is no oath :
Thy George, profan'd, hath lost his lordly honour ;
Thy garter, blemish'd, pawn'd, his knightly virtue ;
Thy crown, usurp'd, disgrac'd his kingly glory.
If something thou would'st swear to be believ'd,
Swear then by something that thou hast not wrong'd.

George Bevis. IV. ii. p.1 ; IV. iii. p.1 ; IV. vi. p.1 ; IV. vii. p.23 ; IV. viii. p.1.

Bevis appears in company with John Holland on Blackheath, and they decide to join with Cade in his projected rebellion. He subsequently appears as a staunch follower of Cade, and brings in Lord Say, who has been taken prisoner in the fighting at Smithfield.

Gloucester's body. III. ii. p.149.

Re-enter Warwick *and others bearing* Gloucester's *body on a bed.*

" The stage-direction in the quarto is—Warwick draws the curtaines, [*i.e.* draws them open] and shows Duke Humphrey in his bed. In the folio—A bed with Gloster's body put forth. These are some of the many circumstances which prove, I think, decisively, that the theatres of our author's time were unfurnished with scenes. In those days, as I conceive, curtains were occasionally hung across the middle of the

stage on an iron rod, which, being drawn open,
formed a second apartment, when a change of
scene was required. The direction of the folio,
' to put forth a bed,' was merely to the property-
man to thrust a bed forwards behind those
curtains, previous to their being drawn open."
Malone.

Gloucester's Garden.

The Scene of Act I., Scene iv. Shows the
arrest of the Duchess of Gloucester, Margery
Jourdain, the witch; Hume, Southwell and
Bolingbroke for practising witchcraft. [Courte-
nay states :   " For the prophecies which the
conjurors extract from their spirits I find no
authority. An insinuation that the charge
against Eleanor was part of the scheme of
' persons near about the king,' is found by
Fabyan. It certainly came opportunely to
bring the Duke into disrepute ; but ' he bore all
things patiently, and said little.' . . . Whatever part Beaufort may have had in this affair,
Queen Margaret certainly had none. Though
Suffolk in the play announces it to the Queen as
a contrivance to get the Duchess out of her way,
it really occurred three years before she came to
England."]

Gualtier. IV. i. 37, 38.

Suf. Thy name affrights me, in whose sound is death.
    A cunning man did calculate my birth,
    And told me that by water I should die :
    Yet let not this make thee be bloody-minded ;
    Thy name is Gualtier, being rightly sounded.
Whit. Gualtier or Walter, which it is, I care not.
                    [IV. i. 33–38.]

The French form of " Walter." In Queen
Margaret's letter to this Duke of Suffolk, by
Michael Drayton, we read :

    I pray thee, Poole, have care how thou dost pass,
    Never the sea yet half so dangerous was,
    And one foretold, by *water* thou should'st die.

The best account we have of Suffolk's death is
No. 93 of the Paston Letters :

          A.D. 1450, 5 May.
    William Lomner to John Paston.
To my ryght worchipfull John Paston, at
           Norwich.
    Ryght worchipfull sir, I recomaunde me
to yow, and am right sory of that I shalle
sey, and have soo wesshe this litel bille with
sorwfulle terys, that on ethes ye shalle
reede it.

As on Monday nexte after May day there
come tydyngs to London, that on Thorsday
before the Duke of Suffolk come into the
costes of Kent full nere Dover with his ij.
shepes and a litel spynner ; the qweche
spynner he sente with certeyn letters to
certeyn of his trustid men unto Caleys
warde, to knowe howe he shuld be res-
ceyvyd ; and with hym mette a shippe
callyd Nicolas of the Towre, with other
shippis waytyng on hym, and by bem that
were in the spyner, the maister of the
Nicolas hadde knowlich of the dukes comyng.
And whanne he espyed the dukes shepis,
he sent forthe his bote to wete what they
were, and the duke hym selfe spakke to
hem, and seyd, he was be the Kyngs
comaundement sent to Caleys ward, &c.

And they seyd he most speke with here
master. And soo he, with ij. or iij. of his
men, wente forth with hem yn here bote to
the Nicolas ; and whanne he come, the
master badde hym, ' Welcom, Traitor,' as
men sey ; and forther the maister desyryd
to wete y͡f the shepmen woldde holde with the
duke, and they sent word they wold not yn
noo wyse ; and soo he was yn the Nicholas
tyl Saturday next folwyng.

Soom sey he wrotte moche thenke [thing]
to be delyverd to the Kynge, but thet is not
verily knowe. He hadde hes confessor
with hym, &c.

And some sey he was arreynyd yn the
sheppe on here maner upon the appeche-
mentes and fonde gylty, &c.

Also he asked the name of the sheppe,
and whanne he knew it, he remembred
Stacy that seid, if he myght eschape the
daunger of the Tour, he should be saffe ;
and thanne his herte fayled hym, for he
thowghte he was desseyvyd, and yn the
syght of all his men he was drawyn ought
of the grete shippe yn to the bote ; and
there was an exe, and a stoke, and oon of
the lewdeste of the shippe badde hym ley
down his hedde, and he should be fair ferd
wyth, and dye on a swerd ; and toke a
rusty swerd, and smotte of his hedde
wythyn halfe a doseyn strokes, and toke
awey his gown of russet, and his dobelette
of velvet mayled, and leyde his body on the
sonds of Dover ; and some sey his hedde

was sette oon a pole by it, and hes men sette on the londe be grette circumstaunce and preye. And the shreve of Kent doth weche the body, and sent his under shreve to the juges to wete what to doo, and also to the Kenge whatte shalbe doo.

Guards. I. iii. p.176 ; I. iv. 41 ; II. iii. p.1.

Hall of Justice. [St. Stephen's Chapel, Westminster].

The Scene of Act II., Scene iii. The trial of the Duchess of Gloucester and her confederates for practising witchcraft has already taken place when this scene opens. The Duchess is condemned to undergo public penance and subsequent banishment to the Isle of Man, while the others are condemned to be executed. The scene closes with the duel between Peter and his master. See also Eleanor, Duchess of Gloucester.

Hautboys. I. i. p.1.

A wind instrument, sounded through a reed and similar in shape to a clarinet.

Heads of Lord Say and Sir James Cromer. IV. vii. p.128.

See Lord Say and Sir James Cromer.

Henry. I. i. 76, 82 ; II. iii. 34.

King Henry the Fifth.

Henry Bolingbroke, Duke of Lancaster. II. ii. 21.

Afterwards King Henry the Fourth.

Henry's conquest. I. i. 94.

The French conquests of King Henry the Fifth.

Henry the Fifth. IV. ii. 156 ; IV. viii. 17, 34, 56.

Henry the Fourth. II. ii. 23.

Herald. II. iv. p.70.

Summons Gloucester "to his majesty's Parliament, holden at Bury St. Edmunds the first of the next month."

Humphrey, Duke of Gloucester, Uncle to the King. I. i. p.1, 67, 74, 135, 157, 160, 167, 170, 175, 177, 181,

191, 201, 239, 251 ; I. ii. 1, 3, 33, 35, 62, 106 ; I. iii. 46, 77, 95, p.100, 148, p.151, 210 ; II. i. p.1, 32, 43, 49, 158, 185, 196 ; II. ii. 74 ; II. iii. p.1, 18, 22, 26, 40 ; II. iv. p.1, 23, 27, 37, 42, 98 ; III. i. 1, 20, 56, 65, 69, p.93, 95, 139, 202, 204, 217, 222, 225, 233, 250, 260, 321, 382 ; III. ii. 20, 29, 55, 72, 78, 123, 138, 182, 187, 202, 231, 248, 374 ; IV. i. 76 ; V. i. 56.

Gloucester is Protector of the realm, and adviser to the king, a strong and loyal supporter of his monarch. But Suffolk sees in him a stumbling-block to his own ambitions and gathers a party of nobles round him for Gloucester's destruction. The weak king, unable to fathom the deeper projects of his lords, submits to the plot and thus loses his staunchest ally, one who might have provided him with a loyal band of nobles and assured the peace and security of his throne and country.

It is seen in the course of the play that Gloucester's rule during Henry's minority has been of such consummate diligence that those who seek to remove him are at a loss to conceive a charge against him, but his wife Eleanor is his undoing. Her ambition is reckless, and through her desires an opportunity occurs to accuse Gloucester of coveting the crown.

His offer to resign is not sufficient for Suffolk and his followers, and they continue to accuse him before Henry, and Suffolk finally accuses him of treason. Gloucester is then led away to await trial, but before this can take place he is murdered by assassins hired by Suffolk.

Gloucester's deep love of his country is exemplified in the first act of the play ; the abrupt termination of his reading the covenant of peace is a piece of exquisite dramatic force, and in his excuse the dramatist has conveyed in a masterly way his conception of Gloucester as a sincere patriot.

Gloucester is well aware of Suffolk's motives in causing his arrest, and his speech as he is led away to imprisonment expresses this in no uncertain way :

Thus is the shepherd beaten from thy side,
And wolves are gnarling who shall gnaw thee first.
Ah! that my fear were false ; ah! that it were ;—
For, good king Henry, thy decay I fear.
[III. i. 191-194.

Inns of Court. IV. vii. 2.

> others to the inns of court :   [IV. vii. 2.]

See Savoy.

Invitis nubibus. IV. i. 99.

> Advance our half-faced sun, striving to shine,
> Under the which is writ Invitis nubibus. [IV. i. 98–99.]

The device on King Edward the Third's standard was a sun breaking through the clouds, with the motto ' Invitis nubibus ' = ' In spite of the clouds.'

Ireland. I. i. 192.

> And, brother York, thy acts in Ireland,
> In bringing them to civil discipline,   [I. i. 192–193.]

An anachronism. The present scene is in 1445, and Richard, Duke of York, was not appointed Viceroy of Ireland until 1447, and delayed his departure until 1449.

Ireland. I. i. 230.

Ireland. III. i. 282, 310, 312.

> The uncivil kerns of Ireland are in arms
> The temper clay with blood of Englishmen :
>   [III. i. 310–311.]

In *The Contention* the passage runs :

> Madame, I bring you newes from Ireland,
> The wilde Onele my Lords, is vp in Armes,
> With troupes of Irish Kernes that vncontrold,
> Doth plant themselues within the English pale.

Cf. I., i., 192–193.

Ireland. III. i. 329, 348, 360, 380.

For, A Report, drawn up by the chief persons in the County of Kildare, to Richard Duke of York, Lord Lieutenant of Ireland, *see* Jones' *York and Lancaster*, 1399–1485, p. 62.

Ireland. IV. ix. 24 ; V. i. 1.

> The Duke of York is newly come from Ireland,
>   [IV. ix. 24.]

Cf. *Extract* 26 from Holinshed.

Iris. III. ii. 407.

> For wheresoe'er thou art in this world's globe,
> I 'll have an Iris that shall find thee out.
>   [III. ii. 406–4.]

In Greek mythology the messenger of the Gods. Because of her swiftness she is represented with wings, riding on a rainbow. One of her offices was to unloose the souls of women from the chains of the body, *e.g.* when Dido laid violent hands on herself, Juno despatched Iris to loose her soul from her body, as described by Virgil in the *Æneid*, Book IV :

> Then Juno, grieving that she should sustain
> A death so ling'ring, and so full of pain,
> Sent Iris down to free her from the stife
> of lab'ring nature, and dissolve her life. [Dryden's trans.]

Isle of Man. II. iii. 13 ; II. iv. 78, 94.

> Shall, after three days' open penance done,
> Live in your country here in banishient,
> With Sir John Stanley, in the Isle of Man.
>   [II. iii. 11–13.]

Cf. *Extract* 15 from Holinshed.

Jack Cade, a Rebel. III. i. 357, 360 ; IV. ii. 4, p.32, 32, 153, 176 ; IV. iii. p.1 ; IV. iv. 13, 19, 28, 49 ; IV. v, 1 ; IV. vi. p.1, 7, 9 ; IV. vii. p.1, 11 ; IV. viii. p.1, 7, 33, 34, 47 ; IV. ix. 8, 31, 34 ; IV. x. p.1, 65, 66 ; V. i. 62, p.64, 67, 68.

The leader of a mob of rebels, hired by York to raise an insurrection in order to strenghen his hand against the king.

York describes his plot in a soliloquy after news has been brought to the king that the rebellion has broken out :

> I have seduced a headstrong Kentishman,
> John Cade of Ashford,
> To make commotion, as full well he can,
> Under the title of John Mortimer.
>   [III. i. 356-359.]

We first meet Cade at Blackheath, surrounded by his Kentish followers. He makes wild promises of what he will do when he has achieved power, and defies the entreaties of Sir Humphrey Stafford to disperse the mob.

The succeeding scenes depict various phases of the rebellion ; the Staffords are slain, and the rebels capture London Bridge, and Cade, elated by this success, urges his followers to :

>   go
> and set London Bridge on fire, and, if you can,
> burn down the Tower too.
>   [IV. vi. 13-15.]

At Smithfield, Lord Say is brought before Cade and is executed at his command, together with his son-in-law.

Cade next appears at Southwark, at the head of the rebels, exclaiming :

Up Fish Street ! down Saint Magnus' Corner !
kill and knock down ! throw them into Thames !
[IV. viii. 1-2.]

when a parley is sounded and Buckingham and Old Clifford with their forces enter. They offer free pardons to the rebels if they will return to their homes. The mob is won over and Cade, seeing his cause is lost, makes good his escape.

He is later seen climbing over the wall of Alexander Iden's garden, worn out with hunger and desperately seeking food. Iden appears and does not recognise the intruder, but Cade exclaims :

Here 's the lord of the soil come to seize me for a stray,
for entering his fee-simple without leave. Ah, villain,
thou wilt betray me, and get a thousand crowns of the
king by carrying my head to him.   [IV. x. 24–27.]

Iden is surprised at these words, and is loth to accept the vagrant's challenge to fight, but Cade persists, and a duel ensues in which Cade is killed. As he lies mortally wounded he reveals his identity, and Iden rejoices that he has freed the country from so base a traitor.

See Appendix III.

Jerusalem. I. i. 47.

See Reignier.

Joan. II. i. 4.

Yet, by your leave, the wind was very high,
And, ten to one, old Joan had not gone out.
[II. i. 3–4.]

The name of a hawk. The meaning is that the wind was so high it was ten to one that old Joan would not have taken her flight at the game. Johnson remarks : " I am told by a gentleman better acquainted with falconry than myself, that the meaning, however expressed, is, that the wind being high, it was ten to one that the old hawk had flown quite away ; a trick which hawks often play their masters in windy weather."

John Goodman. I. iii. 15.

A man serving Cardinal Beaufort.

John Holland. IV. ii. p.1 ; IV. iii. p.1 ; IV. vi. p.1 ; IV. vii. p.1 ; IV. viii. p.1.

Appears with George Bevis on Blackheath, where they decide to throw in their lot with Jack Cade. Appears in all the rebellion scenes.

John Hume, a Priest. I. ii. p.70, 72, 85, 87, 88, 105 ; I. iv. p.1, 3, 8, p.13 ; II. iii. p.1.

Hume is a priest who takes part in the raising of the spirit in the Duke of Gloucester's garden

He tells the duchess at her house that all the plans have been made with Margery Jourdain the witch, and the conjuror Bolingbroke :

This they have promised, to show your highness
A spirit raised from death of under-ground,
That shall make answer to such questions
As by your grace shall be propounded him.
[I. ii. 78–81.]

and on his departure reveals that he takes part in this from a purely mercenary motive, as his speech shows him to be an agent for Suffolk, who has planned thus to trap the ambitious duchess.

At the appointed hour Hume appears in the garden with Bolingbroke, Southwell and Margery Jourdain, and leaves his confederates to be at the Duchess' side.

Having been arrested with the others he is brought before the king, who orders him to be hanged.

Cf. *Extracts* 11 *and* 14 from Holinshed.

John Mortimer. III. i. 359, 372.

I have seduced a headstrong Kentishman,
John Cade of Ashford,
To make commotion, as full well he can,
Under the title of John Mortimer.   [III. i. 356–359.]

A name assumed by Jack Cade. Cf. *Extract* 20 from Holinshed. Grafton says : " For although Richard Duke of Yorke was in person (as the kings Deputie) in the realm of Ireland, continually resiant ther : yet his breath puffed, and his winde blewe dayly, in many partes of this realme. . . . Vpon this coniecture, the friendes, kinsmen, and allies of the Duke of Yorke, which were of no small number, began to practise the gouernaunce of his title : Infusyng and puttyng into mens heades secretly his right to the Crowne, his politique gouernaunce, his gentle behauiour too all the Irishe Nacion, affirmyng, that he which had brought that rude and sauage nacion to ciuile fashion.

and English maners, would (if he once ruled in the realme of England) depose euill Counsaylors, correct euill Iudges, and reforme all matters amisse, and vnamended. And to set open the flood gates of these deuises, it was though necessary, to cause some great commocion, and ye risyng of people to be made agaynst the king : so that if they preuayled, then had the Duke of Yorke and his complices, their appetite and desyre. And because the Kentishemen he impacient in wronges, disdeyning of to much oppression, and euer desirous of newe chaunge, and newe fanglenesse : The ouerture of this matter was put foorth in Kent, and to the entent that it should not be knowen, that the Duke of Yorke or his friendes were the cause of the sodaine risyng : A certaine yong man of a goodly stature, and pregnant wit, was entysed to take vpō him the name of Iohn Mortimer, although his name were Iohn Cade, and not for a small pollicie, thinkyng that by that surname, the lyne and lynage of the assistent house of the Erle of Marche, which were so small number, should be to him both adherent and fauourable."

John Mortimer. IV. ii. 119.

> To equal him, I will make myself a knight presently.
> [Kneels.]   Rise up Sir John Mortimer. Now have at
> him !   [IV. ii. 118–120.]

Jack Cade knights himself to be equal with Sir Humphrey Stafford. Cf. *The Contention :*

> *Cade.* Why then to equall him, ile make my selfe knight.
>   Kneele downe Iohn Mortemer,
>   Rise vp sir Iohn Mortemer,
>   Is there any more of them that be Knights ?
> *Tom.*   I his brother.   [*He Knights Dicke Butcher.*]
> *Cade.* Then kneele downe Dicke Butcher,
>   Rise vp sir Dicke Butcher.

John of Gaunt, the Duke of Lancaster. II. ii. 14, 22, 54.

See *Extract* 13 from Holinshed.

John Southwell, a Priest. I. iv. p.1, 11 ; II. iii. p.1.

A priest who with Bolingbroke, raises a spirit in the Duke of Gloucester's garden, and for his part in the proceedings is condemned to death on the gallows by the king.

See also John Hume.

Jove. IV. i. 48, 49.

> Jove sometime went disguised, and why not I ?
> *Cap.* But Jove was never slain, as thou shalt be.
>   [V. i. 48–49.]

Jove assumed many disguises. Legends represent him as visiting Danae in a shower of gold ; Leda in the similitude of a swan ; and Antiope in the form of a satyr. As a beautiful white bull he carried off Europa, the daughter of Agenor, King of Phœnicia, and counterfeiting the modesty of Diana corrupted Calista, the daughter of Lycaon, king of Arcadia.

Julius Cæsar. IV. i. 137.

>   Brutus' bastard hand
> Stabbed Julius Cæsar :   [IV. i. 136–137

See Brutus' bastard hand stabbed Julius Cæsar.

Kenilworth Castle.

The Scene of Act IV., Scene ix. Buckingham and Clifford announce to the king that Cade's insurrection has been crushed, and Henry grants pardon to all the rebel's followers, many of whom have been conveyed to Kenilworth with halters round their necks. News is now brought that the Duke of York with an army has arrived with the sole purpose of removing the Duke of Somerset from the king's counsel, and Somerset is committed to the Tower, until York and his army be dismissed.

See also Killingworth.

Kent. IV. i. 100.

> The Commons here in Kent are up in arms.
>   [IV. i. 100.]

Grafton says : " the Queene somewhat fearyng the destruction of the Duke, but more the confusion of herselfe, caused the Parliament, before begon at the black Friers in London, to be adiourned to Leycester, thinkyng there by force and rigor of the lawe, to subdue and represse all the malice and euill will, conceyued agaynst the Duke and her : at which place fewe of the Nobility would appere, wherefore it was againe adiourned to Westminster, where was a whole companie and a full apperaunce. In the which session, the Commons of the nether house, put vp to the king and the Lordes, many articles of treason, misprision and misdemeanour, agaynst the Duke of Suffolke ; " For the Articles proposed by the Commons against the Duke of Suffolke, See Grafton's *Chronicle*, Vol. I., page 638-639.

Kent. IV. ii. 121 ; IV. vii. 54, 55 ; IV. x. 43, 73 ; V. i. 75.

Kent. IV. vii. 60.

> Kent, in the Commentaries Cæsar writ,
> Is termed the civil'st place in all this isle :
> [IV. vii. 60-61.]

" The moſt civiliz'd People among 'em are the Kentiſh Men, whoſe Country lyes altogether upon the Sea-Coaſts ; and their Cuſtoms are much the ſame with thoſe of the Gauls : The Inland People ſeldom trouble themſelves with Agriculture, living on Milk and Fleſh Meat, and are clad with Skins ; but all of 'em paint themſelves blue with Woad, that they may look the more dreadful to their Enemies in Battel ; the Hair of their Heads they wear very long, but ſhave all the reſt of their Bodies, except the upper Lip " ; Cæsar's *Commentary of his War in Gaul.*

Kent. Iden's Garden.

The Scene of Act IV., Scene x. Cade, in a famished condition enters the garden of Alexander Iden, a Kentish squire where, during a fight which follows he is mortally wounded by Iden.

Kerns. III. i. 310, 361, 367 ; IV. ix. 26.

> The uncivil kerns of Ireland are in arms
> And temper clay with blood of Englishmen :
> [III. i. 310-311.]

Cf. *The Contention :*

> Madame, I bring you newes from Ireland,
> The wilde Onele my Lords, is vp in Armes,
> With troupes of Irish Kernes that vncontrold,
> Doth plant themselues within the English pale.

See also Gallowglasses.

Killingworth. IV. iv. 39, 44.

Kenilworth Castle in Warwickshire. During Cade's rebellion Henry the Sixth and Queen Margaret took refuge at Kenilworth. Cf. *Extract* 25 from Holinshed.

King Charles. I. i. 41, 43.

Charles the Seventh, King of France.

King Henry the Sixth. I. i. p.1, 24, 45, 46, 59, 128, 151, 216, 249 ; I. ii. 7, 20, 39 ; I. iii. 45, 52, p.100 ; I. iv. 30, 59 ; II. i. p.1, 172 ; II. ii. 54 ; II. iii. p.1, 23, 30, 32, 39, 44 ; III. i. p.1, 189, 194, 224, 383 ; III. ii. p.15, 35, 38, 121, 131, 289 ; III. iii. p.1 ; IV. i. 50 ; IV. iy. p.1 ; IV. ix. p.1, 18 ; V. i. 2, 17, 31, 48, p.56 ; V. ii. p.72.

The character of Henry is portrayed as the direct antithesis of Margaret his queen ; she is wilful, impetuous and headstrong, while he is weak, and might almost be described as " will-less," and helpless amid the troubles of the times, the jealousies of the nobles and the impending disastrous civil strife between the houses of Lancaster and York.

Suffolk is king rather than Henry at the commencement of this Part, and Gloucester aptly describes him as " the new-made duke that rules the roast."

That Henry is totally unfitted to be king is shown by the manner in which he always allows one of the nobles to make a decision for him. He appears to be totally incapable, or afraid to speak for himself, with the authority he should command. He must turn to Gloucester for advice in such a simple matter as Peter's accusation against his master Horner ; this is but one instance of his entire lack of self-confidence.

The queen soon tires of this weak-minded husband whose mind is

> bent to holiness,
> To number Ave-Maries on his beads " : [I. iii. 54-55.]

and it is small wonder that the nobles are able to do just as they please. A little pleading, even when it is obvious to Henry that he should refuse their request, is all that is necessary to obtain his consent. Gloucester's murder is planned by Suffolk and his followers, and Henry, on hearing their accusations against him, exclaims :

> My lords, what to your wisdoms seemeth best,
> Do or undo, as if ourself were here. [III. i. 195-196.]

and then immediately turning to Margaret says:

Ay, Margaret ; my heart is drowned with grief,

.   .   .   .

Ah! uncle Humphrey, in thy face I see
The map of honour, truth and loyalty. [III. i. 198–203.]

Instances such as this are to be found throughout the play, and Henry remains the plaything of the nobles, swayed from opinion to opinion, from party to party, until finally in the last Act we hear York's challenge :

From Ireland thus comes York to claim his right,
And pluck the crown from feeble Henry's head.
[V. i. 1–2.]

and after the battle of St. Albans, Margaret, who has lost all patience with Henry's utter helplessness exclaims :

What are you made of ? you 'll not fight nor fly ;
Now is it manhood, wisdom and defence,
To give the enemy way, and to secure us
By what we can, which can no more but fly.
[V. ii. 74–77.]

Henry's downfall is assured from the moment he allowed Gloucester to be arrested by his enemies, for Gloucester, in spite of all that Margaret could say against him, was his chief supporter, and Suffolk was crafty enough to see that Henry would be helpless without him.

Responsibility for Gloucester's death must be laid on Henry, and no more striking example could be found to show the utter lack of will-power displayed by this weakling monarch, than his acceptance of Gloucester's arrest and murder, feeling sure all the while, as he must have done, that Gloucester was no traitor.

[King Henry the Sixth is also a character in the *Third Part of King Henry the Sixth* (q.v.).]

King of England's own proper cost and charges. I. i. 59.

On April 9th, 1446, the Commons gave Henry a fifteenth and a tenth, but, in specifying the purposes to which these grants were to be applied, they did not mention the 'costs and charges' of bringing Margaret to England or any other expenses connected with her marriage. Cf. I., i., 130–132 :

A proper jest, and never heard before,
That Suffolk should demand a whole fifteenth
For costs and charges in transporting her !

King of France. I. i. 6.

Charles the Seventh. Mentioned here as being present at Tours at the espousal of Queen Margaret. Cf. *Extract* 1 from Holinshed.

King of Sicil. I. i. 6.

Reignier, Duke of Anjou, father of Margaret, was titular king of Sicily. Present at the espousal of his daughter—Margaret—to Henry the Sixth. Cf. *Extract* 1 from Holinshed.

Lacies. IV. ii. 45.

My wife descended of the Lacies,—   [IV. ii. 45.]

A noted family from which Jack Cade claims his wife to be descended, to which Dick the Butcher [aside] replies : " She was, indeed, a pedlar's daughter, and sold many laces " ; " But now of late," adds Smith the Weaver, " not able to travel with her furred pack, she washes bucks here at home."

Ladies.

Lancaster. I. i. 242, 255 ; II. ii. 29.

The House of Lancaster.

Lancaster. II. ii. 66.

But I am not your king
Till I be crowned and that my sword be stained
With heart-blood of the house of Lancaster ;
[II. ii. 64–66.]

Cf. *The True Tragedie of Richard Duke of Yorke, and the good King Henry the Sixt :*

I cannot weepe, for all my breasts moisture
Scarse serues to quench my furnace burning hart ;
I cannot ioie till this white rose be dide,
Euen in the hart bloud of the house of Lancaster.

Lancaster. IV. i. 51.

Suf. Obscure and lowly swain, King Henry's blood,
The honourable blood of Lancaster,
Must not be shed by such a jaded groom.
[IV. i. 50–52.]

" Suffolk had none of this blood in his veins, according to Blakeway. But Hall says that Suffolk assumed a good ancestry." *Hart.*

Lent. IV. iii. 6.

therefore thus will I reward thee, the Lent shall be as long again as it is ; and thou shalt have a license to kill for a hundred lacking one.
[IV. iii. 5–8.]

The selling of meat in Lent was restricted to those butchers who had secured a special license, permitting them to kill a limited number of animals each week. In Dick's case the number is to be ninety-nine. *Barnwell.* In *The Contention* the passage is :

And thus I will reward thee. The Lent shall be as long againe as it was. Thou shalt haue licence to kill for foure score & one a week.

Shakespeare changed the number to ninety-nine. In the reign of Elizabeth, butchers were strictly enjoined not to sell fresh meat in Lent, not with a religious view, but for the double purpose of diminishing the consumption of flesh meat during that period, and so making it more plentiful during the rest of the year, and of encouraging the fisheries and augmenting the number of seamen.

Lionel, Duke of Clarence. II. ii. 13, 34, 50, 56.

See *Extract* 13 from Holinshed.

London. II. i. 176, 198 ; V. ii. 81.

London. V. iii. 24, 32.

For, as I hear, the king is fled to London, To call a present court of Parliament : [V. iii. 24–25.]

Malone remarks : " The King and Queen left the stage only just as York entered, and have not said a word about calling a Parliament. Where then could York hear this ?—The fact is, as we have seen, that in the old play the King does say, ' he will call a parliament,' but our author has omitted the lines. He has, therefore, here, as in some other places, fallen into an impropriety, by sometimes following and at others deserting his original."

London bridge. IV. iv. 49.

The famous old bridge across the River Thames. The heads of the principal rebels were exposed over the draw-bridge. Grafton says : But this counsayle came to small effect : for the multitude of the rebels draue the Citezens from the stoulpes at the bridge foote, to the drawe bridge, and beganne to set fyre in dyuers houses. Alas what sorrower it was to beholde that miserable chaunce : for some desyring to eschewe the fyre, lept on his enimies weapon, and so died, fearefull women with children in their armes, amased and appalled, lept into the riuer : other doubting how to saue themselues betweene fyre, water, and sworde, were in their houses suffocat and smoldered. Yet the Capteynes nothing regarding these chaunces, fought

on the drawe bridge all the night valyauntly, but in conclusion, the rebels gate the drawe bridge, and drowned many, and slue Iohn Sutton Alderman, and Robert Heysande a hardy Citizen, with many other."

London bridge. IV. vi. 14.

But first, go and set London bridge on fire, [IV. vi. 13–14.]

London bridge was built of wood. When Cade entered London he cut the ropes of the draw-bridge, and the houses on the bridge were set on fire, and many of the inhabitants perished. Cf. *Extract* 25 from Holinshed.

London. Cannon Street.

The Scene of Act IV., Scene vi. Cade and his followers arrive in Cannon Street, and striking his sword on London Stone declares he is ' Lord of the City.' After giving orders to fire London Bridge and to burn down the Tower Cade proceeds to Smithfield to engage the king's forces.

London. The Duke of York's Garden.

The Scene of Act II., Scene ii. In this Scene the Duke of York sets forth in detail his claim to the crown. See *Extract* 13 from Holinshed.

London gates. IV. viii. 23.

Hath my sword therefore broke through London gates, that you should leave me at the White Hart in Southwark ? [IV. viii. 23–25.]

Stowe in his *Survey of London*, says : " Gates in the wall of this city of old time were four ; to wit, Aeldgate for the east, Aldersgate for the north, Ludgate for the west, and the Bridgegate over the river of Thames for the south ; but of later times, for the ease of citizens and passengers, divers other gates and posterns have been made. . . . In the reign of Henry II (saith Fitzstephen) there were seven double gates in the wall of this city, but he nameth them not. It may, therefore, be supposed, he meant for the first, the gate next the Tower of London, now commonly called the Postern, the next be Aeldgate, the third Bishopsgate, the fourth Ealdersgate, the fifth Newgate, the sixth Ludgate, the seventh Bridgegate. Since the which time hath been builded the postern called Moorgate, a postern from Christ's hospital towards St. Bartholomewe's hospital in Smithfield, &c."

See also Harben's *Dictionary of London.*

London. The Palace.

The Scene of Act I., Scenes i. and iii ; Act IV., Scene iv.

Act I., Scene i. Opens with the introduction of Queen Margaret to the king and his court by Suffolk who had been sent to France to marry her as the king's proxy. In the Articles of Contracted Peace ceding the provinces of Anjou and Maine, Courtenay remarks that it is " apparently the composition of the dramatist." The Duke of York and the Earls of Salisbury and Warwick condemn the marriage, affirming that it is unprofitable to the realm, in consequence of which a bitter feud breaks out between the nobles, and the Dukes of Buckingham and Somerset join with the Cardinal and Suffolk to oust Gloucester from his protectorship as being the first step towards their own selfish ambitions. The closing scene shows the ambition of York who threatens to " raise aloft the milk-white rose " and assert his claim to the throne.

Act I., Scene iii. Shows the popularity of the Duke of Gloucester, and the relations between the queen and the Duke of Suffolk ; the alliance against Gloucester for the accomplishment of their own selfish motives and the quarrels which subsequently follow. Petitioners present themselves at the palace with petitions to Gloucester asking for certain abuses to be redressed. Margaret complains of the weakness of her husband, and shows her animosity against the Duchess of Gloucester. A debate takes place whether York or Somerset shall be Regent of France. The episode of the dropped fan and the box on the ear which Margaret gives Eleanor is purely imaginary. Horner the armourer and his man Peter being accused of treason are brought in, guarded, and the king orders a duel to be fought between the two men to establish which of them is in the right.

Act IV., Scene iv. A petition is presented to the king on behalf of Cade, and Henry promises to send—to avoid bloodshed—" some holy bishop " to entreat with Cade. A messenger enters with the news that Cade has arrived at Southwark, and is followed by another messenger who bears tidings that the rebels have captured London Bridge, and Buckingham urges the king to seek safety at Kenilworth, until the insurrection shall be crushed.

London. Smithfield.

The Scene of Act IV., Scene vii. In the fight at Smithfield the king's troops are defeated and Matthew Goffe is slain. Cade orders the Savoy, and the Inns of Court to be demolished. Lord Say and Sir James Cromer are beheaded and their heads are brought on two poles and exhibited in the streets of the city.

London-stone. IV. vi. p.1 ; IV. vi. 2.

The central milliarium or milestone of Roman London, similar to that in the Forum at Rome. It is now built into the street wall of St. Swithin's Church, Cannon Street. Grafton says : " The Capitaine being aduertised of the Kings absence, came first into Southwarke, and there lodged at the whyte Hart, prohibyting to all men, murder, rape, or robbery : by which coulour he allured to him the harts of the common people. But after that he entered into London, and cut the ropes of the draw bridge, striking his sworde on London stone, saiyng : now is Mortimer Lorde of this Citie, and rode in euery streete lyke a Lordly Capitayne." Cf. *Extract* 25 from Holinshed.

Harben in his *Dictionary of London*, records : " A rounded block of stone set in a large stone case, in which is an oval opening through which it can be seen. Built into the south wall of St. Swithin's Church on the north side of Cannon Street.

Earliest mention : Stow says it is mentioned in a Gospel book given by King Athelstan to Christ's Church, Canterbury.

He describes it as on the south side of Cannon Street, where it is shown in Leake's map, opposite the south-west corner of St. Swithin's Church. But it appears from the Vestry Minute Book of St. Swithin's that in 1742 the stone commonly called London Stone was ordered to be removed and placed against the church on the east side of the door.

In 1798 it was again removed and placed in its present position.

It is oolite stone, such as was used by the Romans in their buildings, and Strype tells us that it was much worn away and only a stump remaining, so that to preserve it it was cased over with stone " cut hollow underneath, so that the old Stone might be seen, the new one being over it, to shelter and defend the old venerable one.

Stow tells us that in his time the stone was fastened very deeply into the ground with bars of iron and so strongly set that if carts ran against it the stone remained unshaken.

Many suggestions have been made as to the origin of the stone : That it formed part of a large upright stone, or of a monument or building of the Romans. Camden calls it a " Milliarium " or milestone, from which the British high-roads radiated and from which the distances on them were reckoned, similar to the one in the forum at Rome. Wren agrees with this, but suggests that it was not simply a pillar but a building like the Milliarium Aureum at Constantinople.

Perhaps used for Proclamations, etc., or a monument of heathen worship (Strype).

The stone is frequently alluded to in London records to mark the situation of adjacent houses and property, etc., and appears from early times as a surname of London citizens.

The first Mayor of London was named Henricus Filius Eylwini de Londenestane, 1188, his house being situated near at hand."

PROCLAMATION STONES.—" At Totnes is Brutus Stone, on which the mayor stands to proclaim a new sovereign. London Stone appears from Shakespeare (2 Henry VI., iv., 6), following Holinshed, to have conferred special sanction on a new ruler. On the Coronation Stone the new sovereign receives his crown. At St. Austell is the Maengaw Stone, where proclamations of peace and war and new reigns used to be made. Rev. F. G. Odell (*Notes and Queries*, July, 1919).

See also Jack Cade.

London Streets. IV. viii. 45.

Were 't not a shame, that whilst you live at jar,
The fearful French, whom you late vanquished,
Should make a start o'er seas and vanquish you ?
Methinks already in this civil broil
I see them lording it in London streets.
[IV. viii. 41–45.]

Clifford visualises the French—taking advantage of the civil strife—already in charge of London.

London. The Tower.

The Scene of Act IV., Scene v. The Lord Mayor of London craves the assistance of Lord Scales—who is in command of the Tower—and Scales sends Matthew Goffe with troops to defend the city.

Lord Clifford. IV. viii. p.6, 20, 54 ; IV. ix. p.7 ; V. i. 114, p.123, 123, 125, 127, 132 ; V. ii. i, 5, 6, 9, p.13, 61.

First appears with Buckingham in a parley with Cade and his rebel followers at Southwark. They plead for peace, Clifford exclaiming :

What say ye, countrymen ? will ye relent
And yield to mercy, whilst 'tis offer'd you,
Or let a rabble lead you to your deaths ?
Who loves the king, and will embrace his pardon,
Fling up his cap and say—" God save his majesty."
[IV. viii. 11–15.]

At these words the crowd exclaim :

God save the king ! God save the king !
[IV. viii. 19–19.]

Cade next addresses the crowd, and having heard his speech they signify their intention to follow him ; and Clifford makes another appeal, which causes the crowd to change its allegiance once more, and Cade, seeing his danger makes good his escape.

Clifford next appears before the king at Kenilworth, bringing with him a number of prisoners from the ranks of Cade's followers, and informs Henry that Cade has fled.

He 's fled, my lord, and all his powers do yield ;
And humbly thus, with halters on their necks,—
Expect your highness' doom, of life or death.
[IV. ix. 10–12.]

On Blackheath Clifford next appears, summoned by the queen :

Call hither Clifford ; bid him come amain,
To say if that the bastard boys of York
Shall be the surety for their traitor father.
[V. i. 114–116.]

He kneels before Henry, greeting his sovereign loyally " Health and all happiness to my lord the king ! " but York interposes with " We are thy sovereign, Clifford," to receive the reply " This is my king, York ; I do not mistake " and learning that York intends to claim the throne cries out :

He is a traitor ; let him to the Tower,
And chop away that factious pate of his.
[V. i. 134–135.]

Civil strife having commenced, we next find Lord Clifford opposing the rebel forces at St. Albans. He encounters York, whom he fights, and Clifford falls mortally wounded.

[Thomas de Clifford, twelfth Baron Clifford, a staunch supporter of the House of Lancaster. Killed at the first battle of St. Albans, 22nd May, 1455.]

Lord Mortimer. = IV. iv. 28 ; IV. vi. 6 ; IV. vii. 30 ;

A name assumed by Jack Cade. *See* John Mortimer.

Lord Say. IV. ii. 159 ; IV. iv. p.1, 43 ; IV. vii. 20, p.23.

Dick the butcher, a follower of Jack Cade the rebel, vows to kill Lord Say, exclaiming :

And furthermore, we 'll have the Lord Say's head
for selling the dukedom of Maine.   [IV. ii. 159–160.]

which threat is mentioned by the king, when Say appears before him. Lord Say answers :

Ay, but I hope your highness shall have his.
[IV. iv. 20.]

The next time we meet Say, he is a prisoner in the hands of the rebels, and is brought before Cade, who accuses him of selling Normandy to the Dauphin, " corrupted the youth of the realm in erecting a grammar-school " ; and various other " crimes " of a like nature. Cade orders his execution, and Say exclaims :

Tell me wherein have I offended most ?
Have I affected wealth or honour ? speak.
Are my chests filled up with extorted gold ?
Is my apparel sumptuous to behold ?
Whom have I injured, that ye seek my death ?
These hands are free from guiltless blood-shedding,
This breast from harbouring foul deceitful thoughts.
O ! let me live !   [IV. vii. 96–103.]

Cade answers to this touching appeal :

I feel remorse in myself with his words :
but I 'll bridle it : he shall die, an it be but for
pleading so well for his life. Away with him !
[IV. vii. 104–106.]

Later rebels appear bearing the head of Lord Say, together with that of his son-in-law, Sir James Cromer, and Cade exclaims :

Let them kiss one another,
for they loved well when they were alive. Now part them again, lest they consult about the giving up of some more towns in France.   [IV. vii. 128–131.]

[James Fiennes, Baron Say and Sele ; Sheriff of Kent ; Constable of Dover Castle and Warden of the Cinque Ports, 1447-9. Created Baron Say and Sele, 1447 ; lord chamberlain and privy councillor ; lord treasurer, 1447. Accused of maladministration was imprisoned in the Tower and handed over by the Governor to Jack Cade who had him—along with his son-in-law Sir William Cromer—beheaded.]

Lord Scales, Governor of the Tower. IV. v. p.1.

Appears on the Walls of the Tower, before a number of citizens and demands of them :

How now ! Is Jack Cade slain ?   [IV. v. i.]

but a citizen replies that he is not, but

The lord mayor craves aid of your honour
from the Tower, to defend the city from the rebels.
[IV. v. 4–6.]

To this Lord Scales replies :

Such aid as I can spare you shall command ;
But I am troubled here with them myself ;
The rebels have essayed to win the Tower.
But get you to Smithfield and gather head,
And thither I will send you Matthew Goffe ;
Fight for your king, your country, and your lives ;
And so farewell, for I must hence again.
[IV. v. 7–13.]

[Thomas de Scales, seventh Baron Scales. Served in the French Wars, 1422 ; K.G. 1425 ; Raised a force against Jack Cade ; and was in command in the fight against the rebels at London Bridge. Assisted in the defence of the Tower of London, 1460, and was slain while trying to seek sanctuary at Westminster.]

Lords.

Maine. I. i. 49, 57, 108, 117, 212, 234.

See Anjou and Reignier.

Maine. I. i. 207, 208, 210.

Sal. Then let 's make haste away, and look unto the main.
War. Unto the main ! O father, Maine, is lost !
      That Maine which by main force Warwick did win,
      And would have kept so long as breath did last :
      Main chance, father, you meant ; but I meant Maine,
      Which I will win from France, or else be slain.
[I. i. 206–211

This punning passage is taken from *The Contention* :

Sal. Come sonnes away and looke vnto the maine.
War. Vnto the Maine, Oh father Maine is lost,
    Which Warwicke by main force did win from France,
    Maine chance father you meant, but I meant Maine,
    Which I will win from France, or else be slaine.

See also Anjou and Reignier.

Maine. IV. i. 86.

By thee Anjou and Maine were sold to France,
                        [IV. i. 86.]

Grafton says : " Wherefore they (not mindyng to be more charged, then their backes would beare, and perceiuying that by negligent prouision and improuident pollicie, the affayres and businesse in the partes beyonde the sea, dayly decayed, and more were like to do) began first to make exclamacion agaynst the Duke of Suffolke, affirmyng him, to be the onely cause of the deliuery of Aniow, and Main, . . . The commons of the lower house, not forgetting their olde grudge, beseched the King, that such persons, as assented to the relese of Angeow, and deliueraunce of Maine, might be extremely punished, and tormented : and to be priuie to this fact, they accused, as principall, the Duke of Suffolke, with Iohn Bishop of Salisbury, and sir Iames Fynes, Lord Say, and diuers other."

Maine. IV. ii. 160 ; IV. vii. 65.

And furthermore, we 'll have the Lord Say's head
for selling the dukedom of Maine. [IV. ii. 159–160.]

See *Extract* from Grafton, under Maine, IV., i., 86.

Margaret, Queen to King Henry. I. i. p.1, 4, 17, 37, 46 ; I. ii. 39 ; I. iii. p.6 ; II. i. p.1 ; II. iii. p.1, 198, 207 ; IV. i. 58 ; IV. iv. p.1, 55 ; IV. ix. p.1 ; V. i. 83, p.84 ; V. ii. p.72, 73.

As the play opens, Margaret is led in to meet her husband. Henry receives her graciously, exclaiming :

Her sight did ravish, but her grace in speech,
Her words y-clad with wisdom's majesty,
Makes me from wondering fall to weeping joys ;
Such is the fullness of my heart's content.
                  [I. i. 32–35.]

but to the nobles this marriage symbolises nothing but the loss of England's power in France, the surrender of all that Henry V. had so dearly won, and the speeches of Gloucester, Salisbury and Warwick at the conclusion of the scene typify the general feeling that the marriage was wrong.

Margaret is impetuous and strong-willed, she is jealous of Gloucester's protectorship, and would have the king rule for himself. We first note this trait in her character when petitioners enter, and she says :

" To my Lord Protector ! " Are your supplications
to his lordship ? Let me see them : [I. iii. 13–14.]

and turning to Suffolk exclaims :

My Lord of Suffolk, say, is this the guise,
Is this the fashion in the court of England ?
. . . .
Am I a queen in title and in style,
And must be made a subject of a duke ?
                  [I. iii. 41–48.]

She loses no opportunity of defaming Gloucester, and at the Parliament at Bury St. Edmunds, on the king enquiring the reason for Gloucester's non-arrival, she hints that he is seeking the crown and has won the affections of the people with this in his mind, and later in the scene she exclaims :

This Gloucester should be quickly rid the world,
To rid us from the fear we have of him.
               [III. i. 233–234.]

Margaret turned to Suffolk as her guide and counsellor ; she had implicit faith in him, and on his death was deeply distressed. She sadly mourns his loss, and on hearing of Cade's advance on London, says :

Ah ! were the Duke of Suffolk now alive,
These Kentish rebels would be soon appeased !
               [IV. iv. 41–42.]

On her last appearance in the Play we find Margaret at the battle of Saint Albans, doing her best to encourage Henry to escape while there is yet time, so that they may find security in London.

[Queen Margaret is also a character in the *Third Part of King Henry the Sixth* (q.v.).]

Margery Jourdain, a Witch. I. ii. 75 ; I. iv. p.1, 10 ; II. iii. p.1.

Hume, a priest, arranges for Margery Jourdain

to raise a Spirit before the Duchess of Gloucester, so that she (the Duchess) may learn what the future holds in store.

She appears in Gloucester's garden accompanied by Hume, Bolingbroke (a conjuror), and others, and when the spirit appears in answer to their incantations she addresses it :

> Asmath !
> By the eternal God, whose name and power
> Thou tremblest at, answer that I shall ask ;
> For till thou speak thou shalt not pass from hence.
> [I. iv. 24–27.]

Bolingbroke questions the spirit, and, having replied it is allowed to depart.

Jourdain is later brought to trial with the others concerned and is sentenced to death by the King :

> The witch in Smithfield shall be burned to ashes,
> [II. iii. 7.]

Douce says : " It appears from Rymer's Fœdera, that in the tenth year of King Henry the Sixth, *Margery Jourdemayn*, John Virley clerk, and friar John Ashwell were, on the ninth of May, 1433, brought from Windsor by the constable of the castle, to which they had been committed for sorcery, before the council at Westminster, and afterwards, by an order of council, delivered into the custody of the lord chancellor. The same day it was ordered by the lords of council that whenever the said Virley and Ashwell should find security for their good behaviour they should be set at liberty, and in like manner that Jourdemayn should be discharged on her husband's finding security. This woman was afterwards burned in Smithfield, as stated in the play and also in the chronicles." *See also* Grafton's *Chronicle*, Vol. I., p. 622.

Master.   IV. i. p.1.

The master of the party which captures Suffolk and his friends who are fleeing to France.

He assesses the ransom of the First gentleman at one thousand crowns.

> A thousand crowns, or else lay down your head.
> [IV. i. 16.]

Master's-Mate.   IV. i. p.1.

One of Suffolk's captors.

Matthew Goffe.   IV. v. 11 ; IV. vii. p.1.

The leader of the king's forces against the followers of Jack Cade, the rebel. He appears in the fight at Smithfield where he is slain, and his men put to flight.

Mayor of Saint Alban's.   II. i. p.68.

Appears before the king and his nobles, at the head of a crowd of people in the midst of which is Simpcox, carried on a chair, who claims that he has received his sight by a miracle wrought at the shrine of St. Alban.

Medea.   V. ii. 59.

> Meet I an infant of the house of York,
> Into as many gobbets will I cut it
> As wild Medea young Absyrtus did :   [V. ii. 57–59.]

See Absyrtus.

Medice, teipsum.   II. i. 53.

= " Physician, heal thyself." Cf. *St. Luke*, iv., 23.

Melford.   I. iii. 20.

> " Against the Duke of Suffolk,
> for enclosing the commons of Melford." [I. iii. 19–20.]

Long Melford in Suffolk. Trouble arising from enclosing common land was one of the causes of Kett's rebellion, in 1549.

Messengers.   I. ii. p.56 ; IV. iv. p.26, p.49 ; IV. vii. p.19 ; IV. ix. p.23.

I., ii., p. 56. Conveys the king's orders that the Duke of Gloucester is to repair to St. Albans.

IV., iv., p. 26. Brings news to the king that Cade's forces are in Southwark and that their leader proclaims himself Lord Mortimer and has vowed to seize the crown. He advises the king to flee.

IV. iv. p. 49. Announces the progress of the rebel army ; that they have taken London Bridge and are pressing onward.

IV., vii., p. 19. Brings Cade the news that Lord Say has been captured.

IV., ix., p. 23. Reports to the king the arrival of the Duke of York with his army from Ireland.

Michael.   IV. ii. p.110 ; IV. iii. p.1 ; IV. vi. p.1 ; IV. vii. p.1 ; IV. viii. p.1.

One of Cade's followers. On his first appearance on Blackheath, he warns Cade that Sir Stafford and the royal forces are close at hand.

He also appears in the remaining scenes describing the rebellion.

Miracle, A !   II. i. p.59.

See Saint Alban's shrine.

Morisco.   III. i. 365.

> And, in the end being rescued, I have seen
> Him caper upright like a wild Morisco,
> Shaking the bloody darts as he his bells.
>
> [III. i. 364–366.]

A Moorish, or morris-dancer ; in the Middle ages, a peculiar kind of dance, supposed to have been first brought into England in the reign of Edward the Third when John of Gaunt returned from Spain. In the earliest Morisco dance, a boy came into the hall when supper was finished, with his face blackened, his forehead bound with white or yellow taffeta, and bells tied to his legs. Malone quotes Harris : " *Morrice-dancing*, with bells on the legs, is common at this day in Oxfordshire and the adjacent counties, on May-Day, Holy-Thursday, and Whitsun-ales, attended by the fool, or, as he is generally called, the ' Squire, and also a lord and lady ; the latter most probably the Maid Marian mentioned in Mr. Tollet's note : ' nor is the hobby-horse forgot,' " Cf. Pliny (Holland's translation) : " The Curets taught to daunce in armour ; and *Pyrrhus* the Morisk, in order of battell ; and both these were taken vp first in Crete."

Mort Dieu.   I. i. 121.

= " Death of God."   Cf. Marlowe : *Massacre of Paris* :

> *Mort Dieu* ! were not the fruit within thy womb,
> Of whose increase I set some longing hope,
> This wrathful hand should strike thee to the heart.

Mortimer.   IV. ii. 40.

> My father was a Mortimer,—   [IV. ii. 40.]

Cade claims his father was of the family of Mortimer, to which Dick the Butcher, [aside] replies : " He was an honest man, and a good bricklayer."

See also John Mortimer ; London-stone.

Mortimer.   IV. vi. 1.

> Now is Mortimer lord of this city.   [IV. vi. 1.]

= Jack Cade.   See John Mortimer ; London-stone.

Mounsieur Basimecu.   IV. vii. 28.

A contemptuous term for a Frenchman, applied here by Cade to the Dauphin of France.

Naples.   I. i. 47.

See Reignier.

Naples.   V. i. 118.

> O blood-bespotted Neapolitan,
> Outcast of Naples, England's bloody scourge !
>
> [V. i. 117–118.]
> York's reference to Margaret.

Nell. I. ii. 17, 59; II. iv. 10, 26, 58 67, 74.

= Eleanor, Duchess of Gloucester.

Nell.   III. ii. 26.

> I thank thee, Nell ; these words content me much.
>
> [III. ii. 26.]

King Henry's reply to his wife. Theobald remarks : " There can be no reason why he should forget his own wife's name, and call her Nell instead of Margaret." Reed observes : " It has been observed by two or three commentators, that it is no way extraordinary the King should forget his wife's name, as it appears in no less than three places that she forgets it herself, calling herself Eleanor. It has also been said, that, if any contraction of the real name is used, it should be *Meg*."

Nevil's crest.   V. i. 202.

> Now, by my father's badge, old Nevil's crest,
> The rampant bear chained to the ragged staff,
>
> [V. i. 202–203.]

" This well-known badge of the Neville family came to the Earl of Warwick from the Beauchamps through his marriage with the heiress of Beauchamp, Earl of Warwick. The crest of the Nevilles was a dun bull's head, which is still borne by the Earls of Abergavenny ; the supporters of their arms being two bulls, argent, armed, collared, and chained." *Irving edition.* Cf. French *Shakspeareana Genealogica,* [Earl of Warwick], page 192.

Nevil's parts. I. i. 238.

> And therefore I will take the Nevils' parts
> And make a show of love to proud Duke Humphrey,
> [I. i. 238–239.]

See *Extract* 26 from Holinshed.

Nevils. I. iii. 72 ; II. ii. 8, 80 ; III. ii. 215.

The family name of the Earls of Salisbury and Warwick.

Normandy. I. i. 85.

Normandy. I. i. 112, 213.

> These counties were the keys of Normandy. [I. i. 112.]

> the state of Normandy
> Stands on a tickle point now they are gone.
> [I. i. 213–214.]

Grafton states : " by this pretie cautele and sleight imposture, was the towne of Pountlarche taken and surprised, which towne was the key and passage ouer the Riuer of Some, from Fraunce to Normandie, beyng distant from Roan, onely foure leagues."

See also under Anjou.

Normandy. IV. vii. 28, 65.

> What canst thou answer to my majesty for giving
> up of Normandy unto Mounsieur Basimecu, the
> Dauphin of France ? [IV. vii. 27–29.]

See Maine, IV., i., 86.

Officers, (Sheriff). II. iv. p.17.

Owen Glendower. II. ii. 41.

> This Edmund, in the reign of Bolingbroke,
> As I have read, laid claim unto the crown ;
> And, but for Owen Glendower, had been king,
> Who kept him in captivity till he died. [II. ii. 39–42.]

See under Edmund, II., ii., 38, 39, page 833.

Paris. I. i. 92.

> And hath his highness in his infancy
> Crowned in Paris, in despite of foes ? [I. i. 91–92.]

The coronation of King Henry the Sixth as King of France took place at Notre Dame on the 16th of December, 1430.

Paris. I. i. 213 ; I. iii. 171.

Peter, the Armourer's man. I. iii. p.1, p.176 ; II. iii. 67, 68, 70, 81, 82, 89, 93, 97.

Appears before Suffolk and Margaret bearing a petition against his Master for declaring the Duke of York to be the rightful heir to the throne.

He is led away on Suffolk's instructions, and brought back accompanied by his master Horner. Peter repeats his accusations, and Gloucester orders them to fight a duel. Peter protests, saying he cannot fight, but he is told he must fight or be hanged.

On the appointed day, Peter having promised all his belongings to his friends should he be killed, the duel takes place and Peter is victorious, his master confessing treason as he dies.

See also Thomas Horner.

Petitioners. I. iii. p.1.

Appear at the palace, in London, awaiting the appearance of the Duke of Gloucester.

Suffolk and the Queen enter, and the Duke is mistaken for the Protector. The queen demands to hear the petitions and the first petitioner says :

> Mine is, an 't please your grace, against John
> Goodman, my lord cardinal's man, for keeping my
> house, and lands, and wife, and all, from me.
> [I. iii. 15–17.]

The second presents an accusation against the Duke of Suffolk for enclosing the commons of Melford, and the third petitioner, Peter, presents his petition against his master Horner for declaring the Duke of York to be the rightful heir to the throne.

See also Peter, the Armourer's man.

Philippe. II. ii. 35, 49.

Daughter of Lionel, Duke of Clarence, the third son of King Edward the Third. She married Edmund Mortimer, Third Earl of March. See *Extract* 13 from Holinshed *and under* Roger, Earl of March.

Picardy. IV. i. 88.

> and Picardy
> Hath slain their governors, surprised our forts,
> And sent the ragged soldiers wounded home.
> [IV. i. 88–90.]

An old Province of France. In 1435 by the Treaty of Arras part of the province was ceded to Burgundy, but on the death of Charles the Bold in 1477, the province was united to France under Louis XI.

Plantagenet. IV. ii. 43.

My mother a Plantagenet,— [IV. ii. 43.]

Cade claims his mother was of the house of Plantagenet, to which Dick the Butcher [aside] replies : " I knew her well ; she was a midwife."

Pomfret. I. ii. 26.

Pomfret [Pontefract] Castle in Yorkshire, where, according to Holinshed, Richard the Second was murdered. See *King Richard the Second*, Act V., Scene v.

Pompey the Great. IV. i. 138.

savage islanders
Pompey the Great ; [IV. i. 138.]

Unhistorical. Pompey was killed on the coast of Egypt by two of Ptolemy's soldiers. " The land being a great way off from his Galley, when he saw never a man in the boat speak friendly unto him, beholding *Septimus*, he said unto him : Methinks my friend I should know thee, for that thou hast served with me heretofore. The other nodded with his head but it was true, but gave him no answer, nor shewed him any courtesie. *Pompey* seeing that no man spake to him, took a little book he had in his hand, in the which he had written an oration that he meant to make unto King *Ptolomy*, and began to read it. When they came near the shoar, *Cornelia* with her seruants and friends about her, stood up in her ship in great fear, to see what should become of *Pompey*. So she hoped well, when she saw many of the Kings people on the shoar, coming towards *Pompey* at his landing, as it were to receive and honour him. But even as *Pompey* took *Philip* his hand more easily, *Septimus* came first behind him and thrust him through with his sword. Next unto him also *Salvius* and *Achillas* drew out their swords in like manner, *Pompey* then did no more but took up his Gown with his hands and hid his face, and manly abid the wounds they gave him, onely fighting a little. Thus being

nine and fifty years old, he ended his life the next day after the day of his birth." *Plutarch.*

Pool. IV. i. 70.

Suf.   Thou dar'st not for thy own.
Cap.   [Yes, Pole.
Suf.   Pole !]
Cap.   Pool ! Sir Pool ! lord !
   Ay, kennel, puddle, sink ; whose filth and dirt
   Troubles the silver spring where England drinks.
                     [IV. i. 69–72.]

In *The Contention* the passage is :

Suf.   Thou darste not for thine owne.
Cap.   Yes Poull.
Suf.   Poull.
Cap.   I Poull, puddle, kennell, sinke, and durt,
   Ile stop that yawning mouth of thine.

Hart states : " In Peele's *Jack Straw* (Hazlitt's *Dodsley*, v., 412) similar quibbling on a similar occasion occurs :

   Why, Morton, are you so lusty, with a pox ?
   I pulled you out of Rochester Castle by the *poll* !
   Morton.   And in recompense I will help to set your
      head on a *pole*.
   Wat Tyler.   Pray you, let 's be *poll'd* first."

Post, A. III. i. p.282.

= A Messenger.

'Prentices. II. iii. p.59.

Supporters of Peter who appear with him on the occasion of his duel with his master Horner. To them Peter bequeaths various articles :

   Here, Robin, an if I die, I give thee my
   apron : and Will, thou shalt have my hammer : and
   here, Tom, take all the money that I have. O Lord,
   bless me !   [II. iii. 74–77.]

Queen. II. ii. 25.

   Sent his poor Queen to France, from whence she came,
   And him to Pomfret ;   [II. ii. 25–26.]

Isabella, daughter of King Charles the Sixth of France, and second wife of King Richard the Second. Cf. *King Richard the Second*, V., i., 53–54.

Rebels' Supplication. IV. iv. p.1.

The Rebels' Petition to the king. The following is from Grafton : " And to the entent that the cause of this glorious Captaynes commyng thether, might be shadowed from the king and his Counsail, he sent to him an humble supplicacion, with louyng wordes, but with malicious entent : affirmyng his commyng, not to be against him, but against diuers of his counsaile, louers of themselues, and oppressors of the poore Commonaltie, flatterers to the King, and enemies to his honor, suckers of his pursse, and robbers of his subiectes, parciall to their friendes, and extreme to their enemies, for rewardes corrupted, and for indifferencie nothyng doyng.''

Reignier, King of Naples, Sicilia and Jerusalem. I. i. 47, 109.

Father of Margaret of Anjou. Consents to his daughter's betrothal to Henry VI conditionally that he may peaceable enjoy Anjou and Maine. " This Reiner duke of Aniou named himselfe king of Sicill, Naples, and Ierusalem ; having onelie the name and stile of those realmes, without anie penie, profit, or foot of possession.''

Richard. II. ii. 19, 31.

= King Richard the Second.

Richard. II. ii. 27.

And him to Pomfret ; where, as all you know,
Harmless Richard was murdered traitorously.
[II. ii. 26–27.]

= King Richard the Second. *See* Pomfret.

Richard, Earl of Cambridge. II. ii. 45.

See Roger, Earl of March, page 857, and Earl of Cambridge [*King Henry the Fifth*], page 665.

Richard, England's king. II. ii. 63.

Long live our sovereign Richard, England's king !
[II. ii. 63.]

= Richard Plantagenet, third Duke of York. Killed at the battle of Wakefield, 1460.

Richard Plantagenet, Duke of York. I. i.
p.1, 63, 67, 84, 192, 205, 228, 237, 246, 254 ; I. iii. 25, 69, 96, p.100, 101, 102, 105, 107, 159, 163, 177, 178, 182, 191, 206 ; I. iv. p.41, 76 ; II. ii. p.1, 7, 55, 63, 76, 79, 81 ; II. iii. p.1, 87 ; II. iv. 53 ; III. i. p.1, 39, 158, 244, 245, 293, 304, 305, 309, 318, 321, 330, 331, 375 ; IV. i. 153 ; IV. ix. 24, 31, 35 ; V. i. p.1, 1, 88, 106, 115, 119, 129 ; V. ii. p.8, 16, 19, 51, 57 ; V. iii. p.1, 31.

In a soliloquy at the conclusion of the first scene, we are made aware of the Duke of York's ambitions and his method of obtaining them. He says :

for I had hope of France,
Even as I have of fertile England's soil.
A day will come when York shall claim his own ;
And therefore I will take the Nevils' parts
And make a show of love to proud Duke Humphrey,
And, when I spy advantage, claim the crown,
For that 's the golden mark I seek to hit.
[I. i. 235–241.]

and :

Then, York, be still awhile, till time do serve :
Watch thou and wake when others be asleep,—
To pry into the secrets of the state ;
[I. i. 246–248.]

The news of York's purpose comes to Henry's ears through Peter's accusation of his master Horner, and though York vehemently denies the charge it is evident that Henry suspects its truth.

We next find York in company with Buckingham in the Duke of Gloucester's garden, where they surprise and arrest the sorcerers, and York sends an invitation to Salisbury and Warwick to sup with him the following night.

They meet, and the meal being over, York unfolds his project :

Our simple supper ended, give me leave
In this close walk to satisfy myself,
In craving your opinion of my title,
Which is infallible, to England's crown. [II. ii. 2–5.]

and receiving a favourable reply, goes on to trace his claim to the crown from Edward III, to which Warwick exclaims :

Then, father Salisbury, kneel we together,
And in this private plot be we the first
That shall salute our rightful sovereign
With honour of his birthright to the crown.
[II. ii. 59–62.]

This begins once more the feud between the houses of Lancaster and York, and the Duke advises his followers to bide their time, until Gloucester has been removed.

York is present at the duel between Horner and his man Peter, and we next find him at the Parliament at Bury, when he supports the accusations against Gloucester, alleging that he had received bribes from France and had tortured law-breakers in England. The scene ends with York's commission to proceed to

Ireland to put down a rebellion which has broken out there, and this he accepts without demur, for he has his own use for a body of men such as will be provided for the expedition.

Soon the king is warned of York's rebellious return, Buckingham being sent to meet him, and the first scene of Act V opens with York's cry :

> From Ireland thus comes York to claim his right,
> And pluck the crown from feeble Henry's head :
> Ring, bells, aloud ; burn, bonfires, clear and bright,
> To entertain great England's lawful king. [V. i. 1–4.]†

but on Buckingham enquiring the reason for his armed return, York discreetly covers the truth and says he has come but to preserve the king from Somerset. On being told that Somerset is in prison he disbands his forces and with Buckingham repairs to the king's tent, only to be confronted there by Somerset, and thereupon York denounces Henry.

The strife between the rival factions now breaks out anew, and the final scenes of the play depict the battle of St. Albans. York kills Clifford and the king's forces are defeated. York then decided to pursue Henry to London, and with the cry :

> Saint Alban's battle, won by famous York,
> Shall be eterniz'd in all age to come.
> Sound drums and trumpets ! and to London all :
> And more such days as these to us befall !
> [V. iii. 30–34.]

the play ends.

[Richard Plantagenet, Duke of York, is also a character in the *Third Part of King Henry the Sixth* (q.v.).]

† Upon his return from Ireland the Duke issued from Ludlow Castle a Manifesto to the burgesses of Shrewsbury denouncing Somerset. *See* Appendix II.

Richard, son to Richard Plantagenet, Duke of York. V. i. p.122 ; V. ii. p.66 ; V. iii. p.1, 16.

Richard Plantagenet. who afterwards became Richard III, appears with his brother Edward as surety for his father when he is accused of treason.

See also Edward, son to Richard Plantagenet.

Robin. II. iii. 74.

The name of an apprentice, to whom Peter, the armourer's man, bequeaths his apron :

> Here, Robin, an if I die, I give thee my apron :

In *The Contention* Peter bequeaths to Robin his hammer :

> Here Robin, and if I die, here I give thee my hammer.

Roger, Earl of March. II. ii. 37, 38, 48.

Fourth Earl, son of Edmund Mortimer, Third Earl of March. Grafton says : "And by aucthoritie of the same Parliament, Sir Roger Mortimer Erle of March, and sonne and heyre vnto Sir Edmond Mortimer, and of Dame Philip eldest daughter and heyre vnto Sir Lyonell the second sonne of Edward the thirde, was sone after proclaymed heyre apparaunt to the Crowne of Englande. The which Sir Roger shortly after sayled into Ireland, to suppresse the rebellion & vnquietnesse of the people of his Lordship of Wolster, which he was Lorde of by his aforesayd mother. But while he was there occupied about the same, the wylde Irishe came vpon him in a great number, and slue him and many of his company.

This Sir Roger had issue, Edmond, and Roger, Anne, Alice, and Alianor that was made a Nonne. The two aforesayde soones dyed without issue, and Anne the eldest daughter was maryed to Richarde Erle of Cambridge, which Richard had issue by the sayde Anne, Isabell Ladie Bourcher, and Richard that was after Duke of Yorke, and father to King Edward the Fourth, which sayde Richard Erle of Cambridge was put to death by Henrie the fift at Southhamton." See *Extract* 13 from Holinshed.

Rome. I. iii. 61.

Saint Alban. II. i. 91, 107, 129.

Protomartyr of Britain, and a native of Verulam (St. Albans).

Saint Alban's. II. i. 134.

The City of St. Alban's.

Saint Alban's. I. ii. 57, 83 ; I. iv. 72.

> My lord protector, 'tis his highness' pleasure
> You do prepare to ride unto Saint Alban's,
> Where as the king and queen do mean to hawk.
> [I. ii. 56–58.]

In Hertfordshire where the king and queen were hawking. Staunton quotes from Thomas Nash's *Quaternio, or, Fourefold Way to a Happie Life*, 1633 :—" And to heare an Accipitrary relate againe, how he went forth in a cleare, calme, and Sun-shine Evening, about an houre before the Sunne did usually maske himselfe, unto the River, where finding of a Mallard, he whistled off his Faulcon, and how shee flew from him as if shee would never have turned head againe, yet presently upon a shoote came in, how then by degrees, by little and little, by flying about and about, she mounted so high, until she had lessened herselfe to the view of the beholder, to the shape of a Pigeon or Partridge, and had made the height of the Moone the place of her flight, how presently upon the landing of the fowle, shee came downe like a stone and enewed it, and suddenly got up againe, and suddenly upon a second landing came downe againe, and missing of it, in the downecome recovered it, beyond expectation, to the admiration of the beholder at a long flight."

Where hawking was first exercised is not exactly known but it is mentioned by a Latin writer of the fourth century, and it is considered to have been borrowed by the Romans from the Britons, as early as the reign of Vespasian. Boniface, Archbishop of Mons, who was himself a native of England, presented to Ethelbert, King of Kent, one hawk and two falcons ; and a king of the Mercians requested the same Boniface to send him two falcons that had been trained to kill cranes ; so that at this period the art must have been better understood in France than in England. Harold, afterwards King of England, is painted going on a most important embassy with a hawk in his hand, and a dog under his arm ; and even females of distinction were occasionally thus represented as we know from an ancient sculpture in the church of Milton Abbas, in Dorsetshire, where the consort of King Athelstan appears with a falcon in her fist tearing a bird. In France, hawking seems to have been prosecuted with more ardour, and sustained with still greater state and ceremony than in England. From the capitularies of the eighth and ninth centuries we learn that the *grand fauconnier* was an officer of great eminence ; his annual salary was 4000 florins, he was attended by fifty gentlemen and fifty

assistant falconers, was allowed to keep three hundred hawks, licensed every vendor of those birds, and received a tax upon all that were sold. It was the favourite amusement not only of kings and nobles, but of ladies of distinction, and of the clergy, who attached themselves to it not less zealously than they had done to hunting, although it was equally included in the prohibiting canons of the church. In the reign of Edward III the Bishop of Ely excommunicated certain persons for stealing a hawk that was sitting upon her perch in the cloisters of Bermondsey, in Southwark ; but this piece of sacrilege was committed during Divine service in the choir, and the hawk was the property of the Bishop. To part with the hawk, indeed, even in circumstances of the utmost extremity, was deemed highly ignominious. By the ancient laws and capitularies of France, a knight was forbidden to give up his sword and his hawk, even as the price of his ransom. How highly these birds were appreciated may be gathered not only from the severity of the laws, but from the prices occasionally recorded to have been given for them. At the commencement of the seventeenth century, a goshawk and tassel-hawk were sold for 100 marks, a large sum in those days. In the reign of James I., Sir Thomas Monson gave £1000 for a cast of hawks, and Federigo, the hero of Boccaccio's ninth novel, although he had spent all his substance, refused to part with his favourite hawk. In the book of St. Alban's, the sort of bird assigned to the different ranks of persons are placed in the following order :

The eagle, the vulture, and the merloun for an emperor.
The ger-falcon, and the tercel of the ger-falcon for a king.
The falcon gentle, and the tercel gentle for a prince.
The falcon of the rock for a duke.
The falcon peregrine for an earl.
The bastard for a baron.
The sacre and the sacret for a knight.
The lanere and the laneret for an esquire.
The marlyon for a lady.
The hobby for a young man.
The gos-hawk for a yeoman.
The tercel for a poor man.
The sparrow-hawk for a priest.
The musket for a holy-water clerk.
The nesterel for a knave or a servant.

Saint Alban's.

The Scene of Act II., Scene i. Exhibits the court hawking at St. Alban's ; and renews the quarrel between Gloucester and the Cardinal, in which the Queen takes a decided part against Gloucester. The Cardinal, churchman as he is, agrees to fight a duel with Gloucester; in fact, makes the first overture towards this method of settling the dispute. [There is no known authority for Beaufort's challenge, but the queen's part is from Holinshed.] Buckingham arrives with the news that a number of persons—of which the Duchess of Gloucester is one—have been arrested for practising witchcraft.

Saint Alban's.

The Scene of Act V., Scene ii. A considerable interval of time elapses—approximately five years—from the death of Cade to the First Battle of St. Albans, which was fought on the 22nd of May, 1455, in which Clifford and Somerset are among the slain.

Holinshed describes the battle as follows: " The king enformed hereof, assembled lykewise a great host, and meaning to meet with the duke, rather in the north parts than about London, where it was thought he had too many friends, with great speede, and small lucke, being accompanied with the Dukes of Somerset and Buckingham, the Erles of Pembroke, Stafford, Northumberland, Devonshire, Dorset, and Wiltshire, the Lords Clifford, Sudley, Berneis, Roos, and others, beeing in all above two thousande men of warre, departed from Westminster the twentith, or, as some have, the one and twentith of May, and lay the first night at Wadford. Of whose doings the duke of Yorke by espials having still advertisement, with all his power, being not past three thousande men (as some write), coasted the countrey, and came to the toune of Saint Albons, the third day next ensuing. The king there had pight his standerte in a place called Gosclowe, otherwise Sandiford, in Saint Peeters streete; the Lord Clifforde kept the barriers of the toune, to stop that the Duke, being assembled in Keye field, should not enter the toune. . . . The king, when first he heard of the Dukes approche, sent to him messengers, as the Duke of Buckingham and others, to understand what he meant by his comming, thus furnished after the manner of warre. The Duke of Buckingham, doing his message as hee had in commaundement, was answered by the Duke of York and his complices,

that they were all of them the king's faithfull liege subjects, and intended no harme to him at all: but the cause of our comming (saie they) is not in meaning anie hurt to his person. But let that wicked and naughtie man the duke of Somerset be delivered unto us, who hath lost Normandie, and taken no regard to the preservation of Gascoigne; and furthermore hath brought the realme into this miserable estate: that where it was the floure of nations, and the princesse of provinces, now is it haled into desolation and spoile, not so dreadfull by malice of forren enimie, that indeed utterlie (as yee knowe) seeketh our ruine, as by the intollerable outrages of him that so long ago and even still appeares to have sworne the confusion of our king and realme. If it therefore please the king to deliver that bad man into our hands, we are readie without trouble or breach of peace, to returne into our countrie. But if the king be not minded so to do, because he cannot misse him; let him understand, that we will rather die in the field, than suffer such a mischeefe unredressed.

The king, advertised of this aunswere, more wilfull than reasonable, chose rather to trie battell than deliver the duke of Somerset to his enimies. Whereof they ascertained made no longer staie, but straightway sounded the trumpet to battell, or rather as Hall hath, while King Henry sent forth his ambassadors to treate of peace at the one end of the toune, the Erle of Warwike, with his Marchmen, entred at the other end, and fiercely setting on the king's foreward, within a small tyme discomfited the same. The place where they first brake into the towne was about the middle of saint Peter's street. The fight for a time was ryghte sharp and cruell, for the Duke of Somerset, with the other lords, coming to the succours or their companions, that were put to the worse, did what they could do beate back the enimies, but the Duke of York sent ever fresh men to succour the wearie, and to supplie the places of them that were hurt, by which policie, the king's army was finally brought to confusion, and all the chiefetaines of the fielde slaine and beaten doune. For there dyed under the sign of the Castell, Edmund Duke of Somerset, who, as hath bin reported, was warned long before to avoid all castels: and beside hym laye Henry the second of that name Earle of Northumberland, Humfrey erle of Stafford, son to the Duke of Buckingham, John Lord Clifford, sir Barthram Antwisell knight, a Norman born (who forsaking his native countrie to continue in his loiall obedience to king Henrie, came over to dwell here in England when Normandie was lost), William Zouch, John Boutreux, Rafe Babthorp, with his sonne, William Corwin, William Cotton, Gilbert Faldinger, Reginald Griffon, John Dawes, Elice Wood, John Eith, Rafe Woodward, Gilbert Skarlock, and Rafe Willoughbie esquires, with many other, in all to the number of eight thousand, as Edward Hall saith in his chronicle : if there escaped not a fault in the impression, as 8000 for 800, sith hundreds in verie deed would better agree with the number of the kings whole power, which he brought with him to that battell, being not manie above two thousand, as by writers appeareth.

Humfrey, duke of Buckingham, being wounded, and James Butler, Earle of Ormond and Wiltshire, and Thomas Thorpe lord cheefe baron of the escheker, seeing fortune thus to bee against them, left the king alone and with a number fledde away. Those that thus fled, made the best shift they could to get awaie through gardens and backesides, through shrubs, hedges, and woods, seeking places where to hide themselves, untill that dangerous tempest of the battell were overblowne. Diverse of the kings house also, that could better skill to plaie the courtiers than warriors, fled with the first ; and those of the east parts of the realme were likewise noted of too much lacke of courage, for their speedie withdrawing themselves, and leaving the king in danger of his adversaries, who, perceyving hys men thus fledde from him, withdrewe into a poor mans house to save himselfe from the shot of arrowes, that flew about his eares as thicke as snowe."

" The immediate result of the victory," says Sharon Turner, " was the appointment of York to be the constable of England ; Warwick to be captain of Calais ; and viscount Bourchier, treasurer of England. The duke of Buckingham soon after joined the triumphant party, and the earl of Wiltshire solicited a similar reconciliation." In a foot-note Turner quotes from the *Harleian MSS.*, " The Harl., MSS., distinctly names, besides Somerset, Northumberland, and Clifford 14 squires, 1 gentleman and 4 yeomen,

who fell ; besides 25 more whose names were not known, and makes 48 persons, the whole number buried on the king's part. Yet the romancing Hall states 8000 men to have fallen on the king's side, which is almost double the amount of all the troops, of both parties in the battle. The abbot, who was on the spot, gives the force of York as only 3,000, and the Harleian MSS., states the king's as 2,000 and more. The original letter, in Fenn. i, p. 100 mentions only six score persons to have fallen of the king's men. It was the death of the leaders, not the number of the killed, that made the victory so complete."

The following account is from the *Paston Letters*, No. 239, edited by Gairdner :

A.D. 1455, 21–22 May.

THE BATTLE OF ST. ALBAN'S.

Bellum apud Seynt Albons.

Be yt knowen and hadde in mynde that the xxj. day of May the xxxiij. zere of the regne of Kyng Herry and Sext, our sovereigne Lord Kyng toke his jurnay from Westmynster toward Seynt Albones, and rested at Watford all nyght ; and on the morwe be tymes he cam to Seynt Albones, and wyth him on his partye assembled under his baner the Duyke of Bockingham, the Duke of Somersete, the Erle of Penbrok, the Erle of Northumburlond, the Erle of Devynsshire, the Erle of Stafford, the Erle of Dorsete, the Erle of Wyltsshire, the Lorde Clyfford, the Lord Dudley, the Lord Burneys, the Lord Rose, wyth other dyversse knyghtes, squyeres, and other gentilmen and yemen to the nounbre of ijml [2000] and moo. And upon the xxij. day of the seyde moneth above rehersed assembled the Duyk of Yorke, and wyth hym come yn companye the Erle of Salesbury, the Erle of Warrewyke with diverse knyghtes and squyers unto ther partye into the felde, called the Key Feld, besyde Seynt Albones. Fyrthermore, oure seyd sovereyne Lord the Kyng, heryng and knowyng of the seyde Dukes comyng with other Lordes afore seyde, pygth his baner at the place called Boslawe in Seynt Petrus Strete, whych place was called afore tyme past Sandeforde, and commaundeth the warde and barrers to be kepte in strong wyse ; the for seyd Duyk of York abydyng in the feld aforeseyde frome vij. of the clokke in the morn tyl yt was al most x. without ony stroke smeton on eyther partye. The seyde Duke sende to the Kyng our sovereyne

Lord, be the avyse of his councell, prayng and be sekyng hym to take him as his true man and humble suget ; and to consider and to tender at the reverence of Almyghty God, and in way of charite the true entent of his comyng—to be good and gracyous sovereyne Lorde to his legemen, whech with al ther power and mygth wille be redy at alle tymes to leve and dye with hym in his rigth. And to what thyng shoulde lyke his Mageste Ryall to commaunde hem, yf yt be his worsship, kepyng right of the Croune and welffare of the londe ; ' More over, gracyous Lord, plese yt zour Majeste Ryall of zour grete goodnesse and ryghtwesnesse to enclyne zour wille to here and fele the ryghtwyse partye of us zoure sugettes and legemen ; fyrst, prayng and besechyng to oure Lord Jesus of his hye and myghty power to geve un to zou vertu and prudence, and that thorugh the medyacyon of the glorious martyr Seynt Albon to geve very knowleche to knowe the entent of oure assembleng at this tyme ; for God that is [in] Heven knoweth than our entent is rightful and true. And there fore we pray unto Almyghty Lord Jesus these wordes—*Domine sis clipeus defensionis nostræ.* Wherefore, gracyus Lord, plese it your hyghe Majeste to delyvere such as we wole accuse, and they to have lyke, as they have deserved and done, and ze to be honorabled and worsshept as most ryghtffull Kyng and oure governour. For and we shall now at this tyme be promysed, as afore this tyme ys not unknowen, of promes broken whech ful fayth fully hath ben promysed, and there upon grete othes made, we wyll not now cesse for noon such promysse, surete, ne other, tyl we have hem whych hav deserved deth, or elles we to dye there fore.'

And to that answered the Kyng our sovereyne Lord, and seyde : ' I, Kyng Herry, charge and comaund that no maner persone, of what degre, or state, or condicyon that evere he be, abyde not, but voyde the felde, and not be so hardy to make ony resystens ageyne me in myn owne realme ; for I shall knowe what traytor dar be so bolde to reyse apepull in myn owne lond, where thorugh I am in grete desese and hevynesse. And by the feyth that I owe to Seynt Edward and to the Corone of Inglond, I shal destrye them every moder sone, and they be hanged, and drawen, and quartered, that may be taken afterward, of them to have ensample

to alle such traytours to be war to make ony ruch rysyng of peple withinne my lond, and so traytorly to abyde her Kyng and governour. And, for a conclusyon, rather then they shall have ony Lorde, here with me at this tyme, I shall this day, for her sake, and in this quarrell my sylff lyve or dye.'

Wych ansuere come to the Duke of Yorke, the wheche Duke, by the avyce of the Lordes of hys Counceill, seyde unto hem thise wordes : ' The Kyng our sovereyne Lord will not be reformed at our besechyng ne prayer, ne wylle not understonde the entent that we be comen heder and assembled fore and gadered at this tyme ; but only ys full purpose, and there noon other wey but that he wole with all his power pursue us, and yf ben taken, to geve us a shameful deth, losyng our lyvelode and goodes, and our heyres shamed for evere. And ther fore, sythe yt wole be noon other wyse but that we shall ooterly dye, better yt ys for us to dye in the feld than cowardly to be put to a grete rebuke and asshamefful deth ; more over, consederyng yn what peryle Inglonde stondes inne at thys owre, therefore every man help to help power for the ryght there offe, to redresse the myscheff that now regneth, and to quyte us lyke men in this querell ; preyng to that Lord that ys Kyng of Glorye, that regneth in the kyngdom celestyall, to kepe us and save us this day in our right, and thorugh the helpe of His holy grace we may be made strong to with stonde the grete abomynable and cruell malyse of them that purpose fully to destrye us with shameful deth. We ther fore, Lord, prey to The to be oure confort and Defender, seyng the word afore seyde, *Domine sis clipeus defensionis nostræ.*'

And whanne this was seyde, the seyde Duke of Yorke, and the seyd Erle of Salesbury, and the Erle of Warrewyk, betwene xj. and xij. of the clocke at noon, the broke into the toun in thre diverse places and severelle places of the fore seyd strete. The Kyng beyng then in the place of Edmond Westley, hunderdere of the seyd toun of Seynt Albones, comaundeth to sle alle maner men of lordes, knyghthtes, end squyeres, and zemen, that mygth be taken of the for seyde Dukes of York. Thys don, the fore seyd Lord Clyfford kept strongly the barrers that the seyde Duke of York mygth not in ony wise, with all the power that he hadde, entre ne breke into the toun. The Erle of Warrewyk, knowyng ther offe, toke and gadered his men to gedere and ferosly brake in by the gardeyne sydes betuene the signe of the Keye and the signe of the Chekkere in Holwell strete ; and anoon as they were wyth inne the toon, sodeynly the blew up trumpettes, and sette a cry with asshout and a grete voyce, ' A Warrewe ! A Warrewyk ! A Warrewyk !,' and into that tyme the Duke of York mygth nevere have entre into the toun ; and they with strong hond kept yt, and myghttyly faught to gedere, and anoon, forth with after the brekyng in, they sette on them manfully. And as of Lordes of name were slayn the Lord Clyfford, the Duke of Somersete, the Erle of Northumberlond, Sir Bartram Entuwysselle, Knynght ; and of men of courte, Wyllam Zouch, John Batryaux, Raaff of Bapthorp and hys sone, Wyllyam Corbyn, squyers ; William Cotton, receyver of the Ducherye of Lancastre ; Gylbert Starbrok, squyer ; Malmer Pagentoun, William Botelore, yomen ; Rogere Mercroft, the Kynges messanger ; Halyn, the Kynges porter ; Raufe Wyllerby ; and xxv. mo, whych her names be not yet knowen. And of hem that ben slayn ben beryed in Sent Albonos xlviij. And at this same tyme were hurt Lordes of name—the Kyng, our sovereyne Lord, in the neck with an arrowe ; the Duke of Bukingham, with an arrowe in the vysage ; the Lord of Stafford in the hond, with an arowe ; the Lord of Dorsette, sore hurt that he mygth not go, but he was caryede hom in a cart ; and Wenlok, Knyght, in lyke wyse in a carte sore hurt ; and other diverse knyghtes and squyers sore hurt. The Erle of Wyldsshyre, Thorpe, and many other flede, and left her harneys behynde hem cowardly, and the substaunce of the Kynges partye were dyspoyled of hors and harneys. This done, the seyde Lordes, that ys to wote, the Duke of Yorke, the Erle of Salesbury, the Erle of Warrewyke, come to the Kyng, our sovereyne Lord, and on here knees he soughte hym of grace and foryevenesse of that they hadde doon yn his presence, and be sought hym of his Heynesse to take hem as hys true legemen, seyng that they never attendyde [intended] hurt to his owne persone, and ther fore [the] Kyng oure sovereyn Lord toke hem to grace, and so desyred hem to cesse there peple, and that there shulde no more harme be doon ; and they obeyde hys commaundement,

and lote make a cry on the Kynges name that al maner of pepull shulde cesse and not so hardy to stryke ony stoke more after the proclamacyon of the crye ; and so cessed the seyde batayle, *Deo gratias.*

And on the morwe the Kyng and the seyde Duke, with other certeyn Lordes, come in to the Bysshops of London, and there kept resydens with joye and solempnyte, concludyng to holde the parlement at London, the ix. day of July next comyng.

Letter 240.

A.D. 1455, [22 May].

THE BATTLE OF ST. ALBAN'S.

[From MS. Phillipps, 9735, No. 278.]

The solecytouriz and causerys of the feld takyng at Seynt Albonys, ther namys shewyn her aftyr :—

> The Lord Clyfford.
> Rauff Percy.
> Thorpe.
> Tresham and Josep.

The inony [enemy's] batayle was in the Market-place, and the Kynges standard was pight, the Kynge beynge present with these Lordes, whos namys folwe :

The Duke of Bokyngham.	With many Knyghtes
The Duke Somyrcete.	and Squyeriz, to the
The Erle Devynshire.	noumbre in alle that
The Erle of Northombirlond.	faught that day iijml.
The Erle Stafford.	[3000], and it was
The Erle Dorcete.	done on Thursday
The Lord Clyfford.	last past atwyx xj. and
The Lord Ros.	xij at mydday.

The namys of the Lordes that were on the othir party shewyn here aftyr :

The Duke of York.	
The Erle of Salysbury.	With many otheriz, to
The Erle of Warwyk.	the noumbre of vml.
The Lord Clynton.	[5000] men.
Sir Robert Ocle.	

And Sir Rober Ocle tok vjc. [600] men of the Marchis, and tok the Market-place or ony man was war ; than the larum belle was ronge, and every man yed to harneys, for at that tyme every man was out of ther aray, and they joynid batayle anon ; and it was done with inne di. [*i.e. one half,*] houre, and there were slayn the men, whos namys folwyn :

The Duke Somyrcete.	With many othir men, to
The Erle Northombirlond.	the noumbre of iiij^c [400],
The Lord Clyfford.	and as many or mo hurt.
The Lord Clynton.	The Kynge was hurte with
Sir Bartyn at Wessyll.	an harwe in the necke.
Babthorpe and hese sone.	The Duke of Bukkyng-
Cotton, Receyvour of the	ham hurt, and fled in to
Duchye.	the Abbey. The Erle De-
Gryphet, Ussher of Hall.	vynshire hurt. The Erle
Herry Loweys.	Stafford and Dorcetyr
Wyllyam Regmayde.	gretly hurt. Fylongley
John Raulyns. Asple.	faught manly, and was
Harpour, Yoman of the	shet thorwe the armys in
Groune.	iij. or iiij. placys.

The Duke of Norfolke come a day aftyr the jurney was done with vj^mll. [6000] men.

And the Erle of Oxinford also.	
The Erle of Shrewysbury.	with x^mll. [10,000]
Lord Crumwelle,	men were comynge.
And Sir Thomas Stanley.	

The Kynge with all the Lordes come to London to Westmenstyr on Fryday, at vj. of clocke at aftyr none, and London went a generalle processyon the same day.

Saint Alban's battle. V. iii. 30.

The First Battle of St. Alban's. " The First Battle of St. Albans occurred chiefly in St. Peter's Street. The town was occupied by the Lancastrians under Henry VI., and the Duke of Somerset. The Yorkists attacked the Barriers in Shropshire Lane, now Victoria Street, and at Sopwell Lane leading from Holywell Hill. Warwick, the King-Maker, in the meantime broke through between the gates, his men poured into Chequer Street, and thus cut the Lancastrian force into two parts. They made their way into St. Peter's Street, and here the chief affray occurred. The Duke of Somerset, who had been warned to beware of a Castle, was slain upon the doorsteps of the " Castle " Inn, which stood at the top of Victoria Street upon the left-hand side, and is now a tobacconist's. The King, with an arrow wound in his neck, took refuge in Hall Place, beyond St. Peter's Church, which is seen at the end of the street. North of St. Peter's Church, until quite recently, stood Hall Place, the house where Henry VI. took refuge. The upper portion of St. Peter's Street is termed Bow Gate, or Borough Gate, from the mediaeval Bars which stood there." Burrow's *Official Handbook to St. Albans.* For

accounts of the Battle see *inter alia* Barrett's " Battles and Battlefields in England," 1896. Bayley's " An Account of the First Battle of St. Albans from a contemporary Manuscript [*Archæologia*, vol. xx, 1824]. Gairdner's Houses of Lancaster and York, with the conquest and loss of France." 1927. Ramsay's " Lancaster and York : a century of English History (A.D. 1399–1485) 1892, *and under* Saint Alban's, Act V., Scene ii.,

Saint Alban's shrine. II. i. 63.

Forsooth, a blind man at Saint Alban's shrine,
Within this half hour hath received his sight ;
A man that ne'er saw in his life before. [II. i. 63–65.]

Founded on a story in Sir Thomas More's *Dialogue :* " This Humffrey Duke of Gloucester, descending of the blood royal, was not onely noble and valyant in all his actes and doings, but sage, pollitique, and notably well learned in the Ciuile lawe. And among other his worthy prayses, this follownyg is not to be forgotten, which most liuely and plainely declareth him to be both prudent and wise, & to his great laude and praise is written and set forth by Sir Thomas Moore knight, in a booke of hys, entituled a *Dialogue* concerning heresies and matters of religion, and in the xiiij. chapter of the same booke, in this wise follwyng. In the time of King Henry the sixt (sayeth he) as he roade in Progresse, there came to the towne of Saint Albons a certaine begger with hys wyfe, and there was walking about the towne begging fiue or six dayes before the kinges comming thether, sayeng that he was borne blinde and neuer sawe in all his life, and was warned in his dreame that he should come out of Berwike, where he sayd that he had euer dwelled, to seke Saint Albon, and that he had bene at his Shrine, and was not holpen, and therefore he would go seeke him at some other place ; For he had heard some saye sence he came, that Saint Albons body should be at Colyn, and in dede such a contention hath there bene. But of truth as I am certainly informed (sayth Sir Thomas Moore) he lyeth here at saint Albones, sauing some reliques of him, which they there shewe shryned. But to tell you foorth, when the king was come, and the towne full of people, sodainely this blind man at saint Albones Shryne had his sight, & the same was solempnly rong for a miracle, and

Te deum songen, so that nothing was talked of in all the towne, but this miracle. So happened it then that Duke Humfrey of Gloucester, a man so lesse wise, than also well learned, hauing great ioy to see muche a miracle, called the poore man vnto him, and first shewyng himselfe ioyous of Gods glorie, so shewed in the getting of his sight, and exhorting him to mekenesse, and to no ascribyng of any part of the worship to himselfe, not to be prowde of the peoples praise, which would call him a good & a godly man therby, at the last he looked well vpon his eien, & asked whether he could euer see any thing at al in all his life before. And when as well his wife as himselfe affirmed fastly, no, then he looked aduisedly vpon his eyen agayne, and sayde, I beleue you very well, for me thinketh that ye can not see well yet. Yes Sir quoth he, I thanke God and his holy Martir, I can see now as well as any man : yea, can, quod the Duke, what colour is my Gowne ? Then anone the begger tolde him. What colour quod he is this mans Gowne ? he tolde him also without anye stayeng or stomblyng, and tolde the names of all the colours that coulde be shewed him. And when the Duke sawe that, he bade him walke Faytoure, and made him to be set openly in the stockes : For though he could haue sene sodaynely by miracle the difference be-twene dyuers coloures, yet could he not by sight, so sodainely tell the names of all these coloures, except he had knowne them before, no more then he coulde name all the men whome he should sodainely see, thus farre mayster Moore.''

Saint George's Field. V. i. 46.

Meet me to-morrow in Saint George's field. [V. i. 46.]

See *Second Part of King Henry the Fourth*, III. ii., 190.

Saint Magnus' Corner. IV. viii. 1.

Up Fish Street ! down Saint Magnus' Corner ! [IV. viii. 1.]

See Fish Street. Cf. *Extract* 25 from Holin-shed.

Savoy. IV. vii. 1.

So, sirs. Now go some and pull down the Savoy ; others to the inns of court : down with them all. [IV. vii. 1–2].

The Duke of Lancaster's Palace in the Strand. It was destroyed by Wat Tyler and his followers in 1381. Annexed to the crown by Henry IV it was rebuilt as a hospital by Henry VII about 1505. Cade's suggestion to " pull down the Savoy " is derived from the account of Tyler's revolt. Hart quotes from Fabyan's account of the 1381 rebellion : " They . . . came vnto ye duke of Lancasters place standyng without ye Temple Barre, callyd *Sauoy*, & spoyled that was therein & after set it upon fyre & brent it. . . . Than they entryd the cytie & serchied the Temple and other inns of Court, & spoyled theyr places & brent theyr bokys of lawe, & slewe as many men of lawe & quest-mongers as they myght fynde ; & that done they went to Seynt Martyns ye Graunde, & toke with them all seyntwary men, & the prysons of Newgate, Ludgate, & of bothe Counters, & distroyed theyr registers & bokis, & in lyke maner they dyd with the prysoners of the Marshalse & Kynges Benche in Southwerke.'' Fabyan names the leaders as follows : " In this mayers yere and ende of the thyrde yere of Kyng Richard . . . ye comons arose sodeynly and ordeynyd to them rulers and capytaynys, & specially in Kent and Essex, the whiche namyd theyr leders Iacke Strawe, Wyl Wawe, Watte Tyler, Iacke Shepeherde, Tomme Myller, and Hobbe Carter.'' Cf. *Extract* 25 from Holinshed.

Sea Captain, A. IV. i. p.1.

The captain of the party which intercepts Suffolk and his friends in their flight to France. Bringing the prisoners ashore he exclaims :

Therefore bring forth the soldiers of our prize, For whilst our pinnace anchors in the Downs Here shall they make their ransom on the sand, Or with their blood stain this discoloured shore. [IV. i. 8–11.]

and allots them to the members of his crew :

Master, this prisoner freely give I thee ; And thou that art his mate make boot of this ; The other (*pointing to Suffolk*) Walter Whitmore, is thy share. [IV. i. 12–14.]

He orders Suffolk's execution, saying :

Hale him away, and let him talk no more. [IV. i. 131.]

and then orders that the remainder of the prisoners be released :

And as for these whose ransom we have set, It is our pleasure one of them depart : [IV. i. 139–140].

Sennet. I. iii. p.100 ; III. i. p.1.

A signal call on a trumpet. The word occurs chiefly in the stage directions of old Plays.

Servants. I. iii. p.33.

Serving-men who lead Peter away when he has made an accusation of treason against his master.

Servingman. I. iv. p.79 ; IV. iv. p.1.

A male servant.

Sheriff. II. iv. p.17, 74, 100.

Escorts the Duchess of Gloucester during the performance of the penance imposed upon her by Henry for her part in the sorcery practised in her garden. The penance done, the Sheriff hands her over to Sir John Stanley.

Sicilia. I. i. 47.

See Reignier.

Simpcox, an Imposter. II. i. p.68, 91, 123, 124.

An inhabitant of St. Albans, who appears before Henry accompanied by the Mayor of St. Albans, and a great crowd of townspeople. He says that he was born blind, and,

> being called
> A hundred times and oftener in my sleep,
> By good Saint Alban ; who said, ' Simpcox, come ;
> Come, offer at my shrine, and I will help thee.'
> [II. i. 89-92.]

had obeyed the message, and had miraculously received his sight.

His wife bears out this statement, but the Cardinal, noticing that the man is lame, is sceptical, and asks :

> What ! art thou lame ?
> .   .   .   .   .   .
> How cam'st thou so ?   [II. i. 94-96.]

to receive the reply :

> A fall off of a tree.   [II. i. 97.]

This further arouses the suspicions of the nobles, and Gloucester asks him to name the colour of his cloak and his gown. Simpcox answers correctly, and thus exposes the trick. A beadle is sent for, and to test his lameness

Simpcox is whipped, which causes him to leap over a stool and run away.

Simpcox' wife pleads for mercy, saying :

> Alas ! sir, we did it for pure need.   [II. i. 154.]

but Gloucester commands :

> Let them be whipped through every market-town
> till they come to Berwick, from whence they came.
> [II. i. 155-156.]

Foxe in his *Acts and Monuments*, draws attention to the imposture practised at St. Albans. *See* Vol. III., pp. 712-713 ; and Vol. VI., p. 296.

Sir Humphrey Stafford. I. iv. 52 ; IV. ii. 112, p.121 ; IV. iii. p.1 ; IV. iv. 34.

Leader of a part of the king's forces against the rebel Cade and his followers. With his brother William Stafford, he pleads with the rebels, both their words are disregarded, and in an encounter which follows, both Sir Humphrey Stafford and his brother William are slain.

A messenger to Henry exclaims :

> Sir Humphrey Stafford and his brother's death
> Hath given them heart and courage to proceed.
> [IV. iv. 34-35.]

Sir James Cromer. IV. vii. 110.

> and then break into his son-in-law's
> house, Sir James Cromer, and strike off his head, and
> bring them both upon two poles hither.
> [IV. vii. 109-111.]

It was *William Crowmer*, Sheriff of Kent, whom Cade put to death. Lord Say and he had been previously sent to the Tower, and both, or at least the former, convicted of treason, at Cade's mock commission of oyer and terminer at Guildhall. Cf. *Extract* 25 from Holinshed. *See also* Lord Say.

Sir John. I. ii. 68.

A title frequently bestowed on the clergy. Grafton remarks : " In this new rufflyng, the king easily graunted that Abbots, Deanes, & Curates should be elected frely euery where, so that the lawes of the realme were truely obserued. But against that were the Bishops, alleagyng theyr Canonical decrees, & rules synodall, determinyng the king therein to haue nothing a do, but onely to geue his consent after they had once elected. But among that company, there were some that consented not to that error ; A sort also there were of prelates that time which were not pleased that the landes interdiction should ceasse, till the king had payde all which their Clergie in all quarters of the realme had demaunded without reason : yea euery sawcy Sir Ihon for his part, euen to the very breakyng of their hedges, the stealyng of their Apples, and their other occasionall dammages, demaunded allowance which grew to an incredible summe and impossible to be answered."

Sir John Stanley. II. iii. 13 ; II. iv. p.17, 77, 79, 84, 91, 104.

It is to Sir John Stanley's castle in the Isle of Man that the Duchess of Gloucester is condemned to be sent :

> You, madam, for you are more nobly born,
> . . . .
> Shall, after three days' open penance done,
> Live in your country here in banishment,
> With Sir John Stanley, in the Isle of Man.
> [II. iii. 9–13.]

Sir Pool. IV. i. 70.

See Pool.

Smith the Weaver. IV. ii. 29, p.32 ; IV. iii. p.1 ; IV. vi. p.1 ; IV. vii. p.1 ; IV. viii. p.1.

One of Cade's followers, appearing in all the scenes describing the insurrection.

Smithfield. II. iii. 7.

> The witch in Smithfield shall be burned to ashes.
> [II. iii. 7.]

A district of London, the scene of tournaments, fairs, and cattle markets, and a place of executions and burning of so-called heretics. Margery Jourdain, the witch, was burned to death for sorcery at this place. Stowe says : " There was taken alfo Margery Gurdemaine a witch of Eye befides Weftminster, whofe forcerie and witchcrafte the faid Elianor hadde long time ufed, and by her medicines & drinkes enforced the Duke of Gloucefter to loue her, and after to wedde her, wherefore, and for caufe of relapfe, the fame Witch was brent in Smithfield, on the twentie-feauen day of October."

Smithfield. IV. v. 10 ; IV. vi. 11.

In IV., v., 10 the citizens are ordered " to gather head " at Smithfield and resist Cade ; and in IV., vi., 11–12 Dick the Butcher informs Cade " there 's an army gathered together in Smithfield."

Soldiers. IV. ii. p.121 ; IV. vi. p.7 ; V. iii. p.1.

Southwark.

The Scene of Act IV., Scene viii. Cade and his followers arrive at Southwark. Lords Buckingham and Clifford enter offering pardon to all who lay down their arms. [" This *free pardon*, according to Hall, was brought by the Archbishop of Canterbury, then chancellor of England, and the Bishop of Winchester : ' The archebishop of Canterbury, beyng then chauncelor of England, and for his suerty lyenge in the Towre of London, called to him the bishop of Winchester, whiche also for feare, lurked at Halywell. These two prelates seyng the fury of the Kentish people, by reason of their betyng backe, to be mitigate and minished, passed the ryuer of Thamyse from the Towre, into Southwarke, bringing with them vnder the kynges great seale, a general pardon vnto all the offenders : which they caused to be openly proclaimed and published. Lorde how glad the poore people were of this Pardone (ye more then of the great Jubile of Rome) and how thei accepted thesame, in so muche that the whole multitude, without biddyng farewel to their capitain, retired thesame night, euery man to his awne home, as men amased, and strikē with feare." *Irving edition.*] Being forsaken by many of his followers, Cade seeks safety in flight, and Buckingham offers a reward of a thousand crowns for his capture.

Southwark. IV. iv. 28 ; IV. viii. 25.

A metropolitan borough on the Surrey side of the Thames. Jack Cade the rebel in his march on London entered Southwark on the 1st of July, 1450.

See also London-stone.

Spirit, A. I. iv. p.23.

The spirit which is raised in the Duke of Gloucester's garden to answer questions concerning the king, the Duke of Suffolk and the Duke of Somerset.

Asked what shall become of the king, the spirit replies :

> The duke yet lives that Henry shall depose ;
> But him outlive, and die a violent death.
> [I. iv. 30–31.]

as for the Duke of Suffolk,

> By water shall he die, and take his end.   [I. iv. 33.]

and the Duke of Somerset,

> Let him shun castles :
> Safer shall he be upon the sandy plains
> Than where castles mounted stand.   [I. iv. 35–37.]

Having given these answers the spirit exclaims ;

> Have done, for more I hardly can endure.
> [I. iv. 38.]

and it is commanded thereupon to

> Descend to darkness, and the burning lake :
> [I. iv. 39.]

and amid thunder and lightning it disappears into the ground.

Street, A.

The Scene of Act II., Scene iv. The penance of the Duchess of Gloucester, and the summons of the Duke of Gloucester to attend a Parliament to be held at Bury St. Edmunds.

See also Eleanor, Duchess of Gloucester.

Suffolk's body. IV. i. p.142.

For the account of Suffolk's death *see under* Gualtier.

Sylla. IV. i. 84.

> By devilish policy art thou grown great,
> And, like ambitious Sylla, overgorged
> With gobbets of thy mother's bleeding heart.
> [IV. i. 83–85.]

The Captain here compares Suffolk with C. Cornelius Sulla the Roman Dictator. Sulla was the first to introduce the proscription. In 82 B.C. after his decisive victory over the Samnites and Lucanians under Pontius Telesinus before the Colline Gate of Rome, he drew up a list of proscribed persons, and many thousands were put to death.

Tantæne animis cœlestibus iræ ? II. i. 24

= " Is there such anger in heavenly minds ? " (Virgil's *Æneid*).

Ten Commandments. I. iii. 141.

> Could I come near your beauty with my nails
> I 'd set my ten commandments in your face.
> [I. iii. 140–141.]

A popular expression for the ten fingers. Hudson (Windsor edition) quotes *Selimus, Emperor of the Turks*, 1594 : ' I would set a tap abroach and not live in fear of my wife's *ten commandments*.' Again, in *Westward Hoe*, 1607 : ' Your harphy has set his *ten commandments* on my back.' And in Udal's version of Erasmus's *Apophthegms* : ' When Xantippe had pulled awaye her husbandes cope from his backe, even in the open streete, and his familiar compaignons gave him a by warning to avenge suche a naughtie touche or pranks with his *tenne commandments*." Cf. I., iii., 189 where Peter swears by " these ten bones."

Thames. IV. viii. 2.

The River Thames.

Thomas Horner, an Armourer. I. iii. 24, p.176 ; II. iii. p.59, 59.

Is accused of treason by Peter his man, who alleges that Horner has said that the Duke of York is the rightful heir to the throne and that Henry is a usurper.

Horner is brought before the King, and denies the accusation, saying :

> An 't shall please your majesty, I never said
> nor thought any such matter ; God is my witness, I
> am falsely accused by the villain.   [I. iii. 186–189.]

declaring that he is accused out of pure malice :

> My accuser is my prentice ; and when I
> did correct him tor his fault the other day, he did
> vow upon his knees he would be even with me : I
> have good witness of this :   [I. iii. 197–200.]

Gloucester advises a combat between Horner and his man as the best way to settle the quarrel and this takes place before the king.

Horner, before the duel commences, exclaims :

> Masters, I am come hither, as it were, upon
> my man's instigation, to prove him a knave, and myself an honest man : and touching the Duke of York,
> will take my death.   [II. iii. 85–88.]

York urges them to fight, and in the course of the combat Horner is struck down mortally wounded. As he expires, he confesses his guilt :

> Hold, Peter, hold ! I confess, I confess treason.
>
> [II. iii. 93.]

Thomas of Woodstock, Duke of Gloucester. II. ii. 16.

> The sixth was Thomas of Woodstock, Duke of Gloucester.
>
> [II. ii. 16.]

Thomas of Woodstock was the seventh and last son of King Edward the Third, erroneously referred to here as the ' sixth son ' see *Extract* 13 from Holinshed.

Thump. II. iii. 83, 84.

> *Sal.* Come, leave your drinking and fall to blows. Sirrah, what 's thy name ?
> *Peter.* Peter, forsooth.
> *Sal.* Peter ! what more ?
> *Peter.* Thump.
> *Sal.* Thump ! then see thou thump thy master well.
>
> [II. iii. 79–84.]

The Surname of Peter the armourer's man.

Tom. II. iii. 76.

An apprentice to whom Peter, the armourer's man, bequeaths all the money he has : " and here, Tom, take all the money that I have."

Tours. I. i. 5 ; I. iii. 49.

> I tell thee, Pole, when in the city Tours
> Thou rann'st a tilt in honour of my love,
> And stol'st away the ladies' hearts of France,
>
> [I. iii. 49-51.]

Cf Marlowe : *Edward the Second* :

> Tell Ifabel, the queen, I look'd not thus,
> When for her fake I ran at tilt in France,
> And there unhors'd the duke of Cleremont.

See Grafton's *Chronicle*, Vol. I., page 625 ; and *Extract* 1 from Holinshed.

Tower. IV. v. 5, 9 ; IV. vi. 15 ; IV. ix. 38 ; V. i. 41, 134.

The Tower of London.

Troy. I. iv. 17.

> Deep night, dark night, the silent of the night,
> The time of night when Troy was set on fire ;
>
> [I. iv. 16-17].

An ancient city of Asia Minor, immortalised in Homer's *Iliad*. Cf Peele's *Fall of Troy* :

> It was the time when midnight's sleep and rest
> With quiet pause the town of Troy possess'd . . .
> Now Troy, as was foretold, began to burn.

Troy. III. ii. 118.

> To sit and witch me, as Ascanius did
> When he to madding Dido would unfold
> His father's acts, commenced in burning Troy !
>
> *See* Ascanius.   [III. ii. 116–118.]

Tully. IV. i. 136.

> A Roman sworder and banditto slave
> Murdered sweet Tully.   [IV. i. 135-136].

= Marcus Tullius Cicero, Roman philosopher and orator. On the formation of the second triumvirate was proscribed and put to death. Plutarch states : " But in the mean time came the murtherers appointed to kill him, *Herennius* a Centurion, and *Popilius Lena*, Tribune of the fouldiers (to wit, Colonell of a thoufand men, whofe caufe *Cicero* had once pleaded before the Judges, when he was accufed for the murther of his own father) having fouldiers attending upon them. So *Cicero's* gate being fhut, they entred the houfe by force, and miffing him, they asked them of the houfe what was become of him. They anfwered they could not tell. Howbeit, there was a young boy in the houfe called *Philologus*, a flave enfranchifed by *Quintus Cicero*, whom *Tullius Cicero* had brought up in the Latine tongue, and had taught him the liberal Sciences : he told this *Herennius* that his fervants carried him in a Litter towards the fea, through dark narrow lanes, fhadowed with wood on either fide. *Popilius* the Colonel taking fome fouldiers with him, ran about on the outfide of the lanes to take him at his comming out of them : and *Herennius* on the other fide entred the lanes. *Cicero* hearing him comming, commanded his men to fet down his Litter, and taking his beard in his left hand, as his manner was, he floutly looked the murtherers in the faces, his head and beard being all white, and his face lean and wrinckled, for the extream forrows he had taken : divers of them that were by, held their hands before their eyes, whilft *Herennius* did cruelly murther him. So *Cicero* being threefcore and four years of age, thruft his neck out of the Litter and had his head cut off by *Antonius* commandment, and his hands alfo, which wrote the Orations (called the *Philippians*) againft him. For fo did *Cicero* call the Orations he wrote againft him, for the malice he bare him : and they do yet continue the fame name untill this present time."

Two brave bears. V. i. 144.

Call hither to the stake my two brave bears,
That with the very shaking of their chains
They may astonish these fell-lurking curs :
Bid Salisbury and Warwick come to me.
[V. i. 144-147.]

An allusion to the well-known badge of the bear and the ragged staff. " This well-known badge of the Neville family came to the Earl of Warwick from the Beauchamps through his marriage with the heiress of Beauchamp, Earl of Warwick." Cf. *Third Part of King Henry the Sixth*, V., vii., 10-12 :

With them, the two brave bears, Warwick and Mon-
tague,
That in their chains fetter'd the kingly lion,
And made the forest tremble when they roar'd.

Two Gentlemen, Prisoners with Suffolk. IV. i. p.1.

Appear with the Duke of Suffolk on the sea-shore near Dover. They, with the duke, are intercepted when about to cross to France. The first gentleman asks :

What is my ransom, master ? Let me know.
[IV. i. 15.]

The master replies :

A thousand crowns, or else lay down your head.
[IV. i. 16.]

Suffolk having been killed, the captain orders that all the other captives be freed, and they depart, with the exception of the first gentle-man, who, seeing Suffolk's body exclaims :

O barbarous and bloody spectacle !
His body will I bear unto the king : [IV. i. 144-145.]

Two Murderers. III. ii. p.1.

The murderers of the Duke of Gloucester, hired for the purpose by the Duke of Suffolk.

Vaux. III. ii. p.367, 367.

A messenger who brings news that Cardinal Beaufort is lying dangerously ill, and desires to see Henry.

[Sir William Vaux of Harrowden, Northampton-shire. For his adherence to the Lancastrian

cause he was attainted and his estates confis-cated by Edward IV. in 1461. He was killed at the battle of Tewkesbury, 1471.]

Villiago. IV. viii. 46.

Crying " Villiago ! " unto all thy meet. [IV. viii. 46.]

A coward.

Walter. IV. i. 38.

See Gualtier.

Walter Whitmore. IV. i. p.1, 14, 31, 44, 115, 142.

On his capture the Duke of Suffolk is given into the charge of Whitmore, who exclaims :

I lost mine eye in laying the prize aboard,
And therefore to revenge it shalt thou die ; [To Suffolk]
[IV. i. 25-26.]

On hearing these words Suffolk begs for ransom, and on hearing Whitmore say his name is much alarmed. Being asked the reason, he says ;

Thy name affrights me, in whose sound is death.
A cunning man did calculate my birth,
And told me that by water I should die :
Yet let not this make thee be bloody-minded ;
Thy name is Gaultier, being rightly sounded.
[IV. i. 33-37.]

Whitmore exclaims :

Gaultier or Walter, which it is, I care not ;   [IV. i. 38.]

and seizes Suffolk, who now reveals his true identity in a last endeavour to save himself ;

Stay, Whitmore ; for thy prisoner is a prince,
The Duke of Suffolk, William de la Pole.
[IV. i. 44-45.]

His pleadings, however, are of no avail, and Whitmore kills him, afterwards bringing in his body and leaving it upon the shore exclaiming :

There let his head and lifeless body lie,
Until the queen his mistress bury it.   [IV. i. 142-143.]

Westminster. I. ii. 37 ; IV. iv. 31.

= Westminster Abbey.

White Hart. IV. viii. 24.

A famous tavern in Southwark. Cf. *Extract* 25 from Holinshed.

Wife to Simpcox. II. i. p.68.

Appears with her husband before the king at

St. Albans, and supports his story of the miraculous cure of his blindness, while on a visit to the Shrine of St. Alban.

When their deception is found out she exclaims :

> Alas ! sir, we did it for pure need. [II. i. 154.]

but the Duke of Gloucester orders that the pair be " whipped through every market-town, till they come to Berwick, from whence they came."

See also Simpcox, an Impostor.

Will. II. ii. 75.

An apprentice to whom Peter, the armourer's man, bequeaths his hammer : " and, Will, thou shalt have my hammer " : In *The Contention* Peter bequeaths to Will his apron : " And, Will, thou shalt haue my aperne."

William of Hatfield. II. ii. 12, 33.

See *Extract* 13 from Holinshed.

William of Windsor. II. ii. 17.

William of Windsor was the sixth son of King Edward the Third, erroneously referred to here as the ' seventh and last.' See *Extract* 13 from Holinshed.

William Stafford. IV. ii. 112, p.121 ; IV. iii. p.1 ; IV. iv. 34.

Leader of a force against the rebel followers of Jack Cade, in company with his brother Sir Humphrey Stafford.

The brothers endeavour to plead with the rebels, but their words are unheeded, whereupon William Stafford exclaims :

> Well, seeing gentle words will not prevail,—
> Assail them with the army of the king.
> [IV. ii. 173–174.]

In another part of Blackheath, the rival forces meet, and in a fierce encounter both the Staffords are killed.

Wingham. IV. ii. 23.

A village in Kent.

York. IV. i. 94.

= The House of York.

Young Clifford, son to Lord Clifford. V. i. p.123 ; V. ii. p.31, p.83.

Appears with his father before the king when York has announced his intention of seizing the crown. Lord Clifford declares that the traitors should be executed, and Young Clifford supports his father with the words :

> And so to arms, victorious father,
> To quell the rebels and their complices.
> [V. i. 211–212.]

Later, during the battle of St. Albans, Young Clifford appears, and seeing the dead body of his father lying on the battle-field vows to be revenged for his death, and bears the corpse away.

Son of the Lord Clifford of this Play, and the Lord Clifford of the *Third Part of King Henry the Sixth*, in which Play he figures prominently.

APPENDIX I.

1. [In November, 1444, Suffolk and a splendid retinue] came to the citie of Tours in Touraine, where they were honorablie receiued both of the French king and of the king of Sicill. The marquesse of Suffolke, as procurator to king Henrie, espoused the said ladie in the church of saint Martins. At the which mariage were present the father and mother of the bride ; the French king himselfe, which was vncle to the husband ; and the French queene also, which was aunt to the wife. There were also the dukes of Orleance, of Calabre, of Alanson, and of Britaine, seauen earles, twelue barons, twentie bishops, beside knights and gentlemen. When the feast, triumph, bankets and iusts were ended, the ladie was deliuered to the marquesse, who in great estate conueied hir through Normandie vnto Diepe, and so transported hir into England, where she landed at Portesmouth in the moneth of Aprill.

2. Upon the thirtith of Maie next following, she was crowned queene of this realme of England at Westminster, with all the solemnitie thereto apperteining.

3. One thing seemed to be a great hinderance to peace ; which was, bicause the king of England occupied a great part of the duchie of Aniou, and the whole countie of Maine, apperteining (as was alledged) to king Reiner.
The earle of Suffolke (I cannot saie), either corrupted with bribes, or too much affectioned to this vnprofitable mariage, condescended, that the duchie of Aniou and the countie of Maine should be deliuered to the king the brides father ; demanding for hir mariage neither penie nor farthing : as who would saie, that this new affinitie passed all riches, and excelled both gold and pretious stones.

4. The marquesse of Suffolke, by great fauour of the king, & more desire of the queene, was erected to the title and dignitie of duke of Suffolke, which he a short time inioied.

5. During the time of the truce, Richard duke of Yorke and diuerse other capteins repaired into England ; both to visit their wiues, children, and freends, and also to consult what should be doone, if the truce ended.

6. [Suffolk] with his wife and manie honorable personages of men and women richlie adorned both with apparell & iewels, hauing with them manie costlie chariots and gorgeous horslitters, sailed into France, for the conueiance of the nominated queene into the realme of England. For King Reiner hir father, for all his long stile, had too short a pursse to send his daughter honorablie to the king hir spouse.
The king had not one penie with hir ; and, for the fetching of hir, the marquesse of Suffolke demanded a whole fifteenth in open parlement.

7. [About the year 1448,] began a new rebellion in Ireland ; but Richard duke of Yorke, being sent thither to appease the same, so asswaged the furie of the wild and sauage people there, that he wan him such fauour amongst them, as could neuer be separated from him and his linage ; which in the sequele of this historie may more plainelie appeare.

8. Diuerse articles were laid against him [Gloucester] in open councell, and in especiall one : That he had caused men, adiudged to die, to be put to other execution, than the law of the land assigned. Suerlie the duke, verie well learned in the law ciuill, detesting malefactors, and punishing offenses in seuritie of iustice, gat him hatred of such as feared condign reward for their wicked dooings.

9. [In 1446,] a parlement was called, in the which it was especiallie concluded, that by good foresight Normandie might be so furnished for defense before the end of the truce, that the French king should take no aduantage through want of timelie prouision : for it was knowne, that, if a peace were not concluded, the French king did prepare to imploie his whole puissance to make open warre. Heereupon monie was granted, an armie leuied, and the duke of Summerset appointed to be regent of Normandie, and the duke of Yorke thereof discharged.
I haue seene in a register booke belonging sometime to the abbeie of saint Albons, that the duke of York was established regent of France, after the deceasse of the duke of Bedford, to continue in that office for the tearme of fiue yeares ; which being expired, he returned home, and was ioifullie receiued of the king with thanks for his good seruice, as he had full well deserued in time of that his gouernement : and, further, that now, when a new regent was to be chosen

1. *Shakespeare's Holinshed*, by W. G. Boswell-Stone.

and sent ouer, to abide vpon safegard of the countries beyond the seas as yet subiect to the English dominion, the said duke of *Yorke* was eftsoones (as a *man* most *meet* to supplie that roome) appointed to go ouer againe, as *regent of France*, with all his former allowances.

But the duke of Summerset, still maligning the duke of Yorkes aduancement, as he had sought to hinder his dispatch at the first when he was sent ouer to be regent, (as before yee haue heard,) he likewise now wrought so, that the king reuoked his grant made to the duke of Yorke for enioieng of that office the terme of other fiue yeeres, and, with helpe of William marquesse of Suffolke, obtained that grant for himselfe.

10. Although the duke of Yorke was worthie (both for birth and courage) of this honor and preferment, yet so disdeined of Edmund duke of Summerset, (being cousine to the king,) that by all meanes possible he sought his hinderance, as one glad of his losse, and sorie of his well dooing : by reason whereof, yer the duke of Yorke could get his dispatch, Paris and diuerse other of the cheefest places in France were gotten by the French king.

11. Diuers secret attempts were aduanced forward this season, against this noble man Humfreie duke of Glocester, a far off, which, in conclusion, came so neere, that they beereft him both of life and land ; as shall hereafter more plainelie appeere.

For, first, this yeare, dame Eleanor Cobham, wife to the said duke, was accused of treason ; for that she by sorcerie and inchantment intended to destroie the king, to the intent to aduance hir husband vnto the crowne. . . . At the same season were arrested, arreigned, and adiudged giltie, as aiders to the duchesse, Thomas Southwell priest, and canon of S. Stephans at Westminster, Iohn Hun priest, Roger Bolingbrooke a cunning necromancer (as it was said), and Margerie Iordeine, surnamed the witch of Eie.

The matter laid against them was, for that they (at the request of the said duchesse) had deuised an image of wax, representing the king, which by their sorcerie by little and little consumed ; intending thereby in conclusion to waste and destroie the kings person.

12. Richard, duke of Yorke, (being greatlie alied by his wife to the chiefe peeres and potentates of the realme, beside his owne progenie,) perceiuing the king to be no ruler, but the whole burthen of the realme to rest in direction of the queene, & the duke of Suffolke, began secretlie to allure his friends of the nobilitie ; and priuilie declared vnto them his title and right to the crowne, and likewise did he to certeine wise gouernours of diuerse cities and townes. Which attempt was so politikelie handled, and so secretlie kept, that prouision to his purpose was readie, before his purpose was openlie published ; and his friends opened themselues, yer the contrarie part could them espie : for in conclusion all shortlie in mischiefe burst out, as ye may hereafter heare.

YORK'S CLAIM.

13. *Edward the third* had issue, *Edward prince of Wales ; William of Hatfield*, his *second sonne ; Lionell the third, duke of Clarence ; Iohn of Gant*, fourth, *duke of Lancaster ; Edmund of Langleie, fift, duke of Yorke ; Thomas of Woodstoke, sixt, duke of Glocester ;* and *William of Windsor, seauenth.*

The said *Edward* prince of Wales, which *died* in the life time of *his father*, had issue *Richard*, which succeeded *Edward the third* his grandsire ; Richard died without issue ; *William of Hatfield*, the second sonne of Edward the third, *died without* issue ; Lionell *the third sonne* of Edward the third, *duke of Clarence, had issue Philip* his *daughter* and heire, which was coupled in matrimonie vnto *Edmund Mortimer* [3rd] *earle of March*, and *had issue Roger* Mortimer [4th] *earle of March*, hir sonne and heire ; which *Roger had issue Edmund* [5th] erle of March, Roger Mortimer, *Anne, Elianor ;* which Edmund, Roger, and Elianor died without issue. And the said *Anne* coupled in matrimonie to *Richard earle of Cambridge*, the *sonne of Edmund of Langleie*, the *fift sonne* of *Edward the third*, and had issue Richard Plantagenet, commonlie called duke of Yorke. . . . To the which Richard duke of Yorke, as sonne to Anne, daughter *to Roger* Mortimer *earle of March, sonne* and heire of the said *Philip, daughter* and heire of the said *Lionell*, the third sonne of king Edward the third, the right, title, dignitie roiall, and estate of the crownes of the realmes of England and France, and the lordship of Ireland, perteineth and belongeth afore anie issue of the said Iohn of Gant, the fourth sonne of the same king Edward,

14. Margerie Iordeine was burnt in Smithfield, and Roger Bolingbrooke was drawne to Tiborne, and hanged and quartered ; taking vpon his death that there was neuer anie such thing by them imagined. Iohn Hun had his pardon, and Southwell died in the Tower the night before his execution.

15. [The Duchess of Gloucester] was examined in saint Stephans chappell before the bishop of Canturburie, and there by examination conuict, and iudged to doo open penance in three open places within the citie of London . . . and after that adiudged to perpetuall imprisonment in the Ile of Man, vnder the keeping of sir Thomas Stanlie, knight.

16. [The Queen] disdaining that hir husband should be ruled rather than rule, could not abide that the duke of Glocester should doo all things concerning the order of weightie affaires, least it might be said, that she had neither wit nor stomach, which would permit and suffer hir husband, being of most perfect age, like a yoong *pupill*, to be gouerned by the direction of an other man. Although this toy entered first into hir braine thorough hir owne imagination, yet was she pricked forward to the matter both by such of hir husbands counsell, as of long time had borne malice to the duke for his plainnesse vsed in declaring their vntruth (as partlie ye haue heard), and also by counsell from king Reiner hir father ; aduising that she and the king should take vpon them the rule of the realme, and not to be kept vnder, as wards and mastered orphanes.

What needeth manie words ? The queene, persuaded by these meanes, first of all excluded the duke of Glocester from all rule and gouerance. . . .

17. But, to auoid danger of tumult that might be raised, if a prince so well beloued of the people should be openlie executed, his enimies determined to worke their feats in his destruction, yer he should haue anie warning. For effecting whereof, a parlement was summoned to be kept at Berrie ; whither resorted all the peeres of the realme, and amongst them the duke of Glocester, which on the second daie of the session was by the lord Beaumont, then high constable of England, (accompanied with the duke of Buckingham, and others,) arrested, apprehended, and put in ward, and all his seruants sequestred from him, and thirtie two of the cheefe of his retinue were sent to diuerse prisons, to the great admiration of the people.

18. Oft times it hapneth that a man, in quenching of smoke, burneth his fingers in the fire ; so the queene, in casting how to keepe hir husband in honor, and hir selfe in authoritie, in making awaie of this noble man, brought that to passe, which she had most cause to haue feared ; which was the deposing of hir husband, & the decaie of the house of Lancaster, which of likelihood had not chanced if this duke had liued : for then durst not the duke of Yorke haue attempted to set foorth his title to the crowne, as he afterwards did, to the great trouble of the realme, and destruction of king Henrie, and of many other noble men beside.

19. Although the duke sufficientlie answered to all things against him obiected ; yet, because his death was determined, his wisedome and innocencie nothing auailed.

20. Those that fauoured the duke of Yorke, and wished the crowne vpon his head, for that (as they iudged) he had more right thereto than he that ware it, procured a commotion in Kent on this manner. A certeine yoong man, of a goodlie stature and right pregnent of wit, was intised to take vpon him the name of Iohn Mortimer, coosine to the duke of Yorke ; (although his name was Iohn Cade, or, of some, Iohn Mend-all, an Irishman, as *Polychronicon* saith ;), and not for a small policie, thinking by that surname, that those which fauoured the house of the earle of March would be assistant to him.

21. The duke, the night after he was thus committed to prison, being the foure and twentith of Februarie, was found dead in his bed, and his bodie shewed to the lords and commons, as though he had died of a palsie, or of an imposteme.

But all indifferent persons (as saith *Hall*) might well vnderstand that he died of some violent death. Some iudged him to be *strangled*, some affirme that an hot spit was put in at his funda- ment, other write that he was smouldered betweene two feather-beds ; and some haue affirmed that he died of verie greefe, for that he might not come openlie to his answer.

22. [In 1449–50 people] began to make exclamation against the duke of Suffolke, charging him to be the onelie cause of the deliuerie of Aniou and Maine, the cheefe procuror of the duke of Glocester's death, the verie occasion of the losse of Normandie, the swallower vp of the kings treasure, the remoouer of good and vertuous councellours from about the prince, and the aduancer of vicious persons, and of such as by their dooings shewed themselues apparant aduersaries to the common-wealth.

The queene hereat, doubting not onelie the duke's destruction, but also hir owne confusion, caused the parlement, before begun at the Blackfiers, to be adiourned to Leicester ; thinking there, by force and rigor of law, to suppresse and subdue all the malice and euill will conceiued against the duke & hir. At which place few of the nobilitie would appeare : wherefore it was againe adiourned to Westminster, where was a full appearance. In the which session the commons of the nether house put vp to the king and the lords manie articles of treason, mis- prison, and euill demeanor, against the duke of Suffolke : . . .

23. The parlement was adiourned to Leicester, whither came the king and queene in great estate, and with them the duke of Suffolke, as cheefe councellour. The commons of the lower house, not forgetting their old grudge, besought the king, that such persons, as assented to the release of Aniou, and deliuerance of Maine, might be dulie punished. . . . When the king

perceiued that there was no remedie to appease the peoples furie by anie colourable waies, shortlie to pacifie so long an hatred, he first sequestred the lord Saie, (being treasuror of England,) and other the dukes adherents, from their offices and roomes ; and after banished the duke of Suffolke, as the abhorred tode and common noiance of the whole realme, for tearme of fiue yeares: meaning by this exile to appease the malice of the people for the time, and after (when the matter should be forgotten) to reuoke him home againe.

But Gods iustice would not that so vngratious a person should so escape ; for, when he shipped in Suffolke, intending to transport himselfe ouer into France, he was incountered with a ship of warre, apperteining to the duke of Excester, constable of the Tower of London, called the Nicholas of the Tower.[1] The capteine of that barke with small fight entered into the dukes ship, and, perceiuing his person present, brought him to Douer road, and there, on the one side of a cock bote, caused his head to be striken off, and left his bodie with the head lieng there on the sands. Which corps, being there found by a chapleine of his, was conueied to Wingfield college in Suffolke, and there buried.

24. [The rebels] began to shew proofe of those things which they had before conceiued in their minds, beheading all such men of law, iustices, and iurors, as they might catch, and laie hands vpon, without respect of pitie, or remorse of conscience : alledging that the land could neuer enioy hir natiue and true libertie, till all those sorts of people were dispatched out of the waie.

25. The queene (that bare rule), being of his retrait aduertised, sent sir Humfreie Stafford knight, and William his brother, with manie other gentlemen, to follow the Kentishmen, thinking that they had fled : but they were deceiued, for at the first skirmish both the Staffords were slaine, & all their companie discomfited.

Iacke Cade, vpon victorie against the Staffords, apparelled himselfe in sir Humfreies brigandine set full of guilt nailes, and so in some glorie returned againe toward London : diuerse idle and vagarant persons, out of Sussex, Surreie and other places, still increasing his number.

[Cade] sent vnto the king an humble supplication, affirming that his comming was not against his grace, but against such of his councellours, as were louers of themselues, and oppressors of the poore commonaltie ; flatterers of the king, and enimies to his honor ; suckers of his purse, and robbers of his subiects ; parciall to their freends, and extreame to their enimies ; thorough bribes corrupted, and for indifferencie dooing nothing.

[Cade] came againe to the plaine of Blackheath, & there stronglie incamped himselfe ; to whome were sent from the king, the archbishop of Canturburie, and Humfreie duke of Buckingham, to common with him of his greefes and requests.

These lords found him sober in talke, wise in reasoning, arrogant in hart, and stiffe in opinion ; as who that by no means would grant to dissolue his armie, except the king in person would come to him, and assent to the things he would require. The K., vpon the presumptuous answers & requests of this villanous rebell, begining asmuch to doubt his owne meniall seruants, as his vnknowen subiects, (which spared not to speake, that the capteins cause was profitable for the common-wealth,) departed in all hast to the castell of Killingworth in Warwikeshire, leauing onlie behind him the lord Scales to keepe the Tower of London. The Kentish capteine, being aduertised of the kings absence, came first into Southwarke, and there lodged at the white hart, prohibiting to all his retinue, murder, rape, and robberie ; by which colour well meaning he the more allured to him the harts of the common people.

The Maior and other the magistrats of London perceiuing themselues neither to be sure of goods, nor of life well warranted, determined to repell and keepe out of their citie such a mischieuous caitife and his wicked companie. And, to be the better able so to doo, they made the lord Scales, and that renowmed capteine Matthew Gough, priuie both of their intent and enterprise ; beseeching them of their helpe and furtherance therein. The lord Scales promised them his aid, with shooting off the artillerie in the Tower ; and Matthew Gough was by him appointed to assist the maior and Londoners in all that he might. . . .

[Cade] entred into London, cut the ropes of the draw bridge, & strooke his sword on London stone ; saieng : " *Now is Mortimer lord of this citie ?* "

[The citizens] tooke vpon them in the night to keepe the bridge, and would not suffer the Kentishmen once to approch. The rebels, who neuer soundlie slept for feare of sudden assaults, hearing that the bridge was thus kept, ran with great hast to open that passage, where betweene both parties was a fierce and cruell fight.

Matthew Gough, perceiuing the rebels to stand to their tackling more manfullie than he thought they would haue doone, aduised his companie not to aduance anie further toward Southwarke, till the daie appeared ; that they might see where the place of ieopardie rested, and so to prouide for the same : but this little auailed. For the rebels with their multitude draue back the citizens from the stoops at the bridge foot to the draw bridge, & began to set fire to diuerse houses. . . .

1 *The Nicholas of the Tower* was the name of one of the ships of war which accompanied Henry V., from Southampton to Harfleur.

Yet the capteins, not sparing, fought on the bridge all the night valiantlie : but, in conclusion, the rebels gat the draw bridge, and drowned manie ; and slue Iohn Sutton alderman, and Robert Heisand, a hardie citizen, with manie other, beside Matthew Gough, a man of great wit and much experience in feats of chiualrie, the which in continuall warres had spent his time in seruice of the king and his father.

[The rebels marched to John of Gaunt's] house of the Sauoie, to the which, in beautie and statelinesse of building, with all maner of princelie furniture, there was not any other in the realme comparable ; which, in despite of the duke, (whom they called traitor,) they set on fire, and by all waies and means indeuored vtterlie to destroie it. . . .

Now after that these wicked people had thus destroied the duke of Lancasters house, and done what they could deuise to his reproch, they went to the temple ; and burnt the men of lawes lodgings, with their bookes, writings, and all that they might lay hand vpon.

The common vplandish people, . . . purposed to *burne* and destroie *all records*, euidences, court-rolles, and other muniments, that, the remembrance of ancient matters being remooued out of mind, their landlords might not haue whereby to chalenge anie right at their hands.

[Cade declared] if either by force or policie they might get the king and queene into their hands, he would cause them to be honourablie vsed, and take such order for the punishing and reforming of the misdemeanours of their bad councellours, that neither *fifteens* should hereafter be demanded, nor once anie impositions or taxes be spoken of.

·[Cade] caused sir Iames Fines, lord Saie, and treasuror of England, to be brought to the Guildhall, and there to be arreigned ; who, being before the kings iustices put to answer, desired to be tried by his peeres, for the longer delaie of his life. The capteine, perceiuing his dilatorie plee, by force tooke him from the officers, and brought him to the standard in Cheape, and there (before his confession ended) caused his head to be striken off, and pitched it vpon an high pole, which was openlie *borne before* him *thorough the streets.*

[Cade afterwards] went to Mile end, and there apprehended sir Iames Cromer, then shiriffe of Kent, and sonne in law to the said lord Saie ; causing him likewise (without confession or excuse heard) to be beheaded, and his head to be fixed on a pole ; and with these two heads this bloudie wretch entred into the citie againe, and as it were in a spite caused them in euerie street to kisse togither, to the great detestation of all the beholders.

[The battle] indured in doubtfull wise on the bridge, till nine of the clocke in the morning : for somtime, the Londoners were beaten backe to saint Magnus corner : and suddenlie againe, the rebels were repelled to the stoops in Southwarke, so that both parts being faint and wearie, agreed to leaue off from fighting till the next daie ; vpon condition, that neither Londoners should passe into Southwarke, nor Kentishmen into London.

The archbishop of Canturburie, being chancellor of England, and as then for his suertie lieng within the Tower, called to him the bishop of Winchester, who for some safegard laie then at Haliwell. These two prelats, seeing the furie of the Kentish people, by their late repulse, to be somewhat asswaged, passed by the riuer of Thames from the Tower into Southwarke ; bringing with them, vnder the kings great seale, a generall pardon vnto all the offendors, and caused the same to be openlie published. The poore people were so glad of this pardon, and so readie to receiue it, that, without bidding farewell to their capteine, they withdrew themselues the same night euerie man towards his home.

But Iacke Cade, despairing of succours, and fearing the reward of his lewd dealings, put all his pillage and goods that he had robbed into a barge, and sent it to Rochester by water, and himselfe went by land, and would haue entred into the castle of Quinborow with a few men that were left about him ; but he was there let of his purpose : wherefore he, disguised in strange attire, priuilie fled into the wood countrie beside Lewes in Sussex, hoping so to scape. The capteine & his people being thus departed, not long after proclamations were made in diuerse places of Kent, Sussex, and Southerie, that, whosoeuer could take the foresaid capteine aliue or dead, should haue a thousand markes for his trauell.

The king himselfe came into Kent, and there sat in iudgement vpon the offendors ; and, if he had not mingled his iustice with mercy, more than fiue hundred by rigor of law had beene iustlie put to execution. Yet he, punishing onelie the stubborne heads, & disordered ringleaders, pardoned the ignorant and simple persons, to the great reioising of all his subiects.

26. The duke of Yorke, pretending (as yee haue heard), a right to the crowne, as heire to Lionell duke of Clarence, came this yeare out of Ireland vnto London, in the parlement time, there to consult with his speciall freends : as Iohn duke of Northfolke, Richard earle of Salisburie, and the lord Richard, his sonne, (which after was earle of Warwike,) Thomas Courtneie earle of Deuonshire, & Edward Brooke lord Cobham. After long deliberation and aduise taken, it was thought expedient to keepe their cheefe purpose secret ; and that the duke should raise an armie of men, vnder a pretext to remooue diuerse councellors about the king, and to reuenge the manifest iniuries doone to the common-wealth by the same rulers. Of the which, as principall, the duke of Summerset was namelie accused, both for that he was greatlie hated of the commons

for the losse of Normandie ; and for that it was well knowne, that he would be altogether against the duke of Yorke in his chalenge to be made (when time serued) to the crowne,

[Yorke] assembled a great hoast, to the number of ten thousand able men, in the marches of Wales ; publishing openlie, that the cause of this his gathering of people was for the publike wealth of the realme. The king, much astonied at the matter, by aduise of his councell raised a great power, and marched forward toward the duke. But he, being thereof aduertised, turned out of that way, which by espials he vnderstood that the king held, and made streight toward London ; and, hauing knowledge that he might not be suffered to passe through the citie, he crossed ouer the Thames at Kingston bridge, and so kept on towards Kent, where he knew that he had both freends & well-willers, and there on Burnt heath, a mile from Dertford, and twelue miles from London, he imbatelled, and incamped himselfe verie stronglie, inuironing his field with artillerie and trenches. The king hereof aduertised, brought his armie with all diligence vnto Blackeheath, and there pight his tents.

Whilest both these armies laie thus imbattelled, the king sent the bishop of Winchester, and Thomas Bourchier, bishop of Elie, Richard Wooduile, lord Riuers, and Richard Andrew, the keeper of his priuie seale, to the duke : both to know the cause of so great a commotion, and also to make a concord ; if the requests of the duke and his companie seemed consonant to reason. The duke, hearing the message of the bishops, answered : that his comming was neither to damnifie the king in honour, nor in person, neither yet anie good man ; but his intent was, to remooue from him certeine euill disposed persons of his councell, bloud-succours of the nobilitie, pollers of the cleargie, and oppressours of the poore people.

Amongst these, he cheeflie named Edmund duke of Summerset, whome if the king would commit to ward, to answer such articles as against him in open parlement should be both proponed and proued, he promised not onelie to dissolue his armie, but also offered himselfe (like an obedient subiect) to come to the kings presence, and to doo him true and faithfull seruice, according to his loiall and bounden dutie.

It was so agreed vpon by aduise, for the auoiding of bloudshed, and pacifieng of the duke and his people, that the duke of Summerset was committed to ward, as some say ; or else commanded to keepe himselfe priuie in his owne house for a time.

The duke of Yorke, the first of March, dissolued his armie, brake vp his campe, . . . and came to the kings tent, where contrarie to his expectation, & against promise made by the king (as other write) he found the duke of Summerset going at large and set at libertie, whome the duke of Yorke boldlie accused of treason, briberie, oppression, and manie other crimes. The duke of Summerset not onelie made answer to the dukes obiections, but also accused him of high treason ; affirming, that he with his fautors and complices had consulted togither, how to come by the scepter and regall crowne of this realme.

Whilest the councell treated of sauing or dispatching of this duke of Yorke, a rumor sprang through London, that Edward earle of March, sonne and heire apparant to the said duke, with a great armie of Marchmen, was comming toward London : which tidings sore appalled the queene and the whole councell.

APPENDIX II.

The Manifesto issued by Richard Plantagenet, Duke of York from Ludlow Castle to the burgesses of Shrewsbury, denouncing Somerset, the 3rd February, 1452. [*Historical Letters*, edited by Sir H. Ellis].1

Right worshipful friends, I recommend me unto you ; and I suppose it is well known unto you, as well by experience as by common language said and reported throughout all Christendom, what laud, what worship, honour and manhood, was ascribed of all nations unto the people of this realm whilst the kingdom's sovereign lord stood possessed of his lorship in the realm of France and duchy of Normandy ; and what derogation, loss of merchandise, lesion of honour and villainy, is said and reported generally unto the English nation for loss of the same ; namely [especially] unto the Duke of Somerset, when he had the commandance and charge thereof : the which loss hath caused and encouraged the King's enemies for to conquer and get Gascony and Guienne, and now daily they make their advance for to lay siege unto Calais, and to other places in the marches there, for to apply them to their obeisance, and so for to come into the land with great puissance ; to the final destruction thereof, if they might prevail, and to put the land in their subjection, which God defend. And on the other part it is to be supposed it is not unknown to you that, after my coming out of Ireland, I, as the King's true liegeman and servant (and ever shall be to my life's end) and for my true acquittal, perceiving the inconvenience before rehearsed, advised his Royal Majesty of certain articles concerning the weal and safeguard, as well of his most royal person, as the tranquillity and convervation of all this his realm : the which advertisements, howbeit that it was thought that they were full necessary, were laid apart, and to be of none effect, through the envy, malice and untruth of the said Duke of Somerset ; which for my truth, faith and allegiance that I owe unto the King, and the good will and favour that I have to all the realm, laboureth continually about the King's highness for my undoing, and to corrupt my blood, and to disinherit me and my heirs, and such persons as be about me, without any desert or cause done or attempted on my part or theirs, I make our Lord Judge. Wherefore, worshipful friends, to the intent that every man shall know my purpose and desire for to declare me such as I am, I signify unto you that, with the help and supportation of Almighty God, and of Our Lady, and of all the Company of Heaven, I, after long sufferance and delays [though it is] not my will or intent to displease my sovereign Lord, seeing that the said Duke ever prevaileth and ruleth about the King's person, and that by this means the land is likely to be destroyed, am fully concluded to proceed in all haste against him with the help of my kinsmen and friends ; in such wise that it shall prove to promote ease, peace, tranquillity and safeguard of all this land : and more, keeping me within the bounds of my allegiance, as it pertaineth to my duty, praying and exhorting you to fortify, enforce, and assist me, and to come to me with all diligence, wheresoever I shall be, or draw, with as many goodly and likely men as ye may, to execute the intent above said. Written under my signet at my castle of Ludlow, the 3rd day of February.

Furthermore I pray you that such strait appointment and ordinance be made that the people which shall come in your fellowship, or be sent unto me by your agreement, be demeaned in such wise by the way, that they do no offence, nor robbery, nor oppression upon the people, in lesion of justice. Written as above, etc.

Your good friend,
R. YORK.

To my right worshipful friends, the bailiffs, burgesses and commons of the good town of Shrewsbury.

1 Colby's *Selections from the Sources of English History.*

APPENDIX III.

From *Three Fifteenth-Century Chronicles, with Historical Memoranda* by John Stowe, edited by Dr. James Gairdner. [Camden Society].

And than the comynes of Kent a rose and hade chosen hem a capteyne the whiche namyd hym sylfe John Mortymer, whose very trew name was John Cade, and he was an Iresheman ; and so he come to the Black hethe withe the comynes of Kentt. And the kynge with all his lordis made hem redy with all her power for to with stonde him. . . . And Sir Umfrey Stafford, knyght, and John Stafford, squyer, with her peple went in the forwarde, and they were slayne and myche of her peple. . . . And the Meire of London with the comynes of the cite came to the kynge besekynge him that he wolde tarye in the cite and they wolde lyve and dye with him, and pay for his costes of housholde an halff yere ; but he wold nott, but toke his jorney to Kyllingworthe. And whan the kynge was gone the capteyn with the comynes of Kent came a yene to the Black hethe. And the iijᵗʰᵉ day of Juyll he came to London ; and as sone as thei entred in London they rubbed Phelippe Malpas. And the iiij day of Jule he behedid Crowmer and a nother man at Myle Ende ; and the same day at after none the Lords Say was fett oute of the Toure to the Yelde Hall to for the maire to have jugement, and whan he came befor the meir he saide he wolde be juged by his perys. And then the comenes of Kent toke him from the officers and ledd him to the Standart in Chepe and there smote of his hede. And than the capteyn did do drawe him thorowe London, and over London brige, and so Seint Thomas Watring, and ther he was hanged and quartered, and his hede and Crowmers hede and a nother manes hede were sett on London brige. And after that he smote of ij other menes hedis in Sowthewerke. And the vth. day of Jule at nyght (and beyng Sondaye) the comynes of London sett upon the comynes of Kent, for they began to rubbe. And all the men of Kent that were in London that nyght they went to her capteyne in to Sowthewerke. And the same nyght the Meir and Shoreffes and my Lorde Scalys and Mathew Gowghe and the comynes of London went to London Brygge, and ther they faughte from ix of the cloke at eve till ix on the morowe, and at the laste the capteyne fired the drawe brigge. And forthe withe went the Chaunseler to the capteyne and sessed him and yave him a chartur and his men a nother, and so with drowe hem homward. Than the xij daye of Juyll was in every shire proclamed that whate man that couthe take the forsaide capteyne shulde have a M^1 marke and brynge him to the kynge quycke or dede, and as for any man that longed to him, x marke ; for hit was openly knowe that his name was nott Mortymer, his name was John Cade, and therfor his chartor stode in no streynthe. And so one Alexandre Iden, a squyre of Kent, toke hym in a garden yn Sowthsex the xiij day of Jule ; and in the takynge of him he was hurtt and died that same nyght, and on the morowe he was brought in to the Kynges Bynche, and after was drawe throwe London and his hede set on London brige.

For " A proclamation made by Jacke Cade, Captytayn of ye Rebelles in Kent," and a *Satirical Dirge* " made by the comons of Kent in the tyme of ther rysynge, when Jack Cade was theyr cappitayn."   See *Three Fifteenth-Century Chronicles*, edited by James Gairdner [Camden Society], and Jones' *York and Lancaster,* 1399–1485.

The Third Part of King Henry the Sixth

Written. Uncertain.

Published. 1595, and was known as " The | true Tragedie of Richard | *Duke of Yorke, and the death of* | good King Henrie the Sixt, | *with the whole contention be-tweene* | the two Houses Lancaster | and Yorke, as it was sundrie times | acted by the Right Honoura- | ble the Earl of Pem- | brooke his seruants. | Printed at London by P. S. for Thomas Milling- | *ton, and are to be sold at his shoppe under* | *Saint Peters Church in* | Cornwal, 1595." This version was probably written by Greene, Peele and Marlowe.

In 1600 a reprint appeared under the same title, printed by W. W. for Thomas Millington. Some years later a third edition made its appearance. This edition, instead of a title-page, bears the heading " The Second Part. | Containing the Tragedie of | Richard Duke of Yorke, and the | *good King Henrie the* | *Sixt.* | "

The version known as the *Third Part of King Henry the Sixth* was first published in the first folio of 1623.

Source of the Plot. The *Chronicles* of Edward Hall and Raphael Holinshed[1]

The *Third Part of King Henry the Sixth* covers a period of sixteen years, from the first battle of Saint Albans in 1455 to the death of King Henry in 1471.

Outline of the Play. The First Act opens in the Parliament House in London. York, accompanied by his two sons and several of his followers, enters. Warwick wonders how the king managed to escape their hands. York replies that Henry " slily stole away," while Northumberland, whose war-like ears could never brook retreat, " Cheer'd up the drooping army," and was, with the Lords Clifford and Stafford slain by common soldiers. To this Edward adds that Stafford's father—the Duke of Buckingham—must be " either slain or wounded dangerous " as he had " cleft his beaver with a downright blow " while Montague boasts of having encountered the Earl of Wiltshire. Stepping forward, and throwing down the head of Somerset, Richard—the youngest son of York—grimly bids the gruesome object to speak :

> Speak thou for me, and tell them what I did.

York considers that Richard has done better than all his other sons in slaying Somerset, and Richard replies " Thus do I hope to shake King Henry's head."

Warwick then suggests that York take possession of the throne :

> Victorious Prince of York,
> Before I see thee seated in that throne
> Which now the house of Lancaster usurps,
> I vow by heaven these eyes shall never close.
> This is the palace of the fearful king,
> And this the regal seat : possess it, York ;
> For this is thine and not King Henry's heirs'.

[1] *See* Appendix I.

and York consents, providing Warwick and Norfolk will support him :

> Assist me then, sweet Warwick, and I will ;
> For hither we have broken in by force.

York having seated himself upon the throne, Warwick advises that when Henry arrives, no violence should be offered him, unless he attempts to thrust them out by force, while York remarks that the queen will be surprised when she arrives to find them at her council, where he intends to " win our right " either " by words or blows." Warwick then predicts that unless " bashful Henry is deposed, whose cowardice Hath made us by-words to our enemies," and York be king, this parliament shall be known as the " bloody parliament," and York counsels his followers to stay with him and " be resolute " for he means " to take possession of my right." Warwick then boasts that he will " plant Plantagenet " and dares anyone to try to displace him, and again urges York to claim his right :

> Neither the king, nor he that loves him best,
> The proudest he that holds up Lancaster,
> Dares stir a wing if Warwick shake his bells.
> I 'll plant Plantagenet, root him up who dares.
> Resolve thee, Richard : claim the English crown.

Trumpets sound, and Henry with his retinue enters. On seeing York occupying the throne, Henry denounces him as a rebel :

> My lords, look where the sturdy rebel sits,
> Even in the chair of state ! belike he means,
> Back'd by the power of Warwick, that false peer,
> To aspire unto the crown and reign as king.

Westmoreland suggests that they pluck York from the throne, but Henry counsels patience. To this Clifford remarks that " Patience is for poltroons," and tells the king that York dared not have sat there if his (Henry's) father had been alive, and asks the king's permission—in which he is supported by Northumberland—to remove York by force. But Henry, who does not wish " To make a shambles of the parliament-house ! " replies that " frowns, words and threats Shall be the war which he means to use " and orders York to descend from the throne, and " kneel for grace and mercy," as he is his sovereign. York retorts that he is the lawful king, and a fierce altercation takes place between the opposing parties.

> What title hast thou, traitor, to the crown ?
> Thy father was, as thou art, Duke of York.
> Thy grandfather, Roger Mortimer, Earl of March.
> I am the son of Henry the Fifth,
> Who made the Dauphin and the French to stoop,
> And seized upon their towns and provinces.

remarks Henry, and Warwick retorts : " Talk not of France, sith thou hast lost it all." " The lord protector lost it, and not I : When I was crown'd I was but nine months old," is Henry's reply, and Richard tells him " You are old enough now, and yet, methinks, you lose," and turning to York, says :

> Father, tear the crown from the usurper's head.

Henry declares his title is good,—although aside he confesses his title is weak— since his father was king and his grandfather [Henry IV] king by conquest. " 'Twas by rebellion against his king," answers York. But " Richard resign'd the crown to Henry the Fourth," pleads Henry. "He rose against him, being his sovereign, And made him to resign his crown perforce," is York's retort. Clifford declares that he will fight in defence of Henry be his " title right or wrong," but the weakness of Henry's claim is so apparent that some of his followers begin to waver. Seeing this, York calls upon Henry to resign the crown, and Warwick threatens that unless Henry does so he will

> fill the house with armed men,
> And o'er the chair of state, where now he sits,
> Write up his title with usurping blood.

He stamps his foot and soldiers enter the Parliament house, and turning to Warwick the weak-kneed monarch asks permission to let him during his life-time reign as king, and the crown shall then pass to York and his heirs.[1] Incensed at Henry's feeble-mindedness, Westmoreland, Northumberland and Clifford denounce him. Westmoreland calls him " Base, fearful, and despairing Henry ! " and Clifford suggests that they leave to tell the queen that her son has been disinherited. As they march out of the Parliament-house Westmoreland addressed Henry :

> Farewell, faint-hearted and degenerate king,
> In whose cold blood no spark of honour bides,

and Northumberland :

> Be thou a prey unto the house of York,
> And die in bands for this unmanly deed !

to which Clifford adds :

> In dreadful war may'st thou be overcome,
> Or live in peace abandon'd and despised !

As he sadly watches them take their departure, Henry sighs, not for himself but for his son whom he admits he has unnaturally disinherited, and again repeats his willingness to " entail " the crown to York and his " heirs for ever," conditionally upon York taking an oath to cease the civil strife and to allow him to reign in peace. York agrees to this, and coming down from the throne, embraces Henry, after which they depart ; York to Sandal Castle his residence near Wakefield ; Warwick to " keep London with my soldiers " ; Montague " unto the sea from whence I came," while Henry with a sigh mutters :

> And I with grief and sorrow, to the court.

On the news being conveyed to the queen that her son had been disinherited she was furious, and proceeds forthwith to the Parliament-house. As she enters, seeing the anger betrayed upon her face, Exeter and the king try to steal away :

> *Exe.*   Here comes the queen, whose looks bewray her anger :
>   I 'll steal away.
> *K. Hen.*   Exeter, so will I.

" Nay, go not from me ; I will follow thee," exclaims Margaret. Henry entreats her to be patient, but the queen in anger upbraids him for proving so unnatural a father as to disinherit his only son :

> Who can be patient in such extremes ?
> Ah ! wretched man ; would I had died a maid,
> And never seen thee, never borne thee son,
> Seeing thou hast proved so unnatural a father.
> Hath he deserved to lose his birthright thus ?

[1] This was determined by Parliament, October, 1460. *Cf.* Extract I from Holinshed, and Appendix II.

" Father, you cannot disinherit me. If you be king, why should not I succeed ? "
asks the Prince, and Henry craves pardon as he has been compelled to forfeit his
rights :

> Pardon me, Margaret ; pardon me, sweet son :
> The Earl of Warwick and the duke enforced me.

" Enforced thee ! " shouts Margaret in a rage, " art thou king, and wilt be forced ?
I shame to hear thee speak. Ah ! timorous wretch," and declares that if she had
been in the Parliament-house, Warwick's soldiers would have " tossed me on their
pikes " before she would have consented to such a dishonourable act :

> Had I been there, which am a silly woman,
> The soldiers should have toss'd me on their pikes
> Before I would have granted to that act ;
> But thou preferr'st thy life before thine honour ;

and threatens to divorce him unless

> that act of parliament be repeal'd
> Whereby my son is disinherited.

She reminds him that the northern lords have renounced him for his weakness, but
that they have sworn to follow her, as she intends to raise the royal standard to
uphold the house of Lancaster. " Thus do I leave thee," ejaculates Margaret, and
turning to her son, says :

> Come, son, let 's away ;
> Our army is ready ; come, we 'll after them.

" Stay, gentle Margaret, and hear me speak," pleads Henry, and Margaret retorts :
" Thou hast spoke too much already ; get thee gone." " Gentle son Edward, thou
wilt stay with me ? " asks his father, and the prince replies :

> When I return with victory from the field
> I 'll see your grace : till then I 'll follow her.

Having gone, Henry excuses himself by saying that it is the affection the queen
has for himself and for their only son that made her " break out into terms of rage,"
but as the defection of the Lords Westmoreland, Northumberland and Clifford
torments his heart he will write letters to them and ask for their reconciliation, to
which Exeter adds :

> And I, I hope, shall reconcile them all.

We are now transferred to Sandal Castle. It opens with a discussion between
Richard, Edward and Montague as to who shall " play the orator," when they are
interrupted by York who enquires as to the nature of their quarrel. Edward replies
there is " No quarrel, but a slight contention." Richard informs his father that they
were discussing that

> which concerns your grace and us ;
> The crown of England, father, which is yours.

York reminds Richard that it is not his until Henry is dead, he having taken an oath
that Henry should " quietly reign." Edward declares that " for a kingdom any
oath may be broken," in fact he " would break a thousand oaths to reign one year."
To this Richard adds that " an oath is of no moment," except it be taken " Before
a true and lawful magistrate," and in consequence the declaration which York has
taken is " vain and frivolous," and declaring that he cannot rest until the white

rose he wears is dyed with Henry's blood, reminds his father it is a sweet thing to wear a crown, and therefore appeals to York to assume the diadem :

> Within whose circuit is Elysium,
> And all that poets feign of bliss and joy.

York decides that he will be " king, or die," and forthwith directs Montague to proceed to London, to " whet on Warwick to this enterprise," Richard to the Duke of Norfolk, and " tell him privily of our intent," and Edward to visit Lord Cobham " With whom the Kentishmen will willingly rise " : but they must keep their designs secret in order that neither the king nor any of the house of Lancaster may be " privy to my drift."

At this point a messenger enters with the news that Queen Margaret, accompanied by the " northern earls and lords," is at hand at the head of twenty thousand men. York who declares he has no fear, orders Edward and Richard—his two sons—to stay, and immediately despatches Montague to London to acquaint Warwick, Cobham and the rest to " strengthen themselves " and " trust not simple Henry nor his oaths."

Sir John and Sir Hugh Mortimer now enter and Sir John suggests that it will be better to meet Margaret in the field than be besieged in the castle. " What ! " exclaims York, " with five thousand men ? " " Ay, with five hundred, father, for a need. A woman's general ; what should we fear ? " ejaculates Richard. Drums sound and York gives orders for his men to be set in order, and as they issue forth to battle, he recalls the victories he had won in France against overwhelming odds :

> Five men to twenty ! though the odds be great,
> I doubt not, uncle, of our victory.
> Many a battle have I won in France,
> Whenas the enemy hath been ten to one :
> Why should I not now have the like success ?

The next scene shows us a Field of battle between Sandal Castle and Wakefield. Young Rutland—York's youngest son—with his Tutor enters, and the boy is wondering how he can escape falling into the hands of the foe just as Clifford and soldiers appear on the scene :

> Ah, whither shall I fly to 'scape their hands ?
> Ah, tutor, look, where bloody Clifford comes !

Clifford orders the Tutor away : " Chaplain away ! thy priesthood saves thy life," but as for young Rutland he shall die :

> As for the brat of this accursed duke,
> Whose father slew my father, he shall die.

The Tutor appeals to Clifford to spare the lad :

> Ah, Clifford, murder not this innocent child,
> Lest thou be hated both of God and man !

but Clifford orders the soldiers to take him away. In terror, the lad faints, but regaining consciousness, young Rutland appeals to Clifford for mercy, telling him " Be thou revenged on men, and let me live." Clifford answers that he pleads in vain, for his (Clifford's) " father's blood Hath stopp'd the passage where thy words should enter." " Then let my father's blood open it again : He is a man, and, Clifford, cope with him " is Rutland's reply, but Clifford, who is out for revenge tells him that

> Had I thy brethren here, their lives and thine
> Were not revenge sufficient for me ;
> .   .   .   .
> The sight of any of the house of York
> Is as a fury to torment my soul ;
> And till I root out their accursed line,
> And leave not one alive, I live in hell.

Clifford raises his sword to slay Rutland, who asks to be allowed to pray before being put to death :

> O, let me pray before I take my death !
> To thee I pray ; sweet Clifford, pity me !

" Such pity as my rapier's point affords," replies Clifford.   " I never did thee harm : why wilt thou slay me ? " asks Rutland, and Clifford retorts " Thy father hath." " But 'twas ere I was born," is Rutland's rejoinder, and again appeals to Clifford to spare him :

> Thou hast one son ; for his sake pity me,
> Lest in revenge thereof, sith God is just,
> He be miserably slain as I.

Rutland tells Clifford that he has no cause to put him to death. Clifford in anger retorts " No cause !   Thy father slew my father ; therefore, die," and he plunges his sword in the breast of the lad, who falls mortally wounded, exclaiming " Di faciant laudis summa sit ista tuæ ! "   [The gods grant that this be the culmination of thy glory], and Clifford departs to seek out York, vowing that he will not wipe off his sword the blood of Rutland until it has congealed with the blood of his father.

The concluding scene of this Act shows us another part of the battle-field.   York enters and announces that Queen Margaret's forces have been victorious ; that all his army is scattered and his two uncles slain in rescuing him.   His two sons— Edward and Richard—who fought " Like men born to renown by life or death " he knows not what has become of them, while Richard " Three times made a lane to me " and shouted " Courage, father ! fight it out ! "

> The army of the queen hath got the field :
> My uncles both are slain in rescuing me ;
> .   .   .   .
> My sons, God knows what hath bechanced them :
> But this I know, they have demean'd themselves
> Like men born to renown by life or death.
> Three times did Richard make a lane to me,
> And thrice cried " Courage, father ! fight it out ! "
> And full as oft came Edward to my side,
> .   .   .   .
> Richard cried " Charge ! and give no foot of ground ! "
> And cried " A crown, or else a glorious tomb !
> A sceptre, or an earthly sepulchre ! "
> With this, we charged again : but, out, alas !
> We bodged again :

York's troops being defeated, father and sons are swept apart.   There is an alarum, and York, who is too " faint and cannot fly their fury," finding himself hemmed in by the enemy, mutters :

> The sands are number'd that make up my life ;
> Here must I stay, and here my life must end.

Margaret, with Clifford, Northumberland and the young prince enters ; and Clifford and Northumberland revile York now they have him in their power, but York exclaims that from

> My ashes, as the phœnix, may bring forth
> A bird that will revenge upon you all ;

Clifford is on the point of thrusting his sword through York :

> I will not bandy with thee word for word,
> But buckle with thee blows, twice two for one,

but is restrained by Margaret as she wishes to mock him before he is put to death :

> Hold, valiant Clifford ! for a thousand causes
> I would prolong awhile the traitor's life.

Ordering York to be enthroned on a molehill :

> Brave warriors, Clifford and Northumberland,
> Come, make him stand upon this molehill here,
> That raught at mountains with outstretched arms,

she taunts him :

> Where are your mess of sons to back you now ?
> The wanton Edward, and the lusty George ?
> And where 's that valiant crook-back prodigy,
> Dicky your boy, that with his grumbling voice
> Was wont to cheer his dad in mutinies ?

As Clifford and Northumberland hold the struggling York, Margaret offers him a napkin which has been dipped in Rutland's blood for to " dry his cheeks " :

> Or, with the rest, where is your darling Rutland ?
> Look ! York : I stain'd this napkin with the blood
> That valiant Clifford with his rapier's point
> Made issue from the bosom of the boy ;
> And if thine eyes can water for his death,
> I give thee this to dry thy cheeks withal.

As York bears up under this indignity with so much patience, Margaret exclaims that he cannot speak unless he wears a crown, and a paper crown is brought and set upon York's head :

> A crown for York ! and, lords, bow low to him :
> Hold you his hands whilst I do set it on.

Clifford " for his father's sake " again raises his sword to smite York, but Margaret, who wishes to hear York's supplication, once more stays his hand : " Nay, stay ; let 's hear the orisons he makes," and York fiercely denounces Margaret, describing her as the

> She-wolf of France, but worse than wolves of France,
> Whose tongue more poisons than the adder's tooth !
> How ill-beseeming is it in thy sex
> To triumph like an Amazonian trull,
> Upon their woes whom fortune captivates !
> But that thy face is, vizard-like, unchanging,
> Made impudent with use of evil deeds,
> I would assay, proud queen, to make thee blush :

Reminding her that her " father bears the type of King of Naples, Of both the Sicils and Jerusalem, Yet not so wealthy as an English yeoman " ; that she is an unnatural woman, being everything " opposite to every good," to bid a father wipe his eyes with a napkin dipped in his son's blood, every drop of which cries for vengeance on " fell Clifford and thee, false Frenchwoman." Taking the napkin York wipes his face with it, and then telling Margaret to keep it and boast of it, predicts that the world will cry shame on her when her ruthlessness is known :

> O, ten times more than the tigers of Hyrcania.
> See, ruthless queen, a hapless father's tears :
> This cloth thou dipp'dst in blood of my sweet boy,
> And I with tears do wash the blood away.
> Keep thou the napkin, and go boast of this ;
> And if thou tell'st the heavy story right,
> Upon my soul, the hearers will shed tears ;
> Yea, even my foes will shed fast-falling tears,
> And say " Alas ! it was a piteous deed."

This passionate and indignant protest even moves Northumberland to pity, who remarks :

> Had he been slaughter-men to all my kin,
> I should not for my life but weep with him,
> To see how inly sorrow gripes his soul,

but Margaret, who has no pity, replies :

> What, weeping-ripe, my Lord Northumberland ?
> Think but upon the wrong he did us all,
> And that will quickly dry thy melting tears.

" Here's for my oath ; here's for my father's death," shouts Clifford, and rushing forward runs his sword through York's body. With the remark : " And here's to right our gentle-hearted king," Margaret follows his example, and York falling mortally wounded, exclaims :

> Open thy gate of mercy, gracious God !
> My soul flies through these wounds to seek out Thee.

Margaret then orders his head to be cut off and exhibited on the gates of York :

> Off with his head, and set it on York gates :
> So York may overlook the town of York.

The Second Act opens on a Plain near Mortimer's Cross, in Herefordshire. The forces of Edward and Richard enter. Edward wonders whether his father escaped from " Clifford's and Northumberland's pursuit." At the same time

> Had he been ta'en we should have heard the news ;
> Had he been slain we should have heard the news ;
> Or had he 'scaped, methinks we should have heard
> The happy tidings of his good escape.

and then turning to Richard asks why he is so sad ?   Richard replies that he cannot rest until he knows what had become of his father for when he saw him last he was in the thick of the fight surrounded by foes. At this moment there appears in the sky a strange phenomenon. " Dazzle mine eyes, or do I see three suns ? " exclaims Edward. Richard points out that there are three suns and each one is a perfect sun :

> Three glorious suns, each one a perfect sun ;
> Not separated with the racking clouds,
> But sever'd in a pale clear-shining sky.

which after shining separate for a time form one sun :

> See, see ! they join, embrace, and seem to kiss,
> As if they vow'd some league inviolable :
> Now are they but one lamp, one light, one sun.

Edward considers that this strange phenomenon—the like of which had never been seen before—is a call to the three sons of York to battle, and forthwith decides to adopt " three fair-shining suns " for the cognizance upon his target ;

> 'Tis wondrous strange, the like yet never heard of.
> I think it cites us, brother, to the field,
> That we, the sons of brave Plantagenet,
> Each one already blazing by our meeds,
> Should notwithstanding join our lights together,
> And over-shine the earth, as this the world.
> Whate'er it bodes, henceforward will I bear
> Upon my target three fair-shining suns.

A messenger, whose looks foretell evil tidings, enters, with the news that York has been slain at the battle of Wakefield. " O, speak no more, for I have heard too much," is Edward's remark, on hearing the news, but Richard on the contrary demands to know the full story of his father's death : " Say how he died, for I will hear it all." The messenger therefore tells them how York was surrounded by his foes ; how Margaret mocked him, and when York wept with grief, the ruthless queen gave him the napkin dipped in Rutland's blood to wipe the tears away, and after many taunts ordered his head to be cut off and set over the gates of York. Edward declares that " boisterous Clifford " has slain the " flower of Europe for his chivalry," and so mournful is his father's death to him that he will never " see more joy ! " Richard however exclaims he " cannot weep, for all my body's moisture Scarce serves to quench my furnace-burning heart " ; neither can his tongue tell of his heart's grief, but as Tears are for babes ; " blows and revenge for me ! " he will, as he bears his father's name, either revenge his death or " die renowned by attempting it," and Edward reminds his brother that his father left him not only his name, but also his dukedom and the throne.

Warwick with forces now joins Edward and Richard, and on enquiring " what news abroad ? " is told of York's death. Warwick replies that he learned of the result of the fight at Wakefield ten days ago, and presuming that Margaret's next move would be London to rescue her husband, had gathered together an army and had met the queen's forces at Saint Alban's, where a second battle had taken place, with the result that the Yorkist's had been defeated and that Henry had escaped. Collecting together his scattered forces Warwick had proceeded hither to join with Edward for he had heard that Edward was preparing to fight. After a hurried consultation, Warwick suggests that as Henry took an oath that York should succeed him as king, they march on London and take possession of the city :

> He swore consent to your succession,
> His oath enrolled in the parliament ;
> And now to London all the crew are gone,
> To frustrate both his oath and what beside
> May make against the house of Lancaster.

Richard and Edward fall in with this bold move, and hailing Edward as Duke of York, Warwick promises to proclaim him as King of England as they proceed through all the towns and villages on their way to the capital :

> No longer Earl of March, but Duke of York :
> The next degree is England's royal throne ;
> For King of England shalt thou be proclaim'd
> In every borough as we pass along ;

> And he that throws not up his cap for joy
> Shall for the fault make forfeit of his head.
> King Edward, valiant Richard, Montague,
> Stay we no longer, dreaming of renown,
> But sound the trumpets, and about our task.

Their design is however frustrated, for a messenger enters with the tidings that the queen is advancing with an army, and the Yorkists at once make preparations to give battle.

We are before York in the next scene. There is a flourish of trumpets, and Henry, Margaret, with the Prince of Wales and forces enter. After welcoming her husband, Margaret directs his attention to the head of his " arch-enemy " over the gateway of the city :

> Yonder's the head of that arch-enemy
> That sought to be encompass'd with your crown :
> Doth not the object cheer your heart, my lord ?

and Henry replies that the sight of it " irks my very soul " and appeals to Heaven to " withhold revenge." To this Clifford remarks that Henry is too lenient and tells him that " pity must be laid aside," as " Ambitious York did level at thy crown," and urges him to " steel thy melting heart," and leave the inheritance to his son. Henry admits that Clifford plays the orator very well, " Inferring arguments of mighty force," but reminds Clifford that " things ill got had ever bad success." Margaret then appeals to Henry to " cheer up your spirits," for " this soft courage makes your followers faint," and reminds him that he had promised to knight his son :

> You promis'd knighthood to our forward son :
> Unsheathe your sword, and dub him presently.
> Edward, kneel down.

As the Prince rises, Henry bids him to always " draw thy sword in right," to which the young lad answers that he will draw it as heir to the crown and use it in that quarrel even to the death, words which Clifford considers are " spoken like a toward prince."

A messenger enters with the news that Warwick is approaching with an army of thirty thousand men, and Clifford suggests that Henry leave the field, as the queen " hath best success when you are absent," in which he is supported by Margaret, but the king decides to stay as " their fortune is my fortune too." Northumberland then appeals to Henry to fight with " resolution " and the young prince urges his royal father to encourage those who fight in his defence ; " Unsheathe your sword, good father : cry, ' Saint George ! ' "

York, with Warwick and forces, now appears on the scene, and York calls upon Henry to resign his crown or fight :

> Now, perjur'd Henry, wilt thou kneel for grace,
> And set thy diadem upon my head ;
> Or bide the mortal fortune of the field ?

Margaret calls York a " proud insulting boy," to speak so bold to " thy sovereign and thy lawful king," and York retorts that he is by Act of Parliament the lawful king, and that Henry " should bow his knee."

After a passage of arms has taken place between Clifford and Richard, in which Richard calls Clifford "a butcher" for having killed young Rutland, Warwick demands Henry to resign the crown. Margaret calls him " long-tongued Warwick," and asks how dare he speak seeing he ran away from her at the battle of Saint Albans :

> Why, how now, long-tongued Warwick ! dare you speak ?
> When you and I met at Saint Alban's last,
> Your legs did better service than your hands.

After this altercation has proceeded for some time in which Richard calls Clifford " a coward " for having slain young Rutland :

> Ay, like a dastard and a treacherous coward,
> As thou didst kill our tender brother Rutland ;
> But ere sun set I 'll make thee curse the deed,

Henry, as king, claims the privilege to speak, but Clifford requests him to be silent, as the " wound that bred this meeting here Cannot be cured by words," whereupon Richard bids Clifford to draw his sword and fight it out, although he is of opinion that " Clifford's manhood lies upon his tongue." Once more Edward bids Henry to yield up the crown, " Say, Henry, shall I have my right or no ? " for " A thousand men have broke their fasts to-day, That ne'er shall dine unless thou yield the crown," to which Warwick adds that " their blood is upon thy head " if he denies York justice. To this the Prince of Wales remarks :

> If that be right which Warwick says is right,
> There is no wrong, but every thing is right.

" Whoever got thee, there thy mother stands ; For well I wot thou hast thy mother's tongue," retorts Richard, and Margaret reviles Richard, calling him a " foul mis-shapen stigmatic " who ought to be avoided :

> But thou art neither like thy sire nor dam,
> But like a foul misshapen stigmatic,
> Mark'd by the destinies to be avoided,
> As venom toads, or lizards' dreadful stings.

Describing her as a " shameless callat," Edward retorts that " Helen of Greece was fairer far than thou, Although thy husband may be Menelaus ; And ne'er was Agamemnon's brother wrong'd By that false woman as this king by thee," and reminding her that Henry's father " revell'd in the heart of France, And tam'd the king, and made the Dauphin stoop " ; refuses to wrangle with her any longer and defying her bids the trumpets sound for battle :

> Sound trumpets ! let our bloody colours wave !
> And either victory, or else a grave.

calling her a " wrangling woman," whose " words will cost ten thousand lives this day."

A Field of Battle between Towton and Saxton in Yorkshire, where the fiercest battle in this civil strife was fought, supplies the next scene. There are alarums and excursions, and Warwick enters. Being exhausted with fighting he lies down on the grass " a little while to breathe " :

> Forspent with toil, as runners with a race,
> I lay me down a little while to breathe ;
> For strokes received, and many blows repaid,
> Have robb'd my strong-knit sinews of their strength,
> And spite of spite needs must I rest awhile.

At this moment Edward appears in haste, beseeching heaven for victory, or " strike, ungentle death ! " Immediately after George enters with the news that their " ranks are broke " and asks Edward for counsel, and Edward replies that

> Bootless is flight, they follow us with wings ;
> And weak we are, and cannot shun pursuit.

They are joined by Richard, and reproaching Warwick for having " withdrawn thyself from the fight " tells him that Clifford has slain his brother, who in the pangs of death had cried :

> Warwick, revenge ! brother, revenge my death !

and Warwick swears that this time there shall be no retreat. " I 'll kill my horse because I will not fly, . . . I 'll never pause again, never stand still, Till either death hath closed these eyes of mine, Or fortune given me measure of revenge." Edward and his brothers vow to stand firm with Warwick, and taking farewell of each other they depart either to victory or to death.

Scene four shows us another part of the battlefield. It opens with Richard challenging Clifford to fight :

> Now, Clifford, I have singled thee alone.
> Suppose this arm is for the Duke of York,
> And this for Rutland ; both bound to revenge,
> Wert thou environ'd with a brazen wall.

Clifford, who boasts of having slain Richard's father and his brother Rutland, threatens to treat Richard likewise :

> Now, Richard, I am with thee here alone.
> This is the hand that stabb'd thy father York,
> And this the hand that slew thy brother Rutland ;
> And here 's the heart that triumphs in their death
> And cheers these hands that slew thy sire and brother,
> To execute the like upon thyself ;
> And so, have at thee !

They encounter each other, and Warwick appearing on the scene, Clifford seeks safety in flight, and turning to Warwick, Richard tells him to " single out some other chase ; For I myself will hunt this wolf to death," and forthwith dashes away in hot pursuit of Clifford, on whom he has vowed revenge.

We are in another part of the field of battle in scene five. There is an alarum, and Henry, who has been chided by Margaret and Clifford to leave the field, as they " prosper best of all when I am thence," enters alone. As he rests himself on a molehill watching the ebb and flow of the battle he soliloquises on the carnage which unfolds before his eyes. Contrasting his own position which has brought him nothing but grief and sorrow to the happy humble shepherd whose peaceful calling he so feelingly describes, he longs for death if it were the will of God, in whose keeping rests the destiny of the conflict :

> This battle fares like to the morning's war,
> When dying clouds contend with growing light,
> What time the shepherd, blowing of his nails,
> Can neither call it perfect day nor night.
> .   .   .   .
> Here on this molehill will I sit me down.
> To whom God will, there be the victory !
> For Margaret my queen, and Clifford too,
> Have chid me from the battle ; swearing both
> They prosper best of all when I am thence.
> Would I were dead ! if God's good will were so ;
> For what is in this world but grief and woe ?

> O God ! methinks it were a happy life,
> To be no better than a homely swain ;
> To sit upon a hill, as I do now,
> To carve out dials quaintly, point by point,
> Thereby to see the minutes how they run,
> How many make the hour full complete ;
> How many hours bring about the day ;
> How many days will finish up the year ;
> How many years a mortal man may live.
> When this is known, then to divide the times ;
> So many hours must I tend my flock ;
> So many hours must I take my rest ;
> So many hours must I contemplate ;
> So many hours must I sport myself ;
> So many days my ewes have been with young ;
> So many weeks ere the poor fools will ean ;
> So many years ere I shall shear the fleece ;
> So minutes, hours, days, months, and years,
> Pass'd over to the end they were created,
> Would bring white hairs unto a quiet grave.
> Ah ! what a life were this ; how sweet ! how lovely !
> Gives not the hawthorn-bush a sweeter shade
> To shepherds looking on their silly sheep,
> Than doth a rich embroider'd canopy
> To kings that fear their subjects' treachery ?
> O yes ! it doth ; a thousand-fold it doth.

As Henry meditates, a Lancastrian soldier enters, bearing a dead body which he intends to rob, only to discover to his horror that it is his own father who has fought on the Yorkist side :

> Ill blows the wind that profits nobody.
> This man, whom hand to hand I slew in fight,
> May be possessed with some store of crowns ;
> And I, that haply take them from him now,
> May yet ere night yield both my life and them
> To some man else, as this dead man doth me...
> Who 's this ? O God ! it is my father's face,
> Whom in this conflict I unwares have kill'd.

Asking pardon of God, for " I knew not what I did " and pardon of his father " for I knew not thee ! " the soldier declares that his " tears shall wipe away these bloody marks."

Moved to pity by this spectacle, Henry weeps :

> O piteous spectacle ! O bloody times !
> Whiles lions war and battle for their dens,
> Poor harmless lambs abide their enmity.
> Weep, wretched man, I 'll aid thee tear for tear ;
> And let our hearts and eyes, like civil war,
> Be blind with tears, and break o'ercharged with grief.

Immediately a Yorkist soldier appears, bearing in his arms a dead body :

> Thou that so stoutly hast resisted me,
> Give me thy gold, if thou hast any gold,
> For I have bought it with a hundred blows,

exclaims the soldier, but as his eye falls upon the face of the dead man he recognises his only son who has fought on the Lancastrian side :

But let me see :   is this our foeman's face ?
Ah, no, no, no ; it is mine only son !
Ah, boy, if any life be left in thee,
Throw up thine eye, see, see what showers arise,
Blown with the windy tempest of my heart,
Upon thy wounds, that kill mine eye and heart !

Moved with compassion at the grief of the father, Henry exclaims that he would welcome death if it would only put an end to this strife with all its attendant horrors :

Woe above woe !   grief more than common grief !
O, that my death would stay these ruthful deeds !
O, pity, pity ; gentle heaven, pity !
The red rose and the white are on his face,
The fatal colours of our striving houses ;
The one his purple blood right well resembles ;
The other his pale cheeks, methinks, presenteth :
Wither one rose, and let the other flourish !
If you contend, a thousand lives must wither.

Lamenting over the mournful scene just enacted, the son exclaims that his mother will never forgive him when she knows he has slain his father :

How will my mother for a father's death
Take on with me and ne'er be satisfied !

The father declares that his wife will " shed seas of tears " when she learns the news of her son's death :

How will my wife for slaughter of my son
Shed seas of tears and ne'er be satisfied !

while Henry wonders what the verdict of the country will be when they read of the carnage during his reign :

How will the country for these woeful chances
Misthink the king and not be satisfied !

Taking the body of his father in his arms, the son bears it away :

I 'll bear thee hence, where I may weep my fill ;

Lifting up the body of his son to bear it away, the father mournfully exclaims, that :

My heart, sweet boy, shall be thy sepulchre,
For from my heart thine image ne'er shall go :
My sighing breast shall be thy funeral bell ;

         .   .   .   .   .
I'll bear thee hence ; and let them fight that will,
For I have murder'd where I should not kill,

while Henry in the midst of grief, exclaims :

Sad-hearted men, much overgone with care,
Here sits a king more woeful than you are.

There is an alarum, and Margaret with the Prince of Wales and Exeter enter in haste.   Seeing Henry, the Prince and Margaret urge him to fly for " Warwick rages like a chafed bull " and Edward and Richard " like a brace of greyhounds " are in pursuit, breathless for their lives :

Prince.   Fly, father, fly ! for all your friends are fled,
And Warwick rages like a chafed bull.
Away ! for death doth hold us in pursuit.

> Q. *Mar.* Mount you, my lord ; towards Berwick post amain.
> Edward and Richard, like a brace of greyhounds
> Having the fearful flying hare in sight,
> With fiery eyes sparkling for very wrath,
> And bloody steel grasp'd in their ireful hands,
> Are at our backs ; and therefore hence amain.

Seeing Henry hesitate, Exeter expostulates with him, telling him " make speed, Or else come after," and Henry entreats " good sweet Exeter " to take him with him.

> Not that I fear to stay, but love to go
> Whither the queen intends.

The concluding scene of this Act shows us another part of the battlefield. Having been wounded by an arrow in the neck, and realising that his end is near, Clifford exclaims that he fears Henry's overthrow more than his own death, for if Henry had only ruled as his father and grandfather had done, York would not have triumphed :

> Here burns my candle out ; ay, here it dies,
> Which, whiles it lasted, gave King Henry light.
> O Lancaster, I fear thy overthrow
> More than my body's parting with my soul.
>   .   .   .   .   .   .
> O Phœbus, hadst thou never given consent
> That Phaëthon should check thy fiery steeds,
> Thy burning car never had scorch'd the earth ;
> And, Henry, hadst thou sway'd as kings should do,
> Or as thy father did,
> Giving no ground unto the house of York,
> They never then had sprung like summer flies ;

Owing to loss of blood Clifford faints just as Edward with his forces appear. Giving orders for troops to pursue the " bloody-minded " queen, Edward wonders whether Clifford has escaped to which Warwick replies that it is impossible, as he was severely wounded by Richard in the conflict. As they converse Clifford groans aloud and passes away, and Edward remarks : " Whose soul is that which takes her heavy leave ? " and giving orders to " See who it is : and, now the battle 's ended, If friend or foe let him be gently us'd," they recognise the dead body as that of Clifford. Richard demands that the " doom of mercy be revoked, for 'tis Clifford," and Warwick therefore orders his head to be cut off and placed over the gates of York :

> Ay, but he 's dead : off with the traitor's head,
> And rear it in the place your father's stands.

Warwick then proposes that they proceed to London to crown Edward " England's royal king," after which he will cross over to France to ask for the hand of Lady Bona on behalf of Edward. Edward creates Richard Duke of Gloucester and George, Duke of Clarence. Richard however prefers the dukedom of Clarence, as " Gloucester's dukedom is too ominous," but Warwick describes it as a " foolish observation " and Richard accepts :

> Richard, I will create thee Duke of Gloucester ;
> And George, of Clarence ; Warwick, as ourself,
> Shall do and undo as him pleaseth best.
> *Rich.* Let me be Duke of Clarence, George of Gloucester,
> For Gloucester's dukedom is too ominous.
> *War.* Tut, that 's a foolish observation :
> Richard, be Duke of Gloucester. Now to London,
> To see these honours in possession.

The Third Act opens in a Forest in the North of England. Two keepers with cross-bows enter and conceal themselves in the thicket to await the approach of deer. Henry, disguised, with a prayer-book in his hand, muttering to himself that he has secretly crossed the border from Scotland to greet again his native land, strolls along the glade :

> From Scotland am I stol'n, even of pure love
> To greet mine own land with my wishful sight.
> No, Harry, Harry, 'tis no land of thine ;
> Thy place is fill'd, thy sceptre wrung from thee,
> Thy balm wash'd off wherewith thou wast anointed :
> No bending knee will call thee Cæsar now,
> No humble suitors press to speak for right,
> No, not a man comes for redress of thee ;
> For how can I help them, and not myself ?

He is recognised by the first keeper :

> Ay, here 's a deer whose skin's a keeper's fee :
> This is the quondam king ; let 's seize upon him.

They however forbear for a little while, as they wish to hear more, and Henry *sotto voce* mutters that Margaret and his son have gone to France to seek the aid of the French king, and Warwick too has preceded hither to ask for the hand of Lady Bona for Edward, and knowing what a " subtle orator " Warwick is, and Lewis a " prince soon won with moving words " he is afraid that Margaret's appeal will be in vain :

> My queen and son are gone to France for aid ;
> And, as I hear, the great commanding Warwick
> Is thither gone, to crave the French king's sister
> To wife for Edward. If this news be true,
> Poor queen and son, your labour is but lost ;
> For Warwick is a subtle orator,
> And Lewis a prince soon won with moving words.

Emerging from the thicket, the second keeper questions Henry :

> Say, what art thou that talk'st of kings and queens ?

and Henry replies :

> More than I seem, and less than I was born to :
> A man at least, for less I should not be ;
> And men may talk of kings, and why not I ?

" Ay, but thou talk'st as if thou wert a king," is the keeper's query, to which Henry rejoins " Why, so I am, in mind ; and that 's enough." Being asked where his crown is if he is a king, Henry in slow sad words answers that his crown, which he calls content, is in his heart :

> My crown is in my heart, not on my head ;
> Not deck'd with diamonds and Indian stones,
> Nor to be seen : my crown is call'd content ;
> A crown it is that seldom kings enjoy.

Realising that he is none other than the fugitive Henry, in the name of King Edward to whom they have sworn allegiance, they threaten to arrest him :

> Well, if you be a king crown'd with content,
> Your crown content and you must be contented
> To go along with us ; for, as we think,
> You are the king King Edward hath deposed ;
> And we his subjects, sworn in all allegiance,
> Will apprehend you as his enemy.

Reminding them that they were sworn subjects to him, and now they brake their oaths, the first keeper tells Henry that while he was king they were his subjects, but having been deposed by Edward they had now sworn allegiance to the new monarch. " So would you be again to Henry, If he were seated as King Edward is," is Henry's retort.

They however, " in God's name and the king's " seize upon him, and charge him to accompany them " unto the officers " and Henry in his usual submissive manner obeys, offering to submit to whatever may be the will of God :

> In God's name, lead ; your king's name be obey'd :
> And what God will, that let your king perform ;
> And what he will, I humbly yield unto.

In the second scene we are in the Palace in London. Lady Grey, whose husband had been killed at the battle of Saint Albans, enters, and Edward, addressing his brothers, tells them that she has come to ask for the restitution of her late husband's estates :

> Brother of Gloucester, at Saint Alban's field
> This lady's husband, Sir Richard Grey, was slain,
> His lands then seiz'd on by the conqueror :
> Her suit is now to repossess those lands ;
> Which we in justice cannot well deny,
> Because in quarrel of the house of York
> The worthy gentleman did lose his life.

Gloucester considers that Edward will do well to grant her request :

> Your highness shall do well to grant her suit ;
> It were dishonour to deny it her.

Edward, however, is not inclined to grant her petition forthwith, and Gloucester and Clarence whisper to each other, the latter remarking : " He knows the game : how true he keeps the wind ! " Promising to consider her request Edward tells the lady to come again to know his decision :

> Widow, we will consider of your suit :
> And come some other time to know our mind.

but Lady Grey asks for her request to be considered without delay :

> Right gracious lord, I cannot brook delay :
> May it please your highness to resolve me now,
> And what your pleasure is shall satisfy me.

Gloucester and Clarence then draw aside where they hold a whispered conversation between each other, both agreeing that Edward's intention is to grant the lady's suit. While they are conversing Edward asks Lady Grey how many children she has, and being told " Three, my most gracious lord," Edward remarks it " 'Twere pity they should lose their father's lands." " Be pitiful, dread lord, and grant it them," rejoins Lady Grey, and turning to his brothers, Edward requests that they withdraw while he considers her request. Left alone an animated conversation takes place between Edward and Lady Grey, and as the former ceases the conversation Lady Grey remarks : " Why stops my lord ? shall I not hear my task ? " " An easy task, 'tis but to love a king," is Edward's answer. " That's soon perform'd, because I am a subject," ejaculates Lady Grey, and Edward therefore tells her that her husband's estates are restored to her. Thanking Edward " with many thousand thanks," she drops a curtsy, and Gloucester [aside to Clarence] remarks : " The match is made ; she seals it with a curtsey." She is about to leave but Edward requests her to stay as she has misunderstood his meaning, and after a further conversation has taken place, in which Lady Grey does not fall in with his suggestions, she asks permission to depart, declaring " My suit is at an end " and Gloucester [aside to Clarence] whispers " The widow likes him not, she knits her brows."   Edward, who admires the lady, then suggests that she shall become queen :

> Her looks do argue her replete with modesty ;
> Her words do show her wit incomparable ;
> All her perfections challenge sovereignty :
> One way or other, she is for a king ;
> And she shall be my love, or else my queen.—
> Say that King Edward take thee for his queen ?

Lady Grey thinks he is jesting :

> 'Tis better said than done, my gracious lord :
> I am a subject fit to jest withal,
> But far unfit to be a sovereign.

but Edward tells her not to " cavil " for he means to make her queen of England. Seeing that they have arrived at an agreement, Gloucester and Clarence now approach. and Edward informs them of his decision, a decision which Gloucester considers will be a " ten days' wonder at the least," but Clarence reminds him "That 's a day longer than a wonder lasts," to which Edward remarks : " jest on, brothers."

At this point a nobleman enters and informs Edward that Henry has been taken prisoner :

> My gracious lord, Henry your foe is taken,
> And brought your prisoner to your palace gate.

Edward orders Henry to be conveyed to the Tower, and entrusting Lady Grey to the care of his brothers, bidding them to " use her honourably," all leave with the exception of Gloucester.

Left alone, Gloucester in a long soliloquy [III. ii. 124–195] unfolds his impious motives to seize the crown, and in order to achieve the object he has in view, he will " drown more sailors than the mermaid," " slay more gazers than the basilisk," like Nester he will play the orator ; " deceive more slyly than Ulysses " ; like Sinon, take another Troy, change shapes with Proteus if it be to his advantage ; and even send the " murderous Machiavel to school " :

> Can I do this, and cannot get a crown ?
> Tut ! were it further off, I 'll pluck it down.

We are now transferred to France, the next scene being the French King's Palace. Margaret, who had escaped to France after the battle of Towton, to seek aid from Lewis XI, enters, and Lewis invites her to be seated :

> Fair Queen of England, worthy Margaret,
> Sit down with us : it ill befits thy state
> And birth that thou should'st stand while Lewis doth sit.

but Margaret replies that she " must strike her sail " for although once England's queen, misfortune has " trod my title down " and she must now take a more " humble seat " :

> No, mighty King of France ; now Margaret
> Must strike her sail, and learn awhile to serve
> Where kings command.   I was, I must confess,
> Great Albion's queen in former golden days ;

> But now mischance hath trod my title down,
> And with dishonour laid me on the ground,
> Where I must take like seat unto my fortune,
> And to my humble seat conform myself.

Being asked the reason of this " deep despair " Margaret declares that the cause " fills mine eyes with tears And stops my tongue, while heart is drown'd in cares," but Lewis enjoins her not to " yield her neck to fortune's yoke," and inviting her again to seat herself beside him, promises, if possible, to grant her request :

> Whate'er it be, be thou still like thyself,
> And sit thee by our side : [*seats her by him*] yield not thy neck
> To fortune's yoke, but let thy dauntless mind
> Still ride in triumph over all mischance.
> Be plain, Queen Margaret, and tell thy grief ;
> It shall be eas'd, if France can yield relief.

Encouraged by these words, Margaret takes her seat on the dais :

> Those gracious words revive my drooping thoughts,
> And give my tongue-tied sorrows leave to speak.

and then relates to Lewis, that her husband—who is now an exile in Scotland—has been driven from the throne by Edward, Duke of York, who " usurps the regal title " and she has now crossed over to France to ask succour of the French King :

> Now, therefore, be it known to noble Lewis,
> That Henry, sole possessor of my love,
> Is of a king become a banish'd man,
> And forced to live in Scotland a forlorn ;
> While proud ambitious Edward Duke of York
> Usurps the regal title and the seat
> Of England's true-anointed lawful king.

She is winning Lewis over to her side, but her chances are spoiled by the sudden appearance of Warwick, whom Margaret describes as the " breeder of my sorrow." Welcomed by Lewis " Welcome, brave Warwick ! What brings thee to France ? " Warwick explains that he has been sent by Edward to ask for the hand of the Lady Bona in marriage, and Margaret aside mutters " If that go forward, Henry's hope is done." Turning to Lady Bona, Warwick tells her he is " commanded with your leave and favour, Humbly to kiss your hand " and relates to her how deeply enamoured Edward is with " thy beauty's image and thy virtue." Hearing this Margaret appeals to the King and Lady Bona to hear her speak before they answer Warwick, as his " demand Springs not from Edward's well-meant honest love, But from deceit bred by necessity " ; as tyrants cannot safely govern at home, unless they purchase foreign alliances. " Injurious Margaret !" exclaims Warwick. " And why not queen ? " demands the Prince of Wales, and Warwick retorts by telling the prince that as his father is a usurper he is no more a prince than his mother is a queen. To this the Earl of Oxford—who is in attendance on Margaret—points out that if that is so, Warwick renounces the glory won by John of Gaunt who conquered the greater part of Spain, and the victories won on French soil by Henry the Fifth, from whom Henry the Sixth has lineally descended, and Warwick reminds Oxford that all these conquests and possessions have been lost by Henry. Being asked by Oxford why he speaks against his rightful sovereign, whom he has obeyed for thirty and six years, and whom he now betrays without a blush, Warwick invites Oxford to forsake Henry and acknowledge Edward as king, but Oxford haughtily replies that so long as " life upholds this arm," he will fight for the house of Lancaster :

> No, Warwick, no ; while life upholds this arm,
> This arm upholds the house of Lancaster.

to which Warwick replies " And I the house of York." Lewis then requests Margaret, Prince Edward and Oxford, to stand aside while he has further conference with Warwick, and Margaret sadly mutters that the " Heavens grant that Warwick's words bewitch him not." Addressing Warwick, the French King inquires whether Edward is the lawful heir to the throne of England, and whether he is acceptable to the people, for he cannot link with him unless he has been chosen king by lawful means, and Warwick pawns his credit and his honour that it is so. Lewis next asks if Edward is animated by sincerity and affection in asking for the hand of the Lady Bona, and Warwick replying in the affirmative, Lewis, turning to Lady Bona, asks her opinion on the matter : " Now, sister, let us hear your firm resolve," to which with characteristic modesty, replies she is willing to leave the decision to her brother, and turning to Warwick confesses that she has often heard Edward's " desert recounted " which has caused " her ear " to " tempt judgment to desire." Lewis then gives his consent to the marriage, and orders " Articles be drawn " to which Margaret shall be a witness :

> Then, Warwick, thus : our sister shall be Edward's ;
> And now forthwith shall articles be drawn
> Touching the jointure that your king must make,
> Which with her dowry shall be counterpoised.
> Draw near, Queen Margaret, and be a witness
> That Bona shall be wife to the English king.

to which the Prince retorts : " To Edward, but not to the English king." Margaret hotly denounces Warwick as " Deceitful Warwick " for before he appeared on the scene " Lewis was Henry's friend," and Lewis replies that he is still friend to Henry and Margaret. Telling the French king that " Henry now lives in Scotland at his ease " Warwick, turning to Margaret, describes her as " our quondam queen," and tells her that it is better for her to go home to her father than trouble France. Infuriated at Warwick's words, Margaret tells him to hold his tongue, and hotly reproaches him as being a " Proud setter up and puller down of kings ! " refuses to depart until with " talk and tears, Both full of truth," she has convinced Lewis that Edward's love is false, for both Edward and Warwick are " birds of self-same feather " :

> Peace, impudent and shameless Warwick, peace,
> Proud setter up and puller down of kings !
> I will not hence, till, with my talk and tears,
> Both full of truth, I make King Lewis behold
> Thy sly conveyance and thy lord's false love ;
> For both of you are birds of self-same feather.

At this point, a horn is sounded within, and Lewis remarks : " Warwick, this is some post to us or thee." Entering, the Post hands letters to Warwick, to the king, and to Margaret :

> My lord ambassador, these letters are for you,
> Sent from your brother, Marquess Montague :
> These from our king unto your majesty ;
> And, madam, these for you ; from whom I know not.

As they read their letters—which announce the marriage of Edward to Lady Grey—they are closely observed by Oxford and Prince Edward, and as Margaret smiles and Warwick frowns, and Lewis stamps his foot, Oxford remarks :

> I like it well that our fair queen and mistress
> Smiles at her news, while Warwick frowns at his,

to which the Prince adds :

> Nay, mark how Lewis stamps as he were nettled :
> I hope all 's for the best.

" Warwick, what are thy news ? and yours, fair queen ? " enquires Lewis, and Margaret replies " Mine, such as fill my heart with unhoped joys," and " Mine," adds Warwick, " full of sorrow and heart's discontent." " What ! has your king married the Lady Grey ? " asks Lewis, and now to " soothe your forgery and his, Sends me a paper to persuade me patience ? Is this the alliance that he seeks with France ? Dare he presume to scorn us in this manner ? " and Margaret, who is overjoyed at the news ejaculates " I told your majesty as much before : This proveth Edward's love and Warwick's honesty." Warwick, who is indignant at Edward's prefidy forthwith proclaims that he will renounce allegiance to York, and support Henry. Turning to Margaret, Warwick begs her to " let former grudges pass," and he will be her " true servitor " promising to do his best to restore Henry to the throne, and Margaret accepts his offer :

> Warwick, these words have turn'd my hate to love ;
> And I forgive and quite forget old faults,
> And joy that thou becom'st King Henry's friend.

Warwick then requests Lewis to furnish him with " some few bands of chosen soldiers " which he undertakes to land in England, and urged on by Lady Bona who is out for revenge, Lewis announces that he has firmly resolved to accede to Warwick's request. Lewis then commands the messenger to return to England and inform Edward that " Lewis of France is sending over masquers To revel it with him and his new bride " :

> Then, England's messenger, return in post,
> And tell false Edward, thy supposed king,
> That Lewis of France is sending over masquers
> To revel it with him and his new bride.
> Thou seest what 's past ; go fear thy king withal.

" Tell him," exclaims Lady Bona, " in hope he 'll prove a widower shortly, I 'll wear the willow garland for his sake." " Tell him," announces Margaret, " my mourning weeds are laid aside, And I am ready to put armour on." " Tell him from me," adds Warwick, " that he hath done me wrong, And therefore I 'll uncrown him ere 't be long," and rewarding the messenger bids him to " be gone."

Preparations are at once made for Warwick and Oxford to cross over to England with five thousand men, to be followed by a fresh supply under Margaret and Prince Edward. Warwick then suggests, that if Margaret and the Prince are agreeable, the young Prince marry his eldest daughter, a suggestion in which Margaret concurs. Telling her son that the lady is " fair and virtuous " she bids him to " give thy hand to Warwick " in token of " good faith," and Edward exclaims :

> Yes, I accept her, for she well deserves it ;
> And here, to pledge my vow, I give my hand.

Lewis then give orders for soldiers to be levied and conveyed to England by " Lord Bourbon, our high admiral," hoping shortly to hear that Edward has been dethroned for proposing a " mocking marriage with a dame of France."

All leave, with the exception of Warwick, who soliloquises over the sudden change of events, for although he came to France as " Edward's ambassador " he " returns his sworn and mortal foe " ; " Matter of marriage was the charge he gave me, But dreadful war shall answer his demand," not " that I pity Henry's misery, but to seek revenge on Edward's mockery."

We are again in the Palace in London at the opening of the Fourth Act. Gloucester, Clarence, Somerset and Montague enter. Addressing his brother, Gloucester asks his opinion of Edward's marriage with Lady Grey, and Clarence replies that it would have only been an act of courtesy to have awaited the return of Warwick from France, adding, that he intended to speak plainly his mind on the matter. There is a flourish and Edward, the queen and courtiers appear. Being asked by Edward " how like you our choice," Clarence, who is very pensive, replies :

> As well as Lewis of France, or the Earl of Warwick,
> Which are so weak of courage and in judgment
> That they 'll take no offence at our abuse.

But suppose they do take offence, retorts Edward.

> They are but Lewis and Warwick : I am Edward,
> Your king and Warwick's, and must have my will.

Turning to Gloucester, Edward asks whether he is opposed to the match :

> Yea, brother Richard, are you offended too ?

and Gloucester scornfully replies " Not I " :

> God forbid that I should wish them severed
> Whom God hath join'd together ; ay, and 'twere pity
> To sunder them that yoke so well together.

Telling them to set aside their scorns and their mislikes, Edward requests his brothers, as well as Somerset and Montague, to speak freely what they think about the matter :

> Setting your scorns and your mislike aside,
> Tell me some reason why the Lady Grey
> Should not become my wife and England's queen.
> And you too, Somerset and Montague,
> Speak freely what you think.

To this Clarence affirms that Lewis has become Edward's enemy for " mocking him about the marriage of the Lady Bona " ; Gloucester reminds him that he has dishonoured Warwick whom he sent to France to ask for the hand of the French princess ; Montague is of opinion that an alliance with France would have strengthened them against " foreign storms " ; while Hastings,—who does not favour the idea of an alliance with France—considers it is better to " using France than trusting France " adding that they should put their trust in God, for their safety depends upon the seas, which He hath given as a protection to the country, to which Clarence retorts that for this speech Hastings deserves " To have the heir of the Lord Hungerford."

Edward has however made himself unpopular by the honours he has showered on his new wife's family. Gloucester tells him he has not done right in giving the " heir and daughter of Lord Scales " to his wife's brother, as she would have been more suitable for himself or Clarence, but as he is so absorbed in his new wife he has forgotten his brothers. Clarence considers that Gloucester is quite right, otherwise Edward would not have given Lord Bonville's heir to his wife's son, and leave both him and Gloucester to look elsewhere. Edward observes that Clarence is dissatisfied because he has not provided him with a wife, and promises to rectify the omission :

> Alas ! poor Clarence, is it for a wife
> That thou art malcontent ? I will provide thee.

but Clarence expresses a wish to choose for himself in like manner as his brother has done :

> In choosing for yourself you show'd your judgment,
> Which being shallow, you shall give me leave
> To play the broker in mine own behalf ;

and with this end in view he intends to desert him.

Addressing the nobles the queen reminds them that she is not " ignoble of descent " and although her new title honours her and her family, their " dislikes . . . Doth cloud my joys with danger and with sorrow," but Edward requests her to give no heed to their displeasure, for unless they show respect to her, and obey, as they must obey, their sovereign, " they shall feel the vengeance of my wrath " to which Gloucester [aside] mutters " I hear, yet say not much, but think the more."

At this point a Post enters. Asked by Edward " what letters or what news from France," the post replies " no letters ; and few words " which he dare not relate " without your special pardon." Pardon having been granted the post delivers by word of mouth the messages of Lewis, Lady Bona, Margaret and Warwick. Edward considers Lewis very brave to send him such a message ; Lady Bona he blames not since she has been wronged ; and Margaret he belikes to an Amazon ; but when he is told that Warwick threatens to " uncrown him " Edward breaks out in fury :

> Ha ! durst the traitor breathe out so proud words ?
> Well, I will arm me, being thus forewarn'd :
> They shall have wars, and pay for their presumption.

" Is Warwick friends with Margaret ? " asks Edward, and the post answer is that " they are so link'd in friendship " that Prince Edward is to marry Warwick's eldest daughter. Hearing this Clarence declares he will marry Warwick's youngest daughter, and bidding Edward " farewell," tells him to " sit you fast " for although he himself does not possess a kingdom he will not be inferior to Edward in point of marriage and inviting those who " love him " to follow, leaves the room closely followed by Somerset. Clarence having gone, Gloucester [aside] mutters that as his " thoughts aim at a further matter " he will stay " not for the love of Edward, but the crown."

Edward then orders Pembroke and Stafford to collect together an army to oppose Warwick, and turning to Lords Hastings and Montague—who are by blood related to Warwick—Edward, who prefers " foes than hollow friends " asks whether they intend to remain loyal to him or join with Warwick, and as these two noblemen— as well as Gloucester—gives assurances of their loyalty and fidelity, Edward exclaims :

> then am I sure of victory.
> Now therefore let us hence ; and lose no hour
> Till we meet Warwick with his foreign power.

The next scene shows us a Plain in Warwickshire. Warwick and Oxford with French soldiers enter. Warwick is telling Oxford that numbers of the common people have already flocked to join them, just as Clarence and Somerset appear, and Warwick remarks : " But see where Somerset and Clarence comes ! and demands them to " Speak suddenly, my lords, are we all friends ? " Being assured by Clarence that they have come to join him, Warwick bids them welcome, and after promising to give his daughter in marriage to Clarence, Warwick suggests, that as Edward is only attended by a simple guard, they surprise him in his camp and take him prisoner. Warwick asks those who approve of this action being taken to " Applaud the name of Henry with your leader," and as all present cry " Henry " Warwick remarks :

> Why, then, let 's on our way in silent sort.
> For Warwick and his friends, God and Saint George !

Edward's camp near Warwick supplies the next scene. Three watchmen, who guard the king's tent, enter and hold a conversation. One of them asks why Edward does not go to bed, to which the other one answers that he has " made a solemn vow Never to lie or take his natural rest Till Warwick or himself be quite suppress'd." The third watchman is commenting on the " dangerous honour " of guarding the king, for if only Warwick knew how they were situated he would attack them, just as Warwick, Clarence, Oxford and Somerset with forces appear on the scene :

> This is his tent ; and see where stand his guard.
> Courage, my masters ! honour now or never !
> But follow me, and Edward shall be ours.

remarks Warwick. They are challenged by the watch. " Who goes there ? " demands the first watchman. " Stay, or thou diest," adds the second watchman, and Warwick and his followers cry out " Warwick ! Warwick ! " and set upon the guard who fly, crying " Arm ! Arm ! "

A trumpet sounds, and Warwick and Somerset re-enter, bringing Edward out in his gown sitting in a chair. Gloucester and Hastings seek refuge in flight. Being asked by Somerset " What are they that fly there ? " Warwick replies " Richard and Hastings : let them go ; here is the duke." " The duke ! " exclaims Edward, " Why, Warwick, when we parted Thou call'dst me king ! " to which Warwick replies : " Ay, but the case is alter'd : When you disgraced me in my embassade, Then I degraded you from being king, And come now to create you Duke of York," for as you do not know how to treat your ambassadors you are not fit to govern the kingdom. Seeing Clarence with Warwick, Edward reproaches him for his disloyalty, and Warwick, taking the crown off the head of Edward declares that " Henry now shall wear it And be true king indeed." Warwick then charges Somerset to convey Edward to the safe keeping of his brother—the Archbishop of York—promising to follow, after he had fought with Pembroke. Edward is then lead away forcibly by guards, and Oxford suggests that they proceed forthwith to London, to which Warwick agrees

> To free King Henry from imprisonment,
> And see him seated in the regal throne.

We are at the Palace in London in the next scene. Lord Rivers—brother to the queen—enters and inquires why her majesty is so sad, and the queen tells him that Edward, " Either betray'd by falsehood of his guard, Or by his foe surprised at unawares" has been taken prisoner and committed to the custody of the Archbishop of York. Exclaiming that the news is very distressing, he counsels Elizabeth to bear her misfortune with patience, for Warwick who has won the day may yet be defeated. He then enquires as to the whereabouts of Warwick, and the queen replies that he " comes towards London " to liberate Henry from the tower and again place him on the throne, and fearing violence at his hands she will " forthwith unto the sanctuary "

> There shall I rest secure from force and fraud.
> Come, therefore ; let us fly while we may fly :
> If Warwick take us we are sure to die.

The next scene is enacted in a park near Middleham Castle in Yorkshire. It opens with Gloucester remarking to Lords Hastings and Stanley that the reason he has brought them hither is to assist him in rescuing Edward who is a prisoner in the hands of the archbishop. Edward, who is well treated at the hands of his custodian, is allowed to go out hunting, and Gloucester has by secret means, made arrangements to free him from his captivity. Just then Edward, accompanied by a Huntsman, appears.   He is immediately surrounded by Gloucester, Hastings and the rest, who charge him to make haste for a horse stands ready near by to convey him to Lynn and thence by ship to Flanders.   " Huntsman, what say'st thou ? wilt thou go along ? " asks Edward, and the Huntsman replies " Better do so than tarry and be hang'd " and they forthwith gallop away, Edward remarking as they do so

> Bishop, farewell : shield thee from Warwick's frown,
> And pray that I may repossess the crown.

The Tower of London supplies the next scene.   It opens with Henry enquiring of the Lieutenant—that as God has " turn'd my captive state to liberty—what are the fees due to him.   Turning to Warwick, whom he declares to have been the instrument of God in procuring his liberty, Henry bids him to assume the reins of Government :

> But, Warwick, after God, thou sett'st me free,
> And chiefly therefore I thank God and thee ;
> He was the author, thou the instrument.
>
> .   .   .   .
> Warwick, although my head still wear the crown,
> I here resign my government to thee,
> For thou art fortunate in all thy deeds.

To this Warwick replies that Clarence is more suitable, and has better claim to the protectorship than himself.   On the other hand Clarence considers Warwick more " worthy of the sway " and forthwith Henry commands them both to join their hands and proclaims them joint protectors, announcing that he intends in the future to

> lead a private life,
> And in devotion spend my latter days,
> To sin's rebuke and my Creator's praise.

After Edward has been proclaimed a traitor and all his lands and goods confiscated, Clarence asks that the succession to the crown be settled, and Henry answers that before that is settled the queen and his son be sent for from France with all speed, for until they come hence " My joy of liberty is half eclips'd."   Henry then enquires of Somerset whom the youth is in which he is so much interested and Somerset replies it is " Henry Earl of Richmond."   Declaring he is " England's hope " Henry lays his hand on his head for if the truth is suggested by divination

> This pretty lad will prove our country's bliss.
> His looks are full of peaceful majesty,
> His head by nature fram'd to wear a crown,
> His hand to wield a sceptre, and himself
> Likely in time to bless a regal throne.

At this point a Post enters, with the news that Edward has escaped from the custody of the Archbishop of York—and has fled to Burgundy, and Warwick declares that preparations must be made at once to meet any and every emergency which may arise.

All gone with the exception of Somerset, Richmond, and Oxford, Somerset remarks that the escape of Edward predicts the renewal of the civil strife ere long, at the same time " Henry's late presaging prophecy with hope of this young Richmond did glad his heart," and therefore he has decided to send Richmond to Brittany

> **Till storms be past of civil enmity,**

to which Oxford agrees, for if

> Edward repossess the crown,
> 'Tis like that Richmond with the rest shall down.

We are before York in the next scene. Edward, with Gloucester and Hastings, having collected together an army in Burgundy, land at Ravensburgh and march to York. Finding the gates shut against him, Edward declares that he will enter the city by " fair or foul means," and bids Hastings summon the city to surrender. A parley is sounded and the Mayor and his brethren appear on the walls, and inform Edward that having been apprised of his coming the gates have been closed for safety as the city now owes allegiance to Henry. To this Edward replies that he seeks admission as " Duke of York "

> Why, and I challenge nothing but my dukedom,
> As being well content with that alone.

to which Gloucester [aside] mutters :

> But when the fox hath once got in his nose,
> He 'll soon find means to make the body follow.

Hastings then asks the Mayor " why stand you in a doubt ? " and requests him to open the gates as they are King Henry's friends. Having disarmed all suspicion, the Mayor gives orders for Edward to be admitted, and as he descends from the walls, Gloucester remarks :

> A wise stout captain, and soon persuaded !

to which Hastings adds :

> The good old man would fain that all were well,
> So, 'twere not long of him ; but being enter'd,
> I doubt not, I, but we shall soon persuade
> Both him and all his brothers unto reason.

The gates having been opened Edward orders that they must not again be shut except at night or in time of war, and demanding from the Mayor the keys of the city announces that he will

> defend the town and thee,
> And all those friends that deign to follow me.

At this point, Montgomery with forces appear. Being asked why he comes in arms, Montgomery replies to help Edward to regain the crown. Edward thanks " good Montgomery " and informs him that at the moment he only claims the dukedom, and Montgomery bids him farewell, as he came to serve a king and not a duke. Montgomery gives orders for the " Drummer to strike up, and let us march away," Edward bids him stay awhile and they will debate the matter, but Montgomery replies " What, talk you of debating ! " and reiterates his intention of leaving Edward to his fortune unless he proclaims himself king. Declaring that the crown is his by right, Edward is won over, and a proclamation, proclaiming him king of England and France, and lord of Ireland, etc., is made, while Montgomery throws down his gauntlet, challenging anyone who disputes it to single fight, to which all present shout " Long live Edward the Fourth ! " Edward thanks " brave Montgomery," promising that if fortune attends him, he will repay him for his kindness. He then announces his intention of spending the night in York, and on the morrow will march to meet " Warwick and his mates " and " froward Clarence," for as Henry is no soldier he has no doubt of victory, and turning to his followers proclaims :

> Come on, brave soldiers : doubt not of the day :
> And, that once gotten, doubt not of large pay.

We are again transferred to the Palace in London. The Scene opens with Warwick announcing that Edward has landed in England and is marching on London with a large army :

> What counsel, lords ? Edward from Belgia,
> With hasty Germans and blunt Hollanders,
> Hath pass'd in safety through the narrow seas,
> And with his troops doth march amain to London ;
> And many giddy people flock to him.

To this Henry replies that men had better be levied to give him battle, while Clarence is of opinion that " A little fire is quickly trodden out, Which, being suffer'd, rivers cannot quench." Warwick announces that he has many true-hearted friends in Warwickshire whom he will muster, and bids Clarence to " stir up in Suffolk, Norfolk and in Kent, The knights and gentlemen to come with thee " ; Montague to collect forces in Buckingham, Northampton, and in Leicestershire ; Oxford to gather together his friends in Oxfordshire, while Henry shall rest in London until they return.

Warwick then bids farewell to the nobles and to the king : " Fair lords, take leave, and stand not to reply. Farewell, my sovereign," to which Henry replies : " Farewell, my Hector, and my Troy's true hope." Clarence kisses the king's hand " In sign of truth," Montague bids him to be comforted, while Oxford " Seals his truth and bids adieu," and Henry remarks :

> Sweet Oxford, and my loving Montague,
> And all at once, once more a happy farewell.

All gone, with the exception of the king and Exeter, Henry tells Exeter that he is of opinion that Edward's forces will not be able to encounter the army sent against him, but Exeter replies that Edward may be fortunate to seduce the royal troops from their allegiance, an opinion which Henry does not share.

While they are conversing, there is a shout within : " A Lancaster ! A Lancaster ! " " Hark, hark, my lord ! what shouts are these ? " exclaims Exeter, and forthwith Edward, Gloucester and soldiers burst into the palace. Giving his soldiers orders to seize Henry, Edward orders him to be sent to the Tower, and himself again proclaimed king :

> Seize on the shame-faced Henry ! bear him hence,
> And once again proclaim us King of England.
>
> Hence with him to the Tower ! let him not speak.

He then bids the main body of his army to march to Coventry to give battle to " peremptory Warwick " for

> The sun shines hot ; and, if we use delay,
> Cold biting winter mars our hop'd for hay,

to which Gloucester adds :

> Away betimes, before his forces join,
> And take the great-grown traitor unawares :
> Brave warriors, march amain towards Coventry.

The Fifth Act opens in Coventry. Warwick, the Mayor of Coventry and two messengers appear on the walls. In reply to Warwick's enquiries as to the whereabouts of Oxford and Montague, the messengers inform him that the former is at

Dunsmore and the latter at Daintry, both marching forward with puissant forces. Sir John Somerville appears and tells Warwick that he left Clarence—whom he expects in about two hours' time—at Southam. A drum is heard and Warwick remarks that Clarence must be at hand, but Somerville points out that the sound proceeds from the direction of Warwick as Southam lies in the opposite direction. "Who should that be? belike, unlook'd-for friends," remarks Warwick just as Edward, Gloucester and forces appear. Edward orders a parley to be sounded and Warwick appearing on the walls is summoned to surrender, and acknowledge Edward as king:

> Now, Warwick, wilt thou ope the city gates,
> Speak gentle words, and humbly bend thy knee,
> Call Edward king, and at his hands beg mercy?
> And he shall pardon thee these outrages.

Warwick refuses to surrender, and reminds Edward that he gave him the kingdom, and as he has now dethroned him he has sworn allegiance to Henry. "But Warwick's king is Edward's prisoner," rejoins Edward, and again calls upon Warwick to acknowledge him as king:

> Come, Warwick, take the time; kneel down, kneel down.
> Nay, when? strike now, or else the iron cools.

but Warwick replies that he would rather chop off his hand than submit:

> I had rather chop this hand off at a blow,
> And with the other fling it at thy face,
> Than bear so low a sail, to strike to thee.

and Edward, furious at Warwick's reply, declares he will have his head:

> Sail how thou canst, have wind and tide thy friend,
> This hand, fast wound about thy coal-black hair,
> Shall, whiles thy head is warm and new cut off,
> Write in the dust this sentence with thy blood;
> "Wind-changing Warwick now can change no more."

Oxford with forces now arrives and announcing "Oxford, Oxford, for Lancaster!" is admitted into the city. The gates being opened, Gloucester suggests that they enter too, but Edward considers it more prudent to wait until their foes issue forth and give battle. Montague with forces now appears, and calling out "Montague, Montague, for Lancaster!" he and his troops enter through the gates. As Montague passes through the gates, Gloucester tells him that both "he and his brother— Warwick—shall buy this treason with their dearest blood." Somerset, with forces, now arrives and declaring "Somerset, Somerset, for Lancaster!", Warwick orders him to be admitted into the city. As he passes through Gloucester retorts:

> Two of thy name, both Dukes of Somerset,
> Have sold their lives unto the house of York;
> And thou shalt be the third, if this sword hold.

Immediately Clarence with forces appears on the scene, and Warwick invites him to enter the city and join forces:

> And lo, where George of Clarence sweeps along,
> Of force enough to bid his brother battle;
> With whom an upright zeal to right prevails
> More than the nature of a brother's love!
> Come, Clarence, come; thou wilt, if Warwick call.

Plucking the red rose out of his hat, Clarence tells Warwick that he will not "ruinate my father's house, Who gave his blood to lime the stones together, And set up

Lancaster." Declaring his sorrow for " my trespass made " he, in order to " deserve well at my brother's hands," proclaims himself Warwick's mortal foe, and turning to Edward asks for pardon :

> Pardon me, Edward, I will make amends :
> And Richard, do not frown upon my faults,
> For I will henceforth be no more unconstant.

He is welcomed back by Edward :

> Now, welcome more, and ten times more beloved,
> Than if thou never hadst deserved our hate.

to which Gloucester adds :

> Welcome, good Clarence ; this is brother-like.

Edward then enquires of Warwick whether he will leave the town and fight, and Warwick replies that he intends presently to march to Barnet, where, if Edward dare, he will give him battle, and accepting Warwick's offer, Edward forthwith marches away with his forces, followed by Warwick :

> *K.Edw.* What, Warwick, wilt thou leave the town, and fight ?
> Or shall we beat the stones about thine ears ?
> *War.* Alas, I am not coop'd here for defence !
> I will away towards Barnet presently,
> And bid thee battle, Edward, if thou darest.
> *K. Edw.* Yes, Warwick, Edward dares, and leads the way.
> Lords to the field : Saint George and victory !

Scene two shows us a Field of Battle near Barnet. There are alarums and excursions, during which Edward appears with Warwick, who is mortally wounded. Bidding him to " lie thou there : die thou, and die our fear," Edward hurries away in search of Montague so " That Warwick's bones may keep thine company." Having gone Warwick, who realises that his death is near, asks to be told who is victor, " York or Warwick." As he lies unable to move, he soliloquises on the exalted position he has held in the realm :

> For who liv'd king but I could dig his grave ?
> And who durst smile when Warwick bent his brow ?

with his present utter helplessness :

> Lo ! now my glory smear'd in dust and blood ;
> My parks, my walks, my manors that I had,
> Even now forsake me ; and of all my lands
> Is nothing left me but my body's length.
> Why, what is pomp, rule, reign, but earth and dust ?
> And, live we how we can, yet die we must.

Oxford and Somerset now enter, and the latter tells Warwick that if he were as they are they would recover that which they have lost, for the news has just been received that Margaret has landed in England from France with a puissant power. But Warwick, who is at the point of death, calls for his brother Montague :

> Ah ! Montague,
> If thou be there, sweet brother, take my hand,
> And with thy lips keep in my soul a while.
> Thou lov'st me not ; for, brother, if thou didst,
> Thy tears would wash this cold congealed blood
> That glues my lips and will not let me speak.
> Come quickly, Montague, or I am dead.

but Somerset could only make answer that Montague had already " breath'd his last " but before passing away had asked him to " Commend me to my valiant brother,"

> Ah, Warwick ! Montague hath breath'd his last ;
> And to the latest gasp cried out for Warwick,
> And said, " Commend me to my valiant brother."
> And more he would have said ; and more he spoke,
> Which sounded like a cannon in a vault,
> That mought not be distinguish'd ; but at last
> I well might hear, deliver'd with a groan,
> " O, farewell, Warwick ! "

Hearing this Warwick mutters " Sweet rest his soul " and then bidding farewell to Lords Oxford and Somerset promising to meet them in heaven, he counsels them to seek safety in flight :

> Fly, lords, and save yourselves ;
> For Warwick bids you all farewell, to meet in heaven.

" Away, away, to meet the queen's great power ! " exclaims Oxford, and bearing away the body of Warwick they hastily depart to join forces with Margaret who is on her way to Tewkesbury.

We are in another part of the battlefield in Scene three. A trumpet sounds, and Edward in triumph enters. Addressing his brothers he tells them that although they are " graced with wreaths of victory," there is " in the midst of this bright-shining day, a black, suspicious, threatening cloud " for Margaret with a large army has landed on the south coast. Clarence opines that they will soon defeat her, while Gloucester reminds them that Margaret's army, which numbers thirty thousand strong, has been reinforced by the forces under Somerset and Oxford, in consequence of which her army will be as strong as their own. News having been received that Margaret is marching towards Tewkesbury, Edward give orders for his army to proceed forthwith

> And, as we march, our strength will be augmented
> In every county as we go along.
> Strike up the drum ! cry " Courage ! " and away.

The Plains near Tewkesbury supply the next scene. It opens with Margaret, who has heard of the defeat and death of Warwick at the battle of Barnet. reminding the nobles that

> wise men ne'er sit and wail their loss,
> But cheerly seek how to redress their harms.

In a spirited speech in which she reviews the position she inspires confidence and hope in her followers. Pointing out that although " Warwick was our anchor " and " Montague our topmast " they have still in " Oxford another anchor " and in " Somerset another goodly mast " and exhorts them to courage for " what cannot be avoided 'Twere childish weakness to lament or fear." Being carried away by her intrepid speech they all promise to do their utmost to achieve victory. A moment later a messenger enters with the news that Edward with forces is at hand ready to give battle. Amid a flourish of trumpets Edward appears and addressing his army tells them that the " thorny wood " which " yonder stands Must by the roots be hewn up yet ere night." With tears in her eyes Margaret exclaims that she can scarcely speak, for

> Henry, your sovereign,
> Is prisoner to the foe ; his state usurp'd,
> His realm a slaughter-house, his subjects slain,
> His statutes cancell'd, and his treasure spent ;
> And yonder is the wolf that makes this spoil,

and exhorting them in God's name to " Be valiant " gives the signal for the battle to commence.

Scene five shows us another part of the battlefield. The battle is over and the Yorkists have proved victorious. Edward, Clarence, Gloucester and soldiers enter, bearing with them Margaret, Oxford and Somerset who have been taken prisoners. Edward orders Oxford to be imprisoned in Hames Castle and Somerset to be beheaded. As they are led away, Margaret exclaims :

> So part we sadly in this troublous world,
> To meet with joy in sweet Jerusalem.

Edward then issues a proclamation offering a high reward for the capture of Prince Edward. At this point the prince is brought hither by soldiers and Edward demands to know why he has taken up arms against him :

> Bring forth the gallant : let me hear him speak.
> What ! can so young a thorn begin to prick ?
> Edward, what satisfaction canst thou make
> For bearing arms, for stirring up my subjects,
> And all the trouble thou hast turn'd me to ?

to which the gallant youth replies :

> Speak like a subject, proud ambitious York.
> Suppose that I am now my father's mouth :
> Resign thy chair, and where I stand kneel thou,
> Whilst I propose the self-same words to thee,
> Which, traitor, thou would'st have me answer to.

" Ah, that thy father had been so resolv'd ! " ejaculates Margaret, and Gloucester retorts that if that had been so she would have worn the petticoats and not stolen her husband's breeches. But the young prince who is very scornful exclaims :

> Let Æsop fable in a winter's night ;
> His currish riddles sort not with this place,

and Gloucester tells him that he will " plague ye for that word " while Margaret reminds Gloucester that he was " born to be a plague of men." " Take away this captive scold," demands Gloucester, and the young prince sarcastically rejoins " Nay, take away this scolding crook-back rather " and Edward bids him to be quiet or "I will charm your tongue," while Clarence calls him " Untutor'd lad, thou art too malapert." But the youth tells them he knows his duty, and bitterly denounces the Yorkists as traitors :

> I know my duty ; you are all undutiful.
> Lascivious Edward, and thou perjured George,
> And thou misshapen Dick, I tell ye all
> I am your better, traitors as ye are ;
> And thou usurp'st my father's right and mine.

Incensed at the youth's defiance, Edward draws his dagger and plunging it in the boy's breast remarking as he does so : " Take that, the likeness of this railer here." " Sprawl'st thou ? " sneers Gloucester, " take that, to end thy agony," " And that," adds Clarence, " for twitting me with perjury." Margaret implores them to kill her

too. Gloucester was ready, but Edward bids him hold his hand " for we have done
too much." Sickened at the sight, Margaret faints, and as Edward gives orders
" to use means for her recovery," Gloucester, turning to Clarence, bids him to excuse
him to the king his brother, for he must " hence to London on a serious matter," and
whispering to Clarence " The Tower ! the Tower ! " hurriedly takes his departure.
Recovering her senses, Margaret, bending over the body of her son, implores him to
speak, and denouncing Edward, Clarence and Gloucester as "Butchers and villains !
bloody cannibals !" calls down the vengeance of heaven upon them for having spent
their fury on a child. Edward orders her to be forcibly removed, and Margaret in
agony appeals first to Edward and afterwards to Clarence to kill her. Her appeal
being fruitless she inquires for Gloucester knowing that he would not hesitate to
commit the deed :

> Where is that devil's butcher,
> Hard-favour'd Richard ?   Richard, where art thou ?
> Thou art not here : murder is thy alms-deed ;
> Petitioners for blood thou ne'er put'st back,

but Edward orders the soldiers to take her away.
    Turning to Clarence, Edward enquires "Where 's Richard gone ? " and on being
told that he has gone to London " To make a bloody supper in the Tower," Edward
cynically comments "He 's sudden if a thing comes in his head," and giving orders
for the soldiers to be discharged " with pay and thanks " forthwith proceeds to
London to

> see our gentle queen how well she fares :
> By this, I hope, she hath a son for me.

The Tower of London supplies the next scene, where we find Henry sitting reading
a book, with the Lieutenant in attendance. With a sneering smile Gloucester enters
and on his face the hapless Henry read his doom. The Lieutenant having been
dismissed by Gloucester, Henry remarks :

> So flies the reckless shepherd from the wolf ;
> So first the harmless sheep doth yield his fleece,
> And next his throat unto the butcher's knife.
> What scene of death hath Roscius now to act ?

" Suspicion always haunts the guilty mind ; The thief doth fear each bush an officer,"
retorts Gloucester and Henry replies that the bird which has once been entangled is
suspicious of every bush, and entreats Gloucester to kill him with his sword and not
with words, for his breast is more fit for the dagger's point than his ears are for tragic
history. " Is 't for my life ? " that brings thee hither, enquires Henry, and Gloucester
answers " Think'st thou I am an executioner ? "   " A persecutor, I am sure, thou
art," retorts Henry, and " If murdering innocents be executing, Why, then thou art
an executioner."   " Thy son I kill'd for his presumption," sneers Gloucester, and
Henry enjoins that if he had been killed when first he did presume he would never
have lived to kill his son, and goes on to prophecy that old men and widows, and
orphans with tears in their eyes will curse the day when he was born :

> And thus I prophesy : that many a thousand,
> Which now mistrust no parcel of my fear
> And many an old man's sigh, and many a widow's,
> And many an orphan's water-standing eye,
> Men for their sons', wives for their husbands',
> And orphans for their parents' timeless death,
> Shall rue the hour that ever thou wast born.
> The owl shriek'd at thy birth, an evil sign ;
> The night-crow cried, aboding luckless time,

> Dogs howl'd, and hideous tempest shook down trees ;
> The raven rook'd her on the chimney's top
> And chattering pies in dismal discords sung.
>
> . . . .
>
> Teeth hadst thou in thy head when thou wast born,
> To signify thou camest to bite the world :
> And, if the rest be true which I have heard,
> Thou camest—

"I 'll hear no more," snarls Gloucester as he drew back a space, and drawing his sword plunges it in the heart of Henry, sneering out " die, prophet, in thy speech " : " Ay, and for much more slaughter after this," gasps Henry, and falling to the ground in a dying condition implores the forgiveness of God for his sins, and pardon for his murderer. Bending over the lifeless body of Henry, Gloucester remarks :

> What ! will the aspiring blood of Lancaster
> Sink in the ground ? I thought it would have mounted.

and as he watches the blood drip from his dagger, expresses the wish that " such purple tears be always shed From those that wish the downfall of our house ! " Mad with lust of blood, and determined that no " spark of life " shall remain, Gloucester again thrusts his sword into Henry's body, growling as he does so " Down, down to hell ; and say I sent thee thither."

Soliloquising over the scene Gloucester admits he is devoid of " pity, love and fear " for as he came into the world with a crooked body, he implores hell to make crooked his mind to fashion it. Muttering to himself " I have no brother, I am like no brother : . . . I am myself alone " ; he threatens to be " Edward's death " and counsels Clarence to beware, for now that Henry and his son are out of his way there remains only Clarence and Edward to stand between him and the throne.

The final scene of the Play is enacted at the Palace in London. Amid a flourish of trumpets, Edward, the queen, with Clarence, Gloucester and Hastings, enter, followed by a nurse with the young prince. Taking his seat upon the throne Edward announces that once more he occupies " England's royal throne," which he has "Re-purchas'd with the blood of enemies," and recounts with pride that they have :

> mow'd down in tops of all their pride !
> Three Dukes of Somerset, threefold renown'd
> For hardy and undoubted champions ;
> Two Cliffords, as the father and the son ;
> And two Northumberlands : two braver men
> Ne'er spurr'd their coursers at the trumpet's sound ;
> With them, the two brave bears, Warwick and Montague,
> That in their chains fetter'd the kingly lion,
> And made the forest tremble when they roar'd.

and now they have made their footstool secure they will reap the labours of their gain ; and Gloucester [aside] mutters :

> I 'll blast his harvest, if your head were laid ;
> For yet I am not look'd on in the world.
> This shoulder was ordain'd so thick to heave ;
> And heave it shall some weight, or break my back.
> Work thou the way, and thou shalt execute.

Having kissed his infant son, Edward bids both his brothers to love his wife and kiss their nephew :

> Clarence and Gloucester, love my lovely queen
> And kiss your princely nephew, brothers both.

" The duty that I owe unto your majesty I seal upon the lips of this sweet babe,"
exclaims Clarence, and the queen replies " Thanks, noble Clarence ; worthy brother,
thanks." " And, that I love the tree from whence thou sprang'st, Witness the
loving kiss I give the fruit," exclaims Gloucester as he presses his lips to the child's
forehead, and then turning aside with a cruel smile upon his face, mutters with
deadly meaning :

> To say the truth, so Judas kiss'd his master,
> And cried " all hail ! " when as he meant all harm.

We shall meet this child again in *Richard III*, for it is none other than the little
Edward the Fifth who—along with his brother—was, by orders of his uncle Richard,
Duke of Gloucester, afterwards Richard the Third—murdered in the Tower, one of
those many crimes which blot the pages of English History.

Clarence then enquires what Edward " will have done with Margaret," as her
father " Hath pawn'd the Sicils and Jerusalem " to the King of France, and has sent
the money for her ransom, and Edward orders her to be sent back to France : " Away
with her, and waft her hence to France," and the play concludes with Edward
announcing that in future he intends to turn his thoughts to

> stately triumphs, mirthful comic shows,
> Such as befits the pleasure of the court

and bidding the drums and trumpets sound, bids farewell to " sour annoy "

> For here I hope, begins our lasting joy.

Scene :   During part of the Third Act, in France ; during the rest of the Play, in
England.

CHARACTERS, PLACE-NAMES, ETC.

Æsop. V. v. 25.

> Let Æsop fable in a winter's night ;
> His currish riddles sort not with this place.
> [V. v. 25–26.]

An allusion to the Greek Fabulist who is said to have been humpbacked. Prince Edward here compares Richard—who was deformed—to Æsop.

Agamemnon. II. ii. 148.

> And ne'er was Agamemnon's brother wrong'd
> By that false woman as this king by thee.
> [II. ii. 148–149.]

Brother to Menelaus and commander-in-chief of the Greeks at the siege of Troy. He is one of the chief characters in *Troilus and Cressida* (q.v.)

Alarum. I. i. p.1 ; I. iii. p.1 ; I. iv. p.1 ; II. iii. p.1 ; II. v. p.1, p.54, p.125 ; II. vi. p.1, p.31 ; V. ii. p.1.

A summons to arms, as on the approach of an enemy.

Albion. III. iii. 49.

= England.

Albion's queen. III. iii. 7.

> I was, I must confess,
> Great Albion's queen in former golden days ;
> [III. iii. 6–7.]

= England's queen.

Aldermen. IV. vii. p.17, p.35.

Accompanying the Mayor of York.

Amazon. IV. i. 106.

> Belike she minds to play the Amazon. [IV. i. 106.]

A masculine woman, applied here to Margaret by Edward.

Amazonian trull. I. iv. 114.

> How ill-beseeming is it in thy sex
> To triumph like an Amazonian trull,
> Upon their woes whom fortune captivates !
> [I. iv. 113–115.]

Amazon = In Greek mythology a race of female warriors noted for their bravery. *trull* = a strumpet ; a trollop.

Another part of the field [Barnet].

The Scene of Act V., Scene iii. The Yorkists having gained the victory, Edward in triumph enters and announces that Margaret has landed on the south coast with a large army, and orders his army to march forward towards Tewkesbury, where another battle awaits him. For descriptions of the Battle of Barnet see *exempli gratia* Grafton's *Chronicle* ; Hall's *Chronicle* ; Barrett's *Battles and Battlefields in England* ; Brooke's *Visits to Fields of Battle in England, of the fifteenth century* ; *Chronicles of the White Rose.* To commemorate this battle an Obelisk was erected in 1740 by Sir Jeremy Sambrook at the point where the road northward divides St. Albans and Hatfield, about a mile north from Barnet Church. This monument has since been removed, and now stands on what is considered to have been the actual spot where the conflict took place. The Obelisk, which is often called Hadley High Stone contains the following inscription :

> Here was
> fought the
> famous battle
> between Edward
> the 4th and the
> Earl of Warwick
> April the 14th
> anno
> 1471
> in which the earl
> was defeated
> and slain.

See also Field of battle near Barnet.

Another part of the field [Tewksbury].

The Scene of Act V., Scene v. This scene opens after the battle, in which the Yorkists have been the victors. Margaret, Oxford, and Somerset are brought in guarded by soldiers. [Oxford was not at Tewkesbury. After the battle of Barnet he escaped into Cornwall.

" Also the king found meanes to coom by John Erle of Oxford, who not long after the discomfyture receayved at Barnet fled into Cornewall, and both tooke and kept Saint Mychaels Mount, and sent him to a castle beyond Sea caulyd Hammes, where he was kept prysoner more than xii yeres after." *Polydore Vergil.*] A moment later Prince Edward is brought hither a prisoner, and is questioned by King Edward why he takes up arms against him. Edward answers with boldness and denounces the Yorkists as usurpers and traitors. Drawing his dagger, the king plunges it in the youth's breast, followed by Gloucester and Clarence. Margaret implores them to kill her too, to which Gloucester makes an attempt, but is restrained by Edward. [" It is quite clear," says Courtenay " that there nothing like *evidence* either of Prince Edward's smart reply to the king, or of his *assassination* by *any body* ; and that there is not even the report of one who lived near to the time, of the participation of either of the king's brothers in the assassination, if it occurred. There is little in reason for believing any part of the story, though there is not—as there seldom can be— any proof of the negative. I have already noticed the anachronisms of Shakespeare, dependant upon the *ages* of his heroes. His Richard calls the prince scornfully, *brat* ; the prince was just one year younger than Gloucester ; the one was then about nineteen, and the other eighteen years of age. The presence of Margaret, at her son's examination and death, is a dramatic incident ; as is Gloucester's attempt to murder her. She was taken, kept prisoner for five years, and then ransomed by Louis IX."] Cf. *Extract* 18 from Holinshed. Gloucester hurriedly takes his departure for London, and Margaret calls down the vengeance of heaven upon them for the murder of her son. Edward orders her removal, after which he discharges his army, and forthwith leaves for London.

The battle of Tewkesbury was fought on the 3rd of May, 1471. For descriptions of the battle see *exempli gratia* Grafton's *Chronicles ;* Hall's *Chronicle ;* Brooke's *Visits to Fields of Battle, of England, in the fifteenth century ;* Barrett's *Battles and Battlefields in England ; Descriptive particulars of the Battle of Tewkesbury and of all known local scenes and memorials of the battle, with comprehensive notes on The Wars of the* *Roses. Transactions of the Bristol and Gloucestershire Archæological Society*, Vols. xxvi, and xlvii.

See also Plains near Tewksbury.

Another part of the field [Towton].

The Scene of Act II., Scenes iv, v, and vi.

Act II., Scene iv. Richard challenges Clifford to fight, and as they encounter each other, Warwick appears on the scene and Clifford flees.

Act II., Scene v. Shows Henry alone, he having withdrawn from the fight on the advice of Margaret and Clifford. [Hart quotes from Polydore Vergil : " When at the last King Henry espied the forces of his foes increase . . . he with a few horsemen removing a little out of that place, expected the event of the fight, but beholde, suddenly his souldiers gave the backe, which when he sawe he fledd also."] As he sits on a mole-hill watching the ebb and flow of the battle he soliloquises on the scene which unfolds before his eyes. [Johnson remarks : " This speech is mournful and soft, exquisitely suited to the character of the king, and makes a pleasing interchange, by affording, amidst the tumult and horror of the battle, an unexpected glimpse of rural innocence and pastoral tranquillity."] The Yorkists having proved victorious, Margaret with the Prince and Clifford enters and advises the king to seek safety in flight.

Act II., Scene vi. Clifford, who has been mortally wounded, enters, and soliloquises over the scene. Owing to loss of blood he faints and passes away just as Edward and his forces appear. Orders are given for his head to be cut off and placed over the gates of York. [" Clifford, in his retreat, was beset with a party of Yorkists, when eyther for heat or payne, putting off his gorget, sodainly with an arrowe (as some say) without an hedde [he] was striken into the throte, and incontinent rendered his spirite, and the erle of Westmerlandes brother, and almost all his company were thare slayn, at a place called Dinting-dale, not farr fro Towton." *Ritson.*] Edward creates Richard Duke of Gloucester and George Duke of Clarence. Richard objects to his title as being unlucky, but Warwick describes it as foolish. [These two dukedoms were conferred after Edward had been crowned on the 29th of June, 1461, and not on the field of battle as represented in the play, while Richard's objection to the title of the Duke of Gloucester is suggested by Holinshed.]

This battle, in which the house of York was victorious, was fought on a plain between Towton and Saxton, on the 29th of March, (Palm Sunday), 1461. The royal army consisted of about forty thousand men ; and the young Duke of York's forces were 48,760. In this combat, which lasted fourteen hours, and in the actions of the two following days, 36,776 persons are said to have been killed ; the greater part of whom were undoubtedly Lancastrians.

The following is Hall's narrative of this battle, which decided the fate of the house of Lancaster, and placed Edward on the throne of England. " The same day, about ix. of the clocke, whiche was the xxix. day of Marche, beyng Palm sundaye, bothe the hostes approched in a playn felde, between Towton and Saxton. When eche parte perceyved other, thei made a great shoute, and at the same instante time, their fell a small snyt or snow, which by violence of the wynd was driven into the faces of them, which were of kyng Henries parte, so that their sight was somewhat blemeshed and minished. The lord Fawnconbridge, which led the forward of kyng Edwardes battail (as before is rehersed) being a man of great poleice, and of much experience in marciall feates, caused every archer under his standard, to shot one flyght (which before he caused them to provide) and then made them to stand still. The Northrenmen, feling the shoot, but by reason of the snow, not well vewyng the distaunce betwene them and their enemies, like hardy men shot their schiefe arrowes as fast as thei might, but al their shot was lost, and their labor vayn for they came not nere the Southermen by xl taylors yerdes. When their shot was almost spent, the lord Fawconbridge marched forwarde with his archers, which not onely shot their awne whole sheves, but also gathered the arrowes of their enemies, and let a great parte of them flye agaynst their awne masters, and another part thei let stand on the ground, which sore noyed the legges of the owners, when the battayle joyned. The erle of Northumberland, and Andrew Trolope, which were chefetayns of Kyng Henries vangard, seynge their shot to prevayle, hasted forward to joine with their enemies, you

may besure the other part nothing retarded, but valeauntly foughte with their enemies. This battayl was sore foughten, for hope of life was set on side on every parte and takynge of prisoners was proclaymed as a great offence, by reason whereof every man determined, either to conquere or to dye in the felde. This deadly battayle and bloudy conflicte, continued x. houres in doubtfull victorie. The one parte some time flowyng, and some time ebbyng, but in conclusion, kyng Edward so coragiously comforted his men, refreshyng the wery, and helping the wounded, that the other part was discomfited and overcome, and lyke men amased, fledde toward Tadcaster bridge to save them selfes : but in the meane way there is a little broke called Cocke not very broade, but of a great deapnes, in the whiche, what for hast of escapyng, and what for feare of folowers, a great number were drent and drowned, in so much that the common people there affirme, that men alyve passed the ryver upon dead carcasis, and that the great ryver of Wharfe, which is the great sewer of that broke, and of all the water comyng from Towton, was colored with bloude."

King Edward's account of the battle sent by the king himself to his mother Cecily Duchess of York, widow of Richard Duke of York, daughter to Ralph Nevile, Earl of Westmoreland, will be found in Sir John Fenn's Collection of the *Paston Letters*, and is as follows :

Letter CLXII.

To my master, John Paston, in haste.

Please you to know and weet of such tidings as my Lady of York hath by a letter of credence under the sign-manual of our sovereign lord King Edward ; which letter came unto our said lady this same day Eastern even at xj o'clock, and was seen and read by me, William Paston.

First, our sovereign lord hath won the field ; and upon the Monday next after Palm Sunday,[1] he was received into York with great solemnity and processions. And the mayor and commons of the said city made their means to have grace by Lord Montagu and Lord Berners, which, before the king's coming into the said city, desired him of grace for the said city, which granted them grace.

On the king's part is slain Lord Fitzwalter,

[1] Palm Sunday fell on the 29th of March. This account therefore from the King did not arrive in London till six days after the battle.

and Lord Scroop sore hurt ; John Stafford [*and*] Horne of Kent be dead, and Humphrey Stafford [*and*] William Hastyngs made knights, with others ; Blount is knighted, &c.

On the contrary part, is dead Lord Clifford, Lord Nevile, Lord Welles, Lord Willoughby, Anthony Lord Scales, Lord Harry, and by supposition the Earl of Northumberland, Andrew Trollop, with many others, gentle and commons, to the number of twenty thousand.

Item, King Harry, the queen, the prince, Duke of Somerset, Duke of Exeter, Lord Roos be fled into Scotland, and they be chased and followed, &c. We send no er [*earlier*] unto you because we had none certain till now ; for unto this day London was as sorry city as might ; and because Spordams had no certain tidings, we thought ye should take them a worth [*at their worth*] till more certain.

Item, Thorp Waterfield is yielded as Spordams can tell you.

And Jesu speed you ; we pray you that this tidings my mother may know.

By your brother,

W. Paston.
London,   Th. Playters.
Saturday, Easter Eve,
4th April, 1461. I.E. IV.

On a piece of paper pinned to the above letter, is a list of the names of the noblemen and knights, and the number of soldiers slain at the above battle of Towton, as follow :—

Noblemen.

Henry Percy, Earl of Northumberland.
Thomas Courtney, Earl of Devonshire.
William Beaumont, Viscount Beaumont.
John Clifford, Lord Clifford.
John Nevile, Lord Nevile.
Lord Dacre.

Lord Henry Stafford, of Buckingham.
Lionel Welles, Lord Welles.
Anthony Rivers, Lord Scales.
Richard Welles, Lord Willoughby.
Sir Ralph Bigot, knight, Lord de Malley.

Knights.

Sir Ralph Grey.
Sir Richard Jeney.
Sir Harry Belingham.
Sir Andrew Trollop, with twenty-eight thousand, numbered by the hearlds.

For other accounts of the battle, see *exempli gratia* Barrett's *Battles and Battlefields in England ;* Brooke's *Visits to Fields of Battle, in England, of the fifteenth century ;* The Yorkshire Archæological Journal, Volume 10 ; Weekly Supplement to the Yorkshire Herald, March 5th, and 12th, 1927.

See also Field of battle between Towton and Saxton, in Yorkshire.

Another part of the field [Wakefield].

The Scene of Act I., Scene iv. The concluding part of the battle of Wakefield. The Lancastrians have been victorious. York is captured and is subjected to indignity, a paper crown being placed upon his head, after which he is put to death by Margaret's orders and his head placed over the gates of York city. According to some of the Chroniclers, Shakespeare has on this occasion deviated from history, the paper crown not being placed on the Duke of York's head till after it has been cut off. Rutland likewise was not killed by Clifford, till after his [Rutland's] father's death. [Some write that the Duke was taken alive, and in derision caused to stand upon a *mole-hill,* on whose heade they put a garland instead of a crowne, which they had fashioned and made of segges or bulrushes, and having so crowned him with that garlande, they kneeled downe afore him, as the Jewes did to Christie in scorne. *Malone.*]

The Battle of Wakefield was fought on the 30th of December, 1460. For descriptions of the battle see *exempli gratia* Brooke's *Visits to Fields of Battle, in England, of the fifteenth century ;* Barrett's *Battles and Battlefields in England ;* Tyas' *An Historical narrative of the Battle of Wakefield, in* 1460.

In the additions to Camden's *Britannia* it states that a large stone cross was raised on the spot where the Duke of York fell. This cross was demolished in the civil war. In 1897, to preserve the traditional site there was erected a monument, containing a figure of the Duke. This monument stands in Cock and Bottle Lane now Manygates Lane, which formed the ancient highway from Wakefield and the North to London and bears the following inscription :

Richard x x
Plantagenet
Duke of x x
York x x x
Fighting x   This stone
for the x x   is erected
cause of the   in 1897 x x
White Rose   by some
fell on this   who wish to
spot in the   preserve the
Battle of x   traditional
Wakefield   site
December
30 : 1460 x

x Represents the White Rose of York. I am indebted for this inscription to Mr. J. Charlesworth of Wakefield.

See also Field of battle between Sandal Castle and Wakefield.

Antipodes. I. iv. 135.

Thou art as opposite to every good
As the Antipodes are unto us,   [I. iv. 134–135.]

The region of the earth diametrically opposite to our own.

Archbishop of York. IV. iii. 54.

King Edward, taken prisoner by Warwick, then in arms against him, is sent to Middleham Castle :

See that forthwith Duke Edward be convey'd
Unto my brother, Archbishop of York.
   [IV. iii. 53–54.]

George Neville, fourth son of Richard Neville, first Earl of Salisbury, and the owner of Middleham Castle.

Cf. *Extract* 10 from Holinshed.

Atlas. V. i. 36.

In Greek mythology a Titan, king of Mauritania, condemned by Jupiter to the labour of bearing on his head the heaven he had attempted to destroy. His station was said to be the Atlas mountains in Africa, hence the poetical way of saying that the Atlas mountains, because of their loftiness, prop up the heavens. An ' Atlas,' *i.e.* a book of maps, so-called because it contains the world ; first used in this sense by Mercator, the title-page of his collection of maps having the figure of Atlas with the world on his back.

Attendants. V. vii. p.1.
Ave-Maries. II. i. 162.

Numbering our Ave-Maries with our beads ?
   [II. i. 162.]

Cf. *Second Part of King Henry the Sixth*, I, iii 55, page 824.

Barnet. V. i. 110 ; V. iii. 20.

A town in Hertfordshire, and the Scene of Act V, Scenes ii and ii of this play. Here the Yorkists under Edward the Fourth gained a victory over the Lancastrians under Warwick on the 14th of April, 1471.

Before York. The Scene of Act II., Scene ii ; Act IV., Scene vii.

Act II, Scene ii. Henry and Margaret with the Prince of Wales and Clifford appear before York. [This took place after the battle of Wakefield and before the second battle of St. Albans.] Henry knights Prince Edward. [The Prince was at this time only nine years old, and was knighted after the second battle of St. Albans.] Edward, the new Duke of York appears with his forces, and an angry colloquy ensues. [This is altogether imaginary, but some of the allusions are founded on the *Chronicles*.] York upbraids Henry with perjury, and calls upon him to resign the crown. Courtenay remarks : " No parliament had sat, but Henry had by proclamation declared that the agreement for York's succession to the crown was void." The *Irving edition* quotes from Hall : " On the 4th of March Edward was received as king with acclamation at Baynard's Castle and at Westminster, and lodged in the bishops palace : Dayly makyng prouision, to go Northwarde against his aduerse faccion and open enemies, and on the morrow he was proclaymed kyng . . . throughout ye citie. While these thinges were in doyng in the Southpart, king Hēry beyng in the North-country, thinking because he had slayn the duke of Yorke, the chefe Capitayn of the contrary lynage, that he had brought all thyng to purpose and conclusion as he would, assembled a great army, trusting with litle payne and small losse, to destroy the residew of his enemies. Edward in a few days marched northward to Pontefract ; Henry and the queen lay at York. The fact that Edward had been formally recognized as king before he set out for the north is ignored in the play."

Act IV., Scene vii. Edward, who according to IV., v., had escaped from Middleham Castle and fled abroad, appears before York and demands admittance to the city. Being refused he vows that he seeks admittance as the " Duke of York " and friend to Henry. Having disarmed suspicion he is admitted, and demanding the keys of the gates, becomes responsible for the safety of the city. Courtenay remarks : " Edward rallied, being secretly supported by the Duke of Burgundy, and landed in Yorkshire, —at the very place, Ravenspur, it is said, where the first of the Lancastrian kings had disembarked ; and like him Edward at first disclaimed—though he could scarcely expect to be believed—his pretensions to the crown ; vowing that he sought only his paternal inheritance as Duke of York. It is even said, he raised the cry of " Long live King Henry, and wore in his cap the ostrich feather of the Prince of Wales. Some historians affirm, with doubtful accuracy, that the municipal authorities of York, required him to abjure his pretensions to the crown on the high altar of the cathedral." Montgomery with forces enters, and on hearing that Edward only claims the Dukedom of York, is about to march away, declaring that he came to " serve a king and not a duke," but when Edward boldly claims the crown, Montgomery throws down his gauntlet and challenges to fight anyone who disputes Edward's claim. Cf. *Extract* 14 from Holinshed.

Courtenay remarks : " I apprehend that this is the first scene in which Gloucester, who even now was only nineteen years old, ought to have been mentioned. Until this time he was a boy at the court of Burgundy.

Berwick. II. v. 128.

After the battle of Towton Henry is urged by Margaret to " post amain towards Berwick." Cf. *Extract* 6 from Holinshed.

Belgia. IV. viii. 1.

= Belgium.

Bess. V. vii. 15.

= Elizabeth, queen of King Edward the Fourth.

Bishop of York. IV. iv. 11 ; IV. v. 29.

And, as I further have to understand,
Is new committed to the Bishop of York,
Fell Warwick's brother, and by that our foe.

[IV. iv. 10-12.]

Bishop, farewell : shield thee from Warwick's frown,
And pray that I may repossess the crown.

[IV. v. 29-30.]

= Archbishop of York (q.v.).

Bona, Sister to the French Queen. II. vi. 90 ; III, iii, p.1, 56, 65, 121, 128, 139, 197, 212, 217 ; IV. i. 31, 97 ; IV. iii. 57.

On the conclusion of the battle of Towton, Warwick suggests to Edward that he proceed to France and ask the " Lady Bona for thy queen." " Even as thou wilt, sweet Warwick, let it be " ; replies Edward.

Welcomed by the French king, who enquires " What brings thee to France ?" Warwick replies from " worthy Edward, King of Albion," to " crave a league of amity " and to confirm that amity with nuptial knot, if thou vouchsafe to grant That virtuous Lady Bona, thy fair sister, To England's king in lawful marriage.,

Lewis is favourably inclined towards the proposal, but before giving his consent asks Lady Bona her opinion in the matter, and Lady Bona, while admitting that she has often heard Edward's " desert recounted," which has caused " her ear " to " tempt judgment to desire," is willing to leave the decision to her brother.

Lewis then gives his consent, and orders " articles be drawn " forthwith, just as a messenger arrives with the news that Edward had contracted a secret marriage with Lady Grey.

Lewis is indignant at Edward's perfidy, and asks how " Dare he presume to scorn us in this manner ?" and Warwick " in sight of heaven, And by the hope I have of heavenly bliss," protests that he is " clear from this misdeed of Edward's," while Lady Bona expresses the hope that he will " prove a widower shortly," for which she will " wear the willow garland for his sake."

[The Princess Bona, third daughter of Lewis, first Duke of Savoy, and the younger sister of Charlotte, queen of Lewis XI. She married Galeazzo-Maria Sforza, Duke of Milan.]

Bourbon. III. iii. p.1, 252.

> And thou, Lord Bourbon, our high admiral,
> Shall waft them over with our royal fleet.
>> [III. iii. 252–253.]

Louis, Count of Roussillon, and Lord High Admiral of France, son of Charles, Duke of Bourbon, and grandson to the Duke of Bourbon, a character in *King Henry V.*, taken prisoner at the battle of Agincourt.

He was ordered by Lewis, King of France to " waft over " Margaret and her followers " with our royal fleet."

Hall says : " When the league was concluded, the Frenche kyng lent them shippes, monie, and men, and . . . appoynted the Bastard of Burgoyn, Admirall of Fraunce with a greate nauie, to defende them . . . that thei might the surer saile into England."

Breech from Lancaster. V. v. 24.

> That you might still have worn the petticoat,
> And ne'er have stol'n the breech from Lancaster.
>> [V. v. 23–24.]

A reference to the old saying of a shrewish wife who usurps the prerogative of her husband. Cf. *Second Part of King Henry the Sixth*, I. iii. 145,

Brittany. II. vi. 97.

> And then to Brittany I 'll cross the sea,
> To effect this marriage, so it please my lord.
>> [II. vi. 97–98.]

The Quarto gives ' France.'

Brittany. IV. vi. 97, 101.

> Therefore, Lord Oxford, to prevent the worst,
> Forthwith we 'll send him hence to Brittany,
> Till storms be past of civil enmity. [IV. vi. 96–98.]

Hart quotes from Hall : " When Iasper erle of Pembroke was credibly asserteyned that quene Margarete had lost the battayle of Tewkesburye, and that there was no more . . . reliefe to be had for the parte of poore Kyng Henry . . . thence to Tynbye a hauen toune in Wales, where he getting conuenient shyppes for to transport hym and hys ouer the sea into Fraunce with hys nephew lord Henry erle of Rychemounde, and a few of his familiers toke ship, and by fortunes leadyng, landed in Brytayne." Cf. *Extract* 13 from Holinshed.

Buckingham. IV. viii. 14.

The County of Buckinghamshire,

Burgundy. II. i. 143.

> And when came George from Burgundy to England ?
>> [II. i. 143.]

This is a misstatement. Immediately after the battle of Wakefield, George and his brother Richard were sent into Flanders for safety, and did not return until their brother Edward got possession of the crown. George was only twelve years old and Richard nine at this time.

Burgundy. IV. vi. 79, 90 ; IV. vii. 6.

> My lord, I like not of this flight of Edward's ;
> For doubtless Burgundy will yield him help,
> And we shall have more wars before 't be long.
>> [IV. vi. 89–91.]

> Well have we pass'd, and now repass'd the seas,
> And brought desired help from Burgundy.
>> [IV, vii, 5–6.]

Charles the Bold, son of the Duke of Burgundy in the *First Part of King Henry the Sixth*. Hart quotes from Hall : " when the duke saw that Kyng Eduard upon hope of his frendes, would nedes repaire into England again, he caused priuily to be deliuered to him fiftie M. Florence, of the crosse of Saincte Andrew, and further caused foure greate shyppes to be appoynted for him . . . and xiiij shippes of the Easter-lynges, well appointed . . . to serue him truly. . . . The Duke of Burgoyne as men reported, cared not much on whose side the victory fell, sauing for paiment of his money . . . he was frend to bothe partes and eche parte was frendly to hym." Cf. IV. viii. 1–5 :

> Edward from Belgia,
> With hasty Germans and blunt Hollanders,
> Hath pass'd in safety through the narrow seas,
> And with his troops doth march amain to London ;
> And many giddy people flock to him.

Cæsar. III. i. 18.

> No bending knee will call thee Cæsar now, [III. i. 18.]

Cæsar. V. v. 53.

> They that stabb'd Cæsar shed no blood at all,
> Did not offend, nor were not worthy blame,
> If this foul deed were by to equal it : [V. v. 53–55.]

An allusion to the murder of Julius Cæsar.

Calais. I. i. 238.

> Warwick is chancellor and the lord of Calais ;
>> [I. i. 238.]

Grafton says : " In which Parliament also the Duke of Yorke was made Protector of the

Realme, and the Erle of Salisbury was appoynted to be Chauncelor, & had the great Seale to him deliuered : and the Erle of Warwike was elected to the office of the Capteyne of Calice, and territories of the same."

Cliffords, Two. V. vii. 7.

> Have we mow'd down in tops of all their pride !
> Three Dukes of Somerset, threefold renown'd
> For hardy and undoubted champions ;
> Two Cliffords, as the father and the son ; [V. vii. 4–7.]

Thomas Clifford, 12th Baron. Slain at the first battle of St. Albans.

John de Clifford, 13th Baron, fought at Wakefield. Slain, near Ferrybridge.

Coventry.

The Scene of Act V., Scene i. At the opening of this Act we find Warwick with the Lancastrian forces in possession of Coventry. Edward with his forces appears and ordering Warwick to surrender, tells him that Henry is a prisoner in the tower. [This is inaccurate. Henry was in possession of the government at this time, the Coventry events having transpired before Edward's capture of Henry.] Warwick is joined by his brother Montague, Oxford and Somerset. Clarence and his forces now arrive, and a parley ensues between him and his brothers with the result that Clarence discards his red rose and leaves Warwick. The scene closes with Edward accepting Warwick's challenge to fight at Barnet. [Hart quotes from Hall : " In the meane season Kyng Edward . . . avaunced his power towards Couentrie, & in a playne by the citie he pytched his felde. And the next day . . . he valiantly bad the erle battayle : which mistrustyng that he should be deceaued by the duke of Clarence (as he was in dede) kept hym selfe close within the walles. And yet he had perfect worde ye duke of Clarence came . . . with a great army, Kynge Edward being also thereof enformed, raysed hys campe, & made toward the duke . . . as though he would fight. When eche hoste was in sight of other, Rychard duke of Glocester, brother to them both, as though he had beene made arbiter . . . rode to the duke . . . from him he came to Kyng Edward . . . in conclusion . . . both the bretheren louingly embraced & commoned together . . . thys marchandyse was labored . . . by a damsell, when the

duke was in the French court, to the erles utter confusion . . . Clarence sent diuers frendes (to the earl) to excuse him of the act he had done . . . (and) . . . to take some good ende now while he might with kyng Edward. When the erle had hard paciently the dukes message, lord, howe he destested & accursed him . . . he gaue aunswere . . . that he had leuer be always lyke hym selfe, then like a false & a periured duke, and that he was fully determined neuer to leue wat tyll either he had lost hys owne lyfe, or . . . put under his foes and enemies. Warwick then hurries toward London hoping to overtake and fight King Edward on the way, the latter having proceeded there at once. On his way he learns that he is late and Henry is taken prisoner. He determines therefore to hazard all on one battle and ' pitched his field ' on an hill at Barnet, ten miles distant from both London and Saint Albans."]

Coventry. IV. viii. 32, 58, 64.

In Warwickshire, where Warwick announces he intends collecting his army ; and the Scene of Act V., Scene i., of this play.

Crete. V. vi. 18.

> Why, what a peevish fool was that of Crete,
> [V. vi. 18.]

An allusion to Dædalus (q.v.).

Dædalus. V. vi. 21.

> I, Dædalus ; my poor boy, Icarus ;　　　[V. vi. 21.]

In Greek mythology an architect and mechanic. He was the inventor and constructor of the famous Cretan labyrinth, in which he, and his son Icarus, was confined for furnishing a clue to it to Ariadne. By the help of wings which he constructed he fled across the Ægean sea in order to escape the resentment of Minos.

Daintry. V. i. 6.

Daventry, a town in Northamptonshire. The second messenger reports that Montague— Warwick's brother—would at that time have arrived at Daintry with his forces. The quartos read " at Dunsmore." '

Dauphin. I. i. 108 ; II. ii. 151.

The title of the heir apparent to the French throne.

Dian. IV. viii. 21.

= Diana.

Dick. V. v. 35.

And thou misshapen Dick, I tell ye all
I am your better, traitors as ye are ;   [V. v. 35–36.]

An allusion to Gloucester's deformity.

Dicky. I. iv. 76.

And where 's that valiant crook-back prodigy,
Dicky your boy, that with his grumbling voice
Was wont to cheer his dad in mutinies ? [I. iv. 75–77.]

Richard, Duke of Gloucester, used contemptuously by Queen Margaret.

Di faciant laudis summa sit ista tuæ !
I. iii. 48.

" The gods grant that this be the culmination of thy glory." This line is from Ovid's *Epistle rom Phillis to Demophoon*. The same quotation foccurs in Nash's pamphlet *Have with you to Saffron Walden.*

Diomede. IV. ii. 19.

That as Ulysses and stout Diomede
With sleight and manhood stole to Rhesus' tents,
And brought from thence the Thracian fatal steeds,
                    [IV. ii. 19–21.]

See Rhesus.

Duchess of Burgundy. II. i. 146.

And for your brother, he was lately sent
From your kind aunt, Duchess of Burgundy,
With aid of soldiers to this needful war.
                    [II. i. 146–148.]

Isabel, Duchess of Burgundy, was daughter of John the First, King of Portugal by Philippa of Lancaster, eldest daughter of John of Gaunt. Edward and she were, therefore, no more than third cousins.

Duke of Buckingham. I. i. 10.

Lord Stafford's father, Duke of Buckingham,
Is either slain or wounded dangerous ;
I cleft his beaver with a downright blow :
                    [I. i. 10–12.]

Humphrey Stafford, Duke of Buckingham. Edward Earl of March here boasts of having either slain or wounded him at the battle of St. Albans, but according to the *Chronicle* Buckingham fell at the battle of Northampton

in 1460. The *Irving edition* quotes from Hall : " Humfrey duke of Buckyngham, beyng wounded, & Iames Butler erle of Wiltshire & Ormond, seyng fortunes loweryng chaunce, left the king poste a lone & with a greate numbre fled away. What is said in the text happened after the battle of Northampton, when there " were slayn Humfrey duke of Buckyngham, Ihon Talbot erle of Shrewesbury, a valeant person, and not degenerating fro his noble parent." See also *Second Part of King Henry the Sixth*, page 829. Buckingham was the son of the Lord Stafford mentioned in the *First Part of King Henry the Fourth.*

Duke of Clarence. II. vi. 105.

Let me be Duke of Clarence, George of Gloucester,
For Gloucester's dukedom is too ominous.
                    [II. vi. 107.]

See Gloucester's dukedom.

Duke of Exeter. I. i. p.50, 72, 80, 147,
191, 211 ; II. v. p.124, 137 ; IV.
viii. p.1, 34, 48.

Is present at the Parliament-house in the opening scene. He bids York to come down from the throne, and is charged by Warwick with being a traitor in supporting Henry. Later he admits that his conscience tells him that York is the lawful king, and on the entry of Margaret " whose looks bewray her anger " threatens to " steal away."

Is present at the battle of Towton and urges Henry not to " expostulate " but to escape, for " vengeance comes along with them."

[Henry Holland, Duke of Exeter, son of John Holland, Earl of Huntingdon ; married Anne Plantagenet, sister to Edward IV., but remained a faithful adherent of the House of Lancaster. He was present at the battles of Wakefield where the Lancastrians were successful, and at Towton and Barnet, being severely wounded in the latter battle. He was attainted by Edward IV., and fell into the deepest poverty.]

Duke of Lancaster. I. i. 87, 88.

War. Be Duke of Lancaster : let him be king.
West. He is both king and Duke of Lancaster ;
                    [I. i. 87–88.]

Warwick urges Henry to be " Duke of Lancaster " as a descendant of John of Gaunt, but

Westmoreland retorts that he is both " king and Duke of Lancaster."

Duke of Norfolk. I. i. p.1, 31 ; I. ii. 38 ; II. i. 138, 142, 179, 206 ; II. ii. p.81.

John Mowbray, third Duke of Norfolk.

Enters the Parliament-house and supports York in his claim to the crown, remarking that " he that flies shall die." Later he takes an oath to support Henry, but in 1460 renewed his allegiance to the House of York. He is present at the battle of St. Albans, and fought at Towton in 1461.

Duke of Somerset. IV. i. p.1, 27, 127 ; IV. ii. p.3, 3, 7 ; IV. iii. p.23, p.28, 52 ; IV. vi. p.1, 65 ; V. i. p.72, 72, 73 ; V. ii. p.29 ; V. iii. 15 ; V. iv. p.1, 17, 58 ; V. v. p.1, 3 ; V. vii. 5.

Edmund Beaufort, fourth and last Duke of Somerset ; son of Edmund Beaufort, second Duke of Somerset and brother of Henry Beaufort, third Duke of Somerset.

First appears in the play in IV., i., where he, and other nobles, are requested by King Edward IV., to " set aside their scorns and their mislikes " and " speak freely what you think " of his marriage with Lady Grey.

When Edward IV. is taken prisoner in his tent near Warwick he is given in custody of Somerset who conveys him to Middleham Castle.

He has the charge of " young Henry, Earl of Richmond " and resolves to send him to Brittany " Till storms be past of civil enmity."

Commanded the Archers of the Lancastrian army at the battle of Barnet Field, and fought on the side of Queen Margaret at Tewkesbury, and being taken prisoner, was, in spite of a promise of pardon, beheaded by order of King Edward.

> Away with Oxford to Hames Castle straight :
> For Somerset, off with his guilty head.   [V. v. 2, 3.]

Duke of York. I. i. 105.

> Thy father was, as thou art, Duke of York.
> [I. i. 105.]

A mistake. The father of Richard, Duke of York was the Earl of Cambridge and was never Duke of York. He was beheaded during the life-

time of his elder brother Edward Duke of York who was slain at the battle of Agincourt.

Dukes of Somerset, Three. V. vii. 5.

> Have we mow'd down in tops of all their pride !
> Three Dukes of Somerset, threefold renown'd
> For hardy and undoubted champions ;   [V. vii. 4–6.]

Edmund Beaufort, Second Duke of Somerset. Killed at the first battle of St. Albans, 1455.

Henry Beaufort, Third Duke of Somerset. Defeated the Yorkists at the second battle of St. Albans. Pardoned by Edward the Fourth ; but rejoined Margaret. Taken prisoner at the battle of Hexham and executed.

Edmund Beaufort, Fourth Duke of Somerset. Taken prisoner at the battle of Tewkesbury and executed.

Dunsmore. V. i. 3.

Dunsmore Heath is four miles south-west of Rugby and about half way between Daventry and Coventry. The first messenger reports that the Earl of Oxford with his forces is at this place. The quartos read " at Daintry," *i.e.* Daventry.

Earl of Northumberland. I. i. p.50, 54 ; I. iv. p.27, 27, 53, 66, 172 ; II. i. 3, 169 ; II. ii. p.1, 109 ; V. vii. 8.

In the Parliament-house in the first scene of the Play King Henry reminds Northumberland that he has vowed revenge on the house of York for having slain his father at the battle of St. Albans.

Later in the scene, Henry submits to York's conditions. Northumberland describes this submission as an " unmanly deed " :

> Be thou a prey unto the house of York,
> And die in bands for this unmanly deed !
> [I. i. 185–186.]

and forthwith leaves the room with Clifford and Westmoreland.

He takes part in the battle of Wakefield, and seeing the " inly sorrow " that " grips the soul " of York due to the indignity meted out to him, weeps over his fallen foe.

He led the vanguard of the Lancastrians at the battle of Towton, and fell fighting, sword in hand.

In V., vii., King Edward IV. pays a tribute to his memory.

[Sir Henry Percy, third Earl of Northumberland, son of Sir Henry Percy, second Earl of Northumberland, and grandson of Sir Henry Percy, called " Hotspur."]

Earl of Oxford. III. iii. p.1, 88, 98, 109, 234 ; IV. ii. p.1 ; IV. iii. p.23 ; IV. vi. p.1, 96 ; IV. viii. p.1, 17, 30 ; V. i. 1, p.58, 58, 59, 66 ; V. ii. p.29 ; V. iii. 15 ; V. iv. p.1, 16, 58 ; V. v. p.1, 2.

John de Vere, thirteenth Earl of Oxford, hereditary Lord Chamberlain of England, son of John de Vere, twelfth Earl of Oxford.

A retainer to Queen Margaret when she visits the French Court to solicit aid of Lewis the Eleventh. Asking Warwick how he can "without a blush " oppose Henry, whom he has supported for thirty-six years, Warwick endeavours to draw Oxford over to his side, but Oxford, who has rebelled against Edward for having condemned to death his father and elder brother, replies " while life upholds this arm, This arm upholds the house of Lancaster."

With drum and colours enters Coventry, where he is welcomed by Warwick who has joined Henry in consequence of Edward's marriage to Lady Grey.

Is present at the battle of Barnet, being in command of a wing of King Henry's army ; and fights on the side of Queen Margaret at Tewkesbury. He afterwards defended Saint Michael's Mount, and upon its surrender was taken captive, and imprisoned in Hames Castle for twelve years :

> Away with Oxford to Hames Castle straight :
> For Somerset, off with his guilty head.   [V. v. 2–3.]

[The Earl of Oxford is also a character in King Richard the Third (q.v.)]

Earl of Pembroke. IV. i. p.9, 130 ; IV. iii. 55.

Appears only in two scenes of the play.

In IV., i., he is, with Stafford, commanded by King Edward to " levy men, and make prepare for war " ; and in LV., iii., Warwick, after requesting Somerset to convey Edward to Middleton Castle in the custody of the Archbishop of York, promises to follow when he has " fought with Pembroke and his fellows."

[Sir William Herbert, Earl of Pembroke, Yorkist. Knighted by Henry VI.; created Baron Herbert, 1461 ; K.G. 1462 ; and on the attainder of Jasper Tudor in 1468 created Earl of Pembroke ; defeated and captured by the Lancastrians at the battle of Edgecote, and executed. One of his sons, Sir Walter Herbert, is a character in *King Richard the Third*.]

Earl of Warwick. I. i. p.1, 28, 47, 52, 89, 93, 99, 170, 192, 229, 238 ; I. ii. 37, 56 ; II. i. p.95, 96, 101, 142, 148, 157, 166, 186, 188, 189 ; II. ii. 69, p.81, 102, 131 ; II. iii. p.1, 14, 19, 33, 44 ; II. iv. p.12, 12 ; II. v. 65, 126 ; II. vi. 29, p.31, 89, 99, 104 ; III. i. 29, 33, 42, 48 ; III. iii. p.44, 45, 46, 66, 81, 95, 106, 111, 112, 113, 134, 141, 156, 162, 168, 171, 180, 199, 233, 246, 248 ; IV. i. 5, 11, 15, 16, 32, 34, 107, 115, 117, 120, 123, 136, 137, 149 ; IV. ii. p.1, 6, 29 ; IV. iii. 6, 8, 18, p.23, p.28, 31, 44 ; IV. iv. 4, 11, 25, 35 ; IV. v. 29 ; IV. vi. p.1, 16, 23, 32, 46 ; IV. vii. 81, 85 ; IV. viii. p.1, 59 ; V. i. p.1, 13, 17, 21, 27, 35, 37, 38, 39, 40, 42, 47, 48, 57, 80, 81, 85, 98, 107, 112 ; V. ii. p.1, 2, 4, 6, 22, 29, 40, 41, 47, 49 ; V. iv. 13 ; V. viii. 10.

Warwick, described by Margaret as the " Proud setter up and puller down of kings ! " ends his career in this part.

He is present at the Parliament-house and supports York in his claim to the throne :

> Victorious Prince of York,
> Before I see thee seated in that throne
> Which now the house of Lancaster usurps,
> I vow by heaven these eyes shall never close.
> This is the palace of the fearful king,
> And this the regal seat : possess it, York ;
> For this is thine and not King Henry's heirs.
>   [I. i. 21–27.]

York takes his seat on the throne and King Henry entering, an altercation takes place between the nobles assembled. Warwick demands that Henry resign the crown or he will " fill the house with armed men." Warwick stamps his foot, soldiers enter, and Henry asks permission to let him reign during his life-time, after which the crown shall revert to York and his heirs.

Defeated at the battle of St. Albans by Margaret's forces he meets Edward after the latter had routed the Lancastrian army at Mortimer's

Cross, and suggests marching to London to proclaim Edward king.

He is present before York, where he demands Henry " yield the crown," and is taunted by Margaret :

> Why, how now, long-tongued Warwick ! dare you speak ?
> When you and I met at Saint Alban's last,
> Your legs did better service than your hands.
> [II. ii. 102–104.]

After the battle of Towton, where he killed his horse before he would flee, is commissioned by Edward to proceed to France to ask for the hand of the Lady Bona in marriage. He is successful in his mission, but news being received that Edward has secretly married Lady Grey, Warwick protests to the French king that he is " in the sight of heaven clear from this misdeed of Edward's " and threatens to " revenge his wrong to Lady Bona."

Warwick becomes reconciled to Margaret and agrees to marry his daughter to her son, the young Prince Edward.

Lewis gives orders for " England's messenger " to return, and " tell false Edward, thy supposed king, That Lewis of France is sending over masquers To revel it with him and his new bride, while Warwick for the " wrong he hath done me " will " uncrown him ere 't be long."

Returning to England he surprises Edward and takes him prisoner in his tent near Warwick, and restores Henry VI. to the throne.

With forces he arrives at Coventry, where Clarence, who is opposed to the Lancastrian restoration, goes over to the Yorkist side.

They march away towards London, and join battle at Barnet on the 14th April, 1471, Warwick being defeated and slain.

Margaret addressing her troops at Tewkesbury refers to him as " our anchor," and in the last scene Edward pays a tribute to the bravery of Warwick and Montague, describing them as " two brave bears, That in their chains fetter'd the kingly lion, And made the forest tremble when they roar'd."

Earl of Westmoreland. I. i. p.50, 61, 88.

Appears in the Parliament-house in the first scene of the play.

He suggests " plucking York from the throne," for his anger is so great he cannot endure it, but when Henry submits to York's conditions, calls

him " Base, fearful, and despairing Henry ! and bidding him " Farewell, faint-hearted and degenerate king," leaves the room in company with Northumberland and Clifford.

[Ralph Neville, second Earl of Westmoreland and grandson of Ralph Neville, sixth Baron Neville of Raby, and first Earl of Westmoreland. His first wife was Elizabeth Percy, daughter of Sir Henry Percy, called " Hotspur."]

Earl of Wiltshire. I. i. 14.

> And, brother, here 's the Earl of Wiltshire's blood,
> Whom I encounter'd as the battles join'd.
> [I. i. 14–15.]

James Butler, fifth Earl of Ormonde and Earl of Wiltshire, eldest son of James Butler, fourth Earl. He was a Lancastrian, and fought at St. Albans—where he was wounded—Wakefield, Mortimer's Cross and at Towton where he was captured and beheaded in 1460.

See also Duke of Buckingham. I. i. 10.

Edmund, Earl of Rutland. I. iii. p.1 ; I. iv. 74, 79, 88, 146 ; II. ii. 98, 115 ; II. iv. 3, 7 ; II. vi. 48, 74, 84.

Third son of Richard, third Duke of York. When not yet eighteen years of age was stabbed to death by Lord Clifford at the battle of Wakefield, 30th December, 1460, on the plea that " Thy father slew my father ; therefore die."

Edward, Earl of March, afterwards King Edward the Fourth. I. i. p.1 ; I. ii. p.1, 40, 54 ; I. iv. 11 ; I. v. p.1 ; II. i. 63, 179, 191, 192, 198 ; II. ii. 69, p.81, 130 ; II. iii. p.6, 7 ; II. v. 66, 129 ; II. vi. 7, 16, 29, p.31 ; III. i. 30, 44, 46, 52, 69, 94, 95 ; III. ii. p.1, 89, 124, 129 ; III. iii. 27, 45, 49, 67, 100, 114, 134, 139, 146, 180, 183, 223, 235, 254, 256, 265 ; IV. i. p.9, 15, 65, 77, 93, 126, 144 ; IV. ii. 10, 23 ; IV. iii. 25, p.28, 35, 43, 49, 53, 58 ; IV. iv. 3, 18, 24, 28, 32 ; IV. v. p.14 ; IV. vi. 2, 54, 78, 89, 99 ; IV. vii. p.1, 21, 38, 43, 68, 69, 71, 73, 75 ; IV. viii. 1, 35, 47, p.52 ; V. i. p.16, 18, 23, 28, 39, 100, 111, 112 ; V. ii. p.1, 6 ; V. iii. p.1 ; V. iv. 25, 60, p.67 ;

V. v. p.1, 14, 17, 34 ; V. vi. 24, 87 ;
V. vii. p.1.

In the opening scene of the play, Edward
accompanies York to the Parliament-house,
where he advises his father to seize the crown :
" Sweet father, do so ; set it on your head."

After a compromise has been effected declaring York as heir-apparent, Edward leaves
for the Welsh Marches, and gathering together
a large army defeats the Lancastrians at Mortimer's Cross.

While he and his brother Richard are " wondering " how their father has fared at the battle
of Wakefield, there appears in the sky a strange
phenomenon, just as a messenger enters with
the news that York has been defeated and slain.
He is followed by Warwick, Montague and their
army, and Warwick informs Edward that having
heard the news of York's death ten days ago,
he had gathered together a large force and encountered Margaret's force at St. Albans, where
the Yorkists had been defeated and Henry had
escaped.

In 1461 he proclaimed himself king, and gained
a decisive victory over the Lancastrians at
Towton.

In 1464 he secretly married Lady Grey, widow
of Sir John Grey who was killed at St. Albans
fighting on the side of Lancaster, while negotiations were on foot for a match with the Lady
Bona of Savoy. Offended at Edward's faithlessness, Warwick goes over to the Lancastrian
side, and threatens to dethrone Edward :

Tell him from me that he hath done me wrong,
And therefore I 'll uncrown him ere 't be long.
[III. iii. 231–232.]

Is surprised and taken prisoner by Warwick
in his tent near Warwick, and placed in the
custody of the Archbishop of York. Escaping,
he seeks refuge in Holland, but returning in 1471
at the head of an army, marches south, defeats
and slays Warwick at the battle of Barnet, and
proceeding to Tewkesbury, utterly defeats the
Lancastrian forces under Queen Margaret.

[King Edward the Fourth is also a character
in King Richard the Third (q.v.).]

Edward, Prince of Wales, son to King Henry the Sixth. I. i. p.211, 259 ; I. iv. p.27 ; II. ii. p.1, 60, 61, 175 ; II. v. p.124 ; II. ii. 130 ; III. iii. p.1, 31, 65, 73, 109, 245 ; IV. i.

117 ; IV. vi. 60 ; V. iv. p.1 ; V. v.
9, 11, 12, 51.

The only son of Henry VI. [The Paston Letters,
edited by Gairdner, gives an account of the pre-
sentation of the infant Prince to his father.
See Nos. 195 and 226.]

With his mother enters the Parliament-house,
and after protesting against being disinherited,
leaves in company with the queen, declaring
that he will not see his father again until " I
return with victory from the field."

He is " dubbed " knight by his father, who
bids him to " draw his sword in right," and the
Prince boldly declares he will

draw it as apparent to the crown,
And in that quarrel use it to the death. [II. ii. 64–65.]

After the defeat of the Lancastrian forces at
Towton, escapes with the queen to France to
solicit aid of the French king, where, after
Warwick's defection, he becomes affianced to
Warwick's daughter.

Returning to England he is present at the
battle of Tewkesbury, and being taken prisoner
is brought before Edward who demands to know
" what satisfaction he can make For bearing
arms," and the gallant Prince tells him he must
" Speak like a subject " for he is " now his
father's mouth " and denounces the Yorkists as
traitors. Edward threatens to " charm his
tongue," but the Prince courageously replies :

I know my duty ; you are all undutiful.
Lascivious Edward, and thou perjured George,
And thou misshapen Dick, I tell ye all
I am your better, traitors as ye are ;   [V. v. 33–36.]

Edward, Gloucester and Clarence, enraged at his
defiance, stab him to death. His body
was interred in the Church of the monastery of
the black monks in Tewkesbury.

" Immediately beneath the centre of the tower
is a brass marking the traditional burial-place
of Edward, Prince of Wales, only son of Henry
VI. The inscription is as follows : Hic jacet
Edwardus Princeps Walliae crudeliter interfectus
dum adhuc juvenis anno Domino 1471, mense
maii die quarto. Eheu, hominum furor : matris
tu sola lux es, et gregis ultima spes. (Here lies
Edward Prince of Wales, cruelly slain whilst but
a youth, on May 4th, 1471. Alas, the savagery
of men ! thou art the sole light of thy mother,
and the last hope of thy race.) " A New hand-

book and guide to Tewkesbury Abbey, by Rev. Canon Ernest F. Smith.

Edward's camp near Warwick.

The Scene of Act IV., Scene iii. Being ill-guarded, Edward is surprised and taken prisoner and given in the custody of the Archbishop of York — Warwick's brother — at Middleham Castle, after which Oxford suggests that they proceed forthwith to London and free Henry, who is a prisoner in the Tower, to which Warwick agrees. Cf. *Extract* 10 *and* 12 from Holinshed. [According to Hall, Edward was captured shortly after the battle of Danesmoor.]

Elysium. I. ii. 30.

The happy abode of the blessed, who spent their time in the enjoyment of every species of felicity.

England. IV. i. 40.

Why, knows not Montague that of itself
England is safe, if true within itself ?   [IV. i. 39-40.]

The corresponding passage in *The True Tragedy* is :

Let England be true within it selfe,
We need not France nor any alliance with them.

Cf. *King John*, V. vii. 117–118 :

Nought shall make us rue,
If England to itself do rest but true.

England. I. ii. 9.

The crown of England.

England. I. i. 128, 177 ; I. iv. 70 ; II. i. 143 ; IV. vii. 72.

England's hope. IV. vi. 68.

= Henry, Earl of Richmond (q.v.).

England's messenger. III. iii. 222.

= The Post, who brought letters to Warwick, the King of France and Margaret announcing the marriage of Edward to Lady Grey.

Essex. I. i. 156.

The County of Essex,

Europe. II. i. 71.

O Clifford, boisterous Clifford ! thou has slain
The flower of Europe for his chivalry ;   [II. i. 70-71.]

Grafton says : "The xv. day of Iune was borne the kinges first sonne at Woodstock, and was named Edward, which in processe of tyme did grow to a noble and famous man, and was in his dayes accompted the Flower of all Chyrualrye throughout all the worlde, and also some writers name him the black prince."

Excursions. II. iii. p.1 ; II. iv. p.1 ; II. v. p.125 ; V. ii. p.1.

= Sallies.

A Father who has killed his son. II. v. p.79.

At the battle of Towton enters with a dead body which he intends to rob. He recognises the dead man as his son and bitterly remarks: "O boy, thy father gave thee life too soon, And hath bereft thee of thy life too late !   Henry laments at the father's grief, and wishes " that my death would stay these ruthful deeds ! "

Faulconbridge. I. i. 239.

Stern Faulconbridge commands the narrow seas ;
[I, i, 239].

Grafton says : "After thys battayle, king Edwarde rendred to God hys most humble thankes, and with good diligence returned toward London, for he was enformed how Thomas Neuel, Bastard sonne to Thomas Lorde Fauconbridge the valyaunt capitayne, a man of no lesse courage then audacitie (who for hys euyll conditions was such an apt person, that a more meeter could not be chosen to set all the world in a broyle, and to put the estate of the realme in an yll hazarde) had of newe begon a great commocion. Thys Bastarde was before thys time appoynted by the Erle of Warwike to be Viceadmyrall of the sea, and had in charge so to keepe the passage betwene Douer and Calice, that none which either fauored King Edward or his friends should escape vntaken or vndrowned. And when by the death of the Erle of Warwike, he was brought into pouertie, he robbed both on the Sea and the lande, as well hys enemies as also his friendes : By reason whereof he gat together a great Nauie of shippes, and spoyled on euery side, and at the laste tooke lande in Kent, and gathered together a great company of Kentish men, such as were most meete for hys purpose, and so marched toward London, where the Essex men hauyng wylde whay wormes in their heades, ioyned them wyth him, sauing that their comming and quarell was to deliuer out of captiuity king Henry the sixt, and to bring him to his wife, but whatsoeuer their outward wordes were, their inward cogitations were onely hope of spoyle, & desyre to rob and pill. For the Bastard himselfe assaulted the drawbridge of London, and a Capitayne of his called Spisyng scaled Algate with the Essex men, harnessed in their wyfes Cheesecloutes, which assaults were deadly geuen, and manfully resisted, in so much that on both parte manye were slayne and hurt, but at the last the Citizens put back the rebelles, and slue and wounded a great number of them, and draue the Bastard from all hys pray to hys shippes, liyng at Radclyffe, which hauing a good and prosperous winde, made sayle with all haste, and roued on the Sea, as before he was accustomed. . . . Now to returne to Bastard Faulconbridge, waueryng hether & thether in the doubtfull surges of the Sea, as sure of hys lyfe on the water as on the lande, which eyther thinking that no man would see hym, or that all men were blinde, and could not espie him (and especially in so secret a place) came into the open hauen of Southampton, and there tooke lande, where he was not long vntaken, but shortlie behedded.''

Field of battle between Sandal Castle and Wakefield.

The Scene of Act I., Scene iii. The first part of the battle of Wakefield. Young Rutland— son to the Duke of York—is slain by Clifford. See *Extract* 3 from Holinshed and *under* Tutor. Rutland was born in 1443 and was twelve years old when his father killed the elder Clifford at the battle of St. Albans, and therefore at the time of his death was in his eighteenth year. The chroniclers make him five years younger for each event.

See also Another part of the field. [Wakefield.]

Field of battle between Towton and Saxton, in Yorkshire.

The Scene of Act II., Scene iii. This scene evidently refers to the action at Ferrybridge, which precedes the battle of Towton, where Lord Fitzwalter—brother to the Earl of Warwick—was slain. On being informed of his death, Warwick, who had withdrawn from the fight, swore he would kill his horse rather than again retreat. " The Lord Fitzwater, being stationed by King Edward, to defend the pass at Ferrybridge, was assaulted by the Lord Clifford, and immediately slain, and with hym, the bastard of Salisbury, brother to the earl of Warwycke, a valeaunt yong gentleman, and of great audacitie. When the earl of Warwicke, was informed of this feate, he lyke a man desperated, mounted on his hackeney, and came blowing to kyng Edwarde, saiyng : Syr, I praye God have mercy of their soules, which in the beginning of your enterprise hath lost their lyfes, and because of se no succors of the world, I remit the vengeance and punishment to God our creator and Redeemer ; and with that lighted doune, and slewe his horse with his swourde, saying : let them flye thay wyl, for surely I wil tarye with him that wil tarye with me, and kissed the crosse of his swourde." *Hall.*

See also Another part of the field. [Towton.]

Field of battle near Barnet.

The Scene of Act V., Scene ii. In this battle which was fought on the 14th April, 1471, the Yorkists were victorious, Warwick himself being slain. The scene opens with Edward bringing forth Warwick, who is mortally wounded, and telling him to " lie down and die," goes in search of Montague—Warwick's brother. Oxford and Somerset enter and Warwick, who is at the point of death, moans for Montague. Being told that Montague has " breathed his last " Warwick counsels Oxford and Somerset to save themselves by flight, and passes away, and Oxford and other nobles leave forthwith to meet Margaret, who has landed in England from France at the head of a large force.

See also Another part of the field. [Barnet.]

Flanders. IV. v. 22.

> To Lynn, my lord ;
> And ship from thence to Flanders.   [IV. v. 21–22.]

See Lynn.

Forest in the North of England.

The Scene of Act III., Scene i. There is an interval of over three years between the last scene of Act II. and the opening of the Third Act. After being defeated at Towton, Henry, with the queen and prince, retired into Scotland. From Scotland, Margaret went to France to ask help of the French king. Meanwhile—in 1464—the Lancastrians were defeated at Hedgely Moor and at Hexham. Both of these battles are passed over by the dramatist. In 1465 Henry was arrested in Lancashire.

France. III. i. 28.

> My queen and son are gone to France for aid ;
>   [III. i. 28.]

Cf. *Extract* 8 from Holnshed.

France. III. iii. 20.

> Be plain, Queen Margaret, and tell thy grief ;
> It shall be eas'd, if France can yield relief.
>   [III. iii. 19–20.]

Lewis promises, if possible, to assist Margaret.

France. IV. i. 42.

> 'Tis better using France than trusting France.
> Let us be back'd with God and with the seas
> Which he hath given for fence impregnable,
> And with their helps only defend ourselves :
> In them and in ourselves our safety lies.
>   [IV. i. 42–46.]

Johnson remarks : " This has been the advice of every man who in any age understood and favoured the interest of England."

France. V. ii. 31.

> The queen from France hath brought a puissant power';
> Even now we heard the news.   [V. ii. 31–32.]

The following is from the *Memoirs of Philip de Commines, Lord of Argenton*, edited by Andrew R. Scoble : " The Prince of Wales (of whom I have spoken before) had landed in England before this battle, and had joined his forces with those of the Dukes of Exeter and Somerset, and several others of their family and party ; so that in all (as I have been informed by those who

were in that army) they amounted to above 40,000 men. If the Earl of Warwick had stayed till he had been joined by those forces, in all probability they had won the day. But the fear he had of the Duke of Somerset, whose father and brother he had put to death, and the hatred he bore to Queen Margaret, mother to the Prince of Wales, induced him to fight alone, without waiting for them."

France. I. i. 110, 127 ; I. ii. 73 ; I. iv. 111 ; II. ii. 150, 157 ; II. vi. 89, 92 ; III. iii. 46, 86, 91, 155, 177, 255 ; IV. i. 4, 36, 41, 85 ; IV. vi. 61 ; IV. vii. 72 ; V. iv. 18.

France. The King's Palace.

The Scene of Act III., Scene iii. Margaret appears at the French court to ask aid of Lewis XI. She is winning over Lewis to her side when Warwick arrives to ask for the hand of the Lady Bona, sister to the French king, for Edward. Lewis consents to the marriage, and orders Articles of Contract to be drawn up. A messenger enters with the news of Edward's marriage to Lady Grey, and Warwick renounces his allegiance to Edward, and becomes a zealous Lancastrian. Edward, Prince of Wales becomes betrothed to the eldest daughter of Warwick. [" The Lady Bona, was not the sister of Lewis, but of his queen, Charlotte of Savoy. The story of the Lady Bona, and of Warwick's taking offence, is in Holinshed ; but the meeting between Margaret and Warwick *at this time* at Paris, and its consequences, are Shakespeare's own. The embassy of that earl to obtain for his master the hand of the Lady Bona is assigned to the year 1464, after the battle of Hexham, and he found Louis not at Paris, but at Tours, Margaret was not then in France. With one exception, however, of doubtful authority, there is no ground in contemporary historians, French or English, for Edward's suit to this Lady Bona. It was probably taken from Polydore Vergil. It is remarkable that Hearne's fragment repeats and refutes a story which sends Warwick not to France but to Spain ; to seek in marriage, not Bona of Savoy, but Isabel of Castile. But all such suits, it is added, were fruitless, because the princes of Europe had not confidence in the stability of Edward's throne. . . . It was in

1470 that Margaret and Warwick did unite against Edward, and cement their union, under the mediation of Louis, by the marriage of their children. Prince Edward was betrothed to Anne (not eldest, but), second daughter of Warwick. It does not appear that the French king sent any succours to the Lancastrians at any period after the declaration of Edward's marriage." Courtenay.]

Gallia. V. iii. 8.

= France.

George, afterwards Duke of Clarence. I.
iv. 74 ; II. i. 138, 143 ; II. ii. p.81 ; II. iii. p.9 ; II. vi. p.31, 104 ; III. ii. p.1, 112, 130 ; III. iii. 208 ; IV. i. p.1, 1, 9, 54, 59, 118, 127 ; IV. ii. p.3, 3, 6, 10, 12 ; IV. iii. p.23, 42 ; IV. vi. p.1, 31, 37, 38, 45, 53, 57 ; IV. vii. p.1, 26, 30. 83 ; IV. viii. p.1, 11, 27 ; V. i. 8, 11, p.76, 80, 86, 105 ; V. iii. p.1 ; V. iv. 26, p.67 ; V. v. p.1, 34, 46, 71, 73 ; V. vi. 84, 90 ; V. vii. p.1, 26, 30.

On the death of his father at the battle of Wakefield, was sent for safety to Burgundy, and returning in 1461 on his brother,—Edward's— accession to the crown, takes part in the battle of Towton, being created Duke of Clarence on the battlefield.

Is present at the Palace in London when Edward " makes love " to the Lady Grey, and being asked his opinion of Edward's choice, remarks :

> As well as Lewis of France, or the Earl of Warwick,
> Which are so weak of courage and in judgment
> That they 'll take no offence at our abuse
> [IV. i. 11–13.]

Being opposed to the marriage, he revolts against his brother, and when a messenger enters with the news that, owing to Edward's faithlessness, Warwick has gone over to Henry's side, and that the young Prince Edward has become affianced to Warwick's daughter, declares that

> Clarence will have the younger,
> Now, brother king, farewell, and sit you fast,
> For I will hence to Warwick's other daughter ;
> That, though I want a kingdom, yet in marriage
> I may not prove inferior to yourself.
> You that love me and Warwick follow me.
> [IV. i. 118–123.]

and forthwith leaves the room followed by Somerset.

He is with Warwick when Edward is taken prisoner in his tent near Warwick, but disapproving of the restoration of Henry VI. to the throne, upon his arrival at Coventry removes the " red rose out of his hat," and with four thousand men rejoins his brother :

> Father of Warwick, know you what this means ?
> [*Taking the red rose out of his hat.*
> Look here, I throw my infamy at thee :
> I will not ruinate my father's house,
> Who gave his blood to lime the stones together,
> And set up Lancaster. [V. i. 81–85.]

He is welcomed by Gloucester, " Welcome, good Clarence ; this is brother-like," while Warwick remarks : " O passing traitor, perjured and unjust !

He is with Edward at Barnet, and at Tewkesbury, where after the battle he takes part in the butchery of the young Prince of Wales.

In addressing her troops, Queen Margaret describes him as a " quicksand of deceit."

After the murder of King Henry VI. by Gloucester in the Tower, Gloucester in a soliloquy declares that Clarence must " beware " for as Henry and his son are gone

> Clarence, thy turn is next, and then the rest
> Counting myself but bad till I be best. [V. vi. 90–91.]

[Son of Richard, Duke of York and a younger brother of Edward the Fourth, who created him Duke of Clarence in 1461. He married Isabel Neville, eldest daughter of the Earl of Warwick, the " King-maker."]

[George, afterwards Duke of Clarence is also a character in *King Richard the Third* (q.v.).]

George of Gloucester. II. vi. 106.

> Let me be Duke of Clarence, George of Gloucester,
> For Gloucester's dukedom is too ominous.
> [II. vi. 106–107.]

See Gloucester's Dukedom.

Gloucester's dukedom. II. vi. 107.

> Let me be Duke of Clarence, George of Gloucester,
> For Gloucester's dukedom is too ominous.
> [II. vi. 106–107.]

Hall says : " It seemeth to many men that the name and title of Gloucester hath bene unfortunate and unluckie to diverse, whiche for their honor have bene erected by creation of princes to that stile and dignitie ; as Hugh

Spencer, Thomas of Woodstocke, son to kynge Edwarde the thirde, and this duke Humphrey, [who was killed at Bury ;] whiche three persons by miserable death finished their daies ; and after them king Richard the III, also duke of Gloucester, in civil warre was slaine and confounded ; so that this name of Gloucester is taken for an unhappie and unfortunate stile, as the proverbe speaketh of Sejanes horse, whose ryder was ever unhorsed, and whose possessor was ever brought to miserie." Cf. *Extract* 6 from Holinshed.

Hames castle. V. v. 2.

Hammes Castle near Calais, where the Earl of Oxford was imprisoned for twelve years. Cf. *Extract* 17 from Holinshed.

Hector. IV. viii. 25.

Farewell, my Hector, and my Troy's true hope.
[IV. viii. 25.]

See under Troy.

Helen of Greece. II. ii. 146.

Helen of Greece was fairer far than thou, [II. ii. 146.]

Supposed to have been the most beautiful woman of classical antiquity.

Henry, Earl of Richmond. IV. vi. p.1, 67, 93, 100.

Appears in only one scene of the Play.

King Henry enquires of Somerset " what youth is that Of whom you seem to have so tender care " and being told Henry, Earl of Richmond, Henry, addressing him as " England's hope " lays his hand on his head, and predicts :

This pretty lad will prove our country's bliss.
His looks are full of peaceful majesty,
His head by nature fram'd to wear a crown,
His hand to wield a sceptre. [IV. vi. 70–73.]

Somerset declares that Henry's " presaging prophecy Did glad his heart " and suggests that Richmond be sent forthwith to Brittany till all this " civil enmity be past."

[Henry, Earl of Richmond, afterwards King Henry VII., is also a character in *King Richard the Third* (q.v.).]

Henry the Fifth. I. i. 107 ; III. iii. 85, 90.

Henry the Fourth. I. i. 132, 139 ; III. iii. 83.

Hercules. II. i. 53.

But Hercules himself must yield to odds ; [II. i. 53.]

This proverb is taken from Aulus Gellius. " Ne Hercules quidem contra duos."=" Not Hercules even could struggle against two." Hercules was a mythological Greek hero of great physical strength.

Huntsman, A. IV. v. p.14, 26.

Aids Edward to escape from Middleham Castle, and accompanies him in his flight, as it is " Better to do so than tarry and be hang'd."

Hyrcania. I. iv. 155.

O, ten times more than tigers of Hyrcania. [I. iv. 155.]

See under Hyrcan tiger, page 92, and Hyrcanian beast, page 213.

Icarus. V. vi. 21.

I, Dædalus ; my poor boy, Icarus. [V. vi. 21.]

See Dædalus.

Ireland. IV. vii. 72.

Jephthah. V. i. 91.

To keep that oath were more impiety
Than Jephthah's, when he sacrificed his daughter.
[V. i. 90–91.]

One of the twelve judges of Israel, who, before going to fight against the Ammonites, vowed that if successful, he would sacrifice to the Lord the first thing that met him on his return home. His daughter coming out to welcome him was accordingly offered up, but before her death she went into the wilderness to bewail her virginity.

Jerusalem. I. iv. 122.

Thy father bears the type of King of Naples,
Of both the Sicils and Jerusalem,
Yet not so wealthy as an English yeoman.
[I. iv. 121–123.]

See under Reignier.

Jerusalem. V. v. 8.

So part we sadly in this troublous world,
To meet with joy in sweet Jerusalem.   [V. v. 7–8.]

= Paradise, Heaven.

Jerusalem. V. vii. 39.

Reignier, her father, to the King of France
Hath pawn'd the Sicils and Jerusalem,
And hither have they sent it for her ransom.
[V. vii. 38–40.]

See Reignier.

John of Gaunt. I. i. 19.

Such hope have all the line of John of Gaunt !
[I. i. 19.]

Henry the Sixth was a descendant of John of
Gaunt, his grandfather being Henry Bolingbroke, afterwards King Henry the Fourth.

John of Gaunt. III. iii. 81, 83.

Then Warwick disannuls great John of Gaunt,
Which did subdue the greatest part of Spain ;
And, after John of Gaunt, Henry the Fourth,
[III. iii. 81–83.]

Dr. Law says : " John of Gaunt did conduct
an expedition into Spain, and by right of marriage, laid claim to the Spanish throne, but he
did not ' subdue the greatest part.' His military
success there was merely nominal, and his royal
pretensions were satisfied by his daughter's
marriage to the heir-apparent. In the height
of the feeling against Spain after the destruction
of the Armada, Englishmen were frequently
reminded of John of Gaunt's victories. Kyd's
Spanish Tragedy tells us, contrary to history,
that he took King of Castile prisoner. On May
14, 1594, was entered on the Stationers' Register
*the famous historye of John of Gaunte . . . with
his Conquest of Spaine* ; and in 1601, Philip
Henslowe paid Hathway and Rankins for
writing a play, *The Conquest of Spain by John of
Gaunt.* Boswell Stone remarks : " John of
Gaunt, Duke of Lancaster, claimed Castile in
right of his second wife Constance, elder daughter
of Pedro the Cruel. The Duke, however, failed
to dethrone John I., son of Pedro's bastard
brother Henry II., and obtained but a few
transient successes by his invasion of Spanish
territory."

Jove's spreading tree. V. ii. 14.

The oak-tree which was sacred to Jove or
Jupiter. Cf. Ovid's *Metamorphoses* (Golding's
translation), VII. 802–803 :

This tree (as all the rest of Okes) was sacred unto Jove
And sprouted of an Acorne which was fet from Dodon
grove.

Judas. V. vii. 34.

To say the truth, so Judas kiss'd his master,
And cried " all hail ! " when as he meant all harm.
(V. vii. 33–34.)

Judas Iscariot, who betrayed Christ.

Kent. I. i. 156 ; IV. viii. 12.

The county of Kent.

King Henry the Sixth. I. i. 20, 27, 33, 41, p.50, 70, 73, 81, 120, 131, 153, 159, 164, 178, 189, 202, 204, 248 ; I. ii. 10, 34, 59 ; I. iv. 97, 102, 103 ; II. i. 119, 153 ; II. ii. p.1, 81, 101, 126 ; II. v. p.1 ; II. vi. 2, 7, 10, 14, 34 ; III. i. p.13, 15, 43, 45, 95 ; III. ii. 118, 130 ; III. iii. 24, 31, 58, 72, 73, 79, 87, 89, 100, 118, 143, 151, 190, 194, 198, 201, 214, 264 ; IV. i. 96 ; IV. ii. 27 ; IV. iii. 50, 64 ; IV. iv. 27 ; IV. vi. p.1, 50, 92 ; IV. vii. 4, 19, 20, 28, 66, 82, 84 ; IV. viii. p.1, 52 ; V. i. 38, 45 ; V. iv. 76 ; V. vi. p.1, 69, 89, 93.

The weakness of the King is even more portrayed in this part, than in the two preceding
plays.

In the first scene on entering the Parliament-
house and seeing York seated in the chair of
state denounces him as a " rebel," but when his
followers suggest " plucking York from the
throne," Henry in his usual submissive manner
counsels patience, it being far from his "heart
To make a shambles of the parliament-house ! ",
and finally asks Warwick's permission to allow
him to reign in peace during his life-time, after
which the crown shall revert to York and his
heirs, Thus he was disinheriting his only son.

On being welcomed before York by Margaret
who points out to him the head of his arch-
enemy over the city gates, Henry declares that
the sight " irks his very soul " and implores God
to " withhold revenge, 'tis not my fault."

At the request of the Queen, he knights his son, and bids him to " draw his sword in right." He realises that the conflict is the outcome of past wrongs :

> I 'll leave my son my virtuous deeds behind ;
> And would my father had left me no more !
> [II. ii. 49–50.]

Chidden from the field of Towton he weeps over the carnage which unfolds before his eyes, and longs for death : " Would I were dead ! if God's good will were so ; For what is in this world but grief and woe ? " and appeals to " gentle heaven for pity," and " stay these ruthful deeds."

Arrested and thrown into the Tower where he lies peacefully and contemplatively for a period of four years, he is released by Warwick and proclaimed king, but on the entry of Edward into London is dethroned and sent back to the Tower, where he is stabbed by Gloucester.

He dies praying for forgiveness and pardon for the " undigested and deformed lump " who murders him, and foretells the ultimate downfall of the House of York.

Thus the sin against which Henry the Fifth prayed on the eve of the battle of Agincourt :

> O God of battles ! steel my soldier's hearts ;
> Possess them not with fear ; take from them now
> The sense of reckoning, if the opposed numbers
> Pluck their hearts from them. Not to-day, O Lord !
> O ! not to-day, think not upon the fault
> My father made in compassing the crown.
> I Richard's body have interred new,
> And on it have bestow'd more contrite tears
> Than from it issued forced drops of blood.
> Five hundred poor I have in yearly pay,
> Who twice a day their wither'd hands hold up
> Toward heaven, to pardon blood ; and I have built
> Two chantries, where the sad and solemn priests
> Sing still for Richard's soul. More will I do ;
> Though all that I can do is nothing worth,
> Since that my penitence comes after all,
> Imploring pardon. [*Henry the Fifth*, IV. i. 295–311.]

had come to pass. Retribution, for the usurpation of the crown by his grandfather, Henry IV., and the subsequent murder of Richard II., in Pomfret Castle, had fallen on the House of Lancaster. But the day of reckoning of the House of York was yet to follow.

Bell in his *Tower of London* says : " it is said, King Henry VI., was at prayer when he was murdered, on the very night of Edward IV's arrival in London in triumph, after Barnet and Tewkesbury had been fought, ' between xi and xii of the clock, the Duke of Gloucester being then at The Tower, and many others.' "

King of Naples.   I. iv. 121.

> Thy father bears the type of King of Naples,
> Of both the Sicils and Jerusalem,
> Yet not so wealthy as an English yeoman.
> [I. iv. 121–123.]

See under Reignier.

Lady Grey, afterwards Queen to Edward the Fourth.   III. ii. p.1 ; III. iii. 174 ; IV. i. 2, p.9, 25 ; V. vii. p.1, 15.

Widow of Sir John Grey, killed at the second battle of St. Albans, fighting on the Lancastrian side.

In III., ii., presents a petition for the restitution of her late husband's estates which had been seized by Edward IV., after his victory at Towton.

Edward promises to consider her suit, and requests her to " come some other time to know our mind," but the lady " cannot brook delay " and asks for the matter to be settled forthwith.

After an animated conversation Edward grants her request, and dropping a curtsy, she thanks the king with " many thousand thanks." She is on the point of leaving, but Edward tells her to stay as she has misunderstood his meaning, and after further conversation Edward tells her to " Answer no more, for thou shalt be my queen."

When Edward is taken prisoner by Warwick in his camp near Warwick, in order to " prevent the tyrant's violence,—" she will " hence forthwith unto the sanctuary, To save at least the heir of Edward's right " : for if Warwick " take us we are sure to die."

[Lady Grey—as Queen to King Edward IV.— is also a character in *King Richard the Third* (q.v.).]

Lancaster.   I. i. 23, 46 ; I. ii. 13, 46 ; II. i. 176 ; II. vi. 3 ; III. iii. 107.

The House of Lancaster.

Leicestershire.   IV. viii. 15.

Lewis the Eleventh, King of France. III. i. 34 ; III. iii. p.1, 3, 4, 23, 74, 143, 159, 169, 181, 203, 224 ; IV. i. 11, 15, 29, 34, 91, 94, 96 ; IV. iii. 57.

The eldest son of Charles the Seventh, called "The Victorious," and first cousin, on his father's side, to King Henry VI., and the same relationship on his mother's side, to Queen Margaret.

After the battle of Towton, Margaret escapes to France to seek aid of Lewis who promises her his help, but on the entrance of Warwick to solicit the hand of the Lady Bona for Edward IV., he changes his mind and gives his consent to this proposal. A messenger enters with the news that Edward has secretly married the Lady Grey, and Lewis is so indignant at Edward's having " scorned us in this manner," that he offers to supply Warwick and Oxford with five thousand men for the invasion of England, to be followed by a " fresh supply " under Queen Margaret and Prince Edward. His character is well and fully portrayed by Sir Walter Scott in " Quentin Durward."

Lieutenant of the Tower. IV. vi. p.1, 1, 9 ; V. vi. p.1.

Lieutenant of the Tower on the night of the murder of King Henry the Sixth.

French observes : " From the language used in Act IV., Scene vi., by " master lieutenant " and the reply of Henry VI., to his apology, we may infer that this officer is intended for John Tibetoft, first Earl of Worcester, of that name, who was appointed " Constable of the Tower," by Edward IV., at his accession ; the Earl, who was a zealous Yorkist, was beheaded in 1471, when the Lancastrians were in power for a brief space. His successor was John Sutton, Lord Dudley, K.G., who will be the " Lieutenant," attending in Act V., Scene vi., when he is ordered by Gloucester to leave him alone with the ill-fated Henry VI.,—

Sirrah, leave us to ourselves ; we must confer."

London. I. i. 207.

And I 'll keep London with my soldiers. [I. i. 207.]

Warwick determines to hold London with his forces after agreeing that Henry the Sixth should reign during his lifetime.

London. I. ii. 36.

Brother, thou shalt to London presently,
And whet on Warwick to this enterprise.
[I. ii. 36–37.]

The corresponding passage in *The True Tragedie* reads thus :

And Richard thou to London straight shalt post,
And bid Richard Neuill Earle of Warwike
To leaue the cittie, and with his men of warre,
To meete me at Saint Albons ten daies hence.

London. II. i. 174, 182.

And now to London all the crew are gone,
[II. i. 174.]
Why, Via ! to London will we march amain,
[II. i. 182.]

Hart quotes Hall : " The erles of Marche and Warwycke, hauing perfite knowledge that the kyng and quene with their adherentes were departed from Saint Albons, determined first to ryde to London as the chefe Key, and common spectacle to the whole Realme, thinking there to assure them selfs of the East and West parte of the kingdome [Norfolk and Wales], as King Henry and his faction nesteled and strengthened him and his alies in the North regions and boreal plage : meaning to haue a buckelar against a sword, and a southerne byl to counteruayle a Northern bassard."

London. II. i. 111 ; II. v. 64 ; II. vi. 87, 109 ; IV. iii. 62 ; IV. iv. 26 ; IV. viii. 4, 22 ; V. v. 47, 84, 88.

London. The Palace.

The Scene of Act III., Scene ii. ; Act IV., Scenes i., iv., and viii. ; Act V., Scene vii.

Act III., Scene ii. Opens with a petition by Lady Grey for the restitution of her husband's lands, who was slain at the second battle of St. Albans. [Sir John—not Richard—Grey fell in the second battle of St. Albans fighting—not for the house of York as represented in the play —but on the Lancastrian side, and it was Edward himself who seized his lands after the battle of Towton. Shakespeare has corrected this in *King Richard the Third*, Act I., Scene iii.] The interview ends with Edward expressing his intention to marry Lady Grey. See *Extract 7* from Holinshed. Henry is brought in a prisoner, and is committed to the Tower, and the scene closes with a lengthy soliloquy by Gloucester in which he reveals his secret designs on the crown. Johnson remarks: "Richard speaks here the language of nature. Whoever is stigmatized with deformity has a constant source of envy in his mind, and would counter-balance by some other superiority those advantages which he feels himself to want. Bacon remarks that the deformed are commonly daring; and it is almost proverbially observed that they are ill-natured. The truth is, that the deformed, like all other men, are displeased with inferiority, and endeavour to gain ground by good or bad means, as they are virtuous or corrupt."

Act IV., Scene i. This scene shows the dislike of Edward's brothers to his marriage with Lady Grey, as well as the discontent of the nobles at the favours which Edward has bestowed upon his wife's relatives. The messenger from France enters and delivers his messages as portrayed at the end of Act III., Scene iii. Clarence leaves Edward and joins Warwick, whose daughter he intends to marry. Clarence is followed by Somerset, but Gloucester, Pembroke and Stafford remain faithful to Edward. Montague and Hastings—respectively brother and brother-in-law to Warwick—are suspected, but each gives assurances of his loyalty. [Courtenay observes: "It may be asked how it is that Somerset, who is mentioned in the *dramatis personæ* as a 'Lord on King Henry's side,' and whose predecessor was slain fighting in that king's cause, is placed at King Edward's court. The duke who was slain at St. Alban's, left a son Henry, who fought for Henry VI. at Towton, and escaped. He afterwards made his submission to Edward (in company with Sir Ralph Percy and others), but again revolted to King Henry when Margaret obtained her brief successes in the north. At Hexham he was taken and beheaded. All this was really prior to Edward's marriage and to Warwick's defection; but I can find no other ground for the tergiversation of a Duke of Somerset in the play. The successor of Duke Henry was faithful to the Lancastrian side, and was beheaded after the battle of Tewksbury. Pembroke and Stafford are correctly made faithful to Edward. Montagu was the brother, and Hastings the brother-in-law of Warwick, and they were therefore reasonably suspected."]

Act IV., Scene iv. News arrives at the Palace that Edward has been captured, and Queen Elizabeth takes refuge in the sanctuary at Westminster. [Hart quotes from Hall: " innumerable people resorted to the erle of Warwycke to take his parte, but all kyng Edwardes trusty frendes went to diuers sentuaries, dayly loking . . . to hear of his . . . prosperous return. Emongst other, Quene Elizabeth his wyfe, allmoste desperate of all comfort, took sentuary at Westmynster, and there in great penurie forsaken of all her frendes was deliuered of a fayre sonne called Edward."]

Act IV., Scene viii. Warwick announces that Edward has arrived in England at the head of a large army comprised of " hasty Germans and blunt Hollanders," and Henry orders men to be levied to meet him. Having bidden farewell to Henry, Warwick and the other lords,—with the exception of Exeter—depart for Coventry. Left alone, the king and Exeter are conversing when there are shouts and Edward with soldiers enters the palace, seizes Henry, and commits him again to the Tower, after which the Yorkists proceed to Coventry to meet Warwick. Cf. *Exrtact* 14 from Holinshed.

Act V., Scene vii. This, the final scene of the play shows us Edward seated upon his throne, with Queen Elizabeth and the young prince Edward beside him. In triumph, he recounts the foemen he has slain in the wars. Kissing his young son—the future Edward the Fifth—he bids both his brothers to " kiss their princely nephew " too. The child receives the caresses of both Clarence and Gloucester, and the latter, turning aside, confesses that his is indeed a Judas kiss. Margaret is banished and the play concludes with Edward—who is a great lover of pleasure—announcing that he intends spending his time

> With stately triumphs, mirthful comic shows,
> Such as befits the pleasure of the court.
> Sound drums and trumpets! farewell sour annoy!
> For here, I hope, begins our lasting joy.

Hall says: " Queene Margaret lyke a prisoner was brought to London, where she remayned till kyng Reiner her father ransomed her with money, which summe (as the French writers afferme) he borrowed of Kyng Lewes . . . to repaye so great a dutie, he solde to the French

King & his heires, the Kyngdomes of Naples and both the Siciles, with the county of Prouynce. . . . After the ransome payed, she was conveyed in to Fraunce with small honor."

London. I. ii. 36.

Brother, thou shalt to London presently,
And whet on Warwick to this enterprise. [I. ii. 36-37]

The corresponding passage in *The True Tragedie* reads thus :

And Richard thou to London straight shall post,
And bid Richard Neuill Earle of Warwike
To leaue the cittie, and with his men of warre,
To meete me at Saint Albons ten daies hence.

London. The Parliament House.

The Scene of Act I., Scene i. Opens with the Yorkists entering the Parliament-house, where the Duke of York takes possession of the throne. Henry enters and a fierce altercation takes place between the opposing parties. Henry claims that his grandfather—Henry the Fourth—was lawful king, Richard the Second having resigned the crown in his favour, and his father—Henry the Fifth—was therefore heir. Exeter is of opinion that York is the lawful heir and turns against Henry. [There is no authority for this, as Exeter is named among the nobles who refused to acknowledge the parliamentary settlement of the crown, and fought under Queen Margaret for the house of Lancaster.] A compromise is effected, whereby Henry is to reign during his life-time, after which the crown shall pass to York and his heirs. Grafton says : " After long arguments made, and deliberate consultation had among the Peeres, Prelates, and commons of the realme : vpon the vigile of all Saintes, it was condescended and agreed, by the three estates, for so much as king Henry had beene taken as king, by the space of xxxviij yeres and more, that he should enioy the name and tytle of king, and haue possession of the realme, during his life naturall : And if he eyther died or resigned, or forfeited the same, for infringing any point of this concorde, then the sayde Crowne and aucthoritie royall, should immediately dissende to the Duke of Yorke, if he then lyued, or else to the next heyre of his line or linage, and that the Duke from thenceforth should be Protector and Regent of the land. Prouided alway, that if the king did closely or apertly studie or go about to breake or alter this agrement, or to compasse or imagine

the death or destruction of the sayde Duke or hys bloud, then he to forfeit the crowne, and the Duke of Yorke to take it. These articles with many other, were not onely written, sealed and sworne by the two parties : but also were enacted in the high court of Parliament. For ioy whereof, the king hauing in his company the sayde Duke, rode to the Cathedrall Church of saint Paule, within the Citie of London, and there on the day of all saintes, went solempnly wythe the Diademe on his head in procession, and was lodged a good space after in the Bishops Palace, nere to the sayd Church. And vpon the Saturday next ensuyng, Richard Duke of Yorke, was by the sound of a trumpet, solempnly proclaimed heyre apparaunt to the crowne of Englande, and Protectour of the realme."

For York's Oath see *Extract* 1 from Holinshed,

Margaret appears on the scene and in anger denounces her husband for having acknowledged York as his heir and disinherited their only son. [This is unhistorical.] Grafton says : " The Duke of Yorke well knowyng, that the Queene would spurne and impugne the conclusions, agreed and taken in this Parliament, caused her and her sonne, to be sent for by the king : but she being a manly woman, vsyng to rule and not to be ruled, and thereto counsayled by the Dukes of Excester and Sommerset, not only denyed to come but also assembled together a great armie, intendyng to take the king by fine force, out of the Lordes handes, and to set them to a newe schoole." [There is an interval of five years between the first battle of St. Albans alluded to at the opening of this scene and the parliamentary acknowledgment of York as successor to Henry. During this interval many important events had taken place, including the battles of Blore Heath, 1459, and Northampton, 1460, in both of which the Yorkists were victorious. The same year York claimed the crown and was made heir to Henry by Parliament. In the December following the battle of Wakefield was fought in which York was killed. *See* Scene 4.]

London. The Tower.

The Scene of Act IV., Scene vi. ; Act. V., Scene vi.

Act IV., Scene vi. Warwick and Clarence proceed to the Tower and liberate Henry, who appoints Warwick and Clarence joint protectors of the realm. See *Extract* 12 from Holinshed. At the court in charge of Somerset, is Henry, Earl of Richmond, whom Henry declares is " England's hope." This youth was afterwards Henry VII., grandfather of Queen Elizabeth. [In the *Chronicle* the young Earl of Richmond is introduced by his uncle Lord Pembroke. See *Extract* 13 from Holinshed.] A messenger enters with the news that Edward has escaped from Middleham Castle and has fled to Burgundy; yet in the next scene he appears before York.

Act V., Scene vi. This scene depicts the murder of Henry in the Tower ; the address of the unhappy king to Gloucester—which is taken almost verbatim from *The True Tragedie* —and Gloucester's soliloquy, in which he compares the deformity of his mind to that of his body.

The circumstances attending the death of Henry VI. are involved in deep obscurity. The balance of testimony supports the popular tradition that he was murdered on the night of Edward's entry into London, 21st May, 1471 : " And the same nyghte that Kynge Edwarde came to Londone, Kynge Herry, beynge inwarde in persone in the Toure of Londone, was putt to dethe, the xxj. day of Maij., on a tywesday nyght, betwyx xj. and xij. of the cloke, beynge thenne at the Toure the Duke of Gloucetre, brothere to Kynge Edwarde, and many other ; and one the morwe he was chestyde and brought to Paulys, and his face was opyne that every manne myghte see hyme ; and in hys lyinge he bledde one the pament ther ; and afterward at the Blake Fryres was broughte, and ther he blede new and fresche ; and from thens he was caryed to Chyrchsey abbey in a bote, and buryed there in oure Lady chapelle."

Dr. Warkworth, whose chronicle furnishes the above extract, was a contemporary writer, Master of St. Peter's College, Cambridge, from 1473 to 1498, and a man of learning and ability. Fabyan, a citizen of London in the time of Henry the Seventh, is more explicit : " Of the death of this Prynce dyverse tales were tolde : but the most common fame wente, that he was stykked with a dagger by the handes of the Duke of Gloucester."

On the other hand, the Yorkist party con-

tended that the deposed monarch died of grief and melancholy : " In every party of England, where any commotion was begonne for Kynge Henry's party, anone they were rebuked, so that it appered to every mann at eye the sadye partie was extincte and repressed for evar, without any mannar hope of agayne quikkening : utterly despaired of any maner of hoope or releve. The certainte of all whiche came to the knowledge of the sayd Henry, late called Kyng, being in the Tower of London ; not havynge, afore that, knowledge of the saide matars, he toke it to so great dispite, ire, and indingnation, that, of pure displeasure, and melencoly, he dyed the xxiij day of the monithe of May. Whom the kynge dyd to be browght to the friers prechars at London, and there, his funerall service donne, to be caried, by watar, to an Abbey upon Thamys syd, xvj myles from London, called Chartsey, and there honorably enteryd." *Arrivall of Edward IV.*

[" I quite agree with Walpole as to the improbability of Richard's becoming the murderer of the captive and childless king. On the other hand, it is sufficiently clear, that, from the very first, it was suspected that Henry was murdered, and that the perpetrator was in station so high as to be called *a tyrant*, and that a rumour was prevalent at any early period, but perhaps not until *after Richard's death*, that Gloucester was the murderer." *Courtenay*.]

Lord Aubrey Vere. III. iii. 102.

Eldest son of John, twelfth Earl of Oxford. Holinshed remarks : " The earle of Oxford far striken in age, and his sonne and heire the lord Awbreie Veer, either through malice of their enimies, or for that they had offended the king, were both, with diuerse of their councellours, attainted, and put to execution ; which cause Iohn earle of Oxford euer after to rebell."

Lord Bonville. IV. i. 57.

William Bonville. His daughter and heiress Cicely married Thomas Grey, Marquis of Dorset, son by the first husband, of Elizabeth, queen to Edward the Fourth.

Lord Clifford. I. i. 7.

Lord Clifford, and Lord Stafford, all abreast,
Charged our main battle's front, and breaking in
Were by the swords of common soldiers slain.
[I. i. 7-9.]

This personage is the Lord Clifford in the *Second Part of King Henry the Sixth* (q.v.) slain in combat with York at the battle of St. Albans.

Lord Clifford. p.50, 55, 58, 83, 101, 160, 163 ; I. iii. 2, p.3, 8, 16, 18, 24, 36 ; I. iv. p.27, 27, 44, 51, 54, 66, 80, 149, 167 ; II. i. 3, 12, 58, 63, 70, 103, 126, 169, 201 ; II. ii. p.1, 43, 45, 107, 112, 125 ; II. iii. 16 ; II. iv. p.1, 1, p.12 ; II. v. 16 ; II. vi. p.1, 1, 12 ; II. v. 16 ; II. vi. p.1, 37, 46, 53, 61, 69, 70, 71, 76, 78 ; V. vii. 7.

This personage, the "relentless foe of the House of York" and the son of the Lord Clifford slain at the battle of St. Albans, first appears with the other nobles in the Parliament-house in the opening scene of the play. He vows to fight in defence of King Henry, be his "title right or wrong," and hopes the ground will "gape and swallow him alive" before he will "kneel to him that slew his father."

He takes part in the battle of Wakefield and slays in cold blood the young Earl of Rutland, because "Thy father slew my father," and is the first to plunge his sword in the breast of captive York. "Here's for my oath ; here's for my father's death."

At the battle of Towton he encounters Richard, but Warwick appearing on the scene, he takes to flight. Later in the battle he falls mortally wounded, and his head is cut off and placed over the gates of York.

> off with the traitor's head,
> And rear it in the place your father's stands.
> [II. iv. 85–86.]

[John de Clifford ("Young Clifford" in the *Second Part*), thirteenth Baron Clifford ; ninth Baron of Westmoreland, son of Thomas de Clifford, twelfth Baron Clifford. He was slain in a skirmish at Ferrybridge on the 28th March, 1461.]

Lord Cobham. I. ii. 40, 56.

> You, Edward, shall unto my Lord Cobham,
> With whom the Kentishmen will willingly rise :
> In them I trust ; [I. ii. 40–42.]

Sir Edward Brooke. At the battle of Northampton, 1469, commanded the left wing of the Yorkist forces. Grafton says : "The Duke of Yorke and his adherentes perceiuyng, that neyther exhortacion serued, nor accusement preuayled against the Duke of Sommerset, determined to reuence their quarrell, and obteyne their purpose, by open warre and Marciall aduenture, and no lenger to slepe in so waightie a businesse. So he beyng in the Marches of Wales, associate with his speciall friendes, the Erles of Sarisbury, and Warwike, the Lorde Cobham, and other, assembled an army, and gathered a great power, and like warlike persons, marched toward London."

Lord Hastings. IV. i. p.9, 47, 134, 144 ; IV. iii. 11, p.28, 29 ; IV. v. p.1, 1, 16 ; IV. vi. 82 ; IV. vii. p.1, 1 V. vii. p.1.

When Montague suggests that they seek alliance with France, Hastings declares that "England is safe, if true within itself." He is of opinion that their safety lies in their trust in God, and the "seas Which he hath given for fence impregnable," and in themselves, for it is better to "use France" than "trust France," to which Clarence opines that "Hastings well deserves To have the heir of the Lord Hungerford."

In order to test Hastings' loyalty, Edward asks him whether he "loves Warwick more than me ?" and being assured of Hastings' faithfulness, declares "then am I sure of victory."

He escapes when Edward IV. is taken prisoner in his tent near Warwick, and with the assistance of Gloucester and Stanley helps Edward to escape from Middleham Castle.

He is present before York, when the Mayor is prevailed upon to open the gates of the city to allow York to enter.

[Lord Hastings is also a character in *King Richard the Third* (q.v.).]

Lord Hungerford. IV. i. 48.

> For this one speech Lord Hastings well deserves
> To have the heir of the Lord Hungerford,
> [IV. i. 47–48.]

Johnson remarks : "It must be remembered, that till the restoration the heiresses of great estates were in the wardship of the king, who in their minority gave them up to plunder, and afterwards matched them to his favourites. I know not when liberty gained more than by the abolition of the court of wards."

Sir Thomas Hungerford, eldest son of the third Lord Hungerford. Charged with conspiracy, condemned and executed 17th January, 1469. The heiress of Hungerford was married to the son of Lord Hastings of this play.

Lord of Northumberland. I. i. 4 ; V. vii. 8.

Henry Percy, the second Earl of Northumberland.

Mentioned in I., i., as having been slain at the battle of St. Albans ; and in V., vii., King Edward IV. pays a tribute to his memory.

Lord of Somerset. I. i. 18.

Duke of Somerset. Edmund Beaufort, second Duke of Somerset. He was slain at the first battle of St. Albans, 1455, (see *Second Part of King Henry the Sixth*, V., ii.), but here is represented as having fallen by the hand of Richard Duke of Gloucester, afterwards King Richard the Third. His eldest son Henry, who succeeded him, was captured at the battle of Hexham and beheaded. His second son, Edmund, became the fourth Duke and is the Somerset of this play.

Lord Rivers, brother to Lady Grey. IV. iv. p.1, 1.

Appears in only one scene of the Play, being told by his sister, Queen Elizabeth, that Edward had been taken prisoner by Warwick, and committed to the custody of the Archbishop of York.

[Lord—as Earl Rivers—is also a character in *King Richard the Third* (q.v.).]

Lord Scales. IV. i. 52.

Anthony Woodville, Baron Scales and second Earl Rivers, and brother to Elizabeth, queen of Edward the Fourth. On the death of Edward he was executed for treason.

See under Lord Rivers, brother to Lady Grey.

Lord Stafford. I. i. 6, 10.

Earl of Stafford, son of Humphrey, first Duke of Buckingham.

Mentioned as having been slain at the battle of St. Albans.

Lord Clifford, and Lord Stafford, all abreast,
Charged our main battle's front, and breaking in
Were by the swords of common soldiers slain.
[I. i. 7–9.]

Lord Stafford. IV. i. p.9, 130.

Appears in only one scene of the play, where he is, with Pembroke, commanded by King Edward to "levy men, and make prepare for war ; . . . Myself in person will straight follow you."

[Sir Humphrey Stafford, son of William Stafford. Created Lord Stafford, 1464, and Earl of Devon, 1469 ; sent to oppose the northern rebels, but a quarrel breaking out between him and the Earl of Pembroke, he deserted with all his troops, and Edward IV., ordered his execution.]

Lynn. IV. v. 21.

To Lynn, my lord ;
And ship from thence to Flanders.   [IV. v. 21–22.]

Kings Lynn in Norfolk. It was proposed that Edward the Fourth after his escape from Middleham Castle should proceed to Lynn and take ship to Flanders. Cf. *Extract* 11 from Holinshed.

Machiavel. III. ii. 193.

And set the muederous Machiavel to school.
[III. ii. 193.]

An anachronism. Machiavel was not born till 1469. In the *True Tragedie* the corresponding passage is :

And set the aspiring Catalin to schoole.

March, A. II. i. p.1, p.95 ; II. ii. p.81 ; V. i. p.16 ; V. iv. p.1.

= A movement of soldiers.

Marquess of Montague. I. i. p.1 ; I. ii. p.1, 55 ; II. i. p.95, 167, 198 ; II. ii. p.81 ; II. vi. p.31 ; III. iii. 164 ; IV. i. p.1, 27, 39, 134, 143 ; IV. vi. p.1 ; IV. viii. p.1, 14, 30 ; V. i. 4, 5, p.67, 67 ; V. ii. 3, 34, 39, 40 ; V. iv. 14 ; V. vii. 10.

Enters the Parliament-house in the opening scene, and supports York in his claim to the crown.

After the defeat of the Yorkist forces at St. Albans was imprisoned at York, but was liberated by Edward IV. after Towton.

Reverted to the Lancastrians and with drum and colours enters Coventry crying "Montague,

Montague, for Lancaster ! " to which Gloucester remarks :

> Thou and thy brother both shall buy this treason
> Even with the dearest blood your bodies bear.
> [V. i. 68–69.[

He fights on the side of Queen Margaret at the battle of Barnet, where he is slain.

At Tewkesbury Margaret refers to him as " Montague our topmast," while Edward in the concluding scene of the play pays a tribute to his and his brother's bravery, describing them as " two brave bears."

[Sir John Neville, Marquess of Montague and Earl of Northumberland, third son of Richard Neville, first Earl of Salisbury, a character in the *Second Part of King Henry the Sixth*.]

Mayor of Coventry. V. i. p.1.

A supernumerary. In Act V., Scene i., where the action is laid at Coventry, a town much devoted to the interests of Henry and his Queen, the stage direction is, " *Enter upon the walls* Warwick, *the* Mayor *of* Coventry, *two* Messengers, *and others*." As this occurs, as we learn from the context, just before the battle of Barnet, April 14, 1471, it may be concluded that the Mayor was John Brett, who served 1470–1, and who for his adherence to Henry VI., was deprived of his sword of state by Edward IV., and the citizens had to pay a fine of 500 marks to recover the sword, and their franchise. Four years later, Edward IV., kept the festival of St. George at Coventry, and became sponsor to the infant child of the Mayor. *French*.

Mayor of York. IV. vii. p.17, 20, 27, p.35.

When Edward appears before the City of York, the Mayor refuses to open the gates as they " owe allegiance unto Henry," but being told that Edward seeks admission as " Duke of York " and a friend of King Henry, he gives orders for York to be admitted. " A wise, stout captain, and soon persuaded ! " remarks Gloucester, to which Hastings adds that when they have entered, he has no doubt that " we shall soon persuade Both him and all his brothers unto reason."

[Thomas Beverley, Sheriff of York, 1451, and Lord Mayor in 1460 and again in 1471.]

Menelaus. II. ii. 146.

> Helen of Greece was fairer far than thou,
> Although thy husband may be Menelaus ;
> And ne'er was Agamemnon's brother wrong'd
> By that false woman as this king by thee.
> [II. ii. 146–149.]

The reference is to men who have faithless wives.

In *Troilus and Cressida*, V., i., 58–61, Thersites, speaking of Menelaus terms him the " goodly transformation of Jupiter there, his brother, the bull, the primitive statue, and oblique memorial of cuckolds."

Menelaus was king of Sparta, and husband of Helen, who was carried off to Troy by Paris. Homer represents him as being of a mild disposition. Edward IV., here considers Helen " fairer " and not so false to her husband, as Margaret has been to her husband (Henry VI.).

[Menelaus is a character in *Troilus and Cressida*.]

Messenger. I. ii. p.49.

= Gabriel. *See* Richard Plantagenet, Duke of York.

Messengers. I. ii. p.48 ; II. i. p.43, p.205 ; II. ii. p.67 ; V. i. p.1 ; V. iv. p.60.

Minos. V. vi. 22.

> Thy father, Minos, that denied our course ;
> [V. vi. 22.]

In classical mythology King of Crete who shut up Dædalus and Icarus in the famous labyrinth, hence " denied the course."

Naples. I. iv. 121.

> My father bears the type of King of Naples.
> [I. iv. 121.]

See under Reignier.

Naples. II. ii. 139.

> Iron of Naples hid with English gilt. [II. ii. 139.]

Applied to Margaret by Richard.

Ned. V. iv. 19 ; V. v. 51.

Edward, Prince of Wales, son of Henry the Sixth and Queen Margaret,

Ned. V. vii. 16.

Son of Edward the Fourth and Queen Elizabeth.

Nero. III. i. 40.

Nestor. III. ii. 188.

> I 'll play the orator as well as Nestor, [III. ii. 188.]

Nestor was King of Pylos in Greece and one of the Grecian generals at the siege of Troy. He was distinguished for his wisdom. He is one of the speaking characters in *Troilus and Cressida* (q.v.).

Nobleman, A. III. ii. p.118.

Appears only once in the Play and announces to King Edward that Henry has been taken prisoner.

Probably Sir James Harrington is the nobleman referred to.

Norfolk. I. i. 156, 208 ; IV. viii. 12.

The county of Norfolk.

Northampton. IV. viii. 15.

The county of Northampton.

Northumberlands, Two. V. vii. 8.

> And two Northumberlands : two braver men
> Ne'er spurr'd their coursers at the trumpet's sound ;
>   [V. vii. 8–9.]

Henry Percy, second Earl of Northumberland. Killed at St. Albans.

Henry Percy, third Earl of Northumberland. Killed at Towton.

Nurse with the young prince. V. vii. p.1.

A supernumerary, who enters carrying the young prince Edward, son of Edward and Elizabeth.

Olympian games. II. iii. 53.

> And if we thrive promise them such rewards
> As victors wear at the Olympian games.
>   [II. iii. 52–53.]

The Olympian games were held at Olympia in Elis every four years in honour of Zeus. They were first instituted by Hercules in 1222 B.C.

Oxfordshire. IV. viii. 18.

Park near Middleham Castle in Yorkshire.

The Scene of Act IV., Scene 4. Taken prisoner by Warwick, Edward is placed in the custody of the Archbishop of York at Middleham Castle, but is liberated, while hunting, by Gloucester and others. [Courtenay says : " These improbable events, excepting always as to Gloucester, who is improperly brought into every occurrence, are taken from Holinshed. Some historians disbelieve them, but Lingard, on the authority of one contemporary, and an ambiguous record, gives credence to the statement of the captivity of Edward. The error of the dramatist consist of placing the event after the junction between Margaret and Warwick. There is no authority for the mode of escape, which, on the contrary, is said to have occurred with the consent of the Earl of Warwick. There is, in the whole transaction, a mystery which I cannot solve. When released, Edward did not, as in the play, fly to Lynn, and thence to Flanders ; that flight was in 1470."] [Hart quotes from Hall : " Kyng Edward beyng thus in captiuitie, spake euer fayre to the Archebishop and to the other kepers, (but whether he corrupted them with money or fayre promises) he had libertie diuers days to go on huntynge, and one day on a playne there met with hym syr William Stanley, syr Thomas of Borogh, and dyuers other of hys frendes with suche a great band of men, that neither his kepers woulde, nor once durst moue him to retorne to prison agayn." King Edward then " went streyghte to York, where he was with grete honor receyued . . . from Yorke to Lancaster, where he found the Lord Hastynges hys chamberlayne, well accompanyed. . . . He then . . . came safe to the cytye of London."]

Phaëton. I. iv. 33 ; II. vi. 12.

> Now Phaëton hath tumbled from his car,
> And made an evening at the noontide prick. [I. iv. 33.]

> O Phœbus, hadst thou never given consent
> That Phaëton should check thy fiery steeds,
> Thy burning car never had scorch'd the earth ;
>   [II. vi. 12.]

See also Phaëton, *The Tragedy of King Richard the Second,* page 463, and *Shakespeare's Ovid* [Golding's translation]. Book II.

Phœbus. II. vi. 11.

O Phœbus, hadst thou never given consent
That Phaëton should check thy fiery steeds
Thy burning car never had scorch'd the earth ;
[II. vi. 11–13.]

Malone remarks : "The Duke of York had been entrusted by Henry with the reins of government both in Ireland and France ; and hence perhaps was taught to aspire to the throne."

Phœnix. I. iv. 35.

My ashes, as the phœnix, may bring forth
A bird that will revenge upon you all ; [I. iv. 35–36.]

See *The Tempest*, page 158.

Plain in Warwickshire.

The Scene of Act IV., Scene ii. Warwick and Oxford arrive with French soldiers. They are joined by Clarence and Somerset who both affirm their allegiance to Henry, and after promising his daughter in marriage to Clarence, Warwick suggests that they surprise Edward in his tent and take him prisoner.

Plain near Mortimer's Cross in Herefordshire.

The Scene of Act II., Scene i. Opens with Edward and Richard—neither of whom fought at the battle of Wakefield—wondering whether their father escaped from that battle. [There is some confusion here. Edward was at this time in Gloucestershire raising an army intending to intercept Margaret on her way to London, but being pursued by Jasper Tudor, Earl of Pembroke—half-brother to Henry the Sixth— halted and obtained a victory at Mortimer's Cross, but the battle is passed over by the dramatist.]

The appearance in the heavens of "three glorious suns" is mentioned by the Chronicles.

Edward and Richard hear of their father's death at Wakefield. Warwick and Montague enter and report their defeat by Margaret at the second battle of St. Albans. [Wordsworth says that "this second battle of St. Albans, in which Margaret was victorious, was fought after the meeting at York (see next scene) and not before as represented here.]

The scene closes with a messenger entering who announces that Margaret with forces is at hand, and yet the next scene is placed Before York, without any announcement that the Lancastrians have retreated before the Yorkists.

A Pedestal, erected near the fifth milestone of the turnpike road leading from Leominster to Wigmore, to commemorate the battle of Mortimer's Cross, bears the following inscription :

This Pedeſtal is erected to perpetuate the Memory of an obstinate, bloody, and deciſive battle fought near this Spot in the civil Wars between the ambitious Houses of York and Lancaſter on the 2nd Day of February 1461 between the Forces of Edward Mortimer Earl of March (afterwards Edward the Fourth) on the Side of York and thoſe of Henry the Sixth on the wide of Lancaſter.

The King's Troops were commanded by Jaſper Earl of Pembroke. Edward commanded his own in Perſon and was victorious. The Slaughter was great on both ſides four Thousand being left dead on the Field and many Welſh Perſons of the firſt diſtinction were taken Prisoners among whom was Owen Tudor (great grandfather to Henry the Eighth and a Deſcendant of the illuſtrious Cadwallader) who was afterwards beheaded at Hereford. This was the deciſive Battle which fixed Edward the Fourth on the Throne of England[1] who was proclaimed King in London on the fifth of March following.

Erected by Subſcription
in the year 1799.

1 Brooke comments :—" The inscription is not altogether accurate, in stating that the battle of Mortimer's Cross fixed Edward IV., on the throne of England. He certainly was proclaimed King by his partisans, in London, soon after the battle, but he was indebted to the subsequent battle of Towton, for his being really placed upon the throne. The statute 1st Edward IV., passed in 1461, declared the 4th of March to be the date when Edward IV., commenced his reign ; ' the fourth day of the moneth of Marche last past toke upon hym to use his right and title to the seid Reame of Englond and Lordship and entred into the exercise of the Roiall estate, dignite, preemynence and power of the same coroune, and to the Reigne and governaunce of the seid Reame of Englond and Lordship ; and the same fourth day of March amoeved Henry late called King Henry the Sixt son of Henry, son to the seid Henry late Erle

of Derby, son to the seid John of Gaunt, from the occupation, usurpation, intrusion, reigne, and governaunce of the same Reame of Englond and Lordship.' "

For accounts of the Battle of Mortimer's Cross, see *exempli gratia*, Brooke's *Visits to Fields of Battle, in England, of the fifteenth century;* Barrett's *Battles and Battlefields in England; Historical Collections of a Citizen of London in the fifteenth Century.*

Plains near Tewksbury.

The Scene of Act V., Scene iv. Opens with Margaret delivering a soul-stirring speech to her soldiers on the eve of the battle of Tewkesbury, which the dramatist has immortalised [V. iv. 1 *et seq.*] A messenger enters with the news that Edward is at hand and amid a flourish of trumpets, Edward with Clarence, Gloucester and forces enter, and the scene closes with Margaret again exhorting her followers in " God's name " to " Be valiant." Hall says : " When the Queene was come to Tewkesbury, and knewe that Kyng Edward followed her . . . she was sore abashed and wonderfully amased and determined in her selfe to flye into Wales to Jasper erle of Pembroke. But the Duke of Somerset, willyng in no wyse to flye . . . determined there to tarye, to take such fortune as God should send. . . . When all these battayles were thus ordered and placyd, the Queene and her sonne prince Ednard rode about the field, encouragyng their souldiers promising to them (if they did shew them selfe valyaunt) . . . greate rewardes . . . bootie . . . and renoune."

See also Another part of the field. [Tewksbury.]

Post. III. iii. p.163 ; IV. i. p.84 ; IV. vi. p.77.

In III. iii. p.163, the messenger brings letters to Warwick, the King of France, and Margaret, which announce the marriage of Edward to Lady Grey.

In IV. i. p.84, enters with news from France.

In IV. vi. p.77, that Edward has escaped from Middleham Castle.

Priam. II. v. 120.

Son, for the loss of thee, having no more,
As Priam was for all his valiant sons.

[II. v. 119–120.]

" I having but one son, will grieve as much for that one, as Priam, who had many, could grieve for many." *Johnson.*

Proteus. III. ii. 192.

Change shapes with Proteus for advantages.

[III. ii. 192.]

Called " the prophetic old man of the sea " because he had the power of assuming various shapes. Cf. Ovid's *Metamorphoses* (Golding's translation), viii. 916–922 :

As thou O Protew dwelling in the sea that cleepes the land.
For now a yoonker, now a boare, anon a Lyon, and Streyght way thou didst become a Snake, and by and by a Bull,
That people were afrayd of thee too see thy horned skull.
And oftentymes thou seemde a stone, and now and then a tree,
And counterfetting water sheere thou seemedst oft to bee
A River : and another whyle contrarie thereuntoo
Thou wart a fyre.

Queen Margaret. I. i. p.211, 228, 257 ; I. iv. p.27 ; II. i. 207 ; II. ii. p.1 ; II. v. 16, p.124 ; II. vi. 75 ; III. i. 35, 53 ; III. iii. p.1, 1, 4, 19, 30, 78, 109, 138, 144, 218 ; IV. i. 102, 115 ; IV. iv. p.1 ; IV. vi. 60 ; V. iv. p.1 ; V. v. p.1 ; V. vi. 37.

At the opening of the play enters the Parliament-house and indignantly denounces her husband for having entailed the crown to York and his heirs, declaring

Had I been there, which am a silly woman,
The soldiers should have toss'd me on their pikes
Before I would have granted to that act ;

[I. i. 243–245.]

and threatens to "divorce" herself "Until that act of Parliament be repeal'd Whereby my son is disinherited."

Leaving in company with her son and gathering together an army of " northern earls and lords " defeats and takes prisoner the Duke of York at Wakefield. Clifford the " relentless foe of the House of York " is on the point of stabbing York, but is restrained by Margaret who " would prolong awhile the traitor's life,"

Ordering York to be placed on a molehill, she taunts and mocks him, and declaring that " York cannot speak unless he wear a crown," a paper crown is set upon his head. York fiercely denounces Margaret, calling her a " She-wolf . . . Whose tongue more poisons than the adder's tooth," after which he is stabbed to death and his head cut off and placed over the gates of York.

Appears before York and taunts Warwick for having run away at the battle of St. Albans. Edward calls her a " shameless callet " and defying her, orders the trumpets to sound, and

> let our bloody colours wave !
> And either victory, or else a grave. [II. ii. 173–174.]

averring that " These words will cost ten thousand lives this day."

The Lancastrian forces being defeated at the battle of Towton, she escapes to Scotland with her son, and subsequently proceeds to France to solicit aid of Lewis, the French king. She is on the point of winning over Lewis but is frustrated by the entry of Warwick who has arrived to ask for the hand of Lady Bona in marriage to King Edward. Calling Warwick " Proud setter up and puller down of kings ! " for it is " thy device By this alliance to make void my suit " she declares she will not " hence, till, with my talk and tears, Both full of truth, I make King Lewis behold Thy sly conveyance and thy lord's false love ; For both of you are birds of self-same feather."

A messenger enters with the news that Edward has secretly married Lady Grey. Remarking " I told your majesty as much before : This proveth Edward's love and Warwick's honesty," Margaret is overjoyed, while Warwick protests to Lewis that he is " clear from this misdeed of Edward's," and vows revenge.

Renouncing allegiance to Edward, Warwick and Margaret are reconciled, and Warwick to assure his " constant loyalty " suggests that his eldest daughter marry the young Prince, to which Margaret consents :

> Yes, I agree, and thank you for your motion.
> Son Edward, she is fair and virtuous,
> Therefore delay not, give thy hand to Warwick ;
> And, with thy hand, thy faith irrevocable,
> That only Warwick's daughter shall be thine.
> [III. iii. 244–248.]

Returning to England, and marching to Tewkesbury, where she hears of the defeat and death of Warwick at Barnet, she engages the Yorkist forces under Edward and being defeated is captured and brought to London where she remains a prisoner for five years, until released by the Treaty of Pecquigny and leaves England for ever.

" There are many stories told of what happened to Queen Margaret on the crushing defeat of her troops. Brave and fearless as she had often shown herself, it is easy to believe the historians who say that she was utterly cast down with grief on this occasion, and so found by some monks, who led her away to a place of hiding not far distant from the town. Fabian, who wrote the narrative of the affair under the auspices of Henry VII., states that Margaret and her son, the Prince of Wales, were taken prisoners together, but no corroboration of such an occurrence is forthcoming. All of the other early historians agree in the statement that she found a temporary refuge, where for several days the vigilance of those sent in pursuit of her was eluded.

> ' The Tuesday, vii day of May, the Kynge departed from Tewxbery, towards the citie of Worcester, and, on the way, he had certayne knowledge that Qwene Margarete was founden nat fer from there, in a powre religious place, where she had hyd hir selfe, for the surty of hir parson, the Saturdaye, erlye in the mornynge, after hir sonne Edward, callyd Prince, was gon to the filde, for to withdraw hir selfe from the adventure of the battayle ; of whome also he was assured that she shuld be at his commandment.'

There is every reason for believing that this extract contains a correct statement of fact, so far as Queen Margaret's escape from the field, three days' hiding and eventual capture goes, but, judging of her by the undaunted courage which had in former times been so conspicuous in her behaviour, we may discard the motives given—that she sought safety in flight before the battle began—as an outcome of Yorkist prejudice. After her capture, Margaret was held as a prisoner of state until her father was able to pay her ransom, for which the great sum of fifty thousand crowns was demanded, and provided as a loan to him by Louis XI., of France. She survived her restoration of liberty but a few years. dying in France in 1482."

Descriptive particulars of the Battle of Tewkesbury

and of all known local scenes and memorials of the Battle.

For Queen Margaret's Proclamation for Musters, *see* Appendix III.

[Queen Margaret is also a character in *King Richard the Third* (q.v.).]

Ravenspurgh. IV. vii. 8.

> What then remains, we being thus arrived
> From Ravenspurgh haven before the gates of York,
> But that we enter, as into our dukedom ?
> [IV. vii. 7–9.]

Hart quotes from Hall: " Kyng Edward beyng thus furnished . . . hauying with hym onely ii M. men of warre beside mariners . . . sailed into England and came on the cost of Yorkshire, to a place called Rauenspurr . . . "

See *Historie of the arrivall of Edward IV., in England and the finall recouerye of his kingdomes from Henry VI., A.D. M.CCCC.LXXI.* Edited by John Bruce. (Camden Society).

Reignier. V. vii. 38.

> Reignier, her father, to the King of France
> Hath pawn'd the Sicils and Jerusalem,
> And hither have they sent it for her ransom.
> [V. vii. 38–40.]

Hart quotes Hall: " Queene Margaret lyke a prisoner was brought to London, where she remayned till kyng Reiner her father ransomed her with money, which summe (as the French writers afferme) he borrowed of Kyng Lewes . . . to repaye so great a dutie, he solde to the French King & his heires, the Kyngdomes of Naples and both the Siciles, with the county of Prouynce. . . . After the ransome payed, she was conveyed into Fraunce with small honor."

Rhesus. IV. ii. 20.

In Greek legend, a warlike king of Thrace who went to the assistance of Priam, when the Trojan war broke out. On the night of his arrival before Troy, Diomed and Ulysses attacked and slew him and carried away his white steeds in order to prevent the fulfilment of a prophecy that if they grazed on the Trojan plains and drank the waters of the Xanthus, the city would never be overthrown. Cf. Ovid's *Metamorphoses* (Golding's translation), xiii. 122–124 ; 307–310 :

> Let Dulychius match with theis, the horses whyght
> Of Rhesus, dastard Dolon, and the coward carpetkynght
> King Priams Helen, and the stelth of Palladye by nyght,
> Of all theis things was nothing doone by day nor nothing wrought
> Without the helpe of Diomed.

> Proceeding further too the Camp of Rhesus streyght I went,
> And killed bothe himselfe and all his men about his tent,
> And taking bothe his chariot and his horses which were whyght,
> Returned home in trymph like a conquerour from fyght.

Richard. I. i. 138.

King Richard the Second.

Richard, afterwards Duke of Gloucester.

I. i. p.1, 17 ; I. ii. p.1, 35, 38, 54 ; I. iv. 9, 15 ; II. i. p.1, 87, 151, 198 ; II. ii. p.81 ; II. iii. p.14 ; II. iv. p.1, 5, 129 ; II. vi. 29, p.31, 40, 103, 109 ; III. ii. p.1, 1, 146 ; IV. i. p.1, 19, 145 ; IV. iii. p.28, 29 ; IV. v. p.1, 16 ; IV. vi. 81 ; IV. vii. p.1, 1 ; IV. viii. p.52 ; V. i. p.16, 101 ; V. iii. p.1 ; V. iv. 27, p.67 ; · V. v. p.1, 35, 42, 78, 83 ; V. vi. p.1, 4 ; V. vii. p.1, 26.

At the opening of the play enters the Parliament-house, and throwing down the head of Somerset, remarks :

> Speak thou for me, and tell them what I did.
> [I. i. 16.]

He encourages his father to assume the crown :

> You are old enough now, and yet, methinks, you lose,
> Father, tear the crown from the usurper's head.
> [I. i. 113–114.]

After a compromise has been effected, he accompanies his father to Sandal Castle, and incites him to break his oath of allegiance to Henry :

> An oath is of no moment, being not took
> Before a true and lawful magistrate
> That hath authority over him that swears :
> Henry had none, but did usurp the place ;
> Then, seeing 'twas he that made you to depose,
> Your oath, my lord, is vain and frivolous.
> [I. ii. 22–27.]

With his brother Edward, defeats the Lancastrian forces at the battle of Mortimer's Cross.

He appears before the City of York where he has a fierce altercation with Queen Margaret who tells him :

> But thou art neither like thy sire nor dam,
> But like a foul misshapen stigmatic,
> Mark'd by the destinies to be avoided.
> [II. ii. 135–137.]

At the battle of Towton he encounters Clifford, who flees on the appearance of Warwick. Clifford falls mortally wounded, and his body being discovered on the battlefield, Edward orders ;

> See who it is, and, now the battle 's ended.
> If friend or foe let him be gently us'd. [II. vi. 44–45.]

but Richard demands that the " doom of mercy be revoked, for 'tis Clifford."

Created Duke of Gloucester in 1461 although he prefers to be Duke of Clarence " For Gloucester's dukedom is too ominous."

Is present at the Palace in London when Lady Grey presents her suit for the restoration of her late husband's estates, and in a long soliloquy unfolds his impious motives to seize the crown, for though " many lives stand between me " he will :

> like one lost in a thorny wood,
> That rents the thorns and is rent with the thorns,
> Seeking a way and straying from the way ;
> Not knowing how to find the open air,
> But toiling desperately to find it out,
> Torment myself to catch the English crown :
> And from that torment I will free myself,
> Or hew my way out with a bloody axe.
> (III. ii. 174–181.)

Asked by Edward whether he is " offended " at his marriage with Lady Grey, ironically replies :

> Not I :
> No, God forbid that I should wish them severed
> Whom God hath join'd together ; ay, and 'twere pity
> To sunder them that yoke so well together.
> [IV. i. 20–23.]

With Hastings, takes to flight when Edward is taken prisoner in his tent near Warwick, and accompanies Edward when he escapes from Middleham Castle in his exile to Holland.

Returning, he is present before York and Coventry, and at the battle of Barnet, where Warwick is defeated and slain, commands the left wing of the Yorkist forces.

He led the vanguard at Tewkesbury, and after the battle, takes part in the butchery of young Edward, and forthwith, proceeding to London, enters the Tower and stabs to death King Henry VI., remarking as he does so :

> For this, amongst the rest, was I ordain'd.
> [V. vi. 58.]

In a soliloquy Gloucester declares that as Clarence stands between him and the throne he must " beware " for " I will sort a pitchy day for thee " ; and " buzz abroad such prophecies That Edward shall be fearful of his life " ; and " then, to purge his fear, I 'll be thy death."

> King Henry and the prince his son are gone :
> Clarence, thy turn is next, and then the rest,
> Counting myself but bad till I be best. [V. vi. 90–92.]

In the last scene of the play he kisses Edward's infant son :

> And, that I love the tree from whence thou sprang'st,
> Witness the loving kiss I give the fruit. [V. vii. 31–32.]

and then aside, mutters with deadly meaning :

> To say the truth, so Judas kiss'd his master,
> And cried " all hail ! " when as he meant all harm.
> [V. vii. 33–34.]

[Richard, Duke of Gloucester, afterwards King Richard the Third is also a character in *King Richard the Third* (q.v.).]

Richard Plantagenet, Duke of York.

I. i. p.1, 21, 26, 40, 48, 49, 65, 74, 77, 83, 95, 105, 121, 152, 166, 174, 185, 202, 204, 233, 254 ; I. ii. p.4 ; I. iii. 30, 49 ; I. iv. p.1, 30, 79, 84, 86, 93, 94, 99, 180 ; II. i. 35, 46, 68, 100, 101 ; II. ii. 19, 54, 99 ; II. iv. 2, 6 ; II. vi. 51, 73, 84.

In the first scene of the play enters the Parliament-house and taking possession of the throne, openly claims the crown of England. A compromise is effected, by which Henry is to reign during his life-time, Richard is proclaimed heir-apparent and protector, and forthwith leaves for Sandal Castle, his residence near Wakefield.

On hearing that her son has been disinherited, Queen Margaret assembles a large force of "northern earls and lords." Marching to Wakefield, she joins battle with the forces of York, who is defeated and taken prisoner.

He is derided and mocked by Margaret who orders a paper crown to be set upon his head, after which he is stabbed to death and his head cut off and placed over the gates of York.

> Off with his head, and set it on York gates :
> So York may overlook the town of York.
> [I. iv. 179–180.]

Roger Mortimer, Earl of March. I. i. 106.

See *Second Part of King Henry the Sixth*, page 857.

Roscius. V. vi. 10.

> What scene of death hath Roscius now to act ?
> [V. vi. 10.]

The celebrated Roman tragedian. The allusion here is to Richard's hypocritical character.

Saint Albans. II. i. 114, 120.

> March'd toward Saint Alban's to intercept the queen,
> [II. i. 114.]
> Short tale to make, we at Saint Alban's met,
> [II. i. 120.]

See under London, II. i. 174, 182.

Saint Albans. II. ii. 103.

> When you and I met at Saint Alban's last,
> Your legs did better service than your hands.
> [II. ii. 103–104.]

An allusion to the proverb " One pair of heels is worth two pairs of hands."

Saint Albans field. III. ii. 1.

The second battle of St. Albans, 1455. Cf. *Extract 7* from Holinshed.

Saint George. II. i. 204 ; II. ii. 80 ; IV. ii. 29 ; V. i. 113.

The patron Saint of England.

Sandal—Sandal Castle. I. ii. 63.

The Scene of Act I., Scene ii. The residence of the Duke of York, near Wakefield. For the sake of the crown, Edward and Richard—sons to York—urge their father to disregard his oath of allegiance to Henry. He is won over just as a messenger enters with the news that Queen Margaret is at hand at the head of a large army intending to besiege York in his castle. [It will be no more than justice to York, if we recollect that this scene, so far as respects the oath, and his resolution to break it, proceeds entirely from our author's imagination. Neither the Earl of March nor Richard was then at Sandal ; the latter being likewise a mere child, barely turned of eight years old. His appearance, therefore, and actions in this, and, at least, the two first Acts of the following play, are totally unsupported by history and truth. It may be likewise observed that the Queen was not actually present at this battle, not returning out of Scotland till some little time after.]

Scotland. III. i. 13 ; III. iii. 26, 151.

> From Scotland am I stol'n, even of pure love
> To greet mine own land with my wishful sight.
> [III. i. 13–14.]

After the Lancastrian forces were defeated at Towton, Henry took refuge in Scotland. Hall says : " And on that parte that marched upon Scotlande, he laied watches and espialles, that no persone should go out of the realme to kyng Henry and his company, which then laye soiornyng in Scotlande ; but whatsoever ieoperdy or peryll might bee construed or demed to have insued by the meanes of kyng Henry, all suche doubtes were now shortly resolved and determined, and all feare of his doynges were clerely put under and extinct ; for he hymselfe, whether he were past all feare, or was not well stablished in his perfite mynde, or could not long kepe hymselfe secrete, in a disguysed apparell boldely entered into Englande. He was no soner entered, but he was knowen and taken of one Cantlowe, and brought towarde the kyng, whom the erle of Warwicke met on the waie, by the kynges commaundement, and brought hym through London to the towre, and there he was laied in sure holde."

Sennet. I. i. p.206.

A signal call on a trumpet.

Septentrion. I. iv. 136.

Thou art as opposite to every good
As the Antipodes are unto us,
Or as the south to the Septentrion.   [I. iv. 134–136.]

= North.

She-wolf of France. I. iv. 111.

She-wolf of France, but worse than wolves of France,
Whose tongue more poisons than the adder's tooth !
[I. iv. 111–112.]

This expression is applied to Margaret by
Richard, Duke of York. Thomas Gray in his
ode *The Bard* adopts the same phrase, and
applies it to Isabel of France, Queen of Edward
the Second :

She-wolf of France, with unrelenting fangs
That tearst the body of thy mangled mate,
From thee be born, who o'er thy country hangs
The scourge of heaven.

Sicils. I. iv. 122.

Thy father bears the type of King of Naples,
Of both the Sicils and Jerusalem,
Yet not so wealthy as an English yeoman.
[I. iv. 121–123.]

See *Second Part of King Henry the Sixth,* page
865.

Sicils. V. vii. 39.

Reignier, her father, to the King of France
Hath pawn'd the Sicils and Jerusalem,
And hither have they sent it for her ransom.
[V. vii. 38–40.]

See Reignier, V. vii. 38.

Sinon. III. ii. 190.

And, like a Sinon, take another Troy.   [III. ii. 190.]

A crafty Greek who persuaded the Trojans to
receive the wooden horse into their city. He was
the grandson of Autolycus and a relative of
Ulysses. Virgil in his Æneid says that " by
his false words and self-inflicted wounds obtained for the wooden horse, in which armed
Greeks were hidden, admission into Troy."

Sir John Montgomery. IV. vii. p.40, 40, 42, 45, 51, 76.

This personage should be Sir Thomas Montgomery, brother to Sir John.

On his arrival at York, Gloucester refers to
him as our " trusty friend." He is welcomed
by Edward who enquires " why come you in
arms," and Montgomery replies to help King
Edward gain the crown as " every loyal
subject ought to do."

Thanking him for his loyalty Edward reminds
him that he only " claims the dukedom till God
please to send the rest." " Then fare you well,"
remarks Montgomery, " I came to serve a king
and not a duke," and giving orders " Drummer,
strike up," is about to march away, but is requested by Edward to stay and they will talk
over the best means to recover the crown.
Proclaiming himself as " Edward's champion,"
he throws down his gauntlet, and challenges to
single fight whoever disputes " King Edward's
right." Edward thanks " brave Montgomery,"
and promises that " If fortune serve me, I 'll
requite this kindness."

Sir John Mortimer.
Sir Hugh Mortimer. Uncles to the Duke of York. I. ii. p.62, 62.

These two characters, who appear in only one
scene of the play, were, according to Mr. T. P.
Courtenay, the illegitimate sons of Anne Mortimer. They were both killed at the battle of
Wakefield, 30th December, 1460.

Sir John Somerville. V. i. p.7, 7.

Appears in only one scene of the Play.

Asked by Warwick as to the whereabouts of
Clarence, Somerville replies that he left him at
Southam with his forces, and expects him in
about two hours' time.

Sir Richard Grey. III. ii. 2.

Brother of Gloucester, at Saint Alban's field
This lady's husband, Sir Richard Grey, was slain,
[III. ii. 1–2.]

Sir John Grey, who was killed at the second
battle of St. Albans in 1461 fighting on the
Lancastrian side. Cf. *Extract 7* from Holinshed.

Sir William Stanley. IV. v. p.1, 1, 24.

Appears in only one scene of the Play. With
Gloucester and Lord Hastings assists Edward in
his escape from Middleham Castle.

[Sir William Stanley, brother of Sir Thomas Stanley, first Earl of Derby, and also of Sir John Stanley, a character in the *Second Part of King Henry the Sixth*. Is mentioned in *King Richard the Third*.]

Soldiers. I. i. p.1 ; I. iii. p.3 ; I. iv. p.27 ; II. i. p.1, p.95 ; II. ii. p.81 ; II. vi. p. 31 ; IV. ii. p.1 ; IV. iii. p.23 ; IV. vii. p.1 ; IV. viii. p.52 ; V. i. p.16 ; V. iv. p.1, p.67 ; V. v. p.1, p.12.

A son that has killed his father. II. v. p.54.

At the battle of Towton entering with a dead body which he intends to rob, he recognises the dead man as his father. Asking forgiveness of God for " I knew not what I did," and his father for " I knew not thee," he declares that " My tears shall wipe away these bloody marks." Henry laments over the scene enacted " O piteous spectacle ! O bloody times ! . . . Weep, wretched man, I 'll aid thee tear for tear."

Southam. V. i. 9.

At Southam I did leave him with his forces,
And do expect him here some two hours hence.
[V. i. 9–10.]

About seven miles south-east of Leamington. Sir John Somerville tells Warwick that he left Clarence with his forces at this place.

Southam. V. i. 12.

It is not his, my lord ; here Southam lies :
The drum your honour hears marcheth from Warwick.
[V. i. 12–13.]

" The Warwick road entered Coventry on the south-west by Greyfriars Gate : that from Southam appears to have entered by New Gate. From either this or Gosford Gate—outside which Edward is elsewhere said to have encamped—Warwick would be looking eastwards. On coming up from Warwick Edward must be supposed to have found the Greyfriars Gate closed against him, and to be coming round the city wall. Warwick hears the drum somewhere behind him, whereas the road from Southam, which Somerville points to, is before him." *Irving edition.*

Spain. III. iii. 82.

Then Warwick disannuls great John of Gaunt,
Which did subdue the greatest part of Spain ;
[III. iii. 81–82.]

See John of Gaunt, III. iii. 81, 83.

Suffolk. I. i. 156 ; IV. viii. 12.

The county of Suffolk.

Tewksbury. V. iii. 19.

We are advertis'd by our loving friends
That they do hold their course toward Tewksbury.
[V. iii. 19–20.]

In Gloucestershire. Margaret was at this time marching with her forces in the direction of Tewkesbury.

Thracian fatal steeds. IV. ii. 21.

See Rhesus.

Three Suns. II. i. 25, 26.

Edw. Dazzle mine eyes, or do I see three suns ?
Rich. Three glorious suns, each one a perfect sun ;
[II. i. 25–26.]

This supernatural incident is related by Holinshed as having taken place on the morning of the battle of Mortimer's Cross. Grafton says : " The Duke of Yorke called Erle of Marche, somewhat spurred and quickned with these nouelties, retired backe, and met with his enemies in a fayre plaine, neere to Mortimers crosse, not farre from Herford East, on Candle-masse day in the mornyng, at which tyme the Sunne (as some write) appered to the Erle of Marche like three Sunnes, and sodainely ioyned all together in one, and that vpon the sight thereof, he tooke such courage, that he fiercely set on his enemyes, and them shortly discom-fited : for which cause, men imagined that he gaue the Sunne in his full brightnesse for his Cognisaunce or Badge."

Tower. III. ii. 120.

See that he be convey'd unto the Tower :
[III. ii. 120.]

See under Scotland. Cf. *Extract* 6 from Holinshed.

Tower. IV. viii. 57 ; V. i. 46.

> Hence with him to the Tower ! let him not speak.
> [IV. viii. 57.]

Hall describes Henry's capture ; " When the Duke of Somerset and other of Kynge Henryes frendes, saw the world thus sodaynly changed euery man fled and in haste shyfted for hym selfe, leuyng Kyng Henry alone, as an host that should be sacrificed, in the Bishops palace of London . . . in whiche place he was by Kynge Edward taken and agayne committed to prison and captiuitie."

Tower. V. v. 50, 85.

> To London, all in post ; and, as I guess,
> To make a bloody supper in the Tower. [V. v. 84–85.]

Cf. *Extract* 19 from Holinshed.

Troy. III. ii. 190.

An ancient city of Asia Minor, and the scene of *Troilus and Cressida.*

Troy. II. i. 51, 52 ; IV. viii. 25.

> Environed he was with many foes,
> And stood against them, as the hope of Troy
> Against the Greeks that would have enter'd Troy.
> [II. i. 50–52.]

Hope of Troy = Hector. Cf. IV. viii. 25.

Tutor to Rutland. I. iii. p.1.

At the battle of Wakefield the Tutor pleads for the life of young Rutland who has fallen into the hands of Lord Clifford, and being told the youth must die, expresses a wish to die with him. He is ordered away by Clifford, for thy " priesthood saves thy life."

Sir Robert Aspall, Chaplain and schoolmaster to the young earl of Rutland. Hall remarks : " While this battaill was in fightyng, a prieste called sir Robert Aspall, chappelain and schole master to the yong erle of Rutland ii. sonne to the above named duke of Yorke, scarce of the age of xii. yeres, a faire gentleman, and a maydenlike person, perceivyng that flight was more savegard, then tariyng, bothe for him and his master, secretly conveyed therle out of the felde, by the lord Cliffordes bande, toward the towne, but or he coulde enter into a house, he was by the sayd lord Clifford espied, folowed, and taken, and by reson of his apparell, de-

maunded what he was. The yong gentelman dismaied, had not a word to speake, but kneled on his knees implorying mercy, and desiryng grace, both with holding up his handes and making dolorous countinance, for his speache was gone for feare. Save him sayde his Chappelein, for he is a princes sonne, and peradventure may do you good hereafter. With that word, the lord Clifford marked him and sayde : by Gods blode, thy father slew myne, and so wil I do the and all thy kyn, and with that woord, stacke the erle to the hart with his dagger, and bad his Chappeleyn bere the erles mother and brother worde what he had done, and sayde. In this acte the lord Clyfford was accompted a tyraunt, and no gentleman, for the propertie of the Lyon, which is a furious and an unreasonable beaste, is to be cruell to them that withstande hym, and gentle to such as prostrate or humiliate them selfes before him."

Two brave bears. V. vii. 10.

> With them, the two brave bears, Warwick and Montague,
> That in their chains fetter'd the kingly lion,
> And made the forest tremble when they roar'd.
> [V. vii. 10–12.]

An allusion to the well-known badge of the bear and the ragged staff. " This well-known badge of the Neville family came to the Earl of Warwick from the Beauchamps though his marriage with the heiress of Beauchamp, Earl of Warwick.". Cf. *Second Part of King Henry the Sixth*, V. i, 144–147 :

> Call hither to the stake my two brave bears,
> That with the very shaking of their chains
> They may astonish these fell-lurking curs :
> Bid Salisbury and Warwick come to me.

Two Keepers. III. i. p.1.

Appear in only one scene of the Play. They are awaiting the approach of deer in the forest, when Henry, disguised, enters. They recognise him, and in " God's name, and the king's " seize him and convey him " unto the officers."

Holinshed says : " whether he was past all feare ; or that hee was not well established in his wits and perfect mind ; or for that he could not long keepe himselfe secret, in *disguised* at[t]ire boldlie entred into England. He was no sooner entred, but he was knowne and taken of one Cantlow, and brought toward the king; whom the earle of Warwike met on the way by the kings commandement, and brought him through London to the Tower & there he was laid in sure hold.''

Ulysses. III. ii. 189.

> Deceive more slyly than Ulysses could,   [III. ii. 189.]

During the siege of Troy he distinguished himself as a cunning spy and a prudent and eloquent negotiator. He is supposed to have devised the stratagem of the wooden horse and was one of those who were concealed in it. A speaking character in *Troilus and Cressida.*

Ulysses. IV. ii. 19.

> That as Ulysses and stout Diomede
> With sleight and manhood stole to Rhesus' tents,
>   [IV. ii. 19–20.]

See Rhesus.

Wakefield. II. i. 107.

> After the bloody fray at Wakefield fought,
>   [II. i. 107.]

The battle of Wakefield. The Scene of Act I., Scenes III. and IV.

Warwickshire. IV. viii. 9.

Watchmen. IV. iii. p.I.

York. I. iv. 180.

> Off with his head, and set it on York gates :
> So York may overlook the town of York.
>   [I. iv. 179-180.]

Richard Plantagenet, Duke of York. (q.v.)

York. I. iv. 179, 180 ; II. i. 65.

> Off with his head, and set it on York gates :
> So York may overlook the town of York.
>   [I. iv. 179-180.]

The city of York. Holinshed says : '' After this victorie by the queene, the earle of Salisbury and all the prisoners were sent to Pomfret, and there beheaded ; whose heads (togither with the duke of Yorkes head) were conueied to Yorke, and there set on poles ouer the gate of the citie, in despite of them and their linage.''

York. IV. vii. 8, 78.

> What then remains, we being thus arrived
> From Ravenspurgh haven before the gates of York,
>   [IV. vii. 7-8.]

The city of York. *See* Ravenspurgh.

York. II. ii. 1 ; II. vi. 52.

The city of York.

York. III. ii. 6 ; III. iii. 108, 186 ; V. 1. 74.

The House of York.

APPENDIX I.

1. [On the battle-field of St. Albans,] laie Henrie, the second of that name, earle of Northumberland ; Humfrie earle of Stafford, sonne to the duke of Buckingham ; Thomas lord Clifford ; . . .

Humfreie, duke of Buckingham, being wounded, and Iames Butler, earle of Ormond and Wilshire, . . seeing fortune thus against them, left the king alone, and with a number fled awaie.

Maister *Edward Hall* in his chronicle maketh mention of an oration, which the duke of Yorke vttered, sitting in *the regall seat*, there in the chamber of the peeres, either at this his first comming in amongst them, or else at some one time after : the which we haue thought good also to set downe ; though *Iohn Whethamsted*, the abbat of saint Albons, who liued in those daies, and by all likelihood was there present at the parlement, making no further recitall of anie words, which the duke should vtter at that time in that his booke of records, where he intreateth of this matter. But for the oration (as maister *Hall* hath written thereof) we find as followeth : During the time (saith he) of this parlement, the duke of Yorke with a bold countenance entered into the chamber of the peeres, and sat downe in the throne roiall, vnder the cloth of estate, (which is the kings peculiar seat), and, in the presence of the nobilitie, as well spirituall as temporall (after a pause made), he began to declare his title to the crowne, in this forme and order as insueth.

[When Queen Margaret perceived that] she could attempt nothing against him neere to London ; because the duke was in more estimation there, than either the king hir husband, or hir selfe : . . .

After long debating of the matter, and deliberate consultation amongest the peeres, prelats, and commons ; vpon the vigill of All saints, it was condescended : for so much as king Henrie had beene taken as king by the space of thirtie and eight yeares and more, that he should inioy the name and title of king, and haue possession of the realme during his naturall life. And, if he either died, or resigned, or forfeited the same, by breaking or going against anie point of this concord, then the said crowne & authoritie roiall should immediatlie be deuoluted and come to the duke of Yorke, if he then liued ; or else to the next heire of his linage.

Item, the said Richard duke of Yorke, shall promit and bind him by his solemne oth, in maner and forme as followeth :

" In the name of God, Amen : I, Richard duke of Yorke, promise and sweare by the faith and
" truth that I owe to almightie God, that I shall neuer consent, procure, or stirre, directlie or
" indirectlie, in priuie or apert, neither (as much as in me is) shall suffer to be doone, consented,
" procured, or stirred, anie thing that may sound to the abridgement of the naturall life of king
" Henrie the sixt, or to the hurt or diminishing of his reigne or dignitie roiall, by violence, or anie
" other waie, against his freedome or libertie " : . . .

And vpon the saturdaie [November 8, 1460] next insuing [All Saints' Day,] Richard duke of Yorke was by sound of trumpet solemnelie proclamed heir apparant to the crowne of England, and protectour of the realme.

The duke of Yorke, well knowing that the queene would spurne against all this, caused both hir and hir sonne to be sent for by the king. But she, as woont rather to rule than to be ruled, and thereto counselled by the dukes of Excester and Summerset, not onelie denied to come, but also assembled a great armie ; intending to take the king by fine force out of the lords hands,

[Yorke] assigned the duke of Norffolke, and erle of Warwike, his trutie freends, to be about the king, while he, with the earles of Salisburie and Rutland, and a conuenient number, departed out of London the second daie of December, northward ; and appointed the earle of March his eldest sonne to follow him with all his power. The duke came to his castell of Sandall beside Wakefield on Christmasse eeuen, & there began to make muster of his tenants and freends.

2. [When a Yorkist army was passing] through Kent, there came to them the lord Cobham, Iohn Gilford, William Pech, Robert Horne, and manie other gentlemen ; . . .

The people of that countrie and other parts were altogither bent in their fauor ; and no lesse addicted to doo them seruice both with bodie and goods, than the Irishmen seemed to be at their receiuing of the said duke of Yorke, and his yoonger sonne Edmund earle of Rutland ; whom they so highlie honoured, that they offered to liue and die in their quarrell. . . .

But it is to be read in a late writer, that the commons of Kent . . . sent priuilie messengers to Calis to the foresaid erles ; beseeching them in all hast possible to come to their succour. Wherevpon the said earles sent ouer into Kent the lord Fauconbridge, to know if their deeds would accord with their words : so that anon the people of Kent, and the other shires adioining, resorted to the said lord Fauconbridge in great number.

---

1. *Shakespeare's Holinshed,* by W. G. Boswell-Stone.

[Margaret] determined to cope with him yer his succour were come.

Now she, hauing in hir companie the prince hir sonne, the dukes of Excester and Summerset, the earle of Deuonshire, the lord Clifford, the lord Ros, and in effect all the lords of the north parts, with eighteene thousand men, or (as some write) two and twentie thousand, marched from Yorke to Wakefield, and bad base to the duke, euen before his castell gates.

[The Duke,] hauyng with hym not fully fiue thousande persones, determined incontinent to issue out, and to fight with his enemies ; and all though sir Dauy Halle, his old seruant and chief counsailer, auysed him to kepe hys Castle, and to defende the same with his smal numbre, till his sonne the Erle of Marche wer come with his power of Marchemen and Welshe souldiours, yet he would not be counsailed, but in a great fury saied : " a, Dauy, Dauy ! hast thou loued me so " long, and now wouldest haue me dishonored ? Thou neuer sawest me kepe fortres when I was " Regent in Normandy, when the Dolphyn hymself, with his puissaunce, came to besiege me, " but, lyke a man, and not like a birde included in a cage, I issued and fought with myne enemies, " to their losse euer (I thanke God) and to my honor . . . wouldest thou that I, for dread of " a scolding woman, . . . should incarcerate my self, and shut my gates ? "

3. [Halle relates that, while the battle of Wakefield] was in fighting, a prieste called sir Robbert Aspall, chappelain and schole master to the yong erle of Rutland, (ii. sonne to the aboue named duke ofYorke, sca[r]ce of the age of xii. yeres, a faire gentleman and a maydenlike person,)perceiuyng that f[l]ight was more sauegard than tariyng bothe for hym and his master, secretly conueyd therle out of the felde, by the lord Cliffordes bande, toward the towne ; but, or he coulde entre into a house, he was by the sayd'lord Clifford espied, folowed, and taken, and, by reson his apparell, demaunded what he was. The yong gentelman, dismayed, had not a word to speake, but kneled on his knees, imploryng mercy and desiryng grace, both with holding vp his handes and making dolorous countinance, for his speache was gone for feare. " Saue him," sayde his Chappelein, " for he is a princes sonne, and peraduenture may do you good hereafter." With that word, the lord Clifford marked him and sayde : " by Gods blode ! thy father slew myne, and so will I do the and all thy kyn ! " and, with that woord, stacke the erle to the hart with his dagger, and bad his Chappeleyn bere the erles mother & brother worde what he had done and sayde. In this acte the lord Clyfford was accompted a tyraunt and no gentelman, for the propertie of the Lyon (which is a furious and an vnreasonable beaste) is to be cruell to them that withstande hym, and gentle to such as prostrate or humiliate them selfes before hym. Yet thus cruel Clifforde, and deadly bloudsupper, [was] not content with this homicyde of chyld-kyllyng, . . .

4. [Though York] fought manfullie, yet was he within half an houre slaine and dead, and his whole armie discomfited : with him died of his truetie freends, his two bastard vncles, sir Iohn and sir Hugh Mortimer, sir Dauie Hall, sir Hugh Hastings, sir Thomas Neuill, William and Thomas Aparre, both brethren ; and two thousand and eight hundred others, whereof manie were yoong gentlemen, and heires of great parentage in the south parts : whose kin reuenged their deaths within foure monethes next, as after shall appeare.

[Clifford, not satisfied with Rutland's murder,] came to the place where the dead corpse of the duke of Yorke laie, caused his head to be striken off, and set on it a crowne of paper, fixed it on a pole, and presented it to the queene, not lieng farre from the field, in great despite, at which great reioising was shewed : but they laughed then that shortlie after lamented, and were glad then of other mens deaths that knew not their owne to be so neere at hand. Some write that the duke was taken aliue, and in derision caused to stand vpon a molehill ; on whose head they put a garland in steed of a crowne, which they had fashioned and made of sedges or bulrushes ; and, hauing so crowned him with that garland, they kneeled downe afore him (as the Iewes did vnto Christ) in scorne, saieng to him : " Haile, king without rule ! haile, kind without heritage ! " haile, duke and prince without people or possessions ! " And at length, haiing thus scorned him with these and diuerse other the like despitefull words, they stroke off his head, which (as yee haue heard) they presented to the queene.

After this victorie by the queene, the earle of Salisburie and all the prisoners were sent to Pomfret, and there beheaded ; whose heads (togither with the duke of Yorkes head) were conueied to Yorke, and there set on poles ouer the gate of the citie, in despite of them and their linage.

5. [Edward had begun his march thence when] newes was brought to him, that Iasper earle of Penbroke, halfe brother to king Henrie, and Iames Butler, earle of Ormund and Wilshire, had assembled a great number of Welsh and Irish people to take him ; he, herewith quickned, retired backe and met with his enimies in a faire plaine neere to Mortimers crosse, not far from Hereford east, on Candle masse daie [Feb. 2, 1461] in the morning. At which time the sunne (as some write) appeared to the earle of March like three sunnes, and suddenlie ioined altogither in one. Upon which sight he tooke such courage, that he, fiercelie setting on his enimies, put them to flight : and for this cause men imagined that he gaue the sunne in his full brightnesse for his badge or cognisance.

[When] true report came not onelie to the queene, but also to the citie ; that the earle of March, hauing vanquished the earles of Penbroke and Wilshire, had met with the earle of Warwike (after this last battell at saint Albons) at Chipping Norton by Cotsold ; and that they with their powers were comming toward London.

[Queen Margaret] still came forwarde with her Northern people, entendyng to subuerte and defaict all conclusions and agrementes enacted and assented to in the last Parliament. And so after her long iorney she came to the town of sainct Albons ; wherof the duke of Northfolke, the erle of Warwycke, and other, (whom the duke of Yorke had lefte to gouerne the kyng in his absence,) beyng aduertised, by the assent of yᵉ kyng, gathered together a great hoste, and set forward towarde saincte Albons, hauyng the kyng in their company, as the head and chefetayn of the warre ; and so, not myndyng to differre the tyme any farther, vpon shrouetues.!ay, early in the mornyng, set vpon their enemyes. Fortune that day so fauored the Quene, that her parte preuayled, & the duke and the elre were discomfited, and fled, leauing the king . . .

[The Yorkist] nobles that were about the king, perceiuing how the game went, and withall saw no comfort in the king, but rather a good will and affection towards the contrarie part, . . . withdrew . . ., leauing the king . . .

Now after that the noble men and other were fled, and the king left in maner alone without anie power of men to gard his person, he was counselled by an esquier called Thomas Hoo, a man well languaged, and well seene in the lawes, to send some conuenient messenger to the northerne lords, aduertising them, that he would now gladlie come vnto them, (whome he knew to be his verie freends, and had assembled themselues togither for his seruice,) to the end he might remaine with them, as before he had remained vnder the gouernement of the southerne lords. . . .

[The Lancastrian lords conveyed Henry to Clifford's tent,] and brought the queene and hir sonne prince Edward vnto his presence, whome he ioifullie receiued, imbracing and kissing them in most louing wise ; and yeelding hartie thanks to almightie God, whome it had pleased thus to strengthen the forces of the northerne men, to restore his deerelie belooued and onelie sonne againe into his possession.

[Queen Margaret] caused the king to dub hir sonne prince Edward, knight ; with thirtie other persons, which the day before fought on hir side against his part.

[Queen Margaret was] fortunate in hir two battles [Wakefield and 2nd St. Albans], but vnfortunate was the king in all his enterprises : for where his person was present, the victorie still fled from him to the contrarie part.

6. [In the conflict at Ferrybridge was slain] the bastard of Salisburie, brother to the earle of Warwike, a valiant yoong gentleman, and of great audacitie.

When the earle of Warwike was informed hereof, like a man desperat, he mounted on his hacknie, and hasted puffing and blowing to king Edward, saieng : " Sir, I praie God haue mercie " of their soules, which in the beginning of your enterprise haue lost their liues ! And bicause " I see no succors of the world but in God, I remit the vengeance to him our creator and redeemer." With that he alighted downe, and slue his horse with his sword, saieng : " Let him flee that will, " for suerlie I will tarrie with him that will tarrie with me " : and kissed the crosse of his sword as it were for a vow to the promise.

King Edward, perceiuing the courage of his trustie friend the earle of Warwike, made proclamation, that all men which were afraid to fight should depart : and, to all those that tarried the battell, he promised great rewards ; with addition, that anie souldier which voluntarilie would abide, and afterwards, either in or before the fight should seeme to flee or turne his backe, then he that could kill him should haue a great reward and double wages.

This deadly battayle and bloudy conflicte continued x houres in doubtful victorie, the one parte some tyme flowyng, and sometime ebbyng, . . .

This conflict was in maner vnnaturall, for in it the sonne fought agaynst the father, the brother agaynst the brother, the nephew against the vncle, and the tenaunt agaynst his lord, . . .

King Henrie, after he heard of the irrecouerable losse of his armie, departed incontinentlie with his wife and sonne to the towne of Berwike ; and, leauing the duke of Summerset there, went into Scotland, and, comming to the king of Scots, required of him and his councell, aid and comfort.

[A Yorkist force passed the Aire] at Castelford, three miles from Ferribridge, intending to haue inuironed the lord Clifford and his companie. But they, being therof aduertised, departed in great hast toward king Henries armie ; yet they met with some that they looked not for, & were so trapt yer they were aware. For the lord Clifford, either for heat or paine, putting off his gorget, suddenlie with an arrow (as some saie, without an head) was striken into the throte, and immediatelie rendred his spirit ; . . .

[Edward reached York on March 30,] and first he caused the heads of his father, the earle of Saliburie, and other his freends, to be taken from the gates, and to be buried with their bodies : and there he caused the earle of Deuonshire, and three other, to be beheaded, and set their heads in the same place.

[Edward] returned, after the maner and fashion of a *triumphant* conquerour, with great pompe vnto London ; where, according to the old custome of the realme, he called a great assemblie of persons of all degrees ; and the nine & twentieth daie of Iune was at Westminster with solemnitie *crowned* and annointed *king.*   .   .   .

Also, after this, he created his two yoonger brethren dukes ; that is to saie, lord George, duke of Clarence, lord Richard, duke of Glocester ;   .   .   .

Some thinke that the name and title of Glocester hath beene vnluckie to diuerse, which for their honours haue beene erected by creation of princes to that stile and dignitie ; as Thomas Spenser, Thomas of Woodstoke, sonne to king Edward the third, and this duke Humfreie : which three persons by miserable death finished their daies ; and after them King Richard the third also, duke of Glocester, in ciuill warre slaine.

[Henry,] whether he was past all feare ; or that hee was not well established in his wits and perfect mind ; or for that he could not long keepe himselfe secret, in *disguised* at[t]ire boldlie entred into England.

He was no sooner entred, but he was knowne and taken of one Cantlow, and brought toward the king ; whom the earle of Warwike met on the way by the kings commandement, and brought him through London to the Tower, & there he was laid in sure hold.

7.   [In 1464] there came to make a sute by petition to the king dame Elizabeth Greie, which was after his queene, at that time a widow, borne of noble bloud by hir mother, duches of Bedford yer she maried the lord Wooduile, hir father.

Howbeit, this dame Elizabeth hir selfe, being in seruice with queene Margaret, wife vnto king Henrie the sixt, was maried vnto one Iohn Greie, an esquier, whome king Henrie made knight vpon the field that he had on Barnet heath by saint Albons, against king Edward.   But litle while inioied he that knighthood : for he was at the same field slaine   .   .   .   this poore ladie made humble sute vnto the king,   that she might be restored vnto such small lands as hir late husband had giuen her in iointure.

The king, being on hunting in the forrest of Wichwood besides Stonistratford, came for his recreation to the manor of Grafton, where the duchesse of Bedford then soiourned, wife to sir Richard Wooduile lord Riuers ; on whome was then attendant a daughter of hirs, called the ladie Elizabeth Graie, widow of sir Iohn Graie knight, slaine at the last battell of saint Albons,   .   .   .

This widow, hauing a sute to the king for such lands as hir husband had giuen hir in iointure, so kindled the kings affection towards hir, that he not onelie fauoured hir sute, but more hir person ; for she was a woman of a more formall countenance than of excellent beautie ; and yet both of such beautie and fauour, that, with hir sober demeanour, sweete looks, and comelie smiling, (neither too wanton, nor too bashfull,) besides hir pleasant toong and trim wit, she so allured and made subiect vnto hir the heart of that great prince, that, after she had denied him to be his paramour, (with so good maner, and words so well set as better could not be deuised,) he finallie resolued with himselfe to marrie hir ; not asking counsell of anie man, till they might perceiue it was no bootie to aduise him to the contrarie of that his concluded purpose ;   .   .   .

Whome when the king beheld, and heard hir speake, as she was both faire and of a goodlie fauour, moderate of stature, well made, and verie wise : he not onelie pitied her, but also waxed inamoured of hir.   And, taking hir afterward secretlie aside, began to enter in talking more familiarlie.   Whose appetite when she perceiued, she vertuouslie denied him.

But that did she so wiselie, and with so good maner, and words so well set, that she rather kindled his desire than quenched it.   And, finallie, after manie a meeting much wooing, and many great promises, she well espied the kings affection toward hir so greatlie increased, that she durst somewhat the more boldlie saie her mind ; as to him whose hart she perceiued more feruentlie set, than to fall off for a word.   And, in conclusion, she shewed him plaine, that, as she wist hir selfe *too simple to be* his wife, so thought she hir selfe *too good to be* his *concubine.*   The king, much maruelling at hir constancie, (as he that had not been woont elsewhere to be so stiffelie said naie,) so much esteemed hir continencie and chastitie, that he set hir vertue in the steed of possession and riches : and thus, taking counsell of his desire, determined in all possible hast to marie her.

Now after he was thus appointed, and had betweene them twaine insured hir ; then asked he counsell of his other freends, and that in such maner, as they might then perceiue it booted not greatlie to say naie.

8.   [Henry, being] somwhat setled in the relme of Scotland,   .   .   .   sent his wife and his sonne into France to king Reiner hir father ; trusting by his aid and succour to assemble an armie, and once againe to recouer his right and dignitie : but he in the meane time made his aboad in Scotland, to see what waie his friends in England would studie for his restitution.

The queene, being in France, did obteine of the yoong French king, then Lewis the eleuenth, that all hir husbands friends, and those of the Lancastriall band, might safelie and suerlie haue resort into anie port of the realme of France ; prohibiting all other of the contrarie faction anie accesse or repaire into that countrie.

[In 1464, when Edward had brought England] into a good & quiet estate, it was thought meet by him and those of his councell, that a marriage were prouided for him in some conuenient place ; and therefore was the earle of Warwike sent ouer into France, to demand the ladie Bona, daughter to Lewes duke of Sauoie, and sister to the laide Carlot, then queene of France ; which Bona was at that time in the French court.

The earle of Warwike, comming to the French king, then lieng at Tours, was of him honourablie receiued, and right courteouslie interteined. His message was so well liked, and his request thought so honourable for the aduancement of the ladie Bona, that hir sister queene Carlot obteined both the good will of the king hir husband, and also of hir sister the foresaid ladie : so that the matrimonie on that side was cleerelie assented to, and the erle of Dampmartine appointed (with others) to saile into England, for the full finishing of the same.

The earle of Oxford far striken in age, and his sonne and heire the lord Awbreie Veer, either through malice of their enimies, or for that they had offended the king, were both, with diuerse of their councellours, attainted, and put to execution ; which caused Iohn earle of Oxford euer after to rebell.

Incontinentlie was Edward earle of March, sonne and heir to Richard duke of Yorke, by the lords in the said councell assembled, named, elected, and admitted for king and gouernour of the realme.

On which daie, the people of the earles part being in their muster in S. Iohns field, and a great number of the substantiall citizens there assembled to behold their order, the lord Fauconbridge, who tooke the musters, wiselie anon declared to the people the offenses and breaches of the late agreement, committed by king Henrie the sixt ; and demanded of the people, whether they would haue him to rule and reigne anie longer ouer them ? To whome they with whole voice answered : " Naie, naie ! " Then he asked them, if they would serue, loue, honour, and obeie the erle of March, as their onelie king and souereigne lord ? To which question they answered : " Yea, yea ! " crieng, " King Edward ! " with manie great showts & clapping of hands in assent and gladnesse of the same.

The lords were shortlie aduertised of the louing consent which the commons frankelie and freelie had giuen. Whervpon, incontinentlie, they all with a conuenient number of the most substantiall commons repaired to the erle of Bainards castell ; making iust and true report of their election and admission, and the louing assent of the commons. . . .

After that this prince Edward earle of March had taken vpon him the gouernement of this realme of England (as before ye haue heard), the morow next insuing, being the fourth of March, he rode to the church of saint Paule, and there offered ; and, after *Te Deum* soong, with great solemnitie he was conueied to Westminster, and there set in the hall with the scepter roiall in his hand : whereto people in great numbers assembled. His claime to the crowne was declared to be by two maner of waies ; the first, as sonne and heire to duke Richard his father, right inheritor to the same ; the second, by authoritie of parlement, and forfeiture committed by king Henrie. Wherevpon it was againe demanded of the commons, if they would admit and take the said erle as their prince and souereigne lord ; which all with one voice cried : " Yea, yea ! "

The French king was not well pleased to be thus daillied with ; but he shortlie (to appease the greefe of his wife and hir sister the ladie Bona) married the said ladie Bona to the duke of Millan.

Now when the earle of Warwike had knowledge by letters sent to him out of England from his trustie friends, that king Edward had gotten him a new wife, he was not a little troubled in his mind ; for that he tooke it his credence thereby was greatlie minished, and his honour much stained, nameiie, in the court of France : for that it might be iudged he came rather like an espiall, to mooue a thing neuer minded, and to treat a marriage determined before not to take effect. Suerlie he thought himselfe euill vsed, that when he had brought the matter to his purposed intent and wished conclusion, then to haue it quaile on his part ; so as all men might thinke at the least wise, that his prince made small account of him, to send him on such a sleeuelesse arrand.

All men for the most part agree, that this marriage was the onlie cause, why the earle of Warwike conceiued an hatred against king Edward, whome he so much before fauoured.

When queene Margaret, that soiourned with duke Reiner hir father, heard tell that the earle of Warwike was come to the French court, with all diligence shee came to Ambois to see him, with hir onelie sonne prince Edward.

With hir also came Iasper earle of Penbroke, and Iohn earle of Oxford, which, after diuerse imprisonments latelie escaped, fled out of England into France, and came by fortune to this assemblie. These persons, after intreatie had of their affaires, determined by meanes of the French king to conclude a league and amitie betweene them. And first to begin withall, for the sure foundation of their new intreatie, Edward prince of Wales wedded Anne second daughter to the earle of Warwike, which ladie came with hir mother into France. After which mariage, the duke and the earles tooke a solemne oth, that they should neuer leaue the warre, till either king Henrie the sixt, or his sonne prince Edward, were restored to the crowne : and that the queene and the prince should depute and appoint the duke and the earle to be gouernors & conseruators of the common wealth, till time the prince were come to estate. . . .

The French king lent both ships, men, and monie vnto queene Margaret, and to hir partakers ; and appointed the bastard of Burbon, admerall of France, with a great nauie, to defend them against the nauie of the duke of Burgognie ; which he laid at the mouth of the riuer Saine, readie to incounter them, being of greater force than both the French nauie and the English fleet.

9. The earle of Warwike, being a far casting prince, perceiued somewhat in the duke of Clarence, whereby he iudged that he bare no great will towards the king his brother ; and there-vpon, feeling his minde by such talke as he of purpose ministred, vnderstood how he was bent, and so wan him to his purpose : .   .   .

The erle had not halfe tolde his tale, but ye duke in a greate fury answered : " why, my lorde, " thynke you to haue hym kynd to you, that is vnkynd, yea, and vnnatural to me, beyng his " awne brother ? thynke you that frendship will make hym kepe promise where neither nature " nor kynred in any wise can prouoke or moue him to fauor his awne bloud ? Thynke you that " he will exalte and promote hys cosin or alie, whiche litle careth for the fall or confusion of hys " awne line and lignage ? This you knowe well enough, that the heire of the Lorde Scales he " hath maried to his wifes brother, the heire also of the lorde Bonuile and Haryngton he hath " geuen to his wifes sonne, and theire of the lorde Hungerford he hath graunted to the lorde " Hastynges : thre mariages more meter for hys twoo brethren and kynne then for suche newe " foundlynges as he hath bestowed theim on.   But, by swete sainte George, I sweare, if my " brother of Gloucester would ioyne with me, we would make hym knowe that wee were all three " one mannes sonnes, of one mother and lignage discended, which should be more preferred and " promoted then straungers of his wifes bloud."

The Duke of Clarence, being come to Calis with the earle of Warwike, after he had sworne on the sacrament to keepe his promise and pact made with the said earle whole and inuiolate, he married the ladie Isabell, eldest daughter to the earle, in our ladies church there.

King Edward, hauing perfect knowledge of all the dooings of the earle of Warwike, and of his brother the duke of Clarence, was by diuerse letters certified of the great armie of the northerne men, with all speed comming toward London ; and therefore in great hast he sent to William lord Herbert, whom (as yee haue heard) he had created earle of Penbroke ; requiring him without delaie to raise his power, and incounter with the northerne men.   .   .   .

And, to assist him with archers, was appointed Humfrie lord Stafford of Southwike, named but not created earle of Deuonshire by the king ; in hope that he would serue valiantlie in that iournie : he had with him eight hundred archers.

10. It is almost not to be beleeued, how manie thousands men of warre at the first tidings of the earles landing resorted vnto him.

[After Warwick's landing, in 1470,] he made proclamation in the name of king Henrie the sixt, vpon high paines commanding and charging all men able to bear armor, to prepare themselues to fight against Edward duke of Yorke, which contrarie to right had vsurped the crowne.

[Edward] assembled his power, and was comming toward the earle, who, being aduertised thereof, sent to the duke of Clarence, requiring him to come and ioine with him.   The duke, being not farre off, with all speed repaired to the earle, and so they ioined their powers togither, and vpon secret knowledge had, that the king (bicause they were entered into termes by waie of communication to haue a peace) took small heed to himselfe, nothing doubting anie outward attempt to his enimies.

The earle of Warwike, intending not to leese such opportunitie of aduantage, in the dead of the night, with an elect companie of men of warre, (as secretlie as was possible,) set on the kings field, killing them that kept the watch, and, yer the king was ware, (for he thought of nothing lesse than of that which then hapned,) at a place called Wolnie [? Honiley, Warwickshire], foure miles from Warwike, he was taken prisoner and brought to the castell of Warwike.   And, to the intent his friends should not know what was become of him, the earle caused him by secret iournies in the night to be conueied to Middleham castell in Yorkshire ; and there to be kept vnder the custodie of the archbishop of Yorke, and other his freends in those parties.

[All his] trustie freends went to diuerse sanctuaries, and amongst other his wife queene Eliza-beth tooke sanctuarie at Westminster, and there, in great penurie, forsaken of all hir friends, was deliuered of a faire son called Edward.

King Edward, being thus in captiuitie, spake euer faire to the archbishop, and to his other keepers, so that he had leaue diuerse daies to go hunt.   .   .   .

11. Now, on a daie, vpon a plaine, when he was thus abrode, there met with him sir William Stanelie, sir Thomas a Borough, and diuers other of his friends, with such a great band of men, that neither his keepers would, nor once durst, moue him to returne vpon prison againe.   Some haue thought that his keepers were corrupted with monie, or faire promises, and therefore suffred him thus to scape out of danger.

Accompanied with the duke of Glocester his brother, the lord Hastings his chamberlaine, (which had maried the earles sister, and yet was euer true to the king his maister,) and the lord

Scales, brother to the queene, he departed into Lincolneshire. And, bicause he vnderstood that all the realme was vp against him, and some part of the earle of Warwiks power was within halfe a daies iournie of him, following the aduise of his counsell, with all hast possible, he passed the Washes in great ieopardie, & comming to Lin found there an English ship, and two hulkes of Holland, readie (as fortune would) to make saile.

Whereupon he, with his brother the duke of Glocester, the lord Scales, and diuerse other his trustie friends, entered into the ship. The lord Hastings taried a while after, exhorting all his acquaintance, that of necessitie should tarie behind, to shew themselues openlie as friends to king Henrie for their owne safegard, but hartilie required them in secret to continue faithfull to king Edward. This persuasion declared, he entered the ship with the other, and so they departed ; being in number in that one ship and two hulkes, about seuen or eight hundred persons, hauing no furniture of apparell or other necessarie things with them, sauing apparell for warre.

12. On the fiue and twentith day of the said moneth, the duke of Clarence, accompanied with the earles of Warwike and Shrewesburie, the lord Strange, and other lords and gentlemen, some for feare, and some for loue, and some onelie to gaze at the wauering world, went to the Tower, and from thense brought king Henrie, apparelled in a long gowne of blew veluet, through London to the church of saint Paule ; the people on euerie side the streets reioising and crieng, " God saue the king ! " as though ech thing had succeeded as they would haue had it : and, when he had offered (as kings vse to doo), he was conueied to the bishops palace,' where he kept his household like a king.

When king Henrie had thus readepted and eftsoons gotten his regall power and authoritie, he called his high court of parlement, to begin the six and twentith day of Nouember, at Westminster ; in the which king Edward was adiudged a traitor to the countrie, and an vsurper of the realme. *His goods were confiscat and forfeited.*

Moreouer, . . . the crownes of the realmes of England and France were by authoritie of the same parlement intailed to king Henrie the sixt, and to his heiress male ; and, for default of such heires, to remaine to George duke of Clarence, & to his heires male : and, further, the said duke was inabled to be next heire to his father Richard duke of Yorke, and to take from him all his landes and dignities, as though he had beene his eldest sonne at the time of his death.

13. When queene Margaret vnderstood by hir husbands letters, that the victorie was gotten by their freends, she with hir sonne prince Edward and hir traine entered their ships, to take their voiage into England : but the winter was so sharpe, the weather so stormie, and the wind so contrarie, that she was faine to take land againe, and to deferre hir oiurnie till another season.

Jasper earle of Penbroke went into Wales, to visit his lands in Penbrokeshire, where he found lord Henrie, sonne to his brother Edmund earle of Richmond, hauing not full ten yeares of age ; he being kept in maner like a captiue, but honorablie brought vp by the ladie Herbert, late wife to William earle of Penbroke, . . .

The earle of Penbroke tooke this child, being his nephue, out of the custodie of the ladie Herbert, and at his returne brought the child with him to London to king Henrie the sixt ; whome when the king had a good while beheld, he said to such princes as were with him : " Lo, suerlie this is " he, to whom both we and our aduersaries, leauing the possession of all things, shall hereafter " giue roome and place." So this holie man shewed before the chance that should happen, that this earle Henrie, so ordeined by God, should in time to come (as he did indeed) haue and inioy the kingdome and whole rule of this realme of England.

[Pembroke] was conueied to Tinbie, where he got ships, and with his nephue, the lord Henrie earle of Richmond, sailed into Britaine, where, of the duke, they were courteouslie interteined ; with assurance made, that no creature should doo them anie wrong or iniurie within his dominions.

[The Duke of Burgundy] would not consent openlie to aid king Edward ; but yet secretlie vnder hand by others he lent vnto him fiftie thousand florens of the crosse of S. Andrew, and further caused foure great ships to be appointed for him in the hauen of de Veere, otherwise called Camphire in Zeland, which in those daies was free for all men to come vnto, and the duke hired for him fourteene ships of the Easterlings well appointed, & for the more suretie tooke a bond of them to serue him trulie, till he were landed in England, and fifteene daies after.

14. Kyng Edward, without any wordes spoken to hym, cam peaceably nere to Yorke of whose commynge, when the citiezens wer certefied, without delay they armed themselfe, and came to defend the gates ; sendyng to hym two of the chiefest Aldermen of the citie, whych ernestly admonished hym on their behalfe to come not one foote nerar, nor temerariouslye to enter in to so great ieopardy ; consideringe that they were fully determined and bent to compell hym to retract with dent of swourd. King Edward . . . determined to set forward neither with army nor with weapon, but with lowly wordes & gentel entreatynges ; requyryng moste hartely the messengers that were sent to declare to the citizens that he came neither to demaund the realme of England, nor the superiorities of the same, but onely the duchie of Yorke, his olde enheritance ; the which duchie, if he might by their meanes readept and recouer, he would neuer let passe out

of hys memorie so great a benifite, and so frendly a gratuitie to hym exhibited. And so with fayre wordes and flatterynge speche he dismissed the messengers, and with good spede he and his folowed so quickly after that they were almost at ye gates as sone as the Ambassadors. The citezens, heryng his good answere, that he ment nor entended nothynge preiudiciall to kynge Henry nor his royall authoritie, were much mitigated & cooled, & began to commen with him from their walles, willyng him to conuey hym self into some other place without delay, which if he did they assured hym that he should haue neither hurte nor damage ; but he, gently speakyng to all men, and especially to suche as were Aldermen,(whome he called worshipfull, and by their proper names them saluted,) after many fayre promises to them made, exhorted & desyred them that by their fauourable frendshyp & frendly permission he might enter into his awne towne, of the which he had both his name and title. All the whole daye was consumed in doubtful communication & ernest interlocution. The citiezens, partely wonne by hys fayre wordes, & partly by hope of hys large promises, fell to this pact & conuencion, that, yf kyng Edward woulde swere to entertayne his citiezens of Yorke after a gentell sorte & fashyon, and here after to be obedient and faythfull to all kyng Henryes commaundementes and preceptes, that then they woulde receyue hym in to their citie, & ayde and comfort hym with money. . . . When kyng Edward had appesed the citiezens, and that their fury was past, he entred in to the citie, & clerely forgettinge his othe, he first set a garrison of souldiers in the towne, to the entent that nothyng should be moued agaynst hym by the citezens, & after he gathered a great host, by reason of his money.

There came to him sir Thomas Burgh, & sir Thomas Montgomerie, with their aids ; which caused him at their first comming to make proclamation in his owne name, to wit, of K. Edward the fourth : boldlie affirming to him, that they would serue no man but a king.

[When] the duke of Somerset, and other of kynge Henryes frendes, saw the world thus sodaynly chaunged, euery man fled, and in haste shifted for hym selfe, leuinge kyng Henry alone, as an hoste that shoulde be sacrificed, in the Bishops palace of London adioyninge to Poules churche ; not knowyng of whom, nor what, counsayll to aske, as he which wyth troble and aduersitie was clerely dulled and appalled : in whych place he was by kyng Edward taken, and agayne committed to prison and captiuitie.

15. [Edward] auaunced hys power toward Couentre, & in a playn by the citie he pytched his felde. And the next daye after that he came thither, hys men were set forwarde, and marshalled in array, & he valiantly bad the erle battayle : which mistrustyng that he should be deceaued by the duke of Clarence (as he was in dede) lept hym selfe close within the Walles.

[After Clarence had been reconciled to Edward,] was it concluded emongest the iii. brethren to attempt therle of Warwicke, if by any fayr meanes he might be reconciled or by any promise allured to their parte. To whom the duke of Clarence sent diuers of hys secrete frendes, first to excuse him of the act that he had done, secondarely to require him to take some good ende now, while he might, with kyng Edward.

When the erle had hard paciently the dukes message, lorde, how he detested & accursed him ! crienge out to him that he, contrary to his oth, promise, & fidelitie, had shamefully turned hys face from his confederates & alies. But to the dukes messengers he gaue none other answere but thys : that he had leuer be alwayes lyke him selfe then lyke a false and a *periured* duke ; and that he was fully determined neuer to leue war, tyll eyther he had lost hys owne naturall lyfe, or vtterly extinguished & put vnder hys foes and enemies.

[Warwick sent hastily] for the duke of Clarence to ioyne with hym ; which had conscribed & assembled together a great host about London. But when he perceiued that the duke lyngered, & dyd al thinges negligently, as though he were in doubt of warre or peace, he then began somwhat to suspect that the Duke was of hys bretherne corrupted & lately chaunged ; . . . yet he had perfect worde that the duke of Clarence came forward toward hym with a great army. Kyng Edward, beynge also therof enformed, raysed his campe, & made toward ye duke. . . . When eche host was in sight of other, Rychard duke of Gloucester, brother to them both, as though he had bene made arbiter betwene them, fyrst rode to the duke, and with hym commoned very secretly : from hym he came to kyng Edward, and with lyke secretnes so vsed hym that in conclusion no vnnaturall warre, but a fraternall amitie, was concluded and proclaymed ; and then, leuyng all armye and weapon a syde, both the bretherne louyngly embraced, and familierly commoned together.

16. Kyng Edward, thus beyng [by Clarence's alliance,] furnished of a strong hoste, went without any maner of diffidence or mistrust toward London. Therle of Warwycke, pondering that the gain of the whole battail stode in makyng hast, with al diligence followed his enemies ; hopynge (that yf they wer neuer let so lytle with any stop or tariyng by ye waye) to fight with them before thei should come to London. . . . [After resting awhile at St. Albans] he remoued to a village in the meane waye between London & saynct Albones, called Barnet, beyng tenne myle distaunt from bothe the tounes.

[Towards the close of the battle of Barnet, Warwick,] beyng a manne of a mynde inuincible, rushed into the middest of his enemies, whereas he (auentured so farre from his awne compaignie, to kill & sley his aduersaries, that he could not be rescued) was, in the middes of his enemies, striken doune & slain. The marques Montacute, thynkynge to succor his brother whiche he sawe was in great ieoperdy, & yet in hope to obtein the victory, was likewise ouerthrowen and slain.

17. [Queen Margaret, having heard of Edward's return,] gathered together no small compaignie of hardy and valiaunt souldiours, determined with all haste and diligence, with Prince Edwarde her sonne, to saile into Englande ; but yet once again (suche was her destinie) beyng letted for lacke of prosperous wynde, & encombered with to[o] muche rigorous tempeste, " a daie after " the faire," (as the common prouerbe saieth,) landed at the Port of Weymouth, in Dorsetshire.

[When news of Barnet field came,] she, like a woman al dismaied for feare, fell to the ground, her harte was perced with sorowe, her speache was in maner passed, all her spirites were tormented with Malencoly.

Iohn earle of Oxford, which after Barnet field both manfullie and valiantlie kept saint Michaels mount in Cornewall, either for lacke of aid, or persuaded by his friends, gaue vp the mount, and yeelded himselfe to king Edward (his life onelie saued), which to him was granted. But, to be out of all doubtfull imaginations, king Edward also sent him ouer the sea to the castell of Hammes, where, by the space of twelue yeeres, hee was in strong prison shut vp and warilie looked to.

18. [On May 6, 1471,] was Edmond duke of Somerset . . . behedded in the market-place at Tewkesbury.

After the field was ended, proclamation was made, that whosoeuer could bring foorth prince Edward aliue or dead, should haue an annutie of a hundred pounds during his life, and the princes life to be saued, if he were brought foorth aliue. Sir Richard Crofts [the Prince's captor], nothing mistrusting the kings promise, brought foorth his prisoner prince Edward, being a faire and well proportioned yoong gentleman ; whom when king Edward had well adused, he demanded of him, how he durst so presumptuouslie enter into his realme with banner displaied ?

Wherevnto the prince boldie answered saieng : " To recouer my fathers kingdome & heritage, " from his father and grandfather to him, and from him after him to me, lineallie descended." At which words king Edward said nothing, but with his hand thrust him from him, or (as some saie) stroke him with his gantlet ; whom, incontinentlie, George duke of Clarence, Richard duke of Glocester, Thomas Greie marquesse Dorcet, and William lord Hastings, that stood by, suddenlie murthered : . . .

19. [Henry died on May 21 or 22, 1471. He was] in the Tower spoiled of his life, by Richard duke of Glocester, (as the constant fame ran,) who (to the intent that his brother king Edward might reigne in more suertie) murthered the said king Henrie with a dagger.

APPENDIX II.

" On halmesse evyn, abowt thre after noyne, comyn into the Comowne Howus, the Lordys spiritual and temporal, excepte the Kyng, the Duk of York, and hys sonys ; And the Chawnceler reherset the debate had bytwyn owre soveren Lord the Kyng and the Duk of York upon the tytelys of Inglong, Fraunce, and the Lordschep of Erlond, wyche mater was debat, arguet, and disputet by the seyd lordes spiritual and temporal byfore owre soveren Lord and the Duk of York longe and diverse tymys.   And at the last, by gret avyce and deliberacion, and by the assent of owre soveryn Lord and the Duke of York, and alle the lordes spiritual and temporal ther assemelyd by vertu of thys present parlement, assentyt, agreyt, and acordyt, that owre sovereyne Lord the Kyng schal pessabylly and quyetly rejoys and possesse the crowne of Inglond and of Fraunce and the Lordchip of Irlond, with al hys preemynences, prerogatyves, and liberteys duryng hys lyf.   And that after hys desese the coroun, etc. schal remayne to Rychard Duk of York, as rythe inheryt to hym, and to hys issue, prayng and desyring ther the comownes of Inglond, be vertu of thys present parlement assemylet, to comyne the seyd mater, and to gyff therto her assent.   The wyche comyns, after the mater debatet, comynt, grawntyt, and assentyt to the forseyd premisses.   And ferthermore was granted and assentyt, that the seyd Duk of York, the Erl of March, and of Rutlond, schul be sworne that they schuld not compas ne con-spyrene the kynges deth ne hys hurt duryng hys lyf.   Ferthermore the forseyd Duk schulde he had, take, and reportyt as eyr apparent prince and ryth inheryter to the crowne aboveseyd. Ferthermore for to be had and take tresoun to ymagyne or compas the deth or the hurt of the seyd Duk, wythe othye prerogatyves as long to the prince and eyr parawnt.   And fferthermore the seyd Duk and hys sonys schul have of the Kyng yerly x.Ml., marces, that is to sey, to hemself v.Ml., to the Erl of Marche iijMl., the Erl of Rutlond ijMl. marces.   And alle these mateyrs agreyd, assentyt, and inactyt by the auctorite of thys present parlement.   And ferthermore, the statutes mad in the tyme of Kyng Herry the fowrth, wherby the croune was curtaylet to hys issu male, utterly anullyd and evertyth, wyth alle other statutes and grantys mad by the seyd Kynges days, Kyng Herry the V. and Kyng Herry the vj^{te}, in the infforsyng of the tytel of Kyng Herry the fourth in general."   Rot. Harl. C. 7, Membr. 4, dorso.

1. Warkworth's *Chronicle*, Ed. by Halliwell [Camden Society].

APPENDIX III.

QUEEN MARGARET'S PROCLAMATION FOR MUSTERS.[1]

" Jhesus. Maria. Johannes.

   . . . the most nobylle and Crysten prynce, oure most dradde soverayne Lorde Kynge Hary the syxte, verrey true undoutyde Kynge of Englonde and of Fraunce, nowe beynge in the hondys of hys rebellys and gret en[e]my, Edwarde, late the Erl of Marche, usurper, oppressour, and distroyer of oure seyed Soverayn Lorde, and of the nobylle blode of the reme of Englonde, and of the trewe commenes of the same, by hys myschevus and inordinate newe founden lawes and ordenaunces inconveniant, to the uttyrmoste destruccion of the goode commenes of the seyde reme of Englonde ; yf yt so schulde contenne ffor the reformacion wherof, in especialle for the comenwelle of alle the seyde reme, the rygt hyghe and mygty Prynce George Duke [of] Clarens, Jasper Erl of Penbroke, Richarde Erl of Warewyke, and Johnne Erl of Oxenforde, as verrey and trewe feygtfulle cosyns, subgettes, and liege men to oure seyde soveraine Lord Kynge Harry the syxt, by sufficiante autorite commysyd unto theme in thys behalfe, be the hole voyse and assent of the moste nobylle pryncesse Margaret, Quene of Englonde, and the Rygt Hyge and mygty Prynce Edwarde, atte thys tyme beyng Quene, into thys reme to putte theme in ther moste uttermoste devers to dylyver oure seyd Sopheraine Lord oute of hys grete captivite, and daungere of hys enmyes, unto hys liberte, and by the grace of Gode to rest hym in his rialle estate, and crowne of thys hys seyd reme of Englond, and reforme . . . and amende alle the grete myschevus oppressions, and alle odyr inordinate abusions, nowe raynynge in the seyd reme, to the perpetualle pese, prosperyte, to the comene welfare of thys reme. Also ytt ys fully concludyd and grauntyde that alle mail men within the reme of Englonde, of whatt estat, degre, condicion that they be of, be fully pardonede of alle maner tresoun or trespace imagenyd or done, in eny maner of wyse contrary to ther legeyns, agayne oure soveraine Lorde the Kynge, the Quene, and my Lorde the prynce, before the day of comynge and entre of the sayde Duke and Erles in thys sayde reme ; so that they putte them in ther uttermost dever, and att thys tyme drawe them to the company of the seyde Duke and Erles, to helpe and to fortefy theme in ther purpose and jorney ; excepte suche persons as be capitalle enmyes to oure seyde soferaine Lorde, withowte punyschement of the whyche god pece and prosperite of thys reme cannatte he had ; and excepte alle suche as atte thys tyme make any rescistens ageyns the seyde Duke and Erlys, or eny of theme, or of ther compeny. Also the sayde Duke and Erlys, in the name and behalfe of oure seyde soferaine Lorde Kynge Harry the syxt, chargyne and commawndyne that alle maner of men, that be betwen xvj. yeres and lxti., incontinently and immediatly aftyr thys proclamacion made, be redy, in ther best aray defensabell, to attende and awayte upponne the sayde Duke and Erlys, to aschyst theme in ther jorney, to the entente afore rehercyd, upponne payne of dethe and forfiture of alle that they [may forfeyte], withinne the reme of Englond ; excepte suche persons as be visette with syknesse, or with suche noune poure that they may not go."

1. Warkworth's *Chronicle,* Ed. by Halliwell [Camden Society].

APPENDIX IV.

Extract from the Act of Attainder of the 1st. Edward IV., passed against the Lancastrians who had taken part in the second Battle of St. Alban's, the Battle of Wakefield, and the Battle of Towton.—*Rot. Parl.* I Edward IV. (A.D. 1461), vol. v. p. 476, 477, and 478.[1]

" For asmoche as Henry, late Kyng Henry the sixt, ayenst the honoure and trouth that owe to be stablisshed in every Christen Prynce, dissimilyng with the right noble and famous Prynce Richard Duc of York, to whome it lyked at the grete and speciall instaunce of the same Henry, and of the Lordes Spuelx and Temporelx, and Commyns of the Reame of Englond, solempnely to hym made, and for the tender and and naturall zele and affection that he bare unto the commyn wele, good pollitique, and restful governaunce therof, to take his viage from the Cite of London, toward the North parties of the seid Reame, to represse, subdue and resist the unleefull and inordynat commotion and riotte there bigonne, to the subversion of the seid Coen wele, politique and restfull governaunce : Natheles procured, stered and excited, ayenst his promisse, and the forme of the Convention and Concorde made bitwene hem of and uppon the right and title of the seid Coroune, roiall power, dignite, estate, preemynence and possession of the seid Reame, the murdre of the same Duc. And where the seid Henry Usurpour, dissimilyng the destruction of other lordes and persones of the same reame, by his writts, called to assist hym to attend uppon his persone, to resiste and represse another commocion of people, by his assent and wille gadered, and waged not oonly in the North parties, but also oute of Scotland, commyng from the same parties with Margarete late called Quene of Englond, and hir son Edward, late called Prynce of Wales, extendyng to the extreme destruction of the seid Reame, namely of the South parties thereof, wherof experience sheweth the clerenes, respect had to the spoile by theym of Godds chirch, of Chalesses, Crosses of sylver, Boxes for the Sacrament, and other onourments longyng therunto, of defoulyng and ravisshing religious wymmen, wedowes and maydens, of unmanly and abhomynable entretyng of wymmen beyng in the naturall labour and bataille of travailyng of child, by the moyne therof piteously disperaged, Heven sorowyng the lost therby of the Soules that shuld have been of the felauship of Cristendom and of the blisse of Heven, not abhorryng of unmanly, unnaturall and beestly cruelte to drawe wymmen beyng in childebedde from their bedds naked, and to spoile hem of all her goods, a piteous desolacion. The same Henry, actour, factour and provoker of the seid commocion, and assentyng of covyne with the seid Margarete, Henry Duc of Somerset, and Henry late Erle of Northumberlond, in a battaille to be shewed unto hym, and offered of fraudulent dissimilacion, in a feld beside the toune of Seint Albones, the xvii day of Feverer last past, not joynyng his persone and blode to the defence, tuition and salvacion of the same Lordes and persones commen to assist hym by his auctorite and commaundement, lyke a victorious and a noble captayne, but lyke a disseyvable coward, ayenst princely and knyghtly duetee, sodenly, privately and shamefully refused theym, sufferyng and procuryng to disseivably th'effucion of their blode, and horrible murdre and deth, not havyng therof sorowe, pitee or compassion ; adheryng to the seid Margaret, and to the seid Duc of Somerset, and other Lordes and persones that committed the seid orrible and cruell murdre of the seid Duc of York, and of the Erles of Rutlond and Salesbury, and also of the seid people, in the seid felde beside the seid toune of Seint Albones, yevyng therfor to the seid Duc and other assistyng theym therin, a speciall laude and thank ; from thensforth applyyng to theym and to their outrageous and unlawfull riotts and misgovernaunce ; after that sufferying wilfully thoo worthy and good Knyghtes, William Lord Bonvile, and Sir Thomas Kiryell, for the prowesse of knyghthode approved in their persones called to the order of the Garter, and William Gower Squier, the Berer of oon of his Baners, whom to he made feith and assurans under Kynges word, procedyng from his mouth, to kepe and defend theym there from all hurt, joupardie and perell, to be murdred, and after that tyrannyously heded, with grete violence, withoute processe of lawe or any pitee, contrary to his seid feith and promysse, abhomynable in the heryng of all Christen Prynces. For asmoch also as Henry Duc of Somerset, purposyng, ymaginyng and compassyng, of extreme and insaciate malice and violence, to destroy the right noble and famous Prynce of wurthy memorie, Richard late Duc of York, fader to oure Liege and Soverayne Lord Kyng Edward the fourth, and in his lyf verrey Kyng in right of the reame of Englond, singuler protectour lover and defensour of the good governaunce, pollicie, commyn wele, peas and tranquillite therof ; and also Thomas Courteney late Erle of Devonshire, Henry Erle of Northumberlond, Thomas Lord Roos, John late Lord Nevill, John Whelpdale late of Lychefeld, Clerk, Philip Lowes late of Thouresby in the counte of Lincoln Clerk, Bawdewyn Fulforth Knyght, Alexander Hody Knyght, Nicholas Latymer Knyght, James Loterell Knyght, Edmund Mountford Kynght, Thomas

1. Brooke's *Visits to Fields of Battle, in England, of the fifteenth century.*

Fyndern Knyght, Henry Lewes Knyght, John Heron of the Forde Knyght, Richard Tunstall Knyght, Henry Belyngeham Knyght, Robert Whityngham Knyght, William Grymmesby late of London late Squier, Thomas Tunstall late of Thurland in the shire of Lancastr' Squier, Symond Hammes Knyght, Thomas Dalton late of Lilbourne in the counte of Northumberlond Gentilman, James Dalton late of the same Gentilman, George Dalton late of the same Gentilman, John Clapam late of Skipton in Craven in Yorkshire Yoman, Andrew Trollop late of Guysnes Squier, Antony Noteill Knyght, John Botiller late of Howke in the counte of Dorset Squier, Gawen Lampleugh late of Warkeworth in the shire of Northumberlond, Gentilman, Edmund Fyssh late of York Taylleour, Thomas Frysell late of the same Smyth, John Smothyng late of the same Yoman, John Caterall late of Brayton in the counte of York Gentilman, Thomas Barton late of Helmesley in the counte of York Gentilman, William Fyppes late of Southduffeld in the counte of York Yoman, Henry Clyff th' elder late of Lokyngton in the counte of York Yoman, Robert Tomlynson late of Helagh in the counte of York Yoman, and Thomas Barton late of York Mason ; at Wakefield in the shire of York, on Tywesday the xxx day of Decembr' last past, with grete despite and cruell violence, horrible and unmanly tyrannye, murdred the seid right noble Prynce Duc of York. And where also Henry Duc of Excestr', Henry Duc of Somerset, Thomas Courteney late Erle of Devonshire, Henry late Erle of Northumberlond, William Vicecount Beaumont, Thomas Lord Roos, John late Lord Clyfford, Leo late Lord Welles, John late Lord Nevill, Thomas Gray Knyght Lord Rugemond Gray, Randolf late Lord Dacre, Humfrey Dacre Knyght, John Morton late Person of Blokesworth in the shire of Dorset Clerk, Rauff Makerell late Person of Ryseby in the shire of Suff' Clerk, Thomas Mannyng late of New Wyndesore in Berkshire Clerk, John Whelpdale late of Lychefeld in the counte of Stafford Clerk, John Nayler late of London Squier, John Preston late Wakefield in the shire of York Preest, Philip Wentworth Knyght, John Fortescu Knyght, William Tailboys Knyght, Edmund Mountford Knyght, Thomas Tresham Knyght, William Vaux Knyght, Edmund Hampden Knyght, Thomas Fyndern Knyght, John Courteney Knyght, Henry Lewes Knyght, Nicholas Latymer Knyght, Waltier Nuthill late of Ryston in Holdernes in the shire of York Squier, John Heron of the Forde Knyght, Richard Tunstall Knyght, Henry Belyngeham Knyght, Robert Whityngham Knyght, John Ormond otherwise called John Botillier Knyght, William Mille Knyght, Symonde Hammes Knyght, William Holand Knyght called the Bastard of Excestr', William Josep' late of London Squier, Everard Dykby late of Stokedry in the shire of Ruthlond Squier, John Myrfyn late of Suthwerk in the shire of Surr' Squier, Thomas Philip late of Dertyngton in Devonshire Squier, Thomas Brampton late of Guysnes Squier, Giles Seyntlowe late of London Squier, Thomas Claymond, the seid Thomas Tunstall Squier, Thomas Crawford late of Caleys Squier, John Aldeley late of Guysnes Squyer, John Lenche of Wyche in the shire of Worcestre Squier, Thomas Ormond otherwise called Thomas Botillier Knyght, Robert Bellyngeham late of Burnalshede in the shire of Westmerlond Squier, Thomas Everyngham late of Newhall in the shire of Leycestr' Knyght, John Penycok late of Waybrigge in the counte of Surr' Squier, William Grymmesby late of Grymmesby in the shire of Lincoln' Squier, Henry Ross late of Rokyngham in the shire of Northampton Knyght, Thomas Danyell late of Rysyng in the shire of Norff' Squier, John Doubiggyng late of the same Gentilman, Richard Kirkeby late of Kirkeby Ireleth in the shire of Lancastr' Gentilman, William Ackeworth late of Luton in the shire of Bed' Squier, William Weynsford late of London Squier, Richard Stucley late of Lambehith in the counte of Surr' Squier, Thomas Stanley late of Carlile Gentilman, Thomas Litley late of London Grocer, John Maydenwell late of Kirton in Lyndesey in the counte of Lincoln Gentilman, Edward Ellesmere late of London Squier, John Dauson late of Westmynster in the shire of Midd' Yoman, Henry Spencer late of the same Yoman, John Smothyng late of York Yoman, John Beaumont late of Goodby in the shire of Leyc' Gentilman, Henry Beaumont late of the same Gentilman, Roger Wharton otherwise called Roger of the Halle, late of Burgh in the shire of Westmerlond Grome, John Joskyn late of Branghing in the shire of Hertf' Squier, Richard Litestr' the yonger late of Wakefield Yoman, Thomas Carr late of Westmynster Yoman, Robert Bollyng late of Bollyng in the shire of York Gentilman, Robert Hatecale late of Barleburgh in the same shire Yoman, Richard Everyngham late of Pontfreyt in the same shire Squier, Richard Fulnaby of Fulnaby in the shire of Lincoln Gentilman, Laurance Hille late of Moch Wycombe in the counte of Buk' Yoman, Rauff Chernok late of Thorley in the counte of Lancastr' Gentilman, Richard Gaitford of Estretford in Cley in the shire of Notyngh' Gentilman, John Chapman late of Wymbourne Mynster in Dorset shire Yoman, and Richard Cokerell late of York Marchaunt ; on Sonday called comynly Palme Sonday, the xxix day of Marche, the first yere of his reigne, in a feld bitwene the townes of Shirbourne in Elmett, and Tadcastr' in the seid Shire of York, called Saxtonfeld and Tawtonfeeld, in the shire of York, accompanyed with the Frensshmen and Scotts, the Kynges Ennemyes, falsely and traiterously ayenst their feith and liegeaunce, there rered werre ayenst the same Kyng Edward, their rightwise, true, and naturall liege Lord, purposyng there and then to have distroyed hym, and deposed hym of his roiall estate, coroune and dignite ; and then and there, to that entent, falsely and traiterously moved bataille ayenst his seid astate, shedyng therein the blode of a grete nombre of his subgetts : In the which bataille, it pleased Almyghty

God to yeve unto hym, of the mysterie of his myght and grace, the victorie of his ennemyes and rebelles, and to subdue and avoyde th' effect of their fals and traiterous purpose.   And where also the seid Henry, late called Kyng Henry the Sixt, Margarete his wyf, late called Quene of Englond, and Edward her Son, late called Prynce of Wales, and also Henry Duc of Excestre, Henry Duc of Somerset, Thomas Lord Roos, Thomas Grey Knyght Lord Rugemond Gray, in the fest of Seint Marc Evangelist last past, purposyng and ymaginyng the destruction of oure seid Soverayne Lord Kyng Edward, to depose hym of his roiall astate and dignite, procured of James Kyng of Scotts, and of his subgetts, then ennemyes of our seid Soverayne Lord, their eyde, assistence and armed power, to entre uppon the same oure Soverayne Lord into his seid reame, to put hym from the reigne thereof, and to distroy hym ; and to that entent, convened with the same James Kyng of Scotts, and ayeinst their feith and liegeaunce, delyvered to hym to his possession and obeisaunce, in the seid Fest, the toune and castell of Berwyk, of ourse seid liege Lordes, then beyng their rightwisse, true, and naturall liege Lord, to that ende and effect, that the seid Kyng of Scotts soo than possessed of the seid toune and castell, the key of the Estmarches of Englond, shuld therby have entre, to execute the unjust, untrue, and malicious purpose and entent of the same Henry, Margaret and Edward.   And for asmoch also as the seid Margarete, and also Henry Duc of Excestr' Henry Duc of Somerset, Jasper Erle of Pembroke, James late Erle of Wilteshire, Robert Lord Hungerford, Thomas Mannyng Clerk, John Lax, late Parsoune of Walton in the shire of Somerset Clerk, Henry Lewes Knyght, Robert Whityng-ham Knyght, John Ormond otherwise called John Botillier Knyght, Frere Robert Gasley, of the ordre of the Freres Prechours, and Thomas Cornewayle Squier, have ayenst their feith and liegeaunce, dyvers tymes sith the fourth day of Marche last past, stured laboured and provoked the ennemyes of oure seid soverayne Lord Kyng Edward the Fourth, of outeward landes, to entre into his seid reame with grete bataille, to rere werre ayenst his astate within this seid reame, to conquere the same from his possession and obeysaunce, to depose hym of roiall astate, corounes and dignitie, and to destroy his moost noble persone and subgetts.   And where also the same Margarete, and Edward her son, and also the seid Henry Duc of Excestr', Thomas Grey Lord Rugemonde Grey, Humfrey Dacre Knyght, Edmund Hampden Knyght, Robert Whityngham Knyght, Henry Bellyngeham Knyght, and Richard Tunstall Knyght, adheryng to the Scotts, ennemyes of oure seid soverayne Lord Kyng Edward the Fourth, comvened with the same Scotts, procuryng, desiring and wagyng theym to enter into his seid reame, to make there werre ayenst his Roiall Majeste, bringyng the same Scotts and ennemyes to his cite of Carlile, besegyng and envirounyng it, brennyng the subarbes thereof, distroiyng the howses, habitacions and landes of his subgetts nygh therunto, in manere of conquest ; purposyng, ayenst their feith and lie-geaunce, to have delyvered the seid cite, the key of the Westmarches of Englond, into the possession and obeysaunce of the seid Kyng of Scotts, and to have spoiled the coroune of Englond therof, as they didde of the seid toune of Berwyk.   And over that, where the seid Henry, late called Kyng of Englond the Sixt, and also Thomas Lord Roos, Thomas Gray Lord Rugemond Grey, Humfrey Dacre Knyght, John Fortescu Knyght, William Tailboys Knyght, Edmund Mountford Knyght, Thomas Nevill late of Brauncepath in the Bisshopryke of Durham Clerk, Humfrey Nevill late of the same Squier, and Thomas Elwyke late of Caleys Squier, the xxvi day of Juyne last past, at Ryton and Brauncepath in the Bisshopryke of Durham, with standardes and gyturons unrolled, rered werre ayenst oure seid Lord Kyng Edward, purposyng to have deposed hym of his roiall astate, coroune and dignitie, ayenst their feith and liegeaunce.   And for asmoch also as Henry Duc of Excestre, Jasper Erle of Pembroke, and Thomas Fitz Herry late of Herford Squier, at a place called Tutehill, besid' the toune of Carnarvan in Wales, on Friday next after the fest of Translacion of Seint Edward last past, rered werre ayenst the same oure soverayne Lord, purposyng then and there to have proceeded to his destruction, of fals and cruell violence, ayenst their feith and liegeaunce."

The act then declares Henry, late called King Henry the Sixth, convicted of high treason, and to forfeit all castles, manors, lordships, lands, &c., &c., parcel of the Duchy of Lancaster ; and the said Margaret, late called Queen of England, convicted of high treason ; and the said Margaret, and also the said Edward her son, disabled from having or enjoying any name of dignity, pre-eminence, &c., &c., ; and declares the said Margaret, and Edward her son, to forfeit all castles, manors, lordships, lands, goods, &c., &c., and also declares the noblemen comprised in it disabled from having or enjoying any name of dignity, pre-eminence, &c., &c., and the noblemen, knights, and other persons comprised in the act, convicted of high treason, and to forfeit all their manors, lordships, lands, possessions, &c., to the King ; except such as were within the liberty of the Bishop of Durham, which were declared forfeited to the Bishop, who claimed them in right of the Cathedral Church of St. Cuthbert of Durham ; within which liberty the Bishops of Durham were alleged to have had immemorially the right to all forfeitures of that description.

APPENDIX V.

Extract from the Act of Attainder of 14th Edward IV. passed against some of the Lancastrians who had taken part in the Battles of Barnet, Tewkesbury, &c.—*Rot. Parl.* 14th Edward IV. (A.D. 1475), vol. vi. fos. 144, 145, 146.[1]

" And also where John Veer late Erl of Oxford, late of Wyvenho in the counte of Essex Knyght, George Veer, late of the same toune Knyght, Thomas Veer late of the same toune Knyght, Robert Harlyston, late of Shymplyng in the counte of Suffolk Squyer, William Godmanston, late of Bromle in the counte of Essex, Squyer, John Durraunt, late of Colleweston in the counte of Northampton Yoman, and Robert Gybbon, late of Wyngfeld in the counte of Suffolk Squyer, in the solempne and high fest of Ester Day, the which was the xiiiith day of Aprill, the xith yere of the reigne of our said sovereigne liege Lord, at Barnet in the counte of Hertford, and there and thenne togider assembled theym, with grete multitude of his innaturall subgiettes, rebelles and traytours, felonsle falsle and traiterousle, levied werre agayns Kyng Edward the IIIIth, their naturall liege Lord, his roiall persone then and there beyng, and his baner displayed, entendyng traiterousle then and there the fynall distruction of his said moost roiall persone, purposyng to have distroyd' hym, and deposed hym of his roiall astate, corone, and dignitee, and there and then falsle and traiterousle made and reared werre agayns his astate, sheddyng there the blode of grete nombre of his subgiettes ;   in the which bataill, it pleased Almyghty God to gyf hym victorie of hys annemyes and rebelles, and to subdue the effecte of their fals and traiterous purpose.   And also where Thomas Tresham late of Sywell in the counte of Northampton Knyght, John Delves, late of Uttokeshater, in the counte of Stafford Squyer, and Robert Baynton, late of Farleston in the counte of Wilteshire Knyght, with grete nombre of rebelles and traytours, assembled theym the IIIIth day of the moneth of May, the said XIth yere of the reigne of oure said sovereigne Lord, at Tewkesbury in the counte of Gloucestr', and there and then felonsle falsle and traiterousle levied werre agayns Kyng Edward the IIIIth, their naturall liege Lord, his roiall persone then and there beyng, and his baner displaied, entendyng traiterousle then and there the fynall destruction of his said moost roiall persone."

The act then declares the persons comprised in it convicted of high treason, and all their castles, manors, lordships, lands, &c., forfeited to the King, and also declares that they were disabled from having or enjoying any name of dignity, pre-eminence, &c., &c.

1. Brooke's *Visits to Fields of Battle, in England, of the fifteenth century.*